AMERICAN CONVICTIONS

Also by Charles A. Barker

Henry George
The Background of the Revolution in Maryland
Memoirs of Elisha Oscar Crosby (editor)
Problems of World Disarmament (with others)

Cycles of Public Thought

Philadelphia and New York

AMERICAN CONVICTIONS

1600-1850

by CHARLES A. BARKER

J. B. LIPPINCOTT COMPANY

To Ellen and Catherine

Preface

When I made up my mind to write a general book on the history of thought in America, I recognized with sobriety that I was committing myself to examine no less than three centuries of our people's experience. The decision to begin about 1600 was greatly affected, among many considerations, by my feeling that the Christian component has always been strong in American thought. When American intellectual history is discussed without generous shares of Renaissance and Reformation ideas incorporated, it is in my view deprived of more than lively backgrounds and connections with Europe. It is separated from its primary directions and momentums.

If my dimension in time had to be long, there was no doubt about it, and the decision was readily made. But decision about the dimension in social breadth, the scope of the book, came only after difficulties which required more reconsideration and rewriting than I like to recall. I have never been inclined to venture a topical, ribbon history, long and narrow. Yet, not so different, as a teacher, and as the writer of a biography of one of America's occasional, unofficial tribunes of the people, Henry George, I had found satisfaction in examining achievements in the history of thought which either were inspired by, or else were applied to, the felt needs of the people. But this kind of inner direction represented a taste in work, not a field of work as yet defined by me or by anyone.

As I maneuvered my way into the present task, then, the problem of deciding about the scope of the book reduced itself to identifying men and situations on a field of vision on which I could focus my lens. Naming a field helps to give it character, and I do think that a phrase I began at that time to use with my students, "public thought," has served them and me. I have continued using it in order to speak collectively of main ideas and impulses, loyalties and traditions, which have concerned public-community life in America. The same two words appear on the present title page. They suggest, better than any others I can think of, the burden of all that follows.

To come at the matter another way, the splendid title which Bertrand Russell chose a generation ago for a work on modern Europe, *Freedom versus Organization*, will give us a start. Freedom and organization have of course been the poles of social thought, discourse, and decision-making in America as often as in Europe, the two continents in phase with each other in that respect. The historic defiances which our people have uttered, from the seventeenth century to now, have been spoken in the name of freedom; our historic agreements have committed us to new organizations or reorganizations. Defiances and agreements alike have evoked thought, sometimes forethought and sometimes afterthought; and they have applied ideas to situations. Admittedly, public thought in America has turned on other polarities—on the religious and the secular, on the agrarian and the industrial, on individualism and collectivism, and on the national and the international. In due course we shall consider a good many instances. But freedom and organization is the polarity about which Americans have felt and thought the hardest. To their glory it is a polarity which sometimes, 1789 the best time, they have understood well—well enough to reconcile the two ideals to common advantage.

A preface is no place for an author's imagination to wander, and yet one venture out of bounds is required to see where the bounds actually lie and to keep the reader's expectations inside them. Public thought, as an identifiable field of study, could expand indefinitely. Continuing to think of it as a dimension in breadth, something horizontal on the chart of American history, it has intersected many, perhaps all, the formal and traditional lines of thought, the verticals on the chart. For an example with which we of the later twentieth century are well acquainted, public goals and ideals have often impinged on scientific operations and ideas. Likewise, the other side of the coin, men whose minds were governed by the traditions of science have frequently sought to enter the discourse about what is good for the people. Or, thinking rather of artists than scientists, Plato is remembered to have said things about the relevance of music to the life of the state; ideas of harmony have had a memorable bearing on American political theory. Everyone recognizes that, from Renaissance Florence to contemporary New York and Moscow, public needs have always affected the visual arts, and that artists, following the ideals of their craft, have sometimes subserved and at other times tried to subvert the order of society and politics. Yet, while I have not denied myself occasional freedom to enter these areas, the pages which follow have little to say about the arts, and no great amount about the course of science and technology.

Rather have I thought it right—and appropriate to the history of thought in colonies which were to a great extent self-governing; more appropriate still to the ideas of a republic whose spokesmen were amply aware of the intellectual roots and branches of republicanism—to give principal attention to nearer traditions of thought. This means those vertical lines on our chart which have been most immediately crossed by the thrusts of social necessity. If my count is correct, in the American experience the main lines or traditions of that kind have been four in number. Naming them in the order of their first appearance in the text, they begin with (1) the American colonies' legacy of English social, political, and legal ideas and usages. As early to arrive overseas, not as widespread but more self-conscious, was (2) reformist religious thought, which, to the middle of the eighteenth century, contributed more than any other set of ideas to change in church, state, and society. Hardly separate from these ideas at the time, but due to become more so, (3) economic thought and (4) thought about education, twin concerns for the good of the community, reached the colonies as soon as any. Generally speaking, the mercantilist assumption about the economy, that the units of a national system should be made to support one another, and the Christian supposition about education, that guidance in God's ways of salvation provides also for moral behavior, were the starting points of American traditions in those areas.

Those at any rate are the main lines, the more or less widely spaced verticals on the chart, which may help us visualize beforehand the dimension in breadth of this book. I began with the assumption, which I retain and which needs no explanation, that the four connect and sometimes twist together, and sometimes join yet other verticals. To change the figure of speech, they comprise the two-and-one-half-century-long warp of our web. The cross-strands of public concern are the woof which, as much as the warp, give the web its wovenness, its capacity to take the strains of society.

Remembering the days and years I have needed to assemble my data and to sort and resort my ideas, I should speak first of assistance I have received from sources distant from home. During the academic year 1962–1963, freedom from classroom duty was in half-part made possible by a fellowship of the Social Science Research Council. Three years later a fellowship of the Guggenheim Foundation gave me freedom for a third academic term. Since then a grant from the Lincoln Foundation has made fully available to this work the seven months of two summer vacations, and has borne incidental costs such as library travel. To these three foundations, especially because they have been more helpful to a general work than is customary, I return thanks.

Their gift of stretches of working time, totaling almost two years, has been essential to me.

I am equally aware that, from first to last, I have been thoroughly dependent on support from three sources which flow every year. On that account, once again, I return thanks to my university, Johns Hopkins. After all other reasons for institutional loyalty are considered, the one which, after a quarter of a century, seems to me most splendid about Hopkins is the freedom and confidence it bestows on its members to follow the road of their choice. Specifically in my case, beyond granting those leaves of absence and allowing another term on partial leave, the university has put up with the inconveniences which a long-term enterprise creates. Likewise to J. B. Lippincott Company I render thanks for freedom and encouragement far beyond the call of the clauses in a business contract.

My debts to libraries, librarians, and fellow scholars are numerous, and I think that they will recognize, as I have to, that there would be no grace in trying to mention them all. But I have so long drawn on the patience of the staffs of two libraries, the one at home, the Milton S. Eisenhower Library, and the one which during summers and leaves of absence has become a home away from home, the Baker Library of Dartmouth College, that I must put into words an affectionate thank-you to both. To Jo Ann Robinson, who is now a member of the Department of History at Morgan College but who last winter and spring when she helped me was a graduate student at Hopkins, I owe thanks for library and bibliographical services rendered with an expertise which I myself could not have equaled. She checked nearly all the quotations and citations and, also typing, did much of the work of putting the Bibliographical Notes in order. In the stages of making the manuscript readable and printable, Lilly E. Lavarello and Catherine B. Grover did, with cheerfulness and generosity on which I depended, difficult duty which began as secretarial and ended as many-sided assistance.

Not only from people at Hopkins and at Lippincott headquarters, but also from a wide network of old colleagues, old students, and old friends, I have received suggestions and warnings, all of which I cherish, but many of which would be hard to describe or even to recollect in detail. So, in an order of names which is chosen to avoid gradations of debt or gratitude, which would not be the way I feel, I name the following few: Howard K. Bauernfeind, John H. Berthel, Alfred D. Chandler, Jr., Merle E. Curti, Michael G. Hall, Hugh D. Hawkins, Waldo H. Heinrichs, Louis C. Hunter, Frederic C. Lane, Robert D. Mead, Howard H. Quint, Wilson Smith, George Stevens, and C. Vann Woodward. I return thanks to them individually; I thank them collectively too, for the way in which their names, taken together, will represent other scholars, other librarians, and other publishing men to whom my debts, though perhaps smaller, helped to see me through.

Time and experience have developed in me no capacity to describe the support I receive every working day from my family. Not even listing the kinds of assistance she has rendered the preparation of this book, I simply record more gratitude than ever to the central figure in the family circle, Louise Cottle Barker.

Charles A. Barker

The Johns Hopkins University
January 1, 1970

Contents

ILLUSTRATIONS
follow pages 140, 300 and 460

Part One

TRANSATLANTIC OLD REGIME

1600-1750

CHAPTER I

The Birthright of English Colonies: Freedom and Organization

They change their skies but not their minds who sail across the sea.

Horace

English liberty, because it is cooperative, because it calls for only a partial and a shifting unanimity among living men, may last indefinitely, and can enlist every reasonable man and nation in its service. This is the best heritage of America, richer than its virgin continents, which it draws from the temperate and manly spirit of England.

George Santayana, Character and Opinion
in the United States

1 England: Prime Source of American Thought

ONE of the proud and creative parts of the history of thought in America has been our effort to understand ourselves as a people, to look backward at our experience and to will our way forward into realizing such capacities as we find ourselves to possess. No small fraction of that effort is recorded in the attitudes we have taken toward England, the nation we justly speak of as being our mother country. In our defiances of her, and in our attitudes of sympathy and attachment, we have revealed ourselves.

One main attitude in this respect is the one which Thomas Jefferson voiced in his pamphlet *A Summary View*, which he wrote two years before he wrote the Declaration of Independence. In 1774, while the times still permitted him to think that the American colonies might soon achieve the freedom they wanted, and yet remain—like the nations of the British Commonwealth of the twentieth century—under the Crown of England, Jefferson pointed out that our main principles of government had not been born in America but had come here by ocean passage from England, and that England herself had acquired these principles by way of the Anglo-Saxon migration from northern Europe a millennium before the American colonies were settled. Between Jefferson's day and our own, historians and statesmen and propagandists have assessed from many and opposing viewpoints the nature of this English legacy; and in the pages that follow we shall take up some of the discussion. But at the outset it will help to notice that today's informed opinion, largely purged though it is of a sense of debt to the ancient Anglo-Saxons, sympathizes in a general way with Jefferson's view of 1774. Freedom in America did not so much begin on our soil, we now realize, as come and develop here into the forms we know. Without England's contribution, nearly all Americans acknowledge, it would have amounted to far less than it has. With the legacy from England we have been uncommonly rich.

Yet also, not altogether inconsistently, Americans have entertained other and less grateful attitudes. One of them is the view which Jefferson wrote into the great Declaration itself. Not denying an inheritance from the mother country, yet piling up America's grievances against the English sovereign, the Declaration of Independence speaks about the sources of freedom in universal terms rather than in terms of an exclusive tradition. Independence for America had become "necessary" in the natural "course of human events," reasoned Jefferson this time. The great "unalienable Rights" belong to "all men," he said. This is a universalist view of man and government, reinvigorated in the twentieth century, which opens the sympathies of men toward people everywhere. "There is something in the contemplation of the mode in which America has been settled, that, in a noble breast, should forever settle the prejudices of national dislikes," said Herman Melville in *Redburn*, in 1849 when Americans were uncommonly divided about the meaning of their history. "We are not a nation, so much as a world," this mystic believed. "For who was our father and our mother? Or can we point to any Romulus or Remus for our founders? Our ancestry is lost in the universal paternity, and Caesar and Alfred, St. Paul and Luther, and Homer and Shakespeare are as much ours as Washington who is as much the world's as ours. We are the heirs of all time, and with all nations we divide our inheritance."° *

We begin to come to terms with the question of the main derivation of American thought and feeling when we recognize that in national as in personal development two points of view toward a parent arise: the appreciative one which encourages filial piety and the defiant one which encourages other pieties. Both have truth; neither becomes false unless it be so extended as to close out the other view. In the present undertaking we begin by acknowledging that England as mother country remains important in American public thought, and that a look at England during the epoch of colonization is necessary in order to see in perspective certain directions to which Americans have loyally kept.

The best starting point is the reign of the first Elizabeth. Then for the first time, only a couple of decades before Jamestown was settled, did England achieve a position of power among the rising new nations of Europe. In the history of the conflict of states, the defeat of the

* This symbol is used throughout to refer to Bibliographical Notes.

Spanish Armada in 1588 signifies that beginning. The seventeenth and eighteenth centuries would consolidate England's political leadership; and on the side of commerce by about 1700 England would surpass the Netherlands to become the greatest trading nation of the West. In the history of English culture, although up to the time of Elizabeth the record had been slender compared to Italy and France, there did then occur a splendor which all the world remembers. In the production of poetic drama, the England of William Shakespeare bears comparison with ancient Athens. And in many respects Tudor and Stuart England suddenly came abreast of the lands of southern Europe in the work of the Renaissance, and abreast of northern Europe in the unfolding of the Reformation. During the century or so which followed the accession of Elizabeth to the throne, England reached achievement as high as any nation in Biblical knowledge and theological expression, legal scholarship and thought, the production of new music and of lyric and epic poetry, maritime knowledge and venture, and the insights of the world's new science, with Francis Bacon and William Harvey and Isaac Newton among the seventeenth-century leaders.

The nation where so much occurred was not a small one on the scale of those days. Only France and Spain were larger than the island kingdom, and in many respects they were less well organized. But this does not mean that Elizabethan life was either as simple and homogeneous, or anywhere near as idyllic, as Americans who have a postcard image of old English villages are prone to imagine. Region was separated from region by dialect and by prejudices incorporated into local tradition; and distances from place to place were not yet reduced by any form of rapid communication. Country people in the manor houses were set off from and at the same time connected with country people in the cottages, by feudal and manorial relationships, as they had always been; and in English cities and towns early-modern capitalism was making society more complex and competitive than at any earlier period of history. During the first part of the sixteenth century, under Henry VII and Henry VIII, the enclosure movement, a process in which land magnates enlarged sheep culture at the expense of farming and of displacing farm laborers from their village homes, had increased to the danger point the class of vagrants and criminals. Though time improved that situation, and poor laws were passed and economic expansion reduced the pressures of poverty, Elizabethan England, not softened in this respect by cultural brilliance and energy, remained to the end a bitter place for people of the lower classes.

Success in the politics of power *and* internal social tension, economic expansion *and* an ordeal of poverty, new Christian idealism *and* a commitment to commerce, brilliance in the arts *and* a Protestant element of asceticism—the amazing variety, paradox and contrast, of life and thought in Tudor and Stuart England are the things for the reader to visualize first if he would understand the beginnings of thought in the Anglo-American wilderness. For the tensions and excitements of England would cross the broad waters wherever Englishmen went: colonizers would bear ideas, convictions, and hopes from home to the most outlying places of settlement. The very act of going out could not help becoming a stimulus to economic thought. As surely as settlement in America meant, for instance, tobacco planting in Virginia and the taking of shipmasts from New Hampshire, it meant also thought and legislation about the flow of trade and about controlling the labor force. Departure from home always involved, too, a religious goal: in certain colonies the main object would be the practice of dissent, in others it would be simply missionary, but religion would be an urgent matter in every case. Again, an ocean crossing always signified a draft drawn on the sciences used by mariners and explorers; when new geographic findings were reported or new charts were made, it involved as well an addition to the world's scientific knowledge. Musical and architectural traditions would prove exportable from mother country to colony, and so would the impulse to write. On the other hand the more associative arts and sciences—from drama to medicine to legal scholarship—would be slow to move. Life on the outer edge of civilization would inevitably feed the fires of national consciousness. An Englishman in America could not avoid being an Englishman against the distant Spaniard, against rival neighboring Dutchman and Frenchman, and always against the Indian, whoever got in his way. Under overseas circumstances the colonial fathers would naturally ask themselves basic human questions: What are we doing here? What is our business in America? What is our business in life? How shall we be practical about organizing ourselves, in church and civil state?

To ask such questions was to contemplate answers. To answer was to venture the long road of thought about men in the communities they build: political and religious, economic and educational, local and general—what this book calls "public thought."

2 Factors of Tradition: Language and Social Structure

WHEN Bertrand Russell wrote some years ago an account of modern great issues, he took for title a truly English formula of what is important in history: *Freedom versus Organization.* Ever since the Puritan Revolution and the Glorious Revolution, both during the seventeenth century, the Englishman's belief about what his nation stands for has centered proudly on the idea of freedom under law. Devoted to the unwritten constitution of England as a living and growing thing, the Englishman looks back to the ordeals of the seventeenth century as the experiences through which that constitution, barely escaping destruction, became complex and tough and mature. He remembers sixty years of struggle, revolution and reaction and revolution again. His landmarks are: the tyranny of James I and Charles I and Parliament's answering challenge, the Petition of Right, 1628; the successes of the Long Parliament and the battles and idealisms of the Civil War, from 1639 to 1649; the execution of Charles I and the reorganization of England as a commonwealth under Oliver Cromwell, during the next decade. The Englishman is especially proud of the later resolution of the struggle: the Glorious or "Bloodless" Revolution of 1688, and the Bill of Rights and the Act of Toleration at the end. After this series of crises, freedom and organization were set in operating balance, the Englishman concludes. Through the years since 1688 distinguished thinkers about freedom, Whigs or Liberals in politics—the philosopher John Locke and the historian Thomas Babington Macaulay the best remembered of the lot—have been the traditional spokesmen for this balance of government. But in the twentieth century it has been praised also by admirers of organization, by Labor Party intellectuals, for instance, such as Harold Laski. It has never been conceived more eloquently, either in words or in action, than by the Conservative Winston Churchill, England's spokesman in her critical hour.

If we approach the Tudor and Stuart period as a time when enormous releases of energy introduced much tension and many contrasts into English life, this particular contrast, freedom and organization, is the one which for the purposes of this book requires the most attention. English overseas settlers and American founding fathers, call them by either name, were freedom men and organization men both, and both in unusual degree. They were freedom men the more because they had broken from the mold of customary life at home. As careerists on the growing edge of Western civilization they could not escape having decisions to make which would never have been theirs had they not crossed the Atlantic. In the chapters which immediately follow, every occasion that may come up of, say, the founding of a community or a church or school is to be recognized as an occasion when the colonists acted as freedom men, taking care of a situation for which no closely corresponding precedents existed within their knowledge.

But colonizers by those same tokens were organization men, too. Rather, in this chicken-and-egg problem, it does seem that organization came first, or at least that organization held a kind of priority over freedom in early America. To begin with, no Englishman could venture onto American soil as a colonizer unless he settled on a grant of land

and within a structure of government authorized under the Crown of England. The colonizer was organized within the system of English state and church, within the operations of British economic policy, and within English culture, in essence the same as he was before he went overseas. Many a public decision that the early colonies made, and the making of which amounted to an exercise of the special freedom which colonial life evoked, was yet a conservative, organization-minded decision. In this way the colonies set up their separate militia systems and their courts of justice—freely built structures of power with authority to discipline men, quite like the structures to which they were accustomed at home.

What then were the principal habits of mind in England about 1600, which framed men's thought about human affairs quite generally? What main presuppositions were colonizers drawing on? Into what currents of thought and expression were they drawn when they worked at setting up new communities? Did any characteristics of tradition or conscience dominate English ideas of how people behave and how they should be governed?

There is considerable testimony about this in a phase of national life which is more often taken for granted than examined in history, the growth of the language habits, or (better for our purpose) the discussion habits, of the people. By the sixteenth century the vernacular language had reached the halfway point, or further, in succeeding both Latin, which the monks had brought to England more than a millennium earlier, and court French, which the Normans had introduced as the language of literature and authority. Here England was participating in a process common to all the new nations. As the vernacular took over, there appeared everywhere expression of the people's religious and political restlessness; masters of the new languages found splendid occasion for their talent. Dante's epic and Chaucer's verse, Luther's Bible and Shakespeare's drama, are classical examples from early and late.

In England the growth of the vernacular had been important for a long time before colonization. As early as the fourteenth century the Oxford scholar and priest, John Wyclif, had translated the Bible into English; and, when his convictions called for preaching missions across the land, he and his followers, the Lollards, carried their mission to the people in the people's own tongue. Two centuries later, after the Reformation had come to England, the creation of a prayerbook for the new Church of England made English instead of Latin the language of common devotion. And in 1611 the King James version of the Bible rounded off the work begun by Wyclif the translator, by rendering the font of Christian knowledge available in beauty and strength to all who were able to read.

In less popular directions of language development a similar expansion of English occurred. The slow areas were those where scholarship and tradition clung to the older vehicles of thought. The universities of Oxford and Cambridge—retaining from their medieval origins a monastic quality long after Henry VIII destroyed the monasteries—continued as strongholds of Latin as the language of learning. The ancient language remained also the language of church law and of much theological writing, Protestant as well as Catholic. On the secular side, treatises on law were often written in Latin; and in some part the correspondence of commercial houses (among which an international language came in handy) was carried on in that tongue. The royal courts of law were the places where Norman French hung on. But in the high locations of political power, in the Privy Council and Parliament, where men of rank and wealth who were not characteristically men of learning worked out the nation's policy, the common language served. Since before 1500 English had been used as the language of record for those institutions. To be sure, the affairs of Parliament and of the Privy Council remained very private, and the fact that their documents and proceedings were printed conveyed in Tudor and Stuart days no sense of reporting to the people. (This step on the road to democracy would not come in England until the nineteenth century.) Yet, when a printed record was kept in the common language, the basis of public responsibility was already strengthened.

Outside Parliament, moreover, and outside the councils and departments of royal government, during the reign of Elizabeth, the people's language and literature began to affect in a modern way the making of policy in England. The Reformation provided one principal impetus, and overseas expansion provided another. During the 1580s, while Puritan protest was raising issues of church policy more rapidly than Parliament resolved them, a kind of national debate arose, the first in English history, on the question of whether or not England should venture, like Spain and Portugal, an aggressive course of seizing and occupying territory in America. Nearly a century of inactivity had passed since John Cabot had explored the North American coastline and had claimed great domains for Henry VII. By the later sixteenth century the problem was whether or not to make the effort to validate those claims. The decision was complex, not so much from the nature of the problem, for England had powerful reasons to venture, but because so many sorts and conditions of people were involved. In England members of the royal family, different from Prince Henry the Navigator of Portugal and Ferdinand and Isabella of Spain, did not personally lead in the overseas effort; and within the Church of England the nation of course lacked any such armies of missionaries as the Jesuits, the Franciscans, and the Dominicans supplied the Roman Catholic expansionist nations. If England were to be established as a power in America, it was required that individuals and groups become informed and concerned about opportunities there. This demanded such an effort of propaganda and promotion as had never before occurred. During the final quarter of the sixteenth century many writers arose to undertake this work. Early voyages, like Frobisher's, were reported in detail; and the earliest ventures at colonizing—Raleigh's colony, which perished about 1587, and the Jamestown one, which succeeded but twice almost collapsed—became the objects of famous printed accounts by Thomas Harriot and Captain John Smith. But the most voluminous and influential of the spokesmen for transatlantic enterprise was a clergyman collector-historian-promoter who never crossed the seas. In his many writings, most notably the *Principal Navigations, Voyages, Traffics, and Discoveries of the English Nation*, Richard Hakluyt combined history and legend with hopes reasonable and unreasonable about the benefits to be derived from venturing overseas. The need which American Indians might feel, to purchase English woolens to keep them warm through the rigorous winters, was just one of several things which the writer discussed without much sense of the actualities of life overseas. Hakluyt's volumes and those of Samuel Purchas, his principal successor in the propaganda effort, were published and republished between 1580 and 1630; that is, between the time of the exploratory voyages and the time when the great migration of English settlers to America began.

In propaganda and deed, then, the one impossible without the other, England's decision of decisions was made: to try for national economic success through world power and trade (the Levant Company and the East India Company were founded, respectively, in 1592 and 1600); to establish colonies and to control vast domains in America (the Virginia Companies of Plymouth and London were founded in 1606); and to undertake the Protestant efforts for Christ in the New World (the Pilgrims of 1620 were the earliest representatives of the intensely religious part of the effort). This was a decision bigger than Crown or Parliament, or the two together, could have made for the nation. It represented a vast volunteering of interest, economic and emotional, especially in southeastern England.

Generous habits of speech and discussion prepared well for colonial life in America. The habit at home of blending a national vocabulary out of words of Anglo-Saxon and Latin derivation was extended overseas to mixing in Indian words for unfamiliar objects and to borrowing words used by colonists of other nationalities. Thus *persimmon* is a noun derived from the aborigines; in due time a great many Indian place names were adopted, as today's maps amply testify. The word *scow*, standing for a vessel of utility in the colonies, was pilfered early from the speech of the Dutch on the Hudson. As for the colonies' readiness to develop the national language and to extend the areas of public discussion in the service of political and ecclesiastical impulses, much of what appears in the next few chapters will multiply illustration. But none of it will indicate clean departures from England's own habits of complaint and discourse, which the Puritan Revolution developed while the colonies were young. Sermons which would not have been allowed to be printed in England we shall find printed and discussed in New England. (Sometimes the opposite situation occurred.) The sessional records of the colonial assemblies we shall find becoming public documents, even published occasionally in newspapers, before similar records were released by Parliament. The discussion of colonization which preceded the settling of English colonies was continued at home for two centuries in the literature of mercantilist policy and theory; it was continued in the colonies by writing and debate about local trade policy and resource development to be encouraged. Thus phases of English and Anglo-American history, which we sometimes separate for our own convenience under such headings as Renaissance, Reformation, Commercial Revolution, and constitutional development, become inseparable matters in the history of discussion.

English expression often voiced complaint or defense of the conditions of society, as expression always does in times of energy and new undertakings. But in this respect the central fact of the period of colonization is that, while the nation had embarked on a creative and disruptive expansion of society, the modernization of its ideas about society had only begun. That process would not carry far before the nineteenth century, when the business classes captured Parliament and the working classes won privileges. During the years which now concern us, the social structure and ideals of the nation remained principally feudal, manorial, and patriarchal as they had been for many centuries.

That is to say, the social and political order and ideals of England continued to be based much more largely on the medieval, hierarchical, landholding, farming-and-grazing side of the economy than on the early-modern, urban, and commercial side. Admittedly the men of property in the cities acquired economic stature. Founded both on the older wealth of those whose fortunes traced to the medieval wool trade and on the newer wealth of those whose fortunes were based on such undertakings as the Levant and East India Companies, a new order of economic privilege was rising from the ownership of commercial—as distinguished from landed—property. Such a person as a goldsmith, to illustrate by the field of enterprise of an ancestor of one of the first families of Virginia, might attain considerable wealth and prestige. But though a parvenu did sometimes become better-to-do than most country squires, he seldom achieved equal political and social status. The barrier between the middle classes, to which the goldsmith belonged, and the classes of the landed gentry never ceased to be an obstacle to men on the rise; neither was it raised so high as to be altogether insurmountable. In this respect Renaissance England was more like Renaissance Italy than like France or Spain. Business families, rising in the passage of three or so generations above the status of successful craftsman or local trader, succeeded occasionally in buying their way into manorial landholding and privilege. The Winthrop family of Groton, England, for instance, arrived in the squirearchy by such an ascent. And before the most famous son of that family, Governor John Winthrop, became the first citizen of Massachusetts, his grandfather and father had achieved such gains as would make them and him a kind of object lesson in English social history. From anonymity they had risen to business success, from business success to landholding and a coat of arms, from coat of arms to colonial investment and leadership, all in three generations.

Naturally the upward social mobility of the English middle classes proved a long-run advantage to the stability of England as a nation. As businessmen infiltrated the gentry, the gentry, by having yielded some fraction of their exclusiveness, gained the strength of new membership and ambition. As the landholders' way of life was honored, adopted, and imitated, it was also preserved. To businessmen who had succeeded and risen, no less than to men who had been accustomed for generations to receiving land rents and to being called into the councils of government, old upper-class ideals of hierarchy, rank, and estate seemed worth preserving and sound.

In social ideals what was at stake was the conception, which has a lineage in the history of thought at least as far back as Aristotle, that for all men everywhere a fixed role and rank in life is right. It assumes that human society operates not so much as a congeries of individuals, in the way Americans have had the habit of thinking, but as a system of classes and groups of men, each with its own function. In *Troilus and Cressida*, Act I, Scene iii, Shakespeare gives Ulysses a speech which voices the conception beautifully. The following lines from that speech include a passage John Adams would honor because he loved the idea of social harmony; they include also a passage selected for illustration by a modern scholar who has searched Elizabethan literature for unselfconscious expressions of social attitude.

> *The heavens themselves, the planets, and this centre,*
> *Observe degree, priority, and place,*
> *Insisture, course, proportion, season, form,*
> *Office, and custom, in all line of order. . . .*
> *   O! when degree is shak'd,*

Which is the ladder to all high designs,
The enterprise is sick. How could communities,
Degrees in schools, and brotherhoods in cities,
Peaceful commerce from dividable shores,
The primogenitive and due of birth,
Prerogative of age, crowns, sceptres, laurels,
But by degree, stand in authentic place?
Take but degree away, untune that string,
And, hark! what discord follows. . . .
Strength should be lord of imbecility,
And the rude son should strike his father dead:
Force should be right; or rather, right and wrong—
Between whose endless jar justice resides—
Should lose their names, and so should justice too.°

Every social group and every person, Shakespeare is saying, has an intended and due place; let the intention of nature be disregarded, and all else fails too.

Status was understood by Englishmen as Christians, moreover, in a deeper sense than as a description of how men and the universe ought to work. It was believed to represent the very will of God. The Church of England catechism, for example, called on the Christian "to do his duty in that state of life to which it hath pleased God to call him." Richard Hooker's *Of the Laws of Ecclesiastical Polity*—one of the great books of the Reformation, which achieved an almost canonical importance as expression of the philosophy of the Church of England—developed the thought, while Elizabeth was queen, that the law of a nation derives ultimately from God's intention to have harmony among His creatures and that the study of law must be confined to men of superior wisdom. To quote from Book I of the *Ecclesiastical Polity:* "Of Law there can be no less acknowledged, than that her seat is the bosom of God, her voice the harmony of the world. . . . Laws are matters of principal consequence; men of common capacity and but ordinary judgment are not able (for how should they be?) to discern what things are fittest for each kind and state of regiment [regimen]."° The scholarly Hooker's words are an earlier, more moderate, and less materialistic phrasing of the notion of the social hierarchy which the familiar lines by Alexander Pope in *An Essay on Man* also express:

Order is Heaven's first law, and this confest,
Some are, and must be, greater than the rest,
More rich, more wise.

Of course the gathering point of the Englishman's emotional attachment to the order of society in his nation was fixed in the person of the monarch. While Elizabeth I was queen this seems to have been entirely spontaneous and fitting. Around her clustered statesmen and poets alike, sometimes in the same person. She herself both exercised power and symbolized power with dazzling success. To be sure, this was something which none of her successors, the Stuart monarchs who ruled while the colonies were being founded, neither the tyrannical Kings James I and Charles I before the Puritan Revolution nor Charles II and James II after it, ever came near to matching. Yet, not unnaturally because in both periods the kingship was in actual danger, the reign of Charles I was the time when England's principal apologia for divine-right monarchy was composed, and the reign of James II, the time when it was published. "If we compare the natural duties of a Father to that of a King," said Sir Robert Filmer in that work—*Patriarcha; or the Natural Power of Kings*—"we find them to be all one, without any difference at all but only in the latitude or extent of them." Drawing mainly on the Bible, but taking much also from Aristotle and Plato and from the recent Richard Hooker, Filmer made so extreme a case as to assure for himself unpopularity. He has nevertheless the strength of having said, what modern scholars often say, that a nation and its society grow naturally and unconsciously from the past and that it is not a thing which ever was, or could have been, overtly created by men.

When James II was finally forced out, in the Glorious Revolution of 1688, both Filmer theory and Stuart practice of the divine-right personal kingship had been enormously reduced and would ever remain so. Yet monarchy survived, not without a patriarchal factor and not without a touch of divine-right theory, but with famous constitutional restraints on the king's exercise of power. During the second half of the colonial period, after William and Mary ascended, king, Parliament, and Church of England shared more evenly than before the prestige and leadership of England. The habit and theory of limited monarchy was by that time being reached which would yet gather more glory than any other system of monarchical government in the world. Colonists in America would honor it the same as Englishmen at home.

3   *Factors of Freedom: In Parliament, Law, and Christianity*

As love of order, hierarchy and social harmony, and a conception of all God's creatures linked in what John Adams would call a "great chain of being" were woven into the texture of English thought and feeling, so also, the other side of the cloth, was a Christian sense that men individually are responsible and free. More eloquent on this point than any literature is the roster of the great rebels of the Tudor and

Stuart periods who defied even the royal sovereign on behalf of their faith. High on that list from the generation just preceding Queen Elizabeth appear Thomas More and Hugh Latimer, the first remembered as the author of the *Utopia* which has been more famous than any other in the language, and as a lawyer-statesman and devoted Catholic, and the second as a younger Protestant contemporary who as a bishop in the newborn Church of England became an eloquent leader. Both men were martyred for their religion; both were executed under English law: Thomas More in 1535 at the crisis of Henry VIII's defiance of the Pope and Hugh Latimer twenty years later, when Queen Mary I restored Catholicism to its final moment of power in England. Among hundreds of others, these two represent, as honored martyrs, the ultimate values of the age. Dedication to Christ and to His Church in those days transcended that to king and country and all other loyalties.

Risk of life and fortune for religion and for religion's political goals was ventured repeatedly, on behalf of all the main varieties of faith in England, during the century and a half following Thomas More. As the crisis of the Puritan Revolution came on during the 1630s and early 1640s, and while the great migration was carrying thousands to America, the stay-at-home Puritan squires John Hampden and John Pym earned by risk and sacrifice their rank as heroes in the history of resistance to tyranny. On the royalist side, Charles I himself fought and died in such a way as to show that he honored more than life the conception he held of duty; for his quality and sacrifice some honor him still by calling him "Saint Charles." From the side of revolution, Hugh Peters, a chaplain under Cromwell, wrote: "We have wanted bread, lain in cold fields, constant rain, our Guns sunke in the Sea and recovered, we had a desperate Enemy, and few friends, but a mighty God." If the final expression of freedom is volunteering for principle, the century of colonization was one of freedom's heroic periods.

Thanks to an unusual cluster of Englishmen who, having themselves participated in the revolution of the seventeenth century, wrote books of political philosophy, the crises of that period entered permanently the national tradition of ideas. Sir Edward Coke in his *Institutes* (1628), John Milton in *Areopagitica* (1644) and other essays, James Harrington in *Oceana* (1656), John Locke in the *Second Treatise of Government* (1690), and Algernon Sydney in the *Discourses Concerning Government* (1698) expressed superbly the main conclusions of the logic of freedom: government under law, liberty of expression, the prime authority of the legislature, the right to the ballot—the conclusions Americans of the eighteenth century would honor. Contemporaneously with Cromwell a number of lesser thinkers, Henry Ireton and John Lilburne the least forgotten among them, voiced the more democratic and social-reform implications of revolution. Altogether then, before the first century of English colonial life had ended, and long before the rise of American protest began to promise that the colonies might separate from England, the ideas of the English revolutions had been eloquently placed between the covers of books; and English-language pleas for freedom had become as available for overseas export as anything else England produced.

Fortunately for the ultimate capacity of Englishmen to settle down and live with their convictions, much earlier than the seventeenth century procedures had begun to be adopted which promised that political protest could be voiced without restraint, at least by a few. The most clear-cut development of this sort occurred in the House of Commons. Some practice of free debate had begun there during the Middle Ages, an integral part of the rise of Parliament as a great court becoming the nation's legislature. But speech was often restricted; and there is a long history of demands for freedom being presented by the Commons and of their being accepted in part and refused or thwarted in part by the Crown. By the time of Queen Elizabeth the demands of Parliament had been formulated as four "privileges," and in 1571 the queen, who had a rare capacity for acknowledging the strength of a rival and nevertheless having her way, formally recognized the four. As they were accepted by her, and in later times came to be consistently honored by the sovereigns, the historic privileges or rights of Parliament were and are: (1) *freedom of debate* in the House, so that the elected members of the Commons may speak as they will (except when restricted by rules of order of their own making) on the business before them and cannot be restrained under any laws of the realm such as the law of libel; (2) *freedom from arrest*, a guarantee that, during the period of the sessions and for forty days before and after, members of Parliament may not be arrested by the king's officers for civil offense (M.P.s ask no exception from criminal law); and (3) and (4) guarantees by the Crown that the Commons may always have *free access to the royal person* for official business and that the king will always put *a favorable construction on the proceedings of the House*. The third and fourth privileges amount to a promise that the king will deal honestly with the Commons: that he will neither avoid the demands of the House nor twist them out of their intended meaning. As a cluster of rules, the four parliamentary privileges express the principle that mutual confidence among participators is of the essence of government. One may readily suppose that if James I and Charles I had acted that way, respecting Parliament instead of trying to trick it or even subvert it as they did during the 1620s and 1630s, great crises would have been avoided and two generations of revolution and reaction would have been reduced to conflict less violent and tragic.°

Hardly less significant than parliamentary privilege was a second great assertion of freedom under law, largely the work of the stalwart lord chief justice of England, Sir Edward Coke. An aggressive personality who loved power and wealth and pursued them, a lawyer who sought out technicalities in the law and imposed on the law meanings of his own, an attorney general early in his career who persecuted many subjects under the law of libel, Sir Edward seems an improbable figure to appear in the history of idealism of any variety. But legal idealist he was. To him the law of England, especially the common law as the product of centuries of court decisions, was a revelation of true justice, going on and on; and to him the judges of England, like the judges of the Old Testament Sanhedrin, were givers of the law of God, in their role second to none.

Partly because that kind of philosophy is reinforced from sources honored in the thought of the West—from the Old Testament, from Plato, from Cicero, and from Thomas Aquinas—and more immediately because it is being reasserted in the United States and in the United Nations today, American interest in Sir Edward Coke has recently increased. Legal idealism may be defined as that way of conceiving law which presupposes a divinely ordained moral order, to which the law needs be true. It assumes that justice is something to be reasoned about in large philosophical and traditional, rather than just practical and circumstantial, terms; different from historically and sociologically minded jurisprudence with which moderns are familiar, it believes in absolute right and wrong. It attributes to judges on the bench capacity for distinguishing the one from the other more surely than twentieth-century thinkers often allow to be true.

In making an assertion of that idealism Sir Edward Coke, like our own Supreme Court at times, combined moral conviction with legal knowledge and power. Early in the reign of James I, the king personally received an appeal to remove from the Court of Common Pleas, the highest common-law court in the realm, a case which seemed likely to reduce the jurisdiction of the Court of High Commission. The king believed that all the judges were his own deputies and that he had power to act. Not so, was Coke's response: "The king cannot take any cause out of any of his courts and give judgment upon it himself. . . . The judgments are always given *per curiam;* and the judges are sworn to execute justice according to the laws and customs of England." Monarch as much as subject is bound by the law of the land. This is true not in a general sense only, the justice insisted, but literally in the sense that the king must accept what the judges decide. He told James I to his face: "Law is an act which requires long study and experience before a man can attain to the cognisance of it." He capped the interview by quoting from Henry de Bracton, the thirteenth-century master of English laws and customs: *"Quod Rex non debet nesse sub homine sed sub Deo—et lege,"* the king ought not to be under men, but under God—and the law. After hearing this lecture, according to the historian J. R. Tanner, James I "did not allow himself to be allured by the vision of an English Solomon sitting upon the lion throne to judge causes in person."

This famous contretemps between justice and king occurred in the year of the founding of Jamestown. With similar coincidence with respect to time, twenty-one years later at the point when the Massachusetts Bay Company was about to be chartered, a larger crisis brought forward the same spokesman. On this occasion Charles I was making his effort to collect ship money without authorization by Parliament (taxation without representation, 1628), and English subjects were being thrown into jail without due process of law. The veteran Coke, long since out of judicial office, was now a member of Parliament and was writing his *Institutes of the Laws of England.* A leader in drawing up the Commons' Petition of Right against infractions of the constitution by the king, Coke again gathered eloquence from his knowledge of English history. Magna Carta was being violated and a new stand as decisive as that of the barons of Runnymede was needed, he urged. From a statute of Edward III Coke quoted a line "worthy to be written in letters of gold," he said, " 'Loans against the will of the subject are against reason and the franchises of the land.' . . . What a word is that *franchise!* It is a French word, and in Latin it is *libertas."* And again, in the argument of the part of the *Institutes* published that same year, Coke came out plainly with his sense of law as the protector of individual freedom. "Well may the laws of England be called *libertates, quia Liberos faciunt"*—be called liberties because they make men free. Such was the demanding philosophy of law used by English protest before the Puritan Revolution. It did not differ from what later would be called "liberal," and not from the determination to restrain authority as the first protection of freedom, with which the American Revolution would begin.°

The third and final instance of improvement in the position of liberty, in the seventeenth-century background of English colonial life, affected the mass of the people more immediately than did the first or the second. This was the propagation and early acceptance of the idea of religious toleration. As a product of Reformation conditions, a common-sense response to the necessity that men of opposing Christian beliefs live in forbearance with one another, the idea belonged to no party; it came readily where commerce brought about a workaday contact of minds. Accepting the idea of toleration of course required no Christian believer—were he Anglican or Roman Catholic or dissenter—to doubt that his own faith represented the divine intention and was superior to all other faiths. It simply presupposed that the Church of England had a favor to give; and, while it supposed further that conscience forbade persecuting other Christians or even non-Christians, it did not demand equal treatment for all varieties of faith. Unlike the believer in religious freedom, who demands the separation of church from state and privilege, the early-modern believer in toleration characteristically presumed that liberty of conscience was all that the minorities deserved, or else all they could possibly win, and he supposed that such privileges of responsibility as access to government office and to higher education would be reserved for conformists—in this case for members of the Church of England.

But this merely outlines a growing idea. As of about 1600 the law of newly, not radically, Protestant England was far less generous. With respect to religious heresy the law differed not at all in principle from what it had been during the Roman Catholic Middle Ages. Indeed, by reason of many acts of Parliament against "recusancy," the terms of the subject's conforming with the Church of England—his attendance at worship, his taking the sacraments, and the like—were spelled out in the statutes in such detail as never before. The enforcement of the law varied from severity now and then to a more characteristic laxness. But Roman Catholics were political enemies while Elizabeth was queen, and, although she succeeded in ruling seventeen years without persecuting them, she did not maintain that course. During the 1580s, when the war with Spain renewed the old hatred between Protestant and Catholic, Elizabeth let about two hundred Roman Catholics be put to death as traitors—nearly all of them priests.

Yet this persecution needs comparison both with performance elsewhere and with England's own long-term record. England in the entire sixteenth century suffered no occasion of religious violence to equal St. Bartholomew's Day in France, and at no time in the past had there been persecution to match the inquisitions notorious in the lands of southern Europe. While during the medieval centuries there had occurred some suppressions of heterodoxy by force, old Catholic England had been moderate. Even John Wyclif, after having been condemned for heresy, had been permitted to live out his natural life. And now after 1600, as the settlement of colonies began, England abandoned the worst fanaticism permanently. The persecuting of dissenters, though sometimes threatened, never became large-scale and after 1612 was not once carried to the limit. The burning to death of two Unitarians in that year proved the final event of punishment by death under law for religious nonconformity in England.

On many accounts the times were turning against persecution. The nature of the Church of England as a royal and a national institution always favored the mending (or overlooking) of differences of religious opinion wherever that seemed possible. (Archbishop Laud's demand for Anglican orthodoxy during the 1630s—so extreme as to become a reason for both Puritan colonization and Puritan revolution—is exceptional in the history of the church.) The Elizabethan philosopher of the church, Richard Hooker, had spoken for that point of view. And from the side of secular philosophy, the seventeenth-century testimony against persecution became ever more clear. Francis Bacon, royalist and rival of Coke, wished a plague on both Catholic and Protestant houses of extreme and persecuting faith. The antireligious Thomas Hobbes spoke powerfully for freedom; and John Milton's eloquence in *Areopagetica*, which was mainly intended to justify freedom for authors to state their ideas uncensored, may be understood as speaking in part for freedom of religious expression. Milton's idealizing the written word compares closely with Coke's idealizing the common law. "For books are not absolutely dead things," said the great poet and essayist, "but do contain a potency of life in them to be as active as that soul was whose progeny they are. . . . We should be wary therefore . . . how we spill that seasoned life of man preserved and stored up in books, since we see a kind of homicide may be thus committed, . . . whereof the execution ends not in the slaying of an elemental life, but strikes at that ethereal and fifth essence, the breath of reason itself, slays an immortality rather than a life."

During the seventeenth century, a ground swell of this kind of opinion arose. According to Wilbur K. Jordan, the scholar who has studied it thoroughly, a vast pamphlet literature—then the principal form of political literature—flowed from writers otherwise often unknown. Dissenters contributed more than Anglicans, and laymen more than clergymen, a good many Roman Catholics among them. Upper-class Catholics had been little disturbed during the later Reformation in England, and when they spoke for toleration they were speaking whereof they personally had benefited. The important thing is that every area of Christian loyalty supplied spokesmen and that a civilized idea was gradually taking hold.

As of about 1660, Jordan tells us, the principle of toleration had captured the conscience of all major groups in England. Of course, policy lagged meanwhile: the law of heresy was little reformed, and when we speak of relaxed enforcement we must not forget the harsh treatment meted out to Quakers in England between 1660 and the founding of Pennsylvania. Even so, the improvement from the sixteenth century is plain. Although another generation in time and a second revolution, 1688, would be required to bring the constitutional law of England into line with even a cautious idea of toleration, the old religious hatred had already lost much power.°

IN the political history of England, the three areas of freedom discussed in the preceding section of this chapter waited for the Glorious Revolution and the early reign of William and Mary to be firmly and finally built into government, and to be accepted with large effect.

First, the essential privilege of Parliament, the leading one which the other three supported, was incorporated as section nine of the Bill of Rights, 1689: "That the freedom of speech and debates or proceedings in Parliament ought not to be impeached or questioned in any court or place out of Parliament."

Second, the philosophy of the law and the constitution, so boldly spoken by Sir Edward Coke under James I and Charles I, that king and subjects alike are bound to law ordained by the Creator, became after 1688 the recognized philosophy of the English system of government, and John Locke as the writer of the *Second Treatise of Government* emerged as its most prominent spokesman. Suggestively and eloquently, not fully, Locke voiced the main principles of that philosophy: the social compact, the source of government in the people, the priority of the legislature, natural law and natural rights, and the right of a people when wronged to resume the powers they had delegated to their ruler.

And, third, religious toleration, the impulse toward freedom which the most of any depended on the permission of men in authority, was considerably honored by Parliament's Act of Toleration of 1689. To a modern eye, it is true, the factor of preference for the church establishment which attends the idea of toleration is plainer in the phrasing of the act than is the side of concession and generosity to dissenting groups. Many privileges were reserved to Anglicans; admission to university study and the holding of government office were the ones which counted most. Other discriminations, such as a requirement that non-Anglicans take certain oaths of loyalty, were put into the law. But they stopped short of the old persecution. The Act of Toleration did in fact open a *via media* whereby Catholics and Quakers, Presbyterians, Congregationalists, and Baptists could live, at once in security and in accord with religious conscience, under the law of the land.

As we have seen, the moment when these early-modern liberties were assured to Englishmen was the same moment when the English monarchy matured into its early-modern, constitutionalist form. The double maturation provided a unique national background, a double legacy for the colonies. In 1689, just as the first colonies, conspicuously Virginia and Massachusetts, were becoming stabilized, and new colonies, Pennsylvania and Carolina, were being established, freedom and organization were reaching a more even balance, the one against the other, in England, than anywhere else in the Western world.

CHAPTER II

The Old Order in the New World

*As for monarchy, and aristocracy, they are both of
them clearely approved and directed in scripture.*
John Cotton

1   *English Ways in American Regions*

D URING the first generation of American history, ideas and loyalties differed from place to place as sharply as they would ever differ in the future, the year 1860 included. No illustration is plainer than the religious loyalties of the first four colonies, in that epoch of religious antagonisms. Virginia was Church of England; Plymouth was Separatist, or Independent; Massachusetts was congregationalist though in theory nonseparating from the Anglican church; and Maryland had Roman Catholic leadership, all by 1634. Within a couple of years Rhode Island would start on a religious basis different from any other place in the English-speaking world. Those elusive proud qualities which still make it a personal distinction to be a Southerner or a New Englander or a Middle Westerner, not to say a Vermonter, a South Carolinian, or a Kansan, are many of them to be traced to backgrounds established during the seventeenth century.

Today it seems natural to associate local pride, and local ways of speech and thinking, with geography and climate and with institutions long identified with the regions. But of course during the early-colonial period the particularisms of place derived from differentiations which had matured in the Old World, not the New. This refers us back to disputes about faith which had occurred in nationwide debate in England; it also puts on a transatlantic basis the question of the geographic factor in intellectual traditions. For as the forces gathered which produced the Puritan Revolution, regional alignments of religious ideas occurred prominently in old England. Puritanism and political protest concentrated in south and southeastern England where trade and the towns were, including great London, and where Cambridge supplied leadership in ideas. Conservative Anglicanism and the defense of the Stuarts prevailed in the counties of western, northern, and central England, with an advanced position at Oxford and with outlying strength in Kent, where Canterbury gathered Anglican prestige. And if, remembering the Scots who first came in numbers to America late in the seventeenth century, we widen our vision of mother-country backgrounds to include Scotland and northern Ireland, we are yet better prepared to understand that colonizers came to America not as average or ordinary Britishers, a type which existed nowhere, but as groups of like-minded people who were identified with their places of origin and were impelled by group needs and ideals. Enterprisers in London founded the London Company for Virginia, and that colony would retain ideas that had been at home in the city and in the nearby county of Kent; and a cluster of intense Puritans, who also gathered in London and who determined to set up a new commercial city in America, founded New Haven Colony. For at least a generation a special set of purposes and policies, a little different from those of Boston and Hartford and considerably different from Providence, prevailed in that not very successful port town. So in turn each of the colonies bore its stamp of English ideas and of English local background, the two never separate, and nowhere quick to fade.

But this is not to say that the new and strange American environment failed to have an immediate effect on thought. Before the English established themselves in North America, the ribbon area they would occupy—a thousand-mile-long coastal plain between New France and Spanish Florida—had been settled permanently from Europe only by the Dutch and Swedish traders on the Hudson, Delaware, and Connecticut rivers. The fact of their presence encouraged the English to fan out: at first south into the Chesapeake Bay area, then north to Massachusetts Bay. Only a generation later did they themselves enter the fertile valleys between. Considered as a group, connected by water transport with one another and with the mother country and the settlements in the West Indies, England's continental colonies represented always a magnificent domain and a source of raw materials in overseas competition with Spain and Holland and France. But considered separately according to the way the colonies were founded, in the first phase of their growth they pretty well stayed away from one another, stood on their own religious and organizational feet, and often competed among themselves.

Relocation overseas encouraged strong-minded colonizers to become ever more fussy about their original purposes. This operated at many levels, material and spiritual. Aggressive seekers of land, wishing to build family fortunes, were given incomparable opportunities, from the New Hampshire scene of the successes of the Wentworth family to the Fairfax holdings in Virginia and all the way to Georgia; for the younger sons of landholding families there occurred such chances for property of their own as never opened in England. By transplanting from Boston, England, to Boston, Massachusetts, the Puritans of the Bay Colony made themselves infinitely more safe from their entrenched religious and political opponents, and freer to practise their ideas, than they had ever been at home. In no other colony did the fact of having left England behind prove such a transforming opportunity for ideals to be put into practice as it did in Pennsylvania. Quakers, who were accustomed to the jails of England, were enabled by the Holy Experiment to organize society and to worship as they wished, on reaching the banks of the Delaware.

Beyond the variety of life in the colonies brought about by English emigration, the victory at arms of 1664, which changed New Netherland (including what had been New Sweden) into the provinces of New York and New Jersey, began a second kind of social diversity. The conquest of the middle-seaboard region supplied the first instance of a European power in America incorporating, with equal status of citizenship and with full protection of private property, a population of foreign birth and language and church. From that time forward, and especially by reason of very heavy immigrations during the 1680s and the 1730s, the continental colonies contained a large number of Dutch-speaking and German-speaking people, as well as a good number of French Huguenots who were quick to adopt English ways. Partly because the non-English minorities characteristically were intense and evangelical in their own forms of Protestantism, either as Lutheran or Reformed churchmen or as radical sectarians, they brought into being a large number of communities which cherished their own uniqueness with an almost monastic passion. Thus, as Anglo-Americans have long recognized with pride, social and cultural multiformity became, in contrast with New France and New Spain, a normal and accepted situation. What is less frequently recognized is that, compared to times after the Revolution, there seems to have been little or no xenophobia when the non-English settlers moved in.

Although we notice, from the very beginning, the enormous variety of settlers and settlers' ideals in England's America, quite as in a family of children there appeared among the colonies a kind of natural history, common to all, of their social and intellectual development. The first of the three or four main phases of this we have already glimpsed: the impulse of colonial fathers to advance rapidly from their founding ideals to practical and even extreme applications of those ideals. Doubtless feelings of sacrifice at departure from ancient hearths and altars, and of anxiety to set things fresh and right in the New World, go far account for the hurry. It appeared everywhere in terms of religion; it was by no means peculiar to radical Protestants. During a sermon delivered in England in 1610, an Anglican clergyman, William Crashaw, exhorted the new governor about to depart for Virginia, Lord de la Warr, that his duty included an obligation to the "high and better ends that concerne the kingdome of God" and that the government "should make Atheisme and other blasphemie capitall, and let that bee the first law made in *Virginia*." Although no one was actually executed in Virginia for disbelief, the *Lawes Divine, Morall, and Martiall* which Lord de la Warr instituted, and which held awhile after his brief residence in the colony, did apply a tough supervision of church by state. In the phrasing of that code, the Virginia magistrate was obliged to supervise religious life as well as civil, because he himself is supervised "not onely by his superior officer and Iudge here, but by the Iudge of Iudges, who leaves not unpunished the sinnes of the people, upon the Magistrates, in whose hands the power and sword of Iustice and authority is committed, to restraine them from all delinquences, misdeeds and trespasses."° Even the Roman Catholic clerical element in Maryland dared venture far to implement its goals. During the first few years, the Jesuits there, led by Father Andrew White, pushed missionary efforts among the Indians and at the same time labored to acquire secure land grants which would support the Catholic clergy into the indefinite future. These two conspicuous advances exceeded what Protestant power in any part of the English world would permit and, indeed, what the Catholic lay leadership of the province wanted. They were stopped short. But if Jesuit reach exceeded grasp in this case, Catholic grasp went further in Maryland than it did at the time in England.

The second phase of development common among all the colonists is one which supplements the first, and we may call it the Americanization of the third generation and after. Where to colonial first settlers the fact of living in America involved a series of hardships, such as working unfamiliar soils, eating unfamiliar foods, and bearing climate and insects which often seemed dreadful, to people of a couple of generations of accumulated experience those things came to mean obstacles overcome. Only a generous passage of time gave the colonials a sense of being at home in the New World. This process, especially the part of falling in love with America, did sometimes occur within a single lifetime, but it belonged rather to the third generation than either the first or the second. Cotton Mather of Boston—very different from his father, Increase—represented both the generation and the state of mind when he wrote his history of the founding of New England and undertook social reforms in his beloved native city. Benjamin Franklin represented it, in the contribution he made to philanthropy and civic enterprise when Philadelphia was a half-century old; and Charles Carroll of Carrollton, the Maryland signer of the Declaration—whose father once almost decided to abandon Maryland—represented it, when he, a Catholic, declared fully for religious freedom. The distinction we seek is the one Robert Frost caught with emotion in a poem which has become a national one. "The Gift Outright" is historically accurate:

> The land was ours before we were the land's.
> She was our land more than a hundred years
> Before we were her people. She was ours
> In Massachusetts, in Virginia,
> But we were England's, still colonials,
> Possessing what we still were unpossessed by,
> Possessed by what we now no more possessed.
> Something we were withholding made us weak
> Until we found out that it was ourselves
> We were withholding from our land of living,
> And forthwith found salvation in surrender. . . .

The third and final phase of our natural history of the colonies is really a pair of developments which supplemented each other. The earlier was the rise of major regions of colonial economy and life. Of these there appeared, on the American mainland, three: New England, the Middle Colonies, and the Southern Colonies. Although based on geography, this regionalism meant little during the seventeenth century. But by the eighteenth, when the original sharp edges of difference between neighboring colonies were eroding and local distances were being reduced by land settlement and road systems, the larger economic unities created by production and trade made themselves felt. The second of the twin developments, which occurred principally during the half century after 1680, was political, and it originated in the will of king and Parliament. Thanks to decisions in England, by 1730 every one of the large colonies except Pennsylvania—namely, Massachusetts and New Hampshire, New York and New Jersey, Virginia and the Carolinas—had lost the form of government on which it had been founded, and there had emerged in America a prevailing type of government, the type of the royal province, which placed colonial subjects directly under the king. The two parts of this phase—the one representing economic growth and early maturity, and the other, political reorganization—may be understood together as indicating manifold consolidations in American life. We shall see that without them late-colonial feelings and ideas of loyalty would have been vastly different.

Of the three regions, New England offers the plainest case of the absorption of local differences. During the second half of the seventeenth century New Haven had become part of Connecticut, and Plymouth part of Massachusetts, and in both instances a distinct phase of early Puritanism was submerged in a unified larger colony. Even tiny Rhode Island, the historic home of dissenters against dissenters, though it retained much distinctiveness among its neighbors, could not have been characterized during the eighteenth century in the old way, as "Rogue's Island." New England from the Penobscot to Long Island Sound became more and more homogeneous. In every colony the Puritan type of congregationalist Christianity dominated; every one contained a minority of Anglicans; and Presbyterians, Baptists, and Quakers created other minorities. Before 1775 every New England colony had a college of its own. The economy of the region was compounded of farming, fishing, trading, and primitive industry. With the township as the prevailing unit, New England had achieved more in the way of community of life and mind than any other region.

Second in this respect were the tobacco- and rice-producing staple colonies, from Maryland through Georgia. Though many varieties of Christianity throve there, and only in Virginia had the Church of England been established from the start, during the eighteenth century all the other colonies passed laws which gave that church the privileges and obligations of establishment very much as at home. So far as social system and ideal are concerned, every province of the region, with some exception for Georgia, self-consciously followed the English rural pattern of a hierarchy of gentle and working classes. Although among the Southern Colonies there appeared before the Revolution no such consolidation as would justify calling them "the South" in the way that phrase became justified after 1840, there did prevail there both an English patriarchal and a plantation quality of life which differed from New England and from the Middle Colonies.

If the third cultural region, the last to be occupied, had not had its middle location between the other two, one can imagine that the social elements which settled there might have created an incoherent and little-organized fringe of England's colonial system. Quakers and German pietists, many of them complete pacifists, even in wartime; Dutch who were slow, and Germans who often refused, to speak English; Scots-Irish Presbyterians who proved to be frontier seekers and fighters; tradesmen and investors gathering and growing in New York and Philadelphia; Dutch and English landlords on the Hudson; and in New York a political and military control center of English authority in America: these were social components rich in contrast and poor in capacity to assimilate with one another. But the New York, New Jersey, and Pennsylvania which contained them were central both in colonial strategy and in commerce. The three colonies spread across three of the principal river valleys of the seaboard, the Hudson, the Delaware, and the Susquehanna. This meant wide-open Indian frontiers and acute problems of defense, especially for New York and Pennsylvania. The valleys meant also, what they have meant ever since, a wonderful economic advantage. Colonial New York, Pennsylvania, and New Jersey enjoyed from them immense agricultural wealth and the growth of trade; the splendid harbors at the mouths of the rivers gave special access to ocean commerce and made possible the rise of cities. By about 1750 the Middle Colonies had become—what the Middle Atlantic States have succeeded them in being—the most rapidly growing, the most urban, often the most prosperous and tolerant, but also the least homogeneous and the only multilingual area of the three cultural regions.

2 *The Old Order Brought Overseas*

As it is fair to conceive that English society consisted of a hierarchical order of classes and groups, and that the Crown capped and symbolized that order and the Church of England assimilated with it and moderated it, so also it is fair to think that that order was honored by English colonizers and was carried overseas as far as seemed to them to be practical. "As for monarchy, and aristocracy, they are both of them clearly approved and directed in scripture," wrote John Cotton, who as leading minister of first-generation Massachusetts participated as fully as any colonizer in setting up according to dissenting principles the institutions of a new colony. Yet Cotton and his colleagues never departed from the habit of thought which conceived society as the high and the low bound together, "all parts subordinate to the whole . . . every person occupying a particular status." In that vein his friend and associate, Governor John Winthrop, once told the members of the legislature of Massachusetts that the executive officers of the colony were not to be cowed, because as officers "being called by you" they held their "authority from God, in way of an ordinance, such as hath the image of God eminently stamped upon it, the contempt and violation whereof hath been vindicated with examples of divine vengeance."°

Doubtless in part because no American wrote a memorable literary or philosophical defense of monarchy while we were governed by a monarch, and because since then we have been pleased to discover in colonial times the preliminaries of the Revolution of 1776, Americans have paid little attention to the normal, sometimes even aggressive, royalist sentiment with which colonial loyalty was filled. To be sure the monarch stayed always at home. No wearer of the crown ever visited the colonies, as the King George and the Queen Elizabeth of our century have been enabled by modern transport to do; and, although now and then an earl or a lower nobleman was sent as a governor or a military commander, the highest positions in the colonies were usually held by commoners. But the king always had direct representatives overseas, and the fact that such individuals might not have inherited high rank of their own did not diminish the viceregality of their authority and power. The crown governor always acted in a spectacular way. Elaborate displays celebrated his arrival: proclamations were read, commissions and instructions were opened, the governor appeared on the porch or balcony of the capitol, and loyal toasts were drunk. As visitors at Colonial Williamsburg learn today, the governor of Virginia occupied a handsome residence called a palace, his seat of worship in Bruton Parish Church resembled a throne, and the symbols of royalty appeared everywhere. Only less prominently in New York and Boston and Charleston, where distinguished Anglican parishes and sometimes garrisons of redcoats heightened the effect, the presence of crown government added to the color and feeling of life. The people's part in the celebrations and the ceremonials was enacted just as spontaneously, and their compliance in the legal forms of monarchy occurred with just as much natural acceptance, in the thirteen continental colonies as anywhere else in the English-speaking world.

Nor was this simply a matter of form. Just as in England, so in America, the king completed, surmounted, and legitimatized the systems of society and power. Of course there were bad things about crown government, but Americans have remembered overmuch the few seriously corrupt characters who were sent over as royal governors and the many political fights that the colonial assemblies had with the representatives of the king. The important thing is that from James I to George III royalty had a freer and more active role in governance in the colonies than it had at home and that, on the whole, the colonists found the role of the monarch to be benevolently acted. Few Americans would have differed from the words of the English mercantilist writer, Gerard de Malynes, who in 1601 applied figures of speech taken from the family to the regulation of trade under the Crown: "Neverthelesse (as a commonwealth is nothing else but a great household or family:) yet the Prince (being as it were the father of the family) ought to keep a certain equality in the trade or trafficke between his realme and other countries." Nor, until close to 1776, would many have resisted such a sentiment as a later, like-minded essayist, Charles Davenant, uttered: "Kings are the fathers of their country. . . . The Prince is our common father, and therefore all that tends to his safety, ease and state is due him."° Throughout the whole colonial period, when new charters were wanted, as in the case of Connecticut and Rhode Island after 1660, or when boundary disputes arose between neighboring colonies, or when provincial political abuses required external remedy, the king in council as the font of justice was the figure whom his overseas subjects approached reverently, with sincere hope of being given relief.

In the colonies as in England the people's acceptance of the fact of social hierarchy was naturally much more a matter of daily practice than a matter of eloquent words. Different from loyalty to the Crown, this loyalty involved no organized spectacle. But of course the distinctions of dress between the silk breeches and fine gowns of the few and the Osnaburgs and deerskins of working people, and in time the difference between the town and country mansions of the wealthy and powerful and the cabins of the many, did provide a show of the gradations of property and role.

Quite as the charters of the early colonies—and later and always the commissions and instructions addressed by the Crown to the provincial governors—established English ways of government, they established also English patterns of property holding in America. Of the two main types of property known to English law and usage, the feudal and the commercial, it was of course the commercial which was applied earlier and more aggressively in seventeenth-century expansion. The East India Company of 1600 and the Hudson's Bay Company of 1670 represent the long-term financial success which this type of property holding, under conditions favorable to business, could achieve overseas. But when commercial-company enterprise ventured into settling colonies instead of simply making trades, the investors lost money. The London Company for Virginia and the Massachusetts Bay Company, which were perhaps as important in American history as General Motors and Standard Oil, never paid off. Inappropriate though the fact may seem, during the two centuries of the colonial period the feudal type of property holding, the terms of which are so redolent of the medieval past and sound so archaic in American history, served better the interests of the English founders of colonies, and especially served better their heirs, than did the commercial type of property.

Beginning with the New England Council in 1620, throughout a period of three-quarters of a century, the Stuart kings made a series of seignorial grants which conferred large parts of Maine, New Hampshire, and the lower Connecticut River valley and all of New York, New Jersey, Pennsylvania, Maryland, Carolina, and the northern neck of Virginia to such favorites as Sir Ferdinando Gorges, the Duke of York, William Penn, Lord Baltimore, the Earl of Shaftesbury, Lord Culpeper, and others. These tenants in chief of the king were of course expected to distribute their land in subgrants to colonists who would work them or develop them, and it was entirely to the interest of the tenants in chief to do so. In the classic case of Maryland, the royal charter of 1632 presented Lord Baltimore with a mighty grant—it would be dwarfed fifty years later by Pennsylvania—the terms of which imitated in detail the feudal and manorial privileges granted centuries earlier to the bishop of Durham. For their propriety of Maryland the Lords Baltimore were simply required to make a token annual payment, two Indian arrowheads, and to govern according to their charter under England's law. From their subtenants, who ranked from such famous family holders of many thousands of acres as the Carrolls and Darnalls, the Fitzhughs and the Lloyds, down to working farmers holding fifty acres or less, the later Lords Baltimore received in the form of quitrents, manor rents, and fees very large incomes in sterling.

Tenancy and subtenancy in America amounted to a rejuvenation as well as a transplantation of medieval forms of property rights. From those forms, modified by occasional changes, American land law would slowly develop; and by those forms social class distinctions in the colonies were given their principal meaning. Some of the modifications occurred before the Revolution; and those who see in the American frontier the key to American history like to point out cases in which institutions of feudalism and manorialism withered rapidly in the new environment. The courts leet and baron survived only a few years in Maryland, for example, and the florid plan designed by John Locke for early Carolina—to erect there a territorial aristocracy in ranks to be called caciques and landgraves, with estates to be known as baronies and seignories—deserves the contempt with which it is usually mentioned. This line of interpretation has been reinforced by Louis Hartz's widely accepted argument that, because America was settled too late for Americans to experience the Middle Ages, we lack such a tradition of conservatism, rooted in the habits and ideals of an old feudal hierarchy, as England and the European nations have, and that this best explains the persistence of liberal ideals in our national history.° But we need remember that no modern people has itself experienced the creative Middle Ages; all nations of the West have their feudal and manorial and hierarchical residues and symbols—some have more, and others, less. And if we allow that America is short on symbols we need not forget that no phenomenon in colonial society was more recurrent than what the proprietary grants introduced from England: large holdings to preferred people, the establishment of landed families, and the identification of large possession in land with social and political prestige. Of all the colonies New York, which inherited from New Netherland the great patroonship (or manor) of Rensselaerswyck, was the one most given to lordly estates, many of them established during the governorship of Lord Cornbury; and South Carolina seems to have ranked second in this respect. Yet even Massachusetts had its merchant families which acquired large land grants and sought to have security and privileges similar to the squires of England; and Quaker Pennsylvania, where commercial wealth and town life bore uncommon prestige, had its share of patrician landholders and of course of grant seekers and land speculators. Virginia and Maryland, where colonial-period plantations are legendary, and where patriarchal patterns of life can be traced direct to county families in southern England, actually were middling in the matter of land distribution. The much greater proportion of working farmer proprietors in America than in England, and the greater opportunities for younger sons to become land magnates themselves, did certainly differentiate colonial from mother-country family and property arrangements. But it by no means upset the hierarchical ideal, and in many times and places it gave that ideal new life.

In the historic feudalism of old England the combined identity of the baron as landholder and the baron as warrior and counselor of the king was entirely normal and traditional. In the loosened and modified feudal and manorial tradition of colonial America, the warrior element largely dropped out, but on the same pattern as the country squires at home the connection between landholding and power persisted. The shape of things in the colonial world may be reduced to quite general terms. A provincial governor's authority always included, beside the regular business of civil and military administration, both a control over the land system and a viceroy's normal power to call and to dissolve the legislature of the province. Next to him in power and prestige were his surrounding associates, the members of his council. This dozen or so men included the top judicial and legal officers, the attorney general, treasurer, and so on, and also the men specifically in charge of land affairs, the colonial agent and the commissary general. Because these men sat as the nonelective upper house of the legislature and their commitment to the governor attached them to what was often called the "court party," they bore a similarity to the House of Lords even though their membership never became hereditary. And again, because in other capacities they exercised top executive controls and held the highest judicial authority in the colony, they bore likeness also to the Privy Council in England.

While these analogies between high government at home and high government in the colonies carry only a certain distance into operating detail, the more general analogy between hierarchy and patriarchalism in the mother country and in the overseas possessions does reach the heart of the matter. "I conceive it, my Lord," wrote Governor Tryon of North Carolina to Secretary of State Hillsborough, "good policy to lodge large tracts in the hands of gentry of weight and consideration. They will naturally farm out their land to tenants, a method which will ever create subordination, and counterpoise in some measure the levelling spirit that so much prevails in some of His Majesty's governments." What the governor wanted for North Carolina, one of the less class-ridden provinces, was, more than he seems to have realized, common usage in English America. Men who held large estates were chosen for high office; the high officeholders received preference, of course, when new lands were being granted. As in the counties of England, so in the American colonies, owning families intermarried into a web of privilege and distinction, and of authority in affairs.

While the governors' circles were always the centers around which the web was spun, no more in the colonies than around the king in England was the orbit of privilege cut off sharply with "the court." As was true of the members of the House of Commons, the elected members of the lower houses of the colonial assemblies derived largely, and the leaders derived characteristically, from well-established landed families. Sometimes, as occurred conspicuously in New York, Maryland, and Virginia, a number of the eighteenth-century assemblymen could outweigh members of the council as landholders and as members of old families. The councilors, who were not infrequently newcomers and governor's favorites, were thus in latter days cast as colonial parvenus. Where the councilor commanded the title of "Esquire," the burgess or delegate was ranked as "Gentleman." Often the assemblymen, in close parallel with members of the Commons at home, were the holders of appointive as well as elective office, or had previously been holders: they were justices of the peace, or sheriffs, so designated by their governors; and frequently they were elected vestrymen in the parishes. Despite their habit of carrying on running political fights with the governor and council and their attachment to the "country party," in landholding and social tradition this second-highest element in affairs was well established in the pyramid of power under the king—most distinctly so in New York and the Southern Colonies.

Everything that describes upper-class status and privilege suggests as well lower-class dependency and servitude. In the colonial world the lower classes were often, not always, very low indeed. Only for the long run do events sustain the impression beloved by Americans that for settlers to have crossed the Atlantic westward meant escape from social stratification into a new world of free opportunity and land-ownership. There is no doubt that from the outset the numerically small class of yeomen in England, independent farmer proprietors, set a model of thrift and good citizenship which was honored in English letters and was imitated in the colonies—precursors of Jefferson's ideal of a farmer democracy, the foundation of society and politics. But we do not discover in colonial history a direct transplantation of what had been at home a small and special, not unprivileged, class. The yeomen of England, the actual owner farmers, seem on the contrary to have been like the gentlemen owners of larger lands, not very disposed to emigrate. But as English and colonial history is full of "younger sons," a migratory set of descendants of nobles and squires who were themselves neither titleholders nor landholders in England, so it is full also of people of "yeoman stock" turning up in America—in no other family more famous than in that of the Adamses of Braintree, later of the White House in Washington. Although certain questions about their social history remain unanswered, the likelihood is that most of the colonists who derived from yeoman stock (and they were especially numerous in New England) had been obliged to earn their passage as indentured servants, the only way open to colonizers of any origin who lacked money to pay in advance.

This brings us to the depressing fact of the first installment-purchase operation in American history. In undetermined but considerable numbers, impoverished but otherwise free Englishmen of both farm and city origin were willing to buy ocean transportation by committing their labor for a number of years to creditor employers in the colonies. In much greater numbers unfree Englishmen—convicts in jail and vagrants under detainment—had their services committed willy-nilly for them, to whatever employers or contractors would enter the traffic in labor. Voluntary or involuntary, these bonded or indentured servants received ship passage, and in America they were given by their employers "meat, drink, apparel, lodging, and other necessaries." Finally, after their period of years was served, depending on the going practice in the colony where they resided, they might or might not receive as "headright" fifty acres or so of land in freehold. This was the contractual and the benevolent side of indentured servitude. In principle and in best practice the servants' period of obligation and dependency was limited and it ended in an American yeomanry.

Modern investigations indicate, however, that more often than not the situation of the servant proved worse and ended worse than his contract sounded. Only about one in ten came out of his period of indenture both a free man and a freeholder. Some became free artisans or other wage earners. But many servants ended their terms without either land or goods and had no choice better than an extended indenture. An expert on the subject, Abbot Emerson Smith, estimating that at least half and perhaps two-thirds of all colonists south of New York came as servants, figures that in those regions only one in five survived into any sort of economic freedom. "There was a speedy winnowing of the vast influx of riffraff which descended on the settlements; the residue, such as it was, became the American people."°

The bringing of Negroes to English continental America, which began with the famous shipload to Virginia in 1619 and developed at only a slow rate during the next half century, opened the history of the lowest social status ever to be established in America—and one which in time went to degradations below any in the mother country. At first the unfree blacks were treated so far as we know the same as the unfree whites: they were servants some years of whose time were purchased from the importer. But later, when the heavy slave trade began under the Royal African Company, colonial statutes were passed and court decisions accumulated which rendered the unfree Negro and his children into permanent, hereditary, and almost inescapable servitude.

In what terms, in accordance with what possible moral values or with what pattern in English experience, are we to understand that third- or fourth-generation colonists shackled their fellow men? A helpful discussion of this little-recorded phase of early American history, one which emphasizes the buying, selling, and exploiting of both white servants and Negro slaves, was offered twenty years ago by Oscar and Mary Handlin, prime students of immigration. The colonial legislators and lawyers brought into revived operation the medieval status of unfree workers on English manors, they explained. Known as *villeinage*, this status had fallen into disuse at home but had not been dropped from the Englishman's reservoir of legal and social conceptions; in the seventeenth century it abetted the lowering of the Negroes into chattel slavery.° But recent examinations of the origins of slavery in English America, especially the one Winthrop Jordan makes in the chapter entitled "The Unthinking Decision" in his *White Over Black: American Attitudes Toward the Negro, 1550–1812,* show that general considerations of culture, when brought into play by the arrival of black men in the colonies, had more to do than legal tradition with that sad business. Seventeenth-century Englishmen were not especially race-minded; their religion held that all men were descended from Adam. Nor were they slavery-minded, or even very precise about using the term "slave." On the other hand they were servitude-minded: as we have just seen they vastly expanded a system of bondage in order to solve problems of oversupply of labor at home and undersupply in the colonies. And, generally speaking, as a colonizing and conquering people they appreciated to the full the rights of the victor over the defeated, the seizer over the seized. And, as a Christian people at a moment of high self-consciousness about their faith, they gave entire credence to the common idea that believers hold one place in the scheme of things and that the heathen hold another. Finally, what is harder to understand in our time, largely prior to and apart from considerations of race, Englishmen as sharers of Western culture attached a certain set of meanings to whiteness—innocence, purity, and beauty—and another set to blackness—corruption, uncleanliness, and ugliness.

Affected by these suppositions and others less general—the black man's reputation, as known from the literature of visitors to Africa, for savagery, nakedness, sexuality and similarity to the apes—it would seem inevitable that Negroes brought to America by slave traders dropped to a new status, lower than any white man in the hierarchy of colonial society. Probably Governor Horatio Sharpe of Maryland had both white servants and black slaves in mind when he reported in 1755 as follows: "The Planters' fortunes here consist in the number of their Servants (who are purchased at high Rates) much as the Estates of an English farmer do in the Multitude of Cattle." But the increasing number of slaves—and the increase of the slave trade when the trade in bonded servants diminished—inform the taking-for-granted quality of the governor's observation, its meaning of inhumanity. Thus casually had racism and permanent, hereditary bondage entered Anglo-American life together.°

In sum, although one can by no means say that colonial society contained every important group that English society did, it clearly imitated England's hierarchical model and contained one social-class element which England did not have, a lower one than it had ever had, well below the *villein* of medieval centuries. In noticing that traditional, ultimately medieval, landholding usages, and traditional land-working classes, were put to work in America, we notice also that social expansion led sometimes to the improvement of a class and sometimes to its degradation. English immigrants occasionally received thousands of acres in the colonies; they collected rents like lords, and established families of wealth and power. At the other extreme, the Afro-American villein was becoming a chattel slave.

Because, prior to the American Revolution, only a handful of people resisted these social changes, for the purposes of this book they now have to be put down simply as seventeenth-century dragon's teeth, a forewarning of nineteenth-century dragons. But, as we shall see, as early as 1700 a few Quakers and others, and near and during the time of the Revolution yet others of different mind, would discover in both racism and slavery something morally black—something ominous, corrupt, and impure.

3 English Freedoms Transplanted to Chesapeake Shores

WHAT has been outlined in the preceding section describes situations which occurred, albeit unevenly from place to place, in every part of the colonial world. No colony was exempt from monopolistic and patriarchal landholding; neither did any colony lack large numbers of small-farm owners and workers of their own land. A traveler from Georgia to Maine would have discovered only minor differences in land distribution, colony by colony, until he reached Pennsylvania; in that province and in New England he would have found noticeably more in the way of small and distributed ownership. He would have found Negro slaves in every colony, fewer as he went northward; but he would have found a center of the slave trade in Rhode Island, politically and religiously the freest of colonies. Unfree white servants and the descendants of servants he would have discovered everywhere; and occasionally the descendants would, like the Dulanys of Maryland, have arrived in positions of prominence and power.

The transplantation to America of England's habits of freedom, on the other hand, presents a picture much less readily sketched. Their ancient social relationships and ideas the settlers brought with them from home as they wore their cloaks, something taken for granted; but their political and ecclesiastical innovations they wore like a badge, as by special belief and by place they worked out their own ways. The expression of freedom belongs principally to aggressive proponents of new ideas and, while in the English-speaking world freedom already had traditions, especially the early phases of it in America defy broad description.

We may take hold of the problem by considering Virginia and Maryland as sharers from their beginnings of a common geographic and economic situation and of a common social conservatism, and yet also as enterprises which derived from quite different religious and political backgrounds in England. Charles M. Andrews, the master historian of colonial institutions, characterizes Virginia as the most "normal" of all English colonies. Though settled under the control of a commercial company, it became a royal province sixty years ahead of any other continental colony, and as the "Old Dominion" it took pride in that tradition. On the economic side, the cultivation of tobacco, the first colonial staple wanted in England, began and flourished in Virginia; this agricultural export commanded a return flow of goods, all in line with England's mercantilist policy. And religiously Virginia began and ended the colonial period with the Church of England established in law, at least outwardly quite according to the norm.

Using the same yardsticks of historical measurement, Maryland comes out in large ways similar but with differences which would affect the regional history of freedom. Maryland also based its economy on tobacco and for a long time fitted prosperously into England's mercantilist scheme. Governed as a province—that is, a colony under the immediate control of an authority at home—Maryland was like Virginia; but as a *proprietary* province, directly under Lord Baltimore instead of directly under the king, enough difference occurred to account for a history of late-colonial protest unlike anything that happened in Virginia. Of course the Roman Catholic leadership of the province during the seventeenth century was something unique, and it explains a very famous phase of the history of freedom in English America. But this does not indicate a cultural tradition much different from that south of the Potomac. From the beginning Maryland's Catholics numbered no more than a distinguished minority; it would diminish during the eighteenth century to about one in fifteen, and by that time a law of the province would have established the Church of England with such economic benefits and parish responsibilities as applied in Virginia. Given these positions of similarity and difference between the two Chesapeake colonies, it seems fitting that Virginia, as the oldest English colony, should have made the earliest and most continuous record of free represenative government in America; and equally fitting that Maryland should have come first in achieving practical toleration between the often-warring branches of Western Christianity, ahead of all other places.

Colonial representative government began in Jamestown in 1619, when Virginia was twelve years old. But the initiative in the matter came from England, not from within the colony itself. An order from the London Company for Viginia, which still had a few years to hold on as the owning and governing authority of the province, specified that a general assembly should be called and assigned power "to make, ordain, and enact such general laws and orders" as might be necessary, and that as to procedure the new legislature should "imitate and follow the form of government, laws, customs, and manner of trial, and other ministration of justice used in the realm of England." For choosing members that first time in 1619, a far more democratic-sounding electorate was called upon than was the custom of England or would become the custom of the colony: freeholders were given the vote and so, apparently, were indentured servants as well. When during hot July days the twenty-two who were chosen gathered in the church at Jamestown they were seated with the governor and his council and were given substantial business to decide. *Multum in parvo.* In the miniature work of the Jamestown meeting began the practice of self-government which all the English colonies would follow; and with the practice began the habit of mind which the learned James Madison of Virginia, looking back six generations, would call "the fundamental principle of the Revolution": the principle that Americans had possessed always the right to make their own laws.

On the original decision that the new legislature would be assigned a serious agenda—would have a part in making the main decisions of the province, and not just a minor role concerning a few aspects of affairs—depended much of Virginia's strong start. From the early years the assemblymen were presented with such matters as creating new counties when new settlements demanded, regulating the trade of the province, providing defense against the Indians, and, most important of all, enacting the tax laws of the colony. Sometimes their responsibilities were larger than they could meet with foresight; failure to provide adequate Indian defense lay behind the outbreak of 1676 known as Bacon's Rebellion. But neither the burdens of legislation nor the assembly's early mixture of success and failure should obscure the remarkable thread of self-determination which runs through the story. Nor should it obscure the debt of the colonists to the pattern of England. Not only had a company order called the legislature into existence, but the permissiveness of Stuart monarchs, for all their fondness for autocracy, had made possible the survival of that legislature—which might well have been extinguished during the 1630s when Parliament itself was suppressed.

The Englishness of representative government in Virginia, and in all the colonies in due time, appears, sometimes with rare eloquence, in the lines of the legislative records. The chairman of the 1619 meeting, John Pory, an M.A. of Cambridge who had been an associate of Richard Hakluyt, had been also a member of Parliament; if he was not a unique case he was one of a very small number in all of colonial history who ever served both in the House of Commons and in a colonial assembly. In Jamestown he was elected and given the historic title "Mr. Speaker," and this designation marks the beginning of the bold practice to be followed in all the colonies, of naming and shaping the forms and functions of the legislature after the model of Parliament. When, after about forty years of meeting all together, the elected assemblymen withdrew into a lower house of the legislature and the council in legislative session became the upper house (the governor no longer attending), Virginia had achieved a bicameralism analogous to that caused by the separation of the Commons from the Lords—a withdrawal and reorganization which had required about two centuries to come off during the medieval history of Parliament. The elected members in the colony, to be sure, did not imitate so extravagantly as to call themselves the Virginia House of Commons. The lower house there became the House of Burgesses; likewise the Maryland one became the House of Delegates, the Massachusetts one the House of Representatives, and so on.° But at a later stage of colonial history the South Carolina lower house did dare take the name of Commons House of Assembly; and throughout the colonies generally there seems to have been no holding back on imitating the House of Commons on any point which might give a lower house a political advantage. As they chose their own speakers, the lower houses had also their clerks and sergeants at arms and doorkeepers and other minor officials, and gave them duties to perform and robes to wear, all in the style of Parliament. Especially when the lower-house committees took the names and the functions of the famous seventeenth-century committees of the Commons, notably the Committee on Aggrievances and the Committee of the Whole, they showed as plainly as possible that they conceived themselves to be carrying on historic roles cast in the English tradition of legislative independence.

The risk of all this lay in becoming pretentious—in weakening a position by overstating it. As the attorneys of King George III would insist at a crucial time and with legal correctness, the colonial assemblies could not make themselves into overseas parliaments merely by adopting the habits and language of Parliament. Yet there accrued one phase of the business of drawing on English procedure which amounted to more than simple imitation: this was the assemblymen winning for themselves the four historic privileges of members of Parliament.

It was a conquest which occurred piecemeal in every assembly. When a lower house established a precedent—most particularly when it presented a petition involving freedom of speech in the house, and the governor accepted the petition—a point was fixed that was infrequently if ever reversed. In Maryland, where at least the recording of the matter occurred earlier than anywhere else, the second assembly of record, which met in 1638, made a stunning claim to exercise "power, privileges, authority and jurisdiction" like that of Parliament. Though the immediate effectiveness of this claim is lost in the poorly kept records, the claim may be presumed never to have been rejected; it was taken for granted on the assembly side and at least tacitly accepted on Lord Baltimore's side by the end of the seventeenth century. Virginia's attainment of parliamentary privilege, the early stages of which are obscure, seems to have been more than acknowledged by the governor in 1703, when he promised that the burgesses should enjoy the privileges to which they were accustomed, and that if they could think of others he would make an appropriate recommendation to the monarch. As of about 1700 it seems fair to estimate, in the light of Mary P. Clarke's careful research, that the great English freedom of uncoerced debate in Parliament had been fairly transplanted and rooted in all the colonies. However various were the particular effects of parliamentary privilege in the politics of the separate colonies, privilege represented a splended common gathering point for the building of a liberal tradition in the Anglo-American world.

As for the parallel question of transplanting and developing belief in religious toleration, which though widely accepted in England took time and the Glorious Revolution to be assimilated in the law, the Chesapeake colonies display two phases of advance. The first was the growth in Virginia of the propensity of the Church of England to bear with communicants whose ideas wandered from center, whether toward Puritanism or toward high-church maintenance of Catholic traditions.

This does not overlook the fact that vigor of ecclesiastical discipline, such as William Crashaw had advised and as had been practised during the colony's first dozen years, had a devotee in the governor's office before and after the Puritan Revolution. Pursing a policy which more or less corresponded with that of Archbishop Laud, Governor Sir William Berkeley encouraged clergymen of royalist stripe to settle in Virginia early in the revolutionary period. Later, when Charles II restored him to the governorship after years of being deposed, Berkeley managed church affairs as he did all else, with fanatical vigor in behalf of the royal interest. But, as the governor's management bred the resistance which produced Bacon's Rebellion, it bred ecclesiastical discontent too; there had always been a bit of Puritanism in the parishes. In other words, conditions in England's first colony resembled conditions at home, and ideas of toleration had their quiet appeal.

To be sure, the colony did not produce seventeenth-century eloquence to match that of Milton or Locke at home; Virginia's great declarations for freedom of religion waited for its own revolution and revolutionists, Jefferson and Madison and Mason. But meanwhile, beginning even earlier than Governor Berkeley, the minority of Puritan sympathizers learned to rub along in the parishes without separation from the national church. (Presbyterian and Baptist congregations appeared during the eighteenth century.) While Church of England clergymen brought the liturgy to parishes on the edge of the wilderness, and while vestrymen and churchwardens executed their normal, English, civil and ecclesiastical functions, tensions eased about doctrine. In Virginia, as at home after the Puritan Revolution, Puritanism lost fire. Partly because there was no bishop closer than London, and after Berkeley the governors cared less about church supervision, Anglicanism in the colony became low-church, decentralized in practice and tolerant in spirit. After Parliament enacted the Toleration Act of 1689, the colony with some wavering accepted the policy, and then by an enactment of assembly formally incorporated it in provincial law.°

Much more dramatic, more precedent-breaking and precedent-making than the openness of Virginia Anglicanism to many varieties of religious attitudes, was the Maryland contribution to early religious toleration in the Chesapeake Bay region. This was the effort of English Catholic laymen to have religious peace with their Protestant countrymen. While discussion at home which emanated from a "Spiritual Group" of Catholics was helping render toleration into an accepted principle, two noble and powerful laymen, George and Cecilius Calvert, the first and second Lords Baltimore, were enabled by Charles II to venture applications of that principle in the New World. In his first overseas undertaking, a colony projected but never established on the Avalon peninsula of Newfoundland, the first Lord Baltimore planned to allow freedom of worship to Catholics and Protestants alike. And the second Lord Baltimore, after he had been made by royal charter hereditary lord proprietor of Maryland, instructed the governor and council that they should "treate the Protestants with as much mildness and favour as Justice will permit. This is to be observed at Land as well as at Sea."

Lord Baltimore acted courageously, and his action gives him the honor of having been the first authority to establish religious toleration between Catholics and Protestants in any territory belonging to the Crown of England. In one sense he had no choice: even with the strength of his charter and the friendship of the king, as a Catholic in Protestant England (and in subject, Catholic, Ireland) he knew that he could neither settle Maryland with Catholics exclusively nor retain authority if he discriminated against Protestants. For the very reason that he would provide a refuge for Catholics he invited Protestants as well. The choice he had lay between colonizing Maryland and not colonizing at all, rather than between colonizing English Catholics and colonizing a mixed group of English settlers.

Between 1634, when the *Ark* and the *Dove* brought the original settlers and Father White celebrated the first mass in English America, and 1649, when the assembly passed Maryland's famous Act of Toleration, the province and its proprietor had a straight history of trouble. Political and religious tensions flared up, sometimes to the point of violence which included armed intrusions from Virginia. The margin seems to have been paper thin in England, between Cecilius Calvert keeping and losing his charter, and equally thin in America, between the proprietary officials retaining power and being thrown out of the province. There is no accident in the fact that the historic Toleration Act of Maryland was passed in the year in which Charles I was beheaded. That it was passed at all indicates a desperate effort of common sense and common opinion to countervail a drift toward the collapse of the province, rather than any addition to the theory of toleration.

Yet the enactment of the law—as an expression of determination by elected delegates, provincial council, governor, and proprietor—did increase the commitment. The terms of the famous statute contained neither eloquence nor sweep. They simply guaranteed freedom to worship to all believers in the Trinity. Non-Trinitarians and non-Christians, who might conceivably have turned up in Maryland but do not seem to have done so, would have had no better understanding there than they would elsewhere in the Western world. According to the enforcing provisions of the law, the tongues of blasphemers were to be bored. But again, no instance is recorded. The judgment of Charles M. Andrews seems right: "In no other colony of the period was the experiment even tried of Roman Catholics and Protestants actually living side by side in terms of equality, amity, and forbearance."°

4 An Anglo-American System of Society

IN the second section of this chapter we noticed that England's main institutions and ideas of society—government under a monarch, Christianity within a national church, property rights in land, property rights in goods and in business, property rights in men, society from top to bottom always conceived as organic, its parts connected and dependent each on the others—came to America in a grand-scale expansion of population and national power. Clearly this transportation of usage and habit of mind forms a necessary background for later American thought. From the time of the American Revolution to our own time, convictions of status and hierarchy versus convictions of freedom and equality have made the central confrontation in the nation's democratic discourse.

But when one says simply that institutions and ideas came to America from old England and had a later effect, one avoids the question of whether or not they seriously entered colonial discourse. That question is easier when applied to the matter of the third section of the chapter. Lord Baltimore's policy of toleration, for example, though he went no further in principle than contemporaries both Catholic and Protestant were going at home, represented a fighting position, both aggressive and defensive. Much the same, we may be sure though the earliest colonial assembly records are very brief, was true of the legislatures as they began the imitation of Parliament, and especially as they claimed for their members the privileges of members of the House of Commons. The resolutions of that kind which the lower houses passed had to go to the governor, the same as all others, and go from him to lord proprietor or king, before they were made the law of the colony.

By reason of the same circumstance of politics, it seems wiser not to think of the coming of the institutions and usages of hierarchy as something "given," of the nature of a social monolith brought over in the minds and attitudes of Englishmen. Something of that sort did doubtless occur, particularly in the area of the law of property in land. But in the areas where measures of innovation were enacted, the colonies shared in the creation, or at least the naturalization, of their own old order. American assemblies and courts, not Parliament or courts in England, made and interpreted the new rules in old patterns which defined chattel slavery. Colonial assemblies enacted the legislation which established the Church of England in the Southern Colonies, except for Virginia; the same assemblies regulated the local trade in servants, and set the rules of servitude, and gave or withheld the grants of land made to white servants once their term of obligation was finished. In sum, the definition of social hierarchy was legislative business in America from 1619 to 1776, 157 years. The colonials did not self-consciously create the social hierarchy, any more than did Parliament and the people at home. It grew. But in a more active sense than Englishmen at home American colonials accepted it and—no less because they also amended it—deliberately made it their own.

CHAPTER III

The Puritan
Amendment

Yet when the bellows of thy Spirit blow
Away mine ashes, then thy fire doth glow.
                    Edward Taylor

1 A Reformation of the Old Order

DURING the three centuries and more since Americans began to examine themselves in the mirror of history, the colonial fathers of New England have been seen both great and small, sometimes as heroes and sometimes as driven men but always as something uncommon, according to the eye of the beholder. Seventeenth-century Puritans, as Bible believers who conceived that God had chosen them as He once chose the people of Israel, were themselves the starters of this exercise in evaluation. They had no sooner reached America than they began to speak of themselves as makers of history on whom the world would depend. "It was God who did draw me by his Providence out of my Father's family," wrote a sea captain about his own role in the Puritan migration, "and landed me in health at Nantasket, on the 30th of May 1630." Three-quarters of a century later Cotton Mather as historian elaborated the same thought in words which matched the grand title he gave his book: *Magnalia Christi Americana*. "The God of Heaven . . . carried a nation into the wilderness upon the designs of a glorious reformation," he said. " 'Tis possible that our Lord Jesus Christ carried some thousands of Reformers into the Retirements of an American desert, that he might there, to them first and by them, give a specimen of many good things, which he would elsewhere have his churches aspire unto." After a second three-quarters of a century, while independence from England was pending, New Englanders, though they were seldom strict Puritans any longer, continued to see themselves, the heirs of their founding fathers, as carrying a special responsibility. Now opposing the policies of George III, they remembered the conflict with Charles I as having been the determining event in the lives of their ancestors. "It was this struggle that peopled America," observed John Adams during the year of the Stamp Act.

Such pride through the years has rubbed the wrong way people who were not Puritans or New Englanders; and during the nineteenth century, sectional hatreds, which preceded and followed the American Civil War, borrowed from and at the same time contributed to the contrast of historical opinions about New England. Even in our own century, though much industry and goodwill have been invested to reach a unified vision of colonial history, the ideas and the achievements of New England remain matters of grossly differing opinions. In his famous study of American thought which appeared a generation ago, the liberal Vernon Louis Parrington devoted much space to the colonial Puritans but found them a narrow and archaic lot; at the same time Charles and Mary Beard, writing a two-volume history with a scope and insight not yet surpassed in the discussion of American civilization, were able to dismiss the Puritans with no great amount of attention. In the intensified study of American culture which has occurred since those books were written, a number of interpreters have followed the pattern of the Beards, largely bypassing Puritanism and saying very little about any phase of the thought of the seventeenth century. But during the same quarter century other scholars, conspicuously a group at Harvard, have discovered in seventeenth-century Puritan thought the keys to the American intellect. During World War II an eminent philosopher there, Ralph Barton Perry, examined the relationships between Puritanism and democracy and found the second to depend on the first. Perry Miller, whose works have elevated the study of Puritan history to a new level of precision, has explained in half a dozen volumes that early New England is the place to uncover "the innermost propulsion of America."°

To the present writer the Puritans of New England, as thinkers and doers alike, have always seemed the greatest of colonizers, and in my judgment the long-run influence of their ideas is disproportionate to their numbers. We approach here not simply the history of Puritanism, one of the four or five major *isms* to be found in the whole course of American thought; we approach also the first of just two instances in American history of a dynamic region, influential beyond its borders, being dominated over a long period by a body of beliefs which set it apart from rival regions. The other instance is the South, from about 1830 to the present. Like the recent South, New England, up to 1860 or later, if it is to be well understood, needs to be envisaged as made up of subregions each with habits of mind of its own. Compare the leading role of Massachusetts in one region with the role of Virginia in the other; the dissenting role of Rhode Island with that of North Carolina; and South Carolina's late-blooming orthodoxy with that of Connecticut. Yet, again like the South, the original set of ideas had an ultimately unifying effect. This is simply to say that, all inner divisions to the contrary, the New England way did signify convictions and usages held throughout the region during the colonial period and for about a century longer.

Because Puritanism left a more indelible mark in New England than in old England, it is sometimes hard to remember that the movement as a set of convictions not only was born in the Old World but matured there, well before the great migration of English settlers to America occurred. The present book recognizes the Englishness, and the Old World-ness, of Puritanism by the arrangement of the story which places this chapter in Part One under the title, "Transatlantic Old Regime." To be sure, the Puritans, remembered as men of the Reformation and antagonists of James I and Charles I, were so aggressive an element in Tudor and Stuart society, so closely connected with early-modern commercial enterprise, that their large conformity with older, more traditional and medieval elements in that society is often lost to sight. Yet in the sense in which a reformer in any age bases his effort on the foundation work of the old order he sets out to improve, and conservative reformers offend radical ones by caring more for the old order than for the improvements, the Puritans (except for the Separatist wing) believed in the old order in England. In this frame of thought, though first of all they wished to reform the Church of England, they were also determined—as deeply as Queen Elizabeth was, or Richard Hooker or Archbishop Laud, for that matter—to retain and strengthen that church. Again, although the Puritans are remembered as having been revolutionaries, the main goal of their revolution was to increase the authority of Parliament, an institution now three centuries old, and to protect the property rights of squires against the demands of the kings, which they believed to be contrary to right and subversive of the constitution of England.

In this chapter, then, Puritanism in old and New England will be viewed in the same light as the monarchy, the social hierarchy, and parliamentary privilege and other freedoms have been viewed in the two preceding chapters. Like those factors of English life and in company with them, Puritan ideas came to the colonies as something the settlers had grown up with and cherished. The difference in this case is that we must say that "certain settlers" did. For, though Puritanism embodied the great part of the Protestant Reformation in England, it was a movement of conversion. As at home, so overseas, it prevailed only in certain communities. In others, as was the case in the Chesapeake colonies and in the West Indies, it appeared in small minorities. What we confront, as we approach emigration to New England and the application of Puritan doctrine there, is a rare instance of cultural concentration and selection. Certain overseas enterprisers, who had embraced Puritan belief, took to that region such dedication, and on arrival in America found such freedom to do what they chose, that they created a situation which in the history of thought still looms large.

2   *English Puritan Politics: Recapitulation of Protestant Demands*

NO one can say just where, or just when, Puritanism began. There is strength in the suggestion of the scholar who holds that we discover it in the career of William Tyndale, the Protestant translator of the Bible who was martyred on the continent in 1536. This suggestion underlines Bible faith and scholarship as the center of the movement. Or, if we follow the line of interpretation taken by Wallace Notestein, a student of national character who believes that Puritanism was the most English thing in England during the seventeenth century, we may wisely look back to John Wyclif and the Lollards for its origins. At that point the rising tide of the people's participation in religious affairs, upon which Puritanism occupied a crest, becomes plainly visible.

But for immediate purposes the early years of the reign of Queen Elizabeth are the time at which to start. About 1570 the word "Puritan" entered the English language, and a party or faction of Puritans appeared in the House of Commons. Geographically the movement gathered in the region of East Anglia, on the coast of England open to winds of doctrine blowing across the channel from Holland.° Here Puritan clergymen and teachers were settled in parish and university and were encouraged and protected by estate holders of wealth and power. Boston and Lincoln, towns whose names would be reproduced in New England, were active centers; but no other place was quite so important as the University of Cambridge, where makers of doctrine concentrated, and from which they were sometimes expelled. Early English Puritans believed as spontaneously as future American ones would that they were making history. "I hear that you have erected a Puritan Foundation," Queen Elizabeth accosted Sir Walter Mildmay, the father of the Emmanuel College, Cambridge, which after 1684 took from Christ's College the leadership of Puritan thought. "No, Madam," that gentleman responded. "Farre be it from me to countenance anything contrary to your established Lawes; but I have set an Acorn, which when it becomes an Oak God knows what will be the fruit thereof."°

To notice that during the final quarter of the sixteenth century one of England's two universities became the main location of Protestant protest, and that simultaneously the discourse spread to Parliament and parish alike, is to take account of the change of the Reformation in England after the reign of Henry VIII. The original impulse, heavily mixed with political nationalism and the dynastic problems of the Tudors, had destroyed papal authority in England and had brought into existence the national church. At the stage of the 1570s the Puritans, who were the men best acquainted in the realm with the theory and practice of the Protestants of Europe, especially the Calvinist churches of the Rhineland, put special stress on Protestantizing the forms of worship of the Church of England. They wanted the ritual more simple and the vestments of the clergy changed, to depart conspicuously from Roman Catholic traditions.

By the 1580s the Puritans were seeking and taking positions on the deeper questions which Luther and Calvin had raised. Are the sacraments of the church, as good works, valid means of salvation, as Catholic doctrine held? Or does salvation come from grace, God's gift to the individual and not a thing he can earn, as Luther and Calvin both believed? Is the historic government of the church, hinging on the office of bishop in the line of apostolic succession, the same in the Church of England as in the Church of Rome, the true and Biblical way? Certain answers to these questions indicated extreme Protestantism within the Puritan movement before 1600, as we shall see. But experts in Tudor history tell us that during Puritanism's early decades no large acceptance of reform ideas occurred which might not have been incorporated into the law and practice of the Church of England without changing it much. A. L. Rowse says, further, that the personal opposition of Queen Elizabeth, rather than any exclusive Protestantism among Puritans, was the decisive factor which prevented Parliament from enacting moderate Puritan measures.°

But no condition stimulates so powerfully as does rebuff to make reformers spell out their deeper ideas. This is where the Cambridge scholars had their great effect. The history of Thomas Cartwright, brilliant preacher and (until he was forced out) Lady Margaret professor of theology, tells much of the story of English Puritanism as it first advanced to positions about church government which could not be reconciled, or at least not easily reconciled, with the Anglican church. Sprung from a yeoman family, Cartwright had gifts of mind and spirit which lifted him into the international community of Protestant leaders. As a youth at Cambridge he met and was stimulated by Martin Bucer, visiting theologian who had been an associate of both Luther and Calvin; years later, in his time of being exiled, he himself would lecture at Basel and Antwerp and on the isle of Guernsey. Departing from the more moderate ideas of earlier Puritans, and from John Calvin, whose polity lowered the office of bishop from the heights of Catholic tradition but did not abandon it, Cartwright demanded the elimination of that office. In the history of church theory in England, he became the founder of presbyterianism, a system which proposes an alternative to, not a compromise with, the system of episcopacy.

Yet this does not mean either that Cartwright and the Puritans who agreed with him despaired of reconstructing the Church of England according to their standards or that their ideas belonged to the truly extreme fringe of Protestantism during its first century. The new Church of Scotland led by John Knox became definitely presbyterian in 1581, and this polity was much like that of the Reformed churches on the continent. While rejecting the office of bishop as not being Biblical, presbyterianism conceived true church government (as the Presbyterian churches do today) to call for authority distributed among presbyters and laymen and organized in a system of congregations and of supercongregational meetings—the presbyteries, synods, and national assembly. The designation *presbyter* signified a churchman who, though he lacked the miracle-working gifts of a Roman Catholic priest, was endowed with special authority from God. All presbyters were elected by their congregations and then were sanctified or ordained. The rank included both the professional ministry and the ruling elders who were not professionals but were not laymen either. So conceived, the presbyterian polity contemplated having the English church maintain in the future, not altogether different from the past, a system of religious leadership organized on a national basis. Though by no means voicing democratic theory or practice, it did seek a high degree of the people's participation, the sinners along with the saints; and in its scheme of federation it sought to mix the leaders of the church with the followers and to have high authority chosen by fixed procedures of election. Though Scotland is the only nation ever to have had a permanent church establishment strictly on the presbyterian model, under the Long Parliament of the 1640s England itself adopted the system temporarily. The presbyterian phase of Puritan thinking, then, represented no venture into the politically impossible.°

Neither did presbyterianism prove to be a terminal point in the development of Puritan theory. Once thought concerning religious institutions began to shift from control by lords bishops to control by the people in the congregations, no middle position about church authority satisfied all minds. Among English Puritans, almost as early as Cartwright developed presbyterianism other thinkers pushed further than he did the right of the Christian congregation to govern itself. In this way a new polity was born, or rather was evoked, in England. Congregationalism offers the proposition, which like other polities is defended from the text of the Bible, that the congregation, as the natural gathering for worship wherein Christians can share fully their experiences and convictions, is the correct self-governing unit of the Church of Christ on earth. Within the congregational unit lies not simply the authority to elect church officers but to decide on doctrine and all other questions, the congregationalist argument runs.

Before the recent rewriting of the early New England story, American historians chose to remember very particularly only one of the English founders of this decentralizing theory. The man was Robert Browne, a younger contemporary who attended Cambridge while Cartwright was still there but who came up with quite different ideas. The title of his book, *A Treatise of Reformation without Tarying for Anie*, tells a great deal in one line. Asking that people separate at once from the Church of England, he departed from the intention of his major Puritan predecessors and followers, who wanted to reform that church. Instead of a national establishment supported by the state, he called for self-gathered, self-governing congregations of Christians to assume the guidance of English morals and life. The similarity of "Brownism," as this Separatism is often called, to the practice of the Pilgrims of Plymouth Colony a generation after his book, has won for Robert Browne a higher standing among the thinkers in the European background of American history than he truly deserves. The complete story about him includes the facts that in time he recanted his congregationalism and returned to office in the Church of England and that the Pilgrims took their theory less from him than from their own minister, John Robinson, and from John Smyth, a Baptist. Rather than as a direct contributor to congregationalism in America, the author of *A Treatise of Reformation* deserves remembrance as an English precursor of nineteenth-century "come-outerism," a call to abandon the churches which flared up in a wave of defiance.

If thought about congregationalist polity had stopped growing among the Puritans with such uncompromising declarations of independence from the Church of England as Browne's book was, the influence of congregationalism would never have been great in English America. The event proved different. Very few Puritans of the great migration of the 1630s left home as Separatists. Anglicans they remained, for a matter of years. Except for Roger Williams, nearly all of those whose opinions are known—the founders of Boston and the Massachusetts towns circling Boston, the founders of New Hampshire, of Connecticut and the Connecticut River valley settlements in Massachusetts, and of New Haven—left home and arrived in America as believers in a new English-born system of reform. Known in the history of church polity as nonseparating congregationalism, their position was like that of the Brownists and the Pilgrims except on the point of departing from the national church. Like the presbyterians, who had influenced their thought, they wanted to continue to reside within the national church and to reconstruct it from within, but of course they sought to do this on their own pattern of ideas.

In the entire course of public thought in America we shall discover few programs, whether religious or secular, which will seem at once so bold and so intricate. Nonseparating congregationalism was the principal product of the Puritan intellect during the period from 1600 to 1625. This was a middle period of ferment, between the generation of the openers of Puritan theory, Cartwright and Browne and others, and the generation of the English Revolution, when John Hampden and John Pym, among many at home, and John Winthrop and Thomas Hooker and Roger Williams, overseas, translated Puritan convictions into Puritan deed. It is the period of the growth of the movement which was the most overlooked in historical appreciation until a quarter century ago. Since that time such previously neglected terms as the "federal" or "covenant" theology and "nonseparating congregationalism" have become familiar words in colonial history.

During the 1600 to 1625 generation, as earlier, Cambridge University provided the principal place for the begetting of Puritan thought. Lawrence Chaderton, the stirring preacher who served as master of Emmanuel College through the first forty years of its history, and his successor, John Preston, represent the spiritual and institutional center of the movement; but William Perkins, a fellow of Corpus Christi, and his student, William Ames, achieved more, individually, as writing theologians. Ames's book, *Medulla Sacrae Theologiae—The Marrow of Sacred Theology—*1623, made him, in the words of Perry Miller, "the father of New England church polity." For generations his ideas would be familiar to students at Harvard and Yale, and so to the ministers and members of the congregations throughout New England.

The boldness and complexity of Ames, and of Chaderton, Perkins, and Preston, lay in the argument they offered that congregationalist polity, which goes about as far as theory can in the direction of local and multiple church self-government, could and should be reconciled with the national church, which in the nature of the case sought to have general conformity. To achieve so paradoxical a purpose, the authors of it were ready to be patient. Far from asking reformation without tarrying, they retained as they could their offices in church and university; they were among the influential ones who helped fellow Puritans receive parish and other appointments. Like their older contemporaries of presbyterian persuasion, they counted on religious conversion—God working through selected believers—to bring about the result they thought right. The practical problem of the covenant theologians was the age-old one of maintaining local freedom within a system of central authority; and England, with her justices of the peace for each county, with her parish organizations, her lords of the manor, and her city corporations, was old and wise at making accommodations with localism under the monarchy. But under the Stuarts, with similarities to France and the other national monarchies of the West, England was slipping toward centralization. The Puritans were holding out against royalist and Catholic tendencies in the institution which concerned them most.°

No congregationalists of any variety ever came as close as the presbyterians did to capturing the Church of England. Yet, before we assume that the men who were about to establish Massachusetts, Connecticut, and New Hampshire were lacking in political or social realism, we should glance across the Atlantic. A decade prior to the great migration of Puritans, beginning in 1630, the Pilgrims had quietly put congregationalist theory to work. Besides founding their churches at Plymouth, Duxbury, Barnstable, and other settlements, in the Mayflower Compact (which they signed before making landfall) the Pilgrims had covenanted together politically, each committing himself to all the others to act in concert under the will of God. Not setting up any of the machinery of the Church of England, these Separatists, in their congregational meetings and through their church elders, began at once supplying moral and spiritual guidance—the normal duty of the established church to the people of one sizable peninsula in the domains of their king.

Thus, well before Massachusetts Bay Company was founded, the stabilizing capacity of congregationalist practice in an American settlement, albeit one more radically minded and less wealthy than most later settlements in New England, had already been demonstrated.

3 The Vision of the Puritan: American Glimpses

THE positions on church polity which have been outlined in the preceding section represent less the passion of the Puritan, legalistic though he often was, than what he argued about and arranged. While those positions were being formulated, as specific responses to specific challenges in the national situation, the Puritans concerned themselves also, much as Luther and Bucer and Calvin and Zwingli had done, with more ultimate questions of faith. And, as to the general nature of their ideas about God and His relationship with man and about the purposes and capacities of man, Puritan thought appears, quite as it does when the question concerns church polity, to have belonged by sympathy in the Calvinist branch of the total family of Reformation ideas. But once again we discover Puritans connected with other and older traditions. We find in Puritanism an English growth of the Renaissance and the Reformation, the roots of which extended much further back than the sixteenth century—back into the past of the English nation and into the origins of the Christian religion.

Except for minor amendments from other investigators, the solution of the problem offered nearly three decades ago by Perry Miller holds up today. According to that historian, the Puritan's sense of the nature of God belongs in the stream of Christian expression that descends from Augustine of Hippo, the only church father whom the Puritans chose to call "Saint." The Augustinian stream of piety traces back to St. Paul; it draws particularly from Plato as a reservoir of concepts and mysticism; running from ancient to medieval and modern times, it feeds those flows of Christian feeling which exalt God as a Being of inscrutable will and power. Among the contemporaries of the Puritans, German Lutherans, who thought first of the grace and love of God and who were more nearly Christ-mystics than most other Protestant churchmen, and Swiss and French Calvinists, who spoke more of God's will, were like one another and like the Puritans in that they moved in the Augustinian stream. To shift the figure of speech, Protestants quite generally belonged in this ancient lineage; their spiritual relationship one with another was more like that of cousins, the descendants of a distant common ancestor, Augustine, than like those of the children of a recent parent, John Calvin or anyone else. While family disagreements often turned into bitter quarrels about how the Church of Christ on earth should best be governed, most Protestants remained alike— when compared to the Roman Catholic defenders of the sacraments as a means of salvation—in stressing the belief that men and institutions are insufficient and corrupt and that God alone is mighty and has the power to save.°

To participate in this current of thought required of the Puritans that they find words to discuss what they believed to be ultimately beyond expression—"an incomprehensible, first, absolute Being." That is, they had to borrow or create a theology of their own, somewhat different from the system which the Church of England inherited from medieval scholasticism. So the Puritans, who cherished plain speaking about Christianity and wanted all concerned to understand, often spurned the logic of metaphysics and resorted to figures of speech. They loved to draw similes from nature. In the words of one of the theologians of Cambridge University: "You may look into God's essence and see and admire it; but to think that thou couldest comprehend God is, as if a man should think to hold the whole sea in the hollow of his hand." A similar image occurs in a sermon by Thomas Hooker, a Puritan moderate and founder of Connecticut: "As it is with Rivers, they all go to the Sea, and are swallowed up in the Sea; and yet there is nothing seen but the Sea. . . . So let it be with thy Soul, when they wouldst find mercy and grace." As John Milton, a latter-day Puritan, writing in *Paradise Lost* a Protestant's epic of the rulership of God and the power of Satan, drew from the astronomy of the age of Galileo images to suggest the greatness of the Creator, so these lesser Puritans drew on the faces of nature they were familiar with to intimate the features of God.

Far more habitual in everyday Puritan expression than figures of speech drawn from nature, however, were analogies drawn from politics; and even from trade. The very names which were applied to their theology, "federal" and "covenant," suggest an infusion of thought from politics; and, while the texts of their treatises and sermons were heavily Biblical and studded with citations of chapter and verse, the modern student sees behind the argument, as well as Old Testament knowledge, the belief of Englishmen that good monarchy is the best government given to man. William Ames's *Medulla* pictured God as a sovereign ruler, unlimited in His power and inscrutable in His decisions and at the same time communicative and reliable, a font of law and wisdom and love.

The special and distinguishing things about this English theology is the centrality it gave to the idea of divine covenants—to crucial understandings or contracts offered by the Creator to His children on earth. As God's conversation with Abraham, related in Genesis, Chapter 17, was taken to testify, He makes agreements with the nations He favors. He does so at will; and Englishmen of the covenant theology were persuaded that He contracted with them as He had once done with the children of Israel. "We are the children of *Abraham*," reasoned the founding minister of Concord, Massachusetts, "and therefore we are under Abraham's covenant." In this phase of covenant doctrine God was believed to enter the history of peoples directly and, in the cases of ancient Israel and of contemporary England, to have set a light unto the world.

But the national covenants God made were an Old Testament part of the Puritan's theology and a lesser part of their vision. The covenant of grace, as it phrased their idea of personal salvation, was the more central part; it derived from the New Testament and was more philosophic, more Augustinian and less Hebraic, in derivation and nature. The covenant of grace was a deed of gift and the simplest of all contracts. We may borrow the authority of Perry Miller: "On His own side, God voluntarily undertakes not only to save those who believe, but to supply the power of belief, to provide the grace that will make possible man's fulfilling the terms of this new and easier covenant." To meet, or rather to have met, these terms, a human mortal can present "not a deed but a belief, a simple faith in Christ the mediator."° In the view of the federal theology, salvation happened to a soul. It was nothing a man could win for himself; it was an inexplicable act of God's mercy. Some modern minds find it difficult that so ultimate a matter of God's love should have been phrased as having the nature of a contract. But in this aspect of their thought it would be hard to find the Puritans either illogical or unbiblical; and, when one remembers their sense that even on earth law is something more than human, one recognizes the splendor they felt the doctrine of the covenant of grace to contain.

The reader will have recognized also that, for all its simplicity and its echoes of Old Testament history and of the sound of the English forum, the covenant idea contained a great deal of speculative thought. In England as elsewhere the Reformation helped—as the Renaissance had done in Italy—to loosen the hold of medieval scholastic philosophy on the mind of the West. This meant a shift in the use made by Christianity of the ancient body of Greek metaphysics: not by any means a total abandonment of the Aristotelianism established three centuries earlier by scholars among whom Thomas Aquinas was the most weighty, but a reduction of the monopoly of Aritotelianism; and not a wide swing into the more intuitive idealism of Plato and the neo-Platonists, such as would occur two centuries later in Concord, but an increased fondness for intuitive reason and for Plato, nevertheless. As the Puritans in their theology voiced the idea that the one true Church of Christ, over and above the meetings of congregations, is not of the earth, not a matter of history or of tradition, or of organization or wealth or power, but is a body of immortal souls, they participated in this shift of thought.

There was, then, both practicality and flight of the imagination, religious nationalism and philosophic idealism together, in the range of the Puritan theology. To glimpse these contrasting qualities in the way in which colonizers took them to America and wove them into their own expression, we may choose passages from two poems of the later seventeenth century. The first is from "God's Controversy with New-England" by the Reverend Michael Wigglesworth, which was published in Cambridge, Massachusetts, in 1662. God is made the speaker of the following lines, and the fact that He confronts a failure in New England is no more representative of Puritan thought than the fact that He hopes that the loss may yet be retrieved:

Are these the men that prized libertee
To walk with God according to their light,
To be as good as he would have them bee,
To serve and worship him with all their might. . . .
Are these the fold whom from the brittish Iles
Through the stern billows of the watry main,
I safely led so many thousand miles,
As if their journey had been through a plain? . . .
Are these the folk to whom I milked out
And sweetnes stream'd from consolations brest; . . .
With whom I made a Covenant of peace,
And unto whom I did most firmly plight
My faithfulness . . . ?
Ah dear New England! dearest land to me;
Which unto God hast hitherto been dear,
And mayst be still more dear than formerlie,
If to his voice thou wilt incline thine ear.°

The second poem is far from being so anxious or so prosy. Under the title of "The Ebb and Flow," Edward Taylor, who was also a second-generation clergyman in Massachusetts, still conveys the confidence and the elevation of mind which Puritan belief could sustain:

When first thou on me Lord wroughtst thy Sweet Print,
My heart was made thy tinder box.
My 'ffections were thy tinder in't:
Where fell thy Sparkes by drops.
Those holy Sparks of Heavenly Fire that came
Did ever catch and often out would flame.

But now my Heart is made thy Censar trim,
Full of thy golden Altars fire,
To offer up Sweet Incense in
Unto thyselfe intire:
I find my tinder scarce thy Sparks can feel
That drop out from thy Holy flint and Steel.
Hence doubts out bud for feare thy fire in mee
'S a mocking Ignis Fatuus,
Or lest thine Altars fires out bee
It's hid in ashes thus.
Yet when the bellows of thy Spirit blow
Away mine ashes, then thy fire doth glow.°

4 *Church and State in*
Early New England

IN the Elizabethan years, when they demanded simply that Anglican worship be made more fully Protestant in style, the Puritans had thought that Parliament should make those changes by statute. Their readiness to use the legislature as the means to reform the church placed them in the position known to the history of theory as Erastianism, after the Swiss Protestant theologian Erastus, who attributed to government considerable authority over matters quite strictly religious. This position involved a hard question for the man of the Reformation: What human authority does have the right to shape the Church of Christ in this world? English presbyterians and congregationalists alike wanted the Church of England, once reformed, to become more supervisory of government, and less controlled by it, than they charged the Elizabethan establishment with being. Yet in the nature of the case, Puritans of all varieties except Separatists had to be in some degree Erastian, whether they liked the full implications of that doctrine or not. Just as the Lutheran and Reformed churches on the continent had to come to terms with the monarchical politics of their countries, so the English Puritans had no choice but state action in order to achieve their institutional goals. Government had to have divinity about it, to do the work they wanted done.

No departure, then, from the ancient tradition of Christianity, as a religious institution interwoven with the political institutions of the West, was required when the group of Puritans which most concerns us was suddenly elevated to possession and power in the New World. The charter which Charles I granted the Massachusetts Bay Company in 1629 assigned it a domain larger than the shires of southeastern England, where the Puritans were prominent at home. Although the king's grant allowed them only such limited powers of self-government as he gave to all commercial companies, they were nevertheless placed in a strong position, as the London Company for Virginia had been. The familiar story of the political aggressiveness of the Massachusetts Bay Colony does not require another retelling; the nub of the matter, for us, is that because the colony extended the powers of the company into full self-government—with a legislature, a magistracy, a militia system, taxation, and all the basic operations of sovereignty—congregationalist Puritans were able, in America as never in England, to translate from theory into practice the church-and-state relationship preferred by their own theologians.

One part of what the federal theology contemplated came quickly alive when the Puritans arrived in New England. This was the church covenant. While nonseparating congregationalists remained at home, still members of their Church of England parishes, the most they could do was recognize about themselves their common belief and hope; where bishops ruled they could not create their own congregation, decide on the doctrinal terms of admission, and elect their own officers. All these things they felt obliged to do, once they reached the New

World. Where the other covenants they believed in had the quality of being immaterial—the national covenant being their phrase for God's favor to the people He chose, and the covenant of grace being actually not of this world—the church covenant was a thing realized in paper and ink. "Natural covenantry and confederation of the saints in the partnership of the faith according to the Gospel is that which gives constitution and being to a visible Church," summarized Thomas Hooker.

The process took time and thought. Quite as in the history of each New England colony there appeared a ministerial leader who equaled or more than equaled the governor—John Cotton in Massachusetts, Thomas Hooker in Connecticut, Roger Williams in Rhode Island, John Davenport in New Haven, John Wheelwright in New Hampshire—so in the settlement of townships there were minister founders who matched the laymen leaders in the work of settling the frontier. It was around those men that the new congregations and new towns were first conceived. Immigrants would gather in small groups. Sometimes they did so because they came from the same place in England; sometimes because in mutual admiration for a leader in faith they discovered that they would like to have their future together. (The decision was often made during a waiting period, after debarking in Boston.) No specific size was required of a new congregation, but seven men—after the seven pillars of Proverbs, Chapter 9: "Wisdom hath builded her house, she hath hewn out her seven pillars"—became traditional as the right number to sponsor a church. Discussion and confession were required to satisfy each and all that they were a true "confederation of the saints"; this meant that, as best they could judge, signers of the new church covenant would be also souls covenanted in God's grace. When they felt sufficiently assured to do so, they put down their covenant in writing. It could be shorter than a night letter, Ola E. Winslow observes, citing the Salem covenant: "Wee Covenant with the Lord, and one with another and doe bynd ourselves in the presence of God to walke together in all his waies, according as he is pleased to reveal himself unto us in his Blessed word of truth." It could also be long, with fine points of theology included. The Dorchester one concluded with a commitment of each to all: "And lastly we do hereby covenant and promise to further to our utmost power, the best spirituall good of each other . . . by mutuall Instruction, reprehension, exhortacion, consolacion, and spirituall watchfulness over one another."°

Once a congregation was covenanted it was ready for its mission. In the early years this usually meant locating and assuming spiritual leadership in an outlying settlement; later, as the towns grew, it often meant simply increasing by one more meeting for worship the life of the place of origin. Those who signed the covenant were members; the members elected the elders of the congregation. There were usually two teaching elders, or professional ministers: a pastor, whose duties were consultative and administrative, and a "teacher," who did most of the preaching of sermons. These two "administered the seals" with equal and shared authority; this meant the giving of the two sacraments, baptism and the Lord's Supper, which Puritan belief retained from the traditional seven. During the first generation in New England, the ministers were often ordained priests of the Church of England; those of later generations seldom were. Federal theology made that authorization irrelevant. In the Puritan way of thinking, a clergyman's authority was given opportunity to operate by the congregation which called him; God Himself gave the authority. Though the teaching elders by no means ran the congregations unassisted and never escaped the ultimate capacity of the members of the covenant to terminate their services, they nevertheless had great prestige. They began as being specially chosen, both by God and by the godly; they were educated men where learning was honored. Even in later times, after the mystery of their calling had somewhat waned, they were given such deference as has seldom occurred to a profession in America.

In the custodial work of the congregation the lay elders, known as "ruling elders," in common with the teaching elders had a great deal of work to do. After confession had persuaded them—public confession for men; private confession, which could be written, for women—that the candidate deeply believed in the covenant and had truly received divine grace, they admitted new members to the church. They visited the ill and the backsliders; they admonished any whom they found to be wayward; they passed judgment on breaches of behavior. Their ultimate sanction was excommunication from the church. Far beyond matters which pertained to the churches directly, such as orthodoxy and attendance at worship, the elders in their "holy watching" investigated cases of sexual irregularities among their people, fornication as well as adultery, and other offenses which we now think of as quite secular, such as drunkenness, arson, fraud, and larceny. Thus members of the congregations, albeit by their own decision and through leaders of their own selection, were subject to double scrutiny. Because their misdemeanors were often both sins and crimes, they were subject at once to ecclesiastical and to civil authority. Practically speaking this meant that they could be judged twice by the elite of their communities.°

Not earlier than the Mormon community shall we again discover in a large region so complete an application of doctrine to public life as the early New England application of the church-covenant idea. Commitment to the principle that the chosen of God can be fairly certainly identified on earth makes comprehensible the much-discussed franchise law of Massachusetts, enacted in 1631, when the Bay Colony was only one year old. That law awarded and limited the vote, in choosing representatives for the legislature, to the members of the congregations. This was an unusual limitation; but the unusualness lay in the religious standard of exclusion, not the numbers of possible voters excluded. In the latter respect the townships of Massachusetts were probably less narrow than the town corporations of England, where the franchise was limited to small, local oligarchies. Nor does the law of 1631 set Massachusetts apart from Connecticut and New Hampshire, though these colonies passed no similar statute. Throughout all New England the domination of township affairs by the congregations amounted to an informal control of the franchise: if church members did not approve of a resident they could prevent his being elected freeman of the town and in that way exclude him from voting in colony elections. John Davenport, the strict minister of New Haven, former minister of an influential parish in London, summed up the relationship of congregational meeting and town meeting precisely: "In regular actings of the creatures, God is the first Agent; there are not two several and distinct meetings, one of God, another of the People; but, in one and the same action, God, by the People's suffrages, makes such an one Governor, or Magistrate, and not another."

Thus, having crossed the Atlantic and having changed position from political minority in a great nation to political dominance in infant colonies, these Puritans, so recently Erastian in theory, established a system of their own. Clearly they were practising Erastians no longer. Yet, as one cannot say of them that "state over church" was their working principle, one cannot say either that "church over state" was. Teaching elders did not assume political office; they preached and advised on public matters but did not assume direct civil responsibilities. There was no substitute, in the little capitals, for the Anglican hierarchy. Clergymen did not sit in the council, as bishops did in the House of Lords; and (although modern historical literature is full of reference to the "established church") there was no central church administration or authority which fits the words "church establishment." The colony governments did support the congregations with tax provision, with the enforcement of laws against immorality and blasphemy, and with honor and deference to ministers. The congregations supported the government: local government, with moral oversight of the community; colony government, by designating the voters, by election sermons, and by consultation with the ministers.

In the present writer's judgment the one classifying word which before 1680 accurately fits the New England colony systems, and Massachusetts particularly, is *theocracy*, once often used and as often protested. By definition, theocracy means either rule under God or rule by God. In this principle the Puritans believed. In modern usage the word usually connotes rule by a priesthood—the absolute power in one or a few individuals, as in the history of the papal states and, in America, of the Mormons. The Puritans did not have such autocracy. Yet when their own understanding of church membership is taken at face value, the essential meaning of theocracy does apply. For where the government was not set over the church or church over government but "visible Saints" were made the source of authority in both church and government, the ideal of rule by God was met as fully as it can be.°

5   The Old Order Transvalued

FROM almost all points of view common in the twentieth century, the Puritan theocracy seems to have been too improbable—too impractical, too exclusive and undemocratic and intolerant, too sharp a break from home and home tradition—to be understood very sympathetically. According to Alan Simpson, even the Harvard experts have distorted it in their analyses: they have portrayed its intellectual achievements in such a way as to obscure its emotional essence. More than anything else the history of transatlantic Puritanism is the history of the main event in a century-long religious renewal in England, this scholar goes on, making a point from which few would differ. The revival rose with the early Reformation in England and achieved late power in the Quaker movement after 1660; the Puritans of the early seventeenth century represent the crest of the wave.

Such a view of the matter returns us to the position that Puritanism belongs by origin and main development to the Old World rather than the New. Said the Reverend Francis Higginson, soon to be one of the authors of the Salem church covenant, just before he departed from England: "We will not say, as the Separatists were wont to say at their leaving of England, 'Farewel, Babylon!' . . . but . . . 'farewel the Church of God in England!'" The most solid of all Puritan colonial leaders, Governor Winthrop, and his associates said likewise that they had the honor "to call the *Church* of *England*, from which we rise, our deare Mother. . . . We leave it not therefore, as loathing that Milk with which we were nourished there but, blessing God for the Parentage and Education as Members of the same Body, shall always rejoice in her good."

Looking backward from such expressions of loyalty, one remembers the continuities with the old order, in Puritanism. The "deare Mother" church from which the colonizing Puritans moved away, all the while denying separation, was built on an historical system of hierarchy, culminating in the office of bishop. The congregations also were hierarchical; their system was based not on tradition but on salvation, and on the gift of individuals for acting and speaking according to God's mercy. The Church of England had adopted the vernacular. The congregations were born in discussion and open confession; their worship developed the plain style. The Church of England organized Christianity on a basis of nationality. The Puritans believed in a national covenant; their polity went so far as to assign to the local unit for worship the authority to determine for its members what is right Christian doctrine.

Looking forward in time, on the other hand, toward later America instead of earlier England, one senses in the Puritan work in early New England a change in values which was evidently a product of conversion. Though the first generation in America is too early to speak of democracy, admission to the church covenants and participation in the governments which were built on them depended not on property or birth but on Christian experience which happened unpredictably to men, in any station of life. Though Transcendentalism with its idea of the divinity of human individuals lay two centuries ahead in New England history, and a seventeenth-century Puritan would have been dismayed if he had foreseen it, he yet believed that Divinity entered the souls of men like himself. He believed, moreover, that the whole meaning of life depended on that experience. So persuaded, he could make the wonderful leap to the hope that he himself had received grace and belonged in the covenants.

Part Two

THE SHAPING OF AMERICAN CHRISTIANITY

1630-1760

CHAPTER IV

Orthodoxy and Freedom in Early New England

*There goes many a ship to sea, with many hundred
souls in one ship, whose weal or woe is common,
and is a true picture of a commonwealth, or a human
combination or society. It hath fallen out sometimes
that both papists and protestants, Jews and Turks, may
be embarked in one ship; upon which supposal I affirm,
that all the liberty of conscience ever I pleaded for,
turns upon these two hinges—that none of the papists,
protestants, Jews, or Turks, be forced to come to the
ship's prayers or worship, nor compelled from their
own particular prayers or worship, if they practice any.
I further add, that I never denied, that notwithstanding this liberty, the commander of this ship ought to
command the ship's course, yea, and also command that
justice, peace and sobriety, be kept and practiced, both
among the seamen and all the passengers.*

*Roger Williams to the town of
Providence, 1655*

1 *The Theocracy: From Settlement to Commonwealth*

T HE problem of Part Two of this book is to discover how Christian thinkers in the colonies came to terms with their new situation. We need to know what the long process of settling in America meant to them, as to fresh obligations and ideas. We need know what attitudes governed, as population and settlement growth brought the churches to confront one another. Did the differences of conviction which originally divided Puritans from Anglicans, Separatists from nonseparatists, and so on increase or decrease in effect as churches and sects multiplied? At any time during the colonial period, do we discover sufficient community of faith to speak of there being an "American Christianity"? Or was this identity delayed until after the republic was born?

The Puritans of Massachusetts seem to have been predestined (though not in a Calvinist way) to make heavy intellectual going of any rearrangement of their religious ideas or institutions, once the theocracy was launched. For them there could be no such anonymity and ease in that process as benefited the early-colonial Anglicans. For Virginia tobacco planters the Americanization of the Church of England was largely a matter of waiting out what seemed to be the excesses, first, of Puritan Parliament and commonwealth in England and, later, of royalist Governor Berkeley at Jamestown. Then almost automatically, with no such argument as among the congregationalists, their church adapted to local needs. The situation of the New Englanders contrasts too with that of the non-English settlers, as they appeared in due course, mostly in the Middle Colonies. German Lutheran and Reformed, French Huguenots, and Scots-derived Presbyterians would all gather in their own local communities. But none ever had the opportunity and the burden, like the Puritans, of creating and dominating entire colonies. Anything resembling an immigrant-controlled New Rhineland, or a Reformed New France, or a New Scotland, analogous to New England, remained outside the area of the politically possible. Thus, once the great questions of the Reformation came up for discussion—concerning what beliefs ought to be tolerated and what excluded—there was only one American region where decisions had to be made by elected representatives and enforced by an elected governor and council.

Not surprisingly the first half-dozen years proved to be the most troublesome in those respects. When Puritans arrived in the port of Boston, the excitement of making landfall was always compounded by inquiries not to be avoided in a congregationalist community: "What congregation shall I join?" and "Where will it take me to live?" If the immigrant was a minister, he most particularly had to search his soul and gauge his opportunities: "Into what course shall I lead my people?" Conservative and tough-minded Puritans, such as those who soon founded the settlements of the Hartford and the New Haven areas, made their departures from Boston not in disagreement with the leaders of the theocracy but in determination to do things in their own way nonetheless. An economic impulse to deploy—north to Exeter or Dover or Portsmouth in New Hampshire for some, west into the fertile Connecticut valley for others, into the crescent of towns around Boston for most—matched the centrifugalism of church polity. Meanwhile during the 1630s two desperate external situations added to the pressures and tensions. In England Sir Ferdinando Gorges was petitioning the courts that the Massachusetts Bay Company had overstepped its charter (as indeed it had done). If it were not that months and years were required for the judicial processes, and that Gorges's litigation was interrupted by the preliminaries of revolution in England, the Massachusetts Bay enterprise would have lost its legal existence in 1638. Meanwhile in the New World, the threat of massacre by Indians was made terribly real, by war with the Pequots during 1636 and 1637.

As is well remembered by the names of Roger Williams and Anne Hutchinson, the middle 1630s, when all this hazard and tension piled up, was the time also of the boldest assertions of belief in congregational autonomy and in individual religious freedom which were ever to be made in New England history. We shall return to those two heroes in the next section. But the first problem is orthodoxy; the main thing about early Massachusetts is the discipline the new theocracy was able to exercise. Their many friends notwithstanding, Williams and Mrs. Hutchinson were thrown out of the colony; Mrs. Hutchinson's associates in protest were deprived of their church appointments, and some of them went to New Hampshire. Although Harvard College would have been founded soon in any case, in a short-run sense its being established in 1636, with its dedication to provide for the future an educated, loyal clergy, is attributable to the Hutchinson heresy. In retrospect of the critical years, from 1634 to 1637, John Cotton stated the theocracy's tion; . . . their business was to settle, and (as much as in them lay) to position authentically: "The design of our first Planters was not Tolera- secure Religion to Posterity, according to that way which they believed was of God."

After 1638, as King Charles lost out to Parliament under presbyterian Puritan dominance, and again a decade later, when Cromwell took power, Massachusetts's fears that the mother country might interfere with its congregationalist ways were greatly allayed. The clearest test of this occurred in 1645, when a mixed company of Massachusetts settlers, not covenanted in the congregations but not friendless either, demanded political rights. The situation was the reverse of that during the antinomian heresy; now, men more conservative than the theocrats took the initiative. Over the names of Dr. Robert Child and five other signers who were men of substance there was presented to the Great and General Court of Massachusetts (which had just become a bicameral legislature) a "Remonstrance and humble petition" which purported to represent the grievances of thousands of people in the colony. Massachusetts law debarred "freeborne, quiett and peaceable men, righteous in their dealings," from voting and holding office, the Remonstrance said, even though they attended church services. It demanded that "liberty" be granted "to members of the Church of England . . . to be taken into your congregations . . . or otherwise . . . to settle themselves here in a church way, according to the best reformations of England and Scotland."

The remonstrants had certain strengths. Dr. Child is known to have been presbyterian in conviction and to have been in touch with people in England, and the Church of England mentioned in the Remonstrance signifies the church as it had been presbyterianized by recent act of Parliament. Moreover, there was at least one distinguished signer, Samuel Maverick, who held to traditional, episcopalian Anglicanism. Thus, rather than simply two wings of historic Puritanism in conflict in Massachusetts, the presbyterian one and the congregational one, we see the Massachusetts theocracy challenged by presbyterians and some element, probably small, of old Anglicans and maybe others. When the remonstrants proposed that persons who had not signed the congregational covenants be admitted to church membership and share the sacraments and the vote, they showed not only that they were far from honoring covenant theology in the New England way but also that they were ready to have a degree of religious toleration—at very least a balance and sharing of church power between two forms of Puritanism—in colony practice. But the strategy of the Remonstrance was to announce a position which might win allies in England; the remonstrants did not expect to change the minds of the congregationalist theocrats. Unfortunately for them, their timing was off. The presbyterian Long Parliament had about run its course; no pressure on their side came from England to Massachusetts. The colony legislature rejected the Remonstrance as flatly and as successfully as it had banished Roger Williams and Anne Hutchinson when the colony was new. If the remonstrants were so godly, they would be admitted to church membership and to the general franchise, and if on the other hand they failed to prove godliness they were free to leave Massachusetts and settle elsewhere, they were told. Thanks again to Massachusetts's moving with (and only a little ahead of) the current of revolution in England, the theocracy was able to continue in its special way.°

Encouraged by the same conditions, in 1648 elders from the congregations of Massachusetts and Connecticut gathered in Cambridge to make a consolidated New England statement about church polity. The Remonstrance was still in their ears. Though they called their meeting a synod, only the name they chose resembled the usage of Scotland. Richard Mather and John Cotton, of the most inner circle of clergyman leaders, drew up a Platform of Church Discipline. They restated the old principle of nonseparation from the Church of England; and, to testify that they were "a remnant of the same nation" as England, they endorsed "for the substance thereof" the Calvinist-inspired Westminster Confession of Faith which Parliament had approved for the national church. Yet even as they did this they renewed their own loyalty to the principle of church membership limited to the "visible saints." They asserted for their synod no authority higher than that of voicing opinions commonly held, and they sent the Platform the round of the congregations for approval. The process required three years; but in the end the Cambridge Platform was ratified, in contemporary words, not because "a Synod hath said it, but because the Lord hath spoken it by his Spirit." The Cambridge Platform, then, was both a fresh confirmation of the covenant theology and an endorsement of the operating theocracy by the ministers, at the time when that system was rounding out its second decade.°

During the same year, 1648, lay authority in Massachusetts matched the consolidating work of clerical authority by codifying the colony's law. As early as 1636, the Reverend John Cotton had drafted a code, "Moses His Judicials"; the fact that the Hebraist theologian inserted a great deal of Old Testament law probably accounts for the failure of the colony legislature, which knew that its acts would be scrutinized at home, to enact it. But the idea of a codification which would blend Bible precedent and injunction with English law and Massachusetts statute had a lasting appeal in that colony. Only a couple of years later the Great and General Court invited Nathaniel Ward, a minister who had been trained as a lawyer before he was converted, to prepare a code. Ward believed, as Sir Edward Coke did, that true law is of God. "Morall laws, Royall Prerogatives, Popular Liberties, are not of Mans making or giving, but Gods: Man is but to measure them out by Gods Rule: which if mans wisdome cannot reach, Mans experience must mend: and these Essentialls, must not be Ephorized or Tribuned by one or a few Mens discretion, but lineally sanctioned by Supreame Councels."° Ward made a hundred proposals, and enough of them are of a character to tell us that the code he drew deserved its name, the "Body of Liberties." Although English law still permitted wife-beating, this code forbade it, unless a husband acted "in his own defence, upon her assalt." It forbade the granting of monopolies "but of new Inventions that are profitable to the Countrie, and that for a short time"; it cut back feudal dues on land, such as colonists under proprietary grants had to pay. "All our lands and heritages shall be free from all fines and licenses upon Alienations, and from all . . . Escheats, and forfeitures, upon the deaths of parents or Ancestors." Where English law at the time made about fifty crimes punishable by death, this code allowed only ten. More important than its specific inclusions and exclusions, the code put into law the idea that underlies all guarantees of liberty, namely, that sovereign power must be limited according to rule and principle if it is to be just.°

In the climactic year, 1648, the Great and General Court, by enacting *The Book of the General Lawes and Libertyes of Massachusetts*, enlarged and deepened the codified law. A little like the members of the Cambridge synod, who at once accepted and made reservations about the Westminster Confession, the Massachusetts legislators made preparatory studies in English law and incorporated much. They went as far back as Magna Carta and as close to their own times as *Coke on Littleton* and *Coke's Reports*. But while they enlarged the English factor in Massachusetts law, they continued to improve on tradition according to their own lights. They provided, on the opening page of their text, "That no mans life shall be taken away; no mans honour or good name shall be stayned; no mans person shall be arrested, restrained, banished, dismembred nor any wayes punished; . . . [no man shall be] indamaged under colour of Law or countenance of Authoritie, unles it be by vertue or equity of some expresse law of the Country warranting the same." This is one of several passages which voice firmly the idea of due process. The Bible factor is plain under the heading of "Capital Lawes." To be sure there were fifteen of those in the new code, and they include several forms of sexual irregularity; every capital crime was justified as such from Deuteronomy or from one of the nearby books of the Old Testament—Exodus, Leviticus, or Numbers. Though the code made a capital crime of blasphemy and incorporated a law against heresy, it specifically allowed private meetings for "edification in Religion" by any kind of Christians. And as for freedom to speak and to petition the courts, the guarantee was wide and handsome: "Everie man whether Inhabitant or Forreiner, Free or Not Free, shall have libertie to come to any public Court, Counsell, or Town-meeting, and either by Speech or Writing, to move any lawfull, seasonable or material question."°

Because, as Samuel Eliot Morison says, the *General Lawes and Libertyes* of 1648 brought together all the law there was in Massachusetts, and "not merely some of the law," the enactment of the code signified the legislative independence of the colony. That is, in 1648, a year before Cromwell's England did so, Massachusetts became, by acting like one, unchallenged, a commonwealth—a people's independent sovereignty. In 1652 the Great and General Court formally adopted that very name. (The state constitution of 1780 would readopt it; it remains in use today.) In ways which may be understood as both practical and symbolic, the colony acted accordingly. Coinage has traditionally been an act of political sovereignty; Massachusetts immediately issued the pine-tree shilling. In 1650 the legislature enacted a charter for Harvard. Somewhat cautiously the statute did not go so far as to speak of granting degrees; in English tradition a charter from the Crown was required for that privilege, and only the two universities had it. But Harvard College had been granting degrees for a decade, and it would always do so. To borrow again from Morison, who speaks this time as Harvard's official historian: "Venturing to confer degrees at all was perhaps the boldest thing that President Dunster and his Overseers did; it was almost a Declaration of Independence from King Charles."°

So indeed it was, but it was not an isolated act of academic courage. As we have just seen, in the years around 1650 the congregations of two colonies, represented by the Cambridge synod, declared *their* independence; simultaneously the theocratic corporate colony made itself a commonwealth. The courage, the independence, and the factor of organization turned up everywhere. But so also had the factors of bigotry and exclusiveness, which we can no longer avoid. This returns us to Roger Williams and Anne Hutchinson. For the first-generation climax of Massachusett's colonial independence was equaled by the similarly uncompromising personal independence of the two individuals whom the colony had tried its hardest to quiet and then suppress.

2   *Radical Piety and the Impulse to Freedom*

As it is for twentieth-century historians, it was easy for seventeenth-century contemporaries to make the founders of New England sound like a much more consolidated people than they actually were. "I dare take upon me to be the Herauld of *New England*," wrote Nathaniel Ward, the minister and lawyer, who for present-day exactitude should have said "of Massachusetts" instead, "so farre, as to proclaime to the world, in the name of our Colony, that all Familists, Antinomians, Anabaptists, and other Enthusiasts, shall have free Liberty to keep away from us, and such as will come to be gone as fast as they can, the sooner the better." He warned Familists away, as though Massachusetts were not friendly to family worship and did not have a form of birthright membership in the churches; he condemned Antinomians as though his own people did not place high value on an individual's openness to God; and he named Anabaptists as though adult baptism were foreign to Puritan practice. We understand Puritanism better if we recognize that these and other radical impulses of the Reformation were contained but were not developed within that system. By the same token, we understand better the "Herauld" and all other Puritan conservatives if we read their policy as meaning not that Massachusetts was solidly of a mind against radicals, as they themselves were, but that it had a divided mind and might swing into the Protestant left if they did not put on the brakes.

The father of Rhode Island, who as a minister not yet thirty was the first to disturb the seniors of the Bay Colony, was the son of a merchant tailor of Smithfield, a part of London. In every respect of his origins—social class, education, and personal inclination—he well represents Puritan norms. Newgate prison was in Smithfield, with a bell which tolled once a month for those about to be executed; and Newgate was the place where the unitarian heretic, Legate, was burned, when Roger was about eight years old. We may suppose that the event made an impression on the future advocate of toleration. There were also happier circumstances. Londoners who were active in colonization, Captain John Smith among them, often lived in Newgate or came there to worship in St. Sepulchre's parish church. Before he went up from Charterhouse School to Cambridge, Roger was employed by Sir Edward Coke as a keeper of notes on court hearings; Sir Edward sometimes called him "son." This personal connection, like a much later one with John Milton, seems appropriate, but it is hard to evaluate in William's personal development. When he went to the university in 1624, he attended Pembroke and not Emmanuel College; the mark of the dissenter seems not to have been on him so far. We know that in 1627 at Cambridge he signed the test oaths and the Thirty-nine Articles: this was a step a nonseparating congregationalist of the Cambridge sort could take, as being a true Anglican still; but a Separatist would have refused.

Yet two years later Williams as an ordained Anglican clergyman became chaplain in a Puritan household. There he lived and served through the Petition of Right crisis, which was dominated by his old employer, Coke; and he moved in the same circle as contained John Cotton, John Eliot, and the young Oliver Cromwell. Though not among the very earliest to emigrate, he reached the American Boston in 1631; there he was offered at once the most prominent ministry to which he would ever be called. But to the astonishment of many— perhaps even including himself, for we have no previous indication that he had decided that he was a Separatist—he responded openly that he "durst not officiate to an unseparated people." Yet before further crisis could develop, the congregation at Salem invited him to be its teacher; and Roger Williams became an established clergyman and voter in the colony the prevailing, nonseparating ecclesiastical polity of which he had already begun to disbelieve.

Salem had been settled under Governor Endicott a couple of years earlier than Boston: it retained always a certain distinctiveness. Plymouth too might have supplied him a harbor, and he did accept an invitation to visit and preach; yet there he was judged to be "godly and zealous . . . but very unsettled in judgmente," and the possibility of his staying was closed. In Salem he immediately throve: his congregation favored him, he traded with the Indians, and he became the owner of land. He also renewed the flow of critical ideas with which he had begun his American career. First of all he made himself what Ola E. Winslow, as his biographer, calls the earliest opponent in English America of the white man's imperialism. He denied that Massachusetts could rightfully create property in land, superseding the Indians; and in 1633 he pushed that scruple to the point of protesting to King Charles himself "the Evill of that part of the *Patent* which respects the donation of land." If in our own anticolonial century we can see prophetic rightness in Roger Williams's position, we may recall on the side of king and colony that the rights they asserted in land drew on an ancient tradition. From before the Crusades, Christians had held that the earth belongs to believers in the true God, the Maker of earth, and not to unbelievers.

Simultaneously with denying land titles, Roger Williams returned to the church-state problem. To his recent proposition that the congregations in the colony should break from the Church of England, he added the protest that the colony government as allied with the churches—the Massachusetts theocracy—should cut back the scope of its power. Acknowledging that true to the Bible the colony should punish violations of the second table of the Decalogue—the thou-shalt-not commandments against sins committed by man against man: killing, stealing, false witness, and adultery—Williams denied that it had a right to enforce the first table: the injunctions which concern the honor and worship of God. At this point the great visionary who had yet to mature in Roger Williams begins to appear. If the limitation on government he wanted had been approved by the Bay Colony, notes Miss Winslow, "the bulk of town books and sessions records would have shrunk. . . . Had Roger Williams' view prevailed, the magisterial figure of colonial times would have lost much of its terror, and the Monday morning victims for the whipping post, the stocks and the cage would have dwindled to a minority. . . . The civil magistrates were God's own deputies and to have this upstart cutting the very ground from under their feet was monstrous. Those of Boston became thoroughly aroused."

Effective action to curb the young minister lay with the Great and General Court if with anyone; the other ministers could only debate. His own congregation at Salem could do no more than discharge him, and that it now did. Yet the legislature began gingerly: it examined him, then temporized, and finally drew all the ministers into council, in October 1635. Their wisest and most experienced leaders, John Cotton and Thomas Hooker, who had not yet gone on to Connecticut, tried to persuade him to change his mind. But the end of the matter may be called predetermined: Roger Williams would not be changed. The court ruled that, because he had "broached and divulged dyvers new and dangerous opinions," he must depart from the colony.

The "passionate precipitate" young minister feared that he would be deported to England. So, with a new baby named Freeborn, his little family fled secretly to a winter refuge in the Plymouth jurisdiction; when spring came they went on, according to previous planning with sympathizers, to the head of Narragansett Bay, where he gave the town he founded the lovely name it still bears. Two years later Anne Hutchinson's arrival started the multiplication of heterodoxy around the bay. According to Cotton Mather the place filled up rapidly with all kinds of unorthodox people: "Antinomians, Anabaptists, Sabbatarians, Arminians, Socinians, Quakers, Ranters, everything in the world but Roman Catholics and true believers." The list would lengthen with the years, especially to include Anglicans, Congregationalists, Presbyterians, and Jews.

Thus on an extraordinary foundation of religious variety was built the colony of Rhode Island, and to Providence we may turn for the first application of the principle of toleration in a New England community. Two covenants were drawn up: a covenant of "towne fellow-ship," a secular, political covenant like the Mayflower Compact; and a covenant for the congregation. Under the first, the town governed itself with great liberality: the heads of families voted (a small number, eight or so, at first); land, which was first acquired from the Indians by friendly purchase, was distributed with approximate equality; and the town officers, leaving the first table of the Decalogue to individual conscience, were assigned no burden of enforcing attendance at worship.° About church covenants in general, Roger Williams said frankly that they are made by man and are as subject to rewriting as is any other contract. In this he was consistent with the Puritan idea that covenants are what God expects of His people. "The *Church* or *company* of *worshippers* (whether true or false)," he said, "is like unto a Body or Colledge of *Physitians* in a Citie; like unto a *Corporation, Society,* or *Company* of *East-Indie* or *Turkie-Merchants,* or any other *Societie* or *Company* in *London;* which Companies may hold their *Courts,* keep their *Records,* hold *disputations;* and in matters concerning their *Societie,* may dissent, divide, break into *Schismes* and *Factions,* sue and implead each other at the *Law,* yea wholly breake up and dissolve into pieces and nothing."° The positive satisfaction Roger Williams voiced in disputations, schisms, and factions is the first instance we find in American thought of the idea that religious variety is good and not simply a burden to be tolerated. That members of a church might discover God among differences and conflicts of idea about Him, in the way that physicians and merchants discover the truths that concern them, was as unusual a suggestion in Roger Williams's time as any idea he ever put forward.

The year 1644, when he was obliged to go to London to secure a land grant for Rhode Island, was the time when Roger Williams thought through to his famous conclusions the obligations of religious diversity. As a young man in Massachusetts he had brashly denied the right of his seniors to enforce orthodoxy; he had uttered many defiances. Now past forty and in the midst of the revolution in England, where the decision was being taken whether Rhode Island should be assured independence or be left open to Massachusetts to take over, he had reached a point where defiance would not serve. Fortunately for Rhode Island he was able to represent practice and ideal there in such a way that, though his principles were too advanced to win him political support, they did not prevent him from succeeding. He took back to Providence the grant he wanted.

Much of his pamphlet, *The Bloudy Tenent of Persecution, for cause of Conscience, discovered in a Conference between Truth and Peace,* is (as the title suggests) a dialogue between allegorical speakers. Although a reader of today is likely to be put off by its Puritan-sermon style and its many citations of the Bible, if he persists he will discover that the tension between Peace, as she poses the problems, and Truth, as she answers them, has a modern feeling. It closely resembles the tension Mahatma Gandhi voiced, between *satya* (truth) and *ahimsa* (nonviolence). In Williams's own words, most of them spoken by Truth:

> God requireth not an *uniformity of Religion* to be *inacted* and *inforced* in any *civill state*; which inforced *uniformity* (sooner or later) is the greatest occasion of *civill Warre, ravishing* of *conscience*, persecution of *Christ Jesus* in his servants, and of the *hypocrisie* and *destruction* of *millions* of *souls*. . . . In vaine have *English Parliaments* permitted *English Bibles* in the poorest *English* houses, and the simplest man or woman to search the Scriptures, if yet against their soules persuasion from the Scriptures, they should be forced (as if they lived in *Spaine* or *Rome* itselfe without the sight of a *Bible*) to beleeve as the Church beleeves. . . . *Civill weapons* are most improper and unfitting in matters of the *Spiritual state* and *kingdome*, though in the *Civill State* most proper and suitable. . . . *Love* worketh no ill to his neighbor, therefore *love* is the fulfilling of the Law. . . . There is a *Civill sword*, called the Sword of *Civill justice*, which being of a *materiall civil nature* for the defense of *Persons, Estates, Families, Liberties of a City*. . . . It . . . cannot extend to *Spirituall* and *Soul-causes*, Spirituall and Soule *punishment*, which belongs to that *Spiritual Sword* with two edges, the *soul-piercing* (in *soule-saving* or *soule-killing*) the Word of God.°

Interpreters have urged recently, and with reason, that Roger Williams was a supremely pious man in an age of piety and that he is to be understood in that way, as a passionate Bible-inspired speaker for liberty of conscience and not as an anticipator of the philosophers of the eighteenth century. The difference of mentality is great, the difference between the Reformation and the Enlightenment; but the difference of policy is small. Freedom springs from many sources. Roger Williams believed, practised, and urged that Christianity, which seeks to rule by love, and political sovereignty, the essence of which is force, are deeply different. He loved the "Render unto Caesar" doctrine. By keeping Caesar apart from God in the minds of their troubled servants, the founder of Rhode Island insisted, both will be better served, and so will be truth and peace.

Anne Hutchinson appeared later and more briefly than Roger Williams on the stage of Massachusetts affairs, but she raised an issue closer to the heart of Christian belief. She began as deeply saturated in the Puritan ferment as a woman, to whom the schools and universities of England had of course been closed, could very well be. The daughter of a Church of England clergyman who had Puritan inclinations and the wife of a Lincolnshire Puritan of means, Mrs. Hutchinson arrived in Boston in 1634 with solid connections. She knew a great deal about

John Cotton: she had admired his preaching in his home parish of St. Botolph, and her son had crossed the Atlantic with him months before she and her husband came. It may or may not have been his sermons in England which persuaded her not to become a Separatist as she thought of doing; certainly his stress on the doctrine of salvation through grace influenced and encouraged her own theological bent. She was affected also by her brother-in-law John Wheelwright, the Cambridge-trained future clergyman-pioneer of New Hampshire, who took the congregation at Mount Wollaston (the later Quincy of Adams-family fame) not long after she herself had arrived in the New World.

Mrs. Hutchinson had wit and much knowledge of the Bible and theology. As, also, a generous, energetic friend and counselor of other women, as midwife and nurse, she became in a short time a beloved person in the Boston community. The trouble was that she entertained unusual "women's meetings" in her home, which was situated diagonally across the street from Governor Winthrop's. Up to eighty women gathered regularly to hear her review the sermon of the preceding Sunday. Here the Puritan system of having two ministers—in the Boston congregation, John Wilson as pastor and John Cotton as teacher —showed its weakness. Instead of simple reporting, Mrs. Hutchinson's teaching became commentary and criticism. Consistently, according to common report, she spoke adversely of Wilson, who had been converted by the theologian William Ames and who had had legal as well as ministerial training, and she spoke favorably of Cotton, her friend, who was the older and more eminent man. For the first time in New England history a women's gathering became competitive with the men of the community in their habitual control of affairs.

Mrs. Hutchinson caused a fad and a furor by preaching the covenant of grace. The problem is: how could there have been reason for excitement in a lay discussion of the central idea in the covenant system of thought? It is not enough to say that "antinomian" was a fear word and that when it was attached to Mrs. Hutchinson the effect was much like an accusation of witchcraft. Martin Luther had used the word to indicate those who believed, as he himself did, that when divine grace brings salvation to an individual that person is released from—has no need for—any external regulation of his life. *Anti*, against; *nomos*, law: the antinomian believed that when the Holy Spirit truly entered and governed a soul no church law or regulation had bearing. The doctrine gives personal meaning to the covenant of grace. Besides Mrs. Hutchinson's clergymen friends, important laymen, including William Coddington, an assistant (councilor) of the colony and friend of Governor Winthrop, approved of that line of thought. But the potential of the doctrine for religious individualism is plain; and, in the view of people who see danger in intuition and who cherish religious authority, whether in the form of sacraments, or clerical supervision, or theocracy, antinomianism has ever carried a threat of subversion.

From the two years or so of her teaching the women of Boston, we have no firsthand record of what Mrs. Hutchinson actually said. The testimony we have comes from her opponents; from them we can be sure that this earliest woman-independent in religion had made no such pretensions of partnership with God as in later times Mother Ann Lee, the Shaker, would do, or Mary Baker Eddy, who would claim many divine revelations. We may pick, from the long list of preachments alleged to prove Mrs. Hutchinson's error, the following three, as being as extreme as any.

22. There is no such thing as inherent righteousness.
23. We are not bound to the law, no not as a rule of life.
24. We are dead to all acts in spirituall things, and are onely acted on by Christ.

Stated out of context they do not seem very upsetting, and possibly they would not have been so had they never been applied to particular persons. But when John Wheelwright, whose views were known to sympathize with those of his sister-in-law, voiced publicly the opinion that many of the Massachusetts leaders were not truly covenanted in grace, the argument changed from abstract to personal and political, and the fat was in the fire. In the year of the Pequot War, 1637, this was more than the orthodox could bear. John Wheelwright was banished; others not driven from the colony were driven from office.

Mrs. Hutchinson was brought to trial late in the crisis year. There had just been held a synod, in which the errors of the day had been discussed and defined by the ministers. An election had occurred also: it returned John Winthrop—after the short interval during which the young Henry Vane had held office—to the governorship of the colony. Then the governor, the assistants, and the representatives of the townships convened together, the Great and General Court. As when Roger Williams was tried, the ministers appeared; but they were no more than witnesses, for this was a civil matter. Governor Winthrop, though he was characteristically a moderate and had had experience as a magistrate in England, acted, as his supreme office allowed, in mixed and autocratic capacity as prosecutor and judge.

The early part of the trial has the sound of a very deliberate, very controlled, family quarrel. After a few preliminaries, during which the court politely asked the defendant to be seated, she was charged with having broken the fifth commandment. As was the habit of mind of the time, Mrs. Hutchinson acknowledged the applicability of that commandment to an individual's relations with the fathers of the state. But she parried the point by inquiring, "May I not entertain them that fear the Lord because my parents will not give me leave?" She produced Bible passages to justify an older woman teaching the younger; and, when the court at great length inquired whether her meetings had been public, or private as she insisted, and whether or not she had been disrespectful of the clergy, she defended herself with effect. The governor went beyond his theological depth in examining her. When he ruled that the women's meetings must stop, she acquiesced, as she had no choice but to do. Up to a late and critical point in the trial, there seems to have been every likelihood that she would be let off with an admonition and would be the moral victor.

Then a breaking point did come. At a stage of her responses which to a twentieth-century reader has the sound of delayed hysteria, Mrs. Hutchinson began to speak at length. She told of intense experiences before she left England, in the course of which God had put in her mind passages of Scripture which directed and foretold her history, especially the sixth chapter of Daniel. In the words of the accused: "This Scripture is fulfilled this day and therefore I desire you . . . to look and consider what you do." The court was electrified. Immediately the members saw that the once-guarded defendant was about to confess special revelation, to them a great heresy. She gratified them: she spoke of Abraham, a man of God who, offering to sacrifice his son, had broken a commandment. But Abraham had done so, the court observed, under "an immediate voice" from God. "So to me"—Mrs. Hutchinson gave way—"by an immediate revelation. . . . By the voice of his own spirit to my soul." Having said the crucial thing, she continued: "You have power over my body but the Lord Jesus hath power over my body and soul, and assure yourselves thus much, you do as much as in you lies to put the Lord Jesus Christ from you, and if you go on in this course you begin you will bring a curse upon you and your posterity, and the mouth of the Lord hath spoken it. . . . I look that the Lord should deliver me by his providence."

Then was Mrs. Hutchinson banished from the Massachusetts Bay Colony, not for deeds proven against her in court, and not for previous words, but for having confessed an overruling communication from God. More tragic than the cases of the clergymen, Roger Williams and John Wheelwright, who as exiles became leaders and founders elsewhere, Mrs. Hutchinson became a wanderer for the seven years remaining to her. (After a period in Rhode Island she moved to Long Island Sound, where she was killed in an Indian massacre.) Not until the Transcendentalists of Concord, a round two centuries later, would New England again produce religious individualism so complete; never again, personal sacrifice for Christian belief quite so heroic as hers was.°

Yet the victory of orthodoxy muted rather than eliminated the Puritan voices of mysticism and of congregational independence. We have already met Edward Taylor as a late but representative witness to the Puritan vision; now we may call on him again as the writer of a more literary statement of mystical faith than anyone else's in American Puritanism. In a "Sacramental Meditation" composed in colonial West-field, he voiced the ancient intuition that the sun's light is a vehicle which conveys God's glory to man:

> *When, Lord, mine Eye doth spie thy Grace to beame*
> *Thy Mediatoriall glory in the shine.*
> *Out Sprouted so from Adams typick streame*
> *And Emblemiz'd in Noahs pollisht shrine*
> *Thine theirs out shines so far it makes their glory*
> *In brightest Colours, seem a smoaky story. . . .*
> *Yet let my Titimouses Quill suck in*
> *Thy Graces milk Pails some small drop: or Cart*
> *A Bit or Splinter of some Ray, the wing*
> *Of Grace's sun sprindgd out, into my heart:*
> *To build there Wonders Chappell where thy Praise*
> *Shall be the Psalms sung forth in gracious layes.°*

On the side of thought about polity, the expressive learning of John Wise of Ipswich matches, as to quality and Puritan authenticity, the poetic expressiveness of Edward Taylor, his contemporary. Born in Roxbury in 1652, trained in the township school there and at Harvard, and for forty-five years in charge of a modest congregation, the ex-ternals of John Wise's career seem ordinary. But, a powerful man physically and morally, he was a breaker of molds. He was the first son of an indentured servant to enter Harvard; once, after many years as a clergyman, he ventured and won a wrestling match from a local champion. Although he disliked to be conspicuous, he dealt with public and ecclesiastical crises so seriously as to emerge a public leader and a thoughtful writer of theory.

His first political fight occurred in 1687, when he was thirty-five. For some months Sir Edmund Andros had been governor by royal appointment of all the New England colonies. This famous consolidation, the Dominion of New England, marked the climax of the effort of Charles II and James II to establish effective administration over the unruly region; a most offensive feature of it was the sweeping aside without replacement of the colonial assemblies. In principle the same as the Stamp Act crisis, which was eighty years in the future, the fight occurred over taxation imposed on a people who had not been represented in enacting the tax. Resistance cropped up in Essex County, around Ipswich especially, and John Wise spoke for the resisters. "No taxes should be levied upon the subject without the consent of an assembly chosen by freeholders for assessing the same." In the judgment of the Andros government, Wise's obstructiveness demanded to be eliminated, and he was arrested and brought to trial. The plea he made, to exercise freely the rights of an Englishman on the basis of Magna Carta, did not save him; he was fined and removed from church office. But events intervened with uncommon dispatch. The Glorious Revolution in England and the collapse of the Andros regime removed the penalties and restored the assemblies, and the minister returned to his pulpit. The reverse of what is often the case when a clergyman plunges into affairs, John Wise's political action preceded his having reached his full development in political theory. Only when a quarter century had elapsed following the taxation affair, and then in the field of ecclesiastical polity rather than in secular, did he mature his famous ideas. In 1710, in a satirical pamphlet, *The Churches Quarrel Espoused*, he attacked the presbyterian-like proposals which were hatching in Boston in the interest of unity and discipline among the churches. And seven years later, when he was sixty-five, he brought out his reflective and learned *Vindication of the Government of the New England Churches*. This substantial work put him in the line of succession of the major theorists of congregationalism, from Ames and Robinson on through John Cotton and Roger Williams.

The increment of thought, added by this Yankee minister to the work of the men of nearly a century earlier, was the assimilation of secular ideas into the defense of the church polity of his region. Before his time, the autonomy of the congregation had been justified as being what the Bible demanded; Roger Williams, dissenter against dissenters, reasoned in that same way. John Wise, on the other hand, by no means rejecting the Biblical argument, drew freshly from the ancient Greeks and the Romans who spoke for the natural rights of man. He cited also recent thinkers, including Sir Edward Coke, and he acknowledged in the *Vindication* that "I shall Principally take Baron Puffendorff for my Chief Guide and Spokesman."

This was more than a matter of redoing the footnotes of an argument. It meant changing the premises of it, from Puritanism's absorption with the idea that man is by nature sinful, to greater confidence in man and society. In the words of John Wise himself:

> This then is a Fundamental Law of Nature, that every Man as far as in him lies, do maintain a Sociableness with others, agreeable with the main end and disposition of humane Nature in general. For this is very apparent, that Reason and Society render Man the most potent of all Creatures. And Finally, from the Principles of Sociableness it follows as a fundamental Law of Nature, that Man is not so Wedded to his own Interest, but that he can make the Common good the mark of his Aim: And hence he becomes Capacitated to enter into a Civil State by the Law of Nature; for without this property in Nature, *viz.* Sociable-

ness, which is for Cementing of parts, every Government would soon moulder and dissolve.

It is easy to see foreshadowings of the Enlightenment and of the American Revolution and democracy in the lines of John Wise of Ipswich. But it is safer, and more probable and defensible, to see between the lines the conditions and events of a New England township of the early eighteenth century. By his time the original tensions in the churches had been released, and congregationalism had become established in more than the institutional sense of the adjective. Unlimited confidence in the system of congregational meetings and town meetings which had been John Wise's life work appear in the words which follow: "The right of determining all matters relating to the public safety is actually placed in a general assembly." When the son of an indentured servant at the end of a ministerial career chose to say that "Humane Nature agrees equally with all persons; and . . . no one can live a Sociable Life with another that does not own or Respect him as a Man," the equalizing influence of congregational principles had carried far, with lasting effect, in one corner of the Puritan world.°

3   Puritan Commitment and New England Education

THE final return we need make to the 1630s takes us back to the founders of Massachusetts, not to their inner orthodoxy but to the broadness of their minds. Because the Puritans derived characteristically from England's schools and universities, and from business places and manor houses in the southeastern part of the kingdom, all in touch with the continent, they were familiar with lively elements of Renaissance culture. Recent investigators have been fascinated by their knowledgeability and modernity, and some of the findings have illuminated the core of the New England effort. The service rendered to theology by the logical method of the French humanist and Protestant philosopher, Pierre de la Ramée, is a case in point; European treatises on defending and designing cities, because they were applied in colonial town planning, is a second. New England's beginnings in music and in the arts of design, not so slender a story as is often supposed, and of course the early poetry and prose of the region, often took form from the Renaissance in the Old World.

Yet for our practical study, which seeks out ideas and loyalties which were quickened by their bearing on community affairs, the Puritans' great commitment to education is overwhelmingly the most important aspect of the matter. To express that commitment as being at once of the mind of the Renaissance and of the heart of Puritanism is both necessary and difficult to do. The history of the Anglican colonies suggests that, had the Massachusetts fathers not departed far from the ways of the Church of England, they would have relied more on tradition and ritual and less on the study of Bible, theology, and philosophy. They needed those fundamentals to keep up their defenses; hence they uncommonly needed schools. On the other hand the history of the Quaker colonies suggests that, had New England followed the Antinomians and like the Friends relied quite unreservedly on direct inspiration from God, the need to read and study the world of the past and present would have been less compelling than the theocracy believed. The Puritan position, which was occupied always with organizing the community and keeping the members of it alert but safely in line, contained fixed imperatives. Every child born needed the Bible; future leaders needed all that learning could give.

First and always responsibility for education began in the family circle, but it soon transcended what that unit could yield. The public effort started in Boston; and 1636, the year when the Antinomian storm blew hardest, was the great founding year. The town meeting had decided earlier to employ a schoolmaster, but the result is lost from the records. In 1636 the "richer" people of the town raised a subscription, however; an Emmanuel College man was hired, and Boston Latin School started the work it still continues of giving excellent training to boys.° Before the year was out at least one other school in the immediate vicinity, the one at Charlestown, was launched. Supported by taxes and income from land, this was probably the first public school in America. Meanwhile the most historic action of the year was taken by the Massachusetts legislature. The statute is so short and pregnant that it may be quoted in full: "The Court agreed to give 400 l [£400] to be paid the next yeare, and 200 l [£200] when the work is finished, and the next Court to appoint wheare and what building." Thus was Harvard College founded; and those four hundred pounds equaled about one-fourth of the tax levy of the colony for all purposes during the year of the act.

The earliest schools signified township undertakings purely, or rather a first flowing through township channels of the determination of parents to have their children trained. Beginning in Massachusetts in 1642 and in Connecticut in 1650, however, and soon thereafter in New Hampshire, general statutes passed by the colonial assemblies fixed educational obligations which applied to all the towns in the colony. The law of 1642 demanded that the town selectmen see to it that parents and guardians have every child taught to "read and understand the principles of religion and the capital laws of the country." This first policy act left it to parents to decide how the children would be taught, and to the townships whether or not to set up schools. The single requirement was the basic one, reading; and the only philosophy, that religion and good behavior demand a literate citizenry. The more famous Massachusetts act, the "old Deluder" law of 1647, was truly a school law. "It being the chief project of that old Deluder, Satan, to keep men from a knowledge of the Scriptures" and from the use of languages, the law began, every town of fifty or more households was required to provide a teacher of reading and writing; and every town of one hundred or more households, a Latin grammar school with a master "able to instruct youth so far as they may be fitted for the university." Not legislating school attendance or requiring of the pupils any special achievement beyond literacy, the law stopped shorter than is often supposed of such demands as modern society imposes on a school system. But, while it left to each township the option as to whether its school should be supported by a general tax or by assessments charged to the parents of children who attended, it did demand that schools be maintained for all who would come; and it did open to all a route to higher education. No such widely distributed opportunity then existed in England, or would exist for two centuries.

The instruction which was actually offered in the elementary schools is not fully known. At least in Boston it is clear that "reading and writing" meant something more advanced than the beginning of literacy, even for the youngest pupils, who entered at age seven. In that town a previously established ability to read English was taken for granted; from the outset the children were given practice in that skill and were instructed in writing. Throughout New England reading was commonly taught by the women in their homes: either by mothers to their own children or by the keepers of "dame schools" who for a fee taught the children of the vicinity. Those were the places where study began in the hornbooks and primers, and where in time was introduced the famed *New England Primer*, to which was appended the catechism with the interesting title: *Spiritual Milk for American Babes drawn from the Breasts of Both Testaments for their Souls Nourishment*. The town schools, which opened and closed their seven or eight hours of daily teaching with prayers, had Bible reading twice a day, catechism on Saturdays, and writing, spelling, and arithmetic a great deal of the time. This was practical training for the sons of farmers and storekeepers, craftsmen and seamen, church members and nonmembers, the free and indentured without regard for their station in life.

In the ten or so larger towns in New England which fulfilled the requirements of the law concerning Latin schools, there was no practice of progressing from an elementary school to the Latin one. There was simply a different and higher type of school available; boys who were expected to go on to Harvard entered at seven and were given training which paralleled and surpassed that in the three-R schools. The Latin grammar schools are the institution which most strikingly reveals the Puritan transmission of Renaissance traditions of learning. Because those schools were founded in recollection of the Latin schools of England but were maintained out of township moneys rather than by endowments, as at home, they display the boldness and the public interest of the effort. In Boston, by the fourth year the students were reading Erasmus and Ovid; in the fifth and sixth, Tully and Vergil were added, and probably Caesar and Cicero; and in the seventh year, with more of the same, came Horace and Juvenal, and Greek was undertaken with Hesiod and Homer. Ezekiel Cheever, an Emmanuel graduate who on arriving in America had become one of the seven pillars of the New Haven church and schoolmaster there, and who wound up his career with a thirty-eight-year tenure in charge of the Boston Latin School, had his pupils put Aesop's fables into Latin verse. They were required to speak as well as read and write that language in order to enter the college.°

The casual wording of the statute which called Harvard College into being suggests the inevitability of that decision; and from the records of 1637, when the court passed the enabling legislation, one can almost hear a sigh of relief being taken by the legislators.° The danger from the Pequots was over that year, and heresy was about to be extirpated from the land. In the session which banished Anne Hutchinson the court voted that the college be located at Newtowne and that Newtowne be renamed Cambridge—the place of meandering river and fields which looked like the university location so many Puritans loved. At first a residence in the village was made to serve as college building; unfortunately, the enterprise was placed in charge of a scholar who turned out to be a scoundrel and had to be dismissed. But only two years intervened before there arrived in the colony the gifted Henry Dunster. He was at once elected president, and soon a proper new E-shaped building was erected in the pasture which ever since has been the college "Yard." Meanwhile John Harvard, a little-known graduate of Emmanuel, had come to Massachusetts and died. His collection of about four hundred books (which, tiny as it seems, was two-thirds the size of the Emmanuel College library), and half his estate he willed to the new institution, a bequest worth more than eight hundred pounds. The college gratefully took his name. Although by no means handsomely equipped, Harvard did thus early win both public and private support.

During his nineteen years in Cambridge, Henry Dunster, whom Morison ranks second only to Eliot in service rendered by a president to Harvard, did somehow manage to create an overseas college of English-university quality. The curriculum followed the still unyielding medieval pattern of the trivium and quadrivium. The first and second studies in that series, grammar and rhetoric, meant at Harvard advanced Latin grammar and the reading and analysis of "heathen authors" in both Latin and Greek. As at Oxford and Cambridge, Latin was used in all instruction; the B.A. thesis was written, and the final examination spoken, in that language. The Bible was read in Hebrew and Greek, and the New Testament sometimes in Aramaic and Syriac. After grammar and rhetoric, the trivium called for logic—that is to say, philosophy. "Harvardians philosophize in a sane and liberal manner, according to the manner of the century; in Logic as in Physics they are neither sceptics nor dogmatics," observed President John Leverett a half century after Dunster. "Let the dichotomies of the celebrated Petrus Ramus be admired, but not pursued religiously or too scrupulously. University men examine the Categories, Properties, and Syncategories of Aristotle, but are not bound up by them. . . . Without any manner of doubt whatever, all humane matters must be tested by Philosophy." After this suggestion of how Harvard blended the ancient, medieval, and Renaissance intellect, the twentieth-century reader will not mind learning of his ancestors that, in their adaptation of the old quadrivium, only three subjects remained. Arithmetic, geometry, and astronomy, which had been the matter of M.A. work in medieval curricula, were graduation-year studies in the Harvard B.A. course. The fourth in the series, music, did not appear.

During the beginning years, while there were only fifteen or so students, President Dunster taught all the classes. He used the ancient method of "lecture," reading and explaining a book and later reviewing the material. At first only three years were required for the B.A., which seems to have been more in line with the practice than the statutes of Cambridge and Oxford; but Harvard shifted early to the four-year duration which has been the norm in American colleges ever since. With some expansion of the number of students, a tutor, usually a young graduate, was assigned to each entering class. In a role which might today be called "teaching assistant," the tutor gave all the instruction his class received from arrival until graduation, except what the president continued—the teaching of divinity. (The attaching of a permanent tutor to a group of entering students marks the beginning of the distinctive American, and non-English, habit of creating an academic identity out of the dates of arrival and departure from college.)

The president's practice of reserving to himself the teaching of divinity somewhat reduces the meaning of the fact that during its first century Harvard had no professors. In fact if not in name, the president was a professor. He conducted the lectures in "Divinity Catechicall," which were for decades based on Ames's *Medulla*; he taught Bible; and he trained without assistance the M.A. candidates, who were candidates also for the ministry. This meant that until Yale was founded in 1701 he had a complete monopoly, and after that only one-man competition, in teaching the one area of learning which might have been controversial in an important way. Harvard administration and Harvard faculty could not, in the circumstances, run into disagreement; and the modern phrase "academic freedom" applied to that time simply raises the question of whether Harvard's minister presidents thought freely and decided wisely while, training generation after generation for leadership in the region, they delivered their lectures and sermons and phrased and passed upon examination questions for degrees.

Freedom for anyone's mind, president's or student's, to move and choose at will among the differing religious ideas of the world, and the antireligious ones, would in the nature of the case have been out of bounds at seventeenth-century Harvard. (Even Dunster had to leave when he turned Baptist.) Yet one finds no other area which was closed, and one discovers no protest about that closure. In philosophy we have already heard President Leverett's testimony that wide choices were open to students. At this point, the similar, more eloquent, often-cited words of one of the stiff Puritan presidents of Harvard require quotation again. Addressing a class of graduates about 1700, Increase Mather was trying to strengthen his young men in the ways and beliefs of New England. Turning to philosophy he advised: "To Aristotle some prefer Pyrrho, father of the Skeptics; others Zeno, father of the Stoics; many prefer Plato, father of the Academics. You who are wont to philosophize in a liberal spirit are pledged to the words of no particular master. Yet I would have you hold fast to that one truly golden saying of Aristotle: *Find a friend in Plato, a friend in Socrates* (and I say a friend in Aristotle), *but above all find a friend in* TRUTH."

The Harvard men who heard their president speak those words heard them, of course, in Latin.°

4 *After 1660: From Theocracy
to Tradition*

THE assertion by Massachusetts at mid-century that it had achieved the condition of a commonwealth was matched by a renewal of persecuting the heterodox. During the 1650s, while the "sectaries" were having their day in England, Massachusetts banished Baptists as it had banished Roger Williams twenty years earlier, and it dealt immigrant Quakers harsher treatment than it had dealt to Anne Hutchinson. A number of this newly formed sect of mystics were imprisoned and then expelled; two who insisted on returning, having once been banished, were executed. This introduced the ugly second-generation phase of

Puritan control of New England, which Edmund S. Morgan, in the fullness of special knowledge of Puritan family and faith, calls the "tribalism" of the region.

Once again relations with the outside world helped build up tensions within. But where during the 1630s and the 1640s the founders had taken long political chances and won—when they brazened out court actions against the charter, and when denying the remonstrants they challenged presbyterians in England, too—the later-day Puritans had to realize that the current of politics had turned against them. Instead of Puritan revolutionary England, it was Stuart Restoration England they faced; the former expectation, that in time old England—indeed the world, under God—would follow where New England was leading, had to give way to knowledge that the world was not performing according to Puritan schedule. Traditional Anglicanism, including the bishops, was restored at home; Roman Catholicism, never far from being the preference of Stuart kings, threatened again. For Massachusetts, particularly, the situation was complicated by the charters which Charles II gave to Connecticut and Rhode Island in 1662 and 1663. New England was now threatened by the ancient practice of imperial control: *Divide et impera*.

Also in disturbing condition were New England's foreign relations toward the frontier. Although the Puritans did not undertake major efforts to convert the Indians, neither did they forget that their congregations in the New World, simply by existing, constituted an evangel which would be noticed from all points of the compass. As Cotton Mather would phrase things, they believed that "first and by them" Christ would "give a specimen of many good things, which he would elsewhere have his churches aspire unto." The most famous case in the record of the Puritans converting the aborigines began with a minister first extending pastoral care to the Indians in his vicinity and then helping them set up for themselves in the way of life he believed in for those who hoped to be saved. The Reverend John Eliot, whose evangelism at Roxbury and Natick and throughout New England made him the principal English colonial missionary of the century, was the man. Educated at Cambridge, he had become adept there in languages, including Hebrew; he practised this skill on the Massachusetts frontier. He undertook to preach to the Indians in their own language by 1647, and he translated the Old and New Testaments for them into what became the first Bible to be published—with financial help from England—in America in any language. His preaching and organizing led to the gathering of more than a thousand "praying Indians" into largely autonomous, segregated communities. Their Bible reading, their separateness, and their self-government nicely expressed the Puritan pattern of life. But Eliot's missions broke down during the 1670s, under the terror of King Philip's War. The episode offered frightening testimony—from an external operation of the theocracy, but a critical one—that the Puritans were in for hard times.

Thus the problem of thought and purpose shifted, from maintaining a light toward which the world would soon be drawn, to guarding it lest it be snuffed out. The Halfway Covenant, formulated by a synod in 1662, was the theocracy's first, and basic, reinforcement within. It resolved a problem which had come up during the 1640s but which at that time had been deferred. The trouble was simply that the congregations did not discover converts in sufficient numbers to keep church memberships sizable; this meant a diminishing ratio between the elite, who by reason of having been admitted to a church covenant had the vote in the general elections, and the growing population. In some congregations the problem never became acute. But in many the political aspect of the matter became insistent, and a social idea had to be hit upon which would reconcile the perfectionist theocratic standard of the Massachusetts suffrage law of 1631 with the actual situation.

Before 1662 the children of converted and covenanted "visible saints" had been accepted as "confederate," or halfway, church members. Biblical sustenance for this was taken from Genesis, 17:7: "And I will establish my covenant between me and thee and thy seed after thee in their generations for an everlasting covenant, to be a God unto thee, and to thy seed after thee." The congregations had decided, in Richard Mather's words, that "children that are born when their Parents are Church Members are in covenant with God even from their birth." Birthright members were baptized as children, and when they became adults they had simply "to own the covenant"—that is, accept the obligations of it voluntarily—to become members on the halfway basis and so qualify for the Massachusetts vote. Without experience of conversion and without being accepted as saints they did not receive the Lord's Supper, and they were not eligible to vote for, or to be elected among, the church elders. The Halfway Covenant extended this usage: it admitted the children of birthright members to the same halfway membership. Thus at the time when the leaders of the founding generation had largely disappeared—John Cotton, John Winthrop, Thomas Hooker, and Thomas Shepard all died around mid-century—and when England returned to Anglicanism, the religious base of politics was broadened at last in Massachusetts, and a factor of heredity became a large part of that base.°

Contrary to first appearances, the Halfway Covenant did not bring about a departure from the first principles of the Massachusetts system of church and state. That system was still based on Biblical reasoning and on the covenant theology; the government was still a commonwealth, as before. The Halfway Covenant realigned and reinforced those foundations. On the other hand, the Halfway Covenant weakens our own application of the word *theocracy* to the Massachusetts system after 1662. Some of those who voted were not covenanted in grace. Although, according to their own understanding, the Puritans still governed under God and in covenant with Him, according to that same understanding, most unhappily God's presence was neither as frequent nor as prevailing in New England as it had previously been.

While the Massachusetts system thus carried on, preachers and poets in the colony slipped into a voice of anxiety which outlasted the seventeenth century. Michael Wigglesworth's "Day of Doom" is the earliest and best-remembered poem which conveyed that new tone. It was printed in 1662, the year when his equally gloomy "God's Controversy with New England" was published—the poem which was quoted in the last chapter to illustrate the idea of the covenant—and the year also of the Halfway Covenant. The following stanzas, numbers 197 and 204 of the poem's 224, spoke of the separations which the last judgment would bring:

> *One natural Brother beholds another in this astonied fit,*
> *Yet sorrows not thereat a jot, nor pitties him a whit.*
> *The godly wife conceives no grief, nor can she shed a tear*
> *For the sad fate of her dear Mate, when she his doom doth hear. . . .*
>
> *Oh,* fearful Doom! *Now there's no room for hope or help at all:*
> *Sentence is past which aye shall last, Christ will not it recall.*
> *There might you hear them rent and tear the Air with their out-cries:*
> *The hideous noise of their sad voice ascendeth to the Skies.*°

Four decades later, Cotton Mather's *Magnalia Christi Americana*, with its good qualities as history, marks the climax of Puritan remorse. No other writer has ever known better the events of early New England, and none other has better expressed the nostalgia of a region for the period of its beginnings, than that third-generation preacher did. By his time and in his case, moreover, regret for New England's second-generation failure to maintain first-generation standards was matched by a call to a Puritan rebirth. In that way, Mather was the starter of a New England tradition, a kind of revivalism of institutional life. Before the colonial period ended, Jonathan Edwards in the 1730s and 1740s and John Adams in the 1760s and 1770s, each in his own way as we shall see, would ask his contemporaries to renew their progenitors' deeds.

Meanwhile in 1684 a court decision against Massachusetts, in England, at last annulled the charter of 1629. Immediately Governor Edmund Andros was placed by James II in viceregal charge of all New England. Five colonies—Massachusetts Bay Colony (including Maine), New Hampshire, Plymouth, Connecticut, and Rhode Island (their two charters from Charles II notwithstanding)—were thrown together, without respect for their political identities; before Andros was through, New York and New Jersey were added to his domains. His tyranny, which drew such special fire at Ipswich, meant to New Englanders generally a terrifying upset of commonwealth and theocracy. Although from the beginning there was reason to hope that the Dominion of New England would not last long, there was never much ground for expecting that the charter of 1629—and the theocratic commonwealth of Massachusetts—would be restored as before. Increase Mather, who was president of Harvard and leading citizen of Massachusetts, managed to get to England before the Glorious Revolution took place. While the new sovereigns, William and Mary, received him and his advice was welcomed, the most he could do for his colony was to negotiate the terms which went into the new charter of 1691. It was a modified crown government, more like the government of Virginia than that of Massachusetts before 1684, which Mather brought home. Men of Massachusetts could henceforward pronounce the word *commonwealth* with the old reverence, as John Adams and others would do; but never again before 1776 would they have the same kind of republican independence their grandfathers had had in the 1640s and 1650s. Henceforth the right to vote would be determined by a property requirement; acceptance of the covenants would have no political meaning; synods or other meetings of the clergy would not again advise the government. The theocratic commonwealth would never be restored.

The effect of this on life and thought was most immediate in Boston. A Church of England chapel, the first in New England, was set up, not far from where John Cotton had preached and Anne Hutchinson had lived; King's Chapel provided a place of worship for the governor and his associates in power and before long became the church preferred by many of the elite of the provincial capital. Real religious toleration, even equality between Episcopalians and Congregationalists, appeared at the hub; Harvard College admitted students from both churches. Not rapidly but within a generation, partly due to England's act of 1689, toleration spread. Before 1730, Episcopalians, Baptists, and Quakers in Massachusetts were exempted from taxation in support of the Congregational churches; the Saybrook Platform of 1708 announced toleration for Anglicans in Connecticut, and Baptists in that colony were given the same church-tax exemption as in Massachusetts. Quakers on Nantucket Island, Massachusetts, became, as well as numerous, vocal against the slave trade.

In sum, Puritan political institutions and privileges had been destroyed at their historic center, and the monopolistic congregationalism of the region as a whole (always excepting dissenting Rhode

Island) was gradually giving way. But it is easy to think of the changes as having been more upsetting to Puritan predominance than they actually proved. For some years before and after 1700, Increase Mather, Cotton Mather, and other ministers studied and proposed methods of intercongregational organization which would increase the community leadership of the ministers, even though the old church-state relationship was dead. After having become acquainted in London with the United Brethren, as the working union of presbyterian and congregationalist dissenters styled themselves in the mother country, Increase Mather wanted a similar union in New England. Cotton Mather and others initiated ministerial associations in small areas convenient for meetings and sought to have a "consociation" of all congregations, such as was actually instituted in Connecticut by act of the colony legislature. Such presbyterian-like proposals followed logically enough on the synods and conventions of the half century before 1684. The question was whether or not Puritan strength in affairs could be rebuilt in that way.

Different from the result in Connecticut, in Massachusetts the impulse ended with proposal and talk. The proposers had many opponents, John Wise the strongest and most articulate leader. It does seem that practical politics, as well as congregationalist principle, was on his side. If the synods had been institutionalized, with any substance of church authority given to a supercongregational organization, they would have created a vulnerable target for any Anglican governor sent to Massachusetts who might happen to care. Thus a sizable decision, more practical than theoretical in the making but in line with regional theory, was actually taken when the federating reform proposals for the Puritan congregations were let quietly drop.

Meanwhile other senior clergymen, in and out of Boston, ventured more popular solutions of the problem of how to recover, after having lost political power. Evangelical purpose belonged to the foundation history of Puritanism; moreover, as the case of Cotton Mather shows, interest in intercongregational associationism, to be carried out by the ministers, did not exclude interest in revivalism within the congregations. He himself preached with zeal to make conversions; so likewise did Benjamin Colman, who was his critic and rival in Boston religious leadership, at the Brattle Street church. Among the many changes, the time of open competition between congregations and ideas had come to New England.

But the historic effort of conversion which occurred about 1700 belonged less to the hub than to a westward spoke of the Puritan wheel. The leader was Solomon Stoddard, who was known in his own time, as he is to history, as "Pope" Stoddard, and who, a contemporary of John Wise and Edward Taylor among the second-generation Puritan clergymen, was the equal of those men as to gift of mind and spirit. Born in Boston and trained at Harvard in the covenant theology to which he would always be loyal, he served his college as tutor and librarian before he went to Northampton to stay. His arriving there in 1672 timed his long ministry to bridge many crises and transformations: King Philip's War and the Deerfield massacre occurred early and near; the Andros regime and the fall of the theocracy, during the second of five decades of service; enormous population growth in the Connecticut River valley, which raised his town to become a thriving and favored center, early in the eighteenth century. His was a time and a place to keep the doors of the meetinghouse open to newcomers, if the church were to belong to the community and the minister were to be heard.

Precisely on his determination to keep the doors open and to have the church carry on as the guide of the people, Solomon Stoddard based his influential career. Although his congregation accepted the Halfway Covenant, that device no longer sufficed. After 1684 it lost everywhere its political meaning; in the frontier towns, where children and grandchildren of signers of the covenant were in the nature of the case a small portion of the community, it failed to provide the congregations with sizable memberships. Full members of the church were needed, baptized persons and receivers of the Lord's Supper, who could undertake the responsibilities of the parish. Under pressure of that need, Solomon Stoddard asked a question, to which the consistent answer of the founders of New England had been a resounding No: "Whether such Persons as have a good Conversation and a Competent Knowledge, may come to the Lord's Supper with a good Conscience, in case they know themselves to be in a Natural Condition"—by "natural condition" he meant not covenanted in grace. To this question Stoddard returned the answer which an Anglican or a Presbyterian Scot, but not a New England Puritan up to his own time, would normally have given. "They may and ought to come . . . ; as no man may neglect Prayer, or hearing the Word, because he cannot do it in Faith, so he may not neglect the Lord's Supper."

In making this reversal, Stoddard reasoned about the sacraments as John Wise did about the congregation, socially and morally rather than theologically. In his little book, *The Doctrine of the Instituted Churches*, just quoted, he explained: "If a Christian live in a Town, where there is a Church, he is immediately bound to joyn with that Church; and that Church is bound to govern him . . . but there is no occasion that every Member should Covenant particularly with the Church. . . . This Doctrine of the particular Covenant is wholly unscriptural, is the reason that many among us are shut out of the Church, to whom Church Privildeges do belong."° Thus not a supposition that God had bestowed grace on an individual but an individual's voluntary engagement in the Christian community, and his voluntary acceptance of its discipline, became the requirements of church membership in Northampton and in nearby congregations which accepted "Pope" Stoddard's ideas.

In doctrinal thought, no very great change was at issue; in institutional thought, a sizable change had begun. In the Stoddardian revision of congregational practice, full membership in the church, with participation in the Lord's Supper included, lost its old characteristic of being an indication of grace—that is, of salvation achieved. But membership did not become—in Anglican or Catholic style—a step in a soul's earning salvation: Stoddardianism no more than older Puritanism believed in salvation by good works. Over and above a working commitment to the church of the community, membership simply signified the member's hope for salvation—his effort to discover God, if ever the revelation might be given. Thus there was involved no departure from Puritanism's fundamental covenant of grace and none from the conception of a series of covenants which describe the relationships between God and men.

The change of theory which did occur concerned simply the operation of the church covenant, and so was as close as possible to practice. Opening full church membership to persons in a "Natural Condition" meant filling the lists at last, and numerous attendance at the Lord's Supper; in the case of Solomon Stoddard it meant much popularity and honor for the minister of the town. In an indirect way that affected the inner operations of congregation and town, Stoddardianism was a hierarchical doctrine: it assigned to the elders of the church a more prominent role of leadership than earlier, and it gave to regular members of the church less religious distinction. Yet we should hesitate to reason that the effect was antidemocratic. The new procedure brought the community as a whole much more fully into participation in church affairs; church membership by Stoddard's rules no longer designated an elite of God in charge of each town.

In sum, the direction of New England Puritanism, indicated by this frontier-born theory and practice, was turning toward the later American norm of voluntary Christianity. To be sure no New England colony had ever set up a "church establishment" in the historic sense of that phrase: there had been neither central ecclesiastical authority nor mechanism, unless Connecticut's eighteenth-century synods barely fill that condition. The theocratic church-and-government alliance of before 1684 had, however, brought into being political and economic privileges for the congregations, and ecclesiastical sanctions for the governments. After the Andros regime, when the political alliance remained in ashes, though the taxation privilege was restored, Puritan congregationalists were thrown, with that financial exception, once more on their own. Of course there was no Archbishop Laud in New England in the eighteenth century, but there was always an anxiety that a bishop might yet be sent. Neither was there a Governor Winthrop, nor a situation like the 1630s, 1640s, and 1650s, ever again in New England. Congregationalism's great and saving new situation, the legacy of the two generations of the theocracy, was a fairly homogeneous series of township and congregational communities, now deeply entrenched in every social and intellectual way.

To this situation, Puritan evangelicalism, Cotton Mather's in Boston as well as Solomon Stoddard's to the west, was a response. So also were the new degree of New England toleration and New England's growing effort in education. Harvard became more liberal, as to both studies and student admissions, as the eighteenth century advanced. Yale was founded in 1701, with the blessings of Cotton Mather, as a special home for old Puritan ideas. Thus before it was a century old, New England Puritanism became a tradition of effort, of religious and social and educational achievement—a more complex and a more generous thing than mere orthodoxy.

As such judgments indicate, in the estimation of the present writer the second half-century of Puritanism carries a more cheerful sound than historians have often heard. Yet I admire probably more than many do the logical perfection of the theocratic commonwealth during the middle decades of the seventeenth century: without Puritan belief and discipline Massachusetts would hardly have been more effective culturally than, say, contemporary Virginia. The early independence of the Bay Colony—the autonomy of the townships, the self-government of church and colony, the law codes, the college, the schools, the pine-tree shillings and all else—was unique. Its political and constitutional performance made it truly a utopia in a Calvinist style. By that standard the waning of confidence after 1660 and the breakdown of the system during the 1680s marks an immeasurable let-down for the participators. And the regional synthesis which followed was less coherent; it rendered a less pure New England than the one the theocracy had governed.

Still, I do not think that a historian should judge the situation after the Glorious Revolution—the region under the Puritan tradition as we have surveyed it—to have been less revolutionary than the situation during the 1640s and 1650s. To be sure, more for New England than for old, the accession of William and Mary represented certain gains for institutional conservatism. The permanent establishment of crown government in Massachusetts and New Hampshire and the edging of the Anglican Church into the region were two such gains. Yet by the standards of the old order in Western Christendom, especially by those of England when colonization began, one may wonder which situation was more revolutionary, that of Massachusetts and her neighbors in 1650, or after 1700. The early Massachusetts which consolidated the interdependence of church and state? Or the later Massachusetts which, with whatever adjustments of government, contained two churches and tolerated radical sectarians on Nantucket Island and elsewhere? The Massachusetts which by assertion and defiance achieved a bold moment of theocratic commonwealth freedom around 1650? Or the New England which by way of four governments exercised freely and legally the self-government now allowed to all the colonies? In the wake of 1688, what this books calls the first revolution in America—not the first American revolution—even Massachusetts and Connecticut were freer than they had ever been before, a fairly self-determining part of a freer system of overseas colonies than any other so far in the history of the West.

CHAPTER V

Leveling the National

Churches

Come, my Way, my Truth, my Life!
Such a Way as gives us breath,
Such a Truth as ends all Strife,
Such a Life as killeth Death.
  George Herbert, "The Call"

1   *Unique in the West:*
Six Churches under One Crown

I N the two preceding chapters on the Puritans, we have witnessed the emergence of what may be called a subnational church. Though such a name for it would not have occurred to the New Englanders themselves, in fact they had built a congregationalist system which even after Andros retained enviable privileges and remained uniquely entrenched in the society and culture of the region. Congregationalists organized their churches and preached their convictions with unlimited freedom; they were still free to participate in, and even control, governmental and educational institutions. All this occurred under laws either directly administered by the Crown or, in Connecticut, under a commonwealth which the Crown had once chartered and which after the Andros interruption it had allowed to be fully restored. If such privilege and such freedom had been given the nonseparating congregationalists of the Massachusetts Bay Company by the charter of 1629, their hopes as to church polity would have been essentially met, and they would have had little reason of religion ever to leave England at all.

During the eighteenth century, the congregations carried on much as before. Only gradually, and prior to 1740 only in a few townships, did Anglicans or Presbyterians, or Quakers or Baptists, appear. By 1700 if not earlier, the tradition and like-mindedness of the congregationalists justifies speaking of them in the singular as well as in the plural, as comprising the Congregational Church as well as the Puritan congregations. Their lack of central structure and authority notwithstanding, they had, with their predominance in a large and homogeneous region, a collective identity more substantial than that of a sect; the colleges at Cambridge and New Haven and even the township schools were theirs in all but title. The Congregational Church heads the list of the several churches—including the Latter-Day Saints and the Church of Christ, Scientist—which have been born in America.

More than one church under one sovereign, each enjoying favors from the king, was a situation unusual in Western civilization. The natural comparison is with Britain; one turns the more readily to the mother country because there are many parallels, besides northern location, between Scotland in British history and New England in American history. When, on the death of Elizabeth, James VI of Scotland became James I of England, the monarch who was head of the Church of Scotland, presbyterian, became also supreme head of the Church of England, episcopalian. But the Stuart kings James and Charles had no heart for the Scots church polity which John Knox had designed; they believed that bishops were necessary for kings, and they were soft toward Roman Catholicism long before James II became a Catholic. Thanks to their getting their way with the Scottish Parliament, bishops were reimposed on the Church of Scotland. Only after William and Mary succeeded did that church become permanently presbyterian. From then on, the analogy with New England is close: in both the northern kingdom and the northern colonial region, the Crown not merely tolerated but actively favored a church different from, and in principle of polity opposed to, the Church of England.

For the monarchs of continental Europe, whether at home or in their overseas domains, the habit of the seventeenth and eighteenth centuries followed the doctrine of *cujus regio ejus religio*, which had been formulated for the Peace of Augsburg of 1555. By the time of the Treaty of Westphalia, which reapplied the formula in 1648, the doctrine had come to mean, in practice, that throughout central Europe, where the Reformation had struck first and with the greatest disruptive effect, each prince decided for his own domain which one of three faiths —Lutheran, Catholic, or Reformed—should prevail with government support. The treaty contemplated no fourth choice. This amounted to a highhanded kind of religious freedom for sovereigns; it allowed a checkerboard type of religious diversification for a large part of Europe. It was no respecter of persons. It pressed the individual nonconformist in any principality to become either an emigrant or a subversive.

Generally speaking, the principle that the sovereign determines the religion of his people became more tyrannous in the massive national monarchies, which faced the Atlantic, than it did east of the Rhine. The Roman Catholic exclusiveness of Spain and Portugal, an iron policy forged during the long warfare to expel the Muslim and reinforced by the Inquisition, is legendary; it was rigorously applied in New Spain and Brazil. During the seventeenth century France became no less a Roman Catholic monopoly. Even before 1685, while the Edict of Nantes retained some application at home, Huguenots were excluded from settling in New France. The great distances from, say, Boston and Philadelphia to Quebec and Montreal and to the Spanish Main seem not to have reduced the feeling in the English colonies that their national enemies in the St. Lawrence valley and around the Caribbean were monolithically different from themselves, largely because of their Roman Catholicism and their autocratic governments; the two ideas were closely connected.

In the cases of the two young Protestant nations, Holland and Sweden, which, entering the Atlantic through the North Sea, planted little colonies between Connecticut and Maryland, church-and-state relationships were newly constructed. *Cujus regio ejus religio* almost, but not quite, describes them; the practice of the doctrine was less drastic than in the systems of Spain and France. Sweden was Lutheran, in a wing of that faith which retained the office of bishop; to the tiny New Sweden, which was settled on the lower Delaware shortly after Catholics settled in Maryland, came the first Lutherans to immigrate to America. Yet, even before the Dutch seized the place, Reformed worship was allowed; afterward, and again after 1664 when the English took over, Lutheran churches continued under Swedish ecclesiastical supervision. (Doubtless due to their fondness for the episcopal office, following the American Revolution Swedish Lutherans on the Delaware, instead of consolidating with German Lutherans in Pennsylvania and Maryland, would turn permanently Protestant Episcopalian.)

The case of New Netherland was more complicated and more sizable. During the first half of the seventeenth century, while the Dutch republic was leading Europe in commercial expansion, it led also in religious variety at home. The federated government under the Prince of Orange allowed each province religious autonomy among the main branches of Protestantism. In the city of Amsterdam, moreover, a large number of minor sects were permitted, the Pilgrims, before sailing for America, among them. Even Jews and Muslims were given freedom to worship. Yet Roman Catholics despite their large numbers were suppressed in Holland; no form of Christianity existed there which was governed by bishops.

For New Netherland on the Hudson, the religious exclusiveness of a single Dutch province, rather than the freedom of old Amsterdam, was the policy decreed from home. It was pretty completely practised. No churches other than Reformed were erected by the Dutch; in New Amsterdam and up the Hudson little if any other worship occurred.

On the outer fringes of the colony, however, the options demanded by foreign infiltrations were allowed. When New England Puritans crossed the sound to settle on Long Island they were permitted their own worship, the same as the Swedish Lutherans.

We are now in position to see, at the very time of the Peace of Westphalia, that Europe's policy of *cujus regio ejus religio*, while it demanded religious uniformity within the principalities of Europe, actually contributed to an opposite result on England's American seaboard. Here a situation and not a formula prevailed. When in 1664 soldiers of Charles II conquered New Netherland and the king divided it, as New York and New Jersey, between his Catholic brother, James, and other favorites as lords proprietors, that monarch might have tried to establish the Church of England, if not to the exclusion of all other churches at least with considerable preference. Actually he made no such effort. The war with the Dutch had been commercial and territorial, and very little religious; the treaty which ended it was liberal. In New York and upper New Jersey, where the Dutch element would retain for some time its religious and linguistic majority, the Reformed Church was allowed to carry on as before, ecclesiastically subject to authority in Holland. Only at the close of the century, when under William of Orange and Mary Stuart toleration became England's policy, did the legislature of New York give some preference (short of an establishment) to the Church of England; this was limited to the southern counties of the province.

Thus before 1670, among the eight permanent continental colonies which had been founded—Virginia and Maryland; Massachusetts, Connecticut, Rhode Island, and New Hampshire; New York and New Jersey—five historic churches were firmly settled. In chronological order of their founding in America, they were, of course: the Church of England, the Congregational Church, the Roman Catholic Church, the Reformed Church (Dutch), and the Lutheran Church (Swedish). On the European side, four of them existed each under a prince or several princes, nearly always to the exclusion of all others; congregationalists had no privileges anywhere in Europe. Accustomed to power at home, every one of the five believed that ideally it should sustain, and be sustained by, government. But a shift to dependence on the voluntary loyalty and the gifts of the members, the same institutional self-reliance as the sectaries practised, was required of all non-English churchmen. In the nature of the case it meant a severe experience for the church institutions.

During the second century of colonial life, moreover, the number of adherents of non-English Protestant churches, and the proportion of them in the population, greatly increased. Around 1730 the previously tiny number of Lutherans and the number of Reformed were multiplied by the German immigration, much of it to the Middle Colonies. The coming of the Scots-Irish, and a few Scots from Scotland, again largely to Pennsylvania but in sizable numbers also to New England and the Southern Colonies, meant the founding of Presbyterianism. This increased the number of transplanted churches to six, and the number of Calvinist ones to three. The Scots-Irish Presbyterians were the only churchmen who had experienced before coming to America—during their century in northern Ireland—the institutional transformation of living without state support and of living at a distance from the universities at which their ideas were entrenched.

Among the six churches, the Church of England had overwhelmingly the greatest institutional privileges in the colonies; the Congregational Church came second. The other four were either expatriated institutions or missionary ones. Yet even the Anglicans lacked such law and entrenchment in the colonies as sustained their power and prestige at home; and the fall of the Massachusetts theocracy deprived the Congregational Church of its previous authority, though not of many other advantages.

Besides being somewhat reduced in circumstances, the six churches in eighteenth-century America had the unfamiliar obigation to compete with one another for men's loyalty and support. The competition was such as in business life is called "imperfect": the foreign-language churches competed very little with the English-speaking ones; Congregationalists seldom went out of New England. But Anglicans and Presbyterians, who confronted one another sooner or later in every colony, sought to grow each at the expense of the other. Both competed with other English-speaking churches and sects, wherever their people settled. Altogether six churches under one crown created a situation unique anywhere during the seventeenth and eighteenth centuries.

2   *The Truncated Church of England*

THE one region of the three in England's continental American holdings where, in accord with the custom of Europe, the national church was fully established by law was, of course, the Southern Colonies. But only in the original province, Virginia, had this been true from the very beginning, and only there did the church establishment amount for a considerable time to a religious monopoly. Virginia's neighbors all began as proprietary colonies (among which Georgia's trustee system was late and special), and the legislature of every one of them let pass a generation or more before it enacted a church establishment. Maryland and South Carolina took the step near the turn of the century; North Carolina and Georgia did so only after 1750.

Until the 1730s, however, the prevailing or at least little-contested Anglicanism of the Southern Colonies is clear. From that decade through the remainder of the colonial period, nonconformism multiplied and grew. (During the same third of a century, there was little dissent in England; Wesleyanism there represented a social emphasis and an evangelical passion, but not dissent.) After the Scots-Irish and the Germans settled the southern piedmont areas, Anglicans can have counted no more than a small minority in several counties of Virginia and North Carolina. Unlike Parliament, none of the colonial assemblies insisted that their members be Anglican. Contemporary comment tells us that in the Chesapeake colonies many non-Anglicans were elected; one gathers that possibly one assemblyman in three or four was a Protestant dissenter, but that probably no Roman Catholics were elected.

In the Southern Colonies, the Church of England had substantial sources of support which exceeded not simply what was available to other churches and sects in the region but what was available to the Church of England to the north. During the reign of James II the Anglican hierarhcy at home had been able to do little for the colonial church. But after the Glorious Revolution, for a period of about forty years, the able bishops of London, Henry Compton, John Robinson, and Edmund Gibson, ventured, as far as the special authority the king gave them would allow, to aid and supervise the overseas parishes. Meanwhile, in 1701, was founded the Church of England's missionary society for America, the Society for the Propagation of the Gospel; from the S.P.G. gifts of books and money were sent to the overseas parishes, southern and northern alike. On the American side, once the church was established by provincial statute, considerable benefits were assigned to the parishes, namely, the proceeds of church taxes and grants of land for the clergy. Wherever western areas were settled and new counties were created, new parishes were set up, too; although clergymen there often complained that their effort had to be thinly spread, their financial rewards were sometimes considerable. In Frederick, Maryland, for a conspicuous case, a large taxable community created a high salary for the minister of the parish. Although generally speaking the colonial frontier was not a place where Georgian architecture achieved great elegance, dignified parish churches and chapels there still memorialize the mid-century spread of the church.

In Virginia early and famously, and in the other Southern Colonies in due course, social and intellectual conditions favored low-church habits of worship and loyalty. "Every minister is a kind of Independent in his own Parish," observed Hugh Jones, Oxford graduate, and minister and professor in Virginia, in 1724. He noted that the wearing of surplices was returning, after a period of neglect, but also that in "several Respects the clergy are obliged to omit or alter some minute Parts of the Liturgy, and to deviate from the strict Discipline and Ceremonies of the Church, to avoid giving Offense." In a part of the world where there never was a resident bishop, an energetic clergyman was likely to direct his talents into other than strictly ecclesiastical channels. A Maryland parson, for instance, found time to prepare an excellent edition of the laws of that colony and to run a small school for Negroes; clergymen in Virginia and South Carolina took scientifically useful observations on the plant and animal life around them. A service frequently rendered by Anglican clergymen, quite like their Puritan and Presbyterian counterparts, was preparing young men for college.

Yet it was the work of vestrymen, rather than that of clergymen, which accounts for the special institutional characteristics of Anglicanism in the Southern Colonies. Under the law of Virginia which gave the parishes their authority, the vestrymen came to exercise a great deal heavier responsibility in church management than was the role of vestrymen at home. At the time of regaining his throne, Charles II had assigned to the governor the authority to induct clergymen—that is, to present them with their parish living with tenure. At home this function belonged to the diocesan bishop; he acted on nomination by the patron of the parish (the holder of the "advowson"), who might be the local lord of the manor. But in Virginia, where clergymen were in short supply and no landlord held the advowson, the vestries seized the initiative and themselves nominated the ministers. Doubtless this was a relief to the governors: not only did they habitually accept the nominations but they frequently omitted the formal induction. The uninducted minister had no tenure; he was kept under parish review; his salary was paid by an annual decision of the vestry and could be continued or discontinued. Thus the selection and maintenance of clergymen became a matter of local "hiring" (as the word actually was). Because the vestrymen were the only officials who were chosen by election in the Southern Colonies, the assemblymen alone excepted, and because the elections came to be co-optative rather than parish-wide, church government became firmly fixed in the hands of the gentry of each parish. Altogether, by the eighteenth century, Virginia's church polity was just about as tribal as that of Massachusetts had been under the Halfway Covenant.

The original reasons for all this seem to have been monetary and localistic; in the Southern Colonies there seems to have occurred little early public discussion concerning the nature of the Christian church. Yet the latter practice of the parishes contained more than a germ of defiance of the Church of England's hierarchical principles; now and then it became articulate. On the eve of the Revolution, in a tiny Maryland parish which was situated on the Eastern Shore of Chesapeake Bay close to the Virginia line, there broke out a conflict of ideas which is clearly in point. When the governor of that province—who was not allowed to defer to the vestries, in the style of Virginia—inducted a new clergyman and excluded the man of the vestry's preference, argument and violence flared up. The people themselves are the true source of church government, the vestry of Coventry parish protested, and to their rights all other authority must defer. Of course the episode shows an application to the particular situation of ideas being hotly affirmed everywhere in the wake of the Stamp Act. But it also shows a principled effort by laymen to reduce the pretensions of hierarchical church government. "I profess myself a sincere son of the established church," said Richard Bland, a member of the Virginia House of Burgesses at about the same time, "but I can embrace her Doctrines without approving of her Hierarchy, which I know to be a Relick of the Papal Incroachments upon the Common Law."°

The two sets of authorities which had each some control over the Church of England establishments, the church hierarchy at home and the parishes and assemblies in America, during the 1690s entered the rivalry for authority which now seems to have been unavoidable. Bishop Compton sent to Virginia an energetic, Scottish-born and -educated priest, James Blair. After brief service as rector of a parish near Jamestown, that clergyman was elevated to be commissary of the province—in effect, the bishop's representative and deputy. Blair visited the parishes throughout Virginia; he consulted with the ministers; he convened them for discussion; the religious needs of the colony were elaborately reviewed. Blair, and commissaries elsewhere, had some success in encouraging ways of orthodoxy and regularity in the church. But no commissary ever had—in fact, the bishop of London had no power to give to him—the peculiar authorities of a bishop on which church discipline rests: he could not confirm a member or ordain a minister of the church; neither was he given a share in the governor's power of induction (the bishop's power, at home); nor could he remove a wayward minister from his parish. Thus, though Blair held the office of commissary for more than fifty years, and as college president and member of the governor's council became a figure in affairs, he could never force through ecclesiastical reforms. Authoritative control waited for the resident bishop, who never came.

The one exception to the record of low institutional achievement which was the fate of the Anglican church in the Southern Colonies was the building of William and Mary College. Although the settlers of Jamestown had not founded an Oxford-derived college to precede or match the Cambridge-derived one on the banks of the Charles, they had wanted to do so. In 1690, during his first year as commissary, James Blair, himself an alumnus of Edinburgh, renewed that hope. Visiting London, acting on the request of the colony assembly, he secured the support of Bishop Compton and of the theologian archbishop of Canterbury, John Tillotson. King William and Queen Mary became interested. Besides their name they gave the college a royal charter; their deed of 1696 made William and Mary the only colonial college to have this standing, which put it on a legal footing like that of Oxford and Cambridge. The sovereigns assigned from Virginia sources sizable funds for building and for an income of two thousand pounds a year; they designated James Blair president for life. When the president returned to Virginia, moreover, he bore a gift from Robert Boyle, the chemist—the endowment of "the Brafferton" which would provide for the education of Indians within the college. He brought also the set of drawings with which Christopher Wren had presented him, for the building which still memorializes beautifully the legacy from England to which the college was born.

Although a fire and loss of records prevent us from knowing intimately the early history of the college, the charter and early bylaws establish a kind of turning point between English and American methods of organizing higher education. The charter assigned to the president and faculty, as a corporation, the control of the college's considerable properties as well as the direction of the students. This was a long step toward faculty self-government, on the model of the colleges in the English universities; by the same token it was a step in the opposite direction from Harvard, where fellows of the corporation and overseers, leading citizens (then clergymen) not of the faculty, were taking charge—much like modern American college trustees. But the step went only part way. Another provision of the college charter created a board of governors and visitors and gave it power to elect the president and the professors. The charter provided further—odd though the arrangement seems in a deed of gift from the Crown, approved by bishops in England—that the board itself should be elected by the Virginia assembly. This did not destroy, but it did impose a condition on, the self-government granted to the faculty. It inserted a factor of provincial politics and laymen's control into the constitution of the college; it was much like the vestries' control of the parish churches. The difference between William and Mary and the full self-government of the colleges of Oxford and Cambridge is a measure of the influence of Virginia's colonial situation on the structure of academic life.°

During the eighteenth century, undergraduates in the "philosophy school" of the college were trained, much as at Harvard, in the traditional English curriculum based on trivium and quadrivium. Grammar—

that is, Latin grammar with a real command of the language—was a condition of entrance. Logic and rhetoric, and also ethics, were the teaching assignment made to one professor by the college statutes of 1727. This took care of the trivium. The quadrivium was more loosely adapted: the second professor was assigned physics, metaphysics, and mathematics, an arrangement which was close to the medieval tradition. When Professor William Small came to Williamsburg, about 1760, this assignment meant substantial work in contemporary physical science. By building on these studies, young men were actually prepared for careers in the church, as the founders and givers in England had hoped. But only one religious leader educated at William and Mary before the American Revolution, the future president of the college and bishop of the Protestant Episcopal Church, James Madison (not the U.S. president), is remembered among the colonial alumni, while many lawyer and statesmen alumni are well remembered, Thomas Jefferson at the head of the list.

Finally, William and Mary undertook a good deal of duty which was foreign to its tradition as an English college. This began with the Brafferton, where elementary instruction was sometimes given to Indian and white children together. From the beginning, the college had to provide also a Latin grammar-school department for students who came insufficiently prepared in the classical languages to go ahead with the regular work. Altogether, William and Mary, like many an American college of the future, meeting its student body halfway, had to reduce and defer its hopes for higher education. The dictum of Hugh Jones, a young graduate of Oxford, although it was given in 1724 after a serious fire, touched a perennial problem of hopes deferred: "a college without a chapel, without a scholarship, . . . a library without books." If in many respects William and Mary was a pretty divided institution—governed by English clergymen *and* Virginia men of affairs; seeking to train men for the ministry *but* mainly training them for other callings; chartered for higher education *but* maintaining also elementary and secondary schools—such was the condition imposed by time and place. The college succeeded in meeting many of the needs for education in the oldest and most populous colony, and to a degree did so for the Southern Colonies generally. Not until after political independence would the region have a second college, and not for many years one more advanced in higher learning; after the separation from England, new Episcopalian institutions there would be few and lacking in prominence.

From Maryland northward to the fishing settlements on Newfoundland, through colonies which amounted to about half of England's American domains, no single establishment of the Church of England was ever instituted. Until well into the eighteenth century, there were only four places of Anglican worship: King's Chapel in Boston; Trinity Church in New York, founded in 1697; Christ Church, Philadelphia, far short of its later opulence and architectural grandeur; and a mission church, St. Mary's, in Burlington, New Jersey. The Middle Colonies and New England were the huge exceptions, surely, to *cujus regio ejus religio* anywhere in the New World.

This made them the natural concern of the S.P.G., which represented a truly transatlantic effort to galvanize Church of England energies in the colonies. The Reverend Thomas Bray, Bishop Compton's commissary in Maryland, founded the organization; Archbishop Tillotson sponsored it; merchants in London and crown officeholders in America were prominent among the members and sustainers. While the society did place funds in the Anglican colonies, for instance when it sent theological libraries to southern parishes where scepticism was reported, it tried harder to convert Indian pagans and northern-colonial dissenters than to bring Church of England backsliders into line. One S.P.G. missionary called William Penn a greater anti-Christ than Julian the Apostate had been; others abused Puritans and non-English churchmen. But the humanitarian work of the S.P.G. among Negroes and Indians must have been more eloquent and appealing to contemporaries, as it now is in the society's history, than the name-calling, which seems to have been thoroughly useless. With the passing of years, numbers of colonial Quakers did in fact slip quietly into the Anglican parishes; so did a good many Lutherans, including a minister member of the Mühlenberg family, once they became familiar with the English language and community.

The most dramatic phase of the Anglican advance occurred in New England, at first without connection with the S.P.G. At Yale College during the year when that institution of Puritan orthodoxy turned twenty-one years old (and when the S.P.G. did, too), 1722, Timothy Cutler, the rector, divulged on a public occasion that he preferred the Church of England to the Congregational Church. Daniel Brown, the tutor who at the moment was the one other member of the faculty, joined him; so did Samuel Johnson, a recent tutor who was now the minister of the congregation at West Haven, and four other Connecticut ministers. For these men to say in concert that they had come to doubt the validity of their ordination, without a bishop, was as shocking in their time and place, according to a president of Yale nearly two centuries later, as if the modern "theological faculty of the college were to declare for the Church of Rome, avow their belief in transsubstantiation, and pray to the Virgin Mary." Rector and tutor were speedily "excused" from their positions, and they and Johnson set off for England.° Meanwhile a very young tutor, Jonathan Edwards, was placed in charge of the college.

The Puritan background of these surprising conversions to the Church of England could not have been more true-blue. Cutler was descended from early settlers at Charlestown, Massachusetts; after Harvard he had quickly achieved recognition as a preacher. He had married the daughter of the Yale rector whom he succeeded in office. Johnson was the son of a humble Connecticut family; he had been educated at the township Latin school at Saybrook, and at Yale. The specific influence which changed their minds was neither more nor less than the reading they chose among seven hundred books which had been recently given the college library. Young and serious men, they studied as if with new eyes "our best English poets, philosophers, and divines, Shakespeare and Milton, . . . Boyle and Newton, . . . Tillotson . . . etc.," according to Johnson's account. They examined especially the Church of England theologians; they reconsidered in that light the covenant theology on which they had been reared. Their conclusion came hard and seemed inevitable. Again in Johnson's own words: "They all loved their country, and were beloved by it. . . . It was therefore very grievous to them to think of going into conclusions that they knew would be very distressing to their friends and very grievous to their country. They therefore honestly tried to satisfy themselves if possible to continue as they were; they resolved to examine things impartially and read the best things on both sides of the question." They studied the church fathers in the original. After all their reading and discussion, "The result was, that from the facts in Scripture, compared with the facts of the primitive church immediately after and so downward it appeared very plain that the episcopal government of the church was universally established by the Apostles."°

Cutler and Johnson decided to take Anglican orders. Already entranced by traditional doctrine, they loved on arrival in England the medieval splendor of cathedrals and colleges. Cutler, who was thirty-eight, was made doctor of divinity by both Oxford and Cambridge; on return to New England he began a second prominent career as rector of the new Christ Church in Boston. Samuel Johnson, who was a dozen years younger, returned to Connecticut. He started his own, more circuitous, route to prominence by taking charge under S.P.G. auspices of the first Church of England parish in Connecticut—at Stratford, down Long Island Sound from New Haven.

Different from all but a few of the mid-century clergymen in Virginia, Church of England ministers in New England preached aggressively in behalf of increased conformity and regularity with the church at home. Long before the question of having a bishop in America became politically acute (during the 1760s), Cutler and Johnson preached the benefits of that reform. No bishop, no church, they felt, with a force which southern clergymen seldom shared.° Likewise the converts had a zeal for Anglican ritual; Samuel Johnson voiced this taste, as for "a luxuriant garden," in a sermon, "On the Beauty of Holiness in the Worship of the Church of England."° In Johnson's case Church of England loyalty encouraged—what no Virginia parson ever developed—an intellect productive of abstract ideas about faith. During three decades of parish work at Stratford, he did the most substantial part of the writing which requires, in a modern edition, four solid volumes to print. His most ambitious work, *Elementa Philosophica*, which Benjamin Franklin published in 1752, combined two fields of theory. A work of philosophy, not theology, the part subtitled *Noetica* largely follows the metaphysics of Bishop George Berkeley, whose personal and intellectual friendship Johnson had enjoyed about 1730, when that churchman philosopher (not yet a bishop) was in Rhode Island. The author stood more on his own feet in the part subtitled *Ethica*. Pretty much affected by Arminian doctrine, Johnson came out strongly for individual moral independence. His object throughout was to reconcile Christian faith with Lockian and Newtonian science. While Johnson was still a village parson, Oxford honored him with a doctorate of divinity, in recognition of his writings.°

Meanwhile he had married into a Long Island family of prominence and had made friends with the royal governor of New York. Thus, when in 1754 it was decided to found King's College, the future Columbia University, paths opened easily and naturally for him to become first president. The charter required an Anglican for the position. In Johnson's own announcement about the new undertaking: "the chief thing aimed at in this college is to teach and engage the children to know God in Jesus Christ." He himself gladly conducted the college worship and taught New Testament in Greek to the entering students. The fussy, parental, and pious American college president of the nineteenth century had a prototype in Samuel Johnson.

Yet, as director of a pioneer academic enterprise, he took a moderately liberal course. Not different from William and Mary and the Puritan colleges, to be sure, the Laws and Orders of King's College, dated 1758, laid down a sequence of studies based on the trivium and quadrivium.° But the total curriculum was much broader. During the second, third, and fourth years, the students were assigned, along with logic and mathematics, "all the several branches" of modern "experimental philosophy," with "agriculture and merchandise together with something of the classics and criticism all the while," and with "the chief principles of law and government, together with history, sacred and profane." The scholar, who had tired of old William Ames during his own twenties and had introduced Isaac Newton to his tutorial students in New Haven, now let the students at King's read, for instance, Francis Hutcheson, the contemporary Scot who coined the phrase "the greatest happiness for the greatest number"; such thinkers friendly to freedom as Grotius and Pufendorf were likewise encouraged. As president, not different from his inclination as writer, Johnson proved a tolerant, assimilating, and philosophical guide.

Considered together, William and Mary and King's colleges, in their similarities and differences, represent the best of Anglicanism in the colonies. In the Southern Colonies, the Church of England as a series of establishments did serve society and government practically and well. In the church as transplanted there, the direction of growth was toward the colonies' own condition: less hierarchy, less clericalism, less ornate worship, and higher education less high than in the mother country. On the other hand, somewhat in the Southern Colonies, and distinctly in the northern and middle regions, the Church of England in the eighteenth century ventured its own counter-reformation, with a main effort in education. We take a measure on the church overseas when we consider that, where it had its most creative effect, the leaders, James Blair and Samuel Johnson, were not bishops (though they would have liked to be) but were college presidents instead.

3   The Independent Presbyterians

PRESBYTERIANISM came to the colonies in two waves. First, during the 1630s and 1640s, it struck Massachusetts as a theory of church polity; it stopped very short, that time, of reaching acceptance and power. It came second as Scottish Presbyterian institutions and thought, the dominant loyalty of the Scots-Irish immigrants. This wave lapped America before 1700; it reached crest around 1730. From the point of view of the movement itself, it is too bad that the two did not coincide and combine. In that event presbyterianism might have had an early effect equal to Puritan congregationalism. With luck in getting a royal a Presybterian Church establishment which might or might not have charter, there might have been a real New Scotland in America, with been an extension of the Church of Scotland.

As the waves did come, the Scottish and institutional one far separated in time and place from the English one, presbyterianism deployed. It never controlled more than local communities. But they were numerous. They stretched from Londonderry, New Hampshire, to the settlements on the Watauga in western North Carolina. Presbyterians became a faction in politics in some colonies, conspicuously Pennsylvania; they won occasional political victories and favors, as when the College of New Jersey, the future Princeton University, was chartered. Beyond such gains they did not advance; they nowhere achieved such a joint church establishment as was especially sought in Virginia, one in which the Presbyterian Church and the Anglican church might have shared the product of church taxes in a colony.

The traditionally recognized beginning place of the Presbyterian Church in America is the Eastern Shore of Maryland; and, although the recent scholarship of Leonard J. Trinterud and others now makes clear that the little congregations there were simply one origin among several which occurred at the same time, the old story still represents very fairly the way in which Presbyterianism took root. Francis Makemie, the founder in the Rehoboth and Snow Hill vicinity of Maryland, was born in Ireland and trained at the University of Glasgow. About 1682, in his early twenties, he crossed the ocean to become a missionary, at first a wandering one, in the Southern Colonies. The defense he made of the Westminster Confession, against Church of England officials who opposed him, gave promise of the stress on doctrine which he and his kind would sustain. In Maryland he settled and married and became well-to-do; he used his congregations and his property there as a base from which to visit new congregations, as they were founded, and to weave intercongregational acquaintanceship and connection among them. During a visit to New York in 1707, moreover, the year before he died, Makemie struck a blow for religious freedom. Lord Cornbury, a spendthrift and autocratic governor, disliked his presence as a speaker and called him "a Preacher, a Doctor of Physick, a Merchant, an Attorney or Counsellor at Law, and which is worse of all, a Disturber of Governments." He was thrown into jail on grounds of preaching without a license. Makemie's counsel pleaded in a vein which has some of the characteristics of sociological jurisprudence in our century. Because New York was "made up chiefly of Foreigners and Dissenters, and Persecution would but only tend to the disuniting us all in Interest and Affection, not depopulate and weaken our strength," and because "this Prosecution is the first of this Nature or sort, ever was in this Province," the preacher should be acquitted, the lawyer argued.° Thus, seventy years after the Massachusetts Remonstrance, a Presbyterian spokesman once again declared prominently for religious toleration. Doubtless Makemie's success owed nearly everything to a more favorable environment than Dr. Child had had. England's policy of toleration was now nearly twenty years old. Lord Cornbury was hated by the New York assembly; the next year, when it made protests to the Crown partly on account of Makemie, the governor was put out of office.

Freedom to worship was a need strongly felt by Presbyterians out of Scotland; but federated organization was the operating, inborn principle of their church. In the nature of the case, that principle could not be put instantly to work. With Scots-Irish Presbyterians, as with Puritan congregationalists, establishing the covenanted congregations came first. Yet as the new settlements began to occur within horseback distances of one another, Presbyterian ministers managed to keep in touch. Makemie associated his own congregations with others as far north as New Jersey; in 1706 he and six other ministers established in Philadelphia the first American presbytery. Although the presbytery was the lowest of the three federating institutions of the Church of Scotland— the synod and the national convention were above—it was the essential one. Believers found revelation and confirmation of it in the Book of Acts; its animating function was its governance as to doctrine and appointment. The jurisdiction was small enough so that the ministers could consult in presbyterial session; they could visit one another's congregations and examine troublesome problems; above all, they could supervise and examine young men studying for the ministry and ordain such candidates as they approved. Before presbyteries were established, Presbyterians in America had no choice but to send to Scotland or Ireland for new ministers, as Anglicans and Dutch Reformed and Lutherans were obliged to do. When they had a presbytery of their own, they became as free as any congregationalists were to build new churches, as rapidly as ministers became available.

Presbyteries sprang up north and south. Before the 1740s, when the Great Awakening subdivided the church for some years, half a dozen came into being in the Middle Colonies; one was set up in New Hampshire, the "Irish presbytery" of New England. Between 1740 and the Revolution the number doubled. The new ones included the Hanover presbytery in Virginia, where the superb organizing and preaching of Dr. Samuel Davies, future president of Princeton, created a federation of his own.° Meanwhile, beginning in 1716, only a decade after the founding of the first presbytery, the first synod was established in the same place, Philadelphia. Ministers discussed doctrine in that meeting; but because all enforcing power was left to the presbyteries, the synod acquired little authority. The apex of the Presbyterian structure, a national assembly, waited until after the Revolution to be organized.

Closely related to the urgency the Scots-Irish felt about presbyteries was the determination they displayed to have their ministers well prepared. During their century of living in northern Ireland their choice in the matter had lain between sending their young men back to the Scottish universities for training (or recruiting ministers there) and training them, apprentice style, under their own ministers. In America the choice lay among those same options and a third one, namely, sending the candidates to Harvard or Yale for B.A. and M.A. training. The choice of Scotland was expensive and difficult on other accounts, after two removals from there. The older and more well-to-do congregations around Philadelphia were the ones which cherished Scots education and doctrine so dearly as to insist on having their ministers from that source. Harvard and Yale offered only a more convenient alternative.

Though those colleges remained loyal to the covenant theology, common to Congregationalist and Presbyterian, neither place fitted well Scottish immigrant feeling.

Thus residence in America argued strongly in favor of making their own provisions to educate their young men. The so-called "schools of the prophets" were the first solution of the problem. A little paradoxically, the earliest teaching "prophets" were not immigrants who had previously trained ministers in Ireland but were emigrant New England ministers who, having taken charge of Puritan-derived congregations in northern New Jersey, decided to affiliate with the presbytery of Philadelphia. The Reverend Jonathan Dickinson, who, as a recent graduate of Yale when he was ordained minister at Elizabeth, knew what a young and informal school was like, is the principal case. He took the ideas of Presbyterianism and his residence among the Scots-Irish as an opportunity: he persuaded his own congregation to join the Philadelphia presbytery, and he persuaded his minister colleagues there not to make the Westminster Confession fully required of all congregations. Twice he was elected moderator of the synod; his preaching and his writing won him recognition as a theologian. When he opened his home as a kind of apprentice school for ministerial candidates, students did come; perhaps his group was no smaller than the number of M.A. students at the Yale he had attended, during that college's first decade. Others of like background followed his example. The Reverend Aaron Burr, a son of Connecticut and Yale and the father of his well-known namesake, trained ministers at the Presbyterian manse in Newark, New Jersey.

The spectacle which inheres in the *rapprochement*, about three thousand miles from the university in Glasgow and one hundred miles from the college in New Haven, between later-day New England Puritanism and Scots-derived Presbyterianism is heightened by the school of the prophets which outdid all the others. The "Log College," as it was known at the time, was founded by William Tennent soon after emigrating from Ireland, at Neshaminy, Pennsylvania, near the Delaware River north of Philadelphia. It deserves to be recognized, according to Trinterud, as having been "the most important event in colonial Presbyterianism." Though born in Ireland and educated at the University of Edinburgh, Tennent had begun his ministry in the espicopalian Church of Ireland; then he married a Presbyterian and became one. During his middle fifties, with a numerous family of sons, he crossed to Philadelphia and became a minister there. Within a decade or so, he founded his institution, something a little bigger, more spontaneous and purely Presbyterian, than the Connecticut-derived schools a few miles to the north.

If the Log College was truly a college (and we may give it the benefit of the doubt), then William Tennent was president, board, and faculty; the log house, which gave him four hundred square feet of floor space outside his residence, was his hall of advanced studies. The curriculum included Latin and Greek, Bible and theology. The known alumni, of the decade or so of the college's existence, are impressive. Among Tennent's four sons whom he trained, Gilbert Tennent would become easily the second theological figure of the Great Awakening, after Jonathan Edwards. Other graduates include Samuel Davies and Samuel Finley, who would both serve (after Jonathan Dickinson) as president of the College of New Jersey. (Although that institution ranks, of course, as the culmination of Presbyterianism's colonial achievement in education, we must reserve it for its required place in our story, after the Great Awakening.)

As we come on all this personal and institutional initiative we are dealing, for the first time in this book, with a church completely displaced from political and economic preference throughout its entire American history. Altogether dependent on its people's voluntary effort, the Presbyterian Church gathered enormous loyalty. The gift for community-building which we find among all evangelicals doubtless was here enhanced by the clannishness of the Scots. The following passage comes from an anonymous pamphlet published in 1743. The date identifies it as a product of the Great Awakening, but content and title, *Renewal of the Covenants, National and Solemn League*, identify it also as Scots and Presbyterian, by origin and character.

> We find ourselves under a necessity from the Word of God, and from a true covenanted Reformation and our baptismal vows . . . to declare a defensive War against all Usurpers of the Royal Prerogative of the Glorious Lamb of God. . . . We also declare, that we look upon ourselves as bound by the Law of God, and the Law of Nature, to endeavor to defend our religious Liberties wherewith Christ hath made us free and our Bodies and Goods, from all kind of false Impositions, Intrigues, Snares, treacherous Deceitfulness . . . with our best Skill, Power, bodily Strength and Activity.°

Thus less than a century after their arrival in the New World, the Scots-Irish Presbyterians, federalizers by commitment and educators by tradition, were practicing on a uniquely wide scale the arts of voluntary organization which very soon would be their great gift, conveyed by first example, to America.

4   *Dutch and German Churches Expatriated*

FOR the churches of British origin—Anglican, Congregational, and Presbyterian—location in the New World, though it involved certain restrictions in every case, created, as we have seen, expansive opportunities for spiritual, intellectual, and institutional achievement. The other three churches—Roman Catholic, Lutheran, and Reformed—discovered opportunity for life in the English colonial world, a remarkable fact in itself. But they had to work within bounds much narrower than the British churches.

During the eighteenth century Roman Catholics were excluded from the political life of the one colony, Maryland, which they had dominated in the seventeenth century and where wealth in land still protected a few great families. In America as in England higher education was closed to Catholics—unless possibly a few slipped into the non-religious College of Philadelphia during the last two decades of colonial life. The sons of families like the Carrolls and the Darnalls went to the Jesuit college of St. Omer in Flanders, and sometimes to Paris, for study. Mass was celebrated privately, in family chapels. Maryland's anti-Catholic taxation of the French and Indian War period made Charles Carroll of Doughoregan think seriously of emigrating, perhaps to Louisiana; the inactivity of the few priests of the Jesuit order who were in the province disturbed Father John Carroll during the 1760s, when he returned to Maryland after a period overseas. The pope's world-wide suppression of the Jesuits a few years later brought on the all-time nadir of institutional Catholicism in America. There seems to have been a scattering of Catholic immigrants in the port cities, but until after the Revolution their church life was pretty fugitive.

The second, or German, coming of Lutherans to the colonies began about 1715. In the homeland theirs was the prime Protestant church which, under the system of *cujus regio ejus religio*, attached itself with the most complete dependence on the princes; it depended also on a ministry close to a priesthood in authority. These were characteristics hard to adjust to conditions in the English colonies. But when, slow to move, they did cross the seas, hard times was the main reason and in every way they had to be practical. Most of them stopped in Pennsylvania, often settling west and south of Philadelphia in the Lancaster and York area. Others went on, into the Frederick and Hagerstown area of Maryland and south into the Valley of Virginia and beyond; a famous Salzburger element went to Georgia, direct. They suffered a grievous shortage of ministers. Thus willy-nilly Lutheran laymen were often forced to do what the Puritans had done by preference—gather their own congregations and somewhat democratize their habits of church operation.

Much the same occurred among German immigrants of the Reformed faith. For their church also, the immigration of the eighteenth century, a hundred years after the settlement of New Amsterdam, was a second American beginning. Before the 1740s they received little help from the Dutch Reformed; their widely deployed congregations, like those of the early Scots-Irish, were thrown each on its own. In the absence of classis (about the same as a presbytery) and synod, their congregations had to be more self-organizing than theory and previous experience made easy; in the shortage of clergymen, their laymen too came forward.

Under like frontier conditions, and alike deprived by their distance from German patrons, universities, and church authorities, the German Lutherans and Reformed forgot something of their two-centuries-old rivalry in Europe. In a Maryland frontier community, for example, Lutherans and Reformed arranged to use alternately the same church building. In an eloquent event of a saintly lifetime, Count Nikolaus Ludwig Zinzendorf—mystic, Moravian bishop, and Lutheran minister—tried, while he visited Pennsylvania in 1741 and 1742, to unite all German Protestants in a "Congregation of God and the Spirit." This was an effort to transcend, not to eliminate, prior church loyalties. Though it failed of that goal, Zinzendorf's proposal to convene "union synods" on an interconfessional basis did succeed for a while.°

The more lasting consolidations came at the time of the Great Awakening; they did not override, but followed, old lines of German church theology and polity. At that time able and effective young leaders came from Europe to both the Lutherans and the Reformed. Henry Melchior Mühlenberg, a graduate of the new university at Göttingen and the first of many to bring its influence to America, arrived in 1742. He had enough knowledge of medicine and law to serve his congregation of St. Michael's and Zion's, in Philadelphia, in the practical ways familiar in New England. Saturated with Lutheran theology, and with a pietist's belief in the new German humanitarianism which flowed from Halle, where he had taught, Mühlenberg became a kind of German Cotton Mather. Because his talents included a gift for languages, he traveled and preached in English and Dutch as well as in German. He founded the first Lutheran ministerium in this country. As this body assumed the authority to ordain new ministers, his parenthood of it makes him the real father of the Lutheran Church in America.

Mühlenberg's opposite number in the Reformed Church, Michael Schlatter, came to America as a missionary of the church in Holland. But he was Swiss born and was trained in a German university, Helmstedt, as well as at Leyden; he arrived probably as well equipped as anyone could have been to bridge the gap of history, language, and higher and lower social classes, between the Dutch Reformed of the Hudson valley and the German Reformed to the south. He visited about fifty congregations. The Dutch, some of whom were restless and defiant of their church's dependence on authority in Holland, had set up a coetus, which assumed that it had the right to ordain ministers. Schlatter helped organize another, among the Germans, although they did not yet seek church autonomy. Not until 1793, when a Reformed synod of unquestionable authority was organized, can that church be counted as fully independent in America, in that respect equal to the Congregationalist and Presbyterian churches.

Neither of the two German churches made as urgent a matter of higher education in America as did the British churches. Yet, more a Dutch effort than a German one, the Reformed did have their apprentice-style training of ministers, like the Presbyterians. From the little school of a Dutch "prophet," John Frelinghuysen, member of a family of divines, Queen's College, the present Rutgers University, was launched in 1771—with barely time and life enough to graduate four students before the Revolution delayed things further.° German Lutherans, whose ministers were extraordinarily loyal to their home universities, and who kept up lively correspondence with pietist leaders at home, founded no college until 1787. Then they located it at Lancaster, Pennsylvania, and named it Franklin College, for a friend. Gotthilf Ernst Mühlenberg, son of Henry Melchoir Mühlenberg, himself a graduate of Halle and a strong humanitarian preacher, a good botanist and friend of science too, became the first president. (In 1853, when Franklin College by a merger became Franklin and Marshall, the combined institution became more Reformed than Lutheran.)°

While the two early Dutch and German church colleges in America were probably less specifically intended for preparing ministers than were Harvard and Yale and the predecessors of Princeton, they shared fully the first impulse of all the colonial colleges (except Philadelphia) to rear their young men in the ways of faith and national tradition to which they had been born.

5   *Church Leveling and*
    Christian Voluntarism

Religion always sides with povertie," said George Herbert at about the time when a number of his fellow graduates of Cambridge University, in an undertaking very different from any of his own, were founding the colony of Massachusetts Bay. His words now seem prophetic of all six of the churches transplanted from Europe to England's America.

Yet, while every one of them suffered a phase of impoverishment, they were all creators of institutional structure and wealth. Along a thousand miles of American coastline, where in 1600 there had not been a single building for Christian worship, in 1760 there were hundreds. A few churches in every colony were both handsome and costly. By that time there were flourishing, also, two Congregationalist colleges, two Anglican ones, and one Presbyterian one, all of them placing considerable stress on preparation for the ministry. Before the end of the eighteenth century, besides those five and the two German Protestant colleges, the Catholic Church also would have a college, Georgetown, and a Sulpician seminary, St. Mary's in Baltimore. If, omitting the Church of England as a special case, we list the historical churches in the presumable order of their wealth—the Congregational Church, the Presbyterian Church, the Reformed Church, the Lutheran Church, the Roman Catholic Church—we have also the probable order of their numbers and the order of their effort in education.° This order is the exact reverse of the order of their political and economic entrenchment in Europe.

Where, in the three sections preceding this one, we have examined the salient and characteristic differences among the six churches, now in conclusion it is time to note the similarities, besides spread of settlement and physical accumulation. We have seen all the churches affected, after the shock of separation from their political and economic privileges in Europe, by the condition of competition, each with one or more of the others. In every case the churches' important new institutions and practices were the self-perpetuating ones: their congregation building, their habits about communion, their ways of obtaining ordained ministers, their provisions for education. In all regions of colonial America the voluntary Christian church became a massive habit, well before political independence was achieved.°

CHAPTER VI

The Expansion of Pietist Faith

Great is their peace who know a limit to their ambitious minds, that have learned to be contented with the appointments and bounds of providence, that are not careful to be great, but being great are humble and do good.

William Penn, No Cross, No Crown

We should all then, like the quakers, live without an order of priests, moralise for ourselves, follow the oracle of conscience, and say nothing about what no man can understand, nor therefore believe; for I suppose belief to be the assent of the mind to an intelligible proposition.

Thomas Jefferson to John Adams,
August 22, 1813

1 *Mysticism, Pietism, and Sectarianism*

ASTERN and Western Christianity alike have occasionally produced belief of the kind which Rufus Jones, the Quaker historian and philosopher, called "spiritual religion." It is the mystical strain of Christian piety. Believing that God enters human hearts through their love of Jesus Christ, the spiritual religionist believes further that God guides history whenever men are governed by that love. English Quakers of the seventeenth century, the earliest and the principal bringers of the strain to America, cherished especially the first chapter of the Gospel of St. John. Like John the Baptist, they saw their purpose as "to bear witness of the Light, that all men through him might believe." The ninth verse of the same chapter—"That was the true Light, which lighteth every man that cometh into the world"—may be called the Quaker verse; probably it sums up better than anything else the intuition around which the mind of the spiritual religionist revolves.

This vein of thought and feeling is so much a matter of what individuals apprehend privately that it appears in various contexts. The two clear cases of spiritual religion, among persons prominent in this book so far, were both Massachusetts Puritans. The earlier one, Anne Hutchinson, was a figure of controversy and persecution; the other, Edward Taylor, a teaching elder in a place and a time so quiet that, except for his poems of passion for Christ which were kept secret so long, we should hardly know of his having existed. The gentle Francis of Assisi represented spiritual religion during the period when medieval Catholicism contained its greatest variety of Christian faith. Martin Luther, the fighter, had much of it in him too, when, three centuries after St. Francis, he shattered the medieval church.

Over the centuries the characteristic of the Christian mystic which has now and then drawn him, as it did both Luther and Mrs. Hutchinson, into public prominence has been his capacity for standing alone. "*Secessi de popolo*"—"I have seceded from society"—said Tertullian, the theologian of Carthage who, having served the early Latin church superbly, withdrew into a mystical heresy; Tertullian requires to be counted as one of the beginners of spiritual religion. Another of his phrases, which helps us approach the English Quakers, is household wisdom still: "The blood of the martyrs is the seed of the church."

The line which distinguishes the more deviant persons of spiritual religion from people who are simply weird or deranged distinguishes between persons who have spiritual and intellectual integrity, within the terms of their Christian profession, and those who do not. It distinguishes the anchorite from the mere recluse, the saint who preaches to birds from the psychotic who thinks he is one. But the line is often unclear, even to friendly judges; in the nature of the case, orthodoxy, whether it be Roman Catholic, Protestant, or other, is suspicious of the type. Yet beside the strength spiritual religionists are given by the Bible, they regularly have recourse to the font of ancient philosophy. Wherever some form of logic, Aristotelian or other, supplies a church establishment with weapons with which to try to drive them into line, a philosopher or philosophy of the Platonic lineage seems to turn up to give them comfort. This has happened over and over, from Plotinus to Emerson. "Antinomian" is usually an accurate designation for the spiritual religionists, though it is not always applied; their brand of faith has refused through the centuries to be held at bay and destroyed.

So much could be derived from the long record, without regard for the English and German mystics who began about 1650 a century of immigration to the colonies. What the Quakers and German pietists— radical sectarians, much like the Quakers, and Lutherans who were affected by the movement at Halle—brought to America with them which was new in the history of Western Christianity was spiritual religion, gathered and organized on its own terms and rapidly becoming free to act as it would. Before 1700, when mystics gathered, they had usually done so with permission, under the discipline of the Catholic Church; this was the case, for example, with St. Francis and the early Franciscans, and with the Brethren of the Common Life at Deventer, of whom Thomas a Kempis was one. In cases when the mystics had been heretical and defiant, as was true of the ancient Montanists to whom Tertullian seceded, and was true of the Waldenses of the very time of

St. Francis, they had been isolated and persecuted severely. But by the second half of the seventeenth century spiritual religion was spreading widely. To be sure, in the form preached at Halle, which had a sizable following among churchmen, it was mild and humanitarian. Quakers were harshly treated for three decades in England; so were the sects in the Germanies. But like certain Puritans of the 1630s, a certain Quaker of the 1680s was suddenly given favors by the king; and toleration, some time before the law of 1689 was enacted, became generally available to Friends in England. Much more than toleration—real freedom and political power—became available to those who accepted William Penn's invitation and settled in Pennsylvania.

Thus when opportunity came, it arrived with an unfamiliar great rush. And when the Quakers, who were truly radical religionists, settled in the valley of the Delaware River, the door was opened as widely to new devotional and moral undertakings as could possibly be.

2 English Friends and American Colonies

In 1647, at the age of twenty-three, George Fox began preaching in central England the religion of the indwelling Christ to which he felt called; because his followers trembled when they worshiped, they became known as "quakers." Bizarre procedures, such as interrupting the worship of church congregations with strongly worded appeals and refusing to remove hats in the presence of civil and ecclesiastical officers, made Fox's people subject to misunderstanding. (Removing the hat, in stone-cold parish churches, was an honor Quakers paid only to God.) Fox gave many reasons which were not bizarre, however, for taking his message seriously. Inner knowledge of the Holy Spirit is more important than reading knowledge of the Bible, he insisted; it is the one true revelation. Not changes in church and state, such as Reformation and revolution were working, but social and moral transformation is God's requirement, he preached.

Fox was the son of a weaver, a churchwarden in Drayton, Leicestershire, who was known as a "Righteous Christer," a Puritan. Living in the grazing country of central England, he himself was apprenticed as a boy to a wool raiser; although his home was above poverty level and there was talk of his studying for the ministry, the necessary university education seems not to have been a serious possibility. His preaching as a young man, and much of it throughout his life, was directed to country people. The historical interpretation of the character of English Protestantism, which points out that beginning with Wyclif English farmers acquired a habit of heterodoxy, helps explain why George Fox quickly won a large following.° Concerning his feeling about doctrine, we know that he resisted the Puritan predestinarianism of the minister of Drayton and that for his own associates he preferred Seekers and Anabaptists to Puritans—as Roger Williams, visiting England, also did.

During its first, or middle-century, phase, Quakerism belonged to the working people. In this respect it contrasts with Puritanism, a generation earlier. Where the leaders of that movement were accustomed to property and power and were seeking more, George Fox and most of his associates derived from subpolitical classes; they mocked power in ways that stung. Their *thee*'s and *thou*'s, the intimate second person in place of the honorific *you*, signified their belief in the equality of men, in the eyes of God and in their own. Offending against the laws which penalized blasphemy and sustained conformity, Quakers went often to jail. Fox was brought into court some sixty times and was jailed eight times, as frequently during the Commonwealth period as after Charles II was restored. Altogether he spent six years in prison. In 1680 William Penn told king and Parliament that 10,000 Quakers had been imprisoned and that 243 had died there.° In Fox's case the detentions impaired his health, seriously at least once, but they never broke him; every time he returned to preaching in a more ambitious way.

Meanwhile, as the movement broadened, its rural and working-class character yielded to something more composite. The most conspicuous early upper-class convert was Margaret Fell, the wife of a judge who sympathized with the movement; after his death, Mrs. Fell married Fox, when he was forty-five. Her loyalty put her home, Swarthmore Hall, at the disposal of Quaker organizers. The work which they did there, conferring and writing advice to distant sympathizers, is one sign among many that by constant effort the Friends (as they decided to style themselves) were building up a moral and spiritual community of great inner loyalty. In 1671 Quakers in London, by establishing the Yearly Meeting there (somewhat like a presbytery), put the movement on an advanced basis of organization. In that same year Fox went overseas to preach in the West Indies and the continental colonies. As we know from the Puritan persecution of Quakers in Boston, this mission followed by fifteen years the earliest Quaker arrivals in the colonies; Fox's visit coincided rather with the beginning of Quaker investment overseas—first of all, in New Jersey—than with the beginning of Quaker immigration. In sum, before Pennsylvania was settled, the Quakers had passed into their second-generation phase of being accepted outside the social class of their origin in England, and they had more than begun to gain converts in the New World. But they had not quite outlived their ordeal by persecution and so far they had no colony which was fully their own to develop.

William Penn, himself, represents the reach of the movement into the upper classes at home. He was converted in 1667, just before he turned twenty-three; at the time he was administering family estates in Ireland. His early life seems to have prepared him both for heterodoxy and for the affairs of property and state. At the age of twelve he had an intense religious experience; while a student at Oxford he rebelled against required attendance at prayers and was expelled from the university. Later, when his father, Admiral Sir William Penn, sent him to France to study, he enlarged his theological reading. But he was by no means averse to all upper-class responsibilities and amenities. After travel on the continent he studied long enough at Lincoln's Inn to acquire a practical knowledge of law and a Whiggish admiration for the security English law gave to an Englishman's freedom. Yet he had been no longer than months in charge of his father's property at Shangarry when he attended a Quaker meeting and was thrown in jail for doing so; soon afterward he acknowledged his adherence to Quakerism. Estrangement on that account, then reconciliation, alternated between father and son for the remaining few years of the admiral's life; it ended with a deathbed reconciliation in 1670. Soon after that Penn married a girl of his own class who was sympathetic. Thus he found himself, and gained the strength of independent wealth and family devotion, well before he became thirty years old.

Even earlier he demonstrated his loyalty to his new faith. In 1668 he was thrown into the Tower of London for having published his *Sandy Foundation Shaken*, a Bible-studded attack on orthodox belief; during his nine months in jail he wrote *No Cross, No Crown*, his most important book. Because it voices brilliantly the Quaker condemnation of life without illumination and states the conviction which animated the founding of Pennsylvania, it must be quoted. As to the Christianity of his own age, Penn issued a string of adjectives which could hardly have been more condemnatory:

> We find a Christendom now that is superstitious, idolatrous, persecuting, proud, passionate, envious, malicious, selfish, drunken, lascivious, unclean, lying, swearing, cursing, covetous, oppressing, defrauding, with all other abominations known to earth.

How can the condition of man be improved?

> The cross mystical is that divine grace and power which crosses the carnal wills of men . . . and that constantly opposeth itself to the inordinate and fleshly appetite of their minds, and so may be justly termed the instrument of man's holy dying to the world, and being made conformable to the will of God. . . . Where does this Cross

appear? . . . In the heart and soul. . . . The heart of man is the seat of sin. . . . How . . . is the Cross to be daily borne? . . . The way is an inward submission of the soul to the will of God, as is manifested by the light of Christ in the consciences of men: though it be contrary to their own inclinations. . . . How hard it is to be a true disciple of Jesus! The way is narrow indeed. . . . And they that cannot endure the Cross must never have the Crown. To reign, it is necessary first to suffer.°

In *A Brief Account of the Rise and Progress of People Called Quakers*, Penn addressed himself to the question of what the possibilities are of meeting the moral demands of the spirit in the actual course of human history. He thought that little had been gained by the Reformation of Luther and Calvin. "The children of the reformers, if not the reformers, betook themselves, very early, to earthly policy and power. . . . For worship there was for the generality more of man in it than of God." But now that the "Light," or the "Seed," was having effect, moral improvements were actually occurring. He offered the following examples, among others, of changes being brought about by Friends: truth-speaking (without taking oaths) as Matthew, Chapter 5, enjoins; loving enemies and resisting war, a specifically Quaker commitment; refusing alcoholic drink, as leading to evil; refusing to pay church taxes and giving voluntarily instead—"Freely you have received, freely give."° His measurements of moral advancement show what William Penn thought it reasonable to hope for, whenever Quakers might settle in the New World.

He received as lord proprietor the charter for wilderness Pennsylvania in 1681. The simple fact of receiving it of course depended on the rare personal history and personal quality required for a man to be at once a friend and favorite of Charles II and a Quaker. The deed of royal gift by no means lessened the complexity of his life. As a colonial proprietor, Penn became landlord (as the king's tenant in chief) of all recipients of land titles in Pennsylvania; he became permanent governor and captain general of the province; his office and his property were hereditary, in the seignorial tradition. The most ironical part of his authority for a Quaker to exercise was the power of making war. In the phrasing of the charter he was empowered "to levy, muster, and train all sorts of men . . . and to pursue . . . enemies and robbers . . . even without the limits of the said province, and by God's assistance, to vanquish and take them, and being taken to put to death, by the laws of war, or to save them."

Although there is moral drama and paradox that the pious second figure of Quakerism should be also the lordly colonizer who would collect quitrents from other Quakers, the time (though not far in the future) had not yet come when Quaker protest would say that the financial privileges of landlords violate Christian ideals. In Penn's day,

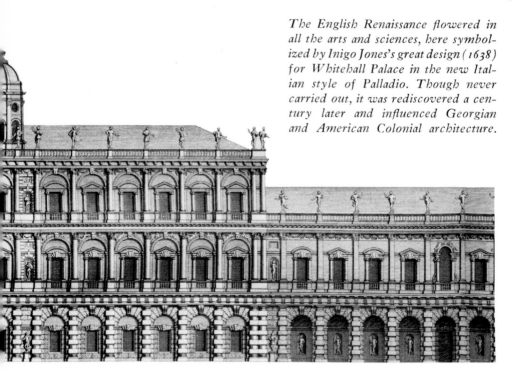

The English Renaissance flowered in all the arts and sciences, here symbolized by Inigo Jones's great design (1638) for Whitehall Palace in the new Italian style of Palladio. Though never carried out, it was rediscovered a century later and influenced Georgian and American Colonial architecture.

Here and on the following page, we see a panoramic view by Wenceslaus Hollar of London as it was when the colonists sailed for America, often from below the Tower (far right). The date of the design is 1666, the year of the Great Fire, but early in the century the city was already being rebuilt to continental tastes by Inigo Jones and other architects (the Fire accelerated that process and gave Christopher Wren his opportunity). Yet London still retained its medieval skyline—churches, Bridge, the Tower —spread along about a mile and a half of the Thames estuary. (over)

The Tower

The Bridge

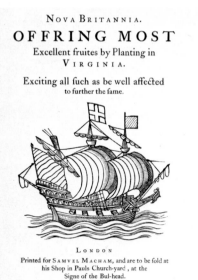

NOVA BRITANNIA.

OFFRING MOST

Excellent fruites by Planting in
VIRGINIA.

Exciting all such as be well affected
to further the same.

LONDON

Printed for SAMVEL MACHAM, and are to be sold at
his Shop in Pauls Church-yard, at the
Signe of the Bul-head.
1 6 0 9.

Title page of Nova Britannia, a tract written to encourage colonization. The ship, clumsily built but with sails and flags flying, typifies the lively seamanship and expansionism which entered the British mentality early and bore fruit in the decision, soon after the Armada, to trade in Asia and the Indies and start colonies in America.

In the 1630s, at the time of the Puritans' Great Migration, the population of Greater London was probably about 170,000, including such outlying parishes as Westminster, the seat of Government, upstream (left) in Hollar's engraving below. Many colonists thus went from urbanism to wilderness when they departed from Britain. In America, it would be two centuries before any city reached a comparable size, and by the time New York achieved that distinction, London's population would be more than one million.

Cathedral of S. Paul

By *1610*, as the title page of Edward Wright's superb book shows, English voyages of discovery had already made possible quite detailed and accurate knowledge of the world's coasts. Besides the Mercator world chart (bottom), the page depicts (from lower left) essential navigational instruments: mariner's rings for correcting variations in instrument reading; a quadrant, for measuring angles; an astrolabe, for sighting the stars; an armillary sphere; a cross-staff; a sea astrolabe; and a compass-like dip circle.

A detail from a chart probably made for the Virginia Company, between 1606 and 1608. It shows and names both "James Towne" and "C[ape] Kod" but otherwise testifies to the poverty of the cartographer's knowledge of the coast between the French and Spanish possessions. Hudson knew no more when in 1609 he made his great third voyage to the Hudson River and Chesapeake Bay.

I-4

O horrable Murder

Portrait of Charles I at his execution, from a Royalist broadside issued at the time of the Restoration (1660). Although the colonies' management was never so much in the hands of the monarch as in New Spain and New France, England's revolution directly affected them. In that sense, Puritan settlement in New England and Puritan Revolution in old England were but two sides of the same historical coin.

An early and probably veracious portrait of the Scottish reformer John Knox, published in 1580 by Calvin's associate Theodore Beza, who knew and admired Knox. The Scot's influence entered American life mainly in the eighteenth century with the Scotch-Irish immigrants, whose clannishness and Presbyterian polity made them sympathetic to American nationalism.

The burning of Protestant bishops Latimer and Ridley at Oxford in 1555, from Foxe's Book of Martyrs (1563). Politically and intellectually, they had been strong leaders in the effort to reform Henry VIII's separated national church, but despite the reaction which destroyed them under Henry's Catholic daughter Mary, the religious passion which they represented would continue to mature for another forty years until it issued in the Puritanism that colonized New England. After the religious violence under Henry and Mary, a kind of tolerance grew up under Elizabeth I, who demanded observance of outward forms but would "make no window into men's souls." But the Protestant spirit continued to grow within the official English church until it found expression in separatism, revolution—and in emigration to Puritan New England.

The three chief buildings of Virginia's capital, Williamsburg, as drawn (probably) by the Philadelphia naturalist John Bartram about 1740: from left, the provincial capitol; the rear elevation of William and Mary College; the royal governor's "palace." Though shown here in artificial relationships, they represent Virginia's vitality — both its independence and its imitativeness of England.

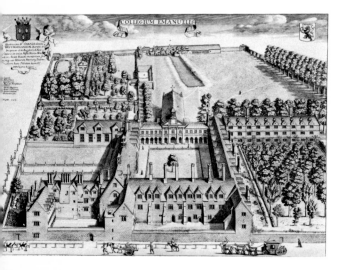

Emmanuel College, Cambridge, as it appeared in 1688, a Puritan foundation (1584) within the otherwise medieval university. It was a fount of that theological and political Puritanism which, when it emigrated to America, regathered its forces in Cambridge, Massachusetts.

Harvard College about 1725, named for its benefactor John Harvard, Puritan minister and Emmanuel College graduate. The three halls pictured here, built between 1675 and 1720, recall the Renaissance character of the college's spiritual counterpart in Cambridge, England.

A prospect of Boston in 1758, engraved from a drawing by Governor Thomas Pownall; the view is to the west across the harbor. With a population nearing twenty thousand (one-thirtieth of London's), Boston, though losing out to Philadelphia as English America's most numerous city, was sufficiently large and culturally independent to breed great confidence in America's future.

Musician and music from an important early collection, 1616. Colonization, like the arts, expressed the great flowering of the society's creative energies.

Early Methodist George Whitefield (1739), who preached in every colony, often outdoors. His superlative evangelism was the first to make the characteristic American appeal across denominational lines.

George Fox, founder of the Society of Friends, preaching at Flushing, Long Island, in 1672. Though he was the only important leader of the late Reformation to visit America, it remained for William Penn to give the Quakers their grand opportunity.

and in his person, Quaker faith characteristically cherished rural life as being the simplest and least corrupt. In his meditative writing, *Some Fruits of Solitude*, Penn said such things about living on the soil as Jefferson is better remembered for. In his own words: "The country life is to be preferred, for there we see the works of God; but in cities little else but the works of men. And the one makes a better subject for our contemplation than the other." Penn anticipated the attitude of the Quaker botanists of the mid-eighteenth century when he observed that the country supplies the philosopher with both "garden and library, in which he reads and contemplates the power, wisdom, and goodness of God." In his attitude toward inferiors on his lands, Penn honored the benevolent traditions of the English squirearchy. Christian morality to him involved economic and social responsibility, including care to preserve the bounty of earth; it required very little changing of economic institutions.°

At this point, where we shift from Penn's particular view of matters to those of Quaker colonizers more generally, comparison with the founders of New England supplies a perspective. No point of resemblance between the two is more conspicuous than the conviction, held by Quakers as firmly as by early Puritans, that conversion precedes membership in the religious community. The fact that Quakers abandoned the sacraments of baptism and communion which to Puritans symbolized membership does not reduce the inner resemblance; to Quakers and early Puritans alike, the quickening of the spirit was the essential criterion of membership. Likewise the special effort of Quakers to make their daily behavior follow the demands of Christian conscience seems like an extension of Puritanism toward ideals of perfectibility. On the institutional side, Quaker weekly meetings resembled Puritan congregations as to intimacy of worship and spiritual acquaintanceship; Quaker monthly meetings, which combined several weekly ones where that was convenient but sometimes involved just one congregation, had the decisive functions of admitting and dismissing members and of electing elders. The Quaker hierarchy of meetings —weekly, monthly, quarterly, and yearly—bears at least a formal likeness to the presbyterian hierarchy of church authority.

Yet, about 1680, on the eve of settling Pennsylvania, the differences of intellect between the two movements becomes prominent. Neither George Fox nor William Penn had any such inclination for a logical system of theology and polity as the nonseparating congregationalists had had. Although in Robert Barclay Quakerism had a scholarly Platonist as its principal theologian, he developed no equivalent for the federal theology;° Quaker settlers, when they reached the site on which they built Philadelphia, lacked any such blueprint as Ames's *Medulla* to guide them while they established a new set of relations between religion and government. Instead of a closely knit group of leaders (like the ministers of the New England congregations) to work out a pattern together, they had, of course, one peerless leader (usually absent from Pennsylvania) and many followers. Penn offered most encouragement to Quakers, and people like Quakers, to immigrate; but far from trying to exclude others, he made all welcome who cared to come. Doubtless the Pennsylvania mixture of English and German nationalities, and of pietists and nonpietists, helps explain why that province failed to develop ideas of its being a chosen people under a national covenant. Behind that difference from the Puritans, however, lay an essential part of the mysticism and morality of the Quakers. Though they cherished their new life in America as a God-given blessing, they thought of themselves as equals and brothers among all the children of earth, and not as a people specially chosen and privileged.

William Penn's solution to the problem of finding a basis for political concurrence in Pennsylvania was to infuse commonwealth principles into the operations of the province under the charter. This did not mean antimonarchical sentiment on his part. To his way of thinking— much the same as John Adams's way, a hundred years later—the essential thing was to have government under law. Where power was so conceived, those who exercised it would do right; the governed would have their freedoms. In the Frame of Government of 1682, which was Penn's first formal gift of political authority to the people of Pennsylvania, he himself phrased a doctrine of power. "The powers that be are ordained of God. . . . This settles the divine right of government beyond exception. . . . So that government seems to me a part of religion itself, a thing sacred in its institution and end."° Divine right, though it sanctioned the proprietary system of government of his province, excluded the practice of autocracy, Penn believed. He thought that assurances of freedom for individuals, and of regularity in the operation of government, accorded with the divine will. Guarantees in behalf of the people, such as frequent periodic elections and the right of habeas corpus, which his friend Algernon Sydney advised, he gave his people as their due. Government, he observed in one of his booklets, "is a just and equal constitution where might is not right but laws rule and not the wills nor power of men; for that were plain tyranny." To William Penn, mystic and lord proprietor of a province containing men in many grades of life, the conviction that government resolves social differences came naturally and with hope.

Yet he was not allowed to hold that belief without strain and cause for doubt. The charter of Pennsylvania required that there be a legislature. Penn implemented that provision, at a time when he was much affected by Harrington's *Oceana*, by establishing a very large elective assembly. But immediately and unfortuately that institution became aggressive in a way which indicates political inexperience and lack of discipline among the members as plainly as it does their ambition and power. "I am sorry at heart for your animosities," Penn responded during an early collision. "For the love of God, me, and the poor country be not so governmentish."° Yet he never retreated from his early liberalism. In 1701, though reluctantly, he issued the Charter of Privileges which became his final grant of constitutional power. The clumsy legislature of the first twenty years was replaced by a small one of thirty-six members; it was a one-house body, the only assembly of that kind in America. Because the franchise was restricted to "freemen," in the sense of freeholders of land, the colony cannot be said to have moved into a state of democracy by reason of becoming unicameral. Yet, because land was relatively easy to obtain, during the early eighteenth century (before complications arose) Pennsylvania's government belonged more largely to the people than did that of any other large province.

One peculiarity of public thought and practice in Pennsylvania, which is as attributable as anything else is to Quakerism, is the lightness of responsibility assigned to local government. Where, in Virginia, the justices of the peace and the members of the vestry carried the weight of local government and, in New England, township and congregational officers shared them, in Pennsylvania the Quaker monthly meetings did. Or rather, since Quakerism separated institutions for worship from institutions for power, it is better to say that the monthly meetings exercised for Quakers certain functions which, elsewhere, were exercised by government. The meetings assisted the poor in the community; they admonished the delinquent; they even undertook to act as tribunals to settle disputes over property in which Quakers were involved.° The German congregations did likewise. In farming areas, where these usages prevailed, local government under the lord proprietor had only minimum functions to serve; only where the nonpietist elements in the population prevailed were the mechanisms of English local government much developed.

William Penn's commitment to unusual freedom was of course greatest on the point of religious liberty. From his teens his hatred for enforced orthodoxy had led him into open protest; at the time of being disciplined at Oxford he had appealed to the vice-chancellor of the university. While he was a young man he wrote to several of the Rhineland princes, asking them not to persecute the sectarians. Although his argument for religious freedom was less sweeping than Roger Williams's had been, for he omitted the Rhode Island man's plea to tolerate Jews and Muslims, it was no less courageous. During years when the threat of a Catholic conspiracy to take over England had basis in fact, Penn had wanted Parliament to change the law so that Catholics could worship legally in their own way. He did say that Catholics might reasonably be required to disavow the claim that the pope had power to absolve English subjects of allegiance to the king. In 1677, as one of the proprietors who had bought part ownership of West New Jersey, he had joined in a declaration that freedom of conscience there had laid "a foundation for after ages to understand their liberty as men and Christians. . . . No person to be called in question or molested for his conscience, or for worshipping according to his conscience." Thus, four years before his own province was founded, Penn had accepted a colony policy. In December 1682, the founding year, the legislature of Pennsylvania enacted, as the first article of its famous Great Law, a provision that no believers in the "one Almighty and Eternal God . . . the Creator, Upholder, and Ruler of the world" should be "molested or prejudiced for their religious persuasion or practice in matters of faith and worship; nor shall they be compelled at any time to frequent or maintain any religious worship, place, or ministry whatever."° Finally, in the Charter of Privileges two decades later, he gave a like guarantee. This later law did require a profession of belief in Jesus Christ by all holders of office. The phrasing was so loose, however, that apparently no one was excluded by reason of his beliefs or lack of them, from holding office; certainly Benjamin Franklin was not, though he was a deist, and materialistic in his philosophy. Pennsylvania colonial law never tolerated (and does not seem ever to have needed to contemplate) the believer or unbeliever outside of Christianity; the question of admitting him to vote or to officeholding did not enter public discourse before 1776, when the first state constitution admitted all who acknowledged "the being of a God."

As close as religious freedom to the heart of Quakerism when Pennsylvania was new, but not a matter so much tied up in Penn's personal history, was the moral objection to war. William Penn had been an infant during the civil wars in England which had grieved George Fox; Penn said little about the matter until the time of the War of the League of Augsburg (King William's War in the colonies), when he published his still-famous *Essay Towards the Present and Future Peace of Europe*. Penn thought that wars occurred because sovereigns wished either to keep, recover, or add some bit of territory with which their pride was involved; to him it was usually—maybe not always—a vain and foolish recourse. Editing George Fox's journal, he endorsed Fox's attitude. In his own words: "if the costs and fruits of war were well considered, peace with its inconveniences is generally preferable."° In 1691, two years before his *Peace of Europe* was published, he wrote to fellow Quakers: "We are here in a troubled sea and almost ready to sink under the weight of wars which fill poor Europe with misery, and particularly Ireland and Flanders with desolation; and where things will pitch and Christendom will have peace, God alone knows."

For the world at large, Penn wanted a confederation of nations. As an international sanction against any makers of war, he proposed the use of force, according to an international agreement. For the New World he hoped that Europe's habit of bloodshed could be avoided. Like Roger Williams, he succeeded better than his neighbors in making treaties with the Indians. He simply acknowledged that they had rights, made straightforward contracts with them on that basis, and regularly gave them gifts. Fortunately for him and for Pennsylvania, when dynastic and imperialistic wars came, between 1689 and 1697 and again after 1702, the French and Indians did not raid south of the Mohawk River. Although this series of wars lasted more than two decades, the Crown did not insist firmly on having much intercolonial action. Penn was thus enabled to get by with simple permissiveness: he permitted a Colonel Markham to raise volunteer troops; he permitted Quakers and other pasifists to carry on as in time of peace, politically and otherwise undisturbed by military obligation. Occasionally the legislature raised a little money for the Crown; either it insisted that the appropriation was not for military use or else it did not try to control the spending. Isaac Norris, a Quaker assemblyman, wrote to James Logan, Penn's agent, in 1711 that there was nothing inconsistent with Quaker principles in giving money to the queen, "notwithstanding any use she might put it to, *that* being not our part but hers."° Altogether during his lifetime, which ended in bankruptcy and nervous breakdown soon after Queen Anne's War was over, William Penn succeeded in avoiding collision with the sovereign on the point of his war duties under the charter. He, and some of his people, had been ambiguous; it is one of the less clear-cut passages of Pennsylvania's early moral history.

3   German Sectarian Pietists

AMONG the Quakers in Pennsylvania, the constant, welcome, and tempting invitation was to enter the world of administration and politics. Over and above what the monthly meetings did in respect of local government, Friends pretty well controlled the upper structure of government. James Logan, scholar, humanitarian, and fortune builder, Penn's alter ego in America who served half a century in various posts, represented at fullest the American Quaker's venture into public affairs. At one time or another he was secretary of the province, commissioner of proprietary revenues, senior member of the council, and mayor of Philadelphia. Less a mystic and less a pacifist than Penn was, Logan thought that no Quaker should seek election for the assembly whose conscience would not permit him to vote for measures of military defense. Yet both pacifists and nonpacifists sought and won seats. From 1682 until 1756, Quakers dominated the legislature by comfortable majorities.

Among the Quaker-like German sectarians who were the first non-English people to immigrate to Pennsylvania, no equal assimilation into affairs occurred. Yet there were conspicuous individual cases. Francis Daniel Pastorius, the lawyer leader of the Mennonites who settled Germantown, became a councilor of the province; Christopher Sower, also of Germantown but a generation later and a Dunker, made himself, by way of the German-language journal he printed, a force for many causes—antislavery and pacifism, for two examples. But generally speaking the sectarians, like most of the other German settlers, became farmers, often in isolated places; this and other nonreligious considerations—the slowness of the naturalization process, the immigrants' own attachment to the German language, their political inexperience and indifference—reinforced their religious inwardness and their separateness from the English-speaking elements.

Of the main groups, the Mennonites came during the 1680s, in the first wave of immigration to Pennsylvania; the Brethren or Dunkers, the Schwenkfelders, and the Moravians arrived about 1730, in the same wave as brought most of the Lutheran and German Reformed Church people and most of the Scots-Irish Presbyterians. In a short course of time the sects proliferated: the Ephrata community derived from the Brethren; the Amish from the Mennonites; the Moravians established good schools and music societies in the towns of Bethlehem and Nazareth.

All groups of spiritual religionists had a vital kinship with the monastic strain in Christianity. To be sure, by the visual tests, this does not show up clearly among the Quakers: they married and propagated abundantly; though they dressed plainly as a matter of principle, they wore no habits; though they lived simply, they built no convents. Yet their withdrawing into voluntary, autonomous, community self-discipline does conform with the monastic tradition; their close connection of work with vocation and worship was kin to the Benedictine rule: *Orare et laborare*. On all counts, the German sectarians went much further into similarity with monasticism. In the Ephrata Cloisters of the 1720s, 1730s, and 1740s (just parallel in time with the Great Awakening in the Calvinist churches), there appeared, indeed, the one true instance of Protestant monasticism in the colonies. Conrad Beissel, mystic and composer of a thousand hymns, gathered a community of his fellow Baptists to live in strict discipline under the high gables of the famous *Saal* they built at Ephrata, near Lancaster. The order grew to several hundred: both sexes were admitted, the Solitary Brethren and the Order of Spiritual Virgins. All wore hoods; they confessed weekly in writing to Beissel; they printed books and made illuminated manuscripts. They devoted themselves especially to religious music. They sang in many-part harmony, an unusual skill in America; their hymnal, largely of Beissel's own composing, *The Turtle Dove*, was printed in German by Benjamin Franklin.

Next to the Ephrata community, the Moravians—more properly called *Unitas Fratrum*—went furthest, though only for a short time, into communal practices similar to monasticism. Their familiar name connects them with the distant origins of their sect: it was descended direct from Jan Hus of Moravia, a century before Luther. Despite a form of organization which retained the office of bishop, and despite a dedication to learning comparable to that of the Calvinists, the Moravians had dwindled almost to the vanishing point when Count Zinzendorf, whom we have met as being also a Lutheran and a pietist and the founder of the Congregation of God and the Spirit, rejuvenated them. At the time of starting fresh in Pennsylvania, the Moravians reorganized along lines which all but took the place of family life.

Now strongly bent on missionary work, they organized their people into what they called "choirs," groups determined by age and sex. There were choirs for married people, widows, widowers, bachelors, spinsters, older boys, older girls, and young children. Each choir lived together; each was organized for work or training for the common commitment; all were governed by the elders of the church. Communal living so systematized meant great attention to rearing the young, and what amounted to boarding schools. The Bethlehem Female Seminary was founded by Count Zinzendorf's daughter; from it the present long since nationally recognized Moravian College for Women is descended. Beside their functions in respect of education and work, the Moravian choirs served also as groups for worship, notably for musical worship, as befits their name. They were the bringers to the New World of German church music, for which the choirs of Bethlehem are famous today.

The other pietist groups, although they were less monastic in organization than either the orders at Ephrata or the choirs at Bethlehem, yet displayed much of the intensity and the corporateness which goes with monasticism. The highly mystical Schwenkfelders, followers of the German theologian, Kaspar Schwenkfeld, stressed the sacraments of the inner life and disregarded the ancient forms, much like the Quakers; they went further than the Quakers did, in acknowledging that revelation from the Holy Spirit and revelation through Holy Scripture sometimes differ, and in preferring the direct opening to God. The other two sects, the Mennonites and the Dunkers, were alike as holders of Anabaptist beliefs and as practitioners of congregationalist church government. The Dunkers insisted that adult baptism should be by three immersions face down; they refused to give or take interest on money lent; they were pacifists.

In living out their convictions, the Germans carried their ascetic practices far. Long beards, plain dress, nun-like bonnets, love feasts, unyielding dedication to farm life, and to their special beliefs about sexual and social morality, were to them requirements of God. Where to most colonials—to many Quakers and especially to Anglican and Calvinist churchmen—their Christian life meant ever more entering the world, adjusting their practices, founding their schools, and imposing their institutional ideas, the German sectarians differed. Quite consistently, they withdrew from the world. Their moral goals retained their original perfectionism. Meanwhile they made joyful, musical noises unto the Lord and reverently worked the soil.

4 *Spiritual Religion Applied to Society: John Woolman*

WHEN the Massachusetts theocracy declined during the later seventeenth century, one of the reasons was the lack of stability in the church-membership and colony-franchise foundation on which it rested. A system constructed from theological and political ideas tempered like steel, it depended on the close articulation of its parts—on community regulation by the congregations, on the administration of the sacraments, on local and colonial elections, on the work of the schools and the college. By contrast the Pennsylvania system was loose. It was three systems connected, rather than one: Quaker way of thinking, proprietary method of government, Whiggish design of people's freedom and rights. The inner tensions which troubled Penn were built into the triangle, and they increased with time: there was always political conflict over the economic privileges of the lord proprietor; the incompatibility between the military obligations of the government and the pacifism of the sectarians of mystical faith, though often muted, was never eliminated. Yet the three parts of the Pennsylvania system had their separate strengths. After the death of William Penn, in 1718, and after the proprietorship passed to successors who were neither Quaker nor idealistic about the colony, the Quaker meetings did their work, and the legislature performed, much as they had before. Because there was no orthodoxy and no need for conformity, one does not find decline where cross-purposes appear, as one does in New England.

In Pennsylvania, instead of statutory provisions to maintain schools, or even half steps in that direction, there developed what modern parlance knows as a confessional system of education. Each church or sect had its own schools, or none. The Friends School and the Episcopal Academy of Philadelphia, and the Moravian schools, became the most important and permanent. Because English and German spiritual religionists, alike, gave little value either to theology or to higher education, no explanation is required that Pennsylvania produced no early colleges; by the same token, none is needed to indicate why, when Benjamin Franklin launched the College of Philadelphia on a non-denominational basis with civic and scientific interests dominant, Quakers gave it support.

After the death of Penn and after Queen Anne's War, the three decades of peace and then King George's War, which hardly affected the colonies south of Massachusetts, eased but never eliminated the strain on Quaker scruples about the military obligation of the province. Quakers controlled the assembly; consistently they refused to provide military defenses. With equal consistency, the proprietary governors, the Scots-Irish of the frontier (who, in that location, were practically disfranchised), and indeed most elements except the Germans, objected to the assembly policy. Yet that policy was not purely pacifist. By regularly voting to give presents to the Indians, the legislature sustained Penn's practical method of dealing with them. This did not prevent the same assembly from voting to provision the king's regiments in America—as it did for Braddock's expedition.

The showdown came during the year 1756, a time of Indian raids and of much anti-Quaker resentment in the province. When the year opened, though the Quakers now numbered only one-fifth of the population (sympathetic Germans numbered one-half) they held twenty-six of thirty-six seats in the assembly. The election of that year reduced them to seventeen, a minority for the first time; and, when governor and council offered bounties for Indian scalps—130 dollars for males, 150 dollars for females—four of the seventeen resigned. Only eight Quakers in good standing in their meetings finally remained as legislators. Never again would there be a Quaker, or a pacifist, majority in any American legislature; indeed, not again until India was led by Gandhi did a great political unit come as close as colonial Pennsylvania had to being committed to government without practices of violence.°

In our own day colonial historians have been prone to read Pennsylvania's long refusal of military performance as indicating aberration and failure by the Quakers as colonizers. "No commonwealth has ever existed that has not been protected by those willing to preserve it with their lives. . . . The Quakers wanted to live in an orderly society that would protect them, their wealth, and also their right to refuse to protect themselves as well as others from public enemies," says Lawrence H. Gipson in his multivolume history of the mid-eighteenth-century empire; Daniel J. Boorstin is much less gentle in adverse judgment on the Quakers as accepters of responsibility.° But such estimations are addressed to the question: How well or poorly did the Quakers perform in England's overseas system—that is, in a system of mercantilism, a nationalist, expansive, and navalist empire? The question inherent in Part Two of this book is different; it is addressed, rather, to the question: What does Quaker history and Pennsylvania history tell us about the capacity of spiritual religion to carry on in America? Having pretty well dropped out of politics, Pennsylvania Quakers after 1756 present a parallelism with the Roman Catholics of Maryland: both had come to America as escapees from religious disadvantage at home to advantage in a proprietary colony; both lost political control of their colony; both survived in high social position and without harsh persecution. The question becomes: Did the Quakers, like the Catholics, sustain their original religious position? Did they continue to nourish their monk-like dedication to peace and human brotherhood, and to work and prayer?

Of course the answer to that question involves the whole history of Quakerism after 1756. Yet the history of John Woolman, a third-generation American Quaker, during the two decades before independence, takes us toward an answer. Grandson of one of the Quaker proprietors of West New Jersey, and the son of a man of substance in the farming community of Rancocas, Woolman himself was a tailor. He seems to have shared the thrift and virtuosity in craftsmanship which Frederick B. Tolles and others discover to have been characteristic of Quakers; at any rate, he felt that he had to guard against making more money than he needed, which sometimes to his embarrassment he did. Diaries or journals have been the prime form of Quaker literary expression, and no American religious writing of that sort has been more treasured and read than the *Journal of John Woolman*. Partly because in that record there are passages which recall the young William Penn, we may quote one which describes Woolman's early efforts to speak in meeting for worship:

> Feeling the spring of Divine love opened, and a Concern to speak, I said a few words in meeting in which I found peace; this, I believe, was about six weeks from the first time, and as I was humbled and disciplined under the Cross, my understanding became more strengthened to distinguish the pure spirit which inwardly moves the heart, and which taught me to wait in Silence sometimes many weeks together, until I felt that rise which prepares the creature to Stand like a Trumpet, through which the Lord Speaks to his flock.

Among the many likenesses between Woolman as renewer of the Quaker passion and Jonathan Edwards as renewer of the Puritan one is the factor of time. Woolman's "trumpetings" in meeting which justify speaking of his becoming a Quaker minister began in 1743, a dozen years after Edwards's leadership began, to be sure, but at the height of the Great Awakening in the Calvinist churches. During the next decade, at just about the time when Quakers lost control of the Pennsylvania legislature, he launched his personal, though not singlehanded, war against slavery. He had observed that institution firsthand in the Chesapeake colonies; he had traveled there as Quaker ministers did, going from meeting to meeting and from home to home, a mendicant of their own kind. He tells how his conscience became aroused. "When I eat, drank, and lodged free-cost with people who lived in Ease on the hard toyl of their slaves I felt uneasie, and as my mind was inward to the Lord, I found, from place to place, this uneasiness return to me," he recorded in his journal for 1746.°

Religious objection to slavery in America was about as old as the institution. Roger Williams had criticized it; around 1700 Judge Samuel Sewall, an otherwise conservative Puritan, had written an antislavery pamphlet. Quakers on the island of Nantucket objected, especially to the slave trading of merchants in Newport, Rhode Island; picking up the excuse that Negroes deserved slavery because they were ignorant and wicked, one islander responded, "If that plea would do, I do believe that [the traders] need not go so far for slaves as now they do." But antislavery never provoked much public thought or inspired much action, until John Woolman and Anthony Benezet, a Huguenot-descended Quaker who joined him, began to publish and organize. In 1754 Woolman brought out Part I of a major pamphlet, *Some Considerations on the Keeping of Negroes*; he completed it during the next decade. Meanwhile Benezet, who had come to believe in the capacity of Negroes by the route of having taught them in school, made the first step of gathering antislavery sentiment for action. "Finally, brethren," he reasoned before the Philadelphia Yearly Meeting, "we intreat you in the bowels of Gospel love, seriously to weigh the cause of detaining them in bondage. If it be for your own private gain, or any other motive than [the Negroes'] good, it is to be feared that the love of God, and the Holy Spirit, is not the prevailing principle in you, and that your hearts are not sufficiently redeemed from the world."° Thus in a Quaker meeting the movement against slavery, which never got into colonial politics and would have such difficulty finding opportunity in state and national politics after 1787, was quietly launched.

From the beginnings during the middle 1750s, successes accumulated piecemeal over a generation. John Woolman, visiting New England, preached against Quaker slave traders in Rhode Island. During the early 1770s, just before he died, he went to England, making his plea. He had a stunning effect. Alfred North Whitehead credits him, while in England, with having founded the international antislavery movement of modern times. In 1754 and 1755 the Philadelphia and New Jersey meetings required their members to abandon the slave trade, and by 1770 a Maryland Eastern Shore meeting and New England meetings had done the same thing. In 1776 the Philadelphia Yearly Meeting abolished slavery within its membership—that is, it disavowed the slaveholders; before the Treaty of Paris, meetings in Maryland, North Carolina, and Virginia took the same difficult step. As we shall see when we examine the Enlightenment and the domestic reforms proposed and enacted during the Revolution, antislavery did enter politics with some effect at that time. But, while state legislation restricted slavery where it was already weak, and ended slave trade where it was no longer considerable, Quaker abolitionism outside politics had its effect (among Quakers) in places where the institution was economically strong.

In the period before the American Revolution, as in our own times, religious and reformist minds which were concerned to improve race relations were often concerned also to eliminate war. After 1756, when war taxes were being levied in Pennsylvania as elsewhere, Woolman, as he says in his *Journal*, "was often affected with the thoughts of paying such Taxes." When he was told that in England Friends paid such taxes and that prominent colonials were ready to do so likewise, his anxiety was eased. Yet he retained, he said, "in the depth of my mind a scruple which I could never get over"; he concluded that "the Spirit of Truth required of me as an individual to suffer patiently the distress of goods, rather than pay actively." The problem became personal when British officers came to Mount Holly and offered money to quarter two soldiers in his home. Again in his own words, "I expected they had legal authority for what they did and after a short time I said to the officer, 'If the men are sent here for entertainment I believe I shall not refuse to admit them into my house, but the nature of the Case is such that I expect I cannot keep them on hire.'" He accompanied this decision with the thought that the early Friends who had "had little or no Share in Civil Government" had been quite "separated" from the spirit in which wars are made, but that his own contemporaries who shared the obligations of government had approached "so near [to fighting] as that the distinction would be little else but the name of a peacible people."° Woolman thenceforward gave almost as much attention to protest against war as to protest against slavery. Again Benezet joined him, and in this cause outdid him. In 1776, four years after Woolman died, Benezet became the author of the antiwar pamphlet, *Thoughts on the Nature of War*. During the War of Independence, now an aging man, he helped to keep Quaker pacifism alive. Modern scholars estimate that in that civil conflict probably a majority of Quakers and about all the radical German sectarians held to their conviction for peace; not different from the fate of the Quakers in England just a century earlier, many of them paid statutory penalties for their conscience.°

Woolman's major pamphlets are the more important because, over and above applying to American social and moral situations the Quakers' particular tenets of love, he informed his ethics with economic argument. This is true of *Some Considerations on the Keeping of Negroes*; it is true also of his *A Plea for the Poor*, which was published in 1763 (and republished as a Fabian Tract in 1897). Well over a century before Thorstein Veblen coined the telling phrase "conspicuous consumption" in criticism of American parvenus, Woolman, writing against slavery, observed that "we cannot go into superfluities . . . without having connection with some degree of oppression, and with that spirit which leads to self-exaltation and strife." If in the fundamental vein of Quaker thought he attributed war to sinfulness, now in this second phase of his reasoning he presented economic aggressiveness, waste, and gross inequality of possessions as the social expression of this sinfulness. Again his words demand to be quoted:

> If we consider the numerous Oppressions in many States, and the Calamities occasioned by Nation contending with Nation in various Parts and ages of the world, and remember that Selfishness hath been the Original Cause of them all. If we consider what great numbers of people are Employed in . . . preparing the materials of war, and the Labor and Toyl of armies set apart for protecting their respective Territories from the Incursion of others, and the Extensive miseries which attend their Engagements, . . . can we remember the Prince of Peace. Remember that we are his disciples . . . without feeling an earnest desire to be disentangled from everything connected with selfish customs in Food, in Raiment, in Houses and all things else? . . . Oh! that we who declare against wars, and Acknowledge our trust to be in God only, may walk in the Light, and therein examine our Foundation and motives in holding great Estates!

With considerable similarity to nineteenth-century reformers, Woolman said that certain of the accepted usages of economic life quietly exploited labor. He objected especially to three: investment and labor applied for useless or immoral purposes, the taking of rent on land, and the collection of interest on capital. Personally opposed, as Penn had been, to drinking "strong liquor," Woolman said, of the economics of that habit, that it gave employment to men for doing work not morally worthy; in addition, the product reconciled workers to overwork and deprivation which were themselves unjust. From his own experience with the high rentals charged farmers for the use of land, he reasoned (as Henry George would reason) that the "Creator of the earth is the owner of it" and that rent paid to landlords led, not to the reward of labor, but to the consumption (and the production) of needless products "contrary to the Gracious designs of Him who is the true owner of the Earth." In line with an ancient tradition of Christian economic thought, Woolman objected likewise to the taking of interest, as being in fact a deprivation of labor, and unjust.° Many of Woolman's points sound like social-gospel and socialist argument, and it is not surprising that reformers of the later nineteenth century cared more for his economic thinking than his contemporaries did.

Thus, where William Penn tried to make English-style government work and to have trade succeed, considering both to be sympathetic with Quaker ideals, John Woolman thought and worked to have reform take place through Christian rather than secular effort and discovered that accepted economic operations were sometimes evil. Yet he resembled the founder of Pennsylvania, as he combined secular reasoning with Quaker suppositions. Casting his effort on the critical side, and lacking any character as a Whig (or a Tory), he made himself an analyst of society in the vein of the Enlightenment. With a sweet soul he combined a probing mind, one as dedicated to reducing injustice as Roger Williams had been or Thomas Jefferson would be.

CHAPTER VII

The Great Awakening

It is God's manner of dealing with men, to lead them into a wilderness, before he speaks comfortably to them, and so to order it that they shall be brought into distress, and made to see their own helplessness, and absolute dependence on his power and grace, before he appears to work any great deliverance for them. . . .

Those affections that are truly holy, are primarily founded on the loveliness of the moral excellency of divine things. . . . The word "moral" is not to be understood here, according to the common and vulgar acceptation of the word . . . meaning an outward conformity to the duties of the moral law. . . . The moral excellency of an intelligent being is . . . holiness. . . . Holiness comprehends all the true virtue of a good man, his love to God, his gracious love to men, his justice, his charity, and bowels of mercies, his gracious meekness and gentleness. . . .

The tendency of grace in the heart to holy practice is very direct, and the connection most natural close and necessary. True grace is not an unactive thing. . . . Holy practice is as much the end of all that God does about his saints as fruit is the end of all the husbandman does about the growth of his field or vineyard.

Jonathan Edwards, Religious Affections

1 *A Situation for Religious Renewal*

I N the modern history of the West, movements in certain areas of society and thought have occurred so conspicuously in cycles that they seem to have a natural history of their own, almost independent of events in other areas. We think in this mode most habitually, and with the most encouragement from experts, in the field of economics; we now have a record of business cycles which covers the last two hundred years and we believe that future cycles are in certain respects as predictable as seasons. Historians and political scientists sometimes speak in the same way about national politics: they see a long-run regularity in the alternations of reform and conservatism and of Democratic Party and Republican Party dominance. A similar principle of history may be applied to literary and artistic styles which are often understood as recurrent.°

One or two modern economic depressions aside, the most recognized cyclical event in American history so far is the Great Awakening of the 1730s and 1740s. At that time a wave of feeling and decision making rose in the Middle Colonies which swept rapidly north and slowly southward and affected all regions profoundly. A renewal of religious devotion, it gave special drive to Christian educational undertakings; it filled the churches to overflowing; it disturbed the equilibria of church and state, which had been established colony by colony. Not only was the Great Awakening powerful; it came first among all the cyclical occurrences of any kind in American society. It preceded by about a generation the earliest general business depression, the hard times of the 1760s; by the same token it preceded the first national wave of political protest, the Stamp Act crisis. Its short-run political effects were local. But the Second Great Awakening would coincide with the national political change-over of 1800. Again, with the third national wave of revivalism which accompanied the Jacksonian swing into working democracy, and still again, with the fourth, which just preceded the secession of the South, revivalism and political upset kept close company. At least for the period covered by this volume—from the separations represented by emigration from England to the separation of the South from the North—religious excitement and political excitement were never distant the one from the other.°

Qualitatively the Great Awakening was part of the international volunteering of evangelical effort of the early eighteenth century; we shall find that it was affected by, and that it affected, the work of the pietists in Germany and the Wesleyans in England. But quantitatively, the background condition which helps best to explain the extent of American revivalism is the simple, solid fact of population growth. At the end of Queen Anne's War, 1715, there were still less than half a million people in all the continental colonies. But at the beginning of King George's War, thirty years later, the number had increased to a million and a half; on the eve of the Revolution, there were probably two and a half million. That is, the population was doubling every twenty or twenty-five years, and the numbers were great enough so that change at that rate made great differences in how the people lived and how they associated with one another. Seventeenth-century port towns were becoming true cities. The population of the large ones, Boston, Philadelphia, and New York, reached about twenty-five thousand each, around the middle of the eighteenth century. If that seems tiny, either by the standards of today or by the populations of London and Paris, which were then not far from a million, the three main colonial cities were nevertheless as large as any in Great Britain except the capital. New towns were rising, moreover; they were usually a little inland, toward the farming hinterland of the colony, or else in a favorable coastal location to gather the trade of that area. Worcester and Northampton, in Massachusetts; Lancaster and York, Pennsylvania; Baltimore and Frederick, Maryland; and Norfolk, Virginia, are cases in point.°

We have already noticed Presbyterians, Reformed, Huguenots, and Lutherans in many towns. Though not everywhere in the same proportions, these late-comers to America turned up in all three colonial regions, without much regard for the church-and-state situation which preceded them. In New England, Boston, which a century earlier had been so solidly Puritan, by the middle of the eighteenth century became as religiously diversified as Providence and Newport. Likewise Baltimore, Norfolk, Charleston, and Savannah, in provinces where there were Church of England establishments, had many citizens who were not Anglicans, including German Protestants in variety. Thus once again, as is familiar in the West's long history, in the fluid cities—and on the fluid frontier—more than in established rural areas, religious loyalties became uncommonly complicated and sometimes antagonistic to one another.

Largely for that reason, throughout all the colonies the old solidarities of the people, in attachment to the faiths of the founding fathers, diminished more rapidly than the simple attrition of time would account for. This enlarged the condition of religious freedom. It also stimulated anxiety, lest cherished beliefs be neglected.

2 Galvanizing the Calvinist Churches: The Middle Colonies

AN inconspicuous town, New Brunswick, in upper New Jersey, was the original home of the Great Awakening. Yet, because Europe preceded America in producing the flows of religious enthusiasm of the period, and because upper New Jersey was truly a crossroads of migrating churches and churchmen from both Europe and the nearby colonies, it seems a more natural starting place for revivalism than one of the cooled-off centers of spiritual ferment would have been—say, Boston, or Providence, or Philadelphia.

The Reverend Theodorus Jacobus Frelinghuysen crossed the ocean in 1719 to take charge of Dutch Reformed congregations which were languishing in New Brunswick. The twenty-eight-year-old son of a minister had already behind him theological training in Dutch and German universities and about a year of experience in a parish of his own. An uncommonly gifted speaker, he was preaching in the two languages of his church; soon he would be preaching in English as well. Although he came from near the center of Reformed authority in Holland, he told his congregations to free themselves from their old dependency on ecclesiastical authorities there. As a trainer of candidates for the ministry, using apprentice-style methods like those of the Presbyterian "prophets," he contributed to the Americanization of his church. But earlier than he could have had much effect in these directions, Domine Frelinghuysen, very much like Solomon Stoddard, cultivated among his people a passion for participation in the life of the church and the community; no such outlay of effort had occurred earlier among the Dutch Reformed, either before or after the English captured New Netherland. If, like Stoddard, he had been called to an out-of-the-way congregation, he might well have become, in time, the "pope" of a subregional movement in the church to which he was born.°

Instead he became the starter of an interchurch, intercolonial insurgency. Frelinghuysen made the connection which would ignite things, when Gilbert Tennent, the eldest son of William, also settled in New Brunswick. In that region the older, Reformed, congregations sometimes lent church buildings to Presbyterian newcomers; Frelinghuysen befriended Tennent, who was a younger contemporary and preached with him in his pulpit. The older man supplied a spark, but the younger man, from the Log College, was ready tinder. In 1729 Gilbert Tennent began the vigorous, traveling evangelical work which he would sustain for fifteen years or longer. He reached peak effectiveness about 1740. During that year, visiting the little Presbyterian center at Nottingham, on the Maryland–Pennsylvania boundary, he delivered a sermon, which would be many times preached and printed, on "The Danger of an Unconverted Ministry." (His echoing a problem raised by Antinomians a century earlier in New England was surely unconscious.) By denouncing the "old formalist," or "high Presbyterian," element, Tennent made a fighting front of what had been for some years a line of cleavage within American Presbyterianism. By the time of the sermon, church parties were already becoming recognizable: Tennent and his associates in protest were the "New Sides" and were mostly graduates of the Log College and other schools of prophets; they had caught the evangelizing spirit. The other side became, in accepted public parlance, the "Old Sides." The controversy between them was phrased in bitter language. "Our LORD will not make Men Ministers, till they follow him," Tennent insisted. "Pharisee-teachers, having no Experience of a special Work of the Holy Ghost, upon their own Souls, are therefore neither inclined to, nor fitted for, Discoursing frequently, clearly, and pathetically, upon important Subjects." Such preachers tended to discuss law and duty, he specified, which suggested salvation by works. "If it be inquired, What is the Call?" said Samuel Finley, who was a disciple of Gilbert Tennent, "I answer in brief, the ordinary call of God is to be gathered from the sincere and ardent desires of serving him in the Ministry of the Gospel, which he puts in the Heart."°

Thus graduates of the Log College advanced, as a matter of doctrine, what they believed they had learned from the experience of conversion. They asked that young men who felt they had been called to the ministry be taken at their own evaluation, subject, of course, to the tests of the presbyteries. Even before Tennent preached at Nottingham, the revivals, which had begun small-scale with help from Domine Frelinghuysen in New Jersey, had spread to Pennsylvania's outlying settlements, where Scots-Irish congregations without ministers were especially ready for Log College trainees and their kind. Yet the Old Sides, by keeping the upper hand in the presbyteries, managed to prevent many ordinations of colony-educated candidates; only the New Brunswick presbytery, among the several in the Synod of Philadelphia, went over to the New Sides. If nothing more had come into play than the evangelizing and Americanizing forces within Presbyterianism, aided and abetted by like-minded Dutch Reformed ministers, the Great Awakening in the Middle Colonies might have slowed to a stop at that

But in the late fall of 1739, and again during the warm season of point—with the insurgents in control of just one presbytery.

1740, George Whitefield entered the pulpits of the Middle Colonies. Most unusual among all the itinerant preachers in America, he was a priest of the Church of England, one who had been trained at Oxford. At the university he had known well John and Charles Wesley; during their absence he had been the leader of the Holy Club, as they called it, of "methodists." Though only twenty-four when he came to America, Whitefield had already suffered and recovered from serious illness; this probably explains his harping on a person's need to achieve a "new birth" in God. In the colonies, first traveling from south to north, he associated in Georgia with the group of Protestant immigrants from Salzburg; later he preached with, and in aid of, almost all varieties of colonial Christianity, but conspicuously little with his own. Whitefield was a preacher, not a creative theologian at all; yet one of the judgments he made, which helps explain his success with American hearers, was a theological judgment. About 1740 he shifted from preaching Arminian free-will doctrine—which Methodists everywhere liked—to greater reliance on Calvinist belief, of course including the doctrines of predestination and grace. With that new emphasis he was ready for the Middle Colonies and New England, as being tuned to their pitch.

There is no room to doubt Whitefield's enormous gift, emotional, vocal, and verbal, as an orator. No temperament or mind could have been more different from his than Benjamin Franklin's. Yet at Whitefield's call to a public meeting, that sage emptied his pockets and observed that it was "wonderful to see the change soon made in the manners of our inhabitants." Whitefield preached everywhere, in every circumstance: in and out of churches and meetinghouses, under the trees, and on the steps of courthouses. In New York an outdoor platform was put up for him, and in Philadelphia a tabernacle was built which doubled as a charity school. No one has estimated totals, but on some days thousands attended Whitefield's meetings. Along the way he befriended Domine Frelinghuysen; he met and assisted Quakers and Baptists.

His greatest effect was on Presbyterians. Where, before his preaching, the New Sides had failed to break the hold of the Old Sides on the presbyteries, his preaching added the needed extra force. In the 1740 and 1741 phase of the awakening, the need for new ministers increased again; it brought on new demands and new decisions. Many laymen, who had not been trained in Scotland or in any college, preached; hundreds of persons were converted, quite outside the accepted procedures of church worship and counsel. New congregations were formed, and old ones were enlarged; if they could not get a full-time minister, they would often settle for part-time services. Under such pressures the Presbyterian hierarchy of authority cracked and became in fact two churches. In the one, the Old Sides retained control of the original presbyteries; in the other, the New Sides, building around the New Brunswick presbytery, set up a rival system, the Conjunct Presbyteries. Rapidly they became the stronger element. The Old Sides themselves fell short of clergymen; in Philadelphia, conservative Presbyterians sometimes slipped over (as later-generation Quakers did) into the Anglican communion. Meanwhile the New Sides advanced in frontier missionary work. When, after seventeen years, in 1758, the schism was mended, they dominated both the policy and the spirit of the Presbyterian Church in the colonies.

Less than halfway through the period of the separation, and shortly after the crest of the conversions, New Sides men, principally, launched the first permanent Presbyterian college in America. Much as, during the 1720s, the model and the assistance of Domine Frelinghuysen had helped Gilbert Tennent begin Presbyterian revivalism, during the middle 1740s close support from old Puritans and others helped bring the College of New Jersey, the future Princeton University, into being. Early in the undertaking, political action was needed; in this respect the Presbyterians were lucky. Two successive governors of New Jersey, both Anglicans but one a Scot and the other a son of Harvard, helped their cause. Under Jonathan Belcher, the Harvard man, the royal government of the province issued a charter in 1746 (and a supplementary one in 1748) which authorized the granting of degrees. (This was an advantage not yet conceded to the educationally equal "dissenting academies" in England.) The Crown's condition for the gift of institutional life was that the College of New Jersey admit students without regard for their church attachment; likewise, by decision of the provincial council written into the charter, the first board of trustees was made to contain a sizable minority of non-Presbyterians. Episcopalian, Dutch Reformed, and Quaker members were appointed. The group contained laymen and clergymen: nine graduates of Yale, four of

Harvard, William and Gilbert Tennent, and at least one other Log College graduate. Yet probably seventeen of the original twenty-three were Presbyterians, and of these more than half were clergymen. The trustees were given the election of president and professors, and of their own successors; they controlled both personnel and property of the college in the emerging American practice. With an early touch of public-relations genius, they first planned to name their splendid Georgian stone building Belcher Hall (not John Knox Hall or Calvin Hall); then, on the governor's insistence, they changed and named it Nassau Hall, in honor of William III of glorious memory.

The first presidents were Yale graduates who had had distinguished evangelical and teaching careers. Jonathan Dickinson, the New Sides moderator who had taken the idea of the college to the governors of New Jersey, came first but served only five weeks before suddenly dying; next came Aaron Burr, who brought the college to life and settled it in Nassau Hall; third and last of the presidents from Yale was Jonathan Edwards, who lived only weeks in office but attached to the place the name of the Great Awakening's superb theologian. Thereafter, as befitted the work of the Log College in quickening both the new Presbyterianism and Presbyterian education, Samuel Davies and Samuel Finley, evangelizers both, succeeded in office. For the first two decades of the life of the college, the New Sides element fully prevailed.

Then in 1768, a decade after the church schism was mended, college and church drew a draft, at last, on Presbyterian resources in Scotland. With luck which must have exceeded the capacity of the trustees for foreknowledge, they called over the minister of Paisley, John Witherspoon, to take charge of the college. To look to Scotland at all of course followed an Old Sides preference. But the man was known to be a censorious opponent of Arminian doctrine, and in that way he was in line with New Sides ideas; most important of all for the future, he brought to America an interest in the things of the Scottish Enlightenment, modern science and moral philosophy. His service as a trainer of students in divinity would be to introduce them—and to introduce in America—the new Scottish "common sense" philosophy. We shall return in later connections—of revolutionary thought, and of Christian thought in the young republic—to certain meanings and developments of this variety of moral intuitionism. For present purposes we need go no further than to notice that President Witherspoon's philosophic effort placed him in one way in parallel with his older contemporary, President Johnson of King's College: both of these new church-college presidents made a great effort to reconcile eighteenth-century science and learning with the Christian tradition they served, for the peace of mind of their students.°

When the American Revolution broke, John Witherspoon, though an immigrant of only eight years, would become the most eminent Patriot among all the college presidents in the colonies and, perhaps it is fair to say, among all the clergymen too. He would sign the Declaration of Independence; he would serve on more than one hundred committees; he would attend, and urge toward the affirmative decision, the New Jersey state convention of 1787, which was the third (after Delaware and Pennsylvania) to ratify the federal Constitution of the United States. Meanwhile he would have led the Presbyterian Church in becoming the first church to organize on a national basis, and in becoming the principal case of a federated church institution, then or later in the New World.

These anticipations of our story are intended to indicate that the evangelical assertiveness of middle-colony Calvinists would carry over into the political assertiveness of the Revolution and the postrevolutionary period. They are intended in addition as a reminder of almost a century of Scots-derived Presbyterianism, and one generation of intensive Presbyterian growth, in America. The speed with which that church learned to live principally on its own American resources, to develop its own tradition of ideas and structure and yet to keep up a home connection, outdid that of other churches. Yet its forced autonomy and maturity, brought on very early by the Great Awakening, was a response to conditions which were common to all branches of American Christianity.

3   The New England Way Divided: Eighteenth-century Puritanism

IN New England a lecture sermon by Jonathan Edwards, in 1731 in Boston, marks the coming of the Great Awakening. Although this was an early occasion, among many, on which that speaker addressed people who hung on his words, it was not a time for making conversions. Edwards spoke to a gathering of clergymen: a graduate of Yale, before an audience of Harvard men; a countryman in the city; the grandson and successor of Solomon Stoddard, who had equaled and rivaled Increase and Cotton Mather as leader in the Puritan community, standing before the quiet men who were now in charge of the spiritual life of Boston and the nearby towns. The insiders were testing the parvenu, and they heard a disturbing lecture.

The title was "God Glorified in Man's Dependence," and by the measurements of a century of Puritan orthodoxy there was nothing new and nothing wrong about it. Nor would there be anything wrong or new about the sermon Edwards delivered at home, in Northampton, two years later, "A Divine and Supernatural Light, Immediately Imparted to the Soul by the Spirit of God, Shown To Be both a Scriptural and a Rational Doctrine." It beautifully rounded out what had been said in Boston; we can see now that the two sermons very nearly encapsulated Edwards's lifetime message. The central doctrine was God's complete and uncompromised sovereignty; from that insight derived, as always, man's complete dependence on Him for grace, or salvation. This was the idea which the covenant of grace, main and beloved conception of a century earlier, had expressed for the founding fathers. A first-generation Puritan might well have said what Edwards said in Boston: "As grace is at first from God, so it is continually from him, and is maintained by him, as much as the light in the atmosphere is all day long from the sun, as well at at first dawning, or at sun-rising." And, because of Edward Taylor, one thinks of second-generation Puritanism when one reads the "Divine and Supernatural Light" sermon. Edwards wrote sermon prose, not verse, and his style was not as specialized an instrument of mystical feeling as Taylor's was, but in his lines the religious meaning of "light" seems to be much the same as Taylor's had been: "God, in letting in this light into the soul, deals with man according to his nature, or as a rational creature; and makes use of his human faculties. But yet this light is not the less immediately from God for that; . . . [the] notion that there is a Christ, and that Christ is holy and gracious, is conveyed to the mind by the word of God: but the sense of the excellency of Christ by reason of that holiness and grace, is, nevertheless immediately the work of the Holy Spirit."°

The thinker, still under thirty, who preached the two sermons spoke with quiet precision, always to the main point. He had the arresting eloquence which absorption in the logic and meaning of the business in hand gives to a clear thinker; pallor and height added to the public effect of asceticism and concentration. The argument of the sermons, considered in the light of his later development, tells us that he was already far advanced in the reading and selection of ideas on which he would build his ultimate system. Today's scholarship makes plain that the preacher's silent treatment of the proliferation of covenants with which the federal theology is filled signifies that he had departed from that traditional Puritan method of discussing (and quietly indicating that there are bounds on) the absolutism of God's sovereignty. We recognize also that his words about the beauty of nature, and about the nature of thought, reveal his having already absorbed much of what Isaac Newton propounded concerning the structure of the universe and of what John Locke said about the operations of the mind. In fact Jonathan Edwards had already, in the early 1730s, gone further than

Cotton Mather or any other New Englander had gone, in learning and accepting the main ideas on which the Enlightenment was then being built. In truth he spoke basic doctrine to the elders, and did so in fresh context. But his hearers had both lost sympathy with the old doctrine and failed to come up to date with the new context. By the time the "Divine and Supernatural Light" sermon was printed, in 1734, Edwards's historic work of transforming church life and thought had, as he said, "surprisingly" begun, not in Boston but in his own rural New England.

The man who stood then at a crossroads belonged, so far as ancestry had power to connect, to the first orthodoxy of Massachusetts. On his mother's side, which means through the Stoddards, family ties interwove with the early Mathers and Winthrops. His father, Timothy Edwards, derived from less distinguished Puritans in England and America; yet some of that family became well to do, and, unfortunately, certain seventeenth-century members of it developed more than streaks of insanity and scandal. Timothy himself was completely steady: once the librarian of Harvard College and long the minister at East Windsor, near Hartford, he provided his one son and several daughters with a home situation which combined life on a valley farm and leadership in the village with piety and learning. Esther Stoddard Edwards, mother of eleven and woman of vigor who lived to be ninety-eight, is said to have confessed conversion only after years of being married to Timothy. If conviction of grace actually waited so long, the fact may be put down as confirming her reputation for having a mind of her own; also it exhibits Solomon Stoddard's principle that unconverted members will discover salvation while already within a church.

By every indication, the home and the church of Timothy Edwards surrounded the future theologian with all possible piety and training, and he never rebelled. Not inconsistent with that, we have Edwards's own testimony that he sensed from childhood that inculcation is not the way of salvation; he seems to have believed always that faith must be found, God's gift, within. More unusual among Puritans, he seems to have grown up—a natural Lockian—thinking that the human senses, as the receivers of impressions from creation, are truly the transmitters of messages from Creator to creatures of His own truth and beauty. The farm at East Windsor was the place of the touching story he tells of a religious experience when he was seventeen, already a graduate of Yale. To be sure, the experience followed a wave of conversion in the community and an intimate talk with his father, but he describes it as a personal meeting of man with nature.

> I walked abroad alone, in a solitary place in my father's pasture, for contemplation. And as I was walking there, and looking up on the sky

and the clouds, there came into my mind so sweet a sense of the glorious *majesty* and *grace* of God, that I know not how to express. I seemed to see them both in a sweet conjunction; majesty and meekness joined together; it was a sweet, and gentle, and holy majesty; and also a majestic meekness; an awful sweetness; a high, and great, and holy gentleness. . . . God's excellency, his wisdom, his purity and love, seemed to appear in every thing; in the sun, moon, and stars; in the clouds, and blue sky; in the grass, flowers, trees; in the water, and all nature; which used greatly to fix my mind.

This vision of God in nature, which Edwards placed in his "Personal Narrative," has been persuasively interpreted as being evidence, from early in his life, of similarity and kinship in thought between him and the New England Transcendentalists a century later. But also the passage is reminiscent of the early Puritans, who especially loved the sea as giving a sign of God's vastness; nature helped Edwards, as it had helped his ancestors, to believe in the old Augustinian vision. "From my childhood up," he says in an earlier part of the same passage, "my mind had been full of objections against the doctrine of God's sovereignty, in choosing whom he would to eternal life, and rejecting whom he pleased." But now, without being able to explain, "my reason apprehanded the justice and reasonableness of it. . . . Absolute sovereignty is what I love to ascribe to God. But my first conviction was not so."° His enchantment with nature grew. As the young minister who loved to walk the banks of the Hudson, and as the aging one outdoors in northwestern Massachusetts, Edwards never ceased to extrapolate from earth and sky and water meanings which reinforced his belief in God. He did not do this in the ordinary way of his own century; creation was not a mechanical thing, and God never a watchmaker. To him, nature gave intimations, not patterns, of divinity. This is the turn of mind which connects him, not alone with the nineteenth-century future, but simultaneously with the seventeenth-century past, of New England thought; it helps us begin to see him as a central and pivotal figure in American religious intuition.

After training which had all taken place at home, Edwards went to Yale College in 1716, just before he became thirteen. He took the B.A. in 1720 and the M.A. in 1723. The fall and winter of 1722–1723 he spent as minister of a tiny waterfront Scots-Irish Presbyterian congregation in New York; this was more a part of his being educated than becoming a leader; it supplied him with his first experience of Calvinism as an intercolonial and international movement. Because during his undergraduate years Yale had not yet settled at New Haven and lacked stability either as to faculty or place, one might suppose that even a book-loving, disciplined student would have been slow about getting work done. Yet Edwards's years in college were the time when he drafted his "Notes on the Mind," much admired by twentieth-century scholars, and his "Notes on Natural Science." Showing a precocious mastery of Locke and Newton, they have been interpreted to indicate that Edwards might well have spent his life as a scientist or scientific philosopher, and not as preacher and theologian. No such choice occurred to him. Nor did he later, in his years of theological study for the M.A., show any taste for a second deviation which seems more in the area of the probable. As a student of divinity he must have had access to the works of literature and history and theology which at that very time and place changed the minds of the Reverends Timothy Cutler and Samuel Johnson; he may have read them, more or less. Because he was given virtual control of Yale College after they left, he must have known well the intellectual and emotional thrusts which upset college and colony in 1722. In this direction, too, he was entirely steady. So far as we can tell, the early 1720s were a time of consolidating and informing his convictions—the effort he would never abandon, and which would keep him in line with his regional Puritan Congregationalist origins.

An external situation to which he had to respond, if "external" is the word for it, came when he decided, about 1730, as the new pastor of Northampton, that the work of his grandfather was being quietly undone. He loyally believed that Solomon Stoddard's preaching and converting and church building had been essentially right; he believed that that effort, and Stoddard's having organized a supercongregational association of churches in the Connecticut valley, was what accounted for there being a purer religious life around Northampton than in the coastal towns. But disturbingly, evil had somehow entered the garden. In the very area of family and community life which Stoddard had especially cultivated, sins of omission and commission suddenly became conspicuous. "Look over your past life," Edwards urged his people, "how little regard you have had for the Scriptures. . . . What wicked carriage you have been guilty of to your neighbors. . . . How some of you have vaunted yourselves in your apparel! . . . Others in their knowledge and their abilities!" Many young people, he later explained, had been "very much addicted to night walking, and frequenting the tavern, and lewd practices, wherein some by their example exceedingly corrupted others. It was their manner very frequently to get together in conventions of both sexes, for mirth and jollity, which they called frolicks; and they would often spend the greater part of the night in them, without any regard to order in the families they belonged to: and indeed family government did too much fail in the town."°

Edwards's response to the situation outdid his grandfather Stoddard's evangelism. He preached in Northampton and in the surrounding towns; for a while penitents came to his study at a rate of thirty a week. In 1735, after nearly two years, revivalism prevailed the length of the settled valley, from Deerfield to Saybrook; it extended along Long Island Sound, including New Haven and Yale College. (Rector Clap's famous resistance came later.) New congregations gathered, and new meetinghouses were built. According to the leader in Northampton, both behavior and belief improved. Weddings became "spiritual mirth," not frolics, he recorded, and there appeared "tokens of God's presence in almost every house." Edwards early "moved to the young People that they should set up Religious meetings, on Evenings after Lectures, which they complied with. . . . About that Time began the Great noise that there was in this Part of the Countrey about Arminianism, which seemed strangely to be overruled for the Promoting of Religion. . . . A Concern about the Great things of Religion began, about the Latter End of December, . . . till in a very Little Time it became universal throughout the Town, among old and young, and from the highest to the Lowest. . . . Those that were wont to be the vainest, and Loosest Persons in Town seemed in General to be seized with strong convictions." The change in persons, Edwards specified, did not exalt their opinion of themselves, but of God: they complained "that they can do nothing, they are poor Impotent Creatures, utterly Insufficient to Glorify their Creatour and Redeemer. . . . I never saw the Christian spirit in Love to Enemies so Exemplified, in all my Life as I have seen it within this Half year."°

The Connecticut valley revivals of 1734 and 1735 were intercolonial in the sense that they occurred throughout sizable parts of Massachusetts and Connecticut. Yet they spread over only a somewhat larger area than Solomon Stoddard's revivals had done. It was only after Edwards had written about them in *A Faithful Narrative of the Surprising Work of God in the Conversion of Many Hundred Souls in Northampton and the Neighboring Towns and Villages* that he and his work came to be interregionally and internationally known. The little book was published in Boston and London and in due course became a textbook for revivalists in the English-speaking world. At least as early as the autumn of 1740, when George Whitefield came to New England, Edwards's success made Northampton a recognized inner citadel of New England faith.

In the phrasing of military strategy, Whitefield's invasion from the sea and Edwards's position in the interior subjected the people of New England to a pincers movement from southeast and northwest. Whitefield landed in Newport; with the reluctant consent of the rector, he began his preaching at the Anglican church in that city. Then he moved up the coast. Drawing crowds by the thousands, many in outdoor meetings, he evangelized his way north to Portsmouth and back to Boston; thence he went to Northampton, where he preached in Edwards's own pulpit; from there he proceeded south to New Haven and the smaller towns along the sound. Whitefield was followed by Gilbert Tennent, who preached several times in Boston. The Presbyterian had printed in that city his sermon on an unconverted ministry; the topic offended antirevivalists, as it had once offended the opponents of Anne Hutchinson. But Whitefield and Tennent, the first an ingratiating orator and the second a rasping one, spread the movement of conversion in places Edwards did not reach. Quite unlike the Middle and Southern Colonies, New England was swept by it as a whole; no subregion was left untouched.

Neither was any social class. Recently Edwin S. Gaustad has demonstrated in detail that the old interpretation of the Great Awakening in New England, which found that the revivals belonged principally to frontiersmen and debtors and was little accepted in commercial and creditor locations, does not conform with the facts. The preliminary phase of the movement, of 1734, occurred in the western counties, but did not especially involve the debtor classes; the later phase, of the early 1740s, was eastern and western and involved all classes, Gaustad's revision shows. Too many people of all social types, high and low as Jonathan Edwards himself observed, believed that they were converted for a social-class explanation to bear weight.

But of course revivalism had social results; one of them was a change in religious method and taste. The year of maximum excitement, 1741, was the time when Edwards, who by disposition and habit was an unspectacular preacher, delivered at Enfield, Connecticut, the hell-fire sermon, "Sinners in the Hands of an Angry God," from which he has been most frequently quoted and most disadvantageously represented. As always Edwards had a theological point: the greatness and inscrutability of God and the weakness of men not saved. He laid on the emotion heavily and deliberately. "There is no want of *power* in God to cast wicked men into hell at any moment. . . . They *deserve* to be cast into hell. . . . They are already under a sentence of *condemnation* to hell. . . . There are in the souls of wicked men those hellish *principles* reigning, that would presently kindle and flame out into hell fire, if it were not for God's restraints. There is laid in the very nature of carnal men, a foundation for the torments of hell." According to Eleazar Wheelock, sympathetic minister and future founding president of Dartmouth College, who was present, "There was such a breathing of distress, and weeping, that the preacher was obliged to speak to the people and desire silence, that he might be heard." Yet even in this instance, when he carried a figure of speech to such a degree and application that those present reached the point of hysteria and could all but smell the burning of flesh, Edwards calmly went on. He regarded the release of guilty and fearful emotion as a necessary part of his calling, to help his hearers reach God.°

As the Great Awakening, wherever its procedures were accepted, changed the psychology of Puritan worship, it changed the sociology of the congregations as well. Like the Presbyterians, the Congregationalists divided into parties: the New Lights and the Old Lights. Sometimes that division produced a lasting schism in the community; in such a case, instead of a simple increase of church attendance and church membership, there occurred a split and a multiplication of the number of churches. Next there followed the problem of which of the rival congregations in a township would retain the church tax and property. New Lights, where they were strong as they first were in Jonathan Edwards's own church, sometimes were the ones to keep the old privileges; the Old Lights were sometimes the ones to lose out. Relatively clear-cut decisions were possible and did occur; so also did compromises, whether made to adjust a schism quite locally or enacted in the colony assembly as a reform of the rules. Altogether the situation was compact with the personal and political, as well as with the economic and religious, components of factionalism.

The most radical religious and organizational result appears in the one hundred or so congregations known as "Separates" or "Old Congregationalists." In the cases of a few leaders, among whom James Davenport, minister great-grandson of the founding minister of New Haven, was most prominent, they became pretty fanatical. As to theology, they characteristically carried the doctrine of man's dependence on God to the point of rejecting the Halfway Covenant (now eighty years old) and requiring an experience of conversion for membership in their congregations. On the side of polity, they accepted the old position of complete congregational autonomy, in the lineage of the Pilgrim churches and of Roger Williams and John Wise. As schismatics they received no tax support from the townships; on principle they did not seek it.

Separates often became Baptists. Adult baptism signifies the individual's conviction of being purged of sin, and of being saved, at the moment of receiving that sacrament. Besides this, the laws of Massachusetts and Connecticut by mid-century excused the members of a congregation which avowed itself to be Baptist from paying church taxes. Altogether the denomination was committed to religious individuality and religious freedom. In Connecticut, resistance to the controls and the orthodoxy of the Saybrook Platform had risen well before the Great Awakening, and a son of Connecticut who turned Baptist, Isaac Backus, became a superb speaker for freedom. As long-term pastor of a loyal flock at Middleborough, Massachusetts, not far from

Cape Cod, Backus supplied a strength to the Baptist movement which it had not previously had.

In New England, the Great Awakening in its many manifestations brought out the energy of Christianity, not its peace, and a new impetus to Puritanism's centrifugal principle. Surely as distressing an event as occurred anywhere in that category was the one which put the principal leader of the revivals out of his church, some years after the revivals had quieted. In 1744, after nineteen years in Northampton and a full decade of incomparable success as evangelist, Jonathan Edwards asked his congregation to restore the ancient rule of the Puritan churches that the communion table be reserved for visible saints and that all others be excluded. After a delay of four years, he pressed for a decision. Accepting the recommendation would have reversed the policy of Solomon Stoddard and meant defeat for a powerful church faction. It would have honored Edwards's own total regard for God's grace as the sole source of salvation, and the evidence of inward transformation as the test of grace having been received. The congregation voted refusal.

Edwards was offered a church in Connecticut, and the possibility arose of an invitation to Scotland. But the call he accepted took him just thirty-five miles westward, a mountain range away, across the Berkshires, to the tiny village of Stockbridge. Thus the magisterial intellect, which had been earliest and keenest in America to grasp deeply both Locke and Newton, undertook, as probably its final assignment, the task of transmitting Christianity to a handful of frontier Indians.

4   *Religious Renewal and Religious Enlightenment: The System of Jonathan Edwards*

IN a series of sermons in 1739, and again in his unfinished posthumous *History of the Work of Redemption*, Edwards set down some of the meanings he found in man's history on earth. Except for quite recent events, his history was much like William Penn's: where the founder of Pennsylvania believed that the Quakers were the present great doers of the work of the Lord, the preacher at Northampton thought that the renewals of the 1730s and 1740s might introduce the millennium of Christ's rule on earth. Both Puritan and Quaker had a cycle theory of development; back of both, and enjoying no less conviction in them than it had in their medieval predecessors for centuries, was a tradition of Christian historiography. From Adam's fall to the coming of Christ had been a long period of spiritual failure; the Savior had turned that tide; since His lifetime, periods of gain, such as when the gospels were revealed and when saints had delivered their message, had alternated with periods of darkness. For Edwards the Reformation was of course one of the greatest events. Where modern scholars think of cycles of employment and unemployment, or of party voting, for instance, or even of waves of religious excitement and lassitude, as helping to explain human destiny, Edwards thought of cycles in which men seek and receive the mercy of God as yielding the historical meaning of life.°

Just before he was forced out at Northampton, Edwards had occasion to preach on the question, related to the significance of history, of the nature of the good life. When young David Brainerd, a New Light minister who had served as missionary to the Indians, died at his home in 1747, Edwards praised the virtues of sympathy and expressiveness: "He had extraordinary knowledge of men, as well as of things; and an uncommon insight into human nature. He excelled most whom I ever knew in the power of communicating his thoughts; and had a peculiar talent at accommodating himself to the capacities, tempers, and circumstances, of those whom he would instruct or counsel." A few months later when Edwards's uncle and partisan, Colonel John Stoddard, died, he had similar things to say. A "great man" of affairs— Colonel Stoddard had been councilman of the province—needs experience of the people and their condition; he needs uncommon natural insight; he must be able to distinguish the true from the false report. Where the minister had praised the young man for his work with his parishioners, he praised the old one for having founded (in 1734) the Indian mission at Stockbridge. At Edwards's own hard moment, of saying farewell to Northampton, he measured himself by like standards. With all his people before him, he addressed them group by group. Obliquely, he asked each and all to acknowledge that he had been true to their needs: "spiritual father" to the "professors" of godliness, active to warn those who remained in a "christless, graceless condition," energetic in caring for those who had come "under some awakenings," a bearer of "peculiar concern for the souls of young people." In sum, Edwards thought of his people, the leaders and the led, as being greatly different from one another, yet all needing his guidance, and every one of them being measured by the spiritual effort they made or failed to make.°

When, during the final dozen years of his life, Edwards poured into five books most of his ideas about Christianity, he addressed himself throughout to questions of what the capacity of the individual is to serve God truly and well. The earliest of the books, *A Treatise Concerning Religious Affections*, was published in 1746, two years before he left Northampton. Time and place are clearly marked in the book, and in its history. First, because it was an apologia, a defense of the author against attackers, and because the argument is buttressed with heavy citations from Protestant writings, an impression arises that the work needs to be studied like a lawyer's brief. Giving weight to this half-truth is the fact that Edwards wrote with a special critic in mind: the Reverend Charles Chauncy of the First Church of Boston, who, during the earlier 1740s, used sermon and open letter, commencement address at Harvard, and, most particularly, a sharp pamphlet, *Seasonable Thoughts on the State of Religion in New England*, to denounce the Great Awakening. Condemnation had been late in coming, even in Boston; but when it came, after the Whitefield and Tennent visits, it described revivalism as if it were a disease, as if it put the social order in danger.

Second, as regards the mark of time on the *Religious Affections*, Edwards had a point of theology to make. In it he inveighed against Arminian doctrines, which accompanied eighteenth-century science and rationalism; on that account the book has sometimes been put down as an old-style Puritan work, against the modernists of the period. Under the heading Arminianism, Edwards designated, here and elsewhere in his writings, not simply theological ideas descended from Jacobus Arminius, a sixteenth-century reviser of Calvinism, but also the growing disposition everywhere, especially in Boston, to reduce emphasis on doctrines of salvation by grace and predestination and to permit belief in complete freedom of the will and in salvation by works. In this respect, though Edwards did build his argument from the Bible as his forefathers had built theirs, and though his drafts on their theology (especially on his grandfather Stoddard's) were numerous, the book departed from Puritanism in the old style. Edwards was now cool, as always, toward federal-theology ideas which moderated one's sense of God's power; and what he said about the psychology of revivalism came straight from his familiarity with Locke's *Essay Concerning Human Understanding*, the work from which the modern science of psychology was at that very time beginning to develop. Actually Edwards understood better, and was more exact in drawing on Locke, than were his detractors.°

But the *Religious Affections* is memorable because it is a great deal more than a masterpiece of self-defense. It was the third and last in a series of Edwards's writings about the Great Awakening; it generalizes and interprets, as the earlier writings do not. The *Narrative of Surprising Conversions*, from which we drew bits of description of the revivals of 1734 and 1735, had preceded it by a decade; a revised version of that essay had included the famous account, still psychologically interesting, of the conversion of Phoebe Bartlett. The *Surprising Con-*

versions is the first of all Edwards's writings to exhibit his extraordinary clinical capacity for observing and interpreting religious transformations. In 1742, during the most fanatical period of the Great Awakening, after Whitefield had departed New England and while Davenport and other Separates were performing conspicuously, the author published his second description, *Some Thoughts Concerning the Present Revival of Religion in New England.* Worried on his own account, and stung by denunciations composed in Boston—the word of attack, "enthusiast," was an insult to a man of mind and orthodoxy—Edwards responded that the Great Awakening must not "be judged of *a priori,* but *a posteriori.*" It was Jonathan Edwards, not a modern historical pragmatist, who insisted that, to be just to the movement, "We are to observe the *effect* wrought; and if, upon examination of that, it be found to be agreeable to the word of God, we are bound to rest in it as God's work." In this second book, Edwards asked those who might be "full of concern about the involuntary motions of the fluids and solids of men's bodies," at the time of conversion, not to judge too quickly; bodily reaction might, or might not, be an indication of spiritual change. He detailed the social gains of revivalism: increased church attendance, sobriety in the community, improved morality among adolescents, and so on. In view of his admiration for David Brainerd and John Stoddard, his account of one set of improvements especially needs to be quoted:

> And, under the influences of this work, there have been many of the remains of those wretched people and dregs of mankind, the poor Indians, that seemed to be next to a state of brutality, and with whom, till now, it seemed to be to little more purpose to use endeavours for their instruction and awakening, than with the beasts. Their minds have now been strangely opened to receive instruction, and been deeply affected with the concerns of their precious souls; they have reformed their lives, . . . particularly . . . their drunkenness. . . . And many of the poor Negroes also have been in like manner wrought upon and changed.°

The *Religious Affections,* Edwards's climactic and largest discussion of revivalism, is, like the other two, highly readable and evocative of his own experience and dedication. It also differs: the argument is topical, analytical, and general; the "distinguishing marks of solitary piety," which are the object of the study, are approached without case studies of Phoebe Bartletts or Indian alcoholics but through logical classifications of types of feeling and behavior which appear in all kinds of people. The phrase *religious affections,* in Edwards, is close to meaning "religious passions." But it does not signify emotion to the exclusion of all else. The word *affection,* as he uses it, connotes also thought, and decision-making for action; it expresses the inclination of the soul to discover its loyalties. In Edwards's account, love is at once a particular affection and the source of all other affections. Early in the work, the "natural love" of persons for other persons is recognized as being something close to divine: "not every thing which in any respect appertains to spiritual affections is different from what natural [unconverted] men can conceive of, and do experience." But natural love fails to prepare the soul adequately for God's visitation, the author said; it does not induce the Christian affections of humility, loveliness, and so on, which are necessary to holiness in an individual. At the close of the work, "Christian practice" is recognized as the ultimate religious affection and as being the most probable indication of divine grace in a man. The author must have calculated his discussion of the point to change readers from an Arminian turn of mind to his own; he makes plain his belief that (though good works can never win a soul's salvation) Christian deeds are blessed and holy. "When a natural man denies his lusts, lives a strict religious life, and seems humble, . . . 'tis all force against nature; as when a stone is violently thrown upwards. . . . But if the old nature be indeed mortified, and a new and heavenly nature infused; then may it well be expected, that men will walk in newness of life, and continue to do so to the end of their days."°

Edwards was saying in this masterwork that the sincere and sustained practice of virtue depends always on faith. Christian merit is not a campaign to win a privilege, but a voluntary effort made by a God-seeking soul. Not until 1902, when William James in *The Varieties of Religious Experience* drew his descriptions of tender-minded and tough-minded believers, would a second American observer write with psychological and religious authority equal to that displayed in the *Religious Affections*. Probably no other book ever written tells us so much about the emotional activism of the Christian evangel, as practised in this country, as does this treatise.°

Shortly before he left Northampton, Edwards told a minister friend that his next writing would be a work to destroy Arminian doctrine. Actually, during his eight years of teaching Indians at Stockbridge, he worked on six books and finished four; the total product would hardly have been possible if it had not all derived from the accumulation of his preaching years. The first of the series, the one concerning which he made the promise and, of course, the most famous of all his writings, *The Freedom of the Will*, has the greatest theoretical interest for our history of public thought, because of the nature of the philosophical problem. But the three minor writings he completed—on *Original Sin*, published in 1758, and on *The Nature of True Virtue* and *The End for Which God Created the World*, published together in 1765—have specific importance for us too. As a group they demonstrate about the author that, though he had recently done so much to upset the equilibrium of the New England churches, he remained to the end of life what he had begun, essentially true to the Puritan tradition and a conservator of it.

In the trio of his less-known writings, the little posthumous work on *The Nature of True Virtue* testifies to Edwards's, and to Puritanism's, essential and continuing Platonism. In it the author renewed philosophical ideas he has mastered while an undergraduate, and had placed with amazing skill in his "Notes on the Mind." Saying now that the nature of virtue is to be understood by examining the nature of beauty, and then distinguishing particular beauty ("a few notes in a tune") from general beauty (a grand harmony), Edwards went on to say that "True virtue most essentially consists in Benevolence to Being in general. Or perhaps to speak more accurately, it is that consent, propensity, and union of heart to Being in general, that is immediately exercised in a general good will."° *The Doctrine of Original Sin Defended* and *Dissertation Concerning the End for Which God Created the World* are convenient places to observe both that Edwards's estimation of natural man resembled that of his ancestors and that it anticipated the dark estimations of our own times. To illustrate from *Original Sin*, the earlier work:

> When man sinned and broke God's covenant, and fell under his curse . . . God then left him. . . . Thus man was left in a state of darkness, woeful corruption and ruin; nothing but *flesh* without *spirit*. . . . Man did immediately set up *himself*, and the objects of his private affections and appetites, as supreme; and so they took the place of *God*.

And from the later work:

> God aims at satisfying justice in the eternal damnation of sinners, which will be satisfied by their damnation, considered no otherwise than with regard to its eternal duration. But yet there never will come that particular moment, when it can be said, that now justice is satisfied. But if this does not satisfy our modern freethinkers, who do not like the talk about satisfying justice with an infinite punishment; I suppose it will not be denied by any, that God, in glorifying the saints in heaven with eternal felicity, aims to satisfy his infinite grace or benevolence, by the bestowment of a good infinitely valuable, because eternal, and yet there never will come the moment when it can be said, that now this infinitely valuable good has been actually bestowed.°

As we approach the book everywhere known as *The Freedom of the Will*, we will be helped by selecting from the author's full eleven-line title a more faithful short title, *That Freedom of Will Which Is Supposed to Be Essential to Moral Agency*.° The two words *supposed* and *moral* are crucial. That freedom is a supposition to be examined and refined, not a certainty to be taken for granted, is a belief which underlies the book; that the aspect of freedom which is moral is the one important aspect of the matter is equally firmly assumed. There is no mention of, say, physics and chemistry, or economics, in the book; no question of materialistic determinism, in any sense of that adjective, arises. Further, to the peace of mind of readers not expert in metaphysics, as Edwards takes off from points of departure in Locke's *Essay Concerning Human Understanding*, he assures us "that the Will (without any metaphysical refining) is plainly, that by which the mind chooses anything. The faculty of the will is that faculty or power or principle of mind by which it is capable of choosing: an act of the will is the same as an act of choosing or choice." Pages later he says:

> But one thing more I would observe concerning what is vulgarly called liberty; namely, that power and opportunity for one to do and conduct as he will, or according to his choice, is all that is meant by it. . . . Let the person come by his volition or choice how he will, yet, if he is able, and there is nothing in the way to hinder his pursuing and executing his will, the man is fully and perfectly free, according to the primary and common notion of freedom.

The *if he is able* phrase in this passage notwithstanding, no reader need be persuaded that Edwards believed a man to be less than free, for example, to seek in marriage the girl of his choice or to cast his vote according to his personal preference.

The true reservation expressed by the *if*, which recurs throughout the book, is that, though the will is free to make choices, there remains always the question of what determines the will. "If the will be determined, there is a determiner." Early in the work, Edwards looked at the matter psychologically, affected by the chapter in the *Essay Concerning Human Understanding* on "Power." Among other determinants, Edwards examined "moral necessity" and "moral inability." To illustrate the first, he observed that it would be "absurd to suppose the same individual will to oppose itself"; to illustrate the second, "A child of great love and duty to his parents, may be thus unable to kill his father." The author reached his problem of criticism in Part II, where he tackled the Arminian position, which affirmed, in Edwards's words, "a self-determining Power in the will." If the will—or person, or soul— actually "determines all its own free acts," he reasons, "then every free act of choice is determined by a preceding act of choice, choosing that act." Thus Edwards found that his Arminian contemporaries, while they were asserting that human choice is ultimately free, were snarling themselves in a chain of poor logic which upset their main proposition.

All his life Edwards had preached the sovereignty of God, a governance described always in terms of ultimates—of His freedom, His power, His goodness and grace. The supremacy of the Almighty was again Edwards's recourse, and indeed he had no other, in solving the problem of free will. "God's moral government over mankind," he said in the conclusion of *The Freedom of the Will*, "his treating them as moral agents, making them the objects of his commands, counsels, calls, warnings, expostulations, promises, threatenings, rewards, and punishments, is not inconsistent with a determining disposal of all events, of every kind, throughout the universe, in his providence, either by positive efficiency, or permission." This grim sentence is followed by similar sentences, which were calculated to push the Arminians to the wall. For example: "The things which have been said, obviate some of the chief objections of Arminians against the Calvinistic doctrine of the *total depravity and corruption of man's nature*, whereby his heart is wholly under the power of sin, and he is utterly unable, without the interposition of sovereign grace, savingly to love God, believe in Christ, or do anything that is truly good and acceptable in God's sight."

The more because *The Freedom of the Will* closes with a thrust of logic against the Arminians, with no effort at moderation or compromise, adverse readers have been ready to say of the later Edwards, as Parrington did in 1927, that he broke "wholly with the social tendencies of his age and world, and that in the end his method of reasoning was unseasoned by any saving knowledge of human nature." Indeed, for about a century before Parrington (the second century after Edwards), Jonathan Edwards's writings were little known outside professional theological circles, and when they were considered by non-Calvinists were characteristically put down as having been anachronistic in his own day of the early Enlightenment and all but unreadable by modern men. Only since Parrington, and especially since World War II, has the tide of appreciation turned. The new response comes chiefly from scholars who are neither theologians nor Calvinists but who share the feeling of our time that now, once again as during and after the Reformation, awareness of evil and frailty in men must be incorporated into philosophical, and public, discourse. In this spirit (and for many reasons) a complete edition of Edwards is now being edited and handsomely published; already, to students of American literature, comparison seems natural and right between Edwards and twentieth-century disturbers of belief in progress, and in human sufficiency to deal rationally and well with humanity's needs. On such a basis Edwards again becomes interesting to readers; it is easy today to say how mistaken Parrington was, when he said that Edwards lacked knowledge of human nature.

But to understand Edwards, and Americans and others who were affected by him in his own century and the next, we must not go far in linking his pessimism with our pessimism which rises in the wake of moral dilemmas and under threat of destruction. When moderns discuss human nature they speak, as far as they are able, of the natural experience of man; they include, as well as man's capacity for evil, man's capacity for good, even The Good. But to Edwards, as to Christian thought traditionally, "natural man," about whom his anxiety gathered, signified the physical and social, earthbound qualities of men —the appetites and the propensities for self-love and for love of other individuals. By common understanding "natural man" was a limited phenomenon. As Edwards's previous life and writings testify and *The Freedom of the Will* testifies again, he was far from saying that holiness never comes to man; he simply said that it never comes to him from his appetites and his love for his own. When it does come, a man is a "natural man" no longer. Not in the slightest compromising the point that natural men cannot win salvation on merit, and very stern on the point that few are saved, *The Freedom of the Will* richly renews the assurance that men can seek salvation and find it—but must seek it as a gift, within.

Altogether then, although the term is often applied, Edwards's theology should not be called determinism at all. Determinisms are usually ways of thinking about groups or societies. They do not apply to individuals when governed by justice or love. Man's one true freedom, in *The Freedom of the Will*, is a share of God's freedom; in the argument of that book there are other kinds, but no other kind which counts. God-given freedom and God-given commands are alike compelling and inscrutable to man. Edwards said this in the final paragraph of his treatise, by quoting I Corinthians 1: 27-29: "But God hath chosen the foolish things of the world, to confound the wise: and God hath chosen the weak things of the world, to confound the things that are mighty: and base things of the world, and things which are despised, hath God chosen: yea, and things which are not, to bring to nought things that are; that no flesh should glory in his presence."°

5 *American Christianity Rough-hewn*

ONE of the quiet aspects of the Great Awakening in New England, which would hardly be noticeable if the American Revolution had not followed so soon, is its indifference to problems of civil and ecclesiastical polity. Revivalism tore congregations and townships apart. But, excepting Connecticut, where church associations were sanctioned by statute and where new laws during the 1740s restricted unlicensed preaching and for the time being reversed the current toward religious freedom, little effort was made to sustain the church-state relationship as a matter of loyalty and principle. Theology had succeeded polity as the main object of public religious concern. After the elaborate conceiving and interweaving of Puritan institutions during the seventeenth century, so that state would sustain church and church would guide state and society, and both hold up a pillar of light to the world, the eighteenth-century emphasis amounted to a reversal. By the same token there is contrast and irony that the descendant of Mathers and Winthrops, who was the genius of Puritanism a century after them, began and ended his career as a quite nonpolitical thinker.

This difference, which contrasts Edwards and most of the New Lights with the founders of Massachusetts, also contrasts him with his contemporaries and brothers in evangelization, wherever they were in a minority, or in a politically dependent, position. In New England the Baptists had to be politically articulate enough to fight for their freedom from church taxation and for their freedom to worship. Among Presbyterian New Sides, everywhere, the need to build their church according to the Scots pattern of federalism among congregations, presbyteries and synods, was never out of mind. After the antagonism between New Sides and Old Sides was absorbed in the reunion of 1758, evangelical Presbyterianism's main problems of freedom and equality shifted southward, to Virginia and her neighbors, where Scots-Irish settlements were growing but Anglicans had the privileges.

By the 1740s, Samuel Davies, Log College graduate and eloquent evangelizer, had gone from Delaware to Hanover County, in western Virginia; he opened his ministerial career by fighting in court and winning the right to preach. He helped to found Presbyterian churches well into North Carolina; the presbytery he established and based at Hanover was energetically New Sides. In the wake of this expansion, much as in the wake of New Lights in New England, Baptists and Baptist congregations volunteered. Some of them derived from the Baptist movement in England; others were started by immigrants from New England. In either stream, Baptists were the earliest sectarians in any number, south of New England, to follow the congregationalist polity. Finally, although the Church of England was slower in America than at home to produce its own, inner, movement of evangelism, the Southern Colonies became the region, as well as of Presbyterians and Baptists, of Methodists in two or three clusters. In Virginia, the Reverend Devereux Jarratt, a colony-born Anglican priest who had been converted by a New Sides preacher, was the founder of the movement. During the decade before the Revolution, gatherings in the vicinity of Baltimore became, more than those in any other location, the American base of the future Methodist Church.

Although none of the evangelical elements in the Southern Colonies established a college in the region, Presbyterianism there contributed money and students and President Davies to the College of New Jersey. Likewise the Baptists contributed to the College of Rhode Island, the future Brown University, which was founded in 1764 and was, as truly as Princeton, an intercolonial and interregional institution. Presbyterian academies, which would grow into the future Hampden-Sydney (named for John Hampden and Algernon Sydney) and Washington and Lee colleges, were launched in western Virginia before the Revolution; Hampden-Sydney became a college in the year of the Peace of Paris, 1783.

Gaustad is plainly right when, concluding a review of the theological results of the New England awakening, he says that increased devotion among the people was the principal thing. "Personal piety, the animating force of religion," he observes, "was the legacy of the Great Awakening to those of its heirs who loved to ascribe absolute sovereignty, above all others, to God."° This proposition could be safely ascribed to all three colonial regions; finally there could be added the amendment, thanks to Edwards principally but not alone, that besides the fact of increased devotion, the Great Awakening brought increased consciousness of devotion. After the 1740s, much more than before, active dedication and service to Christ and to church became an expected norm, not for the few but for the many, in America.

Individualism in any of the senses in which that word has modern meaning—political, economic, or even religious—was hardly a part of the movement. But an impulse to express personal and congregational particularity, either or both, was surely of the essence of the new piety. It is supremely illustrated in Jonathan Edwards and George Whitefield alike, each with his own originality of religious style and method. And, in Edwards's case, while his insisting on individual conversion as a condition of being admitted to church membership recalls the early theocrats, there is considerable difference between having conversion serve as the token of conformity and entering the governing elite (as the theocrats arranged things) and having it serve as the token of a certain kind of congregation (as Edwards wanted in Northampton). In his individual, emotional stress and his self-confidence, there is great similarity between Edwards's concentration on salvation by divine grace and the Antinomians of the 1630s.

After Edwards, and because of him and the Great Awakening, the religious intellect of New England would never regain its century-old coherency. The oppositions over the Halfway Covenant, over Stoddardianism, and over the more and less strict congregationalist theories of, say, John Wise, the Mathers, and the authors of the Saybrook Platform had been serious. But now the new varieties of faith in the Puritan lineage became numerous, attached to faction and interest, and before long deeply entrenched in area, congregation and town, and college. The Congregationalists around Boston, for one main cluster, whose Arminianism and rationalism Edwards had principally attacked, somehow never troubled to respond to the theological fire he hurled during the 1750s, after the awakening had subsided. Charles Chauncy, who before 1741 and his annoyance with Edwards had been an orthodox Puritan, later quite abandoned Calvinism. He and younger contemporaries, conspicuously Jonathan Mayhew of West Church, Boston, proceeded on the course of development which is marked by the Dudleian lectures at Harvard, and which brought them into liberal Congregationalism and close to Unitarianism, before the Revolution. At the opposite wing of religious feeling, the most disturbed New Lights, including James Davenport and John Cleaveland, produced some bizarre theology. Davenport is said to have terrified his congregation by announcing the coming, physical end of the world. Samuel Hopkins, Edwardsian theologian of "disinterested benevolence," went further than his master had done in preaching that the millennium was near; he is reported to have felt spiritually "at home" in that period.°

In their colonial habit of erecting a college to support each broadly held phase of Christian belief, the liberals were too much sustained by their alma mater, Harvard, to want a new institution. The most extreme New Lights were not fond of learning. But Eleazar Wheelock's school for Indians, which migrated from Lebanon, Connecticut, to Lebanon, New Hampshire, and in 1769 became Dartmouth College at Hanover, institutionalized a New Light interest which changed. So did the Baptist College of Rhode Island.

For a period of years after the Great Awakening, still opposed to each other but then reconciled in the way in which New Sides and Old Sides were reconciled in Presbyterianism, were the "Old Calvinists," the least disturbed element in the Congregational churches, and the "New Calvinists," or moderate followers of Edwards. The theological work of reconciliation was begun, before Edwards's death, principally by his two disciples, Joseph Bellamy of Connecticut and Samuel Hopkins of Rhode Island. Both were adjusters and interpreters of Edwards's ideas; both were voluminous writers, as well as preachers, of theology. Hopkins, especially, trained a large number of ministers at his home, probably about seventy. Thus was born and nurtured the New Theology, finally called the New England Theology. Yale College, from which Bellamy and Hopkins had graduated, and which had a checkered history in relation to the awakening, gave the New England Theology a home. Timothy Dwight, who became Yale's president in 1795, was a grandson of Jonathan Edwards, and himself a writing and preaching Edwardsian. Soon after the turn of the century the regional tradition, in this form, returned to the Boston area, flanking and defying Harvard, at the Andover Theological Seminary.

Altogether, throughout the continental colonies, religious leaders had their say and their way, during the generation preceding the Revolution, and the Revolution did not terminate their dialogue. In the Middle Colonies, and wherever else the sects appeared, the sects became more like churches—accepted, institutionalized, and practically free. Everywhere the churches became independent of authority in Europe: the Presbyterians completely so, the Reformed and Lutherans almost as much. The Congregationalists had begun free and now proliferated; the Anglicans became more than ever congregationalized in the Southern Colonies. In bits and pieces, the churches became more like sects—intense, sometimes local and exclusive. All became more layman controlled than in Europe; they were more so at the middle of the eighteenth century than they had been at the middle of the seventeenth.

Little of this was cast into political terms or referred to the legislatures for any kind of action. But much of it was independence-seeking for persons, congregations, sects, and churches. All of it meant to participators the most important independence men could exercise. Many religious actions took a free, or nearly free, society for granted. In their turn, political impulses, seeking greater freedom, would gain by what Christian thinkers and churchmen had done. Within voluntary church organizations great steps were being taken toward democracy.

Part Three

THE ENLIGHTENMENT AND THE REVOLUTION: THE EMERGENCE OF NATIONAL CONVICTIONS

1740-1800

CHAPTER VIII

The Enlightenment
in America

We may say that the Eighteenth Century, nothwith-standing all its Errors and Vices has been, of all that are past, the most honourable to human Nature. Knowledge and Virtues were increased and diffused, Arts, Sciences useful to Men, ameliorating their condi-tion, were improved, more than in any former equal Period.
    John Adams to Thomas Jefferson, November 13, 1815

1   *With the Enlightenment at Peak in Europe*

URING the eighteenth century English-speaking America shared with all the world of the West in that quickening, broadening, and emancipating movement of the intellect which we call the Enlightenment. One of the most exhilarating—and philosophically and socially critical—passages ever to occur in the history of thought, the Enlightenment stirred into action or reaction every sort of participator in the life of the mind. The following types of men, principally, took part in America: scientists, a small group of professionals in the colleges and a number of accomplished amateurs who made themselves truly acquainted with the science of Europe; printers of newspapers and almanacs, who were often the operators of lending libraries as well and who had business advantage to gain from circulating new enthusiasms; city craftsmen and traders who, either with or without substantial acquaintance with science and thought, had a lively interest in technological improvement; gentlemen planters who, by reason of their importing and exporting, had regular correspondence with England, intellectual correspondence included; and clergymen who, for any of a variety of reasons—sometimes because, in their frequent sideline as physicians, they could render a service; sometimes simply because they discovered God's glory in the actual world—gathered new data from nature and gave them active place in their minds.

In its creative locations in Europe, the Enlightenment signified, principally, building on two new foundations of thought. The first and deeper one was the work of science. By 1700 or a little later a body of literature had accumulated which summed up the new physics and astronomy of the age of Galileo and since; by the same time a series of inventions in mathematics, among which the differential and integral calculus were principal items, had given to those who could use them a power to understand and predict the movement of physical bodies far beyond that ever achieved before. Isaac Newton's *Principia Mathematica*, published in 1686 and 1687 at Cambridge, was the most massive embodiment of the new methods and findings. The second foundation of the movement was the work of students of man and society. The seventeenth century produced much historical and political writing; the writers included the English spokesmen for liberty whom eighteenth-century Americans loved: Coke and Harrington, Milton and Algernon Sydney, for example. At the end of the seventeenth century and during the eighteenth, the study of men and peoples widened, and much of the writing, highly critical of conditions past and present, was informed by belief in moral law. Voltaire's *Essays Concerning the English Nation* and Gibbon's *Decline and Fall* represented supremely the new critical spirit. Among the innovations, the origins of modern naturalistic psychology trace to John Locke's *An Essay Concerning Human Understanding*; and early-modern, liberal economics, which stressed emancipating trade and industry from control by the mercantilist state, began in France and England and reached epochal expression in Scotland in 1776, when Adam Smith's *Wealth of Nations* was published. It would be hard to name from any other period of intellectual history a cluster of men more effective, either as the authors of books which would become classics or as critics of the established order of their time, than the men on whose work the Enlightenment was built.

A report on science in the English colonies is mistaken, as Daniel Boorstin correctly insists, if it assumes that American experimenters made discoveries on a par with the epoch-making work in Europe.° And, likewise, no colonial student of society produced anything nearly equal to *The Wealth of Nations* or the *Encyclopédie*. But this does not mean that eighteenth-century colonials missed the tune and beat of their times. In Europe, most of the seminal work of the Enlightenment, on the side of the natural sciences, was done before the eighteenth century began. If we count Linnaeus's basic system of botanical classification to be part of that work, we need bring the time down to 1740. This is the round date, also, which serves best for marking the midpoint of the social thought and criticism of the age. Locke preceded it by half a century. But Montesquieu's *Spirit of the Laws*, Voltaire's early writings, and Lord Bolingbroke's essays on man and history (which would prove strangely influential in America) all appeared about 1740. The work of the Encyclopedists, of Rousseau and Condorcet in France, and that of Adam Smith and the common-sense philosophers in Scotland, followed by three decades, more or less. Because the second third of the eighteenth century is the earliest period during which events permit us to think of the Enlightenment as having become a substantial thing in America, the question is less what the colonies could contribute to the foundation of the movement than how they caught on, and acted in, the spirit of the time.

Since it is an open secret that the decision for American independence from England in 1776 owes much to the intellectual movement we seek, we may enjoy from the beginning the irony that the early Enlightenment in America was very much a selection from the interests of the Enlightenment at home, as they were carried across the sea. Ocean routes were open to this export traffic, but only certain elements transported well. The Royal Society illustrates better than anything else the openness of English science to American colonial participation. The society was founded in 1662 under the auspices of Charles II; it was the first nationalizing of the English scientific community. During the hundred years which followed, writers of scientific papers from New England to the West Indies succeeded in getting them published in the *Philosophical Transactions* of the society; in the same period, about twenty-five colonials were elected into its fellowship, a great distinction then as now. The Puritan bad odor of New Englanders at home did not prevent Governor John Winthrop, Jr., and Cotton Mather from being elected early to fellowships; neither did the passage of time come to exclude eighteenth-century Americans from being chosen. During the generation before the Revolution, Benjamin Franklin and Professor John Winthrop, the first and perhaps the second most creative scientists in the colonies, were privileged to sign themselves "F.R.S."

But availability to scientific recognition did not reduce the sea miles from the main centers of scientific growth—from the cities, courts, and universities of Europe, where scientists gathered in mutual self-help and where a certain amount of financial support could be found. Except for small clusters of enthusiasts in or near Philadelphia and Boston, colonial workers in science were quite isolated. They did correspond with one another and with scientists overseas. Their situation compares with that of colonial writers; sometimes the two situations combined in one man. For the most telling example, Benjamin Franklin trained himself, while a teen-age printer's apprentice, to write in the manner of the *Spectator*; similarly, during his forties, he instructed himself sufficiently to carry out his experiments in electricity. But there were limits to such independent work. Not even a Franklin could make a magazine succeed in the colonies; and, during the colonial period, no American printer, though he published newspapers, almanacs, volumes of sermons, and a few volumes of poetry and history, published a single volume of American fiction. Although a taste for that new genre existed and many novels were imported from England, there were no American writers or publishers of them before independence. In much the same way, colonials of scientific bent could go so far as to collect botanical specimens and write up their findings; they could teach themselves mathematics, and a very few did; they could conduct agricultural experiments. They could not do very much more. In science and literature alike, there simply were not enough contributors and readers or beneficiaries, or enough centralization, for a great effort to be made. Only two or three Americans reached major creativity and made international reputations in the field of science they entered.

On the other hand, location on the periphery of the culture of the West did enhance certain kinds of scientific observation and record keeping. Colonial development promoted explorations, map making, and Indian study. Though what we know as historical or institutional economics was not an intellectual discipline of that time, the Crown regularly demanded from the governors reports of the population, the resources, the economic promise and growth of the colonies. Surveys of regional situations, of which Thomas Jefferson's *Notes on Virginia* after the Revolution would be the classical case, early became an American habit.

The differential and integral calculus, invented by Newton and Leibnitz late in the seventeenth century, remains today the unique symbol it was during the Enlightenment for the capacity of that age for analysis. Though on the American side no such stellar invention was made, new ways of looking at things, harder and more knowingly than before, were frequently needed and found. They were developed and utilized, colonial region by region, according to the region's wants and habits of mind.

2   *Scientific and*
Humanistic Interests in the
Plantation Colonies

SIR Walter Raleigh was responsible for the first scientific work done by an Englishman on the American seaboard, and the work proved to be as brilliant as the Roanoke colony, which it was intended to serve, proved dismal. Sir Walter designated Thomas Harriot, a twenty-five-year-old M.A. and mathematician of Oxford who had been a member of his household and his own tutor in mathematics, to go with the expedition of 1685. The young man made a map of the Roanoke area. He sent to England animals and birds never seen there before: an opossum, a raccoon, a black bear, an otter, a skunk, a bald eagle, and a turkey. Another member of the expedition made drawings. Not neglecting botany and the possibilities of agriculture, Harriot described American trees and shrubs, including the witch hazel and the sassafras, to which he attributed medicinal properties. He reported how the Indians fished, and what varieties of fish they consumed. He noted the presence of sandstone, limestone, iron ore, and copper ore. Raleigh himself was keen on the discovery of Indian corn and tobacco, which Harriot had smoked with the Indians.

No less because the colony totally disappeared soon after he returned to England, Thomas Harriot's work has a classical quality. As to flair for knowledge, it outdid the surveying and reporting which accompanied the settlement and growth of the permanent colony of Virginia, a quarter century later. Captain John Smith, with his explorations, map making, and rendering of accounts in the *True Relation . . . of Virginia*, did similar work; and John Rolfe, the successful innovator of tobacco production, represents some of the same concerns. But, looking for a perspective on the history of science on the American frontier, we can see in the Raleigh and Harriot story, as nowhere else, a first start on experimentation in soil resources and agriculture under government auspices; we can glimpse also a suggestion of a thing which would be rare but important in times to come: founders and investors in a new area of occupation providing science beforehand for the development of the region. This would happen again in the later nineteenth century, but not much during the three centuries intervening.

Between the arrival of Thomas Harriot, mathematician, at Roanoke and the coming of Dr. William Small, one hundred eighty years later, to be professor of mathematics at William and Mary, except for a small number of physicians there seem to have been no career scientists in Virginia or in any other of the Southern Colonies. Active amateur science came little and late, as a diversion of well-educated men. Before the end of the seventeenth century the Reverend John Banister, a graduate of Magdalen College, Oxford, studied the plants of the region of his home on the Appomattox River; he did not live to complete a manuscript on the natural history of Virginia, but several articles by him on Virginia insects, snails, and other "curiosities" were published in the *Transactions* of the Royal Society. A generation later William Byrd II, great landholder and high official, qualified for membership in the same society by writing a paper on an albino Negro. Outside Virginia, Dr. Alexander Garden of Charleston, South Carolina, a physician who had studied at the university and in the botanical gardens of Edinburgh, was the man who did the best scientific work in the colonies south of Pennsylvania. He discovered plants with medicinal value; he collected eels, snakes, and a variety of unusual fauna; his name was bestowed on the gardenia. He became a fellow of the Royal Society, and, through the good offices of Linnaeus, he was elected to the Royal Society of Upsala as well.

From first to last in the Southern Colonies, where life was decentralized and economically and culturally imitative of England, science was decentralized and imitative, too. The single exception to decentralization occurred at William and Mary College during the the 1760s. Dr. Small managed to assemble there what was probably, after Harvard's, the second-best collection of scientific equipment in the colonies; he had also the wonderful luck to have Thomas Jefferson as a student and to open that mind to an area of knowledge and speculation which it would always love. The professor and his student were made welcome at the Williamsburg palace by Governor Francis Fauquier, who himself belonged to the Royal Society. The three studious men talking together in Williamsburg supply our canvas with a candlelit detail of the early Enlightenment in America—its source in England, its reception by a young lover of learning, its effect in the lasting orientation of a mind.

More available to southern-colony squires in general, however, than serious knowledge about science was the educational and literary culture of the age, in the Renaissance tradition still. Here again the colonials depended on the mother country, but the intellectual imports which were needed moved readily across the sea. Anglican and (in time) Presbyterian clergymen carried skill in Latin into the countryside, and there they were ready to teach. We have no school or literacy statistics, but the impression comes through that, among southern-colonial planters of few acres, and certainly among the unpropertied and dependent classes, few children were taught to read. For the children of well-to-do landholders, however, though the plantation school and tutor of southern legend did occur in actual history, the clergymen seem to have borne most of the burden.° They instructed boys of their vicinity, often individually, in Latin and mathematics, sometimes in Greek and in modern languages, to the point of being ready for college. Thomas Jefferson was prepared for William and Mary by ministers near his western home. An occasional clergyman, such as Dulany Addison of Upper Marlboro (whose name suggests connections with two high families of Maryland), maintained a small residence school while he kept up his parish duties. For sons of the well-to-do who did not get ample instruction on or near their home plantation, the colonial capitals offered resources. The advertisements in the gazettes there indicate, especially in Charleston, a number of teachers ready to give instruction in areas which spread from Greek to vocational subjects, like accounting and surveying, and to social ones, like music and dancing. At the end of the colonial period, college work at William and Mary was held back, as Thomas Jefferson the student complained, by the necessity of maintaining a sizable preparatory department in the college.

Library gathering was a phenomenon of the historic Renaissance in Europe, and one measure of the fondness of eighteenth-century planters for that tradition, as Louis B. Wright has demonstrated, is to be found in the book collecting and reading habits they followed. Advertisements in the papers and inventories contained in wills give substance to the impression that educated planters often bought books in numbers. Young Charles Carroll of Carrollton, who had the advantage of having gone to school on the continent and of having trained for law in the London Inns of Court, kept a standing order in England to have sent to him regularly new works in many categories (which included the writings of Voltaire). The best and most numerous library in Virginia, that of our fellow of the Royal Society, William Byrd II, supplies one of the very few statistics we have: he had more than 3,600 books at Westover and kept a librarian in charge. Other families known to have sizable collections are the Dulanys of Maryland and the Lees, the Fitzhughs, and the Carters of Virginia. One scholar's estimation is that the southern planter's library early in the eighteenth century characteristically numbered from two to three hundred books and, later, about four hundred. Any impression of a very low ceiling on plantation reading is shattered when one runs into Henry Callister, a young merchant on the Eastern Shore of Maryland, who, on being called upon to give advice about starting a commercial library, said that he thought that the 1,700 volumes under consideration were so widely known as to make the venture dubious.

What kinds of books were purchased and read in America? In line with the Puritan-influenced Anglicanism of early Virginia and Maryland, more works of theology appeared on southern bookshelves, with greater similarity to those in New England, than might be expected. On the Renaissance side, quite according to expectation, there was more Latin than Greek. Cicero, Seneca, Pliny, Quintilian, and Vergil were favorite classics; Plato and Aristotle were not, but Plutarch was. Besides the ancient writings, sometimes present in the original language and sometimes in English, modern histories of the ancients turned up. Montesquieu's *Causes of the Greatness and Decadence of the Romans* was a favorite.

The books in southern libraries written during, or about, the sixteenth and seventeenth centuries represented a variety of points of view. The Earl of Clarendon's royalist *History of the Rebellions* (the Puritan Revolution) was sometimes present; so, very frequently, was Samuel Butler's burlesque of the Puritans, *Hudibras*. (Probably *Hudibras* was more frequently read, as it certainly was more frequently imitated, than any Elizabethan dramas were, those of Shakespeare included.) But when the seventeenth-century book was political thought, choices fell on the revolutionary, not the royalist, side: often on Harrington, Locke, and Algernon Sydney. Robert Filmer's *Patriarcha*, the main apologia for the monarchy of the seventeenth century, seems to have been the forgotten book in the Old Dominion—the author's connections with early Virginia families notwithstanding. William Robertson's histories of Charles V and of Scotland at the time of the Reformation, works of Scottish Presbyterian origin, were frequently imported and praised during the fifteen years before the Revolution when they were new.

Works on English law were a large component in the plantation owner's library. Books in that field stretched from Henry de Bracton of the thirteenth century to the *Commentaries* of William Blackstone, which reached America at publication, just after the Stamp Act. In the lower colonies as in New England, Sir Edward Coke was the English writer on law more honored than any other. Among non-English and postclassical writings on law and politics, Montesquieu's *Spirit of the Laws* was widely distributed; the German natural-rights theorist Pufendorf and the Swiss one, Burlamaqui, who introduced the idea that the happiness of the citizen is a criterion of political institutions, were imported too.

The possession of books on a working plantation (or anywhere) is one thing; the reading and study, not to say mastery, of them is another, and a hard matter to gauge. As in more modern instances, the most optimistic reports are too good to credit easily; certainly they are too few in number to bear generalizing statements. Yet the young Thomas Jefferson's very long studying day, from before breakfast to after dinner, probably does not exaggerate his case; from the preceding generation, though we know about William Byrd's bawdiness and his cross temper, those data neither reduce the fact of his reading in several languages nor change the record of his having been fond of theology and verse. It does seem reasonable to suppose that for most planters the handbooks they bought were the books they studied hardest. For the state service they were habitually called on to render, that of justice of the peace, Michael Dalton's *Country Justice* was a standard guide. They kept medical compendia ready. They must have derived as much pleasure as guidance from English texts they imported, on the proper conduct of gentlemen and ladies.

At this point the neat distinction made by Howard Mumford Jones, that colonial "North America was of the Renaissance, but not in it," helps to keep the meaning of our data in view.° Concerning the fact of the Renaissance spirit of southern-colonial upper-class culture, there is no room for doubt. Besides the region's tradition of education and letters there is the lovely outdoor testimony of architecture, domestic and public alike. From the colonial years the Georgian residences and public buildings, with columns and Palladian windows, are accurate reminders of continuing Renaissance taste; so also, with a new accent on Roman forms, are the classical revival buildings of the early republic. But the "not in it" part of Jones's judgment, which denies to the colonies creative energy in the Renaissance tradition is hard to accept all the way. Of course, when he tells us that the colonies produced no Milton and that it derogates nothing "from the genial culture of the Byrd family to say that no member of it quite suggests Marsilio Ficino," we cannot help but agree. Yet the notion will not be downed that rural gentlemen of the Chesapeake region and southward, actually affected by their knowledge of the historical and literary past, did take positions of their own which were appropriate to the idea of rebirth and which, as voiced by their leaders from 1774 to 1788, achieved such dedication to nationality as truly belongs in the lineage of Rienzi and Machiavelli.

The early indications, to be sure, are spotty, and they testify rather to the fun of intellectual exercise than to any Ficino-like fondness for Greek philosophy. (Plato had been important in seventeenth-century American culture and would be again in nineteenth; yet even in New England his hold weakened during the Enlightenment.) Early in our period was written a satirical piece of current history, the story of fixing the intercolonial boundary between Virginia and North Carolina, "The History of the Dividing Line Run in the Year 1728," by William Byrd II himself. The manuscript which Byrd composed (and which would not be published until 1841) contained a participator's account of the diplomacy and the field work and of what the surveyors observed. The passage least likely to be forgotten is the one which describes a North Carolina couple who lived Indian style in a bark-covered "bower" and who covered themselves by provision of nature, the man with his beard and the woman with her length of untidy hair. But the more telling thing about William Byrd as author is that he made fun of the origins of his fellow Virginians, as freely as he did of the laziness of North Carolinians. Jamestown was founded, he said, by "about an hundred men, most of them reprobates of good families." They were perverse, he went on: "Like true Englishmen they built a church that cost no more than fifty pounds, and a tavern that cost five hundred." For wives, they waited for women to arrive from England, when they would have done better to take Indian girls.

> Morals and all considered, I can't think the Indians were much greater heathens than the first adventurers who, had they been good Christians, would have had the charity to take this only method [marriage] of

converting the natives to Christianity. . . . A sprightly lover is the most prevailing missionary that can be sent among these, or any other infidels. Besides, the poor Indians would have had less reason to complain that the English took away their land, if they had received it by way of portion with their daughters. . . . Nor would the shade of the skin have been any reproach at this day; for if a Moor may be washed white in three generations, surely an Indian might have been blanched in two.°

The "History of the Dividing Line" was one man's venture in self-amusement and perspective. A yet more revealing manuscript in history and irony, the "History of the Tuesday Club of Annapolis," still unpublished, may be put down as the authentic voice of an upper-class and business-class group in Maryland. Composed about mid-century by Dr. Alexander Hamilton, the author of the amusing *Itinerarium*, perhaps with contributions from another physician and from Jonas Green, the colony printer, the "History" tells of the tastes and attitudinizing of fifteen men at the center of affairs in the province. Though their identities are shrouded by club pseudonyms, it is clear that several were lawyers and some were leaders—of both "country party" and "court party"—in politics. One of their rules required that, if any conversation were started concerning colony politics or administration or other "unwelcome" matter, the society should wait until the speech was ended and then laugh loudly. Another rule required that no fresh liquor be produced after eleven o'clock. By the drawings which accompany the manuscript, the club had wonderful and tipsy meetings, sometimes with song or original verse and often with mock trials or wranglings.

The following lines are drawn from the close of the Tuesday Club's history.

Histories are no farther Instructive, than as they display to us human nature in a true picture, and as a picture is not compleat without the coloring and shading to fill up the design or outline, so history is not compleat without observations remarks and reflexions Interspersed or Interluded with the bare narrative of facts. . . . [As to] the bare narrative of facts and occurrences, there is really a trifling difference between the histories of the smallest Clubs and those of the Greatest Empires and Kingdoms. We find in the Latter a parcell of mortals denominated Emperors, Kings, potentates, and princes, contending and scrambling about little parcells and portions of this terrestrial ball, we find state politicians racking their Invention to bring about Certain Schemes, and still like a parcel of earth moles countermining and undermining one another, we find Generals, or rather licensed banditty, leading forth great armies, pillaging and laying waste vast Countries, burning towns and cutting throats, and all to acquire for themselves, or master, a certain perishable power. . . . In fine, we find the whole world in an uproar about certain matters, in themselves abstractedly of a very mean consideration and of a perishing transitory nature.

The writer concluded by renewing his proposition that the history of a club may display human nature as well as that of an empire, and by saying that he had done his best to salt and season his own history. But if he has failed he will not "care one single farthing, and, notwithstanding, I believe I shall sleep as sound as usual Remembering that golden maxim of Epictetus, never to make myself over solicitous or uneasy about matters that lie Intirely in the power of another, and altogether out of my reach or command."°

Satire as a literary mode—from its classical origins to the great English satirists whom the colonials knew well: Butler, Dryden, Pope, Addison—had ever and always depended more immediately on having readers than other forms of literature had done. A lyric or an epic (and some essays and novels) can wait, but a satire calls for laughter at once. Colonial satirists seem to have gotten their response. Concerning their effectiveness in the Southern Colonies, about all that is certain is that the newspapers published their prose and verse regularly, and little else which pretended to be literary, and the newspapers flourished. The *Maryland Gazette* was founded in 1726, and the South Carolina and Virginia ones shortly afterward; in all three, local contributors burlesqued the manners and morals of all classes, and sometimes the wielders of power. Hennig Cohen has found the *South Carolina Gazette* uncommonly full of that kind of writing. That journal printed a nice instance of satire, in June 1740, when a New Sides evangelical believer responded to satire on the New Sides in his own appropriate verse:

> *Then it will be known who are Deceivers,*
> *Those who preach Original Sin*
> *And the lost State that we are in,*
> *And do maintain that one and all,*
> *Are void of Grace by Adam's Fall,*
> *Or those that love to lol in Chaise*
> *And freely think that Heavens Ways*
> *Are wide enough so that they in Sin*
> *May whip their horse and so ride in!*

In the columns of the Maryland and Virginia gazettes, pseudonymous essayists poked fun, now and then, in the direction of the local politicos —sometimes at the cost of the provincial administration and sometimes at that of the elected lower house of assembly.°

Covert political comment was all that law and habit would allow in print. Though the practice of licensing printers lapsed in the colonies about 1730 as had happened in England, and though the printer might be a successful and respected man, as Jonas Green was in Maryland, he was still short of being the free editor or free publisher who would appear during the next century. The common law of seditious libel hung over him always; as Leonard W. Levy has shown, the lower houses of assembly were proving readier to invoke it, as a mode of demanding respect for themselves, than were the officers of the Crown.° The printer was subject also to financial compulsions, which were strong enough to influence him: he had to have the goodwill of his governor and his assembly if he were to obtain the public printing which kept him in business. Under such circumstances he had ample incentive to choose what was moderate or sly, when he made his selection for the weekly gazette among essays and verses which were critical. To a reader of eighteenth-century papers today, he discovered those qualities remarkably often.

Thus drawing on a vein of satire and irony which was familiar in England, the first generation of printing in the Southern Colonies found ways to voice its annoyances, its wit, and its confidence. Although not productive of memorable writings, that generation does help make intelligible the plain-spoken independence of the next generation—the generation of Jefferson and Patrick Henry and George Mason in Virginia, and of Carroll of Carrollton, the Pinckneys, and the Rutledges in neighboring colonies. In that sequence the generation of about 1725 to 1760 seems the experimental phase of a people finding itself, in thought and expression.

3 Scientific and Secular Thought in the Northern and Middle Colonies

IN *Science and the Modern World* Alfred North Whitehead tells us that Christianity's ancient assertion that the universe is orderly and good helped bring modern science to birth. At this point of returning to the old Puritan and Quaker colonies we shall do well to remember that throughout history unorthodox believers have frequently been the ones to contribute to scientific knowledge. Sometimes the fact of being a dissenter seems to have encouraged a thinker to look at some part of the universe, as he did at Christianity, differently from prevailing habits, and to venture revisions; sometimes a factor of mysticism, heightening his sense of the wonder of creation, had the same effect. During the Middle Ages, for instance, Franciscan friars, who following their founder of Assisi went in the direction of mysticism, outdid in science the Dominicans who had the stronger tradition as educators and philosophers.

Interest in science appeared in New England with second-generation

Puritans soon after the Restoration. In the case of John Winthrop, Jr., son of the Massachusetts governor and himself governor of Connecticut, the identification was rather with enterprise than with religious feeling. Trained in law, informed about medicine, and ready to make investments, he undertook operations in salt and bog-iron mining and in the refining of ore. He wrote papers on technological matters and on astronomy; he became the first colonist to be elected to the Royal Society.° Meanwhile Increase Mather gathered a considerable collection of old and new books on science and during the 1680s studied astronomy seriously. In 1682, when Halley's comet stimulated him in that direction, he preached at first in the ordinary way about God's having sent an astronomical message by special delivery; then he wrote his little book, *Kometographia*, which, though not based, modern style, on firsthand observations, was founded deeply on the European literature. Meanwhile Harvard had set up a little observatory with a telescope given by Governor Winthrop, and the study of astronomy was beginning to have a practical effect in the community.° Students were enabled by their training to calculate almanacs (which were probably Harvard's first technological contribution to the people) and to prepare diagrams and essays explaining the still unorthodox Copernican cosmology, which they were accepting. Altogether the Boston community of learning achieved a fairly advanced sophistication in science before 1700. Interest in science produced a little philosophical society for discussion; it was a factor which helped to cool off the witchcraft episode in Salem.

After the beginnings had culminated in the work of the 1680s, a second intensification of scientific development occurred during the 1720s. Then and thereafter science in New England became more, what the eighteenth century loved, a matter of steady gains. In the shift into new confidence, Cotton Mather, whom we know already as the most filiopietistic of latter-day Puritans, led the way. Among his many activities, building on his father's collection he assembled the largest private library in New England, probably the largest in the colonies; he wrote the papers which won him election to the Royal Society; he corresponded with distinguished European scientists. In 1721, when he was almost sixty, he made a defense of inoculation as a method of medicine, which has marked him ever since as a beginner of immunology and a great friend of science in the service of man. The event does not prove that Mather, or the physician he defended, Zabdiel Boylston, used the best judgment, for the treatment had been little tested. But when an epidemic threatened Boston, the minister acted boldly; he made available data about inoculation which were contained in publications of the Royal Society; he justified his position in a sermon booklet, *The Angel of Bethesda*. With the good luck of having succeeded and of having spoken on the side of the future, his performance as an alert and confident applier of knowledge from the world community of science is unequaled in colonial history up to that time.

The graduate of Yale, the Reverend Jared Eliot, who was the one conspicuous achiever in science in later-colonial Connecticut, did work which compares with that of ministers and physicians in the Southern Colonies. Eliot was both a minister and a physician. The journeys he was called upon to make, as an eminent medical man, help account for his taking detailed observations on the land resources and the farming of New England. An essay by him, on refining iron from the "black sand" he discovered on Long Island Sound, won a medal of the Royal Society. From years of making experiments on his own farm and from knowledge of other men's methods, he published piecemeal during the 1750s a sizable *Essay on Field Husbandry in New England*. It won recognition and circulation as being a sound and useful book. Jared Eliot, grandson of John Eliot, and Cotton Mather, grandson of Richard, were exactly alike in being descended from leaders second to none in bringing the Puritan faith to New England; they were alike also in the services they rendered, turning the science of their time to the aid of the people.

But it was the colleges of New England which, far more than individuals on their own, gave the region distinction in science. As the story is almost exclusively Harvard's, we may notice at the start that Yale's president at mid-century, the Reverend Thomas Clap, a stiff Calvinist who was also a mathematician, did seek to include Newton's *Principia* in the curriculum and actually included Locke's *Essay Concerning Human Understanding*.° But such modernism about philosophy gave Yale neither money nor professor nor equipment to move into scientific activity in the way of the eighteenth century. In those respects Harvard had all the luck. In 1720 Thomas Hollis, a Baptist merchant of London, gave the college its first professorship, the chair of divinity which still bears his name. This in itself created a considerable change in the institution, for, where up to then the president of the college had been the only member who had the authority of a master in a field of learning, once the new professor came he acquired a peer in the college. Scarcely a couple of years after this arrangement, Thomas Hollis, on being persuaded by an enthusiastic young alumnus, doubled his gift. Because this time he created a chair of natural philosophy (which today might be called "general physical science"), he more than doubled the factor of innovation. A professor of theology could be expected to second the president in his own field, serving as a kind of coadjutor (as did occur); but a professor of science, besides committing the college to a new field of study, introduced the likelihood of religious skepticism and some conflict with authority. The second Hollis professorship, the gift and the acceptance, was the first decision for substantial multiformity of thought in an American college.

After an initial misjudgment when, appointing the alumnus who had brought home the endowment from London, Harvard got a lightweight scientist and a drunkard on the faculty, the college acted wisely. The second appointment went to John Winthrop IV, who at twenty-four was a publishing scientist and already more than promising. As he was a recent alumnus, and his distinguished name signified the great-great-grandson of the founding governor, Harvard took no great risk of offending people when it invited him. But he was known to be a theological liberal, and the overseers made a decision for academic freedom when, examining him for the professorship, they refrained from asking him about his belief. (Years later he ridiculed an overseer, who was also a leading minister and a writer of Massachusetts history, for having published a silly piece about earthquakes.) Professor Winthrop did in time become a molder of the thought and work of Harvard. He introduced algebra into the curriculum and established the first experimental laboratory in an American college. Thanks to Thomas Hollis, he and his students had the use of a splendid collection of scientific instruments. How it all struck the students is suggested, and probably exaggerated, in a verse of 1744 printed in Benjamin Franklin's *American Magazine* (which failed), as the "Harvard Student's Lament."

> *Now algebra, geometry,*
> *Arithmetic, astronomy,*
> *Opticks, chronology, and staticks,*
> *All tiresome parts of mathematicks,*
> *With twenty harder names than these*
> *Disturb my brains and break my peace. . . .*
> *We're told how planets roll on high*
> *How large their orbits and how nigh;*
> *I hope in little time to know*
> *Whether the moon's a cheese, or no.°* -

Thus Harvard changed style, after a century of teaching; and higher education in the Puritan tradition incorporated new interests.

John Winthrop's career, moreover, became big enough to have more than a Harvard meaning. For forty years he pursued his investigations and his publishing: sunspots, the transits of Mercury and Venus, the orbit of Halley's comet, and the theory of comets were all grist for his mill. Turning down college presidencies, including Harvard's, in order to carry on with his work, he received honorary degrees and became the only teacher in the colonies elected to the Royal Society. A research professor in fact, Winthrop anticipated a type of American intellectual who would begin to appear frequently about a century later, the academic expert as a leader of thought, widely influential outside his own institution.

In the Middle Colonies, where, thanks to the brilliant emergence of Philadelphia, the new science developed with more effect than elsewhere in America, the work was done sometimes in the way of New England, in close connection with college, church, and city, and sometimes in the way of the Southern Colonies, by individuals widely separated from one another. Lieutenant Governor Cadwallader Colden of New York, the one man of scientific distinction in his province, operated in the latter way. A graduate of Edinburgh and a London trainee in medicine, the governor utilized his estate, Coldengham, not far from Albany, for studying the Iroquois Indians, for examining and classifying the plants of the region, and for philosophical speculation on the theory of gravitation. In the city of New York, shortly before the Revolution, King's College put a student of Winthrop's on the faculty and established the study of medicine; in New Jersey, the college at Princeton appointed a professor of mathematics and gradually developed an interest in science, as President Witherspoon wanted. But those colleges, like Yale, failed to turn up their Thomas Hollis, and if their faculties contained such a talent as John Winthrop's, they did not give it equal opportunity.

But comparison with the older regions, south and north, stops short of reaching the heart of the matter. This was the exuberant growth and cultural energy of Philadelphia, on no pattern but its own, during the second third of the eighteenth century. During the late 1750s, when its population, surpassing 20,000, outdid both New York and Boston, the city which William Penn had planned for God's quiet rule became the largest in the colonies and the most lively and interesting place. Though peace and reconciliation are not the words for the mid-century relationships, in Pennsylvania, among the province's numerous churches and sects—Quakers and Presbyterians; Anglicans, German Reformed, and Lutherans; the pietist sectarians and the small groups of Roman Catholics and Jews—there never occurred any breach of the original policy of religious freedom. Every branch of faith was free to grow and was growing. Much the same was true in politics. While the Quaker experiment in government fell into such cross-purposes as to threaten its own existence, it opened politics to many types of people. Altogether Pennsylvania was caught up in expansion and prosperity and energy; and Philadelphia, which by now was more Franklin's city than Penn's, concentrated many amenities. Before the Revolution the magnificent capitol of the province, which the world would learn to honor as Independence Hall, raised a monument to the taste, as well as to the survival, of the proprietary government. The city's many other good buildings, predominantly brick—meetinghouses and churches, mansions and small residences, shops, offices, and taverns, many of them uncovered during the city rehabilitation of the 1950s and 1960s—proclaimed its well-being and pride.

William Penn once said that, as God should be contemplated as being "the fountain as well of Reason as of Light," common judgment should acknowledge that "it were happy if we studied nature more in natural things, and acted according to nature whose rules are few, plain, and most reasonable." His words may be called prophetic of American Quakerism's eighteenth-century contributions to science in general and of the Philadelphia botanists in particular. The words are only dimly suggestive, however, concerning James Logan, the principal introducer of scientific and humanistic interests into Pennsylvania, who was more a patron of learning than a mystic. Logan was the son of a Scottish schoolmaster and the receiver of a classical education; a Quaker convert, he had come to the colony in 1699 in company with William Penn and in a role as adviser and agent. A favored grantee of large landholdings, he placed a generous share of his money in buying a library. Acquiring about three thousand volumes, he selected and balanced his collections beautifully—probably more carefully, but not very differently, from Byrd of Westover. The ancient classics and modern works on history, law, politics, and science were the principal categories. His collection in science was probably the strongest private one in the colonies. He kept his library in a special building and opened it to readers freely; after his death it went into a public library. Because of his connection with the proprietor and the government, Logan needs be regarded as something more than an individual patron: what he did gives to the proprietary system of Pennsylvania itself a look of benevolent paternalism.

On the farmer side of Pennsylvania life we come closer to the affinity between Quaker faith and interest in science. As Frederick B. Tolles has explained, Friends seek religious faith firsthand, and scientists go direct to nature for their findings; the coincidence between the two has been so marked, in England and America, that Quakerism must be credited with having been a regular source of commitment to science.° Certainly the story which survives about John Bartram, a Quaker farmer deciding to follow a new calling, helps that thesis. He was resting in a field one day when he noticed a flower he had destroyed, and the beauty and wonder of it seized him. He at once began learning Latin, for the sake of the plant names; James Logan helped him; he studied Linnaeus. In due course he developed the botanical garden, the most sizable one of the few in the colonies, which is now part of the Philadelphia park system and still carries his name. His work brought him, in that spacious age of letter writing, into correspondence with Peter Collinson, Quaker merchant and horticulturalist of London, with scientists at Oxford and in Holland, and with the master of his science in Sweden. In the year of the Stamp Act, John Bartram was appointed botanist to the king and was given a modest stipend. He sent to England roots or seeds of honeysuckle, laurel, and sugar maple; he received in return, and cultivated, such flowers as cyclamens, crocuses, lilies, tulips, roses, and snapdragons. He broadened his collecting to include birds, fish, and other wildlife, and he made and proposed geological studies. He developed into a kind of a scientific movement. His son and trainee, William, became in time a more precise naturalist than he was, and the author of *Travels through North and South Carolina, Georgia, . . . Florida* (1791), a classic. One of their associates, Dr. Adam Kuhn, became the first professor of botany (and materia medica, at the College of Philadelphia) in America. Much as John Winthrop IV was the precursor of an academic type in America, John Bartram's profile in history displays a great deal in common with nineteenth-century students of outdoor nature—with Thoreau and Muir and the young Asa Gray, for instance.°

Benjamin Franklin, who has been called both a secular Puritan and a secular Quaker, began his sixty-five-year citizenship of Philadelphia in 1723 when he was seventeen. He was much younger than James Logan, who helped him and whose writing on Cicero he printed, and seven years younger than John Bartram, with whom he made friends. He outdid them both as scientist and as philanthropist, but he built on what they, and what Quaker culture more generally, had established. He could not have timed better his coming to town; the equipment he brought from Boston, as a printer and a writer, met the needs of Philadelphia precisely. Before he reached twenty-five he had his own business, *The Pennsylvania Gazette*, and before he reached forty he had made himself independent. The steps of his ladder of success rose through his being the subsidized public printer of the colony; then a compiler and printer of almanacs, publisher of books, bookseller, and postmaster; and, finally, investor and adviser to publishing enterprises elsewhere. All this led to his being financially able, for forty years, to do whatever he wanted.

Franklin's history as an influence on other men's thought began, not in a church or college or court of law, but in a club. The Junto of 1727, the parent organization of the American Philosophical Society, was only one of many organizations which gathered in the eighteenth century to ventilate its members' ideas; yet it is one of only about three clubs in American history, the voicing of ideas in which has made a recognizable, serious difference in the history of thought. (The Transcendental Club of Concord and the Metaphysical Club at Harvard, where the pragmatic philosophy was born, are the ones which invite comparison.) Franklin's own story of the Junto, contained in his *Auto-*

biography, describes one member as a surveyor who loved books, a second as a writer of poetry, a third as a self-taught mathematician (a fellow who expected "universal Precision in everything said"), and a fourth, destined to become a judge, who had "the coolest clearest Head, the best heart, and the exactest Morals of almost any man I ever met with." The young men discussed everything. In the founder's proud memory, the debate was "conducted in the sincere Spirit of Enquiry after Truth," and the Junto was truly educational, "the best School of Philosophy, and Politics" in Pennsylvania.

During the four decades between the early days of the Junto and the establishment of the American Philosophical Society on a permanent basis, in 1769, the organization passed through two or three stages about which the record is none too full. Its service of the 1730s was in permitting its little library to be transformed, on Franklin's initiative, into the Library Company of Philadelphia. This was the earliest public subscription library in America; others would appear during the 1750s in New York and Providence, and small lending libraries, more or less commercial, would spring up along the full length of the coast. Originally the Junto had provided for the book needs of its young members; now the undertaking was to provide for all who asked (and who would pay an admission fee of forty shillings and annual dues of ten shillings). A company was organized; James Logan was consulted about selections; a book purchase order was sent to Peter Collinson. Within months the library was a going concern. In 1740 Franklin managed to have it given space in the statehouse. In due course it acquired other libraries, James Logan's included, and became a sizable and enduring institution. When it began, Franklin presented a copy of Magna Carta and a collection of Montaigne's *Essays*; Peter Collinson donated Newton's *Principia* and a dictionary of gardening. The original list of books resembled the colonial gentlemen's libraries. Xenophon and Homer and Dryden's *Vergil* appear; so do Pufendorf, Algernon Sydney, and Bayle's *Critical Dictionary*; and, from nearer the present, *Gulliver*, the *Tatler*, and the *Spectator*. About this library and the libraries throughout the colonies, Franklin would boast in his *Autobiography*: "These libraries have improved the general conversation of Americans, made the common tradesmen and farmers as intelligent as most gentlemen from other countries," and have "perhaps contributed" to the separation from England.

Throughout the 1730s and most of the 1740s Franklin remained primarily a printer. The *Pennsylvania Gazette* was his weekly, important, product; but his annual *Poor Richard's Almanack*, through which he reached his widest audience, was the place where he emerged most conspicuously as sage. One contemporary called it the "Farmer's Philosopher, the Rural Sage, and Peasant's Chronicle," and another, "The

Bible of Shop and Barn." *Poor Richard* was not the first almanac to be published in Pennsylvania, and it was probably not as good as New England's best, the older *Astronomical Diary and Almanack* gotten out by Nathaniel Ames. Franklin's, like all other almanacs, accompanied the basic calendar and seasonal information, which was prepared for farmers, mariners, and merchants, with philosophical underpinning of a kind. In pithy sentences he conveyed the Newtonian picture of the universe: the stars, the planets, and their satellites, always in motion and always united, under the Creator's laws. The almanac was garnished with literary bits and pieces, from such widely separated sources as Dryden and Rabelais, and folk sayings, often of Scottish origin. This last type of wisdom, as winnowed and printed a second time by Franklin in his book, *The Way to Wealth*, after *Poor Richard* had been discontinued, is what has given Franklin his fame as speaker for the workaday virtues. ("A fat kitchen, a lean will.") *Poor Richard* was a wonderful parcel dispenser to the people of wares which occurred in the gentlemen's libraries in complex volumes: cosmology blended with morality, and satire with serious purpose. It puts Franklin at the head of the list of publishers who in later days would get out the "digest" periodicals, and at the head of the list of wise men which would include "Mr. Dooley" and Will Rogers in modern times.

During the later 1740s, as he entered his own forties, Franklin did what I. Bernard Cohen assures us was the best scientific work in America of the century, his investigations in electricity. For years he had been contriving inventions, of which the Franklin stove was the most beneficial to society, and had speculated and written in the *Gazette* on various aspects of natural philosophy. We will sense better the nature of his work if we notice beforehand a bit of meteorology he had propounded a decade earlier. Recipient as journalist of news that an equinoctial northeaster had struck the southern coast before his own city, and that it arrived still later in the northern colonies, he asked himself why. His interpretation is still essentially correct: prevailing winds on the seaboard only seem to blow from the northeast; they suck from the south rather than push from the north; they originate in the Caribbean by reason of the rise of the air there, as heated by the tropical sun. No physical equipment was needed for that kind of science, no consultation with colleagues, and no mathematics. Concern, perhaps informed by some knowledge from the literature of other men's interest in the field, and confidence in reason about nature were the essentials. The meteorology of the eighteenth century, in short, stood on even a simpler footing than its botany; and Franklin's sound thinking required less expertise than did, say, the work of Jared Eliot in Connecticut or Alexander Garden in Charleston.

His work in electricity was a much higher sort of operation. Yet he began without training and without knowledge more than having seen the sparks and other stunts of a wayfaring lecturer on science who visited the colonies. Then Peter Collinson sent him an "electric tube," and he went to work. Now at the stage of retirement from business, he set up a laboratory; there he and those who assisted him made systematic experiments and kept records. Soon he was able to report to England that he had made a distinction which appeared to be useful, between plus and minus electrical charges. He had gotten ahead of European scientists; the distinction he made was a fundamental and original one. Whether by luck or by wisdom, he did not misread the data, as French contemporaries did, to conclude that there are two electricities, not one. What is household knowledge today, as familiar as the two wires in a doorbell circuit, was pure science and a beautiful piece of insight when Benjamin Franklin originated it. It brought him wonderful fame: publication in five English editions; publication in French, German, and Italian (and in 1941 an American commemorative edition was published, a sign that the history of science was being born); immediately a medal of the Royal Society, then election to a fellowship; M.A. degrees at Harvard, Yale, and William and Mary, for the man who had not attended a college.°

Speculating on the fact that Franklin's work on electricity was the highest achievement of colonial science and on a par with the best in Europe, Boorstin argues that American science did not go higher, or more often, into theory because Americans lacked such knowledge and taste for mathematics as was needed, and as Europeans possessed. This interpretation may well help to explain why Franklin himself did not pursue pure science further: at his moment of triumph he may have sensed that he had been more lucky and wise than informed, and have decided not to go on. Yet certainly there were other matters to deter him, and which probably entered his decision. King George's War had just been fought to no conclusion; the fourth (and climactic) war with the French and Indians could be foreseen, with Pennsylvania deeply involved. He personally was being drawn more and more into affairs: into greater responsibilities in the postal service; from being clerk to being member of the provincial assembly; and into increasing civic enterprises in Philadelphia—the founding of Pennsylvania Hospital and of the fire company of Philadelphia, for example. Altogether we find much in the situation of Pennsylvania during the early 1750s to remind us of the national situation of the United States two centuries and more later. Like scientific leaders during our own epoch, Franklin was confronted with shortages of science in society, and he turned his attention from his own laboratory to providing for the future.

Nothing else that Franklin did transmitted so well to young men of the next generation the advantages the men of the Junto had created for themselves as did the college he started in 1755. Although he had made up his mind much earlier that Philadelphia needed such an institution, he deferred action until after King George's War and until after the Presbyterians had launched their college at Princeton. Then in 1749, with the sympathy of friends, he turned out a pamphlet, *Proposals Relating to the Education of Youth in Pensilvania*. The plan at this step went no further than founding an academy for boys; yet, explaining his *Proposals*, he raised questions of goal and reform which extended beyond what a school could possibly manage. Pleasantly saying that for the school curriculum "*every* Thing that is useful and *every* Thing that is ornamental" would be desirable, but that only "the *most useful* and the *most ornamental*" would be taught, he emphasized basic reading, composition, and English grammar and then practical training. Possibly thinking of his own laboratory, he once said that drawing should be taught, as being "a kind of universal language, understood by all nations"; he wanted arithmetic and accounting and a bit of geometry and astronomy. One part of the *Proposals* called for training in geography, history, and morals and religion from an historical point of view. Historical study should make students want to read ancient and modern languages, he reasoned; it should make them curious about the arts and sciences and about how the world is improved. Throughout every stage of the training, there should be "inculcated and cultivated" in the young men, he argued, "that Benignity of Mind which shows itself in *searching for* and *seizing* every Opportunity to serve and *to oblige*, and is the Foundation of what is called GOOD BREEDING." Thus Franklin without defiance turned his back on Latin grammar-school training, which he had never had and in which the Quaker colony had never been rich. He voiced, instead, an environmentalist's conviction about how to prepare boys for life by means of condition, suggestion, and example.°

The school was founded; and almost at once the college, a Siamese-twin institution, appeared. Funds were raised, and in 1755, a year after the founding of King's College in New York, the charter was enacted. The one college before the Revolution to do so, the College of Philadelphia broke completely from the tradition of formal or substantial control by one church. The trustees seem to have been as secular-minded and as religiously mixed a group as could be: only one was a college graduate; the rest were merchants, lawyers, physicians, and Benjamin Franklin. To be sure, the leadership of the college went, with the title of provost, to an Anglican clergyman, William Smith. But Smith was a newcomer to the colonies, a Scot in his twenties, who had attracted Franklin's attention by an essay published in New York in favor of education as preparation for citizenship and in favor of agriculture and history as principal college subjects. The vice-provost was Presbyterian; one of the professors, a Baptist; and the tutors had various church attachments.

During the early years the institution offered much more subject matter that was traditional than Franklin had contemplated in the *Proposals*; before long it also ventured innovations he had not contemplated. In an overlapping of academy and college instruction, provost and vice-provost taught philosophy and the tutors taught Latin and Greek; Latin was required for the B.A. degree. In addition, apparently within the academy but not limited to the younger students, botany, zoology, astronomy, physics, and French were offered. In the school Latin could be omitted. When the college was a decade old, the trustees established the first academic medical training in America. The original professorship was given to Dr. John Morgan, who had graduated in the first class in the college and who had studied in Edinburgh, Paris, and London. When he began teaching at the age of thirty, already a fellow of the Royal Society, he had the courage to give his inaugural lecture on a prophetic topic, "A Discourse on the Institution of Medical Schools in America." A long journey, which would lead many later medical men to Europe for training and would encourage many acts of educational independence at home, was then begun.

4   *The Reach of the Enlightenment in the Colonies*

WE have discovered the root interests of the Enlightenment taking hold in all three of the seaboard regions. They were not distributed very evenly from north to south, but they were absent from no single colony and when they started they grew. About 1700, or in some places earlier, the transit of interests began to bring over the more or less philosophical *isms* of the age with the rest. Deism, which raised resistance from Christians everywhere, became the substantial one in America, and to it we shall need to return. Yet any general opposition, or anything other than broad acceptance of science, technology, and the feeling of progress, is all but unimaginable in the colonies; and no such thing occurred.

Generally speaking, the interests of the Enlightenment took hold earliest in those pockets of society where people were most able and ready to keep abreast with the movements of thought in Europe. Compare Dr. Boylston of Boston with Dr. Garden of Charleston, and compare both with the Quaker botanists: they all drew from, and all contributed to, the Royal Society. But in course of time the working associations of scientists with one another, on the American side, began to count as heavily as transatlantic connections did, or more so. For this second-generation phase, compare the clock and instrument maker of Philadelphia, James Rittenhouse, whose wonderful orrery, modeling the solar system, delighted Thomas Jefferson, with the professor at Harvard, John Winthrop: each had a gift for mathematics, each taught himself, and both were fulfilled as members of working groups of scientific men. Although the Harvard College which gave Professor Winthrop his opportunity would not have welcomed being equated with the Philadelphia Junto, the successor institutions of today, Harvard University and the American Philosophical Society, would probably agree that eighteenth-century science did comparably well within their two memberships and did better in both than anywhere else in America. The frontier individual is not to be thought of as having been lost to scientific eminence; for he would recur and recur, but he was no longer the large part of the story he had been in John Winthrop, Jr.'s, day or the early days of John Bartram.

About the middle of the century, moreover, men of science and their sympathizers were among the first to discover, in their findings about America, that America was finding a life of its own. Michael Kraus, an expert on the intercontinental aspects of Western culture, explains that before the Revolution the intercolonial connections of men of science—their correspondence, their meetings, their knowledge of one another—entered the process of an American national self-awareness being born. Part of the process was tacit, a matter of overlooking old boundaries, geographical and ecclesiastical, and creating new communities of interest. Occasionally, as happened with Franklin, an overt recognition occurred, that the colonials were a people and had a right to expect a future more glorious and more unified than their past had been. In this respect Nathaniel Ames's *Astronomical Diary and Almanack* for 1758, a bit from Mr. Everyman's library, is the most quotable thing we have. New Englanders of the seventeenth century had imagined themselves a new chosen people in a wilderness Zion; this descendant exercised equal imagination concerning American destiny, using the terms of his age. Under the heading, "America, Past, Present, and Future," he said:

> The Progress of Humane Literature (like the Sun) is from the East to the West, . . . and now is arrived at the eastern Shore of America. As the Celestial Light of the Gospel was directed here by the Finger of GOD, it will doubtless finally drive the long! long! Night of Heathenish Darkness from *America*:—So Arts and Sciences will change the face of Nature in their Tour from Hence over the Appalachian Mountains to the Western Ocean. . . . Huge Mountains of Iron Ore are already discovered; and vast Stores are reserved for future Generations.

. . . O! Ye unborn Inhabitants of America! Should this Page escape its destin'd Conflagration at the Year's end, and these Alphabetical Letters remain legible, when your Eyes behold the Sun after he has rolled the Seasons around for two or three Centuries more, you will know that in Anno Domini 1758, we dream'd of Your Times.°

With their confidence high about life in this world, Americans of the Enlightenment, like Europeans, often came up with doubts, or with revisions of their ideas, about the next. This problem returns us to Benjamin Franklin, who, though he was neither the earliest American deist nor altogether a representative one, remains the classical case. He heard about natural religion during his teens in his brother's print shop. He liked it; and the Puritan inculcations of his childhood seem to have built no resistance in him to withstand the new skepticism and new faith. His commitment to deism became a matter of record during his London visit, when he set type on an antideist treatise. That argument so offended him that he wrote his own refutation and printed one hundred copies of it, his first book, *A Dissertation on Liberty and Necessity, Pleasure and Pain.*

This brought him into the discussion during the second phase of the deist movement in England, which Sir Leslie Stephen in his masterly *History of English Thought in the Eighteenth Century* years ago called "critical deism." The earlier stage, "constructive deism," was the one on which the father of the movement, Lord Herbert of Cherbury, and others had built a kind of theology, supplementary to Christian theology, on the science of the seventeenth century. That men could explore creation, and learn and follow its laws, was put down as reason for worshiping the Creator, in addition to revelation in the Bible and to all other reasons. But the critical deism of the eighteenth century, for which Charles Blount and Matthew Tindal (both known in America) were among the spokesmen, shifted from alliance with Christianity to attack on some of its main beliefs. It voiced contempt for miracle, mystery, and revelation, as being incompatible with universal law; its suppositions were mechanistic. All of this young Franklin accepted. In the *Dissertation on Liberty and Necessity* he attributed human action to pleasure-and-pain motivations narrowly. Later he regretted having announced so extreme a position. He destroyed many printed copies and, concerning the naturalistic doctrine at issue, his last word (in his *Autobiography*) was that "though it might be true, it was not very useful."

Benjamin Franklin the thinker, as deist, and deism as a vein of colonial thinking appear in a more representative way in the famous "Articles of Belief and Acts of Religion" which Franklin drew up for personal use in 1728, the year of founding the Junto. As was usual with deists, he believed in a "First Mover and Maker" of the universe;

the universe he envisaged as stars and planets "moving periodically, by uniform laws." Deists did not care for angels, but to Franklin a celestial hierarchy was true. "I believe there is one supreme, most perfect Being, Author and Father of the Gods themselves. For I believe that Man is not the most perfect Being but one, rather that as there are many Degrees of Beings his Inferiors, so there are many Degrees of Beings superior to him." On this scale the planet on which he lived, and the human individual, seemed tiny and "of no sort of Consequence." As if not to expect too much of the ultimate "Father of the Gods," Franklin chose to address his devotions to "the author and owner of our System" (he meant the solar system), to whom he attributed interest in human happiness. "Next to the Praise resulting from and due to His Wisdom, I believe he is pleas'd and delights in the Happiness of those he has created; and since without Virtue Man can have no Happiness in this World, I firmly believe he delights to see me Virtuous, because he is pleased when he sees Me Happy."

Finally, though the calculus of pleasure and pain remained and may have governed Franklin's religious speculations, "Adoration" and moral concern came in. "By Thy power hast Thou made the glorious Sun, with his attending Worlds. . . . Praised be Thy name for Ever! . . . Thou abhorrest in thy Creatures Treachery and Deceit, Malice, Revenge, [Intemperance,] and every other hurtful Vice; but Thou art a Lover of Justice and Sincerity, of Friendship and Benevolence, and every Virtue. Thou art my Friend, my Father, and my Benefactor. —Praised be thy name, O God, for Ever! Amen!" From this divinity Franklin petitioned for help, that he might be "preserved from Atheism & Infidelity, Impiety, and Profaneness," that he might abhor "Treason as much as Tyranny," and that he be granted a dozen other such strengths. He did not forget to give thanks. "For peace and liberty, for food and raiment, for corn and wine, and milk, . . . for useful fire and delicious water,—Good God, I thank Thee! For knowledge, and literature, and every useful art, for my friends and their prosperity, and for the fewness of my enemies. . . . For all thy innumerable benefits; for life and reason, and the use of speech; for health, and joy, and every pleasant hour,—My good God I thank Thee."°

In a passage in the *Autobiography* which follows on the famous description of Franklin's thirteen-point program for individual moral self-development, the author mentions a decision which tells worlds about the nature of deism in Philadelphia and in America broadly. A few years after he founded the Junto, Franklin thought of establishing also, in the form of a secret society, a kind of a rationalist sect. Its members would have subscribed to common beliefs—in the line of his "Articles of Belief"—"that the soul is immortal" and that "God will certainly reward virtue and punish vice, either here or hereafter." But

Franklin decided not to go ahead; instead, he poured his organizing talent into the Library Company and other civic enterprises and his intellectual energy into science and politics. In this restraint we see first the man and the Pennsylvanian: he was a reconciler by nature, rather than a controversialist; though his religious beliefs were as extreme as those of the critical deists he followed, he did not care to argue publicly against Christian doctrine in the way certain Englishmen did. As philanthropist he sought, and was joined by, all kinds of associates. Churchmen as straight in the line of John Calvin as the Old Sides Presbyterians, who supported the College of Philadelphia, joined his enterprises. In all this Franklin honored and fulfilled his province's habit of live and let live in matters of belief. Yet, with the advantage of a little foreknowledge, it is possible to see in Franklin's moderation in expressing his deism a national, as well as a local, habit being developed. Franklin's younger contemporaries in the leadership of the Enlightenment, Jefferson, Madison, and John Adams, would each go far in rejecting the Christian beliefs of his background, but not one would care for controversy about doctrine. Hardly at all before the Revolution, and even during the 1790s not in a way to compare with the anti-Christian impulse in the Old World, did advanced deism turn aggressive in America, either as an organized movement or a literary one.

Restraint of deistic statement at the top of society was matched, however, by extensiveness of deistic belief at lower levels. Among Anglicans, rationalism slipped in with so little controversy that it is hard to pinpoint, though it seems to have reached everywhere. The Society for the Propagation of the Gospel discovered it in outlying parishes and distributed theological works among them, intended as a counterforce. According to Thomas Bacon, the most scholarly clergyman in Maryland, who blamed the reading of Tindal especially, "Infidelity has indeed arrived to an amazing and shocking growth in these parts. And it is hard to say whether 'tis more owing to the ignorance of the common people, the fancied knowledge of such as have got a little smattering of learning, or the misconduct of too many of the clergy. . . . Religion among us seems to wear the face of the country, part moderately cultivated, the greater part wild and savage."° From a parish among great estates on the lower Potomac, of which the Carters of Nomini Hall were members, we have the testimony of Philip Vickers Fithian, a tutor, who observed through evangelical eyes. He found the services there to be altogether casual. Skepticism was one force which was quietly eroding southern-colonial Anglicanism at mid-century. It was preparing the way for secessions into the Methodist movement and in other directions—in the case of the Carter family, into Baptist belief.

Only in New England did deism have a clearly "constructive" phase.

In this connection, for their last appearance in the present history, Increase and Cotton Mather are pivot figures once more. Increase Mather's 140-page *Kometographia* had been the successful effort of the Massachusetts minister leader to grasp astronomical matters which needed to be related to faith; writing it had reinforced his anti-Aristotelian feeling. But, as Michael G. Hall has demonstrated, in order to reach a point where the new science directly sustained Christian faith, a second step needed taking. Cotton Mather took it in 1720, when he brought out his *Christian Philosophy: A Collection of the Best Discoveries in Nature with Religious Improvements*; therein he constructed an argument for believing in God which drew directly on contemporary understanding of the universe. Where the father had used older literature extensively and rigorously, the son drew on a few recent books; where the father wrote dispassionately, the son wrote with the passion of the age. In short, Cotton Mather incorporated observational science directly into his theology. According to I. Bernard Cohen, speaking from the point of view of the history of science, "The result is that Mather's book is a very interesting one and still makes exciting reading. It is imbued with a modernity of feeling, despite the 'quaintness' of the 'religious improvements,' and is characterized throughout by the natural freshness that derives specifically from the fact that Mather intended to present the 'best discoveries.' and actually did so."°

Cotton Mather made his venture into constructive deism, yet holding onto orthodoxy, early in the eighteenth century. From that point the pattern of the next two generations of religious thought in New England, as it was affected by the Enlightenment, becomes broadly visible. In one direction lay the path which led to the mid-century liberal divines, Charles Chauncy and Jonathan Mayhew. Abetted by Arminian principles, and after a while as critics of the New Lights, they deviated from the old Puritanism as Mather had not; from them the path would proceed to the end-of-century Unitarians. This was the course of the moderate and assimilative Enlightenment; theologically it reached no great heights, and its particular religious convictions need not deter us before the Unitarians. Geographically these liberals concentrated in the Boston area, and they were sustained by Harvard. In political voice, the preachers were particularly strong on natural-law and divine-law restraints on power; their anxiety about a possible Church of England bishop being established in America stimulated this attitude.

The direction, intellectually so different from the liberals, which was taken by evangelicals during the quarter century after Cotton Mather, is already familiar. But after the mid-century, following its peak period, the Great Awakening ceased to be quite as evenly distributed a rural and urban movement as earlier. The New Light Congregationalists, and their brothers the Baptists, became more a countrymen's affair;

Edwardsian theology came to belong especially to Connecticut and to frontier New England. In political conviction, where the evangelicals were strong in their congregationalism and often protested the policy of the church-and-government alliance, they kept common direction with the liberals, as critics of power. Otherwise the differences between the two camps continued with the passage of time.

In sum, at the close of the colonial period, in New England and throughout all the colonies there were three religious positions which crossed provincial and church lines and owed their existence to the Enlightenment. The first was advanced deism, which was too quiet to be properly called "critical" in America; but it was radical, and in less known cases, the same as in Franklin's, it moved into real materialism. The second was a moderate rationalism, which does deserve to be called "constructive deism" in Mather's case; it kept steady, if not very compatible, company with orthodoxy among Anglicans and Congregationalists and among some Presbyterians.° The third position was that of the New Sides and New Lights; they opposed the popular *isms*, though not the substance of the science, which came with the Enlightenment.

The culminating act during the colonial period, by American men of science and of the Enlightenment, was their self-organization, during 1769, in the American Philosophical Society. This name had been used first in 1743, for gatherings of Philadelphians who wanted to discuss scientific and related matters. The society carried on; but the active effort of Franklin and his colleagues to institutionalize learning and science was flowing into the Library Company, the academy, and the college during the middle decades of the century. Then in 1766 was born a new American Society Held at Philadelphia for Promoting Useful Knowledge. Three years later occurred the stellar event of the century in scientific coordination, the same in America as in Europe: the planning and executing of widely dispersed observations of the transit of Venus across the sun in 1769. There was been no earlier occasion, since the birth of modern mathematics, when readings could be taken which would yield the distance of the earth from the sun and other planetary measurements. Rittenhouse had charge of the observations in the Philadelphia area, and he produced a mathematical result of astonishing (and apparently lucky) accuracy; Professor Winthrop (who had taken a Harvard expedition to Newfoundland in 1761 for a similar purpose) promoted the observations generally and took them at the Harvard observatory. Throughout the colonies telescopes were set on the sun, time spans were recorded, and the information was brought together. Never before in history had a scientific event been so public.

In that year the old society and the recent one merged their names and functions to become a truly national organization, the American

Philosophical Society Held at Philadelphia for Promoting Useful Knowledge. Its model was the Royal Society. Though its name had American flavor, its publications were entitled *Transactions*, and its patron, though not the king, was a viceroy, the governor of Pennsylvania. The society was divided into six standing committees, of which four took in all that we have called science in America: anatomy and medicine; astronomy, mathematics, natural philosophy, and geography; chemistry and natural history; agriculture and botany. The two other committees were charged with areas of useful knowledge: architecture and mechanics, and trade and commerce. Dr. Benjamin Franklin (his LL.D. from St. Andrews), F.R.S., was chosen first president. Among his close associates in the new society were three Bartrams, David Rittenhouse, and Provost Smith of the college; from nearby were Lieutenant Governor Colden of New York and Daniel Dulany of Maryland; from distant places along the seaboard, Dr. Alexander Garden of Charleston, President Edward Holyoke and Professor John Winthrop of Harvard, and Ezra Stiles, the learned minister of Newport who a decade later would be president of Yale. Honoring its overseas debts, honoring also the special interest of many members, the society elected to original membership Linnaeus and Buffon, the leading naturalists of the world.

The founding of the American Philosophical Society thus drew the threads together, tying the intercolonial and the international connections of scientific interest in America. On the side of American cultural nationalism, the society achieved a "first." Among other intercolonial institutions, one compares the Presbyterian synods; one thinks of the Stamp Act Congress, the only possible comparison with a political organization, but the congress was too ephemeral to be called an institution and too incomplete to have been truly national. The American Philosophical Society, organizing a new community of interest, was the earliest American institution, on a national scope, to come to birth.

Very early in its history, when the Revolution came, politics created tensions within the society. While some members, probably most of them, believed as David Rittenhouse did that American political independence would encourage the free mind in science and that science would serve the nation well, other members were Loyalist, and for several war years—while Franklin was absent—the society omitted its meetings. In the hard year for the Revolution, 1780, when a new act of incorporation was in the making, a *whereas* was inserted which stated precisely a higher than national loyalty: "Nations truly civilized (however unhappily at variance on other accounts) will never wage war with the arts and sciences and the common interests of humanity."

CHAPTER IX

First Gathering
of Political Convictions:
Freedom for Persons
and Peoples

I think too we may add, to the great honor of science and the arts, that their natural effect is, by illuminating public opinion, to erect it into a Censor, before which the most exalted tremble for their future, as well as present fame. With some exceptions only, through the 17th. and 18th. centuries morality occupied an honorable chapter in the political code of nations.
    Thomas Jefferson to John Adams, January 11, 1816

I *The Enlightenment and Concern*
for Public Affairs

FOR all their intellectual versatility which was so different from twentieth-century specialist ways, and for all the absence from their time
of the pressure which swift communication has built into ours, colonials of the Enlightenment sometimes felt that the days and years were
short of time for thinking. At thirty-three John Adams was baffled by
his lawyer's life of "Here and every where," attending court sessions
from Martha's Vineyard to Barnstable to Worcester. "Is it possible to
pursue a regular Train of thinking in this desultory life?" he asked his
diary, then answered, "By no means." Confronting the same problem
at age forty-two, Benjamin Franklin quit printing except as an investment, refused an overture to go deeply into politics, and reordered his
days in favor of freedom and thought.

The following thirty-five years of his life, without interruption
through the Treaty of Paris, supply an allegory on the epoch. In 1748
Franklin moved house, he explained to Governor Cadwallader Colden
at the time, "to be quite a Master of my own Time, and no longer (as
the song has it) *at everyone's Call but my own. . . .* Thus you see I
am in a fair way of having no other Tasks than such as I shall like to
give my Self, and of Enjoying what I look upon as a great Happiness,
Leisure to read, study, make Experiments, and converse at large with
such ingenious and worthy Men as are pleas'd to honour me with their
Friendship or Acquaintance, on such points as may produce something

for the common Benefit of Mankind, uninterrupted by the little Cares and Fatigues of Business."° Never did changed mode of living serve its purpose more immediately, as we know: Franklin did at once his experiments in electricity and very soon founded the college. Yet in 1754, six years after his decision for science, he was Pennsylvania's delegate at the Albany Congress and author of the famous plan for colonial union which was presented there; and in 1783, without having had a break for three decades, he was still in public service. In two letters of that year, when his supremely successful work as diplomat of the Revolution was about to end, he observed that, though "many years" and "more important affairs" had intervened since he had engaged in his "pleasing studies," he did hope soon "to have more Leisure and to spend a part of it in those studies that are more agreeable to me than political Operations."

In sum, public events caught Franklin's interest and evoked his gifts, as they did many persons of similar mind. A sign of the times lies in the writing of colonial history, a prime form of American expression. The history of historical writing in the eighteenth century repeats in a way the development of the seventeenth century: books, each telling the story of one colony, were written which made the present position of those colonies clear. During the generation of colonial settlement, however, the purpose of the historian had been either to describe the colony for readers in England, as in the case of Captain John Smith's *True Relation*, or else, as in the (very private) case of William Bradford's *History of Plymouth Plantation*, with a purpose to praise God through a story of His creatures' deeds. During the eighteenth century, colonial history writing became, as the accumulation of events permitted, what the intellectual interests of the time sought, much more a political matter. Though the author might be discussing quite minute affairs a century in the past, he was yet asking and answering the question, "Where does the colony which concerns me stand in the affairs of today?"

The eighteenth-century production of history in America began in 1702 with Cotton Mather's massive two volumes of history and biography, *Magnalia Christi Americana*. In common with other histories which would appear during the first half of the century, the *Magnalia* voiced simultaneously old concerns and new. Its elaborate and nostalgic detail on the founding of Puritan towns, congregations, and schools was infused with data, still important in the twentieth century, about colonial education and colonial leadership and about the earliest American national sentiment—the "chosen people" theme. Two other large-scale histories were published before the crisis of the 1760s, one in Massachusetts and one in Virginia; both were the work of clergymen, but neither was so filiopietistic as the *Magnalia*—"The Great Deeds of

Christ in America." Thomas Prince, minister of the Old South Church in Boston, was interested in science, and his *Chronological History of New England in the Form of Annals* deserves salute for the exactitude of the narrative. Describing his purpose and method, the author stated a lasting ideal of historianship: "I cite my vouchers to every passage, and I have done my utmost first to find out the truth, and then to relate it in the order. I have labored after accuracy, and yet I dare not say, that I am without mistake." His Virginia contemporary, the Reverend William Stith, matched him as to research, precision, and detail. Neither one got far with his history: Prince brought his to 1630, when Massachusetts Bay was founded; Stith, to 1624, when the Crown took charge of Virginia. Neither book sold well or was continued in a second volume as planned. Yet any examination of these dry-as-dust annals raises the question less why the authors were disappointed commercially than why they hoped to succeed. When writer and printer would venture serial publication, as Thomas Prince did of a later part of his work, the best answer seems to be a taste for regional origins already strongly developed.

At any rate, the writing of history by Massachusetts and Virginia clergymen was matched during the eighteenth century by laymen's writing and by spread of the effort into several colonies. Robert Beverley of Virginia, who belonged to an upper-class family and who had been educated in England, brought out his short and lively *History and Present State of Virginia* in 1705, three years after the *Magnalia*. Irreverent where Cotton Mather had been reverent, Beverley did have in common with Mather the underlying purpose of improving life in his colony. He hoped by writing the *Present State of Virginia* to encourage Huguenots to immigrate there; as the book was published in French, in both Holland and France, and the expatriated French Protestants did come, he probably deserves some of the credit. If Beverley was the author also of an anonymous pamphlet of 1701, as there is reason to believe he was, he rendered a service by his pen to the administering, as he did to the settling, of his province. In other colonies than Virginia and Massachusetts (which neither then nor since, however, have lost their lead in local history), in 1755 Provost William Smith of the College of Philadelphia wrote polemics in the form of history against the Pennsylvania Quakers and their pacifism; twenty years later his namesake in New York did a first-class *History of the Province of New York*, with a description of current conditions.

The final and monumental performance in this sequence of historianship was of course Governor Thomas Hutchinson's *History of the Colony of Massachusetts Bay*, the first volume of which appeared in 1764 (while he was lieutenant governor), exactly at the beginning of the crisis of the British Empire. A descendant of Anne Hutchinson, a graduate of Harvard who relished Latin and French and loved to study history, a fortune builder and admirer of the order of things in which he participated at high level, the governor author held complex loyalties in tension. As could hardly have been different, he made Massachusetts politics the burden and theme of his history. Where Cotton Mather had given first place to congregational events and clerical leadership, Hutchinson opened with chapters on secular affairs. Only after three long chapters on settlement did he get around to a fifteen-page explanation of the ecclesiastical constitution of New England. His own lineage in Congregationalism notwithstanding, he said that if the Church of England had been as mild in the seventeenth century as it became in the eighteenth, there might have been no Puritan settlements; his judgment about the Presbyterian-like synods in New England was that they had not been necessary to the *being*, but had contributed to the *well-being*, of the congregations. As to his political judgment of his most famous predecessor in the governor's office, though he printed in an appendix the whole record of the trial of Anne Hutchinson, his sympathy as he narrated that story lay with Governor Winthrop. He did find fault with Governor Edmund Andros of the Dominion of New England, as having been oppressive; but he let off lightly Andros's predecessor and collaborator, Governor Joseph Dudley, as having been "not very grievous." Altogether, Governor Hutchinson as historian was detached, informed, and judicious about Massachusetts Puritanism. He is often remembered for the pathos of the last few years of his life, a Loyalist in England during the Revolution, thoroughly homesick for his own people and place. But his *History* is not a pathetic piece of work. A stalwart, conservative book by a secular writer, his three volumes contain, with their large body of accurate facts, a great deal of common-sense wisdom; their being published in Boston during the decade before the Revolution indicates considerable sophistication and political complexity in that city.°

In Robert Beverley and Thomas Hutchinson we have, in men separated by a generation in age and by seven hundred miles in distance, handsome representation of the fact that, during the eighteenth century, American leadership and thought often belonged to the lawyers. The two are no less representative, moreover, because they have it further in common that, though both held office as magistrates and were close students of the provincial statutes, their training in law was sketchy and subprofessional. Conditions of economic expansion called for rough familiarity with the law but did not require the most expert knowledge. Wherever land speculation preceded new settlement and town growth, as in the lovely fertile crescent of the "Old West" in Pennsylvania, Maryland, and Virginia, there were titles to be established, and a host of conflicts appeared. Old owners everywhere were

thrown on the defensive. As Charles Carroll of Carrollton once explained in exasperation, planters needed their own knowledge of law
to defend themselves against "petty-fogging" attorneys in the courts.
In the north the situation was different only in circumstances from the
plantation colonies, in the towns only somewhat different from the
country. There were conflicts over forest holdings in New Hampshire;
conflicts over tenements and contracts in the towns called for lawsuits
as urgently as any business on the continent. John Adams rose from
youthful anonymity to prominence and Boston residence with a share
of that kind of practice, during the dozen years before the Revolution.
By that time the City of Brotherly Love had already become a famous
center of legal contentiousness.

Besides the economic stimulation to legal alertness, there grew with
population growth the old public motive of the planters to possess
minimum legal equipment, or more than minimum. Every new county
that was founded required a new panel of justices of the peace, and
every enlargement of society required enlargement of the bench as
well as the bar. So far as the equipment of the practitioners was concerned, the colonial response to all this was twofold. In the first place,
there occurred marked improvements in training. Before 1760 very few
colonials entered the Inns of Court in London; during the next fifteen
years many did so, most of them, numbering about eighty-five, from
South Carolina, Virginia, and Maryland.° Although we know very
little about the subject, it is reasonable to suppose that the usual training of colonial lawyers, apprentice-style in law offices, improved generally during the same period. Certainly it was excellent in some cases:
in George Wythe's training of Jefferson and others in Williamsburg,
while Wythe was a member of the House of Burgesses and mayor of
his city (a dozen years before he became the first American professor
of law); in the training given by John Dickinson to young men in
Philadelphia, made memorable by James Wilson, his trainee; in the
thoughtful supervision, appreciated by John Adams, given in James
Putnam's office in Worcester. The second American response to the
need for lawyers and law was—truly a frontier phenomenon—a vast
simplification of the profession. Even Inns of Court trainees sometimes
did not enter practice; very often little-trained men were the ones who
reached power and distinction at the bar or high appointment on the
bench. The hierarchy in the profession and the assistants of the profession in England, with gradations from barrister down to scrivener,
simply was not reproduced in the colonies.

One result of the rapid and undisciplined growth of legal practice
and the legal profession—more the result of the rapidity than the undis-
cipline—was a supply of men ready to participate vocally in the politics
of the colonial assemblies. Though, in the absence of much nose count-

ing, this process is hard to date and to discuss with precision, it is clear that a real infusion of fighting blood took place. In Maryland, which because of its proprietary institutions was a little precocious in the development of the practice of law, this happened soon after 1715, when Daniel Dulany the Elder, the father of his better-known namesake, became aggressive leader of the House of Delegates. In that province and south of the Potomac, where the London-trained minority of lawyers was greater than to the north and where the office of justice of the peace was thoroughly built into governing-class society as in England, the leadership of the parties in the assembly—the "court" and "country" party in each province—was largely a matter of the rivalry of prominent lawyers. In New York and Pennsylvania, the political emergence of lawyers came little if any later than in Maryland. In Massachusetts, where affairs had been so particularly dominated by clergymen, the first lawyer was elected to the House of Representatives in 1738. But from that time forward it was led always by a lawyer; and Thomas Hutchinson, the last native son to be provincial governor, owed his rise through the ranks to his law, in part, and not at all to his historianship.

At this point of turning to specific conflicts, we need simply note the affinity, social and intellectual, between the eighteenth century's production of colonial history writing, which examined the situation of the provinces, often troubled and unclear, and the prevalence in politics of a new profession which was trained in the study of precedents and was committed to the validation of rights not yet proven and recognized.

2 *Before 1765: Freedom and*
Self-government as Rights

WHEN John Adams and Thomas Jefferson during old age reviewed in their wonderful letters the events and ideas of their time, they believed that before 1763—that is, during the mid-century decades of their childhood and education—the British system had been politically sound and good.

With some reservations, today's scholarship agrees. During the eighteenth century before the prerevolutionary crisis, there did prevail in colonial America such a political equilibrium between authority at home and self-government in the provinces as made the system different from the empires of France and Spain. And, as between metropolis and province, so likewise between government and individual there prevailed a reasonable balance. Voltaire himself discovered and praised this in England; in the New World another French émigré who appreciated freedom, St. John de Crèvecoeur, discovered a rural type that he called "this new man"—the American who combining self-reliance and toleration of others made a wonderful neighbor and citizen.

Recent scholarship reports in detail, however, that, within the British system's broad lines of comparative freedom, a good many laws and practices—over and above the laws of servitude—circumscribed personal liberty in critical areas and were sometimes suppressive. When, more than a decade ago, Leonard W. Levy began his researches in the history of the press, he was astonished, he tells us, to discover the number of libel actions taken against printers by the colonial authorities, and to learn where the initiative lay. Most of the actions came from the lower houses of assembly, not the governors; the people's elected representatives brought their detractors before the bar in order to silence disrespect for themselves and their work. As for discrimination against heterodox Christians and against non-Christians, it is hard to estimate how persecuting, or not, the Puritan and Anglican colonies actually were. Laws and habits of religious toleration to the contrary, taxes and other economic privileges for those churches were discriminatory by nature. The Baptists of New England and Virginia protested, but before the Revolution they were not politically powerful. The discontented could move to Rhode Island or one of the old Quaker colonies. Yet only one man could be Benjamin Franklin, and, though American society was already pretty mobile, few people can have escaped church taxes and church pressures for life as he did, simply by moving from a city where such things existed to a city better for business, where they did not occur. Probably the crowning statutory decision for religious discrimination, anywhere in the English-speaking world during the middle-eighteenth century, was Maryland's triple taxation of Roman Catholics during the French and Indian War—an inversion of that colony's seventeenth-century policy of toleration. But the law applied to a minority which was economically entrenched, and no noticeable emigration of Maryland Catholics occurred.

Only in a few cases before 1763 did protest and discussion of principle rise from these gray areas of colonial restrictiveness. But two of those cases are very telling. By all means the most important case of freedom of printing—the most important in American history before the Alien and Sedition Acts—was that of John Peter Zenger, printer of the *Weekly Journal* of New York. The paper was founded in 1733 and in and out of trouble in 1734 and 1735; it was the instrument of a faction of lawyers who had the merit of being opposed to Governor William Cosby. As royal governor, first in New Jersey and then in New York, Cosby had displayed an unlimited capacity for being absorbed in the perquisites and favors of office; he had arbitrarily removed a chief justice from office. Zenger's *Journal* needled the governor in a variety of ways, one of which was the printing of an essay over the signature "Cato." The pseudonym was borrowed, not directly from the moralist of the Roman republic but—as James and Benjamin Franklin and others had already borrowed it—from the much-admired letter writers to the London *Journal* of a decade earlier, whose contributions, *Cato's Letters, or Essays on Liberty Civil and Religious, and Other Important Subjects*, actually written by John Trenchard and Thomas Gordon, gave lively new voice to English commonwealth theory. At any rate the New York "Cato" and his colleagues soon reached the limits of the royal governor's endurance. Probably the most stinging effort they made was a series of advertisements; four requests pretending to seek the return of stray animals lampooned Cosby's favorite advisers. So too did song sheets from Zenger's press, which all but named the favorites:

> *The pettyfogging knaves deny us rights of Englishmen*
> *We'll make the rascals fly, and ne'er return again.*

Governor Cosby resorted to the frequently used law of seditious libel, the same common-law resource as a decade earlier had put James Franklin in jail in Boston. Yet the action stumbled from the beginning. The governor tried and failed to get a grand-jury indictment; he tried and failed to get the assembly to undertake the prosecution. Finally, he and his council had to initiate the action. The most offensive issues of the *Journal* were publicly burned; Zenger himself was arrested and jailed. When the case came to trial, all that the attorney general of the province expected to have to prove to the jury was the undeniable fact that Zenger had printed the objectionable pieces. Thereafter the responsibility would normally be with the judge to rule on the point of law: whether or not the pieces were libelous—criminally "tending to raise factions and tumults" as charged against them.

But the whole action went out of the administration's control. Zenger, though he spent almost ten months in jail, managed to communicate with his wife "through the Hole of the Door of the Prison," and she kept the paper going. In the courtroom Zenger's lawyer patrons were disbarred. They brought off a coup nevertheless, by bringing into the courtroom the venerable Andrew Hamilton of Philadelphia. As a distinguished man—he had taught school in Virginia, had married well and acquired an estate on the Eastern Shore, had served from there in the Maryland assembly, had been admitted to Gray's Inn, and in about fifteen years of residence in Philadelphia had risen in politics and fortune—Hamilton epitomized the personal and intellectual qualities of the parvenu profession in which he was a leader. In the address to the New York jury which made him famous, Hamilton argued simply that the statements in question, criticizing the government, were not false. To the court's response that they were libelous, whatever their truth or falsehood, he rejoined that if what the court called libel were libel, without regard for truth, the king's subjects had no protection from possible tyranny. In his own words: "It is true in time past, it was a crime to speak truth, and in that terrible court of Star Chamber many worthy and brave men suffered for so doing; and yet even in that court, and in those bad times, a great and good man durst say what I hope will not be taken amiss of me to say in this place, to wit, the practice of informations for libels is a sword in the hands of a wicked king." The Philadelphian acknowledged "that government is a sacred thing" but said that he differed when the king's attorney "would insinuate that the just complaints of a number of men, who suffer from a bad administration, is libelling that administration." Appealing to the jury that "the right of complaining or remonstrating is natural" and that a verdict of not guilty for Zenger would protect "every freeman . . . on the main of America," Hamilton won spectacularly the decision he sought.

In order to render it the jury had to reject an instruction by the judge. It had to resort to a fiction about its own authority, which amounted to a usurpation of the judge's. Richard Morris has correctly called the verdict an act of "civil disobedience."

The short-run responses were as eloquent as Hamilton's speech. The governor was humiliated. The visiting lawyer was given the freedom of the city. John Peter Zenger shared the honors, given him with justice and enthusiasm. He issued and reissued a pamphlet which told the story. In 1738 Benjamin Franklin's paper printed a comment which said of the decision that "If it is not Law it is better than Law, it ought to be Law, and will always be Law wherever justice prevails." At very minimum, a spectacular court action had announced as a natural right the principle that a citizen may criticize his government.

The longer-run consequences and the more ultimate meanings of the Zenger case are not so easy to discover and not so certainly liberal. The New York jury's decision had no automatic power to enter the common law and did not do so. No judge was bound to respect it; not until the state constitution of 1821 did New York law incorporate the principle which Hamilton persuaded the jury to accept, namely, that the falsity or truth of an offensive statement is the measure of its being libelous or not libelous. Finally, as Levy insists, after the question of the effectiveness of the Zenger case as precedent in law, there must be considered also the question of the merit of Hamilton's plea. Was his recourse to natural right, as he bound it up to a jury decision, a true service to freedom? Since he cut radically loose from usage in any case, might he not have done better for freedom and have been equally effective against Cosby if, instead of flouting court rulings, he had flouted the law of seditious libel itself? This would have been hard for a common-law lawyer to do. But if, in place of saying that the jury should (by the "not guilty" fiction) displace the judge in ruling on the question of libel—a position which retained common-law censorship —he had said that the citizen's natural right to criticize the government gives him immunity from court review, Hamilton would have had the distinction of prophesying the position of the revolutionary bills of rights half a century later. The discussion of 1735 stopped considerably short of that position, even on the liberal side of the dialogue.°

Three decades later, just before the Stamp Act crisis, a Virginia conflict known as the "Parsons' Cause" raised other questions of free-dom. The conflict started in low key. Twice during the French and Indian War the assembly in Williamsburg, the governor and council of course assenting, passed a "two-penny act" which commuted the salaries of Anglican clergymen from payment in tobacco to payment in money, two pence for each pound of tobacco due. The law was designed to prevent rises in the price of tobacco from inflating clergy-men's incomes; it fitted well the Old Dominion's fixed habit of keeping the clergy humble and the church dependent on lay government. If the matter had been retained at home, nothing more upsetting than disgruntlement might have followed. But the clergymen, led by a parson of high-church inclination, appealed to the king in council and won; a royal disallowance did away with the two-penny act.

This decision brought Patrick Henry, a back-country lawyer still in his twenties, into history for the first time. When a clergyman brought suit in the Hanover County court to recover his full salary at the market value of tobacco, Henry was the attorney chosen to defend the authori-ties who had paid at the two-penny rate. As well as his clients, Henry's background involved him. His father was an Anglican vestryman and his uncle and namesake, an Anglican parson; both were low-church and antibishop. The family was Scots by origin, and Patrick Henry's mother remained a Presbyterian. In the region of their residence, Samuel Davies, the beloved Presbyterian minister, supplied the young lawyer with the model he followed of the emotional orator. When the case came to trial, Patrick Henry in Hanover County, much like Andrew Hamilton in New York, had community sentiment with him. Addressing a court the very life of which signified local loyalty and the local management of affairs, he argued that the clergymen should willingly accept the government of the legislature of their "country," Virginia. Again like Hamilton, he asked for a jury decision which would ignore—or rather, rise above—accepted law and reject a delib-erate decision made on the authority of the king. Not denying the formal constitutionality of the disallowance of the two-penny act, but arguing that it was a tyrannous, mistaken decision, Henry asked that the unpaid salary be withheld. The plea was infused with "Virginia nationalism," according to the Virginia historian of the episode, Hamilton J. Eckenrode; so also was it infused with appeal to the natural right of representative taxation.

Anglican clergymen, who had come to the trial expecting to witness a triumph, fled from the courtroom. There was no opposition between judge and jury this time; the decision, which made Patrick Henry famous, awarded the plaintiff exactly one penny in damages. The rightness of having a Church of England establishment had not been questioned on principle. Nevertheless, any independence in that institution had been challenged; and, after the court decision the clergymen on the advice of the president of William and Mary decided not to appeal but to bear their humiliation. As for the question more directly raised, whether or not the province had ultimate authority to tax and legislate for itself without restraint from England, the particular issue in Virginia, which involved defiance of the king in council, blended at once with the overwhelming intercolonial issue of 1765, which involved Parliament's power to tax in America. But no defiance of English authority before 1776 would be less compromising than the disobedience which occurred, in an atmosphere heady with legal rhetoric and evangelical feeling, in the Hanover County courthouse.°

The famous law-court events of 1735 and 1763 were moments of insight and excitement in the history of freedom, and in the cumulation of the long tradition they count. But for the shorter-term question of in what way, prior to the Stamp Act, questions of individual and provincial freedom entered the stream of political thought, we find better evidence in Pennsylvania and Maryland than in New York and Virginia, where the Zenger case and the Parsons' Cause occurred. In these next-door provinces the representative elements in the legislature were uncommonly aggressive, largely for a single reason. The two had proprietary governments still, the only ones remaining on the American mainland; as such they were subject to a lord proprietor in England, a Penn and a Calvert, respectively, descendants of the colony fathers. But during the eighteenth century little magic of loyalty remained in the historic families. The original ties of unusual faith, one Catholic and one Quaker, no longer connected at the top; the descendants of the founders had deteriorated into takers of quitrents and dues and givers of favors—land grants and offices—to their friends. In both provinces the assemblies had gathered prestige and confidence. The one-house legislature in Pennsylvania started with unusual powers. Maryland's lower house had been early to win parliamentary privilege; in the background of all conflicts in that colony lay awareness that the charter of 1632, notwithstanding its feudal archaisms, contained a clause which guaranteed that Marylanders should enjoy the rights of

Englishmen forever. Before the middle of the eighteenth century, in both provinces the proprietor, his governor, and appointees had collided headlong with the ambitious assembly. Both legislatures tried and failed to reach the king in council, as the font of English justice, and win, by pleas of unfair treatment, the abolishment of the proprietary system. Their request was for royal government, like Virginia's; their reasoning was that under the Crown the legislatures could more fully have their own way. A committee of the Pennsylvania assembly, of which Benjamin Franklin was chairman, once let drop the following line of political dogmatism, describing a position which the lord proprietor denied: "A natural right, inherent in every man, antecedent to all laws, . . . the assemblies have had the power of disposing of public moneys."

Maryland produced a special yield of doctrine; it was formulated during the so-called "judges' oath" controversy of the 1720s. The goal of the legislature had been to put into the form of statute law the obligation it sought to impose on Maryland judges to incorporate English law with Maryland statute in their rulings. After long disagreements between the House of Delegates, pressing for unlimited acceptance of the laws of England, and the proprietary governor and council, holding back, the two elements reached a phrasing and sent it to England as passed. Lord Baltimore disallowed the statute. The collision between the whole province, politically speaking, and the proprietor was the same as the Hanover County court's would be with the king in the Parsons' Cause. The legislature must have the final word, the lower house said. Against Lord Baltimore's charter authority and all else, "It is we that are the people's representatives for whom all laws are made and government established," the House of Delegates declared.

The ultimate statement of the house's position was made in a pamphlet—prime form of eighteenth-century argument—printed in Annapolis in 1728, *The Right of the Inhabitants of Maryland to the Benefit of the English Laws*. The author, Daniel Dulany the Elder, was the principal lawyer of the province and the leader of the lower house; the printer, William Parks, had recently come to Maryland, through the good offices of another lawyer and delegate, and published (for a a short time) the first *Maryland Gazette*. Altogether the rise of the legal profession, the beginning of printing, the beginning of pamphleteering, and a consolidation of political sentiment were completely connected events in Maryland. We do not know Dulany's library as we do the Byrd and Carter libraries in Virginia or that of Charles Carroll of Carrollton nearby, but the quotations and notations in the pamphlet show that the author, who had studied at the University of Dublin, had access to many classics of political thought. He cited an argument from Grotius that mother country and colonies should have equal freedoms; he quoted Coke and asserted with grandeur that the common law combines into one resource "the Law of Nature, the Law of Reason, and the revealed Law of God." A few sentences, which may fairly be read as voicing the essential thought of the mid-century lawyers for self-government, require quotation:

> It is certainly of the greatest Importance to know, whether a People are to be governed by *Laws*, which their *Mother-Country* has experimentally found, to be beneficial to Society. . . . Or whether, they are to be governed by the Discretion, (as some people softly term the *Caprice*, and *Arbitrary Pleasure*,) of any Set of Men. . . . 'Tis this Law, that will effectually secure every Honest Man, who has the Benefit of it, in his Life, the Enjoyment of his Liberty, and the Fruits of his Industry. 'Tis by Virtue of this Law, that a British Subject, may with Courage, and Freedom, tell the most daring, and powerful Oppressor, that He must not injure Him with Impunity. . . . If we be deprived of any Part of that Right, without our Consent, . . . We may by the same Reason, and Authority, be deprived of some other Part; . . . and our Lives, Liberties, and Properties [rendered] Precarious.

By putting his argument into historical perspective and framing it with honored theory, then offering it to the world in print, Daniel Dulany the Elder did, a half century before the Revolution, what his better-known son would do in the Stamp Act crisis. The author of *The Right of the Inhabitants* and the little book itself deserve a greater reputation than they have had; they may have suffered, in part, because Dulany himself very soon accepted appointment, and much economic preference, from Lord Baltimore. But the book may reasonably be compared with John Wise's *Vindication of the New England Churches*, published eleven years earlier. Wise is appreciated today for having restated the fundamental ideas of congregationalist polity and for having voiced their democratic essence in terms of late-seventeenth- and early-eighteenth-century political thought, as well as for having renewed the Bible terms of the Reformation. Dulany justified the autonomy of the colonial legislature, likewise, in terms larger than the traditional ones, of parliamentary privilege. He drew on the continental literature in terms wider than the Whig understanding of English rights under law. The reach of his argument bears great resemblance, as we shall discover in detail when we reach those crises, to the arguments advanced against the control of the colonies by either Parliament or king, at the ultimate crisis of empire.°

W HEN Crown and Parliament seized the opportunity of the peace of 1763 to overhaul the British system in America, though they had reasons of money and policy (which historians of today often judge to have made good sense), there were few colonial contemporaries who saw things the English way.° Every member of a colonial legislature who had sat during the French and Indian War knew well that the king's system of administration had creaked and cracked under the strain. He knew that if not his own neighbors then people in nearby places had traded with the enemy in the West Indies; he had learned that every colony had been slow about raising men and money for the army when the Crown demanded; he knew that England under William Pitt had contributed heavily to the campaigns in North America and that the colonies had gained enormously when New France fell. Even with that kind of war record, and with Indian massacres a reminder during the year of the treaty that the colonies would continue to need ready defense, the most favorable political reactions in America to Lord Grenville's famous changes in the system were, before the Stamp Act, moderation and slowness in objecting and, during the Stamp Act crisis, hesitation to disobey the law.

The nearest things to American apology for imperial reorganization came from the pens of two governors of Massachusetts, Thomas Pownall and Francis Bernard. Their consecutive administrations, from 1757 to 1769, spanned the years when Thomas Hutchinson (who succeeded Bernard) was lieutenant governor; they suggest a comparison. Where Hutchinson, the English-oriented native of Massachusetts, made himself an historian administrator and understood the crisis of the colonies from his knowledge of New England's past, Governors Pownall and Bernard, Englishmen of American experience and insight, made themselves analysts of the obligations of empire—"government political scientists," they might be called if they served today, where Governor Hutchinson was a government historian.

Bernard was the later governor, but, because he was in Boston during the critical mid-1760s and put his ideas into letters while events were hot, we may consider his suggestions first. He was an all-out Parliament man. He believed that Parliament had ample constitutional authority to legislate for the colonies, as it had when it passed the Sugar Act and Stamp Act, and that it should take certain further drastic steps. Reasoning, not without truth, that Connecticut and Rhode Island acted like free republics and that Massachusetts was re-

fusing to submit to England's laws, he proposed that Parliament legislate out of existence the New England colonial governments and then
consolidate the region under new authorities. Along with such regional
reorganization, he thought that in future the upper houses of the
colonial legislatures should be transformed into miniature Houses of
Lords, and that a provincial nobility should be created to fill the new
seats. Once such conservative transformations had been brought off,
the governor wanted colonial tax autonomy restored to the position
before 1764; he proposed also that the colonies be allotted seats in the
House of Commons, where over-all imperial legislation would be enacted. Bernard's schemes voiced imagination, and knowledge of needs
felt on both sides of the water. But in essence they signified a consolidating program centered in England, and American colonial submission to the rapidly ascending authority of Parliament. The governor's
American experience had taught him no more deference to the colonies' belief in the rightfulness of self-government than Crown and
Parliament themselves were displaying.°

In these regards Governor Pownall did better. Though his administration of Massachusetts began in a hard war year and he was well
acquainted with the centralizing tendencies of Lord Loudoun, the
British commander in chief in the field, he had the sense to honor the
legislative authority, to which Massachusetts was habituated, against
the claims of the military. In that way he succeeded in winning appropriations when others failed. A personal friend of Benjamin Franklin,
and praised by John Adams for having been "the most constitutional
and national governor" ever to represent the Crown in Massachusetts,
he gathered the attitudes which enabled him to write a book, *The
Administration of the Colonies*, published in 1764. He saw, what
twentieth-century scholarship endorses, that great enlargements of colonial administration had to come. He did not exclude the possibility of
Parliament taxing the colonies; in the year during which he published,
that question had risen with the Sugar Act but had not yet become
inflamed. His gift was not so much, however, to propose schemes for
shifting the location of power as to suggest ways of forbearance and
accommodation, while shifts already in train were taking place. He
would have made any possible taxation of the colonies by Parliament
conditional on Parliament first admitting American members. Different
from Governor Bernard, he reasoned that the colonies ought to be
granted a share of responsibility in making the decisions about changing
the nature of the empire, before they had to bear whatever burdens
the decisions would create. Leonard W. Labaree, expert on the constitution of the empire, ranks Governor Pownall "ahead of almost all his
contemporaries in his understanding of the colonial attitude, of the

constitutional issues at stake, and of the adjustment necessary if Great Britain were to retain the loyalty of her maturing colonies."°

But Pownall at the time of writing his book was already a retired colonial administrator at home; the capacity he had for generous perspective was shared by few, and not by the Grenville government which immediately put through the Stamp Act. That measure was not a climax of imperial reorganization, for the goal of reorganization was to improve the administration of the Indian frontier and to tighten up trade regulation. Rather, it was an enabling step in the process, a provision of money. The mode of taxation was familiar and accepted in England, and the rates were not high. In short, the act looked conventional and that is how it slipped through.

But of course great trouble lay in the fact that taxation by Parliament would destroy the believed-in habit of the colonies that Americans taxed themselves in their assemblies and devised their own money bills. If ever a measure called for public thought—for a deliberate probing of constitutional methods and political and economic goals—that measure was the Stamp Act. Yet no full-dress discussion occurred. While the prime minister did notify the agents of the colonies, a year in advance, that a stamp tax was intended, he did not use the channels which might have led to the offering of counterproposals from America; none were offered on either side of the water. The government simply sought a showdown on its own terms and had its own way. The often-noticed fact that the Stamp Act as finally drawn impinged directly on the lawyers and the printers of newspapers in America, by requiring them to use stamped paper (or else stop doing business), amounted to a tactical fillip within a strategy which challenged the most vocal persons in the colonies as well as the assemblies themselves.

The response in America led to thought, but first came a massive people's reaction. Organizations sprang up: the Sons of Liberty, the Stamp Act Congress, and meetings everywhere. The opinions expressed, from north to south and at all levels of responsibility, were so single-minded that they may be called public doctrine: Parliament has no right to tax the colonies, because Parliament does not represent them. American colonials are loyal subjects of the king and are true believers in the authority of Parliament; they acknowledge its power to enact general legislation, the same for America as for England. The colonies have always had the rights of Englishmen; these include, in the words of the Stamp Act Congress, freedom that "no taxes be imposed on them but with their own consent, given personally or by their representatives." Between the early, pace-setting resolutions which were passed by the Virginia House of Burgesses on May 30, 1765, after Patrick Henry had spoken, and the moderate resolutions passed by the Stamp Act Congress in October, only minor variations of thought appeared among the many formulations of opposition. Altogether this very first surge of American opinion was more unanimous than any other which would occur for a century and three-quarters—that is, it was the most unanimous ever until the strike on Pearl Harbor.

To a twentieth-century mind the distinction which colonials made, when they acknowledged that Parliament had authority to legislate general policy for them but denied that it had authority to tax them, is a little unreal. Yet to the protesters this was not so. For a century the colonies had been accustomed to Parliament's Acts of Trade, which embodied mercantilist policy; some of those laws took the form of customs duties—that is, of regulatory but not income-producing taxation. The colonies had not objected earlier, and did not in 1765, either to the old economic policy or to the old enforcing legislation. The point which the protesters now insisted on and reinforced with Lockian argument was that individual rights are, by natural law, inviolable and that rights in property are of that order. Taxation is a special form of legislation, they reasoned, because it seizes the property of the subject; no one has a right to assign that property, to the sovereign or to anyone, except the owner or his representative. This core of the natural-rights and natural-law argument against Parliament's innovations was firmly grasped and used by the colonials. It helped justify their distinction between kinds of legislation; it helped them also to reiterate their belief that all legislative power is subject to limitations. One essay, which was published in Maryland and Pennsylvania newspapers, enlarged on the point with sweep: "No Parliament can alter the Nature of Things, or make that good which is really evil. If they could do this, then they might alter the whole Frame of the Constitution where they are chosen—They might make themselves independent on their Constituents, and be perpetual Dictators—or they might do any Thing—But this cannot be: There is certainly some Bounds to their Power, and 'tis Pity they were not more certainly known."° So completely did lawyers and judges yield to the conviction that Parliament had done wrong that, immediately when November 1 came, they closed court rather than do business; then, after a little, they opened court again and did business without the stamps. Printers in the service of provincial governments likewise stopped the gazettes with the last issue in October. Later they started publication, in flagrant defiance of Parliament's law.

Though doubtless the collision force of American resistance accelerated the decision to repeal the Stamp Act which Parliament reached in 1766, the doctrines which had strengthened colonial defiance to the point of conspicuous and widespread civil disobedience made poor argument to help Parliament find a new course. The immediate and practical need of 1765 and 1766 was to find ideas which would lead to second thinking about the reorganization of the British system. Where the intellectual problem of 1764, when Pownall brought out his book, had been to make affirmative proposals for running the empire, the new problem of the political thinker was how Englishmen and colonials should understand, and on what basis England might withdraw from, the recent terrible blunder.

This service Daniel Dulany the Younger, the son of the author of *The Right of the Inhabitants of Maryland to the Benefit of the English Laws*, was superbly able to render. A lawyer in provincial politics, an officeholder under Lord Baltimore, and a man of huge property in land, the younger Dulany was not too conservative to draw on the bank of natural-law and natural-rights argument against England's taxation policy. But he did not draw as heavily as his father had done, four decades earlier, or as his contemporaries were doing. Mainly, his little book, *Considerations Upon the Propriety of Imposing Taxes on the English Colonies for the Purposes of Raising a Revenue*, was an historical, economic, and moral argument, presented with great force. One of the few leaders of the colonial bar who had been fully trained in England—at Eton, Cambridge, and the Middle Temple—Dulany was uncommonly ready to discuss the operating phases of government and economic life. He knew and disdained Pownall's work on administration; he knew, and took so seriously as to answer, Prime Minister Grenville's secretary, Thomas Whately, who had said in a pamphlet that the absence of Americans from Parliament no more deprived the colonies of representation there than ninety per cent of all Englishmen were deprived. Whately's apology drew from the tradition of the House of Commons that all members speak for the nation as a whole, not for their own constituencies narrowly—the apology known as "virtual representation."

Virtual representation was weak stuff, and Dulany hit it hard. In England, said the American author, "The security of the non-elector is that their oppression will fall also upon the electors and their representatives." Americans lack this assurance, he went on: "Not a single elector in England might be immediately affected by taxation in America. . . . The latter might be oppressed in a thousand shapes, without any sympathy or inciting any alarm, in the former."

Dulany turned his nationalist insight to economics as well as to politics. Even though taxes *in* America might be low, he acknowledged, taxes *on goods produced in America* and sent to England for re-exportation—he was thinking of Chesapeake Bay tobacco—raised revenue as they passed through England, and carried much of the burden of empire. Writing when colonial boycotts were already being organized to bring pressure on Parliament for repeal, Dulany prophesied that

Parliament's taxing the colonies, if sustained, would promote home industry in America. (The prophecy came true after the Townshend duties of 1767.) Colonial industries, Dulany went on, would reduce the earnings of England's manufacturers and shippers and would reduce the government's take from customs duties; the sum of his argument was that the Grenville reforms were creating an economic spiral which would strangle the life of England's commercial system.°

Dulany's pamphlet had brilliance; it brought together law, history, economics, and political philosophy, all focused on the Stamp Act. His telling argument against virtual representation pleased the Earl of Chatham, who borrowed and used it with effect, in aid of repeal. Virtual representation would not enter the Anglo-American dialogue again.

Yet, when the Stamp Act was repealed, Parliament passed the Declaratory Act, which stated its authority to tax the colonies if it wished. The new law helps us understand the position to which colonial protest had come. Effort at reconciliation, which is what Dulany's *Considerations* truly offered, could reach only so far. Much more relevant to the real situation were the fluent denials of Parliament's power which the resolutions of the assemblies and the Stamp Act Congress contained. Before 1765 Lockian argument had been turned against royal judge, colonial governor, lord proprietor, and king in council, on separate occasions; now they had been turned, by a people aroused, against the most honored of all English institutions. Vigor of feeling for freedom in the colonies, and for the equality of the colonial legislatures with the mother of parliaments at home, was being fused with vigor of feeling for America, three convictions thrown together in 1765 into a very hot political crucible.

So much was reasonably apparent at the time. In the retrospect of two succeeding centuries, however, it is fair to notice that England, in its blundering of 1765 and after, was having a hard turn at trying to manage one of the problems which recur in American history, the problem this book identifies as reconstruction. Once previously, after 1688, we have seen Americans—as Englishmen—make deep social and institutional adjustments in order to catch up with a revolution. Before long—during the 1770s and 1780s—they would do so again, this time as a separate people. They would have to reconstruct then because they had not let Britain do it for them after 1763. That in the time we are now considering Crown and Parliament tried to impose a system, rather than allow the colonials to share in the development as after 1688, is doubtless the main reason for the failure of the first British Empire.

4 Independence of Parliament and King: The Ultimate Reasoning

BEGINNING in 1764 and through twelve hard years of imperial politics, five thrusts of new policy by the home government, and five counterthrusts in America, led to the breakdown of empire and to recourse to arms. The first, second, and third thrusts and counterthrusts hinged on taxation and were only somewhat productive of political thought.

The Stamp Act crisis, brought on by Lord Grenville's aggressions and developed by the people of the colonies, made the first cycle. The second began with the Declaratory Act of 1766; the real pressure came when Parliament imposed the Townshend duties—customs duties on British goods entering the colonies, which meant money out of American pockets. The colonial response this time, though neither as unanimous nor as disobedient to law as in 1765, was strong enough to win repeal in 1770. The American victory was about as decisive as the repeal of the Stamp Act. The third taxation effort began at that moment, when the government, now led by Lord North, decided to retain from the series of 1767 just one tax, the duty on tea. This was like the Declaratory Act again, an assertion of Parliament's authority to tax the colonies as a matter of principle and precedent. The tea tax was little objected to by the colonials; they let go their recent boycott and resumed their usual tea-drinking habits. Indeed for five years, 1768 to 1773, Britain's effort at reconstruction made little trouble.

The protest literature of the period was correspondingly moderate. John Dickinson wrote the most effective pamphlet, *The Letters of a Pennsylvania Farmer*, which was published serially in many newspapers. Actually the pseudonym of the author was calculated to win readers but not to identify him; far from being a farmer, Dickinson was a Middle Templar, an inheritor of great wealth, a conservative in politics (as defender of the lord proprietorship, still held by a William Penn descendant), and a reader of history who was well acquainted with the constitutional conflicts in England of the seventeenth century. His particular contribution to the dialogue about taxation, a legalistic but useful point analogous to Dulany's virtual-representation argument, was simply to say that, although the Townshend duties were external (or customs) duties, as was alleged in their favor, they were only in that formal way like the mercantilist duties which the colonies had always accepted. Actually they were revenue duties, in intent and operation, and were at bottom as objectionable as the stamp tax itself. Dickinson, who was a very model of the scholarly lawyer of his age, and who had a talent—which he would display in 1776—for seeing both sides of an issue, indicates the capacity Parliament's taxation policy had for bringing out defiance, even in naturally conservative men.

Around 1770, moreover, while the taxation crisis was tapering down and before spectacular new issues arose, new and different leadership in protest was appearing, and conflicts other than taxation were being felt. On the more doctrinaire and radical wing, Samuel Adams was the driving figure in New England and Patrick Henry in Virginia. These men were neither originators nor developers of ideas but public persuaders. Each had been locally prominent in Stamp Act protest and in the protest of the Townshend duties. Patrick Henry's "Caesar had his Brutus, Charles his Cromwell" speech in the House of Burgesses, against the Stamp Act, introduced the same kind of passion into Virginia's belief in its rights as his Hanover courthouse speech had done in the Parsons' Cause. In Samuel Adams of Boston, whose Harvard thesis had borne the title, "Whether or not it be lawful to resist the Supreme Magistrate, if the Commonwealth cannot be otherwise preserved," a corresponding talent appeared. Adams brought to the parlance and decision-making of common men in the town meeting, where he was a master strategist, the abstractions of natural law and natural rights which, though unfamiliar nowhere, had always mainly belonged in books or else in the speech of ministers, lawyers, and legislators. Sam Adams and Patrick Henry were alike able to make ideas of right burn brightly in their hearers' minds.

It is easier to speak of the fire bringers than the fuel, during the quiet period after the Townshend duties were repealed. Part of the incitement to public feeling at that time lay in local, one-province, controversies. These were exciting matters in Massachusetts, for example, where Governor Hutchinson was involved, and in Maryland, where Daniel Dulany the Younger and Charles Carroll of Carrollton were; often they could be prosecuted in terms of Whiggish and natural-right ideas. But in general, throughout the colonies there was something which transcended local questions and amounted to more than memory of the tax crises. Despite the failure of Parliament to make any of its colonial tax laws stick, the structure and administration of empire had been built up since 1763. During the Grenville period, new machinery for territorial security and for the management of Indian relations had been set up, changes which were hardly subject to complaint; during the later 1760s the mechanisms for administering the acts of trade had been enlarged and (for the first time) somewhat centralized in a customs board in America. This was much more ominous. Meanwhile the often-discussed and (by the ideals of the church) much needed measure of Anglican reform, the creation of a colonial diocese with a resident bishop, became an actual possibility during the years around 1770, at least on the English side. In America, however, the religious merits of the case received little hearing; what the colonials recognized was that a bishopric would mean, besides expense, the political presence of a peer of the realm and the offensiveness of symbols of high-church authority. This threat brought about a raising of minds and hearts in opposition—Congregationalist and Presbyterian minds, schooled to disbelief in bishops; Anglican hearts, set on having lay control of the church—which at least equaled the feeling opposed to any other assertion of English authority, except that against taxation by Parliament.°

Altogether tensions were too high, sustained among the people by too many considerations of feeling, for Parliament to link the old issue of taxation with any other sort of assertion of authority over the colonies without getting a violent reaction. But in 1773, after three years of relaxation on the point of taxes, Parliament awarded a monopoly of the colonial tea trade to the East India Company of London, to the deprivation and distress of colonial dealers. The Tea Act added insult to injury; it put force behind the third thrust of policy, in the series of five which led into the War of Independence. The Boston Tea Party—which Benjamin W. Labaree characterizes as "the perfect crisis"—with Samuel Adams in charge, was the principal counterthrust in this cycle; the more because it was matched by violence in other port cities, it excited people the length of the seaboard. With those defiances by the crowd of two English statutes—Parliament's tea tax and Parliament's regulation of the tea trade—and with those destructions of property, the colonies entered what would become an unbroken spiral of disobedience.

The nature of the conflict between mother country and colonies was suddenly transformed. Pamphlets multiplied; issues merged; fears took over. For ten years the area of Parliament's aggression had been debatable and debated: Did Parliament, or did it not, have a right to tax the colonies? Now Parliament's action—the fourth thrust of reconstruction policy—when it passed the "coercive acts" in May 1774 in response to the Tea Party, bypassed taxation to enter a yet more difficult area. Burke and Chatham did want to hold back; but king and Parliament, overwhelmingly, were determined on action. In four angry laws a program of punishment and control was enacted. The harbor of Boston was closed until recompense should be made to the owners of property destroyed and to the government for taxes not paid; the government of Massachusetts was rendered more appointive and less representative than the charter of 1691 said. Most upsetting of all in New England, Parliament reduced the town meetings of that province from being free gatherings in charge of their own agenda to being electoral and occasional meetings, subject to the governor's permission to convene. One of the coercive laws made legal the quartering of troops in houses, anywhere in the colonies. A fifth law, the Quebec Act, not part of the series, instituted government without representation and with preference for the Catholic Church in that conquered province. Though the law had much justification, to the colonials it seemed ominously authoritanian in principle and threatening in practice, because it stretched the boundaries of Canada so far into the Great Lakes region as to incorporate lands claimed under their charters by both Virginia and Massachusetts. The sum of the enactments of 1774 signified an overwhelming constitutional position: the unlimited sovereignty of the mother country in America, the unlimited subjugation of the colonial legislatures to the legislature in Westminster. In 1765 and since then, the colonials had hoped that Parliament's authority would be (or could be made to be) confined within traditional limits. This hope the coercive laws had disregarded. The colonials' recent expectations had been refused as completely as the Grenville government had refused colonial self-taxation. Once again meetings volunteered and mass feelings rose. Again political thought was called for, this time thought which would conceive Parliament outside the pale of colonial affairs.

The call was bravely met. At once in 1774 three members of the resistance, geographically far apart, one in each of the most populous colonies and in each of the major regions of colonial culture, turned a young and gifted mind to the problem of Parliament: John Adams of Massachusetts, James Wilson of Pennsylvania, and Thomas Jefferson of Virginia. The earliest to publish is today the least remembered of the three, though in due course President George Washington placed him on the United States Supreme Court. Wilson was a native of Scotland, trained at the universities of St. Andrews and Edinburgh and possibly at Glasgow; as a youthful immigrant he had served as tutor in Latin and Greek at the College of Philadelphia; he had prepared for the bar in that city, in the office of John Dickinson; already at age thirty-two he had acquired sizable clientele and property in Carlisle, the town of his residence. It speaks for the aggressiveness of his mind, and also for the way in which the need for the colonies to be emancipated from Parliament could be foreseen, that Wilson drafted his manuscript, which became *Considerations on the Nature and Extent of the Legislative Authority of the British Parliament*, as early as 1768. Quoting Blackstone's proposition that "Acts of Parliament, have, by the British Constitution, a binding force on the American Colonies, they composing a part of the British Empire," he answered with propositions equally unqualified. "No one has a right to any authority over another without his consent. . . . It is repugnant to the essential maxims of jurisprudence, to the ultimate ends of all government, to the genius of the British constitution, and to the liberty and happiness of the Colonies, that they should be bound by the legislative authority of the Parliament of Great-Britain. . . . The Commons of Great-Britain have no dominion over their equals and fellow-subjects in America."

Shifting from denials to affirmations, James Wilson spoke with the same kind of certainty. "All men are by Nature, equal and free." (The great Declaration would borrow that line.) "All lawful government is founded on the consent of those who are subject to it: Such consent was given with a view to ensure and to encrease the happiness of the governed, above what they could enjoy in an independent and unconnected state of nature. The consequence is, that the happiness of the society is the *first* law of every government." To provide a design for the British Empire to operate on these terms, the Pennsylvania lawyer proposed simply—what was then unheard of, anywhere, as practice—complete legislative independence for the colonies, under the Crown. "We have Parliaments of our own," he observed. "A denial of legislative authority of the British Parliament over America is by no means inconsistent with that connexion which ought to subsist between the Mother Country and her Colonies." What connection "ought to subsist"? he asked himself, and answered, the Crown. "To the King is intrusted the direction and management of the great machine of government" on both sides of the Atlantic, and from colonial dependence on him, Wilson reasoned, "arises a strict connection between the inhabitants of Great Britain and those of America. They are fellow subjects; they are under allegiance to the same prince; and this union of allegiance naturally produces a union of hearts."°

Wilson laid down the doctrine of the colonies' legislative equality with England with sharpness and completeness. We may reasonably suppose that he was assisted in the direction of colonial self-government by a native's familiarity with the fact that during the seventeenth century Scotland had had the same royal sovereign as England—the Stuarts, of Scots origin—but had had at the same time its own legislature. At any rate he conceded no single shred of the British Parliament's traditional authority in America. He included the acts of trade and navigation in that judgment. If there needed to be a code of law to take the place of those statutes, he reasoned (in the space of a foot-note, merely), let the king's officers for Britain negotiate, with the king's officers for whichever of the colonies were so disposed, a system of treaties of commerce—the same procedure between mother country and colonies as between separate sovereignties.

John Adams, a lawyer of thirty at the time, had entered the politics of protest during the Stamp Act year. When he introduced resolutions against the tax, in his town of Braintree, he grounded his opposition on the argument that the colonies had not consented. But we learn more about the early political dissent of John Adams from his little book of that same year, his first public writing, which was originally published in installments in the *Boston Gazette*. Somewhat overtitled as *A Dissertation on the Canon and Feudal Law*, it pointed out the coherency, in English law and institutions, among three areas of monopolized wealth and power: concentrated landholding in the feudal tradition; the hierarchy of the national church, with its bishops full members of the House of Lords; and government, always in the hands of the propertied and the privileged.° Nine years later—risen to be a leader of the bar, the owner of a sizable library, a member of the House of Representatives, and, as delegate to what we know as the First Continental Congress, an intercolonial leader of protest against the coercive acts—he began the series of public letters which he signed "Novanglus." There he attacked again the power structure of England. Illuminated still by the perspective on the old regime in England which he had taken in 1765, but driven now by the unlimited grievance of Massachusetts against Parliament, he wrote a little masterpiece.

He did not undertake, as James Wilson had, to prove that Parliament had been constitutionally wrong since 1660, when it passed the principal act of trade. "America has all along consented, still consents, and ever will consent, that Parliament, being the most powerful legislature in the dominions, should regulate the trade of the dominions." The question for Adams was gradations of power again—whether or not the governance of the metropolis justly extended to the colony "in all cases." He consulted ancient and modern history and decided that there had been no general rule or habit. "The practice of nations has been different," he noted. "The Greeks planted colonies, and neither demanded nor pretended any authority over them"; Rome's history contained complications, but it was "the policy of Rome to conciliate her colonies by allowing them equal liberties with her citizens." For the present case Adams reasoned cautiously that "Parliament may be allowed an authority supreme and sovereign over the ocean"; he admitted that the charter of Massachusetts gave the colony "no authority over the high seas." Let the line of colonial self-government be drawn at the western "banks of the ocean, the low-water mark," he proposed, not without humor if he was thinking of the Boston Port Act; "let the colonies be treated like reasonable creatures." As for administering the acts of trade on the American side, those laws might be confirmed as provincial enactments and enforced by province officers or some other mutual management might be reached. He disliked the very idea of a "British Empire." With historical truth, which Charles M. Andrews, the twentieth-century master historian of colonial institutions, would endorse for the epoch before 1763, he insisted that the British government was not an empire. To Adams the right term was "limited monarchy," and even the word "republic" he judged to be accurate.

"If Aristotle, Livy, and Harrington knew what a republic was, the British government is more a republic than an empire. They define a republic to be a government of laws, and not of men. If this definition be just, the British Constitution is nothing more or less than a Republic, in which the King is first magistrate." Farther on in the essay he forecast, as Franklin and others did, that "the time may not be so far off . . . when the colonies may have the balance of numbers and wealth in their favor." He then paid the mother country a compliment: "When that shall happen, if we attempt to rule [Britain] by an American Parliament, without an adequate representation in it, she will infallibly resist us by her arms."°

Thomas Jefferson put down his ideas of 1774 in a memorandum which later became his pamphlet, *A Summary View of the Rights of British America*, before the First Continental Congress assembled. The author, though only thirty-two, had already served five years as a member of the House of Burgesses; he had been associated with Patrick Henry. He first intended the memorandum to be the basis for instructing the Virginia delegates to the congress. In common with Wilson and Adams, he conceived that the coercive acts violated the natural right of the colonies to self-government. "Can any one reason be assigned why 160,000 electors in the island of Great Britain should give law to four millions in the states of America, every individual of whom is equal to every individual of them, in virtue, in understanding, and in bodily strength?" he inquired. (His phrase, "states of America," probably following the "States" of the Netherlands, was unusual in 1774; it indicates a reluctance in Jefferson, like Adams's, to use other words which might have seemed to acknowledge mother-country superiority.)°

Uniquely among the three crisis writers of essays, Jefferson took point of departure, and discovered helpful argument, in the long sweep of England's history. Where John Adams drew on his knowledge of the Greeks and Romans to establish political standards, Thomas Jefferson turned to the ancient Saxons. He argued in behalf of America that, as when the Saxons crossed the North Sea they bore to England the primitive and basic freedoms of the German tribes (known to Jefferson from Tacitus), so when the colonizers settled in America they brought with them the freedom of Englishmen. No more than the Saxon invaders continued in a dependency on Denmark did the colonials continue subject to British power. Jefferson found the same truth to hold for American economics as for politics. He urged that "the exercise of a free trade with all parts of the world" belonged to the colonials "as of natural right," which they could exercise at will. Here Jefferson was saying that the acts of trade were as short of being sound law as the Stamp Act had been; he did not say that they were as objectionable.

The old "violations of our rights were less alarming," he said with reference to those laws, because they were "repeated at more distant intervals than that rapid and bold succession of injuries which is likely to distinguish the present from all other periods of history."

Long ago Randolph G. Adams pointed out that the pamphlets occasioned by the crisis of 1774, so fundamentally critical of coercion, made Adams and Jefferson and Wilson true prophets of the modern British Empire.° His point may well be extended. Because the goal of the three lawyers' argument was multiple legislative sovereignty within a single system of loyalty, their pamphlets may be appreciated as having spoken for the principle of the British Commonwealth of Nations of today, for United States federalism, and even for the United Nations. But to say that the three spoke for the nineteenth and twentieth centuries is to say also how slim their chance was to succeed with the Parliament which concerned them, under the leadership of Lord North. The Continental Congress did not go so far as Wilson and Jefferson wanted, when it sent its addresses to the king and to the people of England in hope of resolving the conflict: it did specify restoring to the colonial legislatures their traditional autonomy, their single control over taxation for revenue included. But there was no chance. By the time Parliament had decided on its fifth round of policy, a mixed offering of conciliatory words and an increase of British armed forces in America, the shots fired at Lexington and Concord had been heard. With that violence, and with the acts of independence taken by the Second Continental Congress, political thought addressed to the question of settling on the right relationship between colonies and mother country ceased to have interest in America—ceased for the years until the United States itself became a mother of colonies. Events of war thrust forward different questions: how to justify full separation from England, and how to organize a free people.

Separation from England meant to deny the authority of the monarch as fully as the authority of his Parliament. For this denial, so different and so much more extreme than the other, the colonials had of course had no other preparation than the simple reading of books. They knew from the seventeenth century that two kings of England had gone down in modern times; they believed, from contract theory, that a king's power is always conditional on his own obedience to law. But, even after a dozen years of crisis, they were accustomed to saying nothing worse about the Crown than that some of its decisions had erred.

How English colonials brought themselves to separate from the Western institution of monarchy remains today a difficult question. But a familiar and an undeniable part of the answer is a little book, *Common Sense*, by an author unknown early in 1776 and since then a household name. Thomas Paine had come to America in 1774, only thirteen months before *Common Sense* was printed. Though unsuccessful as a corset maker, storekeeper, tax collector, schoolteacher, and lobbyist in England, he had managed before leaving home to educate himself remarkably well in science, mathematics included. As immigrant in Philadelphia, he had made friends at once with Benjamin Franklin and had written for the journals. Unlike the Dulanys and the Dickinsons of the 1760s and different from the great pamphleteers of 1774 who wrote for their own kind, Paine wrote for everyman, in everyday terms. "There is something absurd, in supposing a Continent to be perpetually governed by an island," he said. "In no instance hath nature made the satellite larger than its primary planet; and as England and America, with respect to each other, reverse the common order of nature, it is evident that they belong to different systems. England to Europe: America to itself." Paine believed in equality among nations; he believed more deeply in equality among human beings. The Quakerism which had been part of his family background echoes in this branch of his thought. But he spoke unquietly, in such extremes as no earlier controversialist had ventured: "Mankind being originally equals in the order of creation. . . . There is . . . a greater distinction for which no truly natural or religious reason can be assigned, and that is the distinction of men into KINGS and SUBJECTS." Again:

> There is something exceedingly ridiculous in the composition of Monarchy; it first excludes a man from the means of information, yet empowers him to act in cases where the highest judgment is required. . . . The nearer any government approaches to a Republic, the less business there is for a King. It is somewhat difficult to find a proper name for the government of England. Sir William Meredith calls it a Republic; but in its present state it is unworthy of the name. . . . For 'tis the Republican and not the Monarchical part of the constitution of England which Englishmen glory in. . . . Monarchy hath poisoned the Republic; the Crown hath engrossed the Commons.°

According to Edmund S. Morgan, an historian of the American Revolution who is also a specialist in the thought of the Enlightenment, Tom Paine was read when published because he "said superbly all the things Americans were waiting to be told." There is no doubt about the popularity of the book. Before spring 1776, well over one hundred thousand copies went out; during the calendar year it was reprinted in several cities, Boston the most northerly and Charleston the most southerly. But popularity is a different thing from the guidance of thought, and *Common Sense*'s influence toward the decision for independence is doubtful. For one consideration, though the attack on monarchy was new, some skepticism was familiar: what John Adams had said as Novanglus, about the elements of monarchism and republicanism in

English government (the two terms not quite exclusive), was similar to what Paine said, all the difference in tone between the two writers notwithstanding. Thomas Jefferson's words in *A Summary View*, admonishing King George in schoolmaster-like language to do justice for his people, indicate that nothing remained of the *mystique* of monarchy in the mind of that author, and that he took none for granted among his fellow burgesses in Williamsburg. It is hard to guess what strength of attachment to monarchy may have been nurtured among colonial subjects by the ceremonial occasions of government—by the taking of oaths, the making of addresses, the salutes with fire of guns, the royal birthdays, and so on. In the formal documents and the newspaper accounts they seem to have been entirely conventional; if they contained something of the lift of heart which has prevailed in modern Canada and Australia, that feeling is hard to discover. The faith in the king in council which we have noticed was perfectly sincere, but it voiced reliance on the rule-of-law aspect of England's constitution— which Adams and Paine preferred to call "republican"—rather than reliance on the royal personage. Until some historian of loyalties discovers just what feelings latter-day colonials did entertain for their sovereign, it is easier to suppose that during the eighteenth century the persons who signified the stability and dignity of government to Americans were the ones located in the capitals of the colonies more than the one who resided in far Windsor.° One judges also that the excitement of *Common Sense* lay in Tom Paine's saying not simply what readers waited to hear, in order to decide for independence, but what, being already persuaded or nearly so, they enjoyed hearing spoken with verve and without interference by censor.

Quite as Bernard Bailyn suggests, the argument of the American resistance was by now transcending argumentation. It was becoming a preoccupation everywhere in the colonies. And further, as Staughton Lynd adds, feeling—best phrased by a writer of Quaker origins—was mounting to Rousseau-style intensity among a people already quite self-aware.

Certainly when the Continental Congress made the ultimate decision to remain colonials and subjects no longer, it selected no different vein of thought, or different kind of speaker, from the volunteer spokesmanship of 1774. Thomas Jefferson and John Adams were both appointed to the committee to draft the Declaration of Independence; Jefferson's work as principal draftsman developed in line with, and in extension of, the ideas he had put down in *A Summary View*. What the Declaration says about George III is not a recital of what the king had done personally but what he had sanctioned as head of state and was responsible for. "The history of the present King of Great Britain is a history of repeated injuries and usurpations, all having in direct object the establishment of an absolute Tyranny over these States. . . . A Prince whose character is thus marked by every act which may define a Tyrant, is unfit to be the ruler of a free people. . . . These United Colonies are absolved from all allegiance to the British Crown." These were hard words about one monarch and one monarchy. Yet they said no more than that king and kingdom had done wrong; they did not say, what Jefferson and Wilson had said about Parliament, that the Crown had had no right to act for America. At the moment of writing the Declaration, the old title of governor was being retained in the newly born states; the office was being cut down merely as to power and duration of tenure. This current cast up no new kingships. But if, among the political deviations which did occur, one or several states had decided to choose a king instead of a governor, and have throne, crown, scepter, and all but absolutism, that king need not have been embarrassed by the Declaration. He could have discovered in it a guidebook, full of philosophy, injunctions and warnings.

What, when Congress announced the United States to the world, were the convictions upon which it chose to seek approbation? A generation ago Professor Carl Becker of Cornell demonstrated that the Declaration is, under the surface of its eloquent and elegant wording, a closely reasoned syllogism.° The major premise, or starting point, of the logic is the "self-evident" truth of a number of propositions. Human equality, and the equality of peoples (or nations), is the main one. The essential propositions are: that all peoples are entitled to "separate and equal station" with all the rest; that "all men are created equal"; that they have "certain unalienable Rights," and "among these are Life, Liberty, and the pursuit of Happiness"; that governments derive from the consent of the governed; that when a government destroys unalienable rights, the governed have a right and duty "to throw off such Government, and to provide new Guards for their future security." The minor premise of the syllogism is the injuries done the colonies by George III. The objectionable events, from 1763 to 1776, are categorized in twenty-seven generalizing, but sharp and staccato, paragraphs. Many of the injuries mentioned are those which began in Parliament, conspicuously taxation without colonial consent and the coercive acts. Several of them, including the closing of the trans-appalachian frontier to settlement and the use of the royal disallowance, trace to the Crown alone.

By the measure of the first premise, the wrongs stated in the second premise did not have to be borne. The conclusion of the syllogism, and of the logic of the Declaration, is stated in the language of contract dissolved: "That these United Colonies are, and of Right ought to be, Free and Independent States; that they are Absolved from all Allegiance to the British Crown, and that all political connection between them and the State of Great Britain is and ought to be totally dissolved; and that as Free and Independent States, they have full Power to levy War, conclude Peace, contract Alliances, establish Commerce, and do all other Acts and Things which Independent States may of right do."

Thanks to Thomas Jefferson, many suppositions of the Enlightenment about politics were incorporated in the Declaration. American independence was represented to the world as a decision reached by men acting under God's law. Equally the decision was represented as made by men acting in self-reliance, on truths which were evident to them and which they expected the people of the world in reason to accept. Confident denial of a king and his kingdom was matched by confident affirmation of the equal value of all peoples, the world around. Sovereignty and nationality in America were saluted with pride. Yet power was welded to freedom and equality. Separated from those values, the independence asserted in the Declaration would have lost its claim on the opinion of mankind.

CHAPTER X

The Principles of
the Revolution

*The American Revolution was not a common event.
Its effects and consequences have already been awful
over a great part of the globe. And when and where
are they to cease?*

*But what do we mean by the American Revolution?
Do we mean the American war? The Revolution was
effected before the war commenced. The Revolution
was in the minds and hearts of the people; a change in
their religious sentiments of their duties and obligations. . . .*

*The people of America had been educated in an ha-
bitual affection for England, as their mother country;
and while they thought her a kind and tender parent,
(erroneously enough, however, for she never was such
a mother,) no affection could be more sincere. But
when they found her a cruel beldam, willing like Lady
Macbeth to "dash their brains out," it is no wonder
if their filial affections ceased, and were changed into
indignation and horror.*

This radical change in the principles, opinions, sentiments, and affections of the people, was the real American Revolution. . . .

*To unite them in the same principles in theory and
the same system of action, was certainly a very difficult
enterprise. The complete accomplishment of it, in so
short a time and by such simple means, was perhaps
a singular example in the history of mankind. Thirteen clocks were made to strike together—a perfection of mechanism, which no artist had ever before
effected. . . .*
John Adams to Hezekiah Niles, February 13, 1818

I   *Commonwealth Ideas Applied*

B Y the time the Declaration of Independence had been offered to the opinions of mankind, a separation of loyalties had occurred in America, with the Patriots on the side of the convictions we have been following and with the Loyalists, at first about equally numerous, on the side of the king. Although the need of deciding for or against independence was past, other decisions, of similar importance for the fulfillment of belief in equality and freedom, arose immediately and demanded action.

In every state the Patriots were obliged to replace with an appropriate republican government the colonial one which independence had destroyed. They had a kind of precedent, as many leaders knew very well, in England's own revolution. After Charles I had been executed, and when the Long Parliament stumbled at revolution, Oliver Cromwell, intervening by force, had done what Americans were now setting out to do in their own way. He had put into effect a commonwealth constitution, the Instrument of Government. Unfortunately for the precedent, the Instrument lasted less than four years, and its failure helped bring on the restoration of the Stuart dynasty. The American states took that kind of risk. But they did so under conditions which, for the short run at least, were favorable. Relieved of their monarch by an act of the pen, the Patriots had no Cromwell and no Ironsides to force their style; neither, for a period of months in 1776, did they have royalist armies to threaten them. From the end of March, when Sir William Howe evacuated Boston, taking a large number of Loyalists to Canada, until July 4, when he occupied Staten Island, nowhere south of Nova Scotia was there a single governor or general acting for George III. Thus during May and June, while Congress was deliberating about independence, and while the burgesses in Williamsburg were preparing a bill of rights and constitution for Virginia, neither the newly sovereign state governments nor their representatives in Philadelphia were threatened by outside force. Even in 1777 and 1778, when the British held both New York and Philadelphia, the meetings of American legislatures were no worse than sometimes obliged to move to a new location; at no time during the Revolution did a general and his army, either Patriot or royal, dictate to a single one. During dark years for independence, 1779 and 1780, Massachusetts, choosing uncommonly deliberate ways, drafted, debated, and ratified a constitution which would become permanent. Operations in the field may, in certain cases, have delayed or speeded the government-building process. They did not stop it or divert it from its intended channels; rather they gave it purpose and meaning.

"For the first time in the history of the world," observes an expert in constitutional history, Edward S. Corwin, "the principles of revolution were made the basis of settled political institutions."° The men of the 1770s sensed equally well the splendor of their opportunity. "In adopting a plan in some respects similar to this," John Adams urged a southern acquaintance concerning his own ideas for state government, "human nature would appear in all its glory, asserting its own real dignity, pulling down tyrannies at a single exertion, and erecting such new fabrics as it thinks best calculated to promote its happiness." Adams's little book of late 1775, *Thoughts on Government*, prepared in the form of a letter, stated the thrill of the occasion: "You and I, my dear friend, have been sent into life at a time when the greatest lawgivers of antiquity would have wished to live. . . . When, before the present epocha, had three millions of people full power and a fair opportunity to form and establish the wisest and happiest government that human wisdom can contrive?"°

If their product were to square with belief that government derives from the people, whoever gathered to write a constitution had to be able to say either that the authority of the people had been delegated to them or else that the document had been submitted to the people or their representatives and had been approved. In several states before 1780, and in every state at some time early in the history of the nation, meetings which called themselves "conventions" did the work. In the early months of the Revolution these meetings were sessions of lower houses of the colonial legislatures as they had been, which were now convened on their own authority—in defiance of, rather than in the name of, the king. This kind of convention, which was known to English history, wrote the constitution of Virginia and made at least temporary provision of separate, sovereign, republican government in several states. In these cases, however, the delegation of authority from the people was too imperfect to satisfy theory: the voters had not chosen their representatives with a purpose to rewrite government, and old inequalities in the franchise created objections to the standing of the constitution as having derived from the people generally. In mid-July 1776, Pennsylvania made itself the first state to avoid such contradictions. By the state election just preceding, the convention was given a clear mandate both to write a state constitution and to serve as a regular legislature. For the Patriot element in the population—which was clearly less than half the total—this was a truly democratic event. Old property qualifications for the franchise were dropped, and the old underrepresentation of frontier areas of the state was corrected. Theory was still unfulfilled, however, for the Loyalist and undecided parts of the population were excluded from franchise and office. The convention, when it gathered, looked a rough lot to many observers— "a democracy of circumstance rather than theory," a modern expert, Elisha P. Douglass, calls the Pennsylvania system of 1776.

The third and final stage of the evolution of the convention as executor of the people's power was reached in 1778. In New Hampshire, where the Loyalists were too few to make a problem like the one in Pennsylvania, a special election chose the convention; the convention was authorized to prepare a constitution but not to enact general legislation, and it was to dissolve when its work was done. First, it was to compose a draft, to be submitted to the town meetings for approval and suggested amendment; then it was to assimilate the responses and produce the final instrument. The first try with this procedure, beginning with a convention in Concord, failed to achieve the necessary agreement; the towns turned down the convention's draft. The second try, which began with a convention at Exeter in 1781, succeeded, after a labor which required more than two years. The slowness of the procedure notwithstanding, the meetings and formulations which began at Concord—New Hampshire would be overtaken by Massachusetts in these matters in 1780—put into actual practice the suppositions that government derives from the people and that a government is made valid by the people's accepting it. Thus the American institution, and the American meaning of the phrase, "constitutional convention," were brought into being; and theory of democracy, which is found everywhere in the thought of the Revolution, took a long step into practical political life.

The Declaration of Independence, an announcement made by the Continental Congress, is often contrasted with the state constitutions, which were drawn by less renowned bodies. The one was intended to defy an empire and has won permanent honor as a charter of freedom and equality; the others were intended to bring life to new republics, and they are vaguely remembered as having been experimental and impermanent. Yet the philosophical basis of the two was identical, and their purposes, completely reciprocal. Jefferson himself would have chosen, had the choice been a personal one, not to go to Philadelphia in June 1776 but to remain in Virginia, to participate in the convention instead. "In truth the drafting of a constitution is the whole object of the present controversy," he wrote to a fellow citizen, "for should a bad government be instituted for us, in future it had been as well to have accepted at first the bad one offered to us."° Even as he yielded to the wish of his colleagues at Williamsburg and departed for Philadelphia to receive his incomparable assignment, he left behind three drafts of a constitution for the convention to consider.

The Declaration of Independence identified old abuses; the conventions laid down guarantees against future abuses. Seven of the new state constitutions were accompanied by a bill of rights, logically if not chronologically prior to the constitution proper. Named after the great document of 1689, on precondition of accepting which William was given the throne of England, they likewise served the purpose of a precommitment, namely, that the state would honor forever the rights of persons and the historic freedoms of the main branches of government. If the American bills of rights were more protective of individuals than was the English prototype, the phrasing more precise, doctrinaire, and pungent, and altogether more available to the common understanding, those differences accorded with their place and their time.°

No comment could convey these qualities as concisely as sample lines from the Virginia bill of rights, exactly as George Mason phrased it. The document was debated and adopted in June 1776, just early enough to be transmitted to Philadelphia and affect the phrasing of the Declaration of Independence. "A Declaration of Rights," it began, "made by the Representatives of the good people of Virginia, assembled in full and free Convention; which rights do pertain to them, and their Posterity, as the basis and Foundation of Government." Article One pronounced, with an emphasis like that soon to appear in Philadelphia, that "all men are by nature equally free and independent, and have certain inherent rights, of which, when they enter into a state of society, they cannot by any compact deprive or divest their posterity, namely, the enjoyment of life and liberty, with the means of possessing and acquiring property, and pursuing and obtaining happiness and safety." Article Two declared "all power" to be vested in, and consequently to derive from, the people, and the magistrates to be the people's "trustees and servants." Article Five laid down that "the Legislative and Executive powers of the state should be separate and distinct from the Judiciary" and that the first two "should, at fixed periods, be reduced to a private station." The other articles all flowed logically in accord with these three. Always in general terms, the people's right "to reform, alter, or abolish" the government and their right to a broadly based franchise, and to the historic English safeguards against abuses in court justice, were strongly affirmed. Climactically the bill asserted the right of the press to freedom and of "all men" to "the free exercise of religion." These two guarantees mark the first incorporation of contemporary ideals into fundamental law. The pledge of an unlimited press presupposed—but did not fix automatically—the end of the law of seditious libel.

The American bills of rights, of which Virginia's was the first, stated principles which the conventions regarded as essential. The constitutions put down operating foundations, in line with those principles, for doing the business of government. Everywhere the idea of separate powers was honored. The constitution of Virginia was even sharper about this than the bill of rights was: "The legislative, executive, and judiciary departments shall be separate and distinct, so that neither exercise the powers rightly belonging to the other." Generally speaking, the revolutionary constitutions strengthened the legislatures to a point well beyond their greatest strength during the colonial period; correspondingly they weakened the executives. The sought-after separation and equilibrium between the two lay in the provisions that each was chosen in frequent elections and that each had its particular functions, related and balanced against the functions of the other. The judiciary was the branch least altered from colonial times; its separateness was the hardest to institutionalize. In revolutionary constitutions, before popular election was more than proposed for the judiciary (except at the lowest level, in a state or two), the judges were either chosen by the legislature, as in Virginia, or nominated by the executive and approved by the legislature; the legislatures set judicial salaries, and the laws they passed controlled many aspects of the work of the judges. In a formal sense their independence had to be based on appropriate salaries and permanence of tenure.

But of course the independence and dignity of the state judges would depend always on larger conditions. Little professionalized though the lawyer yet was in America, clearly he was more and more accepted and honored—in no way so much so as in the leadership he took in the forging of American goals and ideas during the 1760s and 1770s, and in the leadership he was elected to, in the states and the nation during the late 1770s and after. Where Patriot philosophy voiced the operation of law as being the essence of all government, state judges were sure to be honored—as such great ones as George Wythe and Spencer Roane, James Kent and Lemuel Shaw would richly prove.

THE achievements of state reconstruction varied greatly from place to place. The differences can be explained in part by differences of intellectual life and leadership. Where the revolutionists were reform-minded and strong-minded, as they conspicuously were in Virginia and Pennsylvania, heavier drafts were made on the bank of theory than elsewhere. Maryland, though it was quite as open to winds of doctrine as its neighbors, enacted a conservative constitution but altered its habit of religious discrimination: it gave Roman Catholics freedom to vote and to hold government office on the same basis as Protestants. In this vein of comparison, if we take Virginia's constitution as a kind of norm—sharp in cutting back executive power, strong on building up the legislature, fully republican in quality but not far advanced in democratic practice—Pennsylvania, New Jersey, North Carolina, and Georgia set up the memorably radical instruments of government, going toward working democracy; and Maryland and New York set up the memorably conservative ones, with high property qualifications for voting and the holding of office.

Another way of gauging the power of the ideas of the Revolution to change things is to notice the performance of the states according to the size and nature of issues they tackled. At the lower end of this spectrum, Connecticut and Rhode Island had no need for institutional rebuilding. Their charters of the 1660s had allowed them while colonies to govern themselves practically as free commonwealths; after achieving independence from George III they were satisfied to resume self-government on the familiar basis; only formal amendments were needed to make the old charters work as constitutions. At the opposite end of the spectrum appear the largest and most populous states: Virginia, Pennsylvania, and Massachusetts. Culturally and politically different as those three had been while they were colonies, now that they were states their social and political deficiencies were subject to like examination and treatment, according to the standards of equality and freedom recently proclaimed to the world.

In Virginia under its new constitution, the legislature retained the initiative which it had always held. Nor did the annual elections of members, as now instituted, change the ancient custom of the country of choosing, mainly, gentlemen freeholders, men of family and substance, for members.° While the assemblymen did divide into partisan groups, some more advanced, others less so in their revolutionary goals, no such fragmentation occurred as did in England under the Long

Parliament. They maintained a sufficient unity, as the war situation required. Edmund Pendleton, for instance, who led the more conservative-minded, held the office of speaker while his political strength declined. Patrick Henry and Thomas Jefferson, whom the assembly chose the first and the second state governors, and James Madison and George Wythe, all of the reform side, rose in political importance as the 1770s advanced. Although before the decade was out Jefferson and Henry had fallen into a permanent feud, during that period Jefferson and Madison established a deep partnership of mind and spirit which would last until Jefferson's death.

No aspect of the revolutionary system in Virginia was more vulnerable to criticism than its unclear devolution from the people. Jefferson objected to this in the *Notes on Virginia* in 1781 and would do so forty years later. Madison objected on more than one occasion, saying that the fundamental law of the state had not been written by delegates purposely elected for that duty and that the constitution should have been sent to the people for ratification. Yet neither Jefferson nor Madison ever made practical efforts to democratize the vote. The decision of the state convention of 1776, simply to renew the property qualifications which had been the colonial practice, would stand for half a century. Indeed, when a question of the people's capacity to choose their representatives rose between Jefferson and Edmund Pendleton, Jefferson preferred an indirect election of members of the new state Senate instead of the direct election which was actually adopted. "I have ever observed that a choice by the people themselves is not generally distinguished for its wisdom. The first secretion of them is usually crude and heterogeneous. But give to those so chosen by the people a second choice themselves, and they will generally chuse wise men."°

Once the state constitution was working, Jefferson and his colleagues concerned themselves with the reform of law and society, according to the standards of the Enlightenment, rather than with political procedures. A major part of that effort began in the fall of 1776. The assembly created a board of revisors, on which Jefferson, Madison, and Wythe were three of the five members; its assignment was to amend and codify the law of the state in ways fitting to its new sovereignty and purposes. Much of the work was technical and painstaking. Altogether nine years were required, and the drafting and reporting of 126 bills—of which about one hundred were enacted—to bring the task to completion. One recommendation, which voiced the liberal spirit of the enterprise, called for a downward revision of prison sentences; the preamble of that bill indicates that Jefferson had read and accepted ideas about penology from Beccaria and Montesquieu.° In the same direction, but separate from the work of the revisors, Jefferson sought to have enacted a bill for emancipating slaves. The most the assembly would enact was a bill, of 1778, which stopped the importation of Negroes. (Even so, this law preceded by some years anything equal in other Southern States. And the thought, which Jefferson had voiced, that principles of equality demanded an end to slavery, proved during the next few years to have entered the convictions of a sizable number of Virginians. Many manumitted their Negroes by provision of their wills; these documents sometimes used very touchingly the words "liberty" and "equality.")°

Even though Negro slavery involved an injustice which Jefferson hated and revolutionary thought in general did not comfortably tolerate, it rested on a foundation of law developed by the legislature and courts of Virginia and was pretty impregnable there. By contrast, when Jefferson and his colleagues turned to a second area of social injustice, that of land distribution, the law which was brought into question belonged distinctly to English tradition and seemed archaic in America. The particular objects of reform were the law of primogeniture and the law of entail, two usages which, together and separately, could be invoked to prevent the subdivision of an estate at the death of the owner; they sustained in possession one member, or one branch, of a family to the exclusion of all others, possible inheritors or possible purchasers. Altogether they fortified the privileges of the very few and operated without regard for individual or economic merit. So ran the critical view in Virginia, not different from John Adams's complaint against monopolized power and property in the *Dissertation of Canon and Feudal Law*. The assembly enacted the two repeals: the law of entail went down early in the Revolution, and the law of primogeniture when the revisors reported, in 1785. Recent scholarship has discovered that Virginia patricians had relied very little on the old devices; this helps to account for the ease with which the reforms succeeded.° Jefferson seems in this matter to have won a token victory: he seems not to have upset the landlords but to have taken down an old symbol and to have put up a sign for the future, when he feared that land would be scarce. He spoke of his expectations to Bishop James Madison, about the time when primogeniture was defeated: "The earth is given as a common stock for man to labour and live on. . . . It is too soon yet in our country to say that every man who cannot find employment but who can find uncultivated land shall be at liberty to cultivate it, paying a moderate rent. But it is not too soon to provide by every possible means that as few as possible shall be without a little portion of land. The small holders are the most precious part of the state."°

Different from liberal land distribution as a method of reform, but logically connected with it as an effort to deepen the foundations of citizenship, was Jefferson's program of public education for the people of Virginia. Only in New England, so far, had any colony or state undertaken a fixed policy of maintaining schools at public expense. The need was now felt everywhere. Wherever there were colleges from before 1776, the obligation for educational reform and extension was the more recognized and stated; although all the American colleges were of the foundation type which are today called "private," the states where they were located inherited from the colonial past some habit of public support, usually by provision of the legislature. Jefferson, as an alumnus of William and Mary, inherited these traditions. He was participating in a larger than one-state impulse when he asked the general assembly of Virginia to enact a series of laws which would create a complete system of public education, from primary school to the most advanced and professional training.

For the elementary education of all the people, he wanted reading and writing schools, to be gratis for two or three years. He wanted them to be open to girls as well as boys and to be available in every part of the state. To support this part of the system, Jefferson proposed a gridiron of school districts, six miles square. This part of his planning honored by imitation the New England townships, in their school-maintenance function. Beyond the goal of literacy, however, Jefferson's emphasis differed from the northern pattern. Instead of such a family and religious cast as occurred in New England and is represented by the *New England Primer*, Jefferson stressed preparation for citizenship. In the reading schools history was to be read: Greek and Roman, and English and American, history; from this literature the lessons of freedom were to be taught. Jefferson shared with Franklin and many other contemporaries the belief that the study of history opens the mind to the virtues and vices of men and to good systems and bad; but, perhaps more than any other American education reformer, he believed in starting early with that kind of knowledge and morality.

His scheme for secondary training was more nearly traditional. He wanted state-supported grammar schools. He proposed that Latin and Greek be taught, but also English grammar, advanced arithmetic, and geography; in time he decided that surveying and navigation and a variety of modern languages—French, Spanish, Italian, and German— were necessary. On the side of organization, he proposed twenty such schools for the state, each in its own large district. He intended them to be free, like the elementary schools, for a few students selected from those schools; he thought that students who could pay should do so.

For William and Mary, at the top of the pyramid, Jefferson asked release from church control, and government support more generous than under the colony. His goal was to have his alma mater transformed into an institute for higher training, essentially, where future legislators and administrators would be prepared for politics and others for the professions. His scheme called for admitting ten scholarship winners from the secondary schools. The top five were to continue, at state expense, to the highest training for public service; the second five, not less fully maintained but for a shorter period, were expected to become secondary-school teachers.

No single part of Jefferson's program was enacted by the legislature. In the short run he succeeded in just one respect, curriculum change at William and Mary. As visitor of the college he managed to have dropped old professorships in Hebrew, in theology, and in classical languages, and to have new professorships established in medicine, law, and modern languages. Like his land reforms, however, his program of education had, and would continue to have, suggestive significance which transcended the question of immediate application. For all the utopian quality of its arrangements and assumptions, the program was built on a realistic acknowledgment that economic classes exist and are to be altered only gradually. Jefferson's saying that "twenty of the best geniuses will be raked up from the rubbish" sums up the position. Referring to the graduated system of state scholarships, Dr. James R. Conant said in 1962 that Jefferson's selective principle, "viewed as nationwide scholarship policy," is still good education doctrine and is still unfulfilled.° There is no doubt about the ultimate democracy of Jefferson's educational aims, and he should have the final word: "I know no safe depository of the ultimate powers of society but the people themselves; and if we think them not enlightened enough to exercise their control with a wholesome discretion, the remedy is not to take it from them but to inform their discretion by education. This is the true corrective of abuse of constitutional power."°

In the area of the relations of church and state—a critical matter wherever the thought of the Enlightenment reached political influence —Virginia acted early. Thanks to James Madison's insistence, Article Sixteen of the bill of rights committed the state to full religious freedom: "the free exercise of religion, according to the dictates of conscience." With that principle established, the assembly released non-Anglicans from paying church taxes; that action may be called the end of the Church of England establishment in Virginia. But shreds of the institution remained, critical consciences were alerted, and a host of questions arose. Since heresy remained a common-law crime, did the old obligation of the state to punish it still hold, or did the bill of rights eliminate the criminality? Once the Anglican monopoly on church taxes was broken, dissenters who were usually Presbyterians asked, need all church taxes be foregone? Should not a tax be imposed as before, but distributed to several churches in proportions fixed by the preferences of the payers? Whether or not such a solution—a multiple church establishment—could be reconciled with "the free exercise of religion" was the question. That kind of establishment would have honored the old principle that under God church and state sustain each other and are twin institutions. Among the aggressive revolutionaries of Virginia, Patrick Henry was the one leader who favored such a solution.

Jefferson and Madison took the other direction. Jefferson wrote the bill which became the Virginia statute "for establishing Religious Freedom"; Madison worked it through the legislature. Sometimes opposed by Presbyterians and generally by Anglicans, excepting churchmen like Jefferson and himself who at this stage were pretty deistic-minded, and generally supported by Baptists, Quakers, and unbelievers in Christianity, Madison had a hard fight. But when he and his colleagues won, their victory was as clear-cut and categorical as independence had been. The act contained no single line of compromise.°

Its very brief second section contains the substance of the law: "that no man shall be compelled to frequent or support any religious worship, place, or ministry whatsoever." The key word is "support." The same section elaborates: "nor shall [any man] be enforced, restrained, molested, or burthened in his body or goods, nor shall otherwise suffer on account of his religious opinions or belief." Thus were any and all assured that there never would be religious taxes or penalties of any kind enforced against them or for them; the promise was as good for Catholics as for Protestants, for pietists as for churchmen, as good for Jews, or any others, as it was for Christians.

In the statute for religious freedom, the preamble is important, for the passion of Thomas Jefferson illuminates it brilliantly. First the author put down his belief in the goodness of God and in the freedom and goodwill of His creatures. "Almighty God hath created the mind free; . . . that all attempts to influence it by temporal punishments or burthens, or by civil incapacitations, tend only to beget habits of hypocrisy and meanness, and are a departure from the plan of the holy author of our religion, who being lord both of body and mind, yet choose not to propagate it by coercions on either, as was in his Almighty power to do." Second, Jefferson stated the moral frailty he knew to occur in all governments: "Legislator and ruler, . . . themselves but fallible and uninspired men, have assumed dominion over the faith of others, setting up their own opinions and modes of thinking as the only true and infallible, . . . hath established and maintained false religions over the greatest part of the world and through all time." In a third passage, Jefferson resolved the dilemma. True religion is voluntary, for "to compel a man to furnish contributions of money for the propagation of opinions which he disbelieves and abhors is sinful and tyrannical; that even the forcing him to support this or that teacher of his own religious persuasion, is depriving him of the comfortable liberty of giving his contributions to the particular pastor whose morals he would make his pattern." The same sequence of thought separates public morality, the concern of the state, from religious opinion. "Our civil rights have no dependance on our religious opinions, any more than our opinions in physics or geometry. . . . It is time enough for the rightful purposes of civil government for its officers to interfere when principles break out into overt acts against peace and good order." Finally, in the same sequence, Jefferson introduced the proposition that truth is something to be discovered in the meeting and the conflict of ideas, not something which belongs to authority. "Truth is great and will prevail if left to herself, . . . she is the proper and sufficient antagonist to error, and has nothing to fear from the conflict unless by human interposition disarmed of her natural weapons, free argument and debate; errors ceasing to be dangerous when it is permitted freely to contradict them." The third and final section of the act underwrote what preceded, in a very special way. Though the present law is as subject to future repeal as any other act of the assembly, it said, a repeal would be an error. It would be a departure from the law which underlies the enactments of legislatures and alone validates them: "the rights hereby asserted are of the natural rights of mankind, and that if any act shall be hereafter passed to repeal the present or to narrow its operations, such act will be an infringement of natural right."

While the current of conscience in Virginia widened into a delta of reform yet did not demand the people's own participation in affairs, in Pennsylvania an opposite development occurred. Provision for operating democracy proved to be the main story there. It began with the special election of delegates, four days after independence was declared; unfortunately for the authority of the convention, though economic restrictions in the franchise went down, only about six thousand voters took part. One week later, on July 15, the meeting gathered in Independence Hall and put Benjamin Franklin in the chair.

Besides Franklin, one other member bore a public name equal to those of the leaders in Williamsburg during the preceding month. Yet positive likeness of political situation between James Wilson and Thomas Jefferson ends where it begins, with the background fact that their essays of 1774, the *Considerations* and the *Summary View*, contained essentially the same idea. In June, Jefferson absented himself from his state convention but had telling influence on it; in July, Wilson attended his convention but had little effect and disliked most of what occurred. Other distinguished legal minds were conspicuously absent. John Dickinson, who had contributed handsomely to the debate on parliamentary taxation and who would be a delegate to the convention of 1787, was absent; so was Robert Morris, who would become the financier of the Revolution. The two had been among the few members of Congress to vote against independence; temporarily they were out of line with Patriot politics. As for Dickinson and Franklin, the one who had written for colonial autonomy under the Crown had lost sympathy with his constituency and colleagues, and the one who had behind him a quarter century of insurgency had little time or taste for the work of the convention. Franklin had heavy obligations to Congress, between a diplomatic mission completed to England and one coming up, to France; he was ready to leave state reconstruction to other men.

The way was thus wide open to new leadership; and a new group, which is often put down as radical, took over. David Rittenhouse, the self-made mathematician, is the only member who has been mentioned earlier in this book. The other prominent ones were James Cannon and Timothy Matlock, members of the convention, and George Bryan and Dr. Thomas Young, influential advisers of members. Rittenhouse, Matlock, and Cannon were all Philadelphians and were members of institutions which Franklin had founded. Rittenhouse and Matlock were fellows of the American Philosophical Society; Cannon taught mathematics at the College of Philadelphia, and, according to an anti-democratic contemporary, "having little knowledge of man, and scholastic predilection for the antique in liberty, which generally falls to the lot of a pedagogue, he acted accordingly."° These men's advisers were more men of the everyday world than they themselves were. Bryan was a Philadelphia merchant, and probably the only member of the group who had served before in a legislature. Dr. Young, a Hudson River valley medical man and a rationalist, who had acted against the Stamp Act in Albany and had seconded Sam Adams at the Boston Tea Party, represented to the full the intercolonial mobility and excitement of the epoch.

Pennsylvania, as a Quaker colony and a large one, had offered generous hospitality to a host of immigrants and ideas; its system of government, however confused by conflicts, had retained the old advanced Whiggism built into the legislative side by the first lord proprietor. It seems appropriate and continuous with this background that the constitution of 1776 outdid the provincial system in liberalism. Even if a less inexperienced set of legislators had somehow taken charge of the convention, they could hardly have reversed direction. On the focal question everywhere, the nature of the legislature, the constitution carried on the unique unicameral system. The provincial property restriction on voting was removed for the regular elections, as it had been for the special one; the colonial naturalization requirements, which had placed an obstacle in the way of German and other immigrants' becoming politically assimilated, were likewise lifted. Further on the side of the people's participation, categories of local officers, justices of the peace included, were made elective—a new feature of government in America, outside the town officers of New England. Franklin, who thirty years earlier had joined the fight against the authority of the lord proprietor, came up with a pet scheme for keeping the state executive from ever being autocratic, a twelve-man executive council instead of a governor. The convention accepted it.

The innovation and most special feature of the constitution, however, was an invention to institutionalize the idea that constitutional law governs other law. A Council of Censors was created. Patterned on the officers of the republic of Rome for whom it was named, the council was to be elected on an unlimited franchise every seven years and then to make the crucial inquiry, "whether the constitution has been preserved inviolate in every part; and whether the legislative and executive branches of government have performed their duty as guardians of the people, or assumed to themselves, or exercised other or greater powers than they are intitled to by the constitution."

The constitution of 1776 lasted only fourteen years. The criticisms it received, and the fixed reputation it gained for awkwardness and excess of democracy, came to a head with repeal and replacement in 1790, early in the country's Federalist period. Yet the Council of Censors came into action only once, in 1783, and that occasion neither proved nor disproved the merit of having it. Thanks mainly to Dr. Young, the essentials of the constitution were adopted in Vermont by the convention of 1777; the council of censors in that state was to survive until 1870. The constitutional convention of New Hampshire would surpass the censors as a working device, but nothing would surpass it as a symbol, of the fundamental-law idea.

In Massachusetts the achievement of sovereignty brought forward questions which had much in common both with Pennsylvania's political ones and with Virginia's problem of church and state. But Massachusetts of all states entered the Revolution from a recent time of troubles and with habits, second to none, of being independent and articulate. Boston, which had once been the eruptive, then cooling, center of Puritan ideas, had before independence—from the Boston Massacre and the Tea Party on through the battles at Lexington, Concord, and Bunker Hill—been the continental focus of conflict and violence. During those years the protest leadership of the state had passed from the town-meeting speaker and organizer, Sam Adams, to his scholarly and ambitious lawyer cousin, John—Thomas Jefferson's new friend and intellectual peer in Congress. By every reason of situation and momentum, Massachusetts was sure to take hard the domestic changes excited by the national insurgence.

In the process of state making, Massachusetts started with a gift of time. After General Howe's departure, the British troops never returned or seriously threatened the state; the place most sorely tried by the presence of British forces before independence was least harassed after independence. Quite otherwise than in Pennsylvania, Loyalism never became a serious problem. In a degree like Connecticut and Rhode Island, moreover, when independence arrived, Massachusetts had a ready-made government to restore, and the legislature was satisfied to restore it. But the Massachusetts charter of 1691 was much less perfect as a commonwealth constitution than the older charters of the small states adjoining, and in any case the renewal of an old government by an old legislature failed to meet the demands of theory. That such considerations were important became very clear in 1777, when the legislature, the two houses seated together, drafted a constitution and submitted it to the townships. It was defeated by a resounding vote, and Massachusetts made do with the old system for three years longer.

"Examine with candour, my brethren," demanded a pamphleteer from Salem, the original home of critics of Boston, "and you will find a great deal of contemptible, but superstitiously-worshipped rubbish, both in church and state, which has been swept down to us from heathenism and popery by the great net of time. It is now high time to examine the net, cull out the good fishes and cast the bad away." This seaport author may be matched by a parson in the Berkshires, who preached about government in the language of Locke and Sydney. "We have heard much of government being founded in compact," observed Thomas Allen. "What compact has been formed as the foundation of government in this province?"° With the old self-assurance the town meetings of Massachusetts, still often guided by ministers, made declarations. Some of them were pretty visionary. One township called for a one-house legislature and for unrestricted manhood suffrage; Ashfield "voted that we will take the Law of God for the foundation," presumably meaning the Bible, and will seek "No Govrnor but the Govrnor of the Universe, and under him a states-general to consult with the rest of the U.S. for the good of the whole." The most famous complaint of all, one which bore directly on the point of constitutionalism, came from Concord—already the town of the minutemen, not yet that of the philosopher essayists. Passing resolutions proposed by a committee of a shoemaker, two or three farmers, and a Harvard master of arts, the town meeting charged that Massachusetts, after a half year of independence, lacked any "properly established form of government" at all. "A Constitution in its proper idea intends a system of principles established to secure the subjects in the possession and enjoyment of their rights and privileges"; it reasoned further that a constitution needed to be prepared by a convention elected by the "inhabitants" of the state who were "free and twenty-one years of age and upwards" and that it needed to be submitted to them "for inspection and remarks" before being adopted.°

In 1779 the Massachusetts assembly, with New Hampshire's example a year old, itself shifted to the new style of constitution making. Calling a convention for September, it put into action a series of procedures which became the most democratic action on a large scale in American history and perhaps in the history of the West after Athens, up to that moment. It gave the franchise in the special election to adult males; neither a property qualification nor a religious one held for this most basic of all state business. A large body was chosen: of 293 members elected, about 250 (nearly five times the membership of the federal convention of 1787) attended. Thirty members, an unwieldy number, were placed on the drafting committee. The convention began its work with instructions to submit its draft to the townships for review and approval, before it took the final act of ratification.

The size of the drafting committee invited individual leadership, and this created John Adams's opportunity and Massachusetts's gain. The colleague working with Jefferson on the Declaration of Independence whom Jefferson had called "the pillar of its support on the floor of Congress," Adams had arrived home in 1779 from diplomatic duty in France, barely in time to be elected to the convention. There were few services a Massachusetts man could have rendered his government which he had not already rendered: member of the House of Representatives before the Tea Party, delegate to both the First and Second Continental Congress, after 1776 chief justice of the state's Superior Court of Judicature. Even while the convention of 1779 was meeting, he was assigned a new diplomatic mission, and he departed before the review of the constitution by the towns. Besides his eminence, he brought to the meeting as thorough a mastery of the history and theory of politics as any American had. Late in 1775 when, writing the *Thoughts on Government* for friends who at the moment were more concerned with state building than he was, he referred to his debts in political thought, "the names of Sidney, Harrington, Locke, Milton, Needham, Neville, Burnet and Hoadly" came first to his mind. At that stage, when he considered the always-first question of the legislature, his inclination was democratic, in that he wanted legislators to represent all the people accurately and in detail. Yet he wanted restraint also, as the following passage indicates:

> The principal difficulty lies, and the greatest care should be employed, in constituting this representative body. It should be in miniature an exact portrait of the people at large. It should think, feel, reason, and act like them. . . . Equal interests among the people should have equal interests in it. . . . At present, it will be safest to proceed in all established modes, to which the people have been familiarized by habit.

The next year, in Philadelphia, he told Tom Paine, face to face and "in good humour" he says in his *Autobiography*, that *Common Sense* was "so democratical, without any restraint or an Attempt at any Equilibrium or Counterpoise, that it must produce confusion and every Evil Work." He suffered a like reaction against the Pennsylvania Patriot democrats, Matlock, Cannon, and Dr. Young; he charged them with having led their state into "Systems of Anarchy." Where Paine and the Pennsylvania democrats wanted to activate the people, Adams wanted to match interest against interest in politics and to retain valid tradition, with the thought that this would stabilize government.°

It was precisely along the lines of John Adams's philosophy that the Massachusetts constitution was written. Although, unlike Virginia and Pennsylvania, the assembly was balanced by a strong executive—a governor with a veto and with authority to make judicial and other appointments—it would be wrong to conclude that this signified a weak legislature in Massachusetts. Rather, an unusually spacious government was outlined, and the House of Representatives and Senate, placed at center, were created strong, by reason of their functions. Against John Adams's strong disinclination, the church-state relationship was allowed to continue; according to his wish, Harvard College was guaranteed its old authorities and privileges, and a clause of the constitution specified that government should foster literature and science and "good humour" in the state. Such stipulations kept areas open for state undertakings intended to guide the people—as had been familiar in the epoch of Puritanism and mercantilism and might again prove useful.

After the constitution and a bill of rights much like Virginia's were drafted (and John Adams had sailed for France), they were sent according to instruction to the people in town meeting for discussion and suggestion, approval or disapproval. While the purpose of this procedure is clearly Lockian, as it was designed to act out the contract theory of government, and was democratic in the sense of John Adams's wish to build realistically on the needs and opinions of the people, the procedure itself raised difficulties and paradoxes. It opened the way to receiving multiple and disparate responses from the towns— as did occur—and so to making a muddy contract. An even greater paradox was built into the pyramid of property qualifications which the constitution set for voting and holding office. Joseph Hawley, prominent lawyer and public man of Northampton, put his finger on the contradiction. "The right of enjoying that equality, freedom, and liberty is . . . declared unalienable," he said of the bill of rights, approvingly; then, referring to the unequal suffrage clause in the constitution, he added, "Very strange it would be if others should have a right . . . to take away from any individual that which he could not alienate." The humor of the situation returned from the town of Middleboro, which asked, concerning the thousand-pound property requirement to hold the office of governor, what if the voters chose a governor worth £999?° Across the state all issues were debated and elaborate recommendations to the convention drawn up, town meeting by town meeting, during winter months. The franchise clause drew the most objections, but passed; so did the clause which enabled the legislature to give tax support to several churches, according to the designation of the payers in their townships.

In a large way, the story is a romantic one, of village democracy at a high level of understanding and seriousness. A convention chosen by the people labored; the people considered in detail and, ultimately approving, committed themselves to a strong government. They did so with open self-denial: they chose church taxes when they might have chosen relief from them, and they accepted future property limitations on participating in government. A generation ago, Samuel Eliot Morison, after re-examining the facts, reduced the romantic impression: he discovered that in some cases the official reports from the townships exaggerated the votes taken in favor of approval and that therefore in some degree, perhaps not decisive, the ratification was fraudulent. Recently J. R. Pole has reduced the legend in another way, by saying that the new American states, John Adams's Massachusetts included, persisted in old English habits of deference to authority; he sees that character in the Bay State's commonwealth constitution. And Robert E. Brown has pleaded with effect that property was so distributed in eighteenth-century Massachusetts that the state was born with a substantial degree of economic democracy, and the suffrage requirement— whether just before or just after the Revolution—excluded few adult males from voting. After these kinds of reconsideration, Massachusetts's revolutionary-period ideas of equality and freedom seem more qualified and less demanding than they once seemed, but no less elaborately acted out and confirmed, by making the constitution.°

We may try to summarize in one sentence the efforts of the three largest states to match their fundamental law and policy with the ideas of the Revolution. It does appear: that Virginia, which started with the oldest parliamentary tradition, enacted the least political reform but reached the furthest toward egalitarian changes in law, church, and society; that Pennsylvania, which began with maximum social and religious freedom but with little-consolidated political traditions, tried to bring politics into close line with doctrine and reached beyond firm grasp; and that Massachusetts, which began with the most coherent system of any, in society, religion, and politics, but which had suffered unusual upset from England, founded its new government uniquely deep in the theory and practice of consent, and built the most imposing structure.

3 Federalism and the Control of Power

IN the modern history of the West, the United States Constitution is recorded as one of the great beginning points. Thereafter came those new officers, the presidents, the cabinets and the congresses, the Supreme Court, the army and the navy—first the structure and in time the fulfillment of American power. During the troubled 1930s Alfred North Whitehead stirred young men at Harvard, where he was teaching, about the glory of 1787, by making an unfamiliar comparison. "I know of only two occasions in history when the people in power did what was needed to be done about as well as you can imagine its being possible. One was the framing of your American Constitution. They were able statesmen, they had access to a body of good ideas; they incorporated these principles into the instrument without trying to particularize too explicitly how they should be put into effect; and they were men of immense practical experience themselves. The other was in Rome . . . [when Augustus] called in the 'new men' of new ideas."[o]

The English philosopher was tremendously right when he said that the men of the Philadelphia convention "were men of immense practical experience themselves." Whoever estimates at life size the task of drawing up fundamental law in the states during the 1770s, and who considers that during the 1780s three nationwide churches were organized, each with a constitution, and that territories were set up in the Old Northwest, recognizes that, in the history of putting ideas to work, the federal Constitution, from which so much would follow, itself came at the crest of a wave. Many statesmen who had sat in the state conventions, or who had otherwise contributed to establishing the thirteen new or revised governments, served also in the convention of 1787. A continuity of problem, theory, and solution occurred.

To be sure, as has been said so often that the emphasis has been overdone, several of the major spokesmen for independence in 1776 were not heard from in 1787 or 1788 or were heard in opposition to the Constitution. Samuel Adams, who had served on the drafting committee of the Massachusetts convention of 1779 and had since then been a state senator, was two-minded about federalism; Patrick Henry was opposed. Thomas Jefferson and John Adams were both overseas in 1787 and 1788, but they were no more than physically absent. Adams on Grosvenor Square was greatly concerned about the drift of things at home. He published his hastily composed first volume of the *Defence of the Constitutions of the United States of America*—an elaborate justification from comparative history—early enough in 1787 to make a newspaper splash before the Philadelphia convention. It was a plea for maintaining checks and balances, always; it may have served the members of the convention in somewhat the same way as his *Thoughts on Government* had served friends concerned with state constitutions, but it was not so closely an *ad hoc* argument, and its influence in Philadelphia is doubtful.° Jefferson, whose experience as diplomat had made him alert to his country's need for a national government with strength, and who at this stage was more advanced than Adams as political nationalizer, followed the news from home as closely as he could. The *Federalist* essays and the letters he received from Madison, after the convention was over, were what pleased him most. He would not have been Jefferson if he had not regretted the absence from the Constitution at first of a national bill of rights. But his often-cited words about the instrument when he saw it, "unquestionably the wisest ever yet presented to me," came from the heart.

Besides Madison, three other Virginia delegates to the Philadelphia convention had participated in the state convention of 1776: Edmund Randolph, who introduced the Virginia, or "large state," plan and later wobbled about federalism; George Wythe, who had been chancellor of Virginia and professor of law at William and Mary for nearly a decade and was now firmly federalist in principle; and George Mason, who spoke frequently and well at Philadelphia and influenced the work, but who ended in opposition principally because of the absence of a bill of rights. In the Massachusetts delegation of four, one was Caleb Strong, who had served on John Adams's drafting committee of 1779, and who placed more confidence than Adams did in the people as participators in government. From Pennsylvania, Benjamin Franklin, who had been chairman of the 1776 state convention, was a delegate; so were James Wilson, who had opposed that constitution, and Gouverneur Morris, who had helped make the New York one conservative. From other states: George Read, who had been moderate and central in making the Delaware constitution, spoke for the small states at Philadelphia but ended Federalist; among the South Carolina delegates, John Rutledge, distinguished and conservative lawyer, had served on the committee which prepared the constitution of the state. Besides those who had been state constitution makers or closely involved, eighteen or twenty other members of the Philadelphia convention had served their state in some prominent way, several of them as members of Congress, more an ambassadorial than a legislative assignment. Altogether a majority of the fifty-five men of the 1787 convention had previously counted either as authors or as servants, or both, of the twelve sovereign republics which had sent them—Rhode Island alone held out—to Philadelphia.

Again like the state conventions, the Philadelphia one was overwhelmingly civilian in make-up and mind. Except for Thomas Mifflin of Pennsylvania, who had retired early from the American army and who had none too creditable an administrative record, George Washington was the only general in the convention; there were several war veterans, Alexander Hamilton one of them, but no such thing as a military or veterans' bloc. Three-fifths of the members were lawyers; one-third were farmers, nearly all on a large scale; a scattering were physicians, businessmen, and retired men, including Benjamin Franklin. Their property holdings, real and personal, and the possible bearing of those holdings on the economic clauses which were placed in the Constitution, became the subject, a century and a quarter after the convention, of Charles A. Beard's famous book, *An Economic Interpretation of the Constitution of the United States*. Although Beard's classic was resisted during the Wilson epoch as being too class-conscious and materialistic, then widely accepted during the years between the first and second World Wars, its logic and use of evidence underwent a stiff re-examination during the 1950s, and today it is in reduced situation.° So, at least for the time being, is any economic interpretation of the general purpose and meaning of the Constitution. In that vein we are pretty well down to three propositions: first, that the authors of the Constitution at Philadelphia were chosen almost exclusively from the well-to-do, best-educated, senior, and experienced men available; second, that they were alarmed by the recent insurrections in Massachusetts (Shays's Rebellion), were anxious not to have other such outbreaks occur, and were desirous of making an appearance of economic stability before the world; and third, that they wanted property rights protected and wished the government they were designing to promote economic activity within the prevailing, unquestioned system of business and farming. But of course these three propositions would apply with equal truth to the Virginia convention of 1776 and to several other state conventions. The time has come to abandon any residue of the old exaggeration that, for public men and thinkers, the 1770s were a time for freedom and the 1780s a time for organization. Both needs were felt, at both times. The difference between the intellectual qualities required of constitution makers, in 1776 and in 1787, was more like the difference between the talent which starts an undertaking and that which completes one—between special daring and special determination.

Examining the federal Constitution to discover what large principles of the use of power were drawn on, we find three which underlie all the rest. Two were the same as in the state constitutions: that political power derives from the people; and that power, once brought into the machinery of government, needs to be kept in working equilibrium among the principal branches of government, by the system of checks and balances. The third underlying principle was that sovereign power in the United States, which for a dozen years had belonged to the separate states, should be rationally and permanently divided between the national and the state governments—the principle of plural, or multiple, sovereignty.

Only one theory about where sovereignty comes from was entertained by Americans during the eighteenth century. "We, the people of the United States," said the opening words of the instrument, "do ordain and establish this Constitution." At the end, seven articles later, one short sentence prescribed how the people should actually bring about the ordaining and the establishing: "The ratification of the Conventions of nine states shall be sufficient for the establishing of this Constitution between the States so ratifying the same." Thus the framers of the Constitution referred their work for validation to a series of constituent bodies much like those called into existence by the Revolution in New Hampshire and Massachusetts. The method for making changes in the Constitution, moreover, offered the same recourse. After providing that amendments can be introduced either by a two-thirds vote of Congress or by the concurrence of the legislatures of two-thirds of the states, Article V sets forth that an amendment is enacted when approved in three-quarters of the states, either by their legislatures or by special conventions—the choice of procedure to be made by Congress. In the short time span of revolutionary history, Article V signified there having been incorporated into the Constitution the principle that either the method which Virginia (and other states) had employed in 1776, or the one used in northern New England a few years later, suffices to enact fundamental law. Altogether the Constitution of 1787, which generally speaking is very short on stated theory, is completely committed to the theory of government by consent and to the new convention procedures of establishing what has been consented to.

Yet, compared to the conventions which wrote the state constitutions, the convention at Philadelphia occupied an ambiguous position in which to draw on democratic doctrine. The members of the state conventions of the 1770s were elected by the voters of a familiar constituency, which sometimes was quite democratic. By contrast, before 1787 there was no national constituency in any operating sense at all. The members of the Philadelphia convention had been chosen and instructed by the state legislatures; they voted in state units; they were authorized to prepare amendments to the Confederation, which was a league of states. Narrowly speaking they had no more right to propose an entirely new structure of union than any meeting of citizens might conceivably have claimed. Their justification then as now was that they had made a proposal of merit and importance to the country, and one which accorded with needs and cherished ideals.

In *The Federalist*, number thirty-seven, Madison records the thrill the convention experienced when it discovered that a sufficient agreement had been reached. The fifty-five framers, he tells us, put together their document, finally, "with a unanimity almost as unprecedented as it must have been unexpected"; he thought it "impossible for a man of pious reflection not to perceive in [their work] a finger of that Almighty hand which has been so frequently and signally extended to our relief in the critical stages of the revolution." Doubtless the "We, the people" phrase is to be accounted for, in part, as an expression of patriotic exhilaration. In that reading it accords with the increasing use in America of the word "nation" (which does not appear in the Constitution); it accords also with such neologisms as "Americanism" and "Fellow countrymen!"—which was itself an Americanism.° When James Wilson in a splendid address before the Pennsylvania ratifying convention said, "I consider the people of the United States as forming one great community," he was voicing an intuition of nationality which the Philadelphia convention itself helps justify, though the origins of the convention had been strictly within the framework of state affairs.

Equal to the awkwardness between the original purposes of the Philadelphia convention and its ultimate product, a second and equal awkwardness appears. The preamble and Article V specifically indicate reliance on the people; yet the fathers of the Constitution, most famously the three authors of *The Federalist*, Alexander Hamilton, James Madison, and John Jay, said a great deal which displays reluctance to trust them, up to the point of active mistrust. Though the anxieties of Hamilton have often been overstated and he has been misquoted at times, we do not need to review his special case here;° we come closer to the common denominator of anxiety if we sample Madison's warning about how a people's decisions are made. His *Federalist* essay, number ten, which Beard justly celebrated, conceives the voters as activated by self-interest, primarily economic; he discussed them as a driven, rather than as a reasoning, lot. And in number thirty-seven, just quoted for its testimony of final good feeling in Philadelphia, Madison took a different tone when he discussed what he believed to be the usual course of politics in groups. In his own words: "The history of almost all the great councils and consultations held among mankind . . . is a history of factions, contentions and disappointments, and may be classed among the most dark and degraded pictures which display the infirmities and depravities of the human character." When Madison thought of the masses in politics he took comfort, as John Adams did, from expecting that groups and interests, competing in society, would cancel out one another.

Yet the fear of some of the authors of the Constitution—that government by the people would be likely to mean trouble—does not signify that they disbelieved in the people; it means only that confidence came hard. Benjamin F. Wright, a student of eighteenth-century political ideas in America, has pointed out what a splendid compliment Hamilton, Madison, and Jay paid the people, simply by writing *The Federalist* essays for New York newspaper publication. Addressing the voters and the members of the state's ratifying convention and stating their fears for the future with candor, they produced, in the form of eighty-five open letters, the best treatise yet on federalism. They wrote in a practical vein. About a dozen essays, by Hamilton, concentrated on the presidency, the powerful and unprecedented new headship of state; many of the essays developed the need for defense, the problem which the British Empire had failed to solve; others appealed to commercial and other interests which would gain from interstate union and trade. *The Federalist* essays were written under pressure; the three authors had differences of inclination and little time to consult; nowhere did they attempt a philosophical analysis. Yet the essays voiced the writers' philosophy, in the eighteenth-century sense of that word: their common feeling for history, their belief that power can be created by organization and be used for good, and their special hopes for their country. In one of Madison's more confident passages: "It may be pronounced with assurance that the people of the country, enlightened as they are with regard to the nature, and interested, as the great body of them are, in the effects of good government, will never be satisfied with the vicissitudes and uncertainties which characterize the State administrations."

The crucial evidence on the question of whether the Constitution brought to wider life the principle of consent and the practice of government by the people is to be found, as Wright insists, in the ratifying conventions in the states, which were required by Article VII.° The shortcomings of the conventions, measured on an ideal scale of democracy, were many and complex. With the striking exception of New York, the conventions were elected on the basis of whatever property qualification for the franchise the state had adopted for regular assembly elections; the federalists, who seized the initiative naturally, had advantages of wealth, and of influence on the newspapers, which created pressures far out of proportion to their numbers. Yet when the state ratifying conventions are viewed, as Article V requires that they be, as a national series of elections, debates, and votes on the Constitution, they gain in stature. They were a nationalization and an adjustment of the procedure which New Hampshire and Massachusetts had begun; by the standard of those two states they were short on direct reference to the people but were equal to them in their specific, *ad hoc*, authority. Ratifying-convention debates reached a high level. In Virginia, Madison and Wythe and young John Marshall spoke for ratification; Patrick Henry and George Mason spoke against. The conventions as a series brought off a referendum of the country which, although it was not based on universal suffrage and although its accuracy, as a reflection of what the majority may be supposed to have wanted, is more than questionable, was yet liberal by any known standard and was the first in the history of the West.°

The second grand conception about power which was built into the Constitution, the principle of equilibrium made good by checks and balances, requires no more than mention in this book. Lacking that principle, the Constitution, as a deed of gift of power to the national government, would have been out of character with the state contsitutions and with common belief and would surely have been refused ratification. The objection which Patrick Henry pressed, that the plan of national government aggregated too much power, arose among anti-federalists generally and has been a serious question for thought and debate from 1787 to the present, with a famous climax of the discussion in 1861. Yet by reason of its design for equilibrium among separate, inner, locations of power, the United States Constitution is spared modern criticism of the kind to which twentieth-century power aggregations are so often vulnerable—as being "monolithic," or undifferentiated, in its structure of power.

As is too familiar for many words, main attention in the federal Constitution, as in the state constitutions, is given to the legislative branch. Article I, which instituted Congress, is longer than the six other articles together. The names of the two houses, the Senate and the House of Representatives, followed the Massachusetts precedent of 1780; the powers of Congress, as defined in Section 8 and elsewhere, though circumscribed, were large at the time. On the other side of the principal line of balance, the executive, again as in Massachusetts, was assigned authority to make appointments and was given a veto over bills passed by Congress. These and other high powers, like treaty making, echoed powers exercised by the Crown before 1776. Since monarchy offers the only analogy with the authority designed for the president, the device of the electoral college, which was created to transmit power to him at four-year intervals, seems a particularly vivid enactment of the Philadelphia convention's mixture of confidence and fear about deriving power from the people and placing it in mortal and fallible hands.

On the side of the judiciary, effort was made, as in the state constitutions, to give the judges maximum freedom. The justices of the Supreme Court, and their colleagues on lower courts left to be created, were assigned elevated duties. The authority which the Supreme Court would establish after fourteen years, to invalidate an act of Congress if it were found incompatible with the Constitution, we may agree was implicit in Article III, although it was not spelled out in the Constitution anywhere. All federal judges were given tenure during good behavior. But not being elected they did not have independence on the same footing as the president and Congress. They depended on the president for nomination to office and on Congress for salary schedule and for some of the arrangement of duties.

In sum, the three branches as simultaneously created were each given spacious areas for the exercise of power. The Congress was assigned much more scope than Parliament had ever ventured in America, up to 1774; it was not given such powers as Parliament did venture in that year, to transform or destroy state government. The president was given more power than the Crown had ever practically executed, except that he had no equivalent of the royal authority to appoint provincial officers and disallow provincial laws. The Supreme Court was given wider jurisdiction than the Privy Council had exercised in America, in its role as a court of review. The overwhelming difference between the old system and the new was that in the republic the three branches were specifically planned to check one another—as George III had not checked Parliament; nor Parliament, nor Privy Council, the king.

The third major principle of the Constitution's design for power, also its essence and its great innovation in the history of government, was federalism—variously called "divided sovereignty" and "plural" or "multiple sovereignty." This is the aspect of public thought where the classical and historical learning of the fathers had freest play. That learning had some relevance throughout. One readily supposes, though the point might be impossible to prove, that admiration for Aristotle's *Politics* and *Ethics* help explain the office of president, which especially calls for a gifted and balanced leader. One senses likewise that the fathers' familiarity with Polybius's account of elements of monarchy, aristocracy, and democracy in the politics of the Roman republic contributed to their own belief in checks and balances. But when the question is the constitution makers' knowledge of the relationships of the Greek city-states with one another, and with their colonies, one gets a more definite and specific impression. Long before 1787, colonial and revolutionary-period newspaper essays often expressed the jealous idea that ancient Athens once treated colonies as being politically equal to itself. The Achaean League and the Amphictyonic councils of Greece, the Lycian League of Asia Minor, and so on were known and searched for precedents by Americans.°

This background seems to have helped state the questions to be solved more than it helped to reveal answers to American problems.

One trouble was that the scholarly statesmen knew their Montesquieu as well as they knew their Polybius and their Plutarch. Although they rejected the French scholar's dictum that republican government fits city-states and not large nations, they pretty well made the assumption he did, so far as the lessons of the ancient world could be read. Alexander Hamilton wrote to this point, in his "Continentalist" essays of 1782: "We are laboring hard to establish in this country principles more national and free from all foreign ingredients, so that we may be neither Greeks nor Trojans, but truly American. . . . [It would be] as ridiculous to seek for models in the small ages of Greece, as it would be to go in quest of them among the Hottentots and Laplanders." More than likely their knowledge of the ancient confederations helped Americans not to count too heavily on their own Confederation; it seems to have supplied no suggestion at all about how to weld a system of autonomy and national organization to replace the system they had destroyed.

Lacking precedents ancient or modern, the authors of the Constitution found guidance, Robert Livingston Schuyler has tellingly suggested, from the history of their own failure of 1774.° At the time of that deeply felt crisis, when Parliament set out to topple the government of Massachusetts and coerce the colonies as a whole, and when the lawyers James Wilson, Thomas Jefferson, and John Adams came forward with pamphlets, the idea of multiple sovereignty was born but not named. Its features were clear: one national system (under the Crown), a national legislature with restricted power (Parliament), many other legislatures with equal powers (the assemblies), each one supreme in its own area. For several years the idea had no way to take hold. Before independence, while Parliament insisted on its overseas sovereignty, plural sovereignty was a defeated idea, and it had no service to render. After 1776, independence created multiple sovereignties, one in each state, but no system of multiple sovereignty. Of course the Continental Congress, both before and after the Articles of Confederation were adopted, did in fact exercise substantial authority; but it began and ended as the central body of a confederation, not quite sovereign in practice and not at all so in theory, lacking derivation from the people.

Yet by the middle 1780s a practical exception had entered and was beginning to be fruitful of thought. One of the weightiest aspects of royal sovereignty had been the Crown's control of its huge but unsettled transappalachian domains. Now by process of devolution—that is, by George Rogers Clark's conquest of 1778, by the departure of such royal administration as had been built up after 1763, and by the states' surrendering to the Confederation their charter claims to western lands—the Confederation did in fact become sovereign in the Old Northwest, though not anywhere east of the mountains. A resolution offered by James Madison, as early as 1780, shows the idea of plural sovereignty coming to actual life. He moved the Congress that the western domains "be settled and formed into distinct republican states," which would become members of the United States and have the same rights of sovereignty, freedom, and independence as the seaboard states. The same idea recurred with enlargements in the famous congressional ordinances of 1784, 1785, and 1787. The first was a proposal of Thomas Jefferson to have fourteen new republics, each with a Greek-sounding name, set up in the Old Northwest; the point of the ordinance was equal sovereignty for new states—Greek principle as well as Greek names. The more famous land ordinance of the next year carried to the planning for the Old Northwest some of Virginia's reform ideas: an equitable distribution of land and the assignment of public domain to support schools. But only in the Northwest Ordinance of 1787, the dying act of the Confederation, was the idea of multiple sovereignty fleshed out—plural sovereignty as a national system for the future. There in one liberal document was the commitment: full statehood equal to any, once the Northwest territories were settled and ready; within the entire area, first, tutelage in territorial government, and—in a new society under new law—freedom of worship, jury trial, all the honored usages of due process, equal inheritance among the children of intestate property holders, no slavery. In sum, the Confederation promised future western colonies of the United States such equality and freedom as the original states had themselves been denied when colonies, and had had to fight to begin to achieve.

The Philadelphia convention renewed the commitment and, by reason of its larger work, enlarged the commitment as well. Objections were raised by Gouverneur Morris and Elbridge Gerry from large northern states, but support came from James Wilson, and from George Wythe and other liberal Virginians. By Article IV, Sections 3 and 4, the Constitution made multiple sovereignty more than a compact of recent allies, among themselves and for themselves, and more than a gift to the upper Ohio River valley. It made a promise unlimited in time that new states entering the Union, no matter how far distant from the Atlantic seaboard, would always have sovereignty equal to the old states, and a just representation in the national government, as a matter of fundamental law. As an institutional commitment which marked a clear break with European habits of treating outlying, newly settled domains, this was the most confident act of faith in the people which was taken at Philadelphia.

DURING the 1920s, a decade of revolution in Europe and reaction at home, John Franklin Jameson, then the dean of American historians, in four beautiful lectures advanced the uncommon opinion that the Revolution of 1776 brought about sizable elements of economic and social change. His ideas, published under the general title, *The American Revolution Considered as a Social Movement*, were that the Revolution amounted, more than its beneficiaries had begun to realize, to a domestic transformation, somewhat analogous to the French and the Russian revolutions, and that it needed understanding as something more and other than a violent political schism from England, though that was the principal thing. Jameson's evidence included the separating out of Loyalists, a painful social process; the reduction of feudal elements in landholding; the separation of church from state; and certain humanitarian and literary indications. Following Jameson, in the pendulum way of scholarship, first, before 1940, a sizable body of historical studies introduced much new evidence of social change; and, second, after World War II, interpretation reversed. The gradual social changes of the colonial period helped bring on independence and were confirmed by it, the findings of recent years have said; but the Revolution itself instituted few inner changes in American life. The recent transnational comparative study by Robert R. Palmer, *The Age of the Democratic Revolution*, renders a middle verdict. Measured on the scale of the many revolutionary and reform actions in the world of the West, geographically from Poland to Georgia and chronologically from 1760 to 1800, the American Revolution marks a high degree of democracy and a low degree of sudden change, Palmer finds.°

The problem which Jameson opened could be entitled in the history of history, "How socially revolutionary was the American Revolution?" Our present problem of summarization is a facet of that large problem; it could be restated, using more words than the heading of this section, "How great were the promises of freedom, equality and reorganization, which were written into American law and belief?" Where the scholarly debate has been focused, mainly, on the immediate substance of social change, our need is to consider the dimensions of the new commitments. What did the liberating ideas, built into all the constitutions and bills of rights, actually pledge?

As to the promises of freedom, they were broad and yet not far out of line with the practice of the age. On the point of the relations of the state with religion, Connecticut and New Hampshire joined

Massachusetts in continuing tax support for Congregationalist and other churches designated by statute. In this religiously cultivated corner of the republic the least change occurred. As in late-colonial days, extreme dissenters and unbelievers, who received none of the pecuniary benefits of multiple church support, had at least the minimum benefit of being left alone. In Massachusetts and New Hampshire universal freedom of worship was inscribed in the bills of rights. The full principle of religious freedom would have swept away all church taxes, but though not enacted it had received a wider public hearing than before in Puritan land. Baptists, Quakers, rationalists, and many Congregationalists were now committed to the principle; it would never be quieted until the age of Jackson, when it would be crowned with success. In New York and the Southern States where there had been Anglican church establishments, all except those of Virginia and South Carolina went down in unresisting collapse. In Maryland, by the new bill of rights, religious liberty was granted all Christians. (The phrasing suggests that no other faith was considered; in a practical sense none needed to be, for Maryland deists would hardly have denied Christianity, and unless there were already a few Jews in Baltimore there were probably none anywhere in the state.) With that change Roman Catholics were admitted to politics, as they had not been since the special, and broad, toleration policy of the province before 1689. Although several states retained in law bits of the old preferences—such as the pledge required of officeholders in two states, that they were Protestant—such residues can have worked few actual exclusions from office. Thus, when the national government was launched in 1789 there was much practical force in the argument, used broadly against having a federal bill of rights, that no national guarantee of freedom was needed or appropriate. Yet the promise was nationally made. The phrase of the first amendment, which forbade forever a national "establishment of religion," placed in the federal Constitution a conviction which was widespread; it prohibited nothing which at the time would, without that amendment, have had the remotest possibility of being enacted.°

Less close to accepted use were the pledges in the bills of rights, state and federal alike, which protected freedom of speech and assembly as rights that are universal, belonging to every man. Beginning with the enormous number of public meetings which occurred in 1765 —and with events of that year and later which transformed the producers of colonial newspapers into leaders of opinion—voluntary speech, free assembly, and a voluntary press had been the very life of the revolutionary movement. Freedom of the press, new in history as a constitutional right when it was adopted by Virginia and Pennsylvania in 1776, was incorporated with equal boldness into the first federal amendment. By that decision the fundamental law of the nation, like that of some of the states, rose grandly different from the common law of seditious libel, not with automatic power to destroy that law, but quite contrary to it in spirit. Freedom of the press was a decision of self-denial by the governments which passed it; it indicates a supposition that, once the Revolution was over and America was fully on its own, no restriction of the press would ever be needed again.

The prime application of the doctrine of equality during the Revolution was of course the one in the Declaration, concerning the people, or nation. The American people as an entity demanded to be recognized as being the equal of any other people in the world. The equality of individuals, however, though resoundingly stated in the "All men are created equal" phrase, was a less sought-after and little-institutionalized goal. During the Revolution, as during the nineteenth century and after, that doctrine challenged the status of the Negro. South of Pennsylvania, following Virginia by about a decade, Maryland, North Carolina, and South Carolina, in that order, restricted the slave trade. State action in the region went no further; the federal Constitution denied Congress authority to foreclose the slave trade before the year 1808, a concession to the Southern States. North of Maryland, naturally, the equalitarian idea had more effect. Although the Massachusetts constitution made no specification against slavery, in the famous Quock Walker case when the state government was three years old, the Superior Court heard the argument that the constitution had already eliminated slavery in its "born free and equal" phrase, and decided that way. Vermont excluded slavery by constitutional law. Connecticut and Rhode Island passed gradual abolition laws; so did Pennsylvania, partly because of Quaker persuading. In these ways, well before the Constitution was adopted, the promise of equality began to have its morally leavening effects.

Nor is it too much to say, Winthrop Jordan tells us, that revolutionary thought abraded, as well as American complacence about slavery (and even the life of the institution where there were very few slaves), the component of white racial superiority in the assumptions of that age. The reasons why emancipations and manumissions were limited in number lay less in a lack of sharpness than in a shortness of reach of the cutting-edge idea of equality at that time. Americans of the 1770s and 1780s more often saw what was wrong than foresaw how to do right, concerning the condition of the blacks, who were barely beginning to speak for themselves. Jefferson's uneven notions about the racial talents and limitations of Negroes inhibited rather than altered his antislavery. In *The Federalist* itself, number fifty-four, Madison phrased the unhappy mixture of positions in the Constitution that Negroes as slaves were both persons and property. "They partake of both these qualities. . . . Let the compromising expedient of the Constitution be mutually adopted, which regards them as inhabitants, but *as debased by servitude* below the equal level of free inhabitants, which regards the *slave* as divested of two fifths of the *man*."°

For a final view of how contemporary thought understood the reorganization of English-speaking America—colonies into states, and British colonial system into federal republic—we may turn to *The Federalist*, especially number nine, written by Alexander Hamilton. He and Madison used figures of speech from astronomy. Madison spoke of balance in the system, not simply in the check-and-balance operations within the state and the national governments but along a "line of demarkation" between central and state governments. Hamilton developed elaborate analogies with the solar system. In a passage in number nine, wherein he sought to answer Montesquieu's belief that republics to be true to their nature must be small, he pleaded for "the ENLARGEMENT of the ORBIT within which such systems are to revolve." In a passage on the problem of political stability, which he believed always rises with "every political association which is formed on the principle of uniting in common a number of lesser sovereignties," he anticipated that "there will be a kind of eccentric tendency in the subordinate or inferior orbs, by the operation of which there will be a perpetual effort in each to fly off from the common center." (An accurate prophecy, this was, of the political force of states' rights.) In *The Federalist*, number thirty-one, saying that geometry and politics are alike, Hamilton displayed confidence that rules of equilibrium can be followed in politics. The important thing, in his words, was that "the means ought to be proportioned to the end; that every power ought to be commensurate with its object; that there ought to be no limitation of a power destined to effect a purpose which is itself incapable of limitation."

Twentieth-century readers of politics, nurtured on more than a century of Darwinian evolution with its biological metaphors for social thought, are in good position to see how special a doctrine Hamilton and Madison's astronomical image of politics betrays. That institutions evolve, we are quite sure; that nations and lesser communities have personalities of their own, we frequently say; the growth, maturity—above all the strength, and dominance or subjection—of peoples and governments are our everyday suppositions. Our own thinking responds in sympathy with doctrines from before the Enlightenment which, though they were written in praise of monarchy and social hierarchy, were based on the family. Like our own ideas, those older ideas conveyed the influences of heredity, the sense of growth. The strength of nations in competition is our prevailing concern.

The constitutional fathers often thought that way, but they planned on a different basis. Cherishing separation from the power system of Europe, they were convinced as designers of fundamental law that power needed most of all to be reallocated—to be distributed, channeled, and directed. Their colonial and contemporary background of contract, or covenant, ideas confirmed them in this position. The drafts they drew on legal thought of medieval origin, extending from Magna Carta and feudal contracts to Sir Edward Coke, gave support to their hopes for government according to the model of nature, as their age understood nature in the Newtonian way. Not naïve or inexperienced about political power, or about the reliance of power on physical force, they yet believed that power can be governed as well as govern. To their glory, they put that conviction to work.

CHAPTER XI

The Goals of the Philosopher Statesmen: Hamilton, Adams, Jefferson and Madison

The foundation of our Empire was not laid in the gloomy age of Ignorance and Superstition; but at an Epocha when the rights of mankind, after social happiness, were better understood and more clearly defined, than at any former period, the researches of the human mind have been carried to a great extent, the Treasures of knowledge acquired by the labours of Philosophers, Sages and Legislatures, through a long succession of years, are laid open for our use, and their collected wisdom may be happily applied in the Establishment of our forms of Government. . . . At this auspicious period, the United States came into existence as a Nation, and if their Citizens should not be completely free and happy, the fault will be intirely their own.
—*George Washington*, Circular to the States (*1783*)

1　*More Enlightened than Kings: Philosophers for the New Nation*

EGINNING with the four public men—the principal adviser to the first president and the second, third, and fourth presidents of the United States—whom Americans have come to honor as the philosopher statesmen of the early republic, a dozen or so men from then to now have been the supreme spokesmen of our principal sets of political convictions. Doubtless the maximum recognition of their service is the one sometimes rendered by our national habits of speech. Today, a century and two-thirds after Alexander Hamilton, the household word "Hamiltonian" sounds right for a partisan of business and strong national government; likewise the adjective "Jeffersonian" sounds right for a democrat and a freedom man. The other recognition which is given to past spokesmen for main ideas is the recognition of successor spokesmen and scholars. One of the happy achievements of recent historiography has been the belated discovery that John Adams and James Madison belong among the principal creators of traditions we honor.

It would be agreeable, at the high point to which the close of the eighteenth century has brought us in the history of public thought, to look back to the heroic age of colonial settlement for prototypes. We are familiar with the colonial fathers who made themselves principal transmitters to America of English political ideas, and who contributed to ideas and attitudes which in time became characteristically American. Important as they were, those men of the seventeenth and early eighteenth centuries did not state goals and programs which had bearing after the Revolution. One could coin a term "Roger Williamsite," but it would not be quite right for devotees of freedom today, who lack Roger Williams's piety; "Winthropian" would do no better for sustainers of the modern establishment; nor would "Pennite" or "Oglethorpian" serve for philanthropists of our time. The crop of national idea men began only when the nation began.

Since the philosopher statesmen, three presidents enjoy an enviable fate, like theirs, of having been honored, from their own time to ours, because they voiced and served a program which the people have cherished, which added new value to the American system: Andrew Jackson, Abraham Lincoln, and Franklin Roosevelt. Some would say that Theodore Roosevelt and Woodrow Wilson deserve similar honor, and indeed the word "Wilsonian" survives; but the purposes with which those two presidents are identified have not been equally accepted. Outside the presidency, before the Civil War one Supreme Court justice, John Marshall, and one senator, John C. Calhoun, became first the spokesmen, then the symbols, of lines of thought which have endured. So also did the two philosopher essayists and poets, Ralph Waldo Emerson and Henry David Thoreau. Bridging the nineteenth and twentieth centuries, two philosopher educators, William James and John Dewey, did the same.

The naturally infrequent coincidence, in the capacity of one human being, of political and moral expressiveness of high order and of leadership with long-run effect, makes the more stunning the record of the philosopher statesmen. Every one of the four was given a powerful, studious, observant, and decisive mind. Each bore an unlimited concern for his country; each had foresight in uncommon measure. From the life and thought of the four, the United States has benefited, by having had large positions supremely well stated, about the goals which American government and society should serve. Though at times, between their day and ours, their ideas have been degraded in political discussion and have been too much simplified, they have also been augmented and developed, so that real traditions of purpose and thought have emerged.

2   *Alexander Hamilton: To Create Strength from Weakness*

HAMILTON was the youngest of the philosopher statesmen, and by temperament the least philosophical. He was thirty-two when he attended the Philadelphia convention, at the outer edge of sympathy with much of its work. Madison, who was the principal proponent of the Virginia plan which succeeded and the special genius of the meeting, was thirty-six. Jefferson became forty-four that year; John Adams, fifty-two. Hamilton was the most brilliant of the four, if acuteness and drive are main components of brilliance. He had not yet turned thirty-five when he began the series of reports, as secretary of the treasury, which climax his intellectual and his public achievement and which first introduced large economic reasoning into the public thought of the nation. In 1795, when by resigning the secretaryship he ended his career as statesman, he was only forty and had set a record of precociousness in public service which no one since has surpassed.

Yet to understand what is special about Hamilton's thought, we need start not with the man's unique, meteoric talents but with the differences as to background and orientation which separated him from his older contemporaries. John Adams and the two Virginians were alike in that, when they conceptualized the position of the United States and planned its future, they did so in terms which derived from the state of their birth and enduring loyalty. Jefferson and Madison wanted the nation to be like the Virginia they dreamed of and like the Northwest territory they had helped blueprint: a land of farms and trade, and of freedom and amenity, much like the old Virginia but with republican government fully realized and with considerable equality built into society. Theology aside, Adams hoped and feared for the new nation in much the same terms as his Puritan ancestors had for Massachusetts—in terms of the strengths and weaknesses of the people, and of the obligation of government to keep the people in right paths. Unlike Adams, Hamilton, a son of the West Indies, had no regional tradition to sustain. To him his country was a place he had come to; his people were a people in motion, whose march he was happy to join.

"The bastard brat of a Scottish peddler," as John Adams described his origins, Alexander Hamilton was born on the island of Nevis, probably in Charlestown, during the year 1755. At the age of seventeen, when he had already begun to attract some attention by his writing, he succeeded in breaking free from his job as a store clerk. With the help of relatives and friends, who included a Presbyterian minister, he set out for the mainland to be educated. His introductions led him principally to Presbyterian manses in and out of New York; his first American period of study was at a good academy at Elizabethtown, for just one year. He naturally thought first of the College of New Jersey, and he was taken there to call on the president. Dr. Witherspoon thought well enough of the bright lad to weigh his case carefully, though he was short on preparation. But the application was rejected, and, thanks to that decision, Columbia University now has Alexander Hamilton as its most famous collegiate alumnus, a distinction which, with Madison on its own list, Princeton may or may not have equaled. Broadus Mitchell, Hamilton's fullest biographer, speculates that, if Hamilton had gone to Princeton at this point, he would probably have become in due time a Philadelphian or a permanent New Jerseyite instead of a New Yorker. In those locations he could hardly have discovered such crises to exist during the 1780s as he did find in New York; his career and his writing would have been different, and so would American history.°

The Anglicanism and royalism of King's College, which Hamilton entered in 1773, directed him away from his Scottish and evangelical connections; the college brought him, for the first time, to the threshold of the upper class of New York City and province, wherein he would marry and rise. He became friends with President Myles Cooper of the college, an Oxonian and a natural Loyalist in the crisis; the president observed Hamilton's powers to assimilate and express ideas and could hardly believe that they belonged to a youth in his teens. But his associations at King's did nothing to isolate him from the excitement of the city during the Tea Party year, and they aided his political reading. We know that while in college he read and was early able to speak knowledgeably about the authorities his new countrymen loved—Demosthenes, Plutarch, and Cicero, for example, among the ancients, and Grotius, Locke, and Montesquieu, among modern writers. When word came from Boston of the tea thrown into the harbor, Hamilton made a speech on the side of Samuel Adams. He entered the more serious prerevolutionary discourse in 1774, the critical year. He contributed an essay to the Patriot organ, Holt's *New York Journal*, which in its psuedonymity people attributed to John Jay, who was ten years older and a member of the Continental Congress—and his future colleague in writing *The Federalist*. When the prominent Loyalist, Samuel Seabury, replied, Hamilton wrote a quotable rejoinder which tells us that he had already made natural-rights thinking his own. "The sacred rights of mankind are not to be searched for among old documents or musty. They are written as with a sunbeam, in the whole volume of human nature, by the hand of divinity itself." Entering and enlivening American protest in opposition to the coercive acts, Hamilton so soon, and so youthfully and unknowingly, joined forces with John Adams and Thomas Jefferson, the principal pamphleteers of that crisis.

But after 1776 their courses separated, not to converge closely until the designing and launching of the government under the federal Constitution. During years while Adams, Jefferson, and Madison were wrapped up in politics or diplomacy and, taking their turns at state constitution making, were seeking procedures to restrain power, Hamilton was in the army; as aide to General Washington, he had a commanding view of how power was actually being used. Like the philosopher Thomas Hobbes in the Puritan Revolution, whose *Leviathan* he studied, Hamilton during the Revolution studied how power could be concentrated and applied, not restrained; again like Hobbes, he believed that government is hard, but not impossible, to upset.° In Hamilton's life, the American upset had occurred, or almost occurred, before he entered the act; he had arrived in time for the shouting, but the problem of American independence had not been heavily his own. Problems of command, manpower, logistics, finance, and loyalty were the starting points of his independent thinking, rather than the questions which Adams and Jefferson weighed.

The general's assistant had to write letters and reports. Somehow he found time, also, to study. We learn that in the field—at Valley Forge, for one place—he read economic literature, both standard and recent works. His book knowledge of mercantilist policy and practice, which fifteen years later he would honor by applying, he took in part from Sir James Steuart's *Inquiry into the Principles of Political Economy*, a standard work after 1767, and, perhaps more particularly, from the two-volume *Universal Dictionary of Trade and Commerce* by Malachy Postelthwayt, a work which laid uncommon stress on monetary problems and on the value of freedom to the man in trade. At the opposite pole of economic theory, Hamilton informed himself about the French Physiocrats; their ideas were too doctrinaire free-trade for him and gave too much preference to agriculture. We know also that he read carefully Adam Smith's *Wealth of Nations* and took notes on that work. (The loss of his notes, and the absence of any precise information about his judgment of the book, point by point, are great deprivations to scholars.) Although he ended up opposed to Smith in general, it is more than likely that Hamilton's belief in a detailed, industrial-age kind of division of labor in manufacturing, and his moderation about tariffs, owe a good deal to Adam Smith.°

In 1781, the year when military operations in America ended, Alexander Hamilton sketched for the first time the main lines of the national economic policy with which he is historically identified. That the debt of the United States could be transformed into an asset, in the sense of a demanding and invigorating responsibility for the nation to meet, and so a cause of economic activity, was a proposition he explained in a letter to Robert Morris—whose mind was running in the same direction and who was about to found the Bank of North America. The debt called for a semipublic institution to manage it; such an institution as the Bank of England, if established in America, would speak for the solvency of the United States, Hamilton reasoned, and greatly improve American credit. Even before Cornwallis surrendered, Hamilton enlarged his argument and had it printed in newspaper essays which he signed "Continentalist." Himself a member of the Congress which only weeks earlier had adopted the Articles of Confederation, he so soon asked that that league of states be transformed into "a great federal republic" with sovereign powers of taxation and with real authority over the "petty, . . . jarring, jealous, and perverse" states.

In the connectedness which Hamilton saw between economics and politics, moreover, there appeared in his writings of 1781 a flavor of the determinism for which he is remembered. When he reasoned from the credit needs of America to future institutions he revealed the economic determinism which he would phrase, most pithily, in *The Federalist*, number thirty. "Money is, with propriety, considered as the vital principle of the body politic; as that which sustains its life and motion, and enables it to perform its essential functions." But Hamilton also reasoned the other way around: that political "anarchy" under the Confederation depressed business and that a national government would bring prosperity—in short, that politics determine economics. Altogether it is wiser to say that Hamilton reasoned environmentally and deterministically than it is to call him any particular kind of determinist; there would be no justification at all in supposing that the once-Presbyterian youth had been transformed into some sort of historical predestinarian.

During 1786 and 1787 Hamilton's thinking—he was now a practising lawyer in New York—proliferated in a number of ways, all of them nationalistic or compatible with nationalism. Believing that enlarging and securing interstate trade was one of the prime necessities, he went as delegate from New York to the thinly attended Annapolis convention of 1786, on trade; and when he saw that the meeting lacked energy and would fail, he took the initiative which led to Congress's calling the convention in Philadelphia the next year. As a member of that convention, although he was too impatient with the deliberations to be useful and many days failed to attend, he was nonetheless bursting with notions. He spoke for monarchism, not because he expected a king to be established but to nudge things toward unified power. He opposed the Virginia plan, though it promised strong federalism, because it came to terms with the states as continuing (though limited) sovereignties; he would have liked to have had their autonomy destroyed. As a member of the convention's committee on style, he took special pride in Article III, on the judiciary, even though he must have been intensely aware that it failed to spell out the authority of the Supreme Court to rule on the constitutionality of state and federal statutes. The next year, in *The Federalist*, number seventy-eight, he took the initiative to explain publicly that the court needed to have that crucial power. In his own words: "The interpretation of the laws is the proper and peculiar province of the courts. A constitution is, in fact, and must be regarded by the judges, as a fundamental law. It therefore belongs to them to ascertain its meaning, as well as the meaning of any particular act proceeding from the legislative body."°

Although Hamilton's ideas about government at the time of the Philadelphia convention have been called "philosophy" by a modern biographer, his place among the philosopher statesmen could not be assured on that ground. His proposals, though consistently nationalistic, were at once too extreme and too incomplete to stand the test of system and logic. After the convention, not during it, when he had accepted the premises of the Constitution—its republicanism and its multiple sovereignty—Hamilton entered his period of virtuosity as a political thinker. Before he joined forces with Madison and Jay to write *The Federalist* he could hardly have conceived the analogy of the solar system for the federal scheme of things, which we noticed in the last chapter. A new system was now born for him. For the flavor of conversion in his thought we may go to the last paragraph of the final *Federalist* essay. After quoting from his favorite philosopher, David Hume, to the point that a monarchy and a republic equally need wisdom, he went on: "I cannot entertain an equal tranquillity with those who affect to treat the dangers of a longer continuance in our present situation as imaginary. A NATION without a NATIONAL GOVERNMENT is, in my view, an awful spectacle. The establishment of a constitution, in time of profound peace, by the voluntary consent of a whole people, is a PRODIGY, to the completion of which I look forward with trembling anxiety."

In his commitment to ratification, Hamilton assimilated into his pleas for national strength and stability a good deal of reference to the derivation of law and government from the people. The Constitution is the people's assignment of power to several custodians, his thought ran, and it is the business of all branches of government to honor the people's gift. He put the general position into plain terms, which might be taken as an endorsement of the preamble of the Constitution, in *The Federalist*, twenty-two. "The fabric of American Empire ought to rest on the solid basis of THE CONSENT OF THE PEOPLE. The streams of national power ought to flow immediately from that pure original fountain of all legitimate authority." In the seventy-eighth *Federalist* essay, already quoted, in which he advanced the principle of judicial review, he linked that principle to the idea that fundamental law is the people's own. It belongs to the courts to ascertain the meaning of the Constitution, he reasoned, "as well as the meaning of any particular act proceeding from the legislative body. . . .

The constitution ought to be preferred to the statute, the intention of the people to the intention of their agents"—the legislators.

Thus proceeding from essentially Lockian premises, Hamilton reached a non-Lockian conclusion, namely, that legislatures had been too much trusted and now especially needed to be circumscribed. In common with the other philosopher statesmen, he believed that the majority was always ready to tryrannize the minority; federalists of the 1780s commonly saw in Shays's Rebellion justification for this anxiety and regarded the Constitution as insurance against future uprisings. In the twenty-sixth *Federalist* essay Hamilton discussed the problem. Saying that during the Revolution "the minds of men" had failed to "stop at that happy mean which marks the salutary boundary between POWER and PRIVILEGE, and combines the energy of government with the security of private rights," Hamilton pleaded to his readers that the best assurance for the future lay in utilizing the proposed resources of a national government for stability and security. In a vein to give heart to those who feared a drift into chaos—whether from state legislative action, or state failure of restraint—he said, "The citizens of America have too much discernment to be argued into anarchy. And I am much mistaken, if experience has not wrought a deep and solemn conviction in the public mind, that greater energy of government is essential to the welfare and prosperity of the community." This tells us a great part of what the Constitution promised to Hamilton and what Hamilton wanted it to mean for the country.

Hamilton was wise enough to recognize that the strong central executive, which seemed good to him, signified other things to other people. In the same twenty-sixth essay from *The Federalist,* he undertook to relieve the feelings of those who foresaw and feared possible intrusion into politics by the army and a navy about to be created and about to be placed in unknown hands. The federal system, he reasoned, would not permit the armed forces to become engines of tyranny. "Schemes to subvert the liberties of a great community *require time* to mature them for execution," he pointed out, and such a lapse the states themselves, in their jealousy of federal powers, would prevent. "An army so large as seriously to menace [the people's] liberties could only be formed by progressive augmentations; which would suppose, not merely a temporary combination between the legislature and executive, but a continued conspiracy for a series of time. Is it probable that such a combination would exist at all?"°

The function or service of the Constitution which Hamilton envisaged, as he composed his hopeful portrait of American federalism, he himself called "free government." "Freed government" would be a more descriptive phrase. His prime goal, at any rate, was to have government created and released in America on the basis of the people's full authorization and consent, so that it could act in strength. He thought of freedom for individuals, too, but in an active rather than in a permissive sense. When Jefferson and Madison and other liberals (and Adams more like them than like Hamilton) planned for freedom under government, they conceived fixed safeguards, established by bills of rights and by checks and balances. They protected nonpolitical, as well as political, people. Differing from them not so much in terms as in emphases, Hamilton conceived that freedom meant opportunity to get something done through government: the development of security and welfare, assistance to trade, the protection of minorities, the suppression of violence. Whether we call this "free government" or "freed government," or both, Hamilton's dynamism has a modern ring. It suggests the Presidents Roosevelt and recent determinations "to get America moving again" rather than an eighteenth-century vision of harmony and balance.

When, a little more than two years after the final *Federalist* essay was published, President Washington elevated his former secretary to be United States secretary of the treasury, he created an opportunity for authorship which no one, except possibly Hamilton himself, who had sought the appointment, could have foreseen. Hamilton, if he had stayed out of office and yet had tried to put into published words the essence of what actually went into his reports as secretary of the treasury, would have occupied only a somewhat stronger position than he had as "Continentalist" a decade earlier—he would have been an acute economic writer with a set of traditional, ambitious, debatable, and only somewhat popular ideas. But as the first president's right-hand man, submitting as official reports the plans for economic, fiscal, and administrative growth which he was sure the people needed, he had every right to speak with authority and act with energy—quite in line with the grand design of executive leadership which he had drawn in *The Federalist*.

Within less than two and a half years after taking office, his reports were in, and the crucial ones on credit and banking were accepted by Congress and put into action. As John Adams had gathered detailed information on the content and the history of republican constitutions from ancient Athens to revolutionary Massachusetts, so Hamilton now schooled himself in the methods and procedure of public and private finance. American debts, state and national, were piled up and confused; the problem had been on Hamilton's mind at least since 1781. England in recent years had made a practice of debt funding—consolidating old obligations into long-run, systematized national debt. He studied that procedure. The secretary of treasury's first report on public credit, though it made much political bad feeling, did bring the results which Hamilton wanted. Credit flowed where credit had been lacking; wealth increased and men of wealth gained confidence. The government grew.

Hamilton's "Report on a National Bank" is the one of his writings which clearly substantiates the claim of admirers that he was an economist as well as an economic statesman. His studies in preparation took him back into the late-medieval and early-modern origins of banking, as it had risen in the service of the city-states of Venice, Genoa, and Hamburg and the national states of Holland and England. He examined technical problems: the operations of deposit banking, of investment, and of note issue, for instance. His knowledge enabled him to describe the conveniences and benefits that the government and the business community alike would have, once the Bank of the United States were established and its services made widely available. Again, credit was the nub of the matter, "a mass of credit which will supply the need of a money capital," he said.

The most famous of Hamilton's reports, and the one which lies at the center of the Hamiltonian tradition of later times, the "Report on Manufactures," was less particularly an economist's paper. It may have been prepared in the first place by the assistant secretary of the treasury, Tench Coxe, a Philadelphia lawyer and ex-president of an organization, the Pennsylvania Society for the Encouragement of Manufactures and the Useful Arts, which suggests that the spirit of Franklin was carrying on. At any rate the report contained information about economic developments throughout the country which had been gathered by treasury agents. Like the other reports, it is studded with suggestions from theory and from the history of Europe. There are many quotations from Adam Smith. Like Smith, Hamilton wanted the division of labor in industry to be highly detailed. If productiveness seemed to require the employment of women and children in factories—an ugliness of early industrialism which had already appeared in the Boston and Philadelphia areas—Hamilton recommended that, too. The secretary's principal recommendation for the inner development of new industry was the increased use of machinery, especially water-power machinery to take advantage of the many sites.

Coming at the question of national policy, the report inquired, as to background, what reasons explained the economic success of the Atlantic-facing nations of Europe. Once again England prevailed in Hamilton's mind. It was less the England of 1790 than the England of the middle eighteenth century, the country he could read about and which in a way he had known about as a storekeeper in the West Indies, that he admired: the mercantilist England which had grown to be the first power, and then the first industrial power, in the world. Applying England's record and England's policy to the yet undeveloped and sparsely settled United States, Hamilton made several

The Indian "Towne of Secota" from the 1590 edition of colonist Thomas Harriot's A Briefe and True Report of the New-Found Land of Virginia. . . . As cartography and navigation were necessary to overseas exploration and settlement, accurate observation of the plants, animals, and men—botany, zoology, and anthropology—became a part of colonization in America, and the earliest work was among the best. The engraving, from a water color by colonist John White, shows: (A) a burial house, (B) a place for prayers, (C) a ceremonial dance, (D) a feast, (E) tobacco, (G) cornfields, (H) squash, (K) ceremonial fire.

John Winthrop, here with his James Short telescope in the 1773 portrait by John Singleton Copley, was the professor at Harvard who, descended from his namesake, the original governor of Massachusetts, began the work of making science important in higher education.

The orrery built by Franklin's scientific colleague, David Rittenhouse, in 1767–1771. Driven by clockwork, the device, like a modern planetarium, shows the relative motions of the planets around the sun as well as the day, month, year, and astrological sign.

The reach of Franklin's mind equaled Jefferson's, though different
—greater as scientist and philanthropist, less important in public affairs and education. This 1762 portrait shows Franklin the man of
science and invention. The device at the left is a lightning detector.

Franklin represented supremely the free-lance scientific
activity of the eighteenth century. The drawing above is
for an experiment described in his Experiments and Observations on Electricity . . . , published in London in 1769
—one of many by which, with playful ingenuity, he worked
out the nature and properties of electricity. Here, he
used a glass for insulation, a book incised with gold leaf,
an electrified bottle, and a spring wire which, when brought
near the bottle, caused "a strong spark. . . like. . . lightning."

John Adams (below, in the Gilbert Stuart portrait dated
1815) and (above) his home in Quincy, which he bought at
the close of the Revolution and named "Peacefield." Adams
was the senior among the philosopher statesmen of the republic. His mind, though not scientific like Franklin's
nor artistic like Jefferson's, was probably the most reflective of the age. He bore the burden of reconciling
Puritan ways of thought with those of the Enlightenment.
He became a secularizer of old ideas of sin; and—the
other side of that coin—a moralist among revolutionaries.

Thomas Jefferson, in the Gilbert Stuart portrait known as "the Bow-doin Jefferson" (Stuart painted it, 1805–1807, for James Bowdoin, III, who willed it to Bowdoin College). While John Adams's reputation dates from a little earlier, Madison's from a decade after, Jefferson, beginning with the Declaration of Independence, held for half a century the prime voice of philosophical statesmanship. That tradition makes him still the purest spokesman for the hopes of the young republic. The portrait suggests his work in architecture (see next two pages)—the classical forms by which he sought to connect his country with the free city-states of the ancient world. His taste for order, simplicity, and regularity in architecture was appro-priate to his belief in free worship, education, rational government.

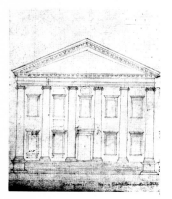

(left, above) The drawing by French architect Clérisseau of the Maison Carrée, a Roman temple at Nîmes, for his Antiquités *(1778), a design Jefferson had studied and which inspired his own plan for the Virginia Capitol at Richmond (left, below, 1785, completed 1792). The Capitol was a major innovation, the first important building in Europe or America on a classical model. In it one sees Jefferson's preoccupation with style, his taste for having things clear, balanced and restrained.*

Architecturally and perhaps in other ways the University of Virginia was Jefferson's masterpiece. At right, below, is his plan for the universally admired original quadrangle, built (1817-1825) under his personal supervision; above, an 1825 engraving of the completed structure, which he first began to plan about 1804. The university, of which Jefferson justly called himself the father, mirrors his ideas about the structure and content of education and its relation to society, as well as his innovative tastes in architecture. At a time when new American colleges were being built around a single building on a showy and expensive scale, his Virginia plan was for a group of smaller structures articulated with each other and with their function. Appropriately, the whole was focused on the library, a rotunda imitative of the Pantheon in Rome, recalling his lifelong occupation with his own domed house, Monticello. The ten "pavilions" on either side of the lawn, protectively joined by porches, intimately housed professors and their families, rooms and dining halls for students, and classrooms. Behind each pavilion was an extensive walled garden, reflecting both Jefferson's theories of public health and his agrarian sympathies.

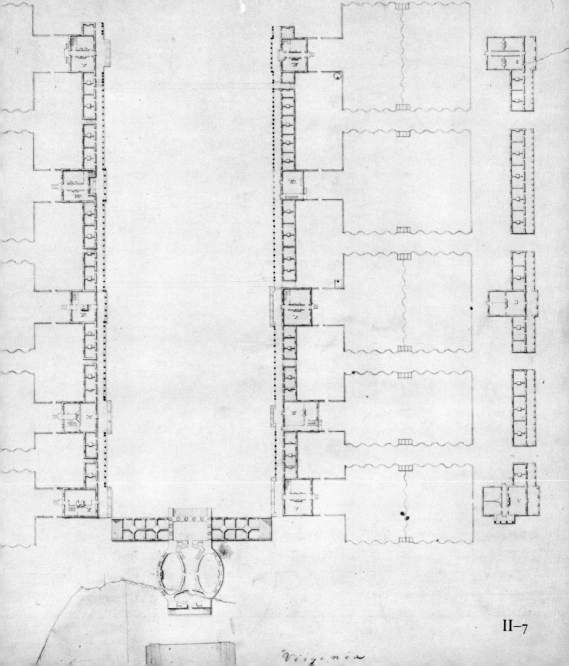

Virginia

II-7

Gilbert Stuart's portrait of Madison, painted (1805-1807) like Jefferson's for James Bowdoin. Youngest of the philosopher statesmen, after 1826 he faithfully executed Jefferson's injunction to take care of him when dead. Yet the moralistic anxiety of his make-up recalls Adams more than other revolutionary Virginians, and his economic-political ideas were strongly nationalist, often close to Hamilton's.

The debater-like pose of Hamilton in this John Trumbull portrait (1805, but from life) fits his role among the philosopher statesmen. He pushed the hardest for centralization and industrialization, and in his day his ideas sounded like mercantilism, a policy somewhat repudiated by the Revolution. Though they went with Hamilton at critical points, the other philosopher statesmen did not greatly honor him.

proposals, first among which was his argument for a protective tariff, mainly the infant-industry argument, which became the classic of its kind. Instead of trade between metropolis and overseas colonies, he foresaw trade among American regions, industrial and agricultural, northern and southern. The report which made Alexander Hamilton the major prophet of industrial growth in America made him prophet also of national economic self-sufficiency and of a protected inner balance of trade.

As for Hamiltonianism becoming a national tradition which would combine the ideas of Hamilton's *Federalist* (his plea for strong executive leadership and for placing power to interpret the Constitution in the judges) with the ideas in his reports (the case for a government-aided, self-sufficient economy), time was of the essence. And the best time came at once: the early years of Hamilton's secretaryship proved to be the one period, for generations, during which the combination would work very well. After the financial success of debt funding and the establishing of the Bank of the United States to the tune of a deal between northern and southern congressmen, the main policy recommendation of the "Report on Manufactures" was in a degree enacted by Congress. The tariffs passed during Washington's administration were not highly protective, but industry was given other advantages. The land policy of the period, in which Hamilton's favoritism for business prevailed, set a high price on western-domain lands to purchasers, in the interest of preventing the labor force from departing the industrial areas and of bringing purchase money into the national coffers. Immediately Hamilton's leadership brought such results as he sought, and brought satisfactions to leader and party and to numbers of people in all sections.°

On the other hand, as Americans remember better than they do most of their history lessons, the political price came high. President Washington's response to resistance to the bank proposal was to seek cabinet opinion. When Jefferson formally challenged the bank as being unconstitutional, the division of ways of thought which was already opening, between strict and loose constructionism of the new Constitution, became at once a fighting matter. The party divisions, Federalist and Anti-Federalist, followed. Ideological and party conflict is something which historical thinking finds inevitable and (usually) healthy. But Hamilton called the terms earlier and more extremely than his own party could take. Out of office, his aggressiveness took the form of intruding on the cabinet's business. His activities succeeded under Washington but under John Adams became outrageous. They split the Federalist administration and party during the later 1790s. Thus Hamilton himself did much to separate Hamiltonian means, executive leadership, from Hamiltonian goals, the national direction of economic life.

What was true of Hamiltonianism during the 1790s has been prevailingly true ever since. Neither Congress nor the economy would often put up with his kind and degree of direction. The tradition has proven schizoid: the country has often had economic growth of the kind Hamilton prophesied, and it has had strong executive leadership, but not the two together in important and intended connection, until the rise of advanced industrialization. The New Nationalism and the New Deal—undertakings of economic reconstruction again—are the clear cases.

Altogether among the philosopher statesmen Hamilton was the most prophetic for the long run, but also the most materialistic as a thinker and the most Machiavellian as a politician. He was also the least trustful of ideas, the least practical combiner of ends and means, and, by those tokens, the least pragmatic of the four.°

3 *John Adams: To Fit Government to Human Nature*

EACH of the philosopher statesmen in his own way took very long views, both backward and forward in time. Compared to contemporaries who were equally philosophical but less mighty as statesmen— the George Wythes, the John Dickinsons, the John Jays of the age— they all had grand success in building their convictions into institutions and habits of mind which would carry on after their century.

When his career is considered as a whole, John Adams is no exception to this rule. But taking the four men in the sequence we follow, the order of their attaining their highest honor and place, Adams did fail to achieve climactic effect in the presidency as he himself was early to say. Not for him such executive glory as Hamilton and Jefferson achieved, each according to his dream: the one made credit flow and industry grow; the other, by acquiring vast new domains for the nation, extended the prospect for agrarian republicanism, his passion, into the indefinite future. John Adams, by contrast, is remembered for decisions he took which were pressed upon him by forces beyond his control. In 1798, under political pressures raised to panic intensity by the undeclared war with France, he signed the Alien and Sedition Acts. In the first round of antiforeignism and antiradicalism in our history, his administration prosecuted two dozen men under the Sedition Act for having criticized the government. Then, in 1800, when with Hamilton's assistance the undeclared war with France seemed about to escalate into something big, he stopped the war in its tracks. His party fell to pieces. "As Hamilton was the Sovereign Pontiff of Federalism," he reminisced in 1809, "all his Cardinals no doubt will endeavor to excite the whole Church to excommunicate and anathematize me. Content. It was time for a Protestant Separation."° There is vista of truth in the story that, when the humiliated ex-president returned from the White House to his beloved farm home in Braintree, he changed its name from "Peacefield," as he had christened it after negotiating the treaty with England, and called it "Stony Field" instead.

But if his duty as president was to say No, during the Revolution he had been a great sayer of Yes; no other statesman of the 1770s, or of any time before 1787 unless it were Jefferson, had been more effective as advancer and institutionalizer of the main ideas of the epoch. In earlier sections of this book we have encountered him on three principal occasions. In the wake of the coercive acts, as "Novanglus" in a Boston paper, he was one of the Americans to propose that the British system could and should contain many legislatures, each with its own area of sovereignty, and yet maintain a desirable common structure and allegiance; his elaboration of this doctrine was more prophetic of the long-run future of American and English institutions than were the like-minded proposals of Jefferson and Wilson. In 1776, at the moment of independence, though Jefferson had the labor and glory of principal authorship of the Declaration, it would be hard to say that anyone else had more effect than Adams in reaching the crucial decision; Jefferson later called him the "Atlas of Independence" in the Continental Congress. The third major occasion of Adams's creativity with the ideas of the Revolution of course occurred at the Massachusetts convention of 1779. Here we see the No-saying side of Adams, the restrainer of the movement toward more participation in government by the people, coming into balance with the Yes-saying side, which spoke for freedom and for commonwealth principles. Going farther than at any other time in his life in acting on democratic theory, John Adams in 1779 favored the plan adopted, of having free manhood suffrage apply in electing members of the convention and of having the constitution submitted to the people for detailed review. He wanted annual elections to the legislature and complete freedom of religion. On the restraining side, he opposed, as if the idea were outrageous, a one-house legislature; he wanted a property qualification for voting in the regular state elections, as had been the law before the Revolution, and a hierarchy of property requirements set up for the holders of state office. There was nothing unusual in his fondness for checks and balances. The uncommon thing was the weight he placed in the executive check on the legislature and the elaborateness with which he conceived the elements of social politics to be always counterpoised, forever holding one another in restraint.

The complex mind, which went so far in directions he chose, then stopped, and always had a reason, and which saw many sides to all problems and yet acted in strength, began and remained deeply persuaded by the idea of a natural order in morals and politics. In common with Franklin and Jefferson, Adams grew up with an interest in science; and the rationalists' inferences from science engaged him deeply. Zoltan Haraszti tells us that, so far as the record shows, Adams commenced his lifelong habit of making marginal notes in the books he read with John Winthrop IV's *A Lecture on Earthquakes*, wherein the Harvard professor differed from the Harvard overseer, the Reverend Thomas Prince. Adams favored the professor. In 1776 John Adams seized on the century's familiar analogy between the operations of a clock and the operations of the universe, including those of the children of earth. "I have long thought an army a piece of clockwork, and to be governed only by principles and maxims, as fixed as any in mechanics; and by all that I have read in the history of mankind, and in authors who have speculated upon society and government, I am much inclined to think that a government must manage society in the same manner; and that this is machinery too."

Eleven years later when, writing his *Defence of the Constitutions*, John Adams was explaining the merits of two-house legislatures, he said that he was as "clearly satisfied of the infallible truth" of that system as he was "of any demonstration in Euclid." To be sure, in 1796, after the United States government had raised a disheartening set of inner conflicts, which he experienced as vice-president, he had his doubts. But he voiced them in his own impulsive, self-critical way; and John Adams, the spokesman for political equilibrium, is the butt of his comment more than the doctrine itself.

> Alas! I am not Amphion. I have been thirty years singing and whistling among my rocks, and not one would ever move without money. I have been twenty years saying, if not singing, preaching, if not playing:
>
> *From various discords to create*
> *The music of a well-tuned state,*
> *And the soft, silent harmony that springs*
> *From sacred union and consent of things,*
>
> but an uncomplying world will not regard my uncouth discourses.

Though his own presidency supplied him no reason to be cheerful, ever again, about the silent harmonies and consent of things, he refused to give up the old assumption. "The Art of Lawgiving is not so easy as that of Architecture or Painting," he told Jefferson, twenty years after retirement. "I may be an Enthusiast. But I think a free Government is necessarily a complicated Piece of Machinery, the nice and exact Ad-

justment of whose Springs Wheels and Weights are not yet comprehended by the Artists of the Age and still less by the People."°

From first to last, then, Adams loved the intuition the Enlightenment
shared, that the cosmos is ultimately on the side of rightness. Although
his notions of human nature had little in common with Franklin's calculus of pleasure, and it would be unthinkable to call Adams hedonist
or materialist, it is fair to call him a moderate deist, as so many descendants of Puritans were. The thought that what men must do is discover
the Creator's laws, and follow them, connected in his mind the question
of what drives the universe with the question of what drives men.
Early and always a reader of religion and philosophy, he noticed that
John Locke, whom Americans everywhere knew as political philosopher but whom only the well read knew to have been much more, had
concerned himself with the study of the nature of man. "In metaphysics, Mr. Locke, directed by my Lord Bacon, has steered his course
into the unenlightened regions of the human mind, and, like Columbus,
has discovered a new world," Adams observed, "a world whose soil is
deep and strong; producing rank and unwholesome weeds, as well as
wholesome fruits and flowers. . . . He has shown us by what cultivation
these weeds may be exterminated, and the fruits raised; the brambles
removed. . . . Here is another hemisphere of science, therefore, abound-
ing with pleasure and profit, too, of which he had but very few, and
we have many advantages for learning."°

When a person who is anxious, as Adams was, probes into that other
"hemisphere of science," the mind, one suspects a streak of neurosis.
Probably John Adams had his share. Yet in his case there were many
external and objective reasons for making estimations of self, and many
occasions to wonder about the causes behind the situations he lived
through. He came from an ordinary family background and believed
himself to be a man of ordinary talents, yet found himself rising
rapidly into public leadership; he loved the ways and traditions of New
England, but knew that New England was changing; for a quarter of
a century he had many trying, responsible occasions to deal with national figures—in Philadelphia, in London, in Amsterdam and Paris—and
this meant seeing and measuring himself by changing standards; as
diplomat, and as vice-president and president, he was in fact often
conspired against, and when he said so he was voicing objective truth,
whether or not also some factor of delusion. A good illustration of
Adams's method of understanding life appears early in his autobiography. His paternal ancestors, he noted with satisfaction, were all buried
in the Congregational churchyard of his own town of Braintree and
had been "all in the middle rank of People in Society: all sober, industrious, frugal, and religious: all possessed of landed Estates, always
unincumbered with debts, and as independent as human nature is, or

ought to be in this World.''° His mother was born a Boylston, a family distinguished for its doctors; his father, a farmer, held town offices, as he himself would do early and late. Only on his father's insistence did he prepare for Harvard or study anything much except science and mathematics, his boyhood enthusiasms. Finally he turned to Latin; in 1775 he graduated from Harvard, ranking fourteenth among the twenty-four men in the class. Though in the long run he would honor and serve the Massachusetts schools and college, a few years after Harvard he said things nearly as complaining about his education as his great-grandson, Henry Adams, would famously say. In his own words: "In consequence of the ignorance of parents and masters, . . . and by reason of the ignorance of my instructors, in the more advanced years of my life my mind has lain uncultured, and at twenty-five I am obliged to study Homer and Horace. Proh dolor!" Besides his share of the self-consciousness which would remain in the family, John Adams had a mitigating sense of humor.

Adams's inclination to seek the *why* of things, as well as their *what* and their *how*, is illustrated in personal terms in a diary entry of 1767, when the immediate matter which troubled him was a question of spending money for books, and the deeper questions were motive and rightness. He was thirty-two at the time: he was three years married to Abigail, two years into public life, and was beginning to make money and to be recognized in his profession. Deeper in the background, but evidently relevant to his way of thinking, was his hard decision of the later 1750s to be a lawyer, not a minister. He had already done a great deal of the fundamental reading of the age, as his diary and his notations in his books bear fascinating testimony. On the literary side, he had read and made some comment on Shakespeare and the English satirists, Pope and Swift. On the side of law, history, and government, Coke, Locke, Milton, and Montesquieu were already familiar to him; he purchased and read Blackstone almost as soon as published. His greatest enthusiasm for an author is also his most astonishing. Personally, Henry St. John, the first Viscount Bolingbroke, essayist on politics and history, represented the things John Adams did not: he was a Tory, a profligate, and a scoffer at religion. But Bolingbroke's deism interested Adams, and his exposition of corruption in politics did more; it seized Adams's imagination as it did also Jefferson's. Bolingbroke's argument, in *The Patriot King* and elsewhere, that factions can be led and one balanced against another, made attractive reading for an intellectual and ambitious young American lawyer. The same ideas about politics would still seem true to Adams, forty year later, when his presidency was over.

"To what Object are my Views directed?" Adams asked himself, when he confronted the question of putting a sizable part of his earnings into the kind of books he loved. "What is the end and Purpose of my Studies, Journeys, Labours of all Kinds, of Body and Mind, of Tongue and Pen? Am I grasping at Money, or Scheming for Power? . . . I find that a great deal of Thought, and Care, as well as Money, are necessary to assemble an ample and well chosen Assortment of Books. —But when this is done, it is only a means, an Instrument. When ever I shall have compleated my Library, my End will not be answered. Fame, Fortune, Power say some, are the Ends intended by a Library. The Service of God, Country, Clients, Fellow Men, say others. Which of these would be nearest to my Heart?" The diarist did not reply.°

But when questions of motive and morality entered a public issue, as they always did with John Adams, he recorded his judgments plainly. His collection of short essays of the Stamp Act year, *A Dissertation of Canon and Feudal Law*, which as an antigovernment pamphlet was indirectly an anti-Stamp Act one, shows that he believed that "love of power" is what drives men, and that that kind of love is often self-love and a source of corruption. Writing about the forces behind English politics, and expressing also a New Englander's reaction to the rising determination of the Church of England to impose a bishop on the American colonies, Adams looked all the way back to the Middle Ages. He attributed to the medieval Catholic Church, specifically to the canon law it created and the hierarchical institutions which ruled it, a power system grown overweening; he charged it with keeping the minds of the people enchained. Likewise the feudal law, which he recognized had once performed necessary military functions, he believed had descended into mere monopolies of power and privilege. The canon and feudal law had overlapped and supported each other in England, Adams explained. Despite Henry VIII's schism from Rome and much else that had liberated England, residues were still entrenched. The Stuart tyranny of the seventeenth century had been based on them, Adams believed, and now once again they threatened evil.°

But Adams's conception of what love of power accomplishes was only half on the side of the entrenched and the authoritarian. The upheaval of the seventeenth century in England, which disturbed but did not destroy the lords spiritual and temporal there, had been brought about by the Puritans. They had been asserters of power and achievers of freedom as well. "Whenever freedom has existed," Adams generalized, love of power has been "the cause of freedom." At this point his thought voiced the American nationalism which underlay it: "It was this great struggle that peopled America," he asserted. "It was not religion alone as is commonly supposed; but it was a love of universal liberty."

Thus the young lawyer of Braintree connected the Puritan Revolution and the settlement of America, a century and a third earlier, with

American protest in 1765. Speaking with what would have been substantial accuracy if he had confined his remarks exclusively to New England, but speaking pretty loosely in his attempt to represent the case of all the colonies, Adams said that the founding fathers, while "very far from being enemies to monarchy," had eliminated the office of bishop and had received their lands direct from the sovereign and not from a lord—that is, that they had escaped from the canon and the feudal law. Their emancipation had given them an inner reward, the writer believed. "In this they discovered the depth of their wisdom and the warmth of their friendship to human nature." Here Adams was paying tribute to the system he had been brought up in and believed in, a system not of an old regime but of a new one. In the words of the *Dissertation:* "And the preservation of the means of knowledge among the lowest ranks, is of more importance to the public than all the property of all the rich men in the country. . . . Let us dare to read, think, speak and write."° Although Adams was a true believer, as we have seen, in his century's mechanistic view of politics and the world, the *Dissertation of Canon and Feudal Law* shows that, at age thirty, he was already much more than that. He was a student of history and a speaker for the tradition of his region; he was moralist and a nationalist; and, a weigher of the motives and values of men, he was himself deeply committed to liberty. The matter may be summed up by discovering in Adams a political thinker with two principal reservoirs of theory: one which belonged to the Enlightenment strictly, drawing heavily on Newtonism and other sources of natural-law ideas, and which served his work of innovation; and one which we may call traditionalist and nationalistic, which helped him justify things American.

If we were to pause again over Adams's crisis writings of the 1770s, the Novanglus papers, the *Thoughts on Government,* and the state constitution, which we have already considered as proposals of innovation, we would find that even during that decade he drew sizable draughts on tradition. In 1774 he thought of monarchy as a natural means for continuing a British empire that would be Americanized, with self-government for all; in 1776 he wanted old usages of colonial government continued in the states, so far as might prove possible; in 1779 he honored Harvard College and the schools by assigning them a fixed tutelary role in the reorganized state. But his later writings are the place, appropriate to the time, where his reliance on tradition gained full voice. The three-volume *Defence of the Constitutions,* published in 1787 and 1788, offered an historical testing, against their remote classical and Renaissance predecessors, of America's state constitutions, now ten or a dozen years old. The author had been alarmed by a published letter written by Baron Turgot, the physiocrat and philosophe;

Turgot had said that a one-house legislature would be more compatible with a people's government than a two-house one. In general the Frenchman wanted power concentrated and responsibility centralized. So far as the legislature was concerned, it was the Pennsylvania (and Vermont) problem again. So Adams did his three volumes of scissors-and-paste history of republican governments to give the bicameral legislature the historical standing he thought to be its just due. One of his annotations on Turgot reads: "Is it possible that any government should exist without equilibrium?" Later, to Jefferson, he described the *Defence*, with its examination of fifty constitutions, as containing "long courses of experiments in political philosophy." He placed himself in the van of political thinkers who were to say that Americans know more about self-government than Europeans.°

The writer of the *Defence* may reasonably be understood to have felt the French Revolution coming; his next writing, his last sizable one and the last one we need consider, appeared after that event had broken out. France's course of violence had quickly polarized feeling in the West; Burke's *Reflections on the French Revolution*, with its denunciations of the philosophes as being doctrinaire and faithless to sense and tradition, was already a year old and in England a runaway best seller. In America, though Citizen Genet had not yet arrived, politics were responding for and against the French Revolution. Adams observed all this and responded in fear, not so much *of* the French Revolution as *for* all revolutions; his point of observation, of course, was the not yet stabilized or influential seat of the presiding officer of the United States Senate.

So he took up his pen, his familiar instrument in time of crisis. To get his historical sights clear this time he turned to the century-and-a-half-old, but excellent, *History of the Civil Wars of France* by the Italian scholar Enrico Caterino Davila; he used the French edition of 1757. For a twentieth-century equivalent the reader must imagine a vice-president since 1919 translating and studying some foreign-language work on Russian authoritarianism two centuries ago, in order to comprehend and attack communist authoritarianism. Adams's background reading accounts for the title he chose, *Discourses on Davila;* such a title as "Revolution and the Control of Affairs" would have been more descriptive. His effort was directed neither to reporting and criticizing Davila, the historian, nor to interpreting the French capacity for civil violence, whether in the sixteenth century or the eighteenth. He sought rather to explain how to avoid that kind of thing—how to have a revolution and avoid chaos. As to the author's supposition that a deep background of history illuminates present events and yields wisdom for participators, the *Discourses on Davila* have much in common with *A Dissertation on the Canon and Feudal Law* and *A Defence of the Constitutions.* As to method they resemble the *Defence,* for once again Adams scissored and pasted other people's writing and added his own comment.

Yet his method is not altogether objectionable, and the *Discourses* give us opportunity to scissors and paste John Adams for his essential ideas—on the side of his traditionalist understanding of men and morals, revolution and thought—after three decades of participation in affairs. Perhaps the bottom question for Adams as witness is: Why do men always struggle with one another? The writer had several answers, of which the prime one is the tension between men being given equal rights under God, and there being no such thing as human equality. (Adams had not carried the "all men are created equal" formula into the Massachusetts constitution; "equally independent" was as far as he had gone.) In the words of the *Discourses:* "Although, among men, all are subject by nature to *equal laws* of morality, and in society have a right to *equal laws* for their government, . . . no two men are perfectly equal in person, property, understanding, activity, and virtue." These are matters beyond human control, Adams said in a much-quoted passage: "Nature, which has established in the universe a chain of being and universal order, descending from archangels to microscopic animalcules, has ordained that no two objects shall be perfectly alike, and no two creatures perfectly equal." But the chain of being does not mean that men are naturally reconciled to one another. "Whenever it becomes disputable between two individuals or families, which is the superior, a fermentation commences, which disturbs the order of all things until it is settled."

In organized society, in what terms does struggle arise? On this point Adams had refined his thought since 1765. Borrowing heavily, though without acknowledgment, from Adam Smith's *Theory of Moral Sentiments,* he explained that men in all conditions of life are driven by needs far beyond the minimum ones of subsistence.° Everyone's "affection for the esteem, the sympathy, admiration and congratulations of the public" he now generalized as the "passion for distinction." This passion succeeded, or rather subsumed, "love of power" in his older view of what men struggle for. Still following Smith, he discovered within the passion a whole series of motives: emulation, ambition (love of power), jealousy, envy, and vanity. In this context he paid his disrespects to wealth: "*Riches attract the attention, consideration, and congratulations of mankind,*" but they do not make men happy. The same is true of those who inherit power. More elaborately than in 1765 but in the same spirit, he gathered his argument by condemning the old regime in Europe. He conceded that art and science had gained in the Old World, by reason of the patronage given them by families of wealth and privilege. But the apex of honor and wealth in Europe was placed in the monarchs; this was too much concentration, and hence the French Revolution. "If a balance of passions and interests is not scientifically concerted, the present struggle in Europe will be little beneficial to mankind, and produce nothing but another thousand years of feudal fanaticism, under new and strange names."

Is there hope in government? John Adams belongs among the believers in progress. He had believed, since he had begun to record his thoughts and we may suppose longer, that his country represented an improvement over Europe, and his age over preceding ages. "The arts and sciences in general," he had said in the preface of the *Defence,* "during the last three or four centuries have had a regular course of progressive improvement. The inventions in mechanic arts, the discoveries in natural philosophy, navigation, and commerce, and the advancement of civilization and humanity have occasioned changes in the condition of the world and the human character which would have astonished the most refined nations of antiquity." As he now said clearly in the *Discourses,* Adams believed in benevolence in human beings ("benevolence" was a rising word in New England theology), but he did not believe that benevolence, unassisted by political arrangement, would suffice to restrain the "selfish affections" of men in society. In sum he found his problem to be what our own problem has often seemed to be in the twentieth century, an obligation to bring the operations of government to a level of responsibility which would accord with the condition of the arts and sciences and "the advancement of civilization."

He did discover grounds for hope. An elder statesman's patriotism shines through the illustrations he picked as signs of encouragement. In spite of universal avarice among men and in spite of the violence and unreason of the revolution in France, he still believed, he said, that knowledge is more equally diffused, that "newspapers, magazines, and circulating libraries have made mankind wiser," and that there lay reason for satisfaction in the fact that "titles and distinctions, ranks and orders, parade and ceremony, are all going out of fashion." Thus Adams was thrown back for comfort, in the end, to increasing indications of equality among men. It frightened him a little, and he exhorted his readers against materialism. He begged Frenchmen and Americans alike to bear in mind that "the perfectibility of man is only human and terrestrial perfectibility." In his own way, he was asking for submission to God; he was asking that people neither believe too much in their individual powers nor place too heavy a reliance on government. "Let the rich and the poor unite in the bands of mutual affection. . . . A balance, with all its difficulty, must be preserved or liberty is lost forever."°

The *Discourses* were published piece by piece, as the vice-president produced them, in Fenno's *Gazette*, the national Federalist paper. The response they received stopped them. To the author's astonishment, they were denounced as being inimical to liberty and favorable to monarchy. (Adams probably never really wanted a king in America, but he did have a lifetime fondness, which became pretty much a love affair at this stage, for the values of paternalism and tradition in monarchy.) At the time when the essays were discontinued, Adams's hard period of being separated from his peers had begun. Though he was then favorable to Hamilton's financial program, he hated such reliance on men of money as the program presupposed, and his hatred of Hamilton would soon develop; he got on well enough with Jefferson at this stage and continued to do so for several years, but the old sympathy was loosening; and the *Discourses* were a factor, on Jefferson's side. In truth, when the time of strain came, Adams's last resource, when speaking for national coherence and solidarity, was traditionalist and sentimental-nationalist, and this did not bridge the crevasses opened by ideology and ambition.

Only recently, when our own age has renewed a sense that man is much governed by his darker passions, has appreciation of the older John Adams risen greatly. Both his epoch in history and ours have had leaders who loved power more than they loved freedom or harmony, and leaders also who, while eloquent for freedom, have yet forgotten harmony. For those two essentials of morality, conceived logically together as necessary each to the other, the second president remains, so far, the country's finest spokesman.

4 *Thomas Jefferson and James Madison: To Fit Government to the Goodness of Man*

THOMAS Jefferson we have met in the three chapters preceding this one; James Madison, in the preceding two. We discovered Jefferson first among the scientific apparatus at William and Mary College, as clearly a child of the Enlightenment as anyone born in America. Madison, who like him belonged to an Anglican family in Virginia's "Old West," attended the Presbyterian College of New Jersey. He emerged appropriately oriented in commonwealthman ideas. In religion he became a moderate deist; what Andrienne Koch says about Jefferson goes equally well for him, "He was a pious man, if the religion of humane morality is recognized as a kind of natural piety."

The two were thrown closely together for the first time in the stirring days of 1776. We have seen that their collaboration of mind and politics began with the great events of Virginia liberalism: writing the state's constitution and the bill of rights, designing its program of social and legal reform, and separating church from state. During the 1780s their duties put the ocean between them, but their affinity carried on. It would be easy to say that, while Jefferson was abroad, Madison acted as his deputy in state and Confederation affairs. The fact is that, though the younger man acted in friendship and loyalty, his judgment was fully his own. Plainly his number-one and number-two services to the Constitution of 1787—fathering it at the Philadelphia convention and defending it by the pen that wrote one-third of *The Federalist* in New York—made him the most independent and creative figure in American affairs for at least a year. Then in 1790, when Jefferson had come home from Europe to be secretary of state and Madison had entered Congress, the two closed ranks again. Their work together included the founding and developing of the Republican-Democratic Party, in which Madison took the greater initiative. By the time Jefferson became president and made Madison his secretary of state, quite as Mrs. Koch says, the most complete collaboration ever in American statesmanship had matured; it would last a second quarter century, until Thomas Jefferson's death.

During the 1780s especially, while Jefferson was in his forties and Madison in his thirties, the services they rendered their country were matched, in both men, by new intellectual growth. Madison, the stay-at-home of the pair, read history and politics industriously, just before he took center on the national stage. Jefferson sent him from Europe large orders of books: works on history and government, religion and morals. While Adams was concentrating on the history of ancient and modern republics, and Hamilton on finance, Madison thought broadly. This period of study, at the time when the need for national reorganization was becoming ever more widely felt, doubtless helps explain why Madison became the one of the philosopher statesmen who had most in common with all the others and, by the same token, had the fewest particularities of his own. Where Hamilton was the one, for example, who, being wrapped up in business and owning-class interests, went the furthest in being deterministic about economic and political affairs, Madison, whose inclination was agrarian, yet made a classic statement about the influence of economics on politics, in *The Federalist*, number ten. Where John Adams dreaded irresponsibility in affairs with a dread like that his Puritan forebears felt, Madison, the son of a pious Anglican household, said about the same things in favor of checks and balances. But none of this separated him from Jefferson. As author in 1790 of the federal Bill of Rights, which Jefferson and other Virginians especially wanted, Madison phrased the same kinds of restraints on the national government as his seniors had placed on the government of Virginia during the year when he first entered politics. The following familiar lines, from the first, ninth, and tenth amendments of the new Constitution, were originally his: "Congress shall make no law respecting an establishment of religion . . . or abridging the freedom of speech or of the press. . . . The enumeration in the Constitution, of certain rights, shall not be construed to deny or disparage others retained by the people. . . . The powers not delegated to the United States . . . are reserved to the States respectively, or to the people."°

While Madison, so to speak, grew up in affairs during the 1780s, Jefferson's going to Europe as diplomat and coming home as an elder statesman—and soon becoming a dissenting one—pretty well fits Arnold Toynbee's pattern of withdrawal and return. Overseas the author of the Declaration, the lineage of whose thought had been so much more English than anything else, had his first considerable saturation in French thought and feeling. He met men of state, such as Vergennes, in the course of duty. He became widely and familiarly acquainted with men and women of rank and cultivation. Benjamin Franklin introduced him to two great ladies of the salons, Madame d'Houdetot and Madame Helvétius. The Marquis de Lafayette and members of his family entertained Jefferson generously. Acquaintanceships with Destutt de Tracy and Du Pont de Nemours, physiocrats and philosophers, led to lifelong admiration and friendships; he became acquainted with other philosophes whose hopes for mankind resembled his own. He attended frequent concerts; he discussed gardening; he learned about wines and wine making; he hired a good chef. In due time, many troubles about money notwithstanding, he rented a splendid house and garden. When things became too thick he escaped for intervals as other important men did, strange as the place seems for him, to a Carthusian monastery in the city, which offered board and lodging and quiet. If the philosophes in Paris shortly before the Revolution be thought of as a club, Jefferson himself was a member, un-French and not as much a lion as Franklin, but more fully a philosophe than any other American.

The intellectual influence which was probably the most exciting of any which affected him in France occurred in the person of another visitor, Dugald Stewart, from Scotland. Stewart was one of the two or three principals of the new "common sense" philosophy of his country; the school was friendly to science and to the study of economics and politics, and it gave special sanction to the belief of the Enlightenment in moral intuition. Apparently the author of the American Declaration —which had justified the birth of the United States on intuitions of equality, freedom, and justice under "the Supreme Judge of the world" —took great satisfaction in discovering a philosopher who bulwarked his own assumptions. In later life Jefferson's appreciation of Stewart seems to have eased his transition, one rather of attitude than mind, from deism into Unitarianism. "The moral sense, or conscience, is as much a part of man as his leg or arm," Jefferson wrote a nephew, from Paris. In 1820, more than three decades later, he wrote John Adams from Monticello that "Stewart is a great man, and among the most honest living. . . . I consider him and Tracy as the ablest metaphysicians living; by which I mean investigators of the thinking faculty of man."°

With all that interested him, however, Jefferson did not become easy in France; he was often homesick for Monticello. The occasions which gave him joy, aside from his affectionate friendship with Maria Cosway, were the artistic and history-seeking ones, and the ones which gave him ideas about the cultivation and the produce of the land. The best of all was his journey to southern France and northern Italy, where the architect in him, which was a generous part of the whole man, had a love affair with the Maison Carreé at Nîmes, and where the admirer of the ancient republics noted with appropriate joy or fury the preservation or the destruction of Roman remains. In 1785, when he was beginning to feel acquainted, he summed up in two sentences the pleasures he was discovering among the French, but even so early he indicated a limit soon reached. "Were I to proceed to tell you how much I enjoy their architecture, sculpture, painting, music, I should want words. It is in these arts they shine. The last of them particularly, is an enjoyment the deprivation of which with us, cannot be calculated. I am almost ready to say, it is the only thing which from my heart I envy them, and which, in spite of all the authority of the Decalogue, I do covet." America had nothing to compensate for French music, but there was no doubt in Jefferson's mind where the better life lay. Also in 1785 he invited a young Virginian, James Monroe, to come to France: "It will make you adore your own country, it's soil, it's climate, it's equality, liberty, laws, people and manners. My God! how little do my country men know what precious blessings they are in possession of, and which no other people on earth enjoy. I confess I had no idea of it myself. While we shall see multiplied instances of Europeans going to live in America, I will venture to say no man now living will ever see an instance of an American removing to settle in Europe and continuing there."°

It would be inappropriate to review in this book the story of the rise, during the early 1790s, of the Federalist and Anti-Federalist parties. But we do have to recognize that in those years, building a party, Jefferson and Madison again had to speak under pressure. Once more they were dissenting. With Hamilton and his Federalist allies now the adversary, instead of Lord North and the Tories of England, they renewed the feeling of the 1770s (which is so foreign to liberal orientation today) that individual freedom is naturally sustained by the states and is naturally endangered by the national government. This was the Anti-Federalist line. Jefferson stated it in 1791, before the party was born. Early in that year, when he wrote for President Washington the first legal opinion to say that Hamilton's plan for a national bank transgressed constitutional law, he fixed, as a line of conflict between Hamilton and himself, the line between loose construction of the Constitution, favorable to national powers, and strict constructionism, favorable to the sttaes. He acknowledged that state governments could be aggressive, but he believed their aggressions not to be dangerous. Writing to Archibald Stuart that year Jefferson observed that the "encroachments of the State governments will tend to an excess of liberty which will correct itself" (for the voters could be relied on to make the correction), "while those of the General Government will tend to monarchy . . . , which will fortify itself from day to day, instead of working its own cure, as all experience shows. I would rather be exposed to the inconveniences attending too much liberty, than those attending too small a degree of it." Jefferson evidently had Europe, as well as Alexander Hamilton, in mind.°

Seven years later the war with France, and the wave of hysteria against political dissent—and some actual subversive activity—gave emotional point to the Jeffersonian and Anti-Federalist position, now called Republican. To be sure, since the Smith Act of 1939 began to pile up our own age's restraints on radical expression, Americans have had an object lesson that the Alien and Sedition Acts were not massive. The Sedition Act, which caused the trouble, for the first time fixed federal fines and terms of imprisonment for persons who wrote or spoke "in a False, scandalous and malicious [way] against the government of the United States, or either house of the Congress of the United States, or the President of the United States, with the intent to . . . bring them . . . into contempt . . . or to stir up sedition." Under these phrases a political speech or an essay could be adjudged criminal, and the author severely punished. A few editors, members of Jefferson's party, were actually jailed. On the mitigating side, the operation of the law was limited to wartime; and, much more important in principle, truth was made admissible in defense. This put the new federal statute out of the class of the English common law of seditious libel; it incorporated the very conception—that what is not false is not libelous—for which the lawyer, Andrew Hamilton, had fought, with a degree of success and a degree of failure, two generations earlier.°

But Jefferson and Madison, and their Republican Party which in 1800 would owe its first national victory to the reaction against the Alien and Sedition Acts, saw nothing forgivable in Congress's action. To them an argument that the offensive law was a war measure and not harsh would have been foolish because irrelevant. The government of the United States had recently begun *tabula rasa* with a new contract, and, as they correctly said, the contract gave no authorization to make, and the first amendment specifically excluded, any abridgment of freedom of speech or of the press by Congress. When Jefferson took office as president he immediately pardoned offenders in jail, without regard to their individual merits. He explained this to Abigail Adams, with whom his relationship while he and the Adamses were in Europe had been especially happy. "I discharged every person under punishment or prosecution under the Sedition law, because I considered and now consider that law to be a nullity as absolute and as palpable as if Congress had ordered us to fall down and worship a golden image; and that it was as much my duty to arrest it's execution in every stage, as it would have been to have rescued from the fiery furnace those who should have been cast into it for refusing to worship the image."° In 1798, participating in the political reaction, Jefferson and Madison drafted the famous resolutions passed by the legislatures of Kentucky and Virginia, which went all the way in defying and denying the Alien and Sedition laws. The resolutions reasoned, as to the substance of the issue, that the laws had been passed by a government which had no power to do so, and that they were void and had no legal force. As to the right of the states to pass judgment, in this "as in all other cases of compact among powers having no common judge, each party has an equal right to judge for itself as well as of infractions as of the mode and measure of redress," wrote Jefferson, in his draft resolutions for the Kentucky legislature; on a different occasion he said that every people "forms a moral person." The Kentucky and Virginia Resolutions have often been read as containing the essence of states' rights argument, as doubtless they do; they have been said also to contain the logic of secession, which is questionable. At any rate secession was the last thing Jefferson and Madison wanted; and it would be more truthful to find in the resolutions an effort to put in the record a manifesto which would help contain the national government, within the letter of the Bill of Rights, than an effort to enlarge anything at all, except the state governments' moral authority. Yet in the contretemps there was clear danger of a break in the federal system. Jefferson personally believed just what the legislature of Virginia declared, that the states themselves should consider any rupture "as among the greatest calamities which could befall them; but not the greatest. There is yet one greater, submission to a government of unlimited powers. It is only when the hope of avoiding this shall become absolutely desperate that future forbearance could not be indulged." When the episode of the Kentucky and Virginia Resolutions is read in Jefferson's way, the proper analogy does not seem to be with South Carolina's defiance of the national government in 1832, which blew up over a question of tariff policy, but with the colonies' defiance of Parliament in 1774, when the question was Parliament's power to destroy constitutional uses and rights long honored in America. This earlier analogy helps us understand why Jefferson's victory of 1800 seemed to him like a second revolution—an American glorious revolution done without violence and brought off, according to fundamental law working in a complicated way (when he himself was finally chosen president by the House of Representatives), by the people and their delegates.

Concerning the use of power in foreign relations, Jefferson's and Madison's thought contained a cautionary attitude, much like their distrust of power at home. Their economies in respect of the military establishment, and their turning to nonimportation and embargo procedures against their adversaries in Europe, beginning in 1806—economic sanctions short of war on the pattern of colonial resistance to Parliament before 1775—represent that side of their feeling. On the other hand there was nothing in their principle of restraint which would hold back the full sovereign force of the United States in foreign relations whenever a valid cause came into play. Indeed the Virginia philosopher statesmen's special sense of the moral superiority of American institutions enhanced their freedom of operation when they dealt with the powers of Europe. Thus Jefferson the president acted in accord with Jefferson the philosophe when, in 1803, Napoleon Bonaparte out of the blue offered to benefit the nation in a way the president cherished. The occasion was of course the incredible offer to sell the Louisiana territory, westward-lying from the Mississippi River to the Rocky Mountains and westward-pointing to the ultimate goal, location on the Pacific coast. The opportunity has a greater piquancy in retrospect, because an incidental factor in the first consul's decision to make the offer had been a push given by certain French liberals. Themselves believing as Napoleon did, and as Americans would happily agree, that France could never develop the trans-Mississippi Eden, they wanted it to come under a republican government—they voiced a physiocratic taste much like Jefferson's own.°

The beginning of the president's belief, phrased in the *Notes on Virginia*, that "those who labour in the earth are the chosen people of God, whose breasts he has made His peculiar deposit for substantial and general virtue," has no date that we know.° His romantic notion of the farm suited his boyhood on Peter Jefferson's holdings and perhaps derived from it. Jefferson always romanticized Monticello, whether he was in Paris or Washington or at home. Two years out of the White House, he wrote Charles Willson Peale that "I have often thought that if heaven had given me a choice of my position and calling, it should have been on a rich spot of earth, well watered, and near a good market for the productions of the garden. No occupation is so delightful to me, as the culture of the earth."° The idea, and even the words, seem to echo a pronouncement of his favorite Latin author, Cicero, who said, on the point: "Of all the occupations by which gain is secured, none is better than agriculture, none more profitable, none more delightful, none more becoming to a freeman." Whatever the literary influences were, we know that Jefferson's agrarian tastes were fixed before he visited France. To him the working owner farmer was always the best type of man and citizen: as man of property, he was responsible; as cultivator he was disciplined, by his commitment to follow the cycle of nature; as rural, he was a person apart from the demagogues and distractions of cities.

Yet his visit to France sharpened and deepened his feeling. After a year and a half there, Jefferson wrote to Madison the famous letter quoted in the preceding chapter, which said that the earth is a gift of the Creator, a "common stock" belonging to all men. In that same letter he moved from principle to policy, including the possibility of the state intervening to correct the maldistribution of land. Observations made while walking in the country near Fontainebleau led him, he explained,

> into a train of reflections on that unequal division of property which occasions the numberless instances of wretchedness which I had observed in this country and is to be observed all over Europe. The property of this country is absolutely concentrated in a very few hands, having revenues of from half a million of guineas a year downwards. These employ the flower of the country as servants, some of them having employed as many as 200 domestics, not labouring. They employ also a great number of manufacturers, and tradesmen, and lastly the class of labouring husbandmen. But after all these comes the most numerous of all the classes, that is, the poor who cannot find work. . . . I am conscious that an equal division of property is impracticable. But the consequences of this enormous inequality producing so much misery to the bulk of mankind, legislators cannot invent too many devices for subdividing property, only taking care to let the subdivisions go hand in hand with the natural affections of the human mind. . . . If for the encouragement of industry we allow [the earth] to be appropriated, we must take care that other employment be provided to those excluded from the appropriation. . . . If we do not the fundamental right to labour the earth returns to the unemployed. . . . It is not too soon to provide by every possible means that as few as possible shall be without a little portion of land. The small land holders are the most precious part of a state.°

Before Jefferson became president, the United States under the Constitution had done little for the small farmer. The government, which had inherited possession of the domain from the Confederation—ultimately, through certain states, from the Crown—had passed two measures of land policy. The first, enacted by Congress under Federalist auspices, had required individual purchasers to buy a minimum of a square mile of land (640 acres) and to pay two dollars an acre; this practically excluded the small owner settler, according to intention. The second policy act, which was passed under Republican pressure, though before Jefferson took office, reduced the minimum to 320 acres; but this was still too large for an owner-operated farm and twice the minimum which frontiersmen wanted. Only in 1804, when an act of Congress made 160 acres the norm and reduced the purchase price to $1.64 per acre with credit, did the distribution of the national domain begin on a basis approaching democracy—though still at a remove from the pre-emption and homestead policies of the middle nineteenth century. Only in this context of policy adjustment, and against the background of the freehold ideal of the eighteenth century, is it possible to sense the magnificence, in contemporary times, of the acquisition of Louisiana. Suddenly the area of the United States was doubled; endless unoccupied acres extended the promise of farm land to sustain a yeoman citizenry; the threat of European nations damming the expansion of republican institutions was removed; boundary lines stopped at the Rockies, but expectations soared over the divide and became boundless in terms of the geography and trade of the time. No wonder that Jefferson regarded the transfer of Louisiana from Old World sovereignty to New World as being, besides a political and economic event, a "philosophical" one too.°

In our industrial and power-seeking twentieth century we have given that purchase, and others which followed, a less flattering name. Historians have fallen into the habit of naming "imperialism" the expansionist phase of United States history which followed on the event of 1803. Gilbert Chinard, Jefferson's sympathetic biographer of 1929, called his hero's trans-Mississippi policy "Protective Imperialism," because United States control of Louisiana saved the nation from what would otherwise have been certain conflict with France or some successor of France in ownership. Charles A. Beard called it, more coolly, "Agricultural Imperialism"; this distinguished it from the commercial, industrial, and navalist kinds but put it on a moral parity with them. Certainly Jefferson and Madison took acquisitive action, and the governance of people not represented was decided upon. This means a French, Spanish-descended, and Negro population of some thousands at the mouth of the Mississippi, and a scattering of Europeans throughout the great river valley. The plains Indians at this time received even less consideration, when the question was government by the people, than Negro slaves did, when the question was human equality. On the other hand, in Jefferson's belief the great area was fated soon to be occupied in any case by migrating Americans, who would have natural rights to the land as good as anyone else's. Probably the scruple which the president himself raised, that the purchase and incorporation of new territory into the United States had no specific constitutional sanction, and his own wish for a constitutional amendment to cover the matter, adds to the suggestion of imperialism in the event, as having been something not compatible with American ideals of self-government. Yet the secretary of state who had been father of the Constitution did not doubt the constitutionality of the action; Congress passed appropriations without objecting.

The first relevant measure after the purchase was President Jefferson's sending his private secretary, Meriwether Lewis, and another army officer, William Clark, with an expedition of thirty men, to cross the new territory and to proceed to the Pacific coast. A vision of national growth was at the heart of the enterprise; but it was a scientific and exploring expedition, not a military or claim-staking one. Within a decade, the populated lower part of the territory, which included New Orleans, became the state of Louisiana, a member of the Union politically equal to any; before 1850, according to Jefferson's expectation, a tier of new states along the west bank of the Mississippi stretched from the Gulf of Mexico to Minnesota. Thus the story which begins with the Louisiana purchase attaches agrarian expansion and enlarged federalism to the thought and policy of Jefferson and Madison. The popular phrase of the 1840s, "Manifest Destiny," seems more descriptive of the process than does the epithet "imperialism" as we now use it. With the one exception—then a tacit matter, now a staring inconsistency—that the plains Indians were considered (rather, unconsidered) as having no political standing within the United States government, the westward expansion of the young republic sought no new inequalities by force. In practice as in inspiration that venture would turn out—for citizens—to be much more an emancipating than a subjugating process.

For the symmetry of the present chapter it would be convenient to say that the Virginia philosopher statesmen, as heads of the national government, found ways to serve their ideals of education, to match their services to the yeoman ideal. Their own preference for strict constructionism did not deter them: both Jefferson and Madison were among the liberals who thought a national university to be desirable for the young republic. But of course it was not until 1862, during the Second American Revolution rather than in the wake of the first, that the United States did much for education over and above the school grants of land which the Confederation had inaugurated in the Old Northwest. Only in our own times, with the policy of awarding national scholarships, has the national government begun to implement Jefferson's ideal of equal opportunity in education.

Not as head of government but as sage and leader in retirement, did Jefferson, still seconded by Madison, round out his philosopher statesmanship, in the service of education. He took hold in 1817 at the point where he had left off, thirty-eight years earlier, with the bill "for the Diffusion of Knowledge" which the revolutionary legislature of Virginia had refused to pass. Reinforced by correspondence and personal association, over the years, with such advanced thinkers about education as Joseph Priestley in America and Du Pont de Nemours in France, impressed especially while overseas with the universities of Edinburgh and Geneva, and above all concerned by the unfulfilled needs of the people while democracy increased, he drew up for the legislature a "Plan for Elementary Schools." The title to the contrary, he put forward a total program for the state. The plan complied, more than the 1779 bill had, with the structure of state government; elementary schools were to be the financial and administrative responsibility of the counties. The proposed secondary schools were made more various than the original plan. Perhaps because he had been to Europe, Jefferson now wanted three modern languages taught. As before, he asked for a system of state scholarships "to avail the commonwealth of those talents and virtues which nature has sown as liberally among the poor as among the rich."

Again as before, the grand scheme failed of support and success. But where earlier his only achievement had been some short-run reforms at William and Mary, this time the University of Virginia was born. Under an act of the legislature, Jefferson himself was made rector; beside him on the board of visitors (or trustees) sat James Madison, President James Monroe, and other distinguished Virginians. Wanting a school for statesmen, Jefferson began with the belief, which doubtless echoed his own breadth of reading, that too early specialization was filling the country "with Blackstone lawyers, Sangrado physicians, a ranting clergy, and a lounging gentry." His own work of love at the drafting board, designing the academic "village," created what is still America's finest monument to the community and the harmony to be sought in intellectual life. As visitors learn today, a handsome brick "pavilion" or family residence in close proximity to his students, was assigned to each professor, facing the university lawn; "hotels," or halls for dining, set in formal gardens, were conveniently and regularly spaced. The whole group of buildings was unified by white colonnades and was enclosed by a serpentine brick wall. On the eminence at the head of the quadrangle, the university father and architect placed the Rotunda, an echo of the Pantheon, which would serve for more than a century as the library of the university.

Above all else the University of Virginia belonged to the Enlightenment, and its ideal and architecture of unity did not inhibit the establishment of specialized higher learning, traditional and professional. The structure of the university was made to resemble more the European universities, with their several faculties, than it resembled the colonial colleges. The student chose among fields of study instead of following a prescribed curriculum; with this multiformity, and yet smallness, the University of Virginia pioneered the American institution of the academic department and the principle of elective studies. Jefferson tried, but failed, to persuade the aging Dugald Stewart to come to Charlottesville to take charge of the work in moral philosophy. The first actual appointment as professor, that of Dr. Thomas Cooper of Philadelphia, son-in-law of Joseph Priestley, tells us a great deal about what Jefferson and his colleagues were up against, as well as about what they wanted. Cooper was at once a lawyer, a chemist, and a Unitarian; Jefferson said that he was "acknowledged by every enlightened man who knows him to be the greatest man in America in the powers of his mind and in acquired information." But Cooper's liberalism proved too much for influential religious opinion in Virginia in 1820, and Cooper resigned before arrival—to go on to South Carolina College in Columbia. After this, one of Jefferson's strong determinations was to have extensive work in law. Four fields were specified: government; the law of nature and nations; common and statute law; and laws civil, feudal, mercatorial, and maritime. For this work, especially, an American scholar was wanted. But not until after Jefferson's death was one found who could do the job, and would do it at an academic salary, valuing it higher than the income and availability to political and judicial office which were the happy destiny of lawyers. Professor John Tayloe Lomax had the dedication but served only a few years. Instead of a liberal, philosophical, and social interest in the law, which Jefferson had contemplated for the university, the young professor discovered that his students were pressed for time and wanted their training to be as practical as possible. Presently he himself decided to accept a judgeship.

If the higher ambitions of Jefferson for the university proved impossible to achieve, either during the few months of his life after the beautiful buildings were opened or soon thereafter, good work was nevertheless started. Scholars from overseas, mostly Englishmen, took charge in modern languages, mathematics, classical languages, and anatomy. Despite the success that the University of London had, as soon as it was founded, in bringing back to England two or three of the new professors at Virginia, fields of learning which would produce traditions at Charlottesville were soundly established. After Jefferson died, James Madison, whom his chief had asked to "Take care of me when dead," became the university rector. He saw through the crisis in law studies, and other academic upsets, as he had so many earlier problems the two had undertaken together.°

On several occasions during the later years, Thomas Jefferson phrased quietly what on the whole he stood for, or wanted to be remembered for. The best reminder of the devotee of freedom and equality is the unforgettable epitaph: "Author of the Declaration of Independence, of the Statute of Virginia for Religious Freedom, And Father of the University of Virginia." The practicality of his mind, or rather his pragmatism (before that word was invented), is beautifully indicated in the fragment of autobiography wherein he records the lasting satisfaction he took from having made navigable the Rivanna, the little river near his home. At seventy-three, for Du Pont de Nemours, the French liberal whom he loved and honored, he summed up:

> We of the United States, you know, are constitutionally and conscientiously Democrats. We consider society as one of the natural wants with which man has been created. . . . We think experience has proved it safer, for the mass of individuals composing the society, to reserve to themselves personally the exercise of all rightful powers to which they are competent, and to delegate those to which they are not competent to deputies named, and removable for unfaithful conduct, by themselves immediately.
>
> We both consider the people as our children and love them with parental affection. But you love them as infants whom you are afraid to trust without nurses, and I as adults, whom I freely leave to self government. . . . I believe with you that morality, compassion, generosity are innate elements of the human construction; that there exists a right independent of force; that a right of property is founded in our natural wants, in the means with which we were endowed to satisfy these wants; . . . that justice is the fundamental law of society; that the majority oppressing an individual, is guilty of a crime, abuses its strength, and by acting on the law of the strongest, breaks up the foundation of society; . . . that all governments are more or less republican in proportion as this principle enters more or less into their composition; and that a government by representation is capable of extension over a greater surface of country than one of any other form.°

5   The Renewal of Organic Thought

THE four philosopher statesmen whom we have just considered, and the new institutions and habits of public thought which they fathered and nurtured, display supremely in the history of the West the conceptions of society and politics which we call Lockian and Newtonian. Nature and man, law and justice, contract and constitution, freedom and rights, and equality were their watchwords. The preoccupations of their age were such always to suggest the moral question: what is right, or what accords with Nature? And, what is wrong, or is out of accord?

Whenever, as when constitutions were being written, public problems could be conceived in terms of contract in the way of John Locke's familiar *Second Treatise of Government*, questions of precedent and innovation, stipulation and reservation, came up most naturally. Society and polity were understood to be in fluid condition, subject to rational rearrangement. The mechanical analogies of the age, in the line of Newton, reinforced that kind of belief: because such images represented the world of politics as it ought to be, rather than as it was, they equally with contract ideas served the cause of change. Thus, constructing his Newtonian figures of speech, Hamilton argued for great weight at the national center; using similar figures, Madison spoke for wide and even dispersal of sovereign authority. Drawing from the same frame of thought, Adams discovered harmony and balance in society.

All this, as we have seen in the last three chapters, contributed equally to the denial of the old order which came to climax in 1776 and to the new constructions of government which followed. An increased sense that the universe is reliable and operates under laws of Nature, and that the affairs of men do too, or rather should do, seems to have been necessary for the break with Crown, administration, and Parliament, when all three performed in ways that were unjust and irregular. The men of 1776 seceded, and did so with thought and conscience; but, allowing an exception for Thomas Paine, they did very little to refute the ideas which traditionally supported monarchy. Hardly anyone spoke for old Robert Filmer; no one tried to refute him. No one essayed to prove that the king was not like a father to his subjects, or that Englishmen on both sides of the Atlantic were not in some sense brothers. Thought which regards a nation as something organic, held together by needs and functions which are mutual, and which speaks of the strength and character of a people, is not demolished by thought which sees society either as a series of contracts or as an area of balance in the tug and pull of contrary forces. In the American Revolution that kind of thought was neglected awhile but never abandoned.

As we have already seen in a good many illustrations, organic social thought breathed new life during the late eighteenth and the early nineteenth centuries. The case of Alexander Hamilton, the only one of the philosopher statesmen whose heart remained heavily mortgaged to mercantilist and monarchist values, is the most obvious one. An innovator of policies which implemented ideas, he was imitator when it came to the ideas themselves. His conviction called for economic growth like England's of the preceding century, and for control and leadership in affairs like England's over a longer period.

The other three philosopher statesmen developed patterns of social growth and strength equally, though more slowly. As occurred between Adams and Jefferson, in the beauty of their friendship and correspondence during their seventies and eighties, the differences among the three diminish with length of perspective. Though Adams was no doctrinaire agrarian like Jefferson and Madison, he had considerable of the farmer in him, not alone in his personal history but in his sense of the character of the people as well. In their expectations for the country, the three, with emphases appropriate to their backgrounds, counted on growth in and from the schools and colleges, and from learning wherever located. They worried about what influence the clergy might again achieve in affairs. Above all they relied on what Jefferson and Adams discussed at length, the "natural aristocracy" of mind and character, which they counted on the goodness of creation to produce. New men, they dared hope, would always be present to assume responsibility as the republic grew older—as they themselves had done at the moment of its birth.

This patriot hope was cherished by many, George Washington included, as the epigraph of this chapter indicates. Yet it would not do to end the part of this book which treats the emergence of national convictions as though a note of solid consensus had been struck, for that is not what the thought of the philosopher statesmen produced. Three quite different though overlapping clusters of ideas had been voiced and made more or less systematic; the conscience of the republic would struggle with them by bits and pieces—accepting, rejecting, and combining ideas and policies—for a long time to come. All three projected into the future the business of reconstructing American society—government and culture—which the disruption of the British system had started and the Constitution had greatly advanced.

Among the differences of ideas, stimulating different expectations of the future, two philosopher statesmen reasoned closely from the realities of American society with which they lived and which they understood, as we have seen, with the help of relevant literature and ideas. This was conspicuously true of Alexander Hamilton's firm and logical set of economic and constitutional ideas. His system was full of discontentment with the present, and of ambitions for time to come. It was hardly less true of John Adams and those who shared with him the burden of giving the cautionary message, that social equilibriums must be discovered and—more than discovered—must be calculated and used in the interest of all. Adams believed in his country with a rare passion; he never cast off his Puritan legacy of thinking that Americans had a special destiny that was good. But he saw the frailties of men—including himself—and his line of thought, though it points far into the future, points less specifically toward growth than do the other two lines.

Jefferson and Madison were more confident. Though, as we shall have need to remember when three chapters hence we reach our discussion of practical democracy, they never wrote up a systematic treatment of their ideas, they had a system nevertheless. Their convictions, which we may call the Jefferson cluster of ideas, we now need to recapitulate from all four chapters of Part Three. They began to have public effect with the master statement of national independence under law and with eloquent contributions to republican government: the priority of the legislature; the independence of all three branches; the unqualified natural freedoms of man. Classical statements and provisions followed at once in favor of manhood suffrage, of the separation of church from state and absolute freedom in religion, of education for citizenship and education for leadership, and of economic security for all in the form of minimum landholding. On top of this program, offered to achieve republican life in Virginia, came Jefferson and Madison's proposals for the nation, some of them enacted for the Old Northwest: the exclusion of slavery, the equality of new states and old in self-government and civil freedom, and the better provision for schools in the new states than the old. Although as president Jefferson had little chance to apply his principles of democracy to the common life, he seized the great occasions he did have—throwing out the Alien and Sedition laws, purchasing the Louisiana territory—with emphasis, explanation, and grandeur.

Thus hardly later than the translation of national independence into a political reality, ideals of equal rights and just opportunities for all in education and landholding were proposed for his fellow citizens by the prime philosopher statesmen. Thomas Jefferson did keep quiet about all this as a total program. Except during the 1770s, he took things a step at a time. Doubtless that is one of the reasons that "Jeffersonian" is usually understood mainly as a political and civil-rights word while "Hamiltonian" is understood to indicate a broad program.

This is a misunderstanding of the record. At least for the period of this volume, Jeffersonianism should signify the biggest public thinking the Revolution and the Enlightenment produced.

Part Four

THE CONSCIENCE OF
THE REPUBLIC

1800-1850

CHAPTER XII

The Reinforcement of
American Christianity

I wish you could live a year in Boston, hear their Divines, read their publications, especially the Repository. You would see how spiritual Tyranny and Ecclesiastical Domination are beginning in our Country: at least struggling for birth.

John Adams to Thomas Jefferson, June 25, 1813

I propose, fellow-citizens, a new sort of union, or, if you please, a Christian party in politics . . . *by adopting, avowing, and determining to act upon, truly religious principles in all civil matters. I am aware that the true Christians of our country are divided into many different denominations; who have, alas! too many points of jealousy and collision; still, a union to a very great extent, and for the most valuable purposes is not impracticable.*

Ezra Stiles Ely, The Duty of Christian Freemen to Elect Christian Rulers *(1827)*

1 *Independence and Constitutions for Churches*

DURING the excitement of the Enlightenment and the Revolution, probably no two main currents of thought diverged more widely from each other than the stream of evangelicalism, which had recently been swelled and channeled by the Great Awakening, from the stream of rationalism, which eroded belief in Christian revelation wherever it flowed. At least up to 1778, when the excitement of Patriot successes closed out much possibility of American reconciliation with England, a New Side or New Light Calvinist was farther apart, intellectually, from the deist who lived next door than Patriot was from Loyalist.

But, a happy thing for America during and after the revolutionary epoch, the religious divergencies of the Enlightenment did not become religious antagonisms or conflicts, not in a degree to resemble the divergencies which had already arisen in Europe and were not to be reconciled. To be sure, the laws enacted by Southern States to terminate the Anglican establishments were anticlerical in the literal sense that they eliminated the ancient privileges of Episcopal clergymen. But little aggressiveness flared up against those parsons. They had already been cut down to size: by 1776 they were either departing their homes and parishes as being Loyalists; or else, being Patriots, they were adjusting to serve their church as a voluntary institution. Thus the century-long process of Americanizing southern Anglicanism ended with minimum discourse—minimum criticism of faith, though the local context of skepticism was ample. Conspicuously in Virginia, the political alliance among those favoring disestablishment—Baptists, Presbyterians, deists, and others—functioned as a bridge between the Bible believers and the religious rationalists.

In the few places where anticlerical, and even anti-Christian, feeling did become a public matter, the preferred church either was too solid to be forced to yield much or was so weak as to resist hardly at all. In 1784 appeared in Vermont a pamphlet, *Reason the Only Oracle of Man*, which Timothy Dwight, who was already eminent throughout New England, characterized as "the first formal publication in the United States openly directed against the Christian religion." Here war Patriot defied war Patriot, for the author of the pamphlet, Ethan Allen, as a Green Mountain Boy had been the hero of Ticonderoga, and Dwight had been a Connecticut Patriot chaplain and poet. In Allen's self-explanation: "My affections are Frenchified. Mankind are too national, and commercial intercourse with foreign nations has a tendency to erase the superstitions of the mind by acquainting them that human nature, policy, and interest are the same in all nations." The burden of the essay, which is more like England's critical deism of the mid-century than American deism, ridiculed the clergy for relying on mystery and miracle; *Reason the Only Oracle of Man* was the most combative piece of American expression of its kind.° Yet the author seems to have been fanning the air. If his practical object was to save his adopted Vermont from entering such a church-state alliance as he had grown up under, the pamphlet was unnecessary; if it was to assist Massachusetts and his native Connecticut to separate church from state—the scission which those two deferred for decades—he had no visible impact.

Yet in a much more decorous New England situation, namely, the formal beauty and patrician atmosphere of King's Chapel, Boston, rationalist ideas did infiltrate and conquer a citadel of traditional Christianity. In the twentieth-century sense of the word "establishment," King's Chapel belonged near the center of the Massachusetts system. The first Anglican parish in all New England, it had been created when royal government succeeded corporate government in the Bay Colony. Throughout the eighteenth century it had been the religious seat of high representatives of the Crown, civil and military, and of many of the social elite of Boston; along with Christ Church, it had been one of the few pulpits in America where the case in favor of establishing a colonial bishopric had been preached and sympathetically heard.° King's Chapel, Boston, compares with Trinity Parish, New York, and Bruton Parish, Williamsburg, as having been uncommonly identified with royalist and traditionalist elements. Given its particular background, of having been Anglican in the old Puritan hub, and given the losses it suffered when British officials, armed forces, and Loyalists withdrew from Boston even before the Declaration, probably it suffered a more severe dislocation by reason of political independence than any other congregation anywhere.

During the war years the rump parish acted as independently as ever a Puritan congregation had, and in much that same style. In 1782 the churchwardens asked James Freeman, who was twenty-three and a Harvard trainee in theology, to conduct their services as a lay reader. Freeman did that and much more. Religious liberal in the style of Mayhew and Chauncy, and also a Patriot, he revised the prayerbook according to his own convictions. Besides deleting prayers for the king, he substituted Unitarian phrasings for the Godhead in place of Trinitarian. Somehow he considered that he was still acting within the frame of his church: although Episcopalian ministers of Boston denounced his work as "subversive" and "unconstitutional," he applied after the war to Bishop Samuel Seabury, America's first bishop, for ordination. He was soundly refused. Yet his congregation sustained him; they printed and followed his prayerbook. Elected parish officials ordained him as "rector, minister, priest, pastor, teaching elder and public teacher"—Episcopalian and Congregationalist titles combined. Though King's Chapel Unitarianism was elder cousin rather than parent in the family of Unitarianism which would mature in eastern Massachusetts during the next forty years, the chapel ranks as the earliest non-Trinitarian church and—as being in the direct lineage of the colonial Church of England—was the most conspicuously anti-traditional church in America.

In New York City and southward a less sustained and less successful effort was made at church building in accord with the critical ideas of the Enlightenment. The preacher leader there, Elihu Palmer, had grown up in western Connecticut and had graduated in 1787 from evangelical Dartmouth College. But as a very young preacher he lost belief in the divinity of Jesus. By the early 1790s he had gone as far as Ethan Allen in critical deism; he inveighed against Bible faith, Christian doctrine, and the acceptance of miracles. Reading Condorcet and other French spokesmen for human progress, and affected also by Tom Paine and by William Godwin's *Political Justice*, he gradually turned toward secular moral affairs; he called his ideas "Theophilanthropism." After some residence and law study in different parts of Pennsylvania, and travels which took him as far as Atlanta, still a preacher at heart he gathered a congregation in New York which became known variously as the Philosophical Society, the Theistical Society, and the Society of Columbian Illuminati. At about the same time, the middle 1790s, and partly in response to his visits and preaching, like-minded societies appeared in Philadelphia, Baltimore, and Newburgh. Palmer kept in touch with them, and they with one another for a while, by weekly journals he put out: for a very brief period, *The Temple of Reason;* for somewhat more than a year, *The Prospect: or, a View of the Moral World.* By that time philanthropy, in the general meaning of the word, had many other voices in America; and deism was quieting down. "Theophilanthropism" as a movement dropped from sight when Elihu Palmer was buried in 1805.°

Congregations which were inspired by rationalist (and essentially non-Christian) ideas, illustrate the range and freedom of church building in America during the 1780s and 1790s. But the main and massive efforts of building, or rather of reconstructing, occurred among the legatees of the national churches of England and Scotland. Like the people of the populous, principal old colonies, Virginia and Massachusetts, the people of the populous, principal old churches, the Anglican Church and the Presbyterian Church, had to have new constitutions which accorded with the spirit and thought of the Revolution—at once with its liberal and its nationalist goals. Thus, soon after the peace, three large churches were founded which derived from the prerevolutionary two: the Methodist Episcopal Church in America, in 1784; the Protestant Episcopal Church of the United States, in 1785; and the Presbyterian Church of the United States, in 1787. The chronological order of their writing their new constitutions is exactly the reverse of the order of the success they had achieved, before 1776, in securing for themselves a practical degree of autonomy.°

Prior to the Revolution, the Methodists, as being members of a movement which was led by an Anglican priest at home, had been organized hardly at all for church freedom. Not long before war broke out, John Wesley had sent Francis Asbury—future Methodist bishop—to America with the function and title of superintendent. During the war years Wesley's own conspicuous royalism put a Loyalist imprint on his American following; moreover, the great number of American Methodists lived in the Middle States where Anglicanism often signified Loyalism and where there was a great deal of both. On the eve of the Revolution, moreover, the Methodists suffered from a problem which had more than once plagued the Puritans: Who should have access to—and also in this case: Who should conduct— the communion service? In the free-will theology which prevailed among them, the Lord's Supper was viewed as an aid to salvation rather than as a symbol (Edwardsian style) of salvation already achieved. It was a means of grace and should be widely available. Notwithstanding that a Virginia Anglican minister, Devereux Jarratt, advised that unordained Methodists be authorized to give the sacrament, John Wesley—who was managerial and in many ways tradition-minded —held back.

Even after the Revolution Wesley continued in his determination to control things and only gradually yielded ground. On the point of organization, he sent a second superintendent, Thomas Coke, to America. Persuaded now that his people should have communion within the organization he fostered, he tried and failed to win the bishop of London to ordain one of the Methodist lay preachers with full and proper authority. Wesley next decided that he himself as a presbyter (or priest) could give that ordination; this time he reasoned from the history of the ancient apostolic churches and came up with a conclusion thoroughly at variance from Anglican church law. In this way two or three clergymen were provided for the American Methodists, and an ecclesiastical continuity—however erroneous by Roman or Anglican standards—was preserved. Wesley also devised an order of service and, from the Thirty-nine Articles of Anglican belief, he drew twenty-four for Methodists in the New World.

So much the octogenarian English leader could send over with success. But he could no longer control American Methodism in detail. Even in a movement where self-government had been lacking, either as idea or as experience, local initiative appeared quickly. The "Christmas Conference," in Baltimore, 1784, was the occasion. As Superintendent Asbury understood beforehand and helped arrange, the lay preachers there strongly insisted—in the style of a state constitutional convention—on enacting their own fundamental law. But Asbury had a fondness for authority which equaled or surpassed John Wesley's own. The upshot of the deliberations in Baltimore was a free church, but one the early self-government of which invites comparison with the Spartas of history rather than with the democratic republics. The conference did not hesitate about performing any and all acts of church government; it made separation from the Episcopal Church altogether complete. It approved the ordination of preachers; "preacher" became the essential ministerial title and office. Beyond his previous ordinations, the conference consecrated Francis Asbury as superintendent, the office Wesley had designated. But this did not suit the man who made himself the actual autocrat of the new church; he promptly pre-empted the title of bishop, and in 1787 that rank was made official. The first ordinations were performed by Coke and others who themselves had been ordained by Wesley in England. Altogether the ordinations and offices, as they were accepted by Methodist believers, eliminated within their new church any of the old doubt about the sacraments. Those and all other essential decisions and positions of the church were authoritatively set forth in a little book which derived from early conference proceedings and was appropriately named *Form of Discipline for the Ministers, Preachers, and Members of the Methodist Episcopal Church in America.* With that book, which included a special injunction—"And remember! A Methodist Preacher is to mind every point, great and small, in the Methodist Discipline!"— and with their Bible and hymnal, the new ministers confronted the world.

Thus was born in bigness, and in system and dedication, a church which rapidly attained nationwide scope. It was a people's church, yet it was neither democratic nor decentralized. On those counts the Methodists departed from the two-century-long trend toward congregational authority which had affected all branches of colonial Protestantism. Among a membership which was characteristically little educated and little privileged, and which was early and numerous to participate in frontier settlement, centralization had enormous advantages. Asbury, who never married and was altogether ascetic, traveled thousands of miles annually by horseback to preach, to ordain, to superintend. His ministers likewise were mainly single and were admonished though not required to remain so; as preachers on horseback they became circuit riders on given assignments and were as ready as Jesuits to undertake a mission on a superior's command. So structured, the church acquired special characteristics of efficiency, expansionism, and vigor in competition with other churches. It was a Bible-studying, hymn-singing, enthusiastic movement; for the first generation or so it would prove less education-minded and less theology-minded than the older churches.

As for the spirit of the enterprise, a few sentences from the *Form of Discipline* of the 1788 edition, the earliest one to be well edited and readable, are instructive.

> What may we reasonably believe to be God's design, in raising up the preachers called Methodists in America? *Answ.* To reform the continent, and spread scripture holiness over these lands. . . . Let us strongly and explicitly exhort all believers to go on to perfection . . . , meaning thereby . . . salvation from all sin, by the love of God and man filling our heart. . . . Is the change gradual or instantaneous? It is both the one and the other. . . . Certainly we should insist on the gradual change. . . . And . . . the more earnestly [believers] expect [the instantaneous change, also], the more swiftly and steadily does the gradual work of God go on in their souls; the more careful are they to grow in grace; the more zealous of good works. . . . Therefore whoever would advance the gradual change in believers, should strongly insist on the instantaneous.

Altogether the Methodists' commitment to personal perfectionism— their belief in good works, combined with their spiritual canniness— and their dedication to missions and the Christianization of nation and continent, were well timed to needs felt by many Americans. As the nation now faced westward, and as also—during the years of Napoleon and Metternich—it had to deal with a very imperfect, seemingly sinful, regime in Europe, increasing thousands of citizens glady accepted Methodist values.°

As Unitarian events at King's Chapel and Methodist ones in Baltimore indicate, the War of Independence caused considerable disintegration within the Church of England in America, well before that church faced up to the schism which was impending between itself and the mother Church of England, in England. Institutionally speaking, American Anglican believers were in a more difficult position in 1783 than the Methodists. The Methodists, though they had to build from the ground, began with a head start in voluntary organization; though they had not early sought institutional independence, when it came their leaders could hardly wait to take charge. The Anglicans, on the other hand, while supplying many of the Southern and Middle State leaders of the Revolution, discovered among those very leaders a low supply of Christian energy. Even where faith was confident, the church had no unified leadership. As before the Revolution, there prevailed in the church (outside Methodism) two moods; the two were geographically somewhat separate, and spiritually were hard to reconcile. The high-church enthusiasts for Anglican traditions of ecclesiasticism were concentrated in Connecticut and New York City; the low-church moderates were numerous in the Southern States. They retained old Virginia ways of ecclesiastical do-it-yourself.

But now that an American bishop would not be an English appointee, sent over like a royal governor, Anglicans of all stripes thought that the time had come for episcopacy in America. Even while the War of Independence was on, meetings of churchmen gathered and the new name, "Protestant Episcopal," came into use. As soon as peace was made, a move toward establishing a bishopric occurred in Maryland. The distinguished but erratic William Smith, formerly head of the College of Philadelphia and now an Eastern Shore rector and president of the new little Washington College, was elected bishop. Apparently it was the reputation he had for excessive drinking which forestalled his being consecrated in England. Much more appropriate than it would have been to have the earliest bishop originate anywhere else, the first successful candidate came from the high-church group in Connecticut. Samuel Seabury, whose father had been one of the early New Englanders to serve as an S.P.G. missionary, had himself been a prominent Loyalist. He was the propagandist with whom Alexander Hamilton crossed pamphlets in 1775; later he had been jailed, a political prisoner in New Haven, and then in 1777 had gone to England and received an honorary degree from Oxford. All this Englishness to the contrary, in 1782 his nearby brothers in the priesthood nominated Samuel Seabury to hold the lordly title of bishop—the office which Connecticut's leading people had rejected and feared from the days of Archbishop Laud.

Here a bit more comparison is in order. The Methodists, in adopting and adapting the episcopate, had decided for the administrative strength of the office but had rejected the supporting theory. According to their *Form of Discipline*, their church believed that "a moderate Episcopacy" would give them "the most excellent mode of church government," but they felt "that the uninterrupted succession of Bishops from the Apostles can be proved neither from scripture nor antiquity." This decision gave them particular advantages: in the immediate situation, it freed them to make the ordinations they did; and in the long-run situation it made them more like dissenters, quite fully Protestant and closer to Presbyterians and others, than they had been at first. A like decision was closed to Episcopalians, "Protestant" though they chose to be called. To have abandoned the apostolic succession would have thrown the high churchmen clear outside the rising American church. (In the future that decision, if it had been taken, would have excluded most American Episcopalians from what has become the Anglican Communion, the common Episcopalianism of the English-speaking world.) Thus there was considerable national importance in the ways and means the Episcopalians found to have the historic episcopacy transplanted at last to America. Their doing this was, with all else, the first reweaving of Anglo-American institutional ties after 1776, a demonstration that transatlantic threads of culture and politics were by no means completely severed.

Bishop-elect Samuel Seabury, who belongs among the most eminent American Anglophiles ever, moved in haste. He arrived in England before Parliament had passed the legislation which would enable English bishops to consecrate a bishop not under the Crown; he proceeded to Scotland, where "non-juring" bishops were free to act. They did so, in Aberdeen, late in 1784. But one bishop does not make a new church; three are normal for consecrations. Back at home, moreover, Seabury's priority in office failed to wipe out his disqualifications for national leadership—his old Loyalism and his New England and high-church particularities. Men better qualified came from the Middle States, where Anglicanism had always been voluntary and unprivileged (or no more than a little privileged) by colonial statute, and where high-church and low-church tastes appeared, each familiar with the other, among neighboring parishes. In 1787 two bishops elect, William White from Pennsylvania and Samuel Provoost from New York, made the necessary voyage; Parliament had now passed the enabling statute, and they were duly and regularly consecrated. As for Virginia, a great deal of church history was reflected in the three more years before 1790, when the Reverend James Madison of Williamsburg, in charge of Bruton Parish and president of William and Mary College, was elected and consecrated the first bishop there. The old colonial capital remained a seat of rationalism and of distrust of power. But meanwhile, indeed from well before the consecration of Bishops White and Provoost and considerably due to their leadership, the way to having a national church, which would be identified at once with American ways and patriotism and with the full legitimacy of the apostolic succession, had been opening.

The decisive deliberations occurred in Philadelphia in 1785, in a convention of forty Episcopalians from seven states, twenty-four laymen and sixteen clergymen. The Reverend Mr. White, who was already bishop elect and in correspondence with members of the Anglican hierarchy, was the elected chairman. Still in his thirties, he was a dozen years along in the sixty-five years he was going to serve Christ Church parish, in Philadelphia; he was a graduate of the College of Philadelphia and had been a Patriot chaplain. More important in 1785, he was the principal spokesman for the mixing of laymen with clergymen in the church's national conventions. This was foreign to Anglican custom, either in the colonies or at home. But White thought of the combination as a desirable way of church government: he conceived of the national church convention as providing a sensible American successor institution to Parliament, as legislative sovereign of the church. With ideas which resembled Presbyterian federalism, he swung Episcopalianism well into line with Protestant habits and republican principles.

The first convention worked White's planning into the basic architecture of the church. Dioceses were created which followed state boundaries. But as in Virginia and different from England, the parishes were considered the prior and basic institution, creators not creatures of the diocese. Patriot representatives, in annual convention, were given the governance of the diocese; the bishop was to guide and preside, and fulfill sacramental functions. The parishes were given full authority to select their own clergymen and to pay them. This perpetuated the autonomy they had won in the colonial establishments and introduced in their new condition a good deal of democracy. The over-all legislative authority of the church was located in the triennial, two-house, national convention. The rank and authority of archbishop was conspicuously avoided. The presiding bishop of the convention was made just that, no more; no bishop was given authority over another bishop. The lower house was composed of mixed lay and clerical delegates from the dioceses. The upper house was made a House of Bishops. There is some irony in all this. Where the Methodists, who were usually little-educated and unprivileged people, had adopted a centrally controlled church government, with great power assigned to their bishops, the Episcopal Church, with upper-class, highly educated leadership and with the claim of divine authority implicit in the apostolic succession, constructed a more leveling system.

Altogether by 1789, the year when the new federal government went into operation, the Protestant Episcopal Church was fully and equally launched. By that time there were three bishops in America, and, after some strain between Seabury on one hand and White and Provoost on the other, they were proving capable of closing ranks sufficiently for organizational purposes. A new prayerbook was published, with some simplifications and with prayers for the officers of the republic. But essentially it was the same as the Church of England one. The ancient rites were maintained; the sacraments, the ordinations and consecrations, all that meant the main tradition of the church, except monarchy and preference by the state, were carried on in the New World. Within such a frame, holding an office carefully pruned of power, the American bishops began their work with restraint and flexibility. In the century and three-quarters intervening since that time, the bishops of the Episcopal Church have gained a reputation for piety and for moderation in all things religious, moral, and political.°

For all its colonial-period accumulations of membership and wealth, the Protestant Episcopal Church after the Revolution retained only about four hundred congregations. This compares with five hundred Presbyterian congregations, widely spread; eight hundred Congregationalist ones, all in the northeastern states; and three hundred Baptist ones. But the tardiness of the Presbyterians about reorganization, compared to the Methodist and Episcopalian successors to the Church of England, derived from a favorable condition: the logic of national independence required little change in a church already on its own. Three decades earlier the New Sides and Old Sides had rejoined in an intercolonial system of presbyteries and synods; before the Revolution the Presbyterian Church had become the most numerous organization in America which appeared in every region. In the War of Independence Presbyterians had nearly all been Patriots: President Witherspoon, their leader, had given them conspicuous political identification. During the war years and down to 1787, the Presbyterian Church supplied the one federal type of institution which was familiar in operation and beloved by many citizens. In that same period, Scots-Irish Presbyterians, who had always been frontier seekers, took prompt and aggressive part in settling and organizing Kentucky and Tennessee, the earliest transappalachian states. More fully than in the case of any other Christian body, the Presbyterian polity paralleled the institutional practices of the United States.

The General Assembly, the church legislature which corresponds to the namesake institution in Scotland, was created in 1789; it became—

what it has remained—the seat of sovereignty within the Presbyterian system. John Witherspoon sat in the chair, as moderator. He was sixty-six, now, and would live only five years longer. Although as a New Jersey assemblyman he was still active in politics, and he was guiding the college at Princeton through a difficult financial period, he found time for leadership in framing the new constitution and in rounding out its confessional and catechetical pronouncements. The collaboration he received from the Reverend John Rodgers of New York testifies to the solidity of what they did. Mr. Rodgers derived from the revivalist wing of the mid-century church: he had been a boyhood convert of George Whitefield; he had been licensed to preach, after study (without college training), by a New Sides presbytery; he had sought to serve with Samuel Davies in Hanover County. Thus in the 1780s, as in the 1760s, Witherspoon and his colleagues brought together the Scottish and the American, the more worldly and the more evangelical, elements in their church. Before the meeting in 1789, four or five years of preliminary study and writing had paved the way. The church now promulgated its pyramid-style constitution: an enlarged system of congregations, presbyteries, and synods, with the new nationwide General Assembly at the top. It formally adopted the Westminster Confession of Faith, which was the confession of the Church of Scotland, as its own. It issued a Longer and a Shorter Catechism and an order of worship for the congregations. If, when we next come upon Presbyterianism, we find it very conservative and prone (again as in the 1740s) to subdivide into schools of thought and structures of organization, we need remember that it had grandly reached a culmination of liberalism and nationalism as to polity, in these respects ahead of all other churches, in 1789.°

Allowing for an important exception among the Congregationalists of Connecticut (to whom we shall return), the remaining two very large Christian bodies, the Congregational and the Baptist ones, did not receive from the Revolution any such stimulation to reorganize as did the Methodists or Episcopalians, or even the Presbyterians. The congregational form of polity, which belonged equally to both, spared them the immediate pressures of nationalization. Interstate connections, especially some coordination of denomination-wide and interdenominational missionary effort, would occur before long. But like the New England townships among political institutions, their congregations did not much seek over-all organization during the critical 1780s. Constitutionally and institutionally speaking, they could and did rest on their oars.

Among the less numerous bodies, the two which were furthest apart in the Christian spectrum, the Roman Catholics and the Friends, were the most changed of all by the Revolution. Or rather, in the Quaker instance, the War of Independence completed the political reduction which the French and Indian War had begun. In 1756 the Quakers had been catapulted out of their control of the Pennsylvania legislature, and very largely out of politics, by the pressures of war. During the Revolution their home city and state had been the place where the decision between Loyalism and Patriotism was most trying, because Philadelphia fell under, and then out of, British control. Quakers were accused of Loyalism, often unjustly; they frequently refused military service for their own good Christian reasons, but this did not endear them with the Patriots, or with the Loyalists either. Thus by the 1780s the American Quakers had pretty well returned to the situation—of being outside affairs—from which they had emerged during the 1680s, on first arrival in the Middle Colonies. John Woolman and Anthony Benezet were dead in 1785. A new time was coming soon for non-political resistance to slavery; the time was coming also for a fresh flow of spiritual religion under Quaker auspices. But until such re-newals actually occurred (in fact beginning about a quarter century after independence), much new work by the Quaker spirit in America would be delayed.°

For the Roman Catholics, entirely the opposite; the conditions of the Enlightenment, independence, and republican government opened doors to participation in affairs. From being alienated in their principal location, Maryland, during the French and Indian War, and from being universally excluded from government, Charles Carroll of Carrollton, the signer, led them into Patriot politics. Meanwhile Father John Carroll, his cousin, took on major responsibilities, first as a Patriot diplomat, later as a builder of the church. Thenceforward there would always be Roman Catholics participating, openly and freely, in the business of church, nation, and state.

But this did not occur in numbers prior to the 1840s, when the heavy Irish immigration came; it could not occur with much effect before the Catholic Church began to match the Protestant churches in education and other public effort. On this account, Father John Carroll rather than Charles Carroll, the priest rather than the statesman, made more considerable early contributions. In 1784 Father Carroll was appointed prefect apostolic, the official representative of the pope in the United States. Five years later he became the first American Catholic bishop; he became the first archbishop in 1808. In Baltimore where he was seated, his diocese erected a splendid cathedral; it was designed by Benjamin Henry Latrobe, the great classical-revival architect of re-publican tastes. Executed in the basilica style but with minaret-like additions, the cathedral preceded by decades any equally monumental cathedral-building by the Protestant Episcopalians. (Not a stone's throw away, Baltimoreans must have enjoyed seeing go up, only a little less grandly, the city's strong Unitarian Church.) Also in Baltimore, the Sulpician Order started immediately its special work of training priests; St. Mary's Seminary there preceded by a decade the founding of any Protestant theological seminary. In Washington, overlooking the Potomac, the Jesuits established Georgetown University in 1815. Some years later the supremely devoted Mother Ann Seton, widowed daughter of Episcopalian parents, founded the first American order of nuns, the Sisters of Charity; she placed the sisters' headquarters at Emmitsburg, Maryland, about fifty miles from Baltimore and Washington. The early missionary effort which was made in Kentucky, with a Trappist monastery in the vicinity (midway between Baltimore and the old French Catholic establishments in St. Louis and New Orleans), was located in what otherwise would have been quite purely Protestant —Presbyterian, Baptist, and Methodist—evangelical country.

Thus quickly did the federal republic entertain Roman Catholic institutions, hierarchy, and symbols. No more than a generation earlier these things had been all but universally regarded as medieval and archaic, and representing bigotry and tyranny in alliance. Now the hierarchy itself, in the person of John Carroll, speedily assured all who would listen that Catholic faith and republican principle are compatible after all. Frequently the Maryland bishop proclaimed his own belief that church should be separate from state and that freedom of religion favored both. He went even further when he said that religious liberty promised, "by giving a free circulation to fair argument, . . . to bring all denominations of Christians to a unity of faith." In such reliance on freedom he took a course which many later American Catholics would refuse to follow—from the time of John Carroll until recent Catholic-Protestant *rapprochements* there has seldom been voiced in America such hope of reconciliation through discourse as the first archbishop put into words.°

Though it would be hard to find an equal statement from a comparably high place among Protestant leaders, belief among them that the new nation belonged to an interchurch Christianity, and vice versa, did sometimes find authoritative voice. In Ezra Stiles, whose presidency of Yale from 1777 to 1795 bridged the Revolution-to-Federalism epoch, and whose thought was more than touched by the modes of the Enlightenment, that belief spoke strongest and best. By disposition a reconciler, as a young clergyman during the French and Indian War in Newport he had preached a sermon, which would be widely distributed and admired, "On Christian Union." The autonomy of the congregations of America, he said, no matter what their church was, opened the way to ample agreement. Stiles generously matched words with deeds: during the 1760s in Rhode Island he helped the Baptists there launch the college which would become Brown University. One of his first acts as Yale president was to make peace between New Lights and Old Lights among faculty and students. Soon he sought, by means of what he called a "fraternal correspondence," to open up a relationship (where there had been none) with Anglican William and Mary. He told President Madison—the future bishop—that their two "infant Seminaries, Colleges, and Universities . . . should cultivate a mutual Intercourse and honorable Friendship with one another." Madison responded warmly: "It belongs to our colleges and Universities to lay the foundation from which the future glory of America shall arise. . . . If America can behold her sons encreasing in Knowledge and in Virtue, then indeed we may, Sir, at least as far as respects ourselves, rejoice in having rendered the most solid advantages to our country."°

During the year peace was made with England, Stiles preached before the state legislature in Hartford his most famous sermon, "The United States Elevated to Glory and Honor." Therein he portrayed in one picture the religious and secular splendors he hoped for in America. Tying economic matters with political and religious, he observed that the country was prospering "in the lively, vigorous exertion of industry"; he recommended trade with Europe on a liberal basis, quite different from the old mercantilism. "The caution with which we are to be treated may occasion and originate a commercial system among the maritime nations on both sides of the Atlantic, founded in justice and reciprocity of interest, which will establish the benevolence as well as the opulence of nations, and advance the peoples of society to civil perfection." More to the point with state legislators (to whose attention he had for years been presenting the financial needs of Yale), Stiles pleaded for such a postrevolutionary flowering of culture as he believed the colleges ready to serve. "The cultivation of literature will greatly promote the public welfare. . . . Travels, biography, and history, the knowledge of the policies, jurisprudence, and scientific improvements among all nations, ancient and modern, will form the civilian, the senator, the patrician, the man of useful eminence in society. The colleges have been of singular advantage in the present day." Stiles's climax was of course a religious one. After praising the revolutionary state governments in America—the other states had now caught up with Connecticut and Rhode Island, he said, as having become commonwealths, too—he reverted to a theme that was very old in New England. He explained the need that government under law has for Christian guidance and the need that the churches have for commonwealth government. "The United States will embosom all the religious sects or denominations of Christendom. Here they may all enjoy their whole respective systems of worship and church government complete."°

If we place Ezra Stiles's quarter century of labor in behalf of Christian nationalism and republicanism alongside Alexander Hamilton's fifteen-year effort in behalf of economic nationalism, the Yale president comes into view as having been, like the secretary of the treasury, a combining social thinker. Quite as we now discern in Hamilton's and Robert Morris's writings simultaneous echoes of old mercantilism and new assertions of national unity, so we may detect in Stiles's pronouncements at once echoes of old Puritan belief in a national covenant and new hope for reconciliation among Christian churches. Events of the coming half century, especially the great waves of Protestant revivalism, would go far to make good Stiles's prophecies regarding cooperation among Protestants.

2 *Widening Goals of Christian Perfectionism*

IN the birth of the Methodist Episcopal Church and its call to sinners to become holy, we encountered in the previous section the first numerous efforts made in America to serve the doctrine best known as "perfectionism." The doctrine never belonged to the Methodists exclusively, but their numbers reinforced its importance. Between the Revolution and the Civil War their church zoomed from zero to twenty-seven hundred congregations, a dozen times as many as Congregationalist or Episcopalian ones, and much the largest denomination in the country.

The idea of perfectionism requires some consideration. In the relevant meaning of the word it signifies emancipation from sin, and guidance by God. Yet it by no means suggests antinomianism, or what we might now call spiritual inner directedness. Certainly the Methodists did not think that church guidance of conduct should wither away for anyone. With them Bible precept and *Form of Discipline*, and the habit of circuit riders to decry the sins of personal behavior, pointed more toward outer direction. On the theological side, the followers of John Wesley had always been mainly free-willers and salvation-by-works believers. While circuit-riding preachers did draw on Jonathan Edwards's manuals on the methods of evangelizing, they worked from a different base. They believed that salvation is given or withheld on a basis of justice, according to an individual's deeds rather than according to the mysterious decisions of God's love. While even among the popular churches any expectation of a Christian millennium (as suggested by the *Book of Revelations*, Chapters 19–21) did not before 1830 come much into voice, that was the direction toward which the search for holiness tended. From that point of view, the institution building of the end of the eighteenth century, organizing new churches or congregations according to conscience, was but the first part of the Christian's duty. Infusing the new organizations with the perfectionist spirit, which meant guiding America toward bringing the Kingdom of God into being on earth, came logically and urgently next.

A second meaning of perfectionism, hardly theological at all, came contemporaneously into American thought. It by no means belonged to the churches but it was near and influential: it was simply the supposition that right reason within right institutions can be made to emancipate society from corruption and injustice. This ideal is sometimes pinpointed as "Post-Christian Perfectionism"; the phrase is mainly applied to the utopias of 1825 and after—that is, to communities like New Harmony and Brook Farm which we will consider four chapters ahead. But the qualifier "Post-Christian" is mistaken. That characterization overlooks the old—secular but not unchristian—habit among Englishmen and Americans of supposing that their national system of law opens roads to higher justice: that it connects with political and social justice, which is close to the intention of God.

Near the beginning of this book, where our business was the early seventeenth century and the problem was to identify those English convictions which bore transplantation overseas, one of the durable transplants was the Englishman's belief that the common law signified divine law, as put into actual operation by the judges. In short, English common law rested on a divine-right theory—belief in God working through judges. From the time of Sir Edward Coke's insisting that the law was higher than James I, that kind of idealism infused English and colonial thought. The Enlightenment altered, but did not transform, the position. To envisage this, we may return to the words Thomas Jefferson addressed to Abigail Adams concerning the Alien and Sedition Acts. Acknowledging "the weakness and uncertainty of human reason," Jefferson told his old friend that "both of our political parties, at least the honest portion of them, agree conscientiously on the same object, the public good: but they differ essentially in what they deem the means of promoting that good. . . . Which is right, time and experience will prove. . . . With whichever opinion the body of the nation occurs, that must prevail. My anxieties on the subject will never carry me beyond the use of fair and honorable means, of truth and reason: nor have they ever lessened my esteem for moral worth."° Thus in the mind of Jefferson the voice of the people seemed to open—albeit not at all quickly in this case—the way to such perfection of justice as is available to men on earth.

Far apart in their working locations in society as the Methodist passion for holiness and the Jeffersonian belief in reason characteristically were, the two brands of perfectionism they stood for—emancipation from sin and emancipation from injustice and corruption—did meet and affect one another in various branches of the American community. Though firsts are hard to establish, efforts which achieved eloquence and success began in Massachusetts and Connecticut. While the Revolution in those states and their neighbors had forced less in the way of church reorganization than elsewhere, the congregations kept up as they could their old habits of supervising the life of the people. In eastern Massachusetts, always culturally the most dynamic part of the region, around the turn of the century Universalists and Unitarian Congregationalists undertook lively ventures into perfectionism which blended Christian and secular values.

Universalism and Unitarianism resembled one another in being impelled by the liberalisms of the eighteenth century: both were optimistic about society, and both rejected the pessimism about the natural condition of man which Calvinism sustained. Of the two, Universalism organized first. The Universalist leaders came from outside Massachusetts and derived from middle to lower conditions of life. John Murray, the founder, settled in Gloucester during the War of Independence, after seven years of wandering from his home in London. Hosea Ballou, the thinker of the movement, was a native of Rhode Island; he circled Massachusetts for decades—preaching from place to place in New Hampshire, Vermont, and New York—before he began (when he was nearly fifty) a very popular thirty-year ministry in Boston.

Murray, who had been a Patriot chaplain and before then a preaching itinerant, established in 1779 the Independent Church of Christ in Gloucester. He preached a distinguishing doctrine, a democratic kind of eschatology, "that *every individual* shall in due time be separated from sin." His idea of salvation for all made his congregation the first Universalist one in America. Ballou was more than a follower. Though too young to have served in the Revolution, he endorsed Murray's democratic theory of salvation and went yet further in ways of separating from New England orthodoxy. Stimulated by deistic reading—Ethan Allen's *Oracle* was one book which affected him—he specifically repudiated many doctrines, of which the Trinity and human depravity were two. In 1803 he drew up the confession of faith which the new church (by now beginning to grow in upstate New York as well as New England) accepted in convention. Only two years later he brought out his doctrinal *Treatise on the Atonement*, the best book of the several he wrote. He insisted that the Bible does not say that God punishes souls after death. Always urging that God bears unlimited love for His children, Ballou reasoned that for eternity there could be none that He would reject.°

The effective emergence of Unitarian convictions among Congregationalists, which occurred about fifteen years after the King's Chapel conversion, included some adopting of Universalist doctrine. As early as 1784 the liberal minister of the First Church, Boston, Charles Chauncy, when he was nearly eighty delivered a sermon, of title and general conception like the preaching of John Murray, on "The Salvation of All Men, the Grand Scheme Aimed at in the Scheme of God." This was the same Chauncy who had criticized Jonathan Edwards's revivalism during the 1740s, and whose earlier preaching had connected him with Jonathan Mayhew as one of the few prerevolutionary clergymen to veer away from Trinitarian belief. Generally speaking, New England Unitarianism would always entertain broad views about salvation; on the other hand, it would not press that issue as much as Universalism did. Since it retained no belief in original sin (while Universalism sometimes did), questions of future rewards or punishments fell outside its area of concern. In underlying conviction and degree of departure from historic Christian traditions, Unitarianism was more radical than Universalism was.

Yet Unitarian Congregationalists had difficulty separating from historic church loyalties; rather, they wished and expected to take control. Their first trial of strength came just after the turn of the century, when the time came for the moderately liberal Hollis professor of divinity at Harvard, David Tappan, to retire. An academic fight occurred. Professors and ministers, the latter including members of the Harvard Corporation and the Board of Overseers, aired the intellectual and personal issues. The decision turned out to be surprisingly clear-cut. When Henry Ware, liberal minister at Hingham, won the appointment, the old college—which was now, after Professor John Winthrop's career, on the way to be a university—risked losing the support of the religiously conservative elements, the very orthodoxy the college itself had done so much to create and then to amend.

Professor Ware would not be the most exciting Unitarian intellect during his thirty-five years as Hollis professor. But he would be one of the most stable and judicious, and an effective consolidator. He would manage the founding of the Harvard Divinity School, and he would help with two crucial appointments which occurred in 1829. In that year Harvard acquired in Josiah Quincy a Unitarian president, the first in the distinguished succession of Unitarians among whom Charles W. Eliot would be the greatest; in that year also it recruited Associate Justice Joseph Story of the United States Supreme Court to be Dane professor of law and central figure of the new Law School. Judge Story made the third Unitarian to take a top place at the university. As to the influence of Unitarianism on Harvard's teaching, it would be hard to name specific changes except in the Divinity School. In that department, the teaching emphasis shifted to Bible scholarship and away from theology proper. But the liberalism characteristic of the university as a whole, while its strength mounted during the nineteenth century, bears over-all the imprint of its scholarly Unitarian leaders.

Meanwhile, and well before the Emersonian 1830s, a cluster of young Harvard-trained clergymen invested Boston Unitarianism with a special, expressive, and humanitarian quality. William Ellery Channing, Joseph Buckminster, and William Emerson (the father of Ralph Waldo)—all of them scholarly and all of them beginning eminent careers in the Congregationalist Church during the opening decade of the nineteenth century—associated in the Anthology Club, which produced the *Monthly Anthology and Boston Review*. In the national history of journalism the *Monthly Anthology* is the worthy predecessor (by ten years) of the *North American Review*; in the literary record the Anthology Club leads to the founding of the Boston Atheneum and anticipates the Transcendentalist Club. Club and magazine help account for what soon became the most literary phase, ever, in American preaching; even though (as the Transcendentalists were soon to protest) Unitarian thought often lost sharpness of edge, Unitarian ministers consistently strove for elegance of composition and modernity of knowledge in their sermons. Then, as Channing and the philanthropically minded Joseph Tuckerman represented best and earliest, organization for the improvement of society appeared with equal spontaneity. The new style of Boston ministers, like their Puritan forebears, found many ways to do good: city missions and a society for the moral improvement of sailors were representative parts of their social effort.

Only the formulation of doctrine came slowly—slowly because reluctantly. To be sure, by definition the word which attached to the movement, Unitarianism, signified a primary conviction, one which echoed Judaism and Islam from a remote past and certain continental and English thinkers on the fringe of the Reformation from more recent times. In Channing's own words, "There is *one God* even the Father, and . . . Jesus Christ is not this one God, but his son and messenger who derived all his powers and glories from the Universal Parent." Nineteenth-century Congregationalist liberals seem to have had no trouble with the idea; they inherited it from their deism-touched fathers. But they wanted to remain Congregationalists—in much the way that their ancestors of the 1630s, the nonseparating congregationalists, had wanted to remain Anglicans. So they deferred separation until clear recognition prevailed. Only in 1819, when Channing preached in Baltimore at the ordination of Jared Sparks—who would soon be the first professor of history in the United States, historical editor and biographer, and president of Harvard—was a statement for the movement made which could be more or less accepted as doctrine. The sermon rejected "excitement" as a method of faith; it denied all authority except the Bible and the free operation of the mind. It rather declared independence of theology than sought to contribute to that literature. According to Channing, a "Liberal Christian," as he and his colleagues liked to call themselves, or a Unitarian, "is disposed to receive as his brethren in Christ all who in the judgment of charity sincerely profess to receive Jesus Christ as their Lord and Master. He rejects all tests and standards of Christian faith, but the word of Jesus Christ and his inspired apostles. He [does not] introduce into the Church creeds of fallible men. . . . He disclaims all exclusive connection with any sect or party, [and] professes himself a member of the Church Universal." In short the Unitarian, in Channing's vision, rejecting creeds, now abandoned all such attitudes of exclusiveness regarding church membership and salvation as his Puritan forebears had cultivated. Thinking better of natural man than their ancestors had, they envisaged goodness, not depravity, in their fellow beings. They continued to profess belief in revelation, however, especially in the moral example of Jesus as set forth in the Bible. Our own age has a bad name for any great reliance on that kind of belief, the "cult of personality"; in due course Ralph Waldo Emerson would criticize Unitarianism on that very account. But the age of Congregationalist Unitarianism—bridging the later Enlightenment and the arrival of Romanticism—placed greater faith than our own age does, or than Emerson did, in the goodness of leaders. Whatever the merits of doing so, the Boston Unitarians voiced their love of the personal Jesus—perfect man, not God, they said—with uncommon devotedness.°

Of course this humanizing of faith offended the orthodox. To them it seemed, rather, a de-Christianizing, carrying no persuasiveness but much challenge to battle. Very appropriately a Yale graduate who was having a distinguished career in Boston—he is still remembered as the founder of the study of geography in America—quickly became the principal attacker. The Reverend Jedidiah Morse, a man well acquainted with Middle State and Southern Presbyterianism, strongly believed in church discipline. In his first round with the Unitarians, he led the inside opposition to the appointment of Professor Ware (Morse was a Harvard overseer). In a second, more public fight, he charged the college with having abandoned belief in the Trinity, an indictment which hurt. Although, almost as early as they began fighting these defensive actions, Morse and his allies turned a good share of their energy into other channels, they never abandoned their battle with liberal religion. Under the title *American Unitarianism*, Morse published in 1815, as a separate pamphlet, a chapter from an English work which displayed Unitarianism as a subversive doctrine and movement. This defiance largely accounts for Channing's giving the doctrinal sermon in Baltimore. Much the same pressure was applied again five years later, in what the public called the "Wood 'n Ware Controversy." This time Morse's associate, the Reverend Leonard Woods, forced into the journals and pulpits the most extensive debate over ideas so far. At last in 1825, in slow motion compared to the usual rapidity of church schisms, the Unitarian congregations formally withdrew from the Congregationalist Association and founded the American Unitarian Association. A new denomination, which some would refuse to call Christian, was thus reluctantly launched in a high and visible place.

The drive against liberal religion by orthodox Congregationalists supplies a dismal page in the history of New England church life, one which matches the region's economic and political misery and its talk of secession while Jefferson was president. Yet, the other side of the coin, those Congregationalists at the same time matched—or, as they were more numerous, more than matched—the humanitarian and philanthropic work of the liberals, and they sustained a parallel intellectual effort. So vigorous were they that a century later their efforts have seemed to scholars to have amounted to an American "Counter Reformation."° Quite in line with the ways of colonial New England (and of the original Counter Reformation), theologians produced a new crop of books. By now the second-generation Edwardsian theologians (principally Joseph Bellamy and Samuel Hopkins) had done their writing and liberals were abandoning the field; in this situation the third generation naturally sought to consolidate and systematize. In Massachusetts Leonard Woods was the principal man; in Connecticut, President Timothy Dwight and Professor Nathaniel Taylor, who together founded the New Haven school of theology and whose thought incorporated perhaps as much from the Scots Enlightenment as the Unitarians did, were foremost. The "One Hoss Shay" symbol notwithstanding, this final, refining period of Calvinist theology in New England was brilliant. Its multivolume products were sufficiently modern to excite young ministers; they exercised much authority.°

Meanwhile the orthodox broadened their appeal to the public. In collaboration with Leonard Woods, Jedidiah Morse launched in 1805 *The Panoplist*, which became the opposite number of the *Monthly Anthology* and, in time, of the later, great Unitarian journal, *The Christian Examiner*. (These three were not quite the earliest religious journals in America, but they are probably the most renowned in that classification.) By 1808 the leaders decided that their cause required a new training school for ministers now that Harvard was lost to them. Again Morse and Woods united: in the academy town twenty-five miles north of Boston they founded the Andover Theological Seminary. As Woods was the candidate sought by two theological factions left over from the Great Awakening, his accepting the professorship of theology pretty well closed a wound. Andover did all it could to keep the faculty solid. One method was a famous oath: professors were obliged to take, and every five years renew, a pledge of orthodoxy based on the Westminster Confession of 1647 (which the American Presbyterians had recently adopted); the requirement held for many decades.

Finally, in character with the goals of a counterreformation, conservative Congregationalists in Massachusetts invested much heart and mind in missionary enterprises. For them missions began at home. The year after the seminary was founded, Morse helped gather and establish the Park Street Congregation in the heart of Boston, across the way from King's Chapel. Although housed in a delicate federal-style brick building, the church gave the name "Brimstone Corner" to the location. To force the fires, a Princeton-trained Presbyterian was brought up from Georgia to be the minister. At the same time, the men of Andover Seminary ventured also as far as possible from the Puritan hub. Even before the controversy over the Ware appointment, Leonard Woods as a journal editor had become spokesman for sending missionaries to the trans-Mississippi West and across the Pacific. Thus we arrive at a synthesis of Christian perfectionism. The testimony of a contemporary, Professor Edwards A. Park, who was an intellectual descendant of Jonathan Edwards (and married to an Edwards great-granddaughter), very well sums up what was involved. God, said Professor Park, exactly echoing Edwards, timed the discovery and occupation of America for the fulfillment of true Christianity:

> He designed this land for the comprehensive and variegated activity of his church; and as he has mingled, so he will continue to mingle in it those diversified elements which coalesce in the richest and most durable character, and the result of which, under a liberal culture, will be a poetry, a philosophy, a theology more capacious, more profound, more soul-stirring than he has vouchsafed to any other people. A character gleaned thus from all nations, will be so versatile, so energetic, as to qualify us for mingling with them all and elevating their religious spirit.°

Thus again was heard in Boston what the old Puritans had said first but now many evangelicals were saying: America chosen by God to lead the world.

In Connecticut's late-Puritan culture things ran in parallel ways. While Harvard had edged consistently farther into the stream of the Enlightenment during the eighteenth century, Yale had swung mainly with the religious tempests. After the ructions within the standing order caused by the Anglican conversions around 1720, the college—and the commonwealth—had been torn between the Old Lights and

New Lights, including a good many Separates (mainly Baptists); during the decades between 1760 and 1800, while Connecticut was in the Revolution but outside the combat area, the parsons often filled their sermons with such a sense of foreboding and failure as had affected Massachusetts a century earlier.° Yet in the foreground of affairs Connecticut did not have such problems of revolution as Massachusetts did. Amending and continuing the charter of 1662, the state drew no new constitution. Although in 1784 it did enlarge the latitude allowed to non-Congregationalists, to place their church taxes in the church of their choice, it avoided until 1818 the strain of deciding in favor of full freedom of religion. In the wake of the Revolution, under President Stiles, Yale students were allowed a good deal of intellectual leeway; some Universalism entered the state, but little or no Unitarianism. All things considered, Connecticut's internal state operations were carried on in a more organic way—by means of close relationships among government, established church, and college—than in any other state in the union.

From all this followed a twenty-year burst of conservative Christian perfectionism. Much of the change is due to a minister college-president leader, Timothy Dwight, of Yale, and to an evangelical-reformist minister, Lyman Beecher, of Litchfield. Dwight, who though born to some wealth in Northampton had chosen Yale for his training and Connecticut for a pastorate rather than the Boston area, began and ended his life as a kind of intellectual prodigy. A grandson of Edwards, he had read the English Bible at four and learned Latin at six; only by stretching out his preparation did he manage to defer college to thirteen. He graduated with top honors and became a tutor in the college during war years, while he was in his twenties. He was thought of for president then; when Stiles was given the job he went off to be a Patriot chaplain, to write "Columbia, Columbia, to Glory Arise" and other patriotic songs, and (after the war) a long epic, "Conquest of Canaan." This work was intended to serve America in the nationalizing and elevating ways he imagined that the *Iliad* and the *Aeneid* had served Greece and Rome. He traced the lineage of American superiority from the ancient Jews of Palestine to revolutionary New England. During the 1780s, while serving a ministry, he entered local politics; simultaneously he kept a school and composed thousands of pentameters. Thus, in the work and thought of a man of infinite drive and a multitude of talents and dedications, we discover united the principal loyalties of Connecticut and of Congregationalism: Puritan orthodoxy, American nationalism, and education.

Dwight's twenty-two years in New Haven, beginning in 1795, spanned, in national affairs, the later Federalist and the Jeffersonian periods; in state affairs it spanned the period of close state-church-college relationships which Richard Purcell once called the state's "transition," before church and state were finally separated. As college president and as public figure—next to John Adams the second Federalist of New England—he acted as though the old order were being restored for eternity. His prime task was to return Yale to the old piety. To this end he preached, and repeated on a four-year cycle so that all students would hear all, a series of sermons; in due course the series became his posthumous five-volume work, *Theology, Explained and Defended*. Not the least or the least significant of his conversions was that of his brilliant young recruit (of 1802) in chemistry. Benjamin Silliman's career at Yale would be the most eminent one in America, in his fields of chemistry and geology. In a way he did for Yale what John Winthrop IV had done for Harvard: he made science influential in the college, and he led and participated in nationwide scientific interests and organizations. He was also different: where Winthrop had been a figure of rationalist and liberal general thought, Silliman, like his chief, was a reconciler of orthodoxy and science. Toward the undergraduates, "Pope Dwight" proceeded in ways paternalist and evangelical: besides giving the sermons, he promoted a secret society to stop the use of profanity and liquor. As to Yale's larger commitments, along with other science Dwight introduced medical studies; as the faculty increased, he brought it into the government of the college. He raised much money, some of it from the state legislature and some of it from individuals. Although Yale had offered Harvard no serious rivalry during its first century, Dwight raised it to doing so, at the time when the older college was having internal divisions.°

In the division of spiritual labor in Connecticut, Dwight specialized in college and regional affairs; Lyman Beecher, in church and local problems. As a public figure, Dwight often concerned himself outside New Haven and Hartford with the conservatives of Massachusetts. Because he was alarmed by the rise of Jeffersonianism, he produced in 1798 a stiffly antidemocratic tract, *The Duty of Americans at the Present Crisis*. When he was aroused by the Boston-area religious controversies, he helped found the Andover Theological Seminary; like his famous grandfather Edwards, a complete believer in missions, he assisted in the organization work of state and national societies.

More on a parish or one-state basis, and in less spectacular ways than Dwight, Lyman Beecher gave himself to the same ultimate goals. Where Dwight's reforms and innovations began with a renewal of orthodoxy at Yale, he began with church revivals and with social reforms. In line with the Moral Society in the college, of which he had been a member, Beecher soon founded the Connecticut Society for the Promotion of Good Morals. His sermons called for personal improvement in many directions: for reducing intemperate drinking and intemperate language; in favor of Bible reading, Sabbath observance, and Sunday School. In the same effort of revival, he helped—but it took especially the organized work of women to succeed—with historic innovations in charity work. In Hartford a group volunteered to provide for the deaf and dumb; the decision led the Reverend Thomas Gallaudet to bring over a skilled instructor from Paris, a Frenchman and a Catholic. Much is revealed about the charity and the uncharity of the Hartford people, by their employing the man on the stipulation that he make no effort to proselytize the mutes. The same wave of benevolence led to the founding of the Hartford Retreat, today an historic and a superior institution; when founded it was (probably) the fifth mental hospital in America. "We view the Asylum for the Deaf and Dumb, the first institution of the kind in this country, and the Retreat for the Insane, two of the distinguished ornaments of our State, and contemplate the immense amount of human suffering they may be made instrumental of relieving," said the speaker at the dedication of the Retreat in 1824. "These are the triumphs of the religion of the Prince of Peace."°

With Harvard and Yale and their constituencies of the spirit we have now viewed the principal academic sources of religious perfectionism in the young republic. In the early century a great deal of religious vigor also showed itself at the Presbyterian headquarters at Princeton. When, after President Witherspoon died, a struggle occurred within the college between defenders and attackers of Enlightenment liberalism, the Princeton Theological Seminary was founded; there, beginning in 1812, Calvinist orthodoxy acquired a new major residence, the third in the country. But where Andover Seminary and the Yale Divinity School were strongly identified with missionary, nationalist, and revivalist goals—and very soon Presbyterian seminaries in the West would likewise be—Princeton Seminary was not. The Presbyterian intellect there centered on theology: Charles Hodge, a systematic scholar and writer of many volumes, in a kind of American-Scottish reaction, became its incomparable spokesman.°

But Princeton conservatism was a matter of a church minority. So far as public thought and early influence were concerned, social perfectionism in its several varieties—romantic, straining, compelling, sometimes liberal and sometimes conservative—was the prevailing religious mode. Largely on that account, but with nonreligious contributions, reform, education, and philanthropy were everywhere on the rise.

HIGH on the list of the concerns of American Protestants was the future of the beckoning West. "Before the millennium, [when] settlements in America may become more numerous millions," said President Stiles in the sermon from which we have been drawing, "how applicable would be the text, when the Lord shall have made his American Israel high above all the nations he had made. in numbers, and in praise, and in name, and in honour."° In those sentences the Yale president said nothing that a Maryland Methodist or a Carolina Baptist, or nearly any other kind of American Christian, might not have said. To be sure, Quakers, German-language pietists and a few others lacked that sort of ambition for the nation; on the other hand all the nationwide evangelical churches thought the transcontinental domain to offer a God-given opportunity, a splendid occasion for duty and growth. If in evangelical estimations faith was declining on the eastern seaboard, a lack of moral discipline and of Christian education was the problem of the West. Though Pope Dwight had ventured no farther frontierward than upstate New York, he was ready to say in his famous *Travels* that the pioneers were "too idle; too talkative; too passionate; too prodigal; and shiftless; to acquire either property or character. They are impatient of the restraints of law, religion, and morality."°

From such ambitions as President Stiles and President Dwight entertained, arose the organized missionary movement. But missions were not in their beginnings the result of fresh organization; rather they were the cause. Timothy Dwight's work of conversion at Yale, for instance, and Morse's and Woods's work in and around Boston, was truly missionary work. It was "home missionary" work in the most immediate sense of a phrase which would soon come to signify missionary work done anywhere within the boundaries of the United States. Likewise the famous camp-meeting revival of 1801 at Cane Ridge, Kentucky, was truly a missionary effort, led by Presbyterians in behalf of themselves and their neighbors. Among Protestants of congregationalist or near-congregationalist polity, only minimum organization was in character. The early Episcopalians were insufficiently united, and insufficiently evangelical-minded after having lost the Methodists, to organize aggressively for expansion. The Methodists were the one Protestant church which was designed as much for large-scale missionary work as it was for the care of established congregations. Thus they made their amazing numerical gains. But, the other side of the coin, as being theologically and culturally apart from the older churches, the Methodists were disqualified for much share in the interchurch aspect of missions. Only the Roman Catholics, with their hierarchy and their missionary orders, could move westward with both central control and experience. Even so, Catholicism accelerated slowly at first. Roman Catholic Church growth, from 56 congregations in 1780 to 124 in 1820, turned out to be small in proportion to Protestant gains. It was during the next forty years, which included the Irish immigration, that a more significant expansion—to about 2,550 parishes in 1860—brought the Catholics numerically even, or somewhat more than even, with the Congregationalists, the Episcopalians, and the Lutherans, each about the same number.°

There was more than just an increase in Protestant numbers, institutions, and geographical spread. Surrounding and impelling that growth, there occurred an increase of emotional intensity. It began in 1797 with a tide of religious renewal—called the Second Great Awakening, it actually was the second of the four or five such cycles which have occurred at roughly half-century intervals in America, beginning with the Great Awakening. We have seen enough of the late eighteenth-century rationalism of Ethan Allen and Elihu Palmer to recognize considerable similarity between the attack on Christian ideas made around 1800 and that of the days of Edwards. In both periods an acceleration of deistic currents eroded confidence in revealed religion; persons and groups departed from Biblical faith. Yet in both periods any such massive collision of faith and skepticism as occurred in Europe was avoided. Christian spokesmen, though counterattacking, exercised moderation; they participated in making accommodations with rationalism, both times. Indeed conservative Congregationalists seem to have been less intolerant toward doubters outside their church than toward liberals inside. Somewhat as his grandfather Edwards had done, though he was less a theologian, Timothy Dwight as college president cultivated modern scientific thought and Christian faith, together and in parallel, as not being ultimately opposed. Again, as Cotton Mather had directed prerevolutionary currents of humanitarianism into Christian channels, Beecher guided benevolent effort under the auspices of their churches. Today William G. McLoughlin and Timothy L. Smith, experts in the history of revivalism, encourage the view that the Second Great Awakening was more complex than the first and entered more deeply into the national experience and character.°

A new style of evangelism was born. Beginning with the extraordinary revivals at Cane Ridge in 1801, the Reverend James McGready took leadership. He was a second-generation Scots-Irishman who had trained in a western Pennsylvania Presbyterian minister's study, and who received his calling to be an evangelist in Hanover County, Virginia, where the Reverend John Blair Smith, the president of Hampden-Sydney College, conducted revivals. During the next decade, as he moved westward, McGready led his congregations to pledge (by covenant) truly heroic efforts of prayer, fasting, and making converts. Then he invented the camp meeting. McGready had a stentorian voice and a compelling personal presence: he may or may not have equaled George Whitefield, sixty years earlier, as a speaker; he had no intellectual superiority. Yet the camp meeting brought results which no other method of revivalism matched. Whitefield, as an itinerant, had preached in whatever places people could gather readily; in due course his congregations dispersed. McGready brought the people to himself. They gathered from isolated farms; they came not for one service but for several; they camped out while they attended; the services sometimes lasted throughout the night. The person who attended such a meeting was pretty well caught from the start.°

The method spread among all the popular churches. The Methodists, whose circuit riders were good managers, and the Baptists, whose spectacular baptisms in wilderness Jordans gave them a dramatic advantage, were the most adept. Camp meetings were scheduled for weekends which began on a Friday and ended on Monday; Thursday to Tuesday was the duration sometimes. Up to twenty-five thousand people attended; sometimes Negro slaves were present. Whether the Negroes met separately as usual, or simply were seated a little apart, African jungle-worship habits had some effect. But the idea was to accept Jesus Christ. The leaders, though not generally undisciplined, were innovators, in a hurry to have results; they had no prayerbook, deacons, or trustees to restrain them. The worshipers were finding a way out of loneliness; they were participating often in the biggest crowds they ever experienced. The singing and the sacraments were exalting. The sermons lashed at their consciences. The converted were encouraged to display signs of the transformation they felt within. Falling prone was understood to signify that the Holy Spirit had entered the body. "The jerks," a shaking of body and flopping of head, and the "holy laugh" or "holy whine," by which converts sought "to tree the devil" as a coon dog trees a coon, sometimes followed. Travelers who witnessed these things with no intention except to observe and perhaps be amused were sometimes themselves carried away.°

Yet to name the extreme phenomena, and not to add that those things happened only occasionally and soon were discouraged by Presbyterians, would be poor history today. The recent studies of Charles A. Johnson show that camp-meeting excesses, whether the religious-psychological displays we have mentioned or the sexual and alcoholic debauches which did occur, tapered down before long. The fair estimation accords with the appreciation rendered by Edward Eggleston nearly a century ago. "More than anyone else, the early circuit preachers brought order out of this chaos. . . . Much as I have laughed at every sort of grotesquerie, I could not treat the early religious life of the West otherwise than with the most cordial sympathy and admiration."° Viewed simply as social phenomena, the camp meetings classify with cabin raisings, militia musters, and political barbecues and conventions among the essential community events of the American farm and forest society. In this perspective the revivalists deserve credit for filling the churches and for reducing the hard-liquor habit of the frontier; moreover, the camp meetings had certain moral, and even intellectual, legacies to leave. Without them the music and the lectures, and even the theater which in due time flowered among Methodists—best at their permanent summer camp-meeting ground at Chautauqua, New York—might not have occurred. The community-building impulse in evangelicalism, which Perry Miller has strongly emphasized, sometimes became a very broad thing.

Revivalism in the United States was much quieter during the fifteen years—of war, political nationalism, depression, and recovery—which followed 1810 than during the equal period preceding. Then about 1825 a much stronger leader than McGready, more like a latter-day Whitefield yet with a considerable touch of Edwards about him because he had power as a theologian, Charles Grandison Finney, appeared. Finney began life in Connecticut and was reared near Rochester, New York. As a student he twice came close to going back to the seaboard, once to Yale and once to Princeton. It is significant that he did not do so. The first decision turned him to apprentice-style law-office training, for what turned out to be a brief but successful young man's career at the bar; the second decision placed him, instead of at Hodge's unevangelical Princeton Seminary, in the minister's study of George W. Gale, the future founder of Knox College. Married to the pious young woman who had aided his conversion, and himself a restless believer, Finney began in the Presbyterian ministry with ways he would never give up. He spoke to his congregations in the second person, much as though he were addressing witnesses, or men under indictment, in court; he used imperative verb forms. His hearers were the persons on trial; the judge being addressed was God Himself. Individuals who recognized their misdeeds being mentioned were often greatly affected. By 1826, only two years after ordination, the Reverend Charles G. Finney was being invited to speak the length of the Mohawk valley, and by 1830 he had become yet another new type of American revivalist.

Had Finney lived in the seventeenth century, or had he in his own time been a frontier dweller, he might readily, like old Solomon Stoddard, have become the dominator of a parish and a region. But he did live in upstate New York, a mixed farm and industrial society; as he visited congregation after congregation, his revivalist inventions found widespread acceptance and he quickly became a regional, an interstate if not a national, leader. The "anxious bench" was one of his contrivances: there he had seated during his services those persons who waited conversion; seated apart from both the converted and the unconverted, they made a cynosure for all members of the congregation. Small meetings for confession, usually if not always restricted to women, was another of Finney's procedures. As McLoughlin points out, where Jonathan Edwards had "prayed down" grace from heaven, in old Northampton, and where frontier revivalists "worked up" conversions in the camp-meeting way, now, in this third variation, Finney pressed conversions out of the worshipers at his services.

Perhaps he deserves the praise he has been given for achieving a "philosophical result of the right constituted means," according to one sympathizer. At any rate, he used his mind and in due course became the principal nineteenth-century theologian of revivalism. Out of his experience he concocted the thesis, quite in line with historic doctrines of salvation by grace, that the saved are given, as well as the comfort of the Holy Spirit, an obligation to direct other men. He articulated this conviction in a six-volume work—which reached six editions by 1836—his *Lectures on Revivals of Religion.*° Next to Edwards's writings, Finney's *Lectures* are the most important work on conversion in the American literature. There is a leadership principle, close to theocracy, in the argument. In Finney, during his upstate New York period, the modern ministry's specialized subprofession, of revivalist, was born in America.

In 1832 Finney accepted a call to New York City, and with that relocation the partly frontier aspect of his leadership faded away. He took charge first of a Presbyterian church; soon he moved to the Broadway Tabernacle, which was created for him. By this time he had lost patience with the restraints which the Presbyterian pyramid of authority placed on ministers. He turned Congregationalist; in the Broadway Tabernacle he trained candidates for the ministry in the ways of conversion he had ventured. Meanwhile Finney enlarged his moral concerns to include public matters. Speaking of slavery, "Christians can no more take neutral ground upon this subject, since it has come up for discussion," said Finney, soon after South Carolina's nullification crisis of 1832, "than they can take neutral ground on the subject of the sanctification of the Sabbath. It is a great national sin." Soon he was saying openly that slaveholders should be excluded from church membership. Methodists had been declaring this from soon after their church was born; nevertheless saying it during Jackson years in New York was something extraordinarily bold. Finney truly believed that an ecclesiastical sanction against slaveholding, a kind of a Protestant excommunication, would have the power to reduce the institution of slavery if ever such a thing were brought to bear.

Meanwhile Finney, having been independent on many subjects—conversion, church polity, and social ethics—developed broadly as theologian. Although in the natural logic of conservative opposition to evangelicalism his preaching and writing had received many critical appraisals, in 1831 he was assured by a group of New Haven ministers that his views and theirs were substantially the same. The reformist position he was taking, like the theology of Nathaniel Taylor of the new Divinity School at Yale, placed high estimation on moral freedom. This was the fork of the road of New England theology which veered away from the doctrines of Samuel Hopkins and Nathaniel Emmons, latter-day Edwardsians who had been popular with ministers at the turn of the century. The new thought was pointing—as Finney's critics were vocal to warn—into perfectionism close to Methodist style, and into millennial expectations of the Kingdom of God on earth. Yet Finney remained sufficiently Calvinist—or Augustinian, or Edwardsian —to voice always a strong sense of salvation by grace. If as theologian he moved far from the Puritan fathers, it was because he believed that God is a generous sovereign, a bestower of His own full freedom on many mortals. In this vein Finney's theology became known as the sanctification theology or (more loosely) as the perfectionist theology. Quite naturally it drew sharp objection from Princeton Seminary and a various reception among Congregationalists, favorable at Yale but elsewhere sometimes unfavorable.

In the third and final phase of his ministerial career, Finney himself and his doctrine obtained a special reinforcement from the westward slope of the Appalachian divide. In 1835 occurred the startling removal, from Lane Theological Seminary, in Cincinnati, to Oberlin College, of a group of divinity students who believed that their antislavery consciences had been denied freedom by the seminary. Faculty action had forbidden them to debate the merits of colonizing American Negroes in Africa and of abolishing slavery by legislative action, state by state. To care for the student seceders, Arthur Tappan, New York philanthropist and abolitionist and supporter of Broadway Tabernacle, provided money for a theology professor at Oberlin. This background accounts for the call which removed the trainer of ministers from tabernacle to college. Academic freedom for students, economic and social freedom for Negroes, and the freedom of men of God to aid and guide their fellow creatures—all these converged in the discourse when Finney took up his western duties.

Institution and professor of theology were equally stimulated. Oberlin College was already pioneering in educational equalitarianism: it admitted women as students, and admitted and gave degrees to Negroes before any other college did. Under sympathetic circumstances, Charles G. Finney performed for thirty-eight years enormous feats of duty. In the town of Oberlin, he served as minister of the First Congregational Church; in Oberlin College, he served until 1851 as professor and then went up to be president. Besides all else he contributed regularly to the *Oberlin Evangelist* and for years edited the *Oberlin Quarterly Review*. It was shortly after he began at the college that he brought out his multivolume *Lectures on Revivals;* within a decade seven or eight other volumes of sermons and lectures, and his biggest thinking, the *Lectures on Systematic Theology*, all appeared. Thus the sanctification theology became known as "The Oberlin Theology." And, as much as any other center of learning in America, new little Oberlin became the bearer of a Protestant theological and moral tradition. Though many of the books appeared after 1840, during a national epoch which lies beyond the main scope of this section and chapter, the character of the Oberlin doctrine derived from the 1820s and 1830s.°

Finally about Finney, and about the impact on public thought and feeling of the Second Great Awakening, we have the telling word of Lyman Beecher. That aging Yankee spokesman for orthodoxy and reform, after six years in Boston which had been less successful than his years in Connecticut, had come to Ohio before Finney had, in 1832. As president of Lane Theological Seminary he had played a regretful, more or less bystanding, role when the divinity students had departed northward. In his autobiography he placed the opinion that the national movement to abolish slavery had been "the offspring of the Oneida denunciatory reforms"—that is, that antislavery as a national cause owed its birth to Finney's evangelism beginning in upstate New York. This opinion is instructive still. Without an emotional habit of believing that one side of a moral issue is (literally speaking) divinely pure and that the other side is satanic, and without a conviction that goals of Christian perfection do attach to social reforms, the antislavery movement would surely have been less passionate than it soon became.°

But any speculation concerning an America without an emotional habit of believing is hypothetical and is intended simply to improve perspective on actual events; it does not at all serve historical description. The essential fact is that evangelical revivalism was a form of behavior leading to commitment which sprang up numerously in every part of the nation. Reforms which were undertaken in that context gained purposefulness; reformers gained association with other reformers.

Unfortunately, while religious expansionism united men in fresh loyalties, those groups ran—it often seems—as much to antagonism as to love. Hearts were stirred in many situations; but heads were turned away from one another. Sometimes collision courses and sometimes separation courses were set.

4   "The Broken Body of Christ":
American Fractures

THE thought, that Americans should be conceived as a Christian people guided by the church on earth, achieved its maximum impact during the Second Great Awakening. Little Connecticut, where Congregationalist and Presbyterian polity fused, after the Revolution served as a seedbed of Christian republican ideas. Connecticut's great neighbor, in this period the builder of the Erie Canal, soon became the main place of early Congregationalist and Presbyterian expansion and co-operation.

The so-called Plan of Union, which in 1801 became a joint enactment of the Presbyterian Church in America and the Congregationalist General Association of Connecticut, and in addition was ratified by the general associations of the other New England states, was a direct product of the Connecticut awakening. Yankee Congregationalists were pouring west, into and across the state of New York; ministers were going as missionaries. In the new locations, as on the frontiers of the 1740s, congregations cried for ministers, and vice versa. One of the most eminent men to become involved illustrates the situation. The Reverend Eliphalet Nott, a Congregationalist who had been educated at the Baptist College of Rhode Island, left his church in New London, Connecticut, to take one in Cherry Valley, New York. Thence he rose to the leading pulpit in Albany, a Presbyterian one, and from there to the presidency of Union College—significantly named—a new institution in Schenectady which had been founded by Dutch Reformed and Presbyterians. According to tradition, when Mr. Nott was a few years along in his upstate career he was the one who negotiated, on behalf of the Connecticut Congregationalists, the Plan of Union; Jonathan Edwards, Jr., who preceded Nott in the college presidency, negotiated for the Presbyterians.

According to that agreement the two churches joined forces for westward expansion. Rather than a full merger they made cooperative arrangements: ministers of either church were ruled to be equally available to serve congregations of the other; the founding of joint Congregationalist and Presbyterian parishes was part of the expected result. During the half century of its operation, Plan of Union congregations were actually established all across New York and in the states and territories of the Old Northwest. Of course, the combination was neither so massive nor so predominating that it prevented the rise of new sects—Mormons and others—or excluded competition from Episcopalians, Methodists, Baptists, and Universalists, or even from Roman Catholics. The plan held in abeyance, rather than prevented, competition between the member churches. Unfortunately for the Congregationalist identity, especially in New York, the plan operated to Presbyterian advantage: joint congregations often became Presbyterian; also, the superstructure of the Presbyterian Church assisted in founding such a number of its own kind of congregations as quite to outdo the Congregationalists. Yet under the Plan of Union great numbers of trained clergymen of Calvinist derivation moved west, and more in the way of intellectual vigor appeared in frontier colleges and seminaries—from Union and Lane to Knox and Beloit—than in new church colleges at any later time. We shall return to them.°

Throughout the decades of the Second Great Awakening, dozens of other commitments were undertaken among the Calvinist-descended churches. Like the Plan of Union, they started largely from New England, often from Connecticut, and characteristically had to do with church expansion. About 1810 a group of Congregationalist ministers-in-training at Andover Seminary made good the expectation of their school to carry the gospel as far as possible. The brief career of Samuel J. Mills, Jr., more than anyone else the founder of the foreign-missionary movement, recapitulates that history. A son of middle Connecticut, a teen-age convert in 1801, and one of a number of Williams College students who were called to be missionaries, he went briefly to Yale and then to Andover. Well before he had finished his studies he joined in the pledges and petitions which prompted Congregationalist authorities first, and soon Presbyterian ones, to launch the permanent American Board of Commissioners for Foreign Missions. On graduation from Andover, however, Mills served first as a home missionary up and down the Mississippi valley; he helped found the interchurch, nationwide American Bible Society and worked for a missionary society of Presbyterian and Reformed membership. Though he helped other missionaries go to India, and himself dreamed of Latin America, he did not go overseas until 1817, when on behalf of the antislavery American Colonization Society he went to Africa. (He died en route home, at age thirty-five.) Meanwhile the Commissioners for Foreign Missions had undertaken to work among the American Indians. More compatibly with the name of the commission, they placed missions the world around, on the Pacific islands, especially Hawaii, and in India, China, Africa, and the Middle East. In the same period, the little-organized Baptists, though with some holding out by certain strict

Calvinist congregations, formed their own missionary societies. So did the Methodists and less numerous denominations.

Foreign missions had the hugeness of the non-Christian world to confront, but organizationally they presented a simpler calling to Americans than did home missions. From Saint Paul to the crusaders and always, Christian faith in most of its varieties has called upon believers to take the gospel to the heathen: move first and arrange later has been the order of things which is almost built into the movement. But American home missions began with uncommon foreknowledge. Not only did the field work among western settlements and the sustaining work to the east—the recruiting, organizing, financing, and placing of clergymen and teachers—have to be prosecuted, but also, according to Kenneth Scott Latourette, "the efforts of Protestant Christianity to hold or win to the faith the older American stock" demanded many collateral activities. Probably closest to the missionary societies, properly so-called, were the American Bible Society, the American Sunday School Union, and the American Tract Society. These three were each broadly interdenominational; each was founded between 1816 and 1825; and each sought to reach all Americans.°

Yet neither the missionary movements nor their cousins, the organizations for Christian education, nor those efforts combined, quite express the full intention of early-century orthodox Protestants, to give Christian attention to the bodies and souls of their fellow men. Along with home missions numerous peace societies appeared. And temperance societies, though the effort had started strong in Connecticut, soon came to belong to outlying communities especially, and to the Methodists and Baptists more than to others. When all aspects of Christian reformism and nationalism are taken together, the evangelical work of Americans to save one another during the first and second generations of the republic challenges comparison with like work done anywhere, at any time, in religious history. During the Jefferson-Jackson period, except for the Democratic Party there was no other instrument of social action to equal the evangelical complex in the numbers of people participating or in interstate and interregional scope.°

Yet by the time of the tapering down of the Second Great Awakening during the 1830s—while Jacksonian politics assumed some of the excitement of millennial feeling—interchurch evangelicalism began to display contradictions of a serious sort. For a geographically remote example, there occurred a *reductio ad absurdum* among American Congregationalist and Presbyterian missionaries in the Turkish Empire. When as evangelicals they failed in their original purpose to win the minds of Muslims—either ruling Turks or conquered Arabs—quite as the crusaders half a millennium earlier had failed to win Mohammedan loyalties, the missionaries shifted to converting, for example, Armenian Orthodox within the upper empire and Copts in northern Africa. They achieved considerable success, but surely more a success of American pride than one of Christian forbearance. Much more famously, disrespect by one kind of Christian for another flared up at home. Though the American Revolution had provided full citizenship, at last, to Roman Catholics, and Catholic leadership had responded in sympathetic terms, by the 1820s Catholics were doing things which touched Protestant nerves. By 1829, when the first grand provincial Council of Catholicity assembled in Baltimore, both sides were ready to be aggressive. Bishops at that council attacked what they called "corrupt translations" of the Bible which were being peddled by Protestants; the American Bible Society and the Protestant evangelical press—this was the time of the Finney awakenings—were quick to fire back. In this book we do not need to retell the sad history of the anti-Catholic terror which rose during the 1830s: the faked reports about life in the convents and the burning of those buildings. We should notice, however, that all that excess of feeling produced little thinking along the way: reserved for much later was any worthy discourse in America concerning the principles—Thomist philosophy, sacramental practice, and so on—which dignify while they separate Catholic from Protestant. Intended and self-conscious forbearance between Catholic and Protestant, such as occurred in early Maryland and during the Revolution, all too plainly lost out under the pressures of the nineteenth century.°

Even so there did exist, and did grow, among certain American churches considerable loyalty to ancient Christian sacramentalism and sacerdotalism. During the first half of the century a mainly northern group of Episcopalians, as inheritors of the high-church tastes of the Reverend Samuel Johnson and Bishop Samuel Seabury, and as people affected by the Anglo-Catholic movement at Oxford University, intensified their devotion to church history. Under a "banner" marked both "EVANGELICAL TRUTH" and "APOSTOLIC ORDER," Bishop John Henry Hobart led that renewal early in the century. Hobart's career in New York combined Protestant-style evangelism—represented by his work as preacher and founder of new schools and parishes—with tastes that impelled him to write reverentially *The Nature and Constitution of the Christian Church, A Companion for the Festivals and Fasts,* and an *Apology for Apostolic Order and Its Advocates.* But in combining evangelism and traditionalism, Hobart proved unusual and a figure of transition. More characteristically, and with the effect of building parties in the Episcopal Church like those in the Church of England, high-church feeling separated from and opposed evangelicalism, as did Bishop Dehon of South Carolina and Bishop Whittingham of Maryland. The other side of the coin, Episcopalian evangelicalism, identified itself with low-church preferences, in the tradition of old Virginia.°

Only toward mid-century did Calvinist orthodoxy anywhere become expressly tradition-minded, apart from filial piety toward the colonial Puritans. The case most like Episcopalian traditionalism occurred on the periphery of orthodoxy, at the new Mercersburg Theological Seminary in south-central Pennsylvania. There, under Reformed Church auspices, gathered a group of scholars of mixed Reformed, Presbyterian, and Lutheran background; John W. Nevin, a theologian who came from Puritan-Presbyterian origins, and Philip Schaff, a church historian from Switzerland, were the principals. Not since the Great Awakening, when the question of who took the Lord's Supper came up for an exciting round of debate in New England, had American Calvinists had much to say about the theory and practice of the sacraments. But now the Mercersburg people examined those problems and studied catechetical questions and church history; in such areas of scholarship their seminary became as important as Oberlin in Christian ethics.° Meanwhile, a contemporary, Horace Bushnell of Hartford, in the heartland of Calvinist orthodoxy, took a parallel course. The most eminent Congregationalist theologian of mid-century, he argued—in the work, *Christian Nurture*, 1847, which has become a classic—the importance of church, home, and school in the attainment of salvation. To Bushnell, a child's being reared in Christian context and an adult's committing himself to the life and service of the church offered a surer route to attain grace than the ways of the preaching evangelists.°

With such newly opened divisions of religious conviction, in addition to all the sectarian ones of long standing, it was the acts of separation and opposition among Protestants which had multiplied by the second quarter of the nineteenth century, far more than the acts of interchurch unity. Besides all else, by the 1840s the question of slavery, which most threatened the integrity of the federal republic and the nation, was already disrupting the large churches. In 1843 the Southern Baptists set up their own association, and a year later the Methodist Church, South, was founded, both of them favorable to slavery; among the Presbyterians, antislavery people in Ohio were the first, in 1847, to separate from their national church on account of the moral issue. Later we shall have to return to these scissions of Christianity by region; for present purposes the lines they make darkly crosshatch the more accustomed lines of conflict between churchman and churchman.

Numbers will help with proportion. In 1780, as the nation was breaking free, the two large Calvinist churches, before they began their cooperation in missions and philanthropy, numbered together, roundly,

1,250 congregations: 750 Congregationalists ones and 500 Presbyterian. Forty years later, with that cooperation increasing, the total figure had more than doubled, to reach 2,800: while the Presbyterians had muliplied by three and one-half, to 1,700, the Congregationalists had by one and one-half, to 1,100. But in that interval, before 1820, directly stemming from the Kentucky revivals, the Cumberland Synod had separated from the national Presbyterian Church. The new synod was the New Sides over again, during the nineteenth century: it organized those who cared more for revivalism and less for clerical training and church discipline. And in 1832, during the second main phase of the awakening, the Presbyterians splintered once more. Liberals under the leadership of the Reverends Thomas and Alexander Campbell set out to establish a church which, down-valuing sectarian differences, intended to absorb all sects. But soon the Disciples of Christ, or Campbellites, became a new—and markedly sectional—western denomination. During the 1780 to 1820 period, the Baptists increased from 450 to 2,700 congregations; the Methodists rose to equal numbers. During that first long generation of the republic the Methodists gained more rapidly than any other church, and they continued to do so. In 1860 there were nearly 20,000 of their congregations, compared to the Baptists' 12,000; together the two most popular and least traditional churches had a generous two-thirds of all the congregations in America.

Their history to this point does not include much theological creativity or much leadership in reform or national affairs. Great in numbers, if not great in mind, they were affected by the divisionism to which the common life, religious and public, was subject. The Baptists present such a record of doctrinal, regional, racial, and organizational variations, and the story is so generally familiar, that we need not try to survey them. Even the Methodists, who loved organization and control, quite apart from the north-south issue suffered certain secessions. One group, the Methodist Protestant Church, founded in 1830, ruled against having bishops. Twelve or fifteen years earlier the African Methodist Episcopal Church was formed in northern coastal cities, for Negroes.°

Probably not a single church or sect in America maintained organizational, or operating, connections with more than a few other churches. Only the most widely deployed churches could venture interchurch cooperation. But to name the widely deployed ones is to call to mind their inward and outward tensions: the Methodists, Baptists, Presbyterians, Episcopalians, and Catholics. Put another way, a minister in a regional church, or in a small one, could lead an active parish life without contact with, perhaps without knowledge of, the existence of a good many churches. A New England Congregationalist could have lived in ignorance of American Lutherans and Cumberland

Presbyterians; so could a Southern Baptist with respect to Disciples, Reformed, and Catholics. Generally speaking, the churches lived separately, not in communion, and they carried on in practical competition more than in practical cooperation with one another.

Of course no other interchurch rivalry equaled the most historic one, between Catholics and Protestants. But as to massiveness and everyday self-consciousness, the rivalries among evangelical Protestants, especially between the newer and more popular churches and the older ones, ran deep and often bitter. The feeling of the Reverend Peter Cartwright, herculean rider of Methodist circuits, says much of attitudes which were natural between the parvenus and the patricians of early-century churchmanship. To Cartwright the ministers of the older churches were "sapient, velvet-mouthed, downy D.D.'s"; about his own kind he acknowledged that many were unable "to conjugate a verb or parse a sentence" but said that they could bring down "a divine unction" and often succeeded.

For visualizing the fragmentation of nineteenth-century American Christianity, finally, no fracture line tells more than the one between Congregationalists and Presbyterians, which was held closed for half a century and then allowed to reopen. Had the Plan of Union been permanently solidified and extended, the common Calvinist orthodoxy of those churches would have been incomparably strong. Under the Constitution, it could not have been much like a national church establishment but would have been something like one. A nationwide church well ahead in higher education, it could have exercised enormous authority. When the Plan of Union broke down, on the contrary, the Congregationalists remained a regional church: though no longer a New England one, it was still altogether northern—in New England, the Old Northwest, and the trans-Mississippi region. The Presbyterian Church, having fragmented profusely, was not to mend quickly again as it had in the 1750s. Thus the complex Calvinist tradition, which is still sometimes called the American orthodoxy, became a thing of minorities and of multiple inward divisions.°

CHAPTER XIII

Working Goals of National Ambition

Our country is called, as it is, practical; but this is the element for intellectual action. No strongly-marked and high-toned literature, poetry, eloquence, or philosophy, ever appeared, but under the pressure of great interests, great enterprises, perilous risks, and dazzling rewards. Statesmen, and warriors, and poets, and orators, and artists, start up under one and the same excitement. They are all branches of one stock. They form, and cheer, and stimulate, and, what is worth the rest, understand, each other; and it is as truly the sentiment of the student, in the recesses of his cell, as of the soldier in the ranks, which breathes in the exclamation,

To all the sons of sense proclaim
One glorious hour of CROWDED LIFE
Is worth an age without a name. . . .

> *Edward Everett,* The Circumstances Favorable to the Progress of Literature in America *(1824)*

1   *Toward a People's "Intellectual Action":*
Bases in Science and Publication

IN the nature of the case, Christian expectations for the future of America contained a degree of perfectionism which economic and political programs failed to equal. Yet great belief in the nation did grow in seedbeds which were not evangelical. Before the eighteenth century ended, poems were composed and novels were written "under one and the same excitement" as impelled American "statesmen and warriors," quite as Edward Everett said. So also, before and after the turn of the century, did less "high-toned" writings state national ideals. Addresses and essays, calling for American ways of speaking and writing, and of educating the young, poured from the presses; pleas for economic development multiplied, many of them in the lineage of Alexander Hamilton's thought; lawyers' briefs, which carried outside as inside the courtrooms, developed our ideas of the Constitution. Judicial decisions which would affect our basic institutions were rendered by masterful judges, some from the federal and some from the state bench. For the first time American lawbooks were written and read. "Intellectual action" became ever more plentiful during the 1820s and 1830s.

Next to their Christian loyalties, the American people's interest in science gave them their most practical intellectual tradition. Unfortunately, three of the four principal custodians of that tradition up to 1776—the American Philosophical Society, the College of Philadelphia, and William and Mary College—had been badly upset by the Revolution; only Harvard College had been little disturbed. But, beginning about 1780, renewals took place. In Philadelphia the Philosophical Society, after reorganizing itself as independence required, elected first David Rittenhouse and then Thomas Jefferson, practical scientists and theoretical republicans both of them, to the presidency in which Benjamin Franklin had come first. In 1785 the Philosophical Society fostered the new Philadelphia Society for Promoting Agriculture. Within the next decade the Chemical Society of Philadelphia, which Benjamin Rush founded before any chemical society had been founded in Europe, and the College of Physicians were organized in the same city. Meanwhile, in 1780, John Adams, who while overseas had admired the French Academy and who disliked to have Philadelphia outdo Boston, took the lead in founding in his own city the American Academy of Arts and Sciences. The charter of this new organization pledged "to cultivate every art and science which may tend to advance the interest, honor, dignity, and happiness of a free, independent, and virtuous people." Like the Philosophical Society it had an interstate and international membership. This included the Englishman Joseph Priestley, who, as well as being a great chemist (as an investigator of the properties of gases), was a major theologian of Unitarianism and settled in America during the 1790s.°

The policies of the national organizations put more weight on technology than on pure science. This had been true of the Philosophical Society earlier. But now, by the measure of the theoretical work being done by Sir William Herschel in England and Baron Cuvier in France, the practicality of American science becomes ever more conspicuous. Among the colleges, the new University of Pennsylvania as successor institution to the College of Philadelphia advanced strongly in medicine; in Professor Rush it had, as well as a superb trainer of students, the greatest physician and psychiatrist in the country. But it would be hard to say that the university and the neighboring scientific societies kept up the pace of discovery and invention which Franklin had started in the city. Likewise Harvard, though it soon began medical work, skipped a generation before it had again a scientific researcher as productive as John Winthrop IV had been; William and Mary College had let wither its larger than regional leadership in science before the Revolution began. Even Yale College, though by reason of Professor Benjamin Silliman's work it became the first American college in science during the early 1800s, waited until 1871, when Josiah Gibbs became professor of physics, to recruit a pure scientist to compare with the masters in Europe.° Probably Joseph Henry, who did epoch-making studies in electromagnetism at Princeton between 1832 and 1844, is the only American, besides Gibbs, from Franklin during the 1740s down to the American psychologists around 1900, who will stand that comparison. Henry's researches opened the way to inventions by Samuel F. B. Morse and others—telegraphs, telephones, and electric motors among them. They paralleled and on some points preceded Sir Michael Faraday's work in the same important field, carried on in the Royal Institution in London.

Broadly speaking, except for the undertakings which began and gradually accumulated in the capital city of Washington, American work in science and for science proliferated during the first two generations of the republic on much the same pattern as effort in education and in the churches. As we have seen, two of the colonial centers of science—Boston and Philadelphia, which remained centers also of branches of Christianity friendly to science—retained most of their old leadership in science and technology. New centers appeared, more numerous than effective. Before 1800 societies to promote agriculture were founded in New Jersey and South Carolina; the Charleston Library Society set up a natural history museum; the Maryland Academy of Sciences was founded. Virginians, some of whom had taken part in the Agricultural Society in Philadelphia, founded an agricultural society in Richmond; two national leaders (at opposite poles of politics), John Marshall and James Monroe, though neither one qualified as much of a scientist, were the first president and vice-president of that society. Among the early state-size efforts, Connecticut did best. Thanks to Yale's presidents Stiles and Dwight, there was launched in the capital city of Hartford the excellent Connecticut Academy of Arts and Sciences. As he himself rose to eminence, Professor Silliman contributed to the state's work in aid of knowledge by publishing the academy's papers in *The American Journal of Science and the Arts,* which was the prime journal of science of the period. Thus locality by locality there appeared, first in the older states, the kind of initiative in science which the state universities of the West would in a later period carry to wonderful fruitfulness. Only after about 1820 in the sense of centralization, but earlier in the sense of geographic spread and the involvement of people, interest in science grew into a national concern.

Quite as American taste in that age ruled that the main purpose of science is practicality, American scientists characteristically placed their effort in discovering, exploring, charting, describing, and conceiving the utilization of the resources of the continent. This encouraged individual effort; it sometimes gave grand opportunity to imagination and art. This is beautifully true of John James Audubon's most famous of all books in ornithology: his stunning *Birds of America* was published over a ten-year period beginning in 1827. His several multi-volume publications of texts and plates, including a five-volume study of American quadrupeds, were completed over a quarter century. Foreigners were welcome to share the exploring and reporting, and many did. Constantine Rafinesque, Turkish-born son of west-European parents, as a professor in Transylvania University, wrote voluminously on the botany of Kentucky and nearby regions; Joseph Nicollet, a French visitor who first studied the geography of the Mississippi valley, was employed by the federal government for surveying, and to train army officers in making maps. Even the earliest and most famous and successful of all federal-government surveys, the Lewis and Clark expedition, depended largely on the personal initiative of Meriwether Lewis, the leader, and on the assistance of the American Philosophical Society. Though Jefferson himself conceived the expedition and put his own secretary in charge, he had few facilities within the government to assist Lewis and Clark. The preparations for the expedition and, when the work was done and the records were in, the expert studies—geographical, ethnological, historical, even astronomical, which the expedition produced—all had to be principally cared for by the society in Philadelphia.

Yet, while the institutionalization of science in most cases amounted to voluntary gatherings of patrons and amateurs, there was always open the possibility—quite the reverse of the situation in respect of a national establishment of religion—that Congress would create a scientific establishment, or otherwise give money to scientific work, and create a close relationship between the national government and the men and organizations of science.° To be sure, after the first four presidents lost out on their wish to have a grand university of the United States in Washington, no national institution which might have equaled the French Academy ever came close to enactment. Even during the first dozen—the Federalist—years of the national government, and still more during the 1820s and 1830s while Jacksonian tastes prevailed, on grounds of economy and states' rights feeling, Congress resisted making sizable appropriations. Yet certain laws did assign work and responsibility to men of science. The United States Mint was put under the directorship of David Rittenhouse; federal patent law required that the government employ able men and exercise careful scientific judgment in that area. In a crisis situation, appropriations were enacted to help fight the yellow-fever epidemic in Philadelphia; this created some precedent for federal public health service. Official weights and measures were authorized. With the Lewis and Clark expedition, the government's employing and serving science shifted to oblique procedures and justifications. Jefferson spoke of that expedition as providing assistance to commerce. The same savant president had first opposed a military academy; later he approved the founding of West Point and liked it because it gave the first formal schooling in engineering ever offered in the United States. Similarly during the 1840s John Quincy Adams, who as president had wanted to establish a national observatory (an American Greenwich), was pleased and half satisfied when Congress provided for the Naval Observatory and for sustained work in astronomy in Washington.° After the Lewis and Clark expedition the government regularly placed western-frontier exploring and information gathering in the hands of the military; before the Civil War the army became proportionately less a fighting organization, and more a scientific and administrative one, in the West. Geology came within its purview when Dr. Melines C. Leavenworth served in the region; geology, ethnology, and natural history did so, when Henry R. Schoolcraft went on expeditions.

Nor did larger possibilities of the relationship between science and the national government—that is, generous support of pure science by government; some share in policy making by scientists—drop altogether from thought. John Quincy Adams, who would prove to be the last nineteenth-century president keen about science, in his first annual message to Congress reverted to the proposal of his father's generation. He asked for a national university and for much else in that vein—a federal observatory, a naval academy, the financing of explorations by sea, and many economic improvements. Observing that the nations of Europe were doing well in science, even though they were "less blessed with that freedom which is power than ourselves," he urged that the United States government be concerned; "moral, political, intellectual improvement are duties assigned by the Author of our Existence to social no less than to individual man." He wanted Congress to provide a new department of government which would direct the nation's work in science and internal improvements. Although Adams's speech induced none of the action he wanted, today it seems very wise. Looking backward to the eighteenth century, John Quincy Adams appears to have restated the affinity of the Enlightenment for our national institutions; looking forward to the twentieth century, he seems to have been a prophet of the modern federal establishment. His proposals were off beat only for a couple of generations, including his own.

Even at that time, moreover, though he failed to get Congress to act, Adams's position represented the feeling of many men. In Washington, while he was secretary of state, he had been one of a body of public and scientific men who had gathered into what Congress incorporated in 1818 as the Columbian Institute. They set out to foster on a voluntary basis "every department of human knowledge." To be sure, their enduring practical contribution amounted to no more (and no less) than founding a botanical garden in Washington (the present National Botanical Garden, in embryo) and starting some work in astronomy. The more important thing is the bridge they threw, and for a while maintained, between science and government. With a number of eminent scientists, such as Charles Wilkes, who explored the south Pacific, Joel R. Poinsett, and Adams himself, they combined about thirty congressmen and half as many senators. Henry Clay, before he formulated the American System; John C. Calhoun, before states' rights became his obsession; and Andrew Jackson, before he got seriously into presidential politics, were all members. Although the Columbian Institute was no more capable of growth than President Adams's program was of being enacted, the sentiment it expressed in Washington helps us understand the benefit which did come to pure science during the 1840s.°

A *deus ex machina* was needed. And, in the person, or rather the estate, of James Smithson, a wealthy English scientist, such a *deus* appeared. During the 1830s, when Congress was otherwise least ready to act, a bequest of a half million dollars came from him to the United States government, to assist "the increase and diffusion of knowledge among men." Acceptance and implementation of the gift met with the usual delays for the usual states' rights reasons, now stated by John C. Calhoun. But happily John Quincy Adams, at this time chairman of a committee of the House of Representatives, could help see the matter through. Thus the Smithsonian Institution was created, in 1844. It was placed under the control of trustees who included the vice-president, the chief justice, and members of Congress; most remarkable of all, the directorship of the Smithsonian was entrusted by the government first, and for three decades, to Joseph Henry, whose sense of duty brought him (from Princeton and the best research in physics in the land) into public administration. To Joseph Henry, "increase and diffusion of knowledge" meant "increase" far more than "diffusion." Under his directorship the Smithsonian began researches which in due course have proliferated into work in ethnology, tropical biology, and astrophysics; the institution's famous series, *Contributions to Knowledge*, and other series have brought such work to all who have cared to read. Meanwhile, as is better known, on the diffusion side, the Smithsonian has developed and supervised the National Museum, including the Gallery of Art in Washington.

Although nationalizing shifts in the language and publishing habits of the American people were much less self-conscious than advancements in science, and had little connection with politics, that kind of change also underlay the "intellectual action" of the republic. What happened to American English during and after the Revolution, and while the transappalachian West was being settled, recalls the expansions and enrichments of language which occurred in England two centuries earlier. English increased then, at the expense of Latin and French, in the discussion of religion and of affairs; it increased now, at the expense of Latin, in scholarship, as John Adams noticed. In the earlier period the processes of colonization had enriched the language: in England, by encouraging discourse about America; in America, by introducing words from unfamiliar languages into English. Now, after 1800, as American settlers moved into the Mississippi valley and beyond, again speakers of English took over words from the Indians and from French and Spanish settlers who had preceded them. America was less subject than England to the localism of dialects, noted one observer of that time, because people moved about so much, and speakers of different origins learned one another's words—"cole slaw," he mentioned, for example. President Witherspoon, of Princeton, who talked to students and churchmen from all parts, himself coined the word *Americanism*, to designate words and usages which were peculiar to the country. In a formal discussion of the matter, he classified Americanisms under eight subheadings. Among many observations, he described two or three special ways in which Americans made contractions, which were not familiar in Great Britain. "I am going to," rather than "I am going to do it," was one of them.° Being forever tense and in a hurry was often put down, during the nineteenth century, as a national characteristic of Americans.

What to Witherspoon and others were a people's habits and worth discussing, very soon became, in the work of a serious Connecticut Yankee, a cause and a career. Noah Webster, who was a contemporary of Alexander Hamilton and who in his own way served, perhaps as well as Hamilton did, the cause of strong nationality, worked on the American language and offered proposals about the schools the people needed. In 1783 when, only five years out of Yale, he brought out the first edition of a spelling book, he struck the main vein he would mine. As a man of the people who knew everyday habits of speech, as a teacher to whom the clarifying of expression was a duty, and as a believer in a national literature, he had many advantages for textbook production. For one particular, he thought that Greek and Roman lore and literature, and even the Bible, were too much used in the schools. "America must be as independent in *literature* as she is in *politics*—as famous for *arts* as for *arms*," he announced in that famous blue-backed speller. "The author wishes to promote the honour and prosperity of the confederated republics of America; and chearfully throws his mite into the common treasure of patriotic exertions."

For more than four decades—while he did many related things: became an ardent Federalist; edited newspapers and an *American Magazine*; wrote on many subjects, including economics; founded Amherst College—Noah Webster constantly expanded his work in American English. Two years after the speller, he brought out a grammar and a reader; in and out of combined editions, the different books blended those three functions of teaching language. When he was approaching eighty, Webster estimated that about fifteen million spellers had been distributed. Meanwhile, during the early 1800s, he had turned to lexicography. Webster's very first dictionary, though entitled "Compendious," was small; but in 1825 appeared in two volumes the first edition of the epoch-making *An American Dictionary of the English Language.* In the expert opinion of Kenneth Murdock, this was "probably the most ambitious publication ever undertaken, up to that date, upon American soil." Therewith the unending series of Webster's dictionaries, rich in scholarship and practicality, at once accurate and flexible, always friendly to enlarging the language, was properly launched.°

The public meaning of language development has never been much discussed by historians. But a generation ago Charles and Mary Beard argued in *The American Spirit* that the ways in which Americans in the young republic used the word "civilization" revealed an important development of civic values. The English Samuel Johnson, those authors explained, had refused in 1772 to insert the word "civilization" in his dictionary; although the word was already in use in two languages, English and French, it appeared first in any dictionary, an English one, in 1775. But Americans were using the word: Jefferson, for one, used it in his *Notes on Virginia,* which compared this country with Europe. It seems fair to interpret American fondness for "civilization," and for other new words such as "nationality" and "peoples," as a sign that in the time of the Revolution and constitution making the people were thinking of themselves as being dedicated to civic effort. Among many words in use around 1800, the following Americanisms have endured: "Fellow countrymen," a phrase which echoes democracy and patriotism; "nationality," a collective noun which suggests attachment and devotion; "backwoodsman," a specially American type of man; "consociation" and "association," New Englandisms derived from church life.°

Broadly considered, the question of national language development pretty well merges with community growth. During the Revolution, newspapers proliferated, more than in proportion to population increase. In a town or a vicinity where an old newspaper favored the Loyalist side, a Patriot paper often appeared; newspapers moved away from the port cities, which the British often controlled. Around 1790 newspapers expanded again: Federalists and Anti-Federalists, both, had to have their journals; and, when Kentucky and Tennessee entered the Union, the transappalachian press was born, along with the new states. During the first third of the nineteenth century, the same kind of multiplication was repeated. The lapse of the Sedition Act, which released political editors from threat of federal censorship, helped; but the main considerations were the settlement of the Misssssippi valley and the rise of the Whig and Democratic parties between 1815 and 1835. In 1801 there were about two hundred newspapers in the United States; in 1833, about twelve hundred. According to the expert in the field, Frank Luther Mott, the "world had never seen" an equal expansion of journalism.° The press of the period is often and justly remembered for political scurrility: in place of the political fables which had obliquely voiced "country party" protest before the Revolution, direct political attack occurred everywhere in republican days, no holds barred. But quality journalism was born, too, in the Jefferson period. For examples: the *National Intelligencer and Washington Advertiser*, which spoke for the three presidents of the Virginia dynasty; the Richmond *Enquirer*, at first Jeffersonian and later Jacksonian; the New York *Evening Post*, founded and controlled by Alexander Hamilton around 1800 but by 1830 attached to radical democracy. High mortality and low profits among newspapers testify to many people sharing in producing them, much the same as in other businesses and other forms of expression.

Even more suggestive of variety and experimentalism in American expression is the proliferation of magazines, from very few and very short-lived before 1780 to probably five to six hundred ventures during the first quarter of the nineteenth century. Before the middle 1790s, the magazines which started and lapsed all but completely imitated the English literary magazines and borrowed from them. Then politics largely took over, and particular specializations began: before 1815 there were at least a half-dozen religious journals, including one each for the Baptists and Methodists; there were three or four scientific journals, including a medical one. During the first decade of the nine-teenth century, the years during which newspapers of quality appeared, good magazines were launched as well. The Philadelphia *Port-Folio*, which was the most important magazine in the country for some years, the New York *Literary Magazine and American Register*, which Charles Brockden Brown edited in the interest of scientific as well as literary matters, and the Unitarian *Monthly Anthology and Boston Review* all belong to that period. The *North American Review*, which in 1815 succeeded the *Monthly Anthology*, was the climax of this early national development of literary journals. The peak of expan-sionism did not come, however, until about thirty years later. During the 1840s and 1850s, the regional-minded epoch which preceded the Civil War, many regionally inspired magazines were founded. Alto-gether about one hundred American magazines were being produced in 1825 and about six hundred in 1850. These last included quarterly reviews, several of them in the South, a multiplication of religious—many of them missionary—magazines, and the new class of women's magazines.°

Finally on the point of the expansion of the press as a precondition of thought and feeling in the nation, literary book publication paralleled, but only roughly paralleled, magazine publication. More than magazines, and a great deal more than newspapers, the book business depended on coastal location and on centrality; transportation costs made decisive differences among publishers competing with one another. Thus during the early nineteenth century, Boston's two-hundred-year head start gave the city little advantage, prior to railroads. Book publication remained decentralized in New England; and, as a region, New England remained until toward mid-century on the periphery of the national market. Only about 1850 did the Boston area's literary productivity manage to join forces with improving transportation, and Boston achieve its permanent second or third place in the book business. Meanwhile Philadelphia's eighteenth-century leadership in all forms of publishing remained fairly stable. In that city the established publishing houses, with the nation-minded Careys at the center, the location there of active work in science, and the concentration of Presbyterian and Episcopalian publication all counted. The main advantage was availability to transportation and to urban buyers; only around 1850 did New York's cheaper accessibility to the West by water begin to pay off in the publishing business.

Already, as the cities got into publishing, an epoch of national literary confidence and literary enthusiasms had opened: book publishers were for the first time competing in a nationwide market. Again for the first time, they were able to discover willing writers to meet their demands: under boom conditions, the profession of creative writing was born in the country. On the purchasing side, all kinds of tastes were having effect, from the taste for social reformism to the taste for agricultural information and improvement. There had always been best sellers in America, from the *Bay Psalm Book* through *Poor Richard* to the Knickerbocker *History of New York*. But best selling had taken on a national dimension only in 1776, when Thomas Paine's *Common Sense* appeared. During the 1820s it took on a different kind of popularity, a kind to produce greater profits: in that decade Walter Scott's splendid novel, *Waverly*, and before long *Ivanhoe*, captured the hearts of Americans. People in all parts of the nation who never read novels before became enthusiasts for Scott.

No one could suppose that Sir Walter's novels introduced Americans to heroic and nostalgic feelings about the past, any more than one could suppose that Tom Paine introduced them to the political feeling of the Enlightenment. Yet the Scots novelist, drawing his drafts on the lives of common men and writing for ordinary readers, did become uniquely a model and inspiration for contemporary Americans who wanted to be literary. In becoming a transatlantic phenomenon, Scott resembled the eighteenth-century essayists, from whom in all else he differed. That is to say, Sir Walter Scott added a thrust of popularity, and a sense of economic success, to the wave of romantic—passionate, often hopeful—expression in America which was already rising to crest.°

2 A Fitting National Literature: Beginnings and Hopes

THERE is no problem of dating the beginning of literary expression in behalf of American nationalism. The hope that the English-speaking New World would produce a splendid literature of its own had always had voices, from the time of settling the colonies. The question, instead of its arrival (when was the hope first stated?), is its nature—what was its quality and force: what kind of national consciousness did it sustain, what expressive result did it achieve? During the years before the Revolution, for one kind of beginning, the little capital of Maryland, Annapolis, styling itself "the Athens of America," stated great civic and cultural pride; in Williamsburg and Charleston to the south and in Boston and Philadelphia to the north, similar pronouncements were made. During the middle-eighteenth century the Ames and Franklin almanacs and gazettes restated the impulse, originally Puritan, of the colonies to create a literature; during the Revolution President Ezra Stiles of Yale represented, more grandly, like-minded Christian republican ambition. In the period after 1815, when writing was becoming a profession and literary publishing a profitable business, the magazines, especially, campaigned for an American literature. Motives like that of the *North American Review*, "to foster American genius, and, by independent criticism, instruct and guide the public taste," prevailed in editors' offices. Though literary nationalism seems to have been more active in Democratic-oriented than in Federalist-oriented journals, it was not very much a political-party phenomenon.

As an otherwise forgotten magazine, *The Portico* of Baltimore, stated, after the Treaty of Ghent America was crowded with literary genius and laziness, and the time had come to produce. *The Portico* called for biographies. Asking first for books on George Washington, it of course went with the times. The George Washington legend, which was early expressed in "Light-Horse" Harry Lee's marvelous phrase in a memorial resolution by Congress, "First in war, first in peace, first in the hearts of his countrymen," had already been somewhat fulfilled. Chief Justice Marshall's five-volume biography helped. The legend had been made yet more legendary by the famous fifth edition of Parson Weems's biography for children—the cherry-tree story and "I cannot tell a lie" edition.° *The Portico*, again in a way which represents the times, called on American writers to produce Indian studies and stories and to compose typically American poems. The writer in *The Portico* could hardly have known, but at the very time he made his plea, fresh and excellent American biographies, Indian stories, and poems were well on the way.°

By a head start, which the business and the traditions of Philadelphia and New York largely explain, the Middle States region produced the major part of early-republican literature. In 1800 the two cities, with populations of 70,000 and 60,000 respectively, were far and away the largest and most prosperous in the country. Boston, with 25,000 people, Charleston, with 18,000, and Baltimore, the growing parvenu city with 13,000, were the only other American cities with a population larger than 10,000. But money and market are only part of the explanation. The Middle States, as the heirs of Dutch colonial and Indian legends and the place where the Revolution was principally fought, had many great advantages in favor of writing verse, history, and fiction.°

Even before the Revolution, remarkable coincidences in student life at the College of New Jersey had stimulated literary activity which would endure. At Princeton about 1769, Philip Freneau, a Huguenot descendant from New York, and Hugh Henry Brackenridge, a Scots-born west Pennsylvanian, became friends; that friendship came to include James Madison of Virginia. The three heard, learned, and discussed together covenant and commonwealth political ideas; they learned the Scottish moral-intuitionist philosophy which President Witherspoon preached and lectured. In 1771 Freneau and Brackenridge composed the commencement poem which would be the first of several collaborative efforts. Though Brackenridge usually wrote humorous verse, they chose a serious subject, "The Rising Glory of America," and put together lines which were sober.

> 'Tis but the morning of the world with us
> And Science yet but sheds her orient rays....
> I see a Homer and a Milton rise
> In all the pomp and majesty of song....
> This is thy praise, America, thy power
> Thou best of climes, by science visited,
> By freedom blest and richly stor'd with all
> The luxuries of life. Hail happy land,
> The seat of empire, the abode of kings,
> The final stage where time shall introduce
> Renowned characters, and glorious works
> Of high invention and of wond'rous art
> Which not the ravages of time shall waste
> Till he himself has run his long career.

Before finishing at Princeton, Brackenridge wrote and recited on the occasion of taking his M.A. a "Poem on Divine Revelation," which traced the spread of Christianity from Palestine to the Massachusetts Bay Colony. Soon after college both men studied theology, but during the later 1770s they turned together to publishing. They brought out in Philadelphia for a time the *United States Magazine*, the first journal to bear that title.

Following the War of Independence, Brackenridge wrote a couple of plays based on Patriot history—one of which was put on by Harvard students. Then, abandoning equally the study of theology and the pursuit of publishing, he studied law with Samuel Chase in Annapolis; he settled, and practised his profession, in Pittsburgh. There Brackenridge's story is reminiscent of Franklin's in Philadelphia; almost equally with Franklin's his career bespeaks the history of a city and region. He helped establish the first newspaper, the first bookstore, and the first academy in that westward-facing city. In 1786 he was elected to the state legislature. By 1787 his position, his writing and speaking, made him the most eminent Federalist in the region. Even so, he was defeated for the Pennsylvania convention to ratify the Constitution. His successful opponent was also very articulate, and the combat returned Brackenridge to pen and publication. First he lampooned the rival in short newspaper pieces; soon he composed a long Hudibrastic poem, "The Modern Chevalier." Finally he broadened his attack—pillorying all frontier buffoons who ventured into politics—into a satiric novel, America's first, *Modern Chivalry*. Considered narrowly, Brackenridge, the nationalist westerner, seems in these ways of expression to have been out of tune with his America: he advanced as writer by shifting from a dated form of English poem to another form of satire, one which he derived from Greek and Latin literature and from Cervantes and Swift. The hero of *Modern Chivalry*, who speaks for the author, was patterned on Don Quixote. Yet, when *Modern Chivalry* is viewed as an occurrence in biography and history, it seems exactly true to time and place. It was the first book about the American West, produced in the West with love for the region; forward, from it into the new century, the vein of frontier humor opens up. In public thought, Brackenridge's satire on crude fellows seeking office points the way—the more poignantly because he himself soon changed into a Jefferson-party man and a devoted, anxious democrat—to a century and more of anxiety among American writers concerning government by the people. He anticipated the doubts which Fenimore Cooper would voice in the 1830s, and even those of Henry and Brooks Adams, and of Henry L. Mencken in our own century.°

Meanwhile, since the Princeton friends had parted, Philip Freneau—always more the man of feeling, and economically freer to do as he pleased—had taken a course eastward and sometimes southward instead of westward. During the middle 1770s, he had declared personal independence by taking a secretaryship with a West Indian planter. On the island of Santa Cruz his native romanticism spoke early in "The House of Night" and other poems; during several Caribbean voyages he began his famous series of sea verses—poetry which no other American has yet surpassed in the same genre. The War of Independence struck personally when English sailors removed him from an American brig at sea. The experience which followed he rendered compactly in "The British Prison Ship," bitter verse which marks his turning completely and permanently Anglophobe. The following lines, the first six from the "Prison Ship" and the others—which were sung to the tune of "God Save the King"—from an "Ode" to honor Citizen Genet in 1793, convey his public passion.

> *Americans! a just resentment shew,*
> *And glut revenge on this detested foe;*
> *While the warm blood exults the glowing vein*
> *Still shall resentment in your bosoms reign*
> *Can you forget the greedy Briton's ire,*
> *Your fields in ruins, and your domes on fire[?]*
>
> *God save the Rights of Man!*
> *Give us a heart to scan*
> *Blessings so dear:*
> *Let them be spread around*
> *Wherever man is found*
> *And with the welcome sound*
> *Ravish his ear.*
>
> *Let us with France agree,*
> *And bid the world be free,*
> *While tyrants fall!*
> *Let the rude savage host*
> *Of their vast numbers boast—*
> *Freedom's almighty trust*
> *Laughs at them all!*

Thus the Patriot mind of Philip Freneau moved with the advance guard of his country's march. But the country did not go with him and his kind, in respect of hospitality for writers who had dogmas to express and career intentions to fulfill. He achieved his maximum recognition during two protest years in Philadelphia, while that was the national capital and while he was editor of the *National Gazette* in the interest of Thomas Jefferson and the Anti-Federalist Party. But this same period earned him President Washington's scornful phrase "that rascal Freneau," and it gave him little opportunity to practise the art of poetry. Freneau formulated the problem in "To an Author," a strong statement of the quarrel he had with society and a prime expression of a protest many American authors were going to make—a resentment close to their ambivalence about democracy.

> *On these bleak climes by Fortune thrown,*
> *Where rigid Reason reigns alone,*
> *Where lovely Fancy has no sway,*
> *Nor magic forms about us play—*
> *Nor nature takes her summer hue*
> *Tell me, what has the muse to do?—*
>
> *An age employed in edging steel*
> *Can no poetic raptures feel;*
> *No solitude's attracting power,*
> *No leisure of the noon day hour,*
> *No shaded stream, no quiet grove*
> *Can this fantastic century move;*
> *The muse of love in no request—*
> *Go—try your fortune with the rest,*
> *One of the nine you should engage,*
> *To meet the follies of the age....°*

Considered in parallel, the careers of Brackenridge and Freneau tell us, first, of the thrust the Revolution gave to literary expression. In their different ways each brought uncommon imagination into play. The writings of both show minds which were stimulated by public situations and convictions and yet were governed by their own creative individuality. There are also shortcomings, which were not strictly literary, to consider. Neither writer produced much, or was much recognized, after 1805. It is not that opportunity, literary or economic, fell away; during the first quarter of the new century, other writers succeeded in the same region. Beginning in 1798, Charles Brockden Brown, a Philadelphian of Quaker background, brought out a series of novels, not political in content, which made him first in several lines of American literary development. One of them was being the first American to have a self-sustaining literary career, something which neither Brackenridge nor Freneau attained and which would have meant everything to Freneau. Still more indicative, during the early 1820s in New York, while Freneau lived on in retirement, Washington Irving and James Fenimore Cooper enjoyed successful careers; and young William Cullen Bryant, on being recognized as a nature poet, was brought down from Boston to begin the career which would prove long and effective as editor, critic, poet, and reformer in the great publishing city.

Thus, in the rise of American literature, the years from about 1800 to about 1815 appear to have been a kind of watershed in the innovating Middle States. Before that time the literary life had had only occasional existence apart from religious or public thought: it had had little autonomy, either in the intellectual sense of authors opening up new subject matter and venturing new modes of expression or in the sense of achieving economic independence. After 1800, and much more definitely after 1820, those freedoms arrived. Sharing the romantic excitement about nature and locale, and about human nobility, heroism, and venturousness, which writers in Europe had already begun to voice, the republic's novelists and poets of the second generation multiplied production and achieved such quality as we still honor.

Much is suggested by the case of Fenimore Cooper, who was the first American novelist to compete seriously with the marvelously successful Sir Walter Scott. Among Scott's advantages with American readers and purchasers, he had a great gift for portraying medieval people, some of them at the lower levels of society. That is, he offered American readers an attractive door of escape into a period of history, the Middle Ages, for which they had previously had little taste. Cooper had a similar advantage of opening windows, though they were faced toward a different and nearer view. His Leatherstocking and his Indians and seamen helped ordinary Americans see themselves agreeably in ways which corresponded with their previous impressions. As we shall see in detail when we reach his conservative polemic, *The American Democrat* of 1838, much of the novelist's feeling about his fellow countrymen was as anxious as anyone else's. But Cooper's feeling involved, first, knowledge and fondness: in his case the early American novel tendered acquaintanceship with the people, without satire or irony, and made romance of their adventures into the wilderness and across the seas.

After the Middle States, New England entered chronologically second into the national current toward literary achievement. Or, to refine the statement, Boston and eastern Massachusetts, the ancient intellectual hub of the region, did so. A first start, though not a long-sustained movement, did occur in Connecticut quite as early as in Pennsylvania. In literature as in religion, most of the story in that state derives from a half-dozen ambitious Yale graduates, men of dedication to the standing order. Though the group is usually called the "Connecticut Wits," the name does not fit well: their performance reached beyond their famous satires to include the writing of epic poems and a successful effort to reform Yale College. Indeed the very weakness of Yale, before the Revolution and before President Stiles, helps account for their thought and work. During the middle 1760s, toward the close of a period of troubles when the undergraduates had protested the curriculum and the teaching, two very able students, John Trumbull and Timothy Dwight, reading and writing independently, very largely educated themselves. They became the earliest wits to produce. In

1772, while tutoring at the college, Trumbull brought out a long poem, "The Progress of Dulness," on the badness of college education and on the goodness of literature. Telling a story, he said, "of Tom Brainless, shewing . . . how he went to College and what he learned there; . . . how afterward he became a Great Man and wore a wig," Trumbull declared the Yale protest opinion—which he borrowed from Lord Kames of the Scottish school of philosophy—that "the *meer* knowledge of ancient languages, of the abstruser parts of mathematics, and the dark researches of metaphysics is of little advantage in any business or profession in life." Modern literature, and composition, he said, was needed in college.° But Trumbull did not remain a Yale tutor. Like his Princeton contemporary, Hugh Brackenridge, he turned to a career in law (studying in John Adams's office) and meanwhile wrote poetry. Ten years after "The Progress of Dulness" he published complete what he had already brought out serially, "M'Fingal," a mock epic of the Revolution. Trumbull ridiculed Loyalists and Patriots both; his caricatures made him popular nowhere during the war. Then the poem caught on: probably no other American poem before "Evangeline" equaled the popularity it reached during the early 1800s. At that time, among New England Federalists especially, it was easy to be condescending and ironical about government by the people; even today, when the Connecticut Wits are hard to read, "M'Fingal" is amusing.

Though they were politically different from each other, both Timothy Dwight, the second wit in order of literary production, and Joel Barlow, the third, knew the Revolution from inside as having been Patriot soldiers, and both wrote long, sober poems honoring the rise of the American nation. As befitted his ministry and his conservatism, Dwight adapted American history to Bible terms: his "Conquest of Canaan," which he truthfully described as "the first epic poem ever to have appeared in America," plainly represents the United States as the land of Canaan, and George Washington as Joshua. His thousands of couplets indicate an amazing investment of time taken from parish and school. This latter-day Puritan renewed the theme of the chosen people, but he did so not so much for New England as for the United States as a whole.

Joel Barlow is remembered as a radical, a minor Tom Paine, and a sport among the Connecticut Wits, but that phase of his writing came late.° When, in the year of Daniel Shays's Rebellion, several of the wits collectively produced a mock epic, the "Anarchiad," Barlow was one of the contributors. The object of pillory, this time, was the Massachusetts insurgents. But simultaneously, and quite in accord with what others in the group were doing, Barlow stated in a long poem his view of America's promise. His "Vision of Columbus" of 1787 differed from "The Conquest of Canaan" in being mainly a secular vision; it became yet more different during the next twenty years, as the author revised and revised, until the poem appeared in final form as "The Columbiad," late during the presidency of Jefferson. The millennial spirit remained. It was not unchristian, but it was governed more by common-sense philosophical notions of a great moral fulfillment by America than by an expectation of the second coming of Christ. So believing, Barlow voiced confidence in the ordinary man—in democracy.

> First, his own powers the man, with care, descries,
> What nature gives, and various art, supplies;
> Rejects the ties of controversial rules,
> The pride of names, the prejudice of schools;
> The sure foundation lays, on which to rise,
> To look thro' earth and meditate the skies;
> And finds some general laws in every breast,
> Where ethics, faith, and politics may rest.

To be sure, letting a seraph speak for him, Barlow prophesied that America would live united and free and that in due course a league of the world would be born.°

When their individual and collaborative output is considered as a whole, all of it public in bearing, the Connecticut Wits give an impression of an extraordinary mixture of qualities. Their national patriotism, the ultimate democracy and ultimate internationalism of at least one of them, and their fondness for satire in British styles a century old, all brought them close to Middle States feeling and writing. The habits of mind which they shared with Scots philosophers were matched, as we have seen in an earlier chapter, by Jefferson and other Virginians; two chapters hence, we shall come upon that intellectual influence again. Yet, much as they shared intellectually with Americans outside New England, the wits seem provincial and immature, even ridiculous at points. Their scolding attitude toward revolutionary-age society resembled in letters President Dwight's attitude toward his students: they found the American people in a phase they were determined to chide and guide. On the literary side, if they so much as considered that to compose an epic equal to the *Aeneid* required more of them than taking time off from regular duty and grinding out pentameters, any such wisdom fails to shine through their lines.

As we come to eastern Massachusetts, of course the most splendid literary region of all from 1815 to 1860, the striking thing after the Revolution is the tininess and tardiness of the literary renewal. Bostonians and Cantabrigians brought out nothing that was sizable and memorable—nothing to equal Freneau or Brackenridge, or Barlow or Noah Webster—until the War of 1812 had passed. Yet by 1800 a seedbed which is remembered more for its second- than for its first-generation product was beginning to sprout. At that time the literary initiative in the region was taken by the young Unitarians of the Anthology Club and journal. A search among conservative Congregationalists for equal literary effort discovers only Jeremy Belknap, who had come to Boston from New Hampshire in 1787 and who then published several volumes of history and biography and founded the Massachusetts Historical Society, all before the century ended. But while orthodoxy quieted down in a literary sense, the young and liberal ministers, of whom the most prominent was William Ellery Channing, delivered much literary energy. Their *Monthly Anthology* often discussed, and often printed in translation form, the literature of ideas in Europe. They shared, and voiced in their own way, the conviction that America lagged. In 1809 Joseph Buckminster of the group, who was a Bible scholar, contributed to the *Anthology* an essay on "The Dangers and Duties of Men of Letters" which reasoned—much as Ralph Waldo Emerson's most famous of all discussions of literary nationalism, *The American Scholar,* would reason three decades later—that to participate in the exchange of modern liberal ideas is a species of religious duty.°

What was taking hold at the ancient hub of New England, ahead of other places in America, was a change in literary taste—indeed in emotional values. The liberals of eastern New England, already emancipated from their regional theology, were simply not of a mind, like their older contemporaries in Connecticut, to phrase their hopes for America in formal and conventionalized verse. In the Anthology Club and surrounding circles the idea was being imported and accepted from Europe that a national literature requires form and substance of writing which fit the style of the people involved. This line of thought introduced into Yankee discourse considerations which America's favorite philosophers, John Locke and the Scots, had not considered. In continental Europe, especially the Germanies under Napoleon, such considerations—call them organic or even functional—were coming alive. The brothers and philosophers, August W. and Friedrich von Schlegel, for principal example, edited their own journal, the *Athenaeum,* from 1798 to 1810. A major instrument of German Romanticism, it published much discussion, historical and philosophical, in favor of such literature as would embody (in the later words of a sympathetic American) "the aggregate mass of symbols, in which the spirit of an age or the character of a nation is shadowed forth." What the German journal helped originate, Massachusetts journals, notably the *Monthly Anthology* and the *North American Review*—and also the *Port-Folio* of Philadelphia— greatly helped to spread: the feeling that a people's literature is an important, passionate, coherent part of the life of the nation.°

In the Boston and Cambridge area the shift to romantic-nationalistic feeling evoked a great deal of pronouncing and promising about American culture. In this respect the keynoter was Edward Tyrrel Channing, younger brother of the more eminent William Ellery Channing, and anticipator of him and of Ralph Waldo Emerson as a prophet of the birth of a great national literature. Writing under the heading "Literary Independence" and using—and probably creating—the phrase "American Scholar," Channing said that an American scholar is one who "chooses his own walks, provides his own nourishment and delight; his pursuit of excellence is enthusiastic." Channing spoke with personal authority: he was editor of the *North American Review* and soon, as professor of rhetoric at Harvard, would be training writers. Between the lines of his essay, a good many current influences in the community can be detected: knowledge of German theorizing about the nature of nationality is present; so is Unitarian belief in personal self-fulfillment.

> We are not indebted to independent minds merely for the enlargement of knowledge;—they are also the formers of national literature. . . . To do away with all foreign influences and establish here what is properly called a national literature is perhaps wholly out of the question. . . . But . . . we may have a perfectly independent one. . . . Let the American Scholar turn homeward a little more, let our own rivers and mountains and valleys and forests be as holy in his fancy, and bring to his mind as burning and rapid associations, as the classical regions, which his young mind made the only land of beauty and brightness. . . . Cultivate domestic literature, that your countrymen, in every part of the Union, may feel a closer, more enlightened and even a more generous intimacy. . . . Cultivate domestic literature as a source of national dignity, a foundation of respect from foreigners. . . . You must find your happiness and your glory in the consecration of every power and attainment to the service of mankind.°

"Let our own rivers and mountains and valleys and forests be . . . holy," exhorted this editor just at the time when William Cullen Bryant's poems were beginning to appear in his own *North American Review*. Channing must have known well that New England writers had been preceded by at least one good poet from another region, Philip Freneau, who had found wild honeysuckle and the honeybee to be proper subjects for verse, and by several prose writers who were able to create frontier and regional characters and build novels around them. But he—his journal and his college—were soon to excel in helping to bring literary performance toward the level of hope. Edward Tyrrel Channing himself "probably trained as many conspicuous authors as all other American instructors put together," said one of the trainees, Thomas Wentworth Higginson, at the end of the century—the others, we know, included Emerson, Thoreau, Oliver Wendell Holmes, Richard Henry Dana, and James Russell Lowell.

Many romantic contemporaries spoke for the organic sense of writing which seeks to match substance with style. William Cullen Bryant made much of the literary challenge laid down by the correspondence between American character and American environment: "Whoever will take the pains . . . will be surprised at the infinite variety of forms of character which spring up under the institutions of our country. . . . The adventurous and roving natives of our sea-coasts and islands are a different race of men from those who till the interior, and the hardy dwellers of our mountainous districts are not like the inhabitants of our rich plains that skirt our mighty lakes and rivers."°

Finally, concerning this age of finding ourselves, before the classical period of American literature between 1835 and 1860, a glimpse through William Ellery Channing's "Remarks on National Literature" will reveal something of the piety of cultural nationalism. "By a national literature," began the most influential of all the Unitarian clergymen critics, "we mean the expression of a nation's mind in writing. . . . We mean the manifestation of a nation's intellect in the only forms by which it can multiply itself at home, and send itself abroad. . . . We regard its gifted men, whether devoted to the exact sciences, to mental and ethical philosophy, to history and legislation, or to fiction and poetry, as forming a noble intellectual brotherhood, and it is for the purpose of quickening all to join their labors for the public good, that we offer the present plea in behalf of a national literature."°

Know yourselves, the two Channings and their kind were saying to all Americans who would listen. Take leadership, they were advising their peers in American society. For, as Unitarians especially believed, self-realization and self-fulfillment evoke the wisdom and strength of a people.

3 *A Resourceful National Economy*

PUBLIC thought in America, as we saw in detail in our colonial-period chapters, has often been centrifugal thought—thought, that is, to justify group departure from old centralizations and norms. The congregational separatism of Puritans, Baptists, Quakers, Germans, and even southern Anglicans amply represents centrifugal thought, and the grand doctrine of the Declaration is, of course, the primary example. After 1776 and well into the nineteenth century, multiple state making and church and community building carried on this same centrifugal force. Every new institution was born to the tune of fresh justifications of being different and separate.

Against the centrifugal tendency, the main counterassertions which were made before Reconstruction derived, on the religious side, largely from theology and interchurch feeling and, on the secular side, from convictions felt in favor of strengthening the nation and the federal system of government. *E pluribus unum*, the national motto, visually associated (in flag and seal) with a field of stars, very neatly sustained the Newtonian vision of the nature of the Union which the founding fathers had loved. Altogether it is fair to say that nationalist sentiment, though it had long been voiced as recognition that Americans are one of the peoples of earth, did not until the later nineteenth century gain any such passion and prevalence as since then the country has known. Unitarian promptings to the contrary, the United States lacked its Fichte or Hegel.

Yet the early nineteenth century did have practical public thinkers whose minds sought to express the unities of American life. In this connection, a school of economists, or at least economic thinkers, came first. Although the political and personal reputation of Alexander Hamilton, their eminent predecessor, declined during the quarter century after his death, Hamiltonian programs gradually gained acceptance in many directions. Even while his old enemies Jefferson and Madison were in the White House and their party ruled Congress, Hamilton's Bank of the United States had been maintained to the statutory limit, 1811. Then, in 1816, the second bank was created; and the tariff law of that same year enacted a truly protectionist policy, more than Hamilton himself had ever obtained. Perhaps the most persuasive tribute ever paid to the economic practicality of Alexander Hamilton was one delivered by Representative John Quincy Adams, seven years after President Jackson had condemned the second bank to death. Speaking at a semicentennial celebration of the inauguration of George Washington, Adams acknowledged that Hamilton—his father's great enemy—had been "one of the first financiers of his age" and truly had saved the nation. In the words of the address: "*Especially the incorporation of the bank*, operated like enchantment for the restoration of public credit; [it] repaired the ruined fortunes of the public creditors, and was equivalent to the creation of many millions of capital, available for the encouragement of industry and the active exertions of enterprise."°

The name and tradition of Alexander Hamilton, then, still had magic, at least among Whigs, even while the mid-century epoch of tragic divisionism in America came on. But continuity and development in economic nationalism depended more on needs felt within the economy than on any tradition from the Federalist age. As early as the 1780s and 1790s, while most of the philosopher statesmen and President Washington himself were either indifferent or opposed to much industrial development, societies formed and launched periodicals. Tench Coxe, who served Hamilton in the treasury department, but later joined the Jeffersonian party, and Mathew Carey, the publisher, both of Philadelphia, became leading promoters of industrialization. The strong Pennsylvania Society for the Encouragement of Manufactures and the Useful Arts, founded in 1787, was their organization, and the *American Museum* was their magazine. Societies with like intentions appeared early in New York and Boston, Baltimore and Providence, and before long in South Carolina and Ohio. Colonel David Humphreys, who was a minor figure among the Connecticut Wits and a major manufacturer of woolens, turned a smiling face toward what was to be—in America as in England—an ugly aspect of a key industry, textile manufacturing:

> *Teach little hands to ply mechanic toil*
> *Cause failing age o'er easy tasks to smile....*
> *So shall the young find employ,*
> *And hearts, late nigh to perish,*
> *leap for joy.*°

The journal which would do the most, between the War of 1812 and the Civil War, to inform and advance the ideas of economic nationalism, *Niles' Weekly Register*, was founded in Baltimore in 1811, apparently without any benefit of direct Federalist Party connection or inspiration. The proprietor editor, Hezekiah Niles, grew up in Wilmington, Delaware, among artisans—in his own words, among "able, industrious and sober *mechanics* (as I trust that some half a dozen of my own sons, by the blessing of PROVIDENCE, will be)." He was educated in the Quaker school there, probably; somewhere he learned Greek and Latin. Like many another, he learned the printer's trade, expertly, in Philadelphia; in the same apprenticeship he became well acquainted with the ways and means of producing journals. About 1800 he returned to Wilmington, now in his middle twenties and married to a Quaker girl. There he was soon elected town clerk and a burgess in the state legislature. "I was the junior member of the first *regular* democratic meeting or 'caucus,' that, as I believe, was ever held in Delaware, with a general view to the organization of the party," he reminisced, much later, about that interval.

Although the first and second starts Niles made on his own in journalism, one in Wilmington and one in Baltimore, are unremarkable, from the launching of the *Weekly Register* he proved timely, useful, and very successful. Both a newspaper and a magazine, the *Register* published a generous supply of public documents: it drew on the semi-official *National Intelligencer* of Washington for congressional papers; in that way it rendered such a service as the *New York Times* does today. In the magazine phase of its operation, the *Register* produced a regular news digest and sometimes devoted whole issues to special topics. In a way a regional paper, it specialized in business matters appropriate to its Chesapeake Bay location. But Baltimore, which was a kind of early-period Chicago, was itself a phenomenon of national growth: the Chesapeake and Ohio Canal and the Baltimore and Ohio Railroad connected the booming city with transappalachian business; its famous clippers (and other sailing vessels) connected it with South American and Pacific trade. Niles's editorial mind, and his journal, seized on all this with enthusiasm.

But the *Weekly Register* was never committed all out to any political party; it was too independently run for that. While consistently nationalist and humanitarian, Niles was also consistently democratic, in line with his personal past. In 1812 he described majority rule "as the first principle of our solemn compact with each other"; four years later he predicted the rise of what we now call Jacksonianism "by the indignant suffrage of a neglected and injured people." In due course he spoke favorably of the rise of workingmen's parties. Concerning nationalism as feeling, during the War of 1812 he wished "that *my* countrymen had the same sense of *national glory* that actuates the *British* nation"; he regretted that "At present, we are semi-*Englishmen*, and have not a national character." But by the summer of 1817 he thought that a clear improvement had come: "It is delightful to see the words 'national character,' 'national feeling,' and the like, coming into *common* use;— and it is, indeed, a luxury to the editor of this paper to believe, that he, as much as any man, has contributed to bring it about. . . . The people are every day more and more convinced that they have a country and a constitution worth defending." In that same year in an open letter to ex-Presidents Jefferson and Madison, Niles sought their endorsement of having American textbooks for American schools, Noah Webster's idea; in the *Register* he gave favorable notice to writings by Washington Irving.°

Naturally economic themes were the ones which Niles most harped on, with the greatest resonance in city and region. In 1812, when the *Weekly Register* was new, he voiced happy astonishment at the speed with which the war was spawning infant industry; in 1815 he devoted an entire volume to the "Manufacturers of the United States whose labors are eminently calculated to build up a National Character and insure the Real Independence of our beloved country." Eight years later, during an anxious time before Clay's tariff of 1824 was enacted, the editor wrote a congressman, with evident reference to Henry Clay, that "Some bill of the sort *must and will* be passed. Is it not possible that a certain man may ride to the presidency upon it?" Once more Niles thought—correctly, so far as the next ten years would tell the story—that he was helping to make the future. "I believe that I am now about the *oldest* public writer—(as we editors are honorably called.) in favor of domestic manufacturers in the United States. I commenced the *campaign* about eighteen years ago, with nearly the same views, and to help bring about nearly the same purposes that I now aim at."° Although Niles did waver in 1828, when the extremely high (and notoriously corrupt) "Tariff of Abominations" was passed, he consistently supported Henry Clay's American System and bank program during the 1830s. As the country's grand publicist for economic nationalism, he ranks with the great men of the bench and bar—Marshall, Story, and Kent; Clay and Webster—among the strong-minded Hamiltonians of the Jacksonian epoch.

Meanwhile in 1820 a second Baltimorean, Daniel Raymond, made a different but equal kind of contribution to economic nationalism. Quite as specifically as Hezekiah Niles's background in Philadelphia and Wilmington prepared him for his career in nationalist journalism, the Federalist-oriented legal training which Raymond received in Judge Reeve's law school in Connecticut prepared him for a more theoretical kind of nationalism. During a briefless period as a young lawyer in Baltimore, he read economics copiously. Before he was thirty-five he brought out *Thoughts on Political Economy*, which was the first treatise on fundamental economics (as distinguished from economic policy) ever to be written in America. His central idea and original idea, which he would develop in later writings, was that the wealth of a nation lies in its capacity to produce and distribute goods and to render services. It lies, that is, in the overlapping, mutually dependent areas of a nation's national resources, the people's labor and technology, their operating capital, and their law and policy. This challenged Adam Smith's *Wealth of Nations*. Smith had conceived that the wealth of a nation, Great Britain or any other, consists of the accumulations of the economy; he had conceived that those accumulations are mainly the possessions of private owners. But Daniel Raymond, reasoning more socially, argued that much which truly represents the wealth of a nation is not private property at all. In sum, national wealth inheres less in things than in capacity—in a people's science and culture, their education and law, their public institutions and policy.

Like Niles, Raymond was affected by the business environment he lived in and by the policies advanced by Federalist-line statesmen in Washington. What he had to say about the usefulness of knowledge corresponds closely to the ideas entertained in the Columbian Institute. Like other nationalists, he saw merit in making known the theory of nationalism. In a second book, *The American System*, accordingly, Raymond expanded, and succeeded somewhat in popularizing, his ideas of the nature of wealth. Here, under the title he borrowed from Henry Clay, appears clearly the continuity between Hamilton's neo-mercantilism of the 1790s and the more social nationalism of the 1820s. Raymond had saturated himself in the economic writings of the first secretary of the treasury. He stated and developed the idea that a public debt can be a blessing, because—stimulating investment, interest payment, and reinvestment—it calls into action the mechanisms of business. To that argument, he added a democratic codicil, namely, the consideration that a public debt, if widely spread among the people as bondholders, avoids the hazard of making the people as taxpayers the payers of tribute to an upper class. Altogether Raymond's logic led in modern directions: toward more banks, more expenditure for internal improvements, even toward military outlay; in sum, toward massive economic acts by government. The same logic carried the author toward certain social emancipations. Where there is no slavery, he said, doubtless thinking of Connecticut, the labor force is more resourceful and productive than where slavery prevails.

Raymond's little books had strength, economic and moral. Henry Clay, himself no theorist, could hardly have had better intellectual endorsement than *The American System*. Hezekiah Niles, though he outdid all others in gathering data and presenting the traditional arguments in favor of a national economy, displayed no such analytical power as Raymond did. Neatly the two Baltimoreans complemented each other.°

Though during the 1810s and 1820s the new and speedily growing city at the head of Chesapeake Bay took the lead in economic-nationalist thinking, after about 1832, when *Niles' Weekly Register* declined and Daniel Raymond dropped from sight as author, Philadelphia resumed its old leadership. Partly this was a phenomenon of economic growth in and around the city. During the 1820s and 1830s Pennsylvania's mighty future in transportation, and in iron and other industry, became increasingly clear. In Philadelphia, moreover, a second generation of promoters and writers emerged. Among these, or rather in nearby Reading but truly a member of the same group, the most important for economic thought was Georg Friedrich List, the German political economist. Dr. List had arrived in America in 1826, after having abandoned at age thirty-seven a post at the University of Tübingen. He brought such an equipment to bear on economic problems as probably no one else in America equaled; his policy inclinations were timely. At home he had been a leader in both national and liberal movements: in behalf of the *Zollverein*, or customs-union movement among the German principalities, he had edited a journal; as a liberal he had been elected to the Diet of Württemberg; he had been jailed on grounds of sedition. Immediately on arrival in America, introduced as a friend of Lafayette, he associated himself with Mathew Carey and others of the Pennsylvania Society for the Encouragement of Manufactures. By his own account it was not his book learning, or even his German political experience, which took over, when almost at once he produced books and addresses in favor of American nationalism. In the United States, Professor List said in retrospect, "I cast all books aside—they would only have tended to mislead one. The best work on Political Economy which one can read in that modern land is actual life. . . . Progress which requires centuries in Europe goes on there before one's eyes. The book of actual life I have earnestly and diligently studied and compared with the results of my previous studies. . . . The result has been (as I hope) the preparing of a system which . . . is not founded on bottomless cosmopolitanism but on the nature of things, the lessons of history, and on the requirements of the nations."°

The short-run effectiveness of List's American observations far outdid Raymond's: they were more elaborate (though not more original), and they won more recognition. He early wrote his *Outlines of American Political Economy*. He addressed the legislature of Pennsylvania; he received many invitations and was offered good appointments; he organized the little railroad which would grow ultimately into the Reading system. His writings succeeded so well as to carry American economic nationalism into the European market of ideas. Soon after returning to Germany he published in 1841 his famous and enduring work, which would be put out in English fifteen years later, *The National System of Political Economy*. Of course it pronounced for the tariff protection of infant industries; it was infused with German-idealist feeling for national existence. Once practically exiled from Germany, List became an accepted contributor to German policy thinking right into the Bismarck epoch. Those who care for the ironies of history may consider his unique experience. His economic thought, beginning in the protest nationalism of the period of Baron Stein, ascended through a phase of being reinforced in America into a final phase of contributing to the German Empire.

Henry C. Carey, son of Mathew and his successor in the Lea and Carey publishing firm in Philadelphia, was the fourth and last of the major expositors of economic nationalism in the Middle States cluster of that school. Where List's special contribution to nationalism was to sophisticate it and enter it in the international exchange of ideas, Carey's was to make it spacious and intellectual among Americans. Not college-educated—among the major economic nationalists of the period, only List was that—but trained by his father both for publishing and for economic observation and thought, the younger Carey read widely in all kinds of English and American literature, the school of Adam Smith of course included. When in future this writer's economic argument took an anticlassical direction, as that of the Irish and Germans among the American economic nationalists did most readily, it nonetheless incorporated large doses of English ways of economic thinking. Henry Carey's definitions, and his logical and systematic reasoning from general position to general position, always borrowed much doctrine and style from the classical economists, even while he rejected their policy conclusions.

Henry Carey's first book, an *Essay on the Rate of Wages*, appeared in 1835, when he was forty-two; it proved to be his least nationalistic one. It appeared in the wake of the unhappy tariff escalation and compromising, from 1828 to 1833; at that time the author did not thoroughly commit himself to protectionism. Writing on wages, he accepted in principle the wages-fund doctrine of the British economists—the position, which had forty years to prevail before being criticized to death by academic economists, that labor depends on funds accumulated by capitalists to make employment possible. Yet he resisted the ordinarily accepted implications of wages-fund doctrine. Rather than wages being a subtraction from capital, or high wages being a loss to capitalists, the Philadelphia economist believed that high wages and high profits might accompany one another. Indeed Carey argued that high wages benefit the whole economy. At the close of the *Rate of Wages*, he defined political economy as being, instead of a dismal science, a study devoted to the happiness of nations, and more particularly as a science of applying *national* labor "so that the laborer can command the greatest amount of comfort with the smallest sacrifice."

During the next quarter century, though he became ever more involved in business, reform, journalism, and politics, Carey produced ten or a dozen volumes. His two major systematic works, *The Principles of Political Economy* and *The Principles of Social Science*, published respectively in 1837–1840 and in 1858–1859, each in three volumes, so far developed his antiorthodox positions, and so amply expressed his nationalism, that—although they are overlong and not very original—they deserve their reputation for being the great monuments of the American economic nationalist movement. *The Principles of Political Economy*, a postdepression book, said in essence that the people should draw on the resources of the national government in times of adversity. Though the second Bank of the United States was dead, Carey argued that banks should be assigned the power of note issue—really a form of control of currency, a function of the central government under the Constitution. Developing the logic in economics of American belief in social harmony, he formulated thirty-seven natural laws of development. Among many passages intended to demonstrate the benevolence of nationalism, he reasoned that population growth and technology should always benefit the laborer, as they would assure him an increasing share of the product of the economy.

During the 1840s, apparently encouraged by the simultaneous fall of the British tariff and rise of the American one and by the appearance of List's *National System*, Carey was converted completely to high protectionism. Besides this, as is evident in his biggest and most generalizing book, *The Principles of Social Science*, he became in other ways most nationalistic. In that book he explained—in the line of Tocqueville—that great voluntary associations would benefit all the people. He particularized about cities. Carey, like the other nationalists, had never liked Malthus's population theory; now openly and uncompromisingly he opposed it. Where the English parson author had found that population growth and pressure meant degradation for labor, Carey, an urban dweller, found that it meant new clusters of labor and advantage to everyone. As the author explained: England had destroyed local industry in Ireland and India; Americans must avoid making any such error. Using figures of speech reminiscent of Alexander Hamilton—the sun and the planets—to refer to American federalism, Carey reasoned that local and national centers of economic attraction and motion needed to be created in the economy. He was saying that new regions must have both farms and industries and that the different economic classes must produce the institutions or associations they need. Carey had truly a grand vision of freedom and organization in harmony in the economic growth of his country.°

4 *A More Perfect Union:*
Convictions about Justice and Peace

ALTOGETHER the prophets and reasoners of American nationality whom we have considered in Chapters XII and XIII so far had little to say about government. Yet from them we have heard echoes of America's political climaxes and crises—the resonances of national events in 1776 and 1787, in 1800 and 1812, and in 1816, 1828, and 1832. Among religious, literary, and economic nationalists, as among those who were more politically minded, the thrill of republican government under law infused every kind of promise which was spoken or written concerning the New World of the coming century.

If we were to review our nationalists by groups and rank them in the order of such concern as they did show toward government, our list would come out as follows: the economic nationalists, first, because they sought to enlarge federal policy; the scientists and friends of science, second, even though the studies they projected had little to say about politics, because they conceived science to serve the organized nation; the religious nationalists, third, because Christian missions were concerned with settling and making secure the frontier and with overseas foreign relations. Doubtless the literary nationalists were the least government-minded of any. Not different from most literary men most of the time, they managed to be very patriotic without being very political. Yet some of them became active party men, and some wrote about society and reform. In New York, James Fenimore Cooper, a Whig, and William Cullen Bryant, first a Democrat and later a Republican, did both.

Very different from today's large number of professions, the members of which actively study or participate in public affairs—economists, political scientists, historians, and so on—the young republic knew only one profession which was customarily concerned with the exercise of power. Quite as lawyers had been the ones who fathered the Revolution, and who had written the constitutions of the 1770s and 1780s and infused the new governments with energy, now, in the nineteenth century, lawyers continued to predominate in affairs. Except for the two minor generals, William Henry Harrison and Zachary Taylor, who captured the presidency for the Whig Party in the 1840s when no other kind of candidate could, all the presidents between General George Washington and General Ulysses S. Grant were lawyers. During those same seventy-two years clearly a high (but unfigured) proportion of the seats in the cabinets and Congresses, and in the state conventions, legislatures, and executive branches, was occupied by lawyers.

The social as well as the political development of the country called for lawyers' services. Quite as in colonial days, population growth and spread of settlement created infinite complexities concerning land grants, claims, and titles. Characteristically the land lawyer, himself often a speculator, made money. It was the same in commercial law. Besides there being on all counts much legal business to do, the newness of America's institutions created uncertainties about how and where to take hold. A question, under the new federal government, arose often: In which of several courts was to be found the authority to act on the matter in hand? This was accompanied by a more difficult question, one which sent lawyers and judges to history and theory for answers: What kinds of law—common law or equity, English law or civil law of Roman lineage—could and should the courts apply?

Until the United States began to conquer land from Mexico, except for Louisiana, which as legatee of the law of France and Spain was special, all the states inherited directly the English common-law tradition. But tradition could be altered by usage and statute, and sometimes was. Around 1804, when the Code Napoleon was promulgated for France and for the areas of Europe where French arms prevailed, lawyers in several states proposed like simplifications for America. As late as 1849, when the state convention at Monterey was writing the constitution of California, the possibility of establishing civil law instead of common law came up for decision, though only to be dismissed. Generally speaking, while the natural tendency to maintain English law prevailed, that tendency bore complexities enough of its own. Where in America, for one frequent question, could judge or lawyer discover appropriate common-law precedents? Books were not plentiful and often were not to the point. Blackstone, though he was more popular in America than at home, reflected early eighteenth-century usage in England and failed to inform many courtroom problems; old Coke—however much still honored by American patriots for having sustained their belief in independence—was not very useful now. The colonial lawyers had written no textbooks. Thus, after the Revolution, the threads of practical legal thought were pretty well unraveled; much reweaving was then in order.

In the logic of the situation, some American codifications of English law as long practised in the country were indicated. This had been part of the Virginia reform program of the 1770s and 1780s, and James Wilson had sought to have a Pennsylvania codification. Robert Livingston wanted a New York one; and Edward Livingston, as congressman from New York in 1795, had moved a little-supported resolution for a codification of United States penal law. This Livingston had great capacity as a codifier, which was improved by knowledge of Jeremy Bentham and perhaps equaled Bentham's own. After the turn of the century, he achieved one of the few successes of codification (on a state basis, not a national one) when he resettled in Louisiana and worked with that state's non-English criminal law. Logical as codification was, however—as a rounding-out of the work of constitution making and as an adjustment of the law to a large and fluid situation—the impulse tapered down. Dean Roscoe Pound's authority assures us that codification simply could not have succeeded at the time. The common law by its nature resists codification; in this case not enough republican law had cumulated, or enough American scholarship, for comprehensive work so soon.°

Before the turn of the century, moreover, a kind of party spirit had entered the discourse about common law. Our postrevolutionary populisms, Shays's Rebellion and the rise of Jefferson's party, encouraged the attitude that the common law, far from being friendly to liberty, was an England-centered international influence which, disfavoring debtors, favored creditors and the taking of lawyers' fees. Simultaneously arose a somewhat technical question as to whether or not the common law belonged in the new federal courts at all. Here in America was a small new hierarchy of courts: it had no certain legacy from England; it was heir to the national habit of natural-law thinking; it drew its being from the Constitution of 1787 and from the statutes Congress passed. Fundamentals were often challenged. Around 1800, between the one adverse attitude and the other—doubt concerning the appropriateness of the common law to democratic republican life; doubt whether that law was even available in the highest courts—the usable content of American law was as unclear as the growth of legal practice was demanding that it be used.

Although in the course of time answers to these doubts were reached mainly through judicial processes, as decisions were handed down by the top state and federal courts, some of them were phrased by Congress and the state legislatures as they set up new court systems and court jurisdictions. Indeed the whole development of thought about the nature of American government and American law, though it is universally remembered as having belonged especially to John Marshall's Court, was in fact a process broadly shared. During the half century after 1800, about as much as during the epoch of the Revolution and the Enlightenment in America, the operations of sovereignty were conceived to be operations under the governance of Nature's own laws. Thus the relationship between government (the operators of sovereignty) and law (the rules of sovereignty) was still conceived to be very intimate. Not only America's judges when they were considering constitutional cases, but thinkers and speakers from the other two branches of government and scholars who spoke from the sidelines, all still used the Enlightenment's language. They spoke of equilibrium and harmony, of the use of power and the restraint of power, and of higher law, very much as Patriot thinkers had done on national occasions in Philadelphia.

The over-all view which such ways of thinking opened up appears in a lecture which was delivered in that same city, before President Washington, Vice-president Adams, the cabinet, the Congress, and members of the Pennsylvania legislature, soon after the government moved there. Associate Justice James Wilson, of the United States Supreme Court, spoke on that occasion in a double capacity: besides being judge, he was freshly appointed professor of law at the University of Pennsylvania, one of two or three such professors in America. Since 1774, the time we last heard much about him, when he had equaled Jefferson and Adams in speaking commonwealth principles, Wilson had been always eminent in the politics of state and nation. Only three years before the lecture, he had rendered heroic service at the constitutional convention, where his ideas coincided with James Madison's. Partly because Wilson was a conceited man, it is perhaps too easy to notice how pretentious was the title of his lecture, "Of Man as a Member of the Great Commonwealth of Nations." Yet the text was a logical synthesis of democratic and nationalist ideas, and it seems wonderfully right for the time and the place.

Wilson, who had been the author of the "We the people" phrase of the Constitution, developed for his eminent audience the continuity in theory from the Declaration to the Constitution. "A revolution principle certainly is, and certainly should be taught as a principle of the constitution of the United States, and of every State in the Union. . . . This revolution principle—that, the sovereign power residing in the people, they may change their constitution and government whenever they please—is not a principle of discord, rancor, or war: it is a principle of melioration, contentment, and peace." He was pleading at once for the principles of 1776, and for solidarity. Using the word *metaphysics*, but meaning what we mean by "psychology," he urged that Americans study metaphysics and history as ways of understanding law. That was the core of the matter. "In free countries . . . that boast the blessing of a common law, springing warm and spontaneous from the manners of the people," Wilson said, using words that anticipated Justice Oliver Wendell Holmes, "Law should be studied and taught as a historical science."°

Among the three branches of the government, the executive had least to do with the practical shaping of the law. To illustrate, neither President Jefferson nor President Madison, who a quarter century earlier had moved together for codification and reform, chose to resume that kind of effort while he lived in the White House. On the other hand, no early president, including the general who served first, could escape making difficult decisions concerning the higher operations of government on the basis of constitutional law. When the validity of the national bank came into question, Washington decided between opinions he sought from Hamilton and Jefferson. The first presidential veto ever cast was one about which Washington took advice from Attorney General Randolph, Secretary of State Jefferson, and Representative Madison—that is, from Virginia's three great philosopher constitutionalists, on a constitutional question. But while this kind of decision making went with the presidency, it did not express the spirit and feeling of the office in any ample way.

The speaking role of the presidents concerning the operations of power often drew from a less technical area of thought. George Washington spoke as a father to the people. "We are a young Nation, and have a character to establish," he had said when the War of Independence ended. A decade later, when during his first administration factions within and pressures without were splitting the cabinet and the Congress, he took the same line. "We may all be considered the children of one common country. We have all been embarked in one common cause." The Farewell Address voiced a like feeling, tactfully:

"Cultivate peace and harmony with all. Religion and morality enjoin this conduct. And can it be that good policy does not equally enjoin it? ... The nation which indulges toward another an habitual hatred or an habitual fondness is in some degree a slave." In offering his "countrymen" his "counsels of an old and affectionate friend," moreover, the retiring first president echoed the Newtonian image of federalism, which Hamilton and Madison, who advised him on the address, had introduced in *The Federalist*. North, South, East, and West, President Washington reasoned, are drawn and held together in channels of trade and advantage, as "directed by an indissoluble community of interest as *one* nation." He pictured Europe as being only somewhat different. Of course the Old World lay outside the American orbit of power, but this did not place it beyond the reach of calculation, commerce, and good will. In the president's own words: "Harmony, liberal intercourse with all nations are recommended by policy, humanity, and interest." Washington's advice, to steer clear of permanent alliances with the nations of Europe, has been the remembered thing about the Farewell Address. But twentieth-century historiography finds the other side of that coin also memorable. To the father of the country—though he recognized that even at home "the current of the passions" might be hard to control—the peoples of Europe moved in an orbit of their own. They and all nations, he believed, are guided by self-interest. Reason and the national interest require Americans to watch all nations carefully and act cautiously. The first president did not regard them as being deeply foreign, or altogether apart, from ourselves.°

Democratic-Republicans seem to have been less given than Federalists to using figures of speech from the family to express belief in the nation. On the other hand, the Newtonian metaphor for federal organization, the solar system, came readily to Thomas Jefferson. While John Adams was still in office, and at the time when his own secret authorship of the Kentucky Resolutions represented Anti-Federalist dissent at high pitch, Jefferson used Newtonian language reminiscent of Hamilton's own. He said that the union is to be compared with "the planets revolving around their common sun" and that the "beautiful equilibrium" of American federalism promised the world "a degree of perfection unexampled but in the planetary system itself." Three years later, well after his "We are all republicans—we are all federalists" inaugural address, Jefferson used the image of a ship in a storm to picture the ordeal the Union had survived. "The tough sides of our Argosie have been thoroughly tried. Her strength has stood the waves into which she was steered with a view to sink her. We shall put her on her republican tack, and she will now show by the beauty of her motion the skill of her builders."°

Thirty years later, when South Carolina's nullification presented the gravest challenge, so far, to the integrity of the Union, and when with that state ready to depart from orbit a Newtonian figure of speech would have been impossible for a nationalist, ex-President Madison gathered his ideas and came up with an ethical and personal figure of speech for the Union. In an essay on "Sovereignty," and in accompanying "Notes on Nullification," the father of the Constitution acknowledged that still, after a half century of American federalism, he found it hard "to argue intelligibly concerning the compound system of government in the U.S." Yet he conceded nothing to the nullifiers. The right of revolution, he said, avails any who find their government to be unjust and who judge that their contract has in that way lost validity. But the right of revolution justifies no disobedience of the law by men who pretend, like the South Carolinians, to remain loyal citizens. On both sides of the nullification argument, Madison found, "the *moral being* created by the social compact" was being called into question; the sovereign authority of the state and the sovereign authority of the nation alike were being defended, he noticed, as "moral persons." Now an octogenarian and the only survivor of the end-of-century philosopher statesmen, Madison had no doubt that the moral being of the United States as a union was a mighty thing and a good one, and that it had a capacity for wise decision making. "A political system which does not contain an effective provision for a peaceable decision of all controversies arising within itself, would be a Gov't in name only. Such a provision is obviously essential; and it is equally obvious that it cannot be either peaceable or effective by making every part an authoritative umpire. The final appeal in such cases must be to the authority of the whole." With this injunction Madison referred his readers to *The Federalist*, number thirty-nine, of his own authorship almost half a century earlier.°

Whatever the early presidents may have had to say about the allocation of power, the first half century of the republic was the epoch when the legislatures, not the executives, did most of the acting which affected that allocation in America. They did so without much need for theory, beyond the foundations laid in the eighteenth century. During the decade while Congress was the Congress of the Confederation, it was of course the state legislatures, not that central one, which exercised the ultimate sovereignty. If at first they did the extraordinary things that revolutionary legislatures always have to do, after the Peace of Paris they carried on, with little break of habit, in ways which resembled their predecessor institutions, the provincial assemblies. Twentieth-century scholars have discovered that early nineteenth-century economic policies adopted by the states were more like eighteenth-century colony policies—regulating, controlling, even participating in economic life—than is usually believed. Much mercantilist-style legislation was passed—to found banks, build roads, and dig canals, for example—which aided and abetted business and the general welfare.°

Parallel in time, Congress under the Constitution displayed a genuine likeness to Parliament in American affairs before independence. Of course the new American national legislature had a greater competency and rendered a more continuous performance than Parliament ever had for the colonies. Institutionally it was sustained by Article I of the Constitution; it was assisted, from the intellectual background of action, by the Lockian and commonwealth belief that the national legislature is the prime seat of power. So Congress had first of all to be practical, and much of its early achievement lay in enacting economic policy. Its principal actions of that kind were, of course: Hamilton's program during the early 1790s; preparations for war, while Adams was president and again under Madison; acquiring, providing for, and distributing the national domains, which trebled the size of the Union under the Virginia presidents; legislating internal improvements, during the later 1810s and the 1820s.

Altogether then, the American legislatures, national and state, like Parliament and the assemblies before 1776, addressed themselves to questions of expansion, organization, and security. Allowing that the Kentucky and Virginia Resolutions represent much more than a ripple, only after 1830 for a while, and after 1848, did north-south issues raise such tidal waves as resembled the collisions between mother country and colonies beginning in 1765. Only in the mid-century crises were congressmen forced to think systematically and defensively about their power and to resort much to theory—either to justify themselves or to crack down on the states. Only at that time (and outside the scope of this volume) did the time come for the deeply nationalist leaders like Webster, and the last-ditch states' righters of whom Calhoun became spokesman, to think and debate afresh the ultimate powers of nation and state.

Meanwhile, before 1830 the judicial branches of the national and state governments had been famously expressive, thoughtful and sharp —more so than presidents and Congresses—about the distribution of sovereignty in America. For the decision making which the Supreme Court assumed in this, the acts of the Privy Council supplied a suggestive background. During the seventeenth and eighteenth centuries that council had occasionally heard appeals from the colonies which resulted in disallowing a provincial statute or a provincial court's decision. But a greater authority than the Privy Council's, the crucial power to disallow acts of the national *and* state legislatures—if they were found on practical test in court to be incompatible with the Constitution—was implied though not phrased, in the federal instrument of

1787, as belonging to the Supreme Court. This authority took time to be court-tested and recognized. Indeed the United States Supreme Court had sat for a dozen years, and Congress had created the federal hierarchy of district and circuit courts under the Supreme Court, before that power was exercised and established as to federal statute. In those years, the Federalism of the administrations of Washington and Adams notwithstanding, and the nation-mindedness of the lawyers whom those presidents appointed chief justice—John Jay, first, and soon Oliver Ellsworth, the author of the federal Judiciary Act—to the contrary, no decision was rendered which established the practice of the Supreme Court reviewing statutes.

Only after John Marshall of Virginia became chief justice in 1801 did the Court act in that way. Man of extended Hamiltonion principles though Marshall soon became, he began differently, a Federalist more in the style of John Adams (who appointed him) than in that of Adams's Federalist rival. As a young Virginian, Marshall had shared, though not richly, in the social and educational advantages of the late-colonial squirearchy. On his mother's side he derived from patrician lineage; through the Randolphs he was a cousin of Thomas Jefferson. During the Stamp Act-to-independence decade, while he was in his teens, Marshall's father was burgess, sheriff, and vestryman. More than likely the young man learned his first law from his father's copy of Blackstone (the earliest American edition), during months surrounding the Boston Tea Party. He joined the Patriot army within one month after the Declaration. George Washington became his idol, and his war service made him a powerful nationalist: "I was confirmed in the habit of considering America as my country and Congress as my government." About one month in 1780 of attending the lectures of George Wythe, trainer of Virginia statesmen, was all the education in college John Marshall ever had; he was admitted to the bar that same year. Being in the state legislature during the early 1780s, and being in the state ratifying convention, 1788, gave him a political education by participation, the usual kind in the squirearchy of the Old Dominion. Though during the 1790s he refused the attorney generalship under President Washington and the secretaryship of war under President Adams, his being in and out of Congress, and serving briefly as secretary of state (1800), gave him inside knowledge of the operation of the republic before he became chief justice.

Scholarship has upset in Marshall's favor the long-lasting legend that he was not a learned lawyer, as his great friend and associate justice, Joseph Story, unquestionably was. On the other hand, Marshall's first great constitutional case, and indeed all three of the decisions which made Court law of the most famous of his constitutional principles— the principle that the Supreme Court can rule on the validity of statute law—derived their strength from another quality than learning. Far above his predecessors in the chief justiceship, John Marshall was gifted with a sharp intuition of where the crux of a power issue lay; this gift was sustained by an equal capacity for logic and leadership in the Court. Thus in 1803, when *Marbury versus Madison* placed before the Court a question of completing or not completing a minor appointment under an act of Congress, the chief justice's obiter dictum became the clear and important thing, not the (still debatable) issue of substance brought in by the plaintiff. In that remarkable dictum the chief justice reasoned from the nature of sovereignty that, in case of incompatibility between a federal statute and the Constitution, the Constitution—on which all else depends—must stand, and that judgment in such issues belongs to the Supreme Court. In essence, his ruling said, there are laws but only one law. Although modern restudy of *Marbury versus Madison* has not excluded the estimation (once common) that something close to trickery on the part of Marshall was needed to derive so large a doctrine from so small a case, the prevailing present-day judgment is that Marshall was correct. The doctrine had been previously stated in *Federalist* propaganda, in Hamilton's famous number seventy-eight. According to Edward S. Corwin, whose opinion is endorsed by Samuel J. Konefsky and others, Supreme Court review of the constitutionality of statutes was an "idea" when the Constitution was written, but at that time no more than "the germ of a possible institution." Probably institutionalization would have come in time, at other hands if not at Marshall's; but the speed, force, and clarity with which it occurred belonged to Marshall alone.°

As it announced the special principle of the obiter dictum, *Marbury versus Madison* also placed new urgency behind the general doctrine of government under law—the foundation idea of constitutionalism in the commonwealthmen's line of theory. But the case did not touch directly the grandest operating phase of the Constitution, the equilibrium to be maintained among America's multiple sovereignties. That question remained in abeyance, so far as the authority of the Supreme Court to review state lawgiving was concerned, for a dozen years. Quite as Article III of the Constitution omitted to spell out that the Supreme Court has authority to rule—in appropriate instances brought before it—on the compatibility of congressional statutes with the fundamental law of 1787, it also omitted to spell out authority to disallow statute law or court law which began in state legislature or court, if and when the Supreme Court might find such law to be incompatible with the Constitution. Yet, if the Court were to be as much umpire in such cases as the Privy Council had been for the enactments of the colonial assemblies and the decisions of the colonial courts, it had to consider state law whenever issues of constitutional limitations came up.

Three famous cases established the Court's authority. In the earliest of them, the very first case in which the Supreme Court upset a state statute, *Fletcher versus Peck*, 1810, Chief Justice Marshall did not draw as heavily as he had in *Marbury versus Madison* on the general and implied power of the national government. Rather the contract clause of the Constitution, which specifically stopped the states from "impairing the obligation of contracts," supplied the foundation for the disallowance. Land grants which had been made, then cancelled, by the legislature of Georgia were the immediate issue in question: the Court ruled that the state could not repudiate its contract with the grantees. The second and third cases, *Martin versus Hunter's Lessee*, 1816, and *Cohens versus Virginia*, 1821, affected the sovereignty of Virginia, the oldest state and the one which was tenderest of all, at that time, about states' rights. The two cases concerned, instead of the authority of the state legislature, the authority of the state courts. Both cases were determined in opposition to the reasoning of Judge Spencer Roane, of the Supreme Court of Appeals of Virginia; that eminent man derived from a personal background much like John Marshall's own, but he entertained principles which resembled those of Thomas Jefferson. "There is a Charybdis to be avoided, as well as a Scylla," Judge Roane observed. "A centripetal, as well as a centrifugal principle, exists in the Government." He warned against the centripetal one: "No calamity would be more to be deplored by the American people, than a vortex in the General Government, which should ingulph and sweep away every vestige of the State Constitutions."°

By the time *Martin versus Hunter's Lessee* came up, the second peace had been made with England and the new economic nationalism had taken hold in Congress. On the Supreme Court itself, much else than Chief Justice Marshall's logic and learning and leadership impelled motion toward the center, or "vortex," of power. Not the least of the centripetal influences was the new and very young associate justice from Massachusetts, who wrote the *Martin versus Hunter's Lessee* opinion. A Republican in politics, he had resented the disloyalty in New England during the War of 1812: "Do not suffer conspiracies to destroy the Union to be found in the bosom of the Union," he had said of the resisters of the nation's effort. When he spoke for the Supreme Court three years later, Joseph Story reasoned again from his wartime anxiety. Should the sovereignty of Virginia now be restricted, he said in the *Hunter's Lessee* case, that is in line with the federal Judiciary Act, and it is a payment of the price which had been agreed to in 1789 for the achievement of a federal Union.

In the Cohens case five years later, Chief Justice Marshall went to the outer limit of that line of thought. Giving the opinion of the Court, the chief justice said that Virginia had contended "that the Nation does not possess a department capable of restraining, peaceably, and by the authority of law, any attempts which may be made by a part, against the legitimate powers of the whole." Unless such a "department" did truly exist and operate, Marshall reasoned, any state which felt that its authority was not being fully respected could reasonably execute its own will by the use of force. Thus the Supreme Court ruled the second time against Virginia. Thenceforward the Court's attitude would be clear and predictable in any such conflict. Highly placed among the national and nationalizing institutions in America's system of multiple sovereignty, the Court would decide for itself about the extent of its own authority—an attitude which expresses the very nature of sovereignty.

Although there is no need in this book to examine all the famous constitutional cases which made the Supreme Court a unique center for thought about the centripetalism and centrifugalism of power, before we follow our subject outside Washington we should notice, though briefly, the intellectual bearings and references of the nationalism of the Court. As Joseph Dorfman has wisely observed, deciding cases with an economic bearing made the Marshall Court a kind of seminar on the American economy and on the relations of economics to government. *McCulloch versus Maryland* called for a crucial ruling about where the powers of taxation lay within the system of distributed sovereignty. This was the area of constitutionalism wherein English thought and policy had so sadly failed between 1764 and 1775. Of equally large importance, down to our own time of Congress regulating commerce fully, was *Gibbons versus Ogden*, the Hudson River steamboat decision. Here the justices considered the nature of commerce and came up with a broad definition. They ruled on problems of jurisdiction in international and interstate water transport and reached a decision which—compared to the failure of Britain's old colonial system to solve similar questions in America—brought off a solid piece of durable law. More on the side of economic institution than policy, the Dartmouth College case ruled on the nature of the corporation—and even on the relationship of state governments to "private" education. By reason of Daniel Webster's elaborate and passionate argument, no other case of the period proved quite so spectacular. In that area the nation's top Court reinforced the corporation as a free institution and reinforced the private (and religious) college.

Modern scholarship acknowledges that the Supreme Court did sometimes slip into "mystifications" to assert its ideas, quite as Jefferson said; it acknowledges that the Court perhaps needlessly offended liberal Virginians whose legal learning was high. Yet today the judgment of Marshall's Court, which finds that the thinking there was big, prophetic, and sound, prevails. Stated in terms of intellectual role and function, as an acting-out of the ideas of the age, the Supreme Court under Marshall curiously resembles the boards of censors which the constitutions of Pennsylvania and Vermont established for those two states. Where those boards were planned to be review boards to test the correctness of state legislation according to the principles of their fundamental law, the Supreme Court now actually passed that kind of judgment. Moreover, it did so on a nationwide, federal-law scale. The difference, of course, was that with the Supreme Court the review process occurred only in specific, practical cases which the Court admitted as being appropriate for litigation, and occurred not at all—as was expected of the Pennsylvania censors—in an over-all way. The nationalism, conservatism, and practicality of the Supreme Court gave it a momentum, a force which in cases carried dangerously far. But such a tendency does not alter the fact that a main current of Enlightenment taste—its aspiration for harmony in society, its hope to have violence and antagonism controlled—was sustained by John Marshall and his associate justices, and that their rulings channeled that taste early into American constitutional law.

Meanwhile, in the state-court area of the federal equilibrium, great bodies of precedent were building and traditions were being established. The upper courts of three large and populous states, Virginia, New York, and Massachusetts, proved the homes of the most magisterial work and thought; three learned chief judges in those states—Spencer Roane, James Kent, and Lemuel Shaw, respectively—proved to be the most influential men. From those three and their peers on the state benches (for instance) of Vermont and Maryland, states' rights sentiment, when it came into play, did not always collide early and headlong with authority at the Washington "vortex." Sometimes more, sometimes less affected by their political convictions, the judges' opinions accumulated a vast corpus of American law and an American-mindedness about law. From state to state, precedents were studied and cited. Especially James Kent's Federalist-style decisions, rendered during his decade as chief common-law judge of the commercial state of New York, were followed—the more because they were well edited and published—in many states. On the great question, about which there had once been doubt, as to whether the United States should follow English common law—whether the federal courts should do so at all, and whether the states should go far or short in that direction— the passage of the first third or so of the nineteenth century yielded a gradualist, selective answer. At maximum the state courts drew heavily on English precedents, even on English decisions which had been handed down after 1776. At minimum, alike in the federal courts and certain state ones, the principles and usages of the common law were introduced, and given a chance to proliferate.

Gradually equity law also put down American roots. Among the myriad expressions of Americanism and experimentalism in law, probably no other is more concise and telling than the observation about equity made by James Kent in his autobiography. It concerns the time, in 1814, when he transferred from being chief justice of the Empire State to being its chancellor. He took charge of the Court of Chancery, he says, "as if it had been a new institution, and never before known in the United States. I had nothing to guide me, and was left at liberty to assume all such English Chancery powers and jurisdiction as I thought applicable under our Constitution."°

Chancellor Kent's sense of history working through himself brings us, finally, to a large threshold in the development of American law. Besides being a judge, Kent was also a scholar, one of the two most influential book lawyers during a great generation of legal scholarship. But naturally his personal and judicial career bore on the more monumental work he did. As a student during the War of Independence—attending Yale College during years which overlapped Noah Webster's as a student there, and with Ezra Stiles coming in as president—he seems to have been already a prodigy in his reading of law. Blackstone thrilled him at that age. During the 1780s he studied in a Poughkeepsie law office; next he served five years as the first professor of law in Columbia College. An advanced Federalist, he was soon elected to the state assembly. In 1798 he became a judge; he remained one for a quarter century, a self-conscious stabilizer of society in an age and place of much social mobility. Chancellor Kent was going strong in 1823, when at the age of sixty retirement overtook him unwilling. Only two years earlier, as a member of New York State's constitutional convention, he had opposed unsuccessfully the move to incorporate manhood suffrage into fundamental law. Just one year later, having returned—for a brief period—to Columbia College, he stated in lectures the main ideas of what after 1830 became famous as Kent's *Commentaries on American Law*.°

The total four volumes amounted to a systematization of American law according to categories of use. Like Blackstone, whose style he imitated, Kent compiled, simplified, and commented across the board. He considered hundreds of cases, American and English. His respect for the common law equaled that of his English predecessor, Coke; it anticipated that of his pragmatist successor, Holmes. "The body of laws that concern the common justice . . . consists of infinite particulars . . . ; and such are the common laws of England, namely the production of much wisdom, time and experience." But Kent did not believe in codifications, and the *Commentaries* were designed to help do without that form of simplification. The work begins at the wide end of the funnel, with a two-hundred-page "part" on the law of nations; it moves next to a slightly longer part on the constitutional law of the United States, an historical and analytical treatment; then, third, it proceeds, in the most concise and generalizing part of the book, to the sources of state law. This includes (a measure of the author's competence) a section on Roman law and a section on equity. Thereafter, in the very long parts, the work is organized according to court-law functions: there are sustained treatments of personal rights, with considerable space to the law of marriage, for example, and of property rights, with a treatment of corporations which is admiring of the Marshall decisions.

The whole is magisterial, imposing in style, in a social way a huge arsenal of deterrence to class insurgency, and in a literary way a book to be compared with Edwards's works on theology or with Webster's *Dictionary*, as the great original of its kind of systematic learning in America. Although Kent is hard to read for other than the purposes of law practice which he set out to serve, and he is not readily quotable in terms of his public intentions, we may nevertheless borrow from Part III a couple of passages which do indicate how loyal author and book were to the Hamilton and Marshall way of thinking. "The Common Law of England," observed James Kent, after having saturated himself in it for decades, "is not the product of the vision of some one man or society of men in any one age; but the wisdom, counsel, and experience and observation of many ages." Again:

> There have been modern theorists [Kent seems to have meant Rousseau] who have considered separate and exclusive property and inequalities of property as the cause of injustice and the unhappy result of government and artificial institutions. . . . Human society would be in a most unnatural and miserable condition if it were possible to be instituted or reorganized upon the basis of such speculations. . . . The sense of property is graciously bestowed on mankind for the purpose of rousing them from sloth. The natural and active sense of property pervades the foundations of social improvement.°

Where James Kent wrote one huge treatise and John Marshall wrote none, the third member of America's top trio of jurisprudents of their age, Joseph Story, wrote nine. Probably some of his productivity may be attributed to his origins. As the son of an eastern Massachusetts physician, he had begun life with many advantages, of which a Harvard education was one. As a member of the famous class of 1798, in which he stood number two behind William Ellery Channing, he was a sharer from the beginning in the rise of the Unitarian intellectual element of Cambridge and Boston; he learned his law in the office of a congressman who bore an ancient judicial name, Samuel Sewall, and who would later be the chief justice of the commonwealth. While

Story was still in his twenties he entered politics: he served first in the state legislature and then, one term, in Congress. Well before President Madison appointed him, at thirty-two, to the Supreme Court, he had especially studied equity procedure, and—lively member of a seaboard community—maritime law. He already had three books to his credit, and had done much work on an unpublished digest of American law, when he went to Washington.

During the first half of his thirty-four years on the Court he wrote dozens of majority opinions. No other achieved greater fame than the federalizing one of 1816, *Martin versus Hunter's Lessee*. But it was during the second half of his tenure, after he became Dane professor at Harvard (and a stage-coach commuter between Washington and Cambridge), that his writings flowed from his desk to the press and the public at a rate seldom if ever surpassed by other scholars of the law. Three volumes of his own series of *Commentaries* concerned his old study, equity; they appeared during the late 1830s. Other volumes concerned varieties of business law, bills of exchange, and the like. His very nationalist work *On the Constitution*, which appeared in the year of nullification, 1833, itself was a three-volume treatise. In the person of Story there was something more in the way of self-conscious, conservative, and nationalist conviction, with an intention to speak to the public, than occurred in Marshall and Kent. As his inaugural address as Dane professor shows, he admired and followed Edmund Burke. Lawyers and judges, he told the young men of Harvard—in words which seem to echo the James Wilson who addressed president and Congress in 1790—are truly a kind of priesthood: they are guardians of society and property. "Upon the actual administration of justice . . . must depend the welfare of the whole community. The sacred rights of property are to be guarded at every point. . . . If they are unprotected, all other rights become worthless or visionary. What is personal liberty, if it does not draw after it the right to enjoy the fruits of its own industry?"°

By Dean Roscoe Pound's authoritative count and comparison, ten American scholars produced twenty-one textbooks in law between 1826 and 1862—where before there had been none. They covered every specialized field. Their works remained standard throughout the nineteenth century; several of them continued so, well into the twentieth century. Kent made a career of nearly two decades out of revising and extending his *Commentaries*. In 1873, a short generation after the author's death, Oliver Wendell Holmes, already a scholar but not yet a professor or judge, produced a new edition which had required three years and became standard; that edition was reissued several times before the end of the century. The *Commentaries* were published also in Spanish and German. Almost as soon as Kent and Story began producing, their peer in scholarship, Henry Wheaton of Boston, brought out in 1836 his *Elements of International Law*. This major work followed a good deal of study in the Germanies and Scandinavia by the author (who was very skillful in those languages) and some writing in the history of German law. His *Elements* was published in English fifteen or more times, the last time in England three decades ago; it was published also in other languages. As being textbook literature, this pre-Civil War "doctrinal" writing—as Dean Pound calls it—supplied America with sizable compensation for the codes which were never put together. It made law available in America, in spite of all the handicaps, and made it usable according to deeply rooted common-law tradition and taste.°

Like American thought about government, and about economics and science and religion, American thought about law was increasingly and consciously nationalistic but not totally so. Judges and legal scholars placed their bets on their vision of a splendid republic and a grand nationality in the making. But, in their several ways, they spoke at times also for state, local community, and person, and sometimes for Europe, even the world.

CHAPTER XIV

The Arrival of Democracy: In Experience and in Thought

I speak for the universal diffusion of human powers,
not of human attainments; for the capacity of progress,
not for the perfection of undisciplined instincts. . . .

The government by the people is in very truth the
strongest government in the world. Discarding the
implements of terror, it dares to rule by moral force,
and has its citadel in the heart. . . .

There is a spirit in man: *not in the privileged few;*
not in those of us only who by the favor of Providence
have been nursed in public schools: IT IS IN MAN:
it is the attribute of the race. . . .

If reason is a universal faculty, the universal decision
is the nearest criterion of truth. The common mind
winnows opinions; it is the sieve which separates error
from certainty. The exercise by many of the same
faculty on the same subject would naturally lead to
the same conclusions.

George Bancroft, The Office of the People in Art,
Government, and Religion *(1835)*

1   *Concerning Democratic Doctrine:*
The American Shortage

THE oration from which the epigraph to this chapter is drawn was delivered in Williamstown, Massachusetts, by the scholar who over the half century from Andrew Jackson to Grover Cleveland was going to be the chief intellectual defender of democracy in America. George Bancroft, who had recently been a minister and was still a schoolmaster in Northampton, Massachusetts, at thirty-five had just published the first volume of what would become a ten-volume *History of the United States* (from colonial origins to federal Constitution). As a Democrat he had already entered politics; this would lead to the secretaryship of the navy and to high diplomatic appointments. But he would be always a writer, and his writings would be more affected by contemporary events, and events would be more affected by his writings, than in the case of any other historian of the nineteenth century. Already as he stood before his audience he must have been consciously striving to lead people into the ways of democracy. Any such broad proposition as he voiced, that "human powers" sufficient for self-government are distributed everywhere among members of the human race, was far from accepted doctrine in 1835. Intellectuals and intellectual communities, especially evangelical ones like the college town he was visiting, were not often so optimistic about democracy as he.

Doctrine was short but conditions were long. By 1835 "Jacksonian Democracy"—republican government with mass participation—

had amply arrived. To be sure the female half of the population, and all but a very few Negroes, were excluded from voting. No grand charter of democracy had ever been drawn or ever would be, nothing nearer than the Bill of Rights. Democratic practice had seeped into the American system by way of state laws, detail by detail. Among the original states, old property-holding requirements for the suffrage had been reduced; in the new states such requirements were either omitted or kept low. Thus by the time of Jackson, but not because of him or any other president, adult white male suffrage had become the practice of the body politic as a whole. Besides this main underpinning of democracy, during the 1820s and early 1830s the political convention—special American institution of the 1770s and 1780s—had undertaken new functions. In place of caucuses attended by congressmen in Washington, a procedure which favored oligarchy, national political-party conventions began to nominate candidates for president and vice-president. By reason of its Jeffersonian heritage, it would seem doctrinally natural for the Democratic-Republican Party to have taken the initiatives toward mass participation. And so it did in part. But the Whig Party, the leaders of which—John Quincy Adams, Henry Clay, and Daniel Webster—held generally to Federalist principles, was a little earlier to act. The striking thing, here, is the similarity of the two. Quite as the states stimulated one another to enact manhood suffrage, the two parties as rivals for members and voters accelerated the movement into mass politics. Part of the same popularization, the legendary extravagances of American politics—the planks and the platforms, the florid orations and journalism, the promises and the compromises, the election parades and the drinking—all as much matters of pleasure as of politics, came during the 1830s and 1840s into their nationwide own.

Parallel with the tumult of democracy as practice, the quietness of the current of democracy as belief poses a problem in the intellectual history of Jacksonian America. Of course there was no shortage of expression of democratic values. We have already found much of that among those literary men who asserted their belief in a people's government; in later chapters we shall often come on equalitarianism as a factor in educational and other reform. But the problem which we have to consider at present, in phase with the people's acceptance of operational democracy, is the coolness of most intellectuals. Allowing a grand exception for George Bancroft with his faith in "a *spirit in man,*" the processes of democracy—as distinguished from its values—were hard for thinking men to believe in. To put the problem historically: never before in the history of the West had any sovereignty larger than ancient Athens come close to the Jacksonian Age's degree of assimilating the people into politics. At this point we may better anticipate that not until after 1900, beginning with the Progressive period in politics and scholarship, would the study of how democracy works truly thrive in the literature of history and political science in America.

Rather than native Americans it was European observers in America who brought the operations of democracy into discussion. During the third of a century after 1815—grand epoch of immigration and western settlement, early industrialization and city growth—the United States was crossed and recrossed by curious, critical, and hopeful inquirers, an amazing number of whom were ready and anxious to publish their findings. The land and its resources, the nation and its politics, the society and its manners and morals, its educational and religious customs, and of course the institution of slavery—all these and many other facets of society gained early the entrance into public concern which being discussed in a book bestows. It was something like the era of Hakluyt and Purchas over again: the promises of American life were up for European appraisal.°

From the whole genre of European travel accounts, the masterwork appeared in two parts at the very flood tide of Jacksonian democracy. The first "part" of Alexis de Tocqueville's *Democracy in America*, which concerned political institutions, was published in 1835; the second, concerning society and thought, came five years later. Part One was immediately translated by Henry Reeve, formerly of the *Edinburgh Review*, and published in London. The earliest American edition appeared three years later, in 1838. From then to now the Reeve translation has been almost as standard as the work itself; no major edition in England or America has more than revised it. After Part Two appeared, the editions multiplied: about twenty American ones were published before the Civil War. There were nearly as many in French, several of them brought out in Belgium. One or two editions were published also in German, Danish, Swedish, Hungarian and Russian; and several in Spanish, in Madrid, Paris, and Buenos Aires.°

What the author found in America—that government and society, thought and taste, had moved out of control by the classes and into control, or at least into the area of participation, by the masses—required a great gift to explain. The subject seized young Tocqueville completely. Already a magistrate when he crossed the ocean, a scholar but not yet an author, he came commissioned to find out how the new republic was managing its problem of crime. (The colleague with whom he traveled, Gustave de Beaumont, came to study Negro slavery.) But by the time he put into New York Tocqueville had decided that, besides doing the expert work for which he had been appointed, he would examine American society broadly. Perhaps the fact that he had once viewed with a sense of tragedy the remains of

Greek civilization in Italy, more surely the fact that he knew the irretrievable losses that the fall of an old order had brought to his own family, impelled him to probe deeper than other visitors.

At any rate he spared himself none of the trouble of travel and study. First, he had many interviews in New York; then he went upstate (of course going to Sing Sing, already famous as a reform-style "penitentiary"); next he crossed the Old Northwest territory the full distance into upper Michigan. Thence he returned east and, working south from Boston, visited the seabord cities. In a final loop he swung west again, but down the Mississippi, and then traversed the South to return by way of Virginia and Washington.

From first to last Tocqueville responded to what he saw with both firmness and flexibility of mind. We may call it the patrician in him which made him dislike New York on arrival. He hated always what he ran into there and elsewhere, the boastfulness of Americans about their country. Yet by the time he returned to Europe he was ready to say that America's kind of commitment to freedom and equality represented the future of the West, the Old World as well as the New. He pictured the United States as the place where that future had already arrived. Assimilating and organizing the data, sifting out his estimations and expectations, composing the two parts, would require seven years. But as Pierre Paul Roger-Collard, a scholar statesman compatriot, said wisely when *Democracy in America* was new, there was "Nothing like it"—nothing of comparable quality had "appeared since Montesquieu."°

The more because all that Tocqueville said was judicial in style, weighing up things good and bad, *Democracy in America* posed ideas and questions to American thought from the day of publication. It began on familiar ground with a discussion of the unique spaciousness of the country. But Tocqueville did this not at all as an economic or geographic determinist. He acknowledged immediately that America's free institutions, a legacy from England, better favored expansion and enterprise than French institutions did. He interpreted America's openness as deriving from an historical coincidence, English freedom and American opportunity. While he kept to economic matters, the author was as optimistic about the New World as a native.

When he shifted to politics his mood darkened. The most anxious passage in Part One's discussion of institutions is his often-cited opinion that majority rule generates tyranny. Tocqueville accepted majority rule as a principle. But the point of the famous Chapter Fifteen on the "Unlimited Power of the Majority in the United States and Its Consequences," including a subsection on the "Tyranny of the Majority," is that where majorities prevail they are likely to be too much respected, and that in America they were already inhibiting the freedom and good judgment of the citizens. Not far removed from this finding, Tocqueville discovered in America's complex race situation a second great cause for anxiety. In the North he noticed the disassociation between Negroes and whites; in the South he learned of the tensions which accompanied slavery. (He visited Virginia soon after the Nat Turner insurrection.) So Tocqueville inserted a grim prophecy: racial antagonism would deepen; emancipation, if that should occur, would not eliminate it; ultimately war between the races was likely. This prophecy deserves appreciation in twentieth-century America equal to what is given Tocqueville's much more noted and quoted prophecy that in future the United States and Russia would become the great rivals for power in the world.°

Selecting from *Democracy in America* such conspicuous judgments as these, one gets an impression of greater pessimism than the work gives as a whole. Besides the optimism of the opening chapters, Tocqueville said in a number of contexts that the United States had been right to develop democratic usages rather than try to be like Europe. Though he thought that America's political parties had gone downhill after 1800, he said they served passably well. (Surprising as it may seem, he had trouble gaining information about them.) He exonerated Andrew Jackson from the charge, familiar in Europe, that the president wanted a military, or at least centralized, control of government. On the contrary, said Tocqueville, Jackson belonged to the decentralizing party and was rather too much than too little pleased with that tendency. The author foresaw—what would happen by the 1850s—that the national government was going to grow weaker and perhaps erode quite away.

"Part the Second, the Social Influence of Democracy," which is the second volume in modern American editions, carried into new spheres the balanced judgment of the first. Close to the political interest of the preceding volume, no passage is more to our concerns than the famous second chapter of the "Second Book," "Of Individualism in Democratic Countries." The moral issue itself was new: the English language lacked the right word to express the national trait Tocqueville delineated. Thus he selected the unfamiliar French noun, "individualisme"; Reeve simply Anglicized the author's word choice. Supplying his own definition, Tocqueville explained that the trait is close to egotism and selfishness. "Selfishness originates in blind instinct; individualism proceeds from erroneous judgment more than from depraved feelings; it originates as much in deficiencies of mind as in perversity of heart." Thus he described an ugly quality; and it comes hard to Americans to see how tellingly Tocqueville identified it with the people—especially the New Yorkers—he visited.°

The four or five pages Tocqueville devoted to individualism contain one of his most explicit distinctions between democracy and the old regime, between France and the United States.

> Among aristocratic nations [he explained more succinctly than a paraphrasing could do] a man almost always knows his forefathers and respects them; he thinks he already sees his remote descendants and he loves them. . . . Men living in aristocratic ages are . . . almost always closely attached to something placed out of their own sphere. . . . They often sacrifice themselves for other men. In democratic times, on the contrary, when the duties of each individual to the race are much more clear, devoted service to any one man becomes more rare; the bond of human affection is extended, but it is relaxed. . . .Thus not only does democracy make every man forget his ancestors, but it hides his descendants and separates his contemporaries from him; it throws him back forever on himself alone and threatens in the end to confine him entirely within the solitude of his own heart.

While Tocqueville never shaded down this condemnation, the seventy-five chapters of Volume Two are full of fact and comment which convey real feeling for American society. He attributed to our general thought ("philosophy") a certain attractive intuitiveness and practicality rather than taste or gift for abstraction; he was gratified that the multiplicity of churches included enough Roman Catholic ones to make him feel sometimes at home. He said also that that very multiplicity—like mass democracy—encouraged a leveling sameness. Even while he observed that pure art and pure science lacked such support in the New World as was given by aristocrats at home, he explained that Americans were devising their own ways of sustaining at least some of the arts and sciences. In the chapter on "Public Associations" (which in good logic is placed close to the one on individualism) he put his finger on an American custom which has flourished since Benjamin Franklin's Junto: voluntary gatherings in aid of philanthropy and learning. The United States had already become a nation of joiners, and, though Tocqueville failed to place a modern valuation on that fact, he was early to remark on it as a national characteristic.

Of course it is impossible to naturalize Tocqueville's treatise—to transform it into being an American book. Yet by virtue of it the author ranks no lower than the number-two thinker, ever, about democracy in America. The number-one thinker, Thomas Jefferson, had been broader. He had been both a spokesman for democratic values (which Tocqueville was not) and a statesman planner who conceived a democratic process. The cluster of liberal goals and policies which we considered in Chapter XI, and will return to in the following subsection, belonged to the Revolution and Enlightenment—Jefferson's combined program of republican government and federalism, manhood suffrage and civil rights, universal education and farm life as far as possible, generous land distribution and opposition to slavery. Tocqueville regarded the same and related phenomena. In judging them, his standards were not very different—not nearly so different as his mood was—from the democratic philosopher statesman. He too believed that democracy was a process and product of history in which America was coming out first.

The actual course of native American thinking about democracy during the middle nineteenth century is represented, rather than by either a program builder or a critic, by the historian with whom this chapter began. George Bancroft, whose first volume preceded *Democracy in America*, had at least one main emphasis in common with Tocqueville, namely, that democracy involves more than voting politics, that it inheres in the mind and character of a people. But Bancroft had reached that conviction during student years in Germany around 1820, especially from the historians Eichhorn and Boeckh, with whom he long kept in touch. The intellectual slant he gained was thus entirely different from Tocqueville's. One of the first Americans to take a Ph.D., Bancroft assimilated a generous dosage of his professors' romantic philosophical belief that every nation, or people, has a spirit and that the history of a people consists in the self-realization of that spirit. Among many lectures during his wandering years in Germany, Bancroft listened to Hegel, the philosopher, and to Schleiermacher, the theologian and education reformer.° Where Tocqueville brought skepticism to the study of people and government, the German university scholars brought passion and faith.

For one early example of how this attitude affected Bancroft, we need look no further than the preface of his first volume. "The maturity of the nation is but a continuation of its youth," he observed. "The spirit of the colonies demanded freedom from the beginning. It was in this period, that Virginia first asserted the doctrine of popular sovereignty; that the people of Maryland constituted their own government; that New Plymouth, Connecticut, New Haven, New Hampshire, Maine, rested their legislation on the popular will; that Massachusetts declared itself a 'perfect commonwealth.' " In Volume Four, as he summed up the situation of 1748, following a paraphrase from Immanuel Kant, Bancroft said in the same spirit: "Each people that has disappeared, every institution that has passed away, has been but a step in the ladder by which humanity ascends towards the perfecting of its nature. . . . It was the office of America to substitute for hereditary privilege the natural equality of man; for the irresponsible authority of a sovereign, a dependent government emanating from the concord of opinion." When he reached the decade between the Stamp Act and 1776, Bancroft developed the story of how the people rose in protest, how they shared in upsetting the provincial governments and in founding the states. For a final illustration of Bancroft's romanticism, almost mysticism, toward the people, the following lines are drawn from his summary of the colonial situation in January 1776. "The declaration of independence was silently but steadily prepared in the convictions of all the people. . . . The spirit of the people far outran conventions and congresses. . . . The common sense of the people now claimed its right to sit in judgment on the greatest question ever raised in the political world."°

Bancroft's books soon became popular. They competed successfully enough in the market, where the sale of fiction had just become a habit; he himself was the first and one of the few writers ever to make money by writing voluminous history. Naturally not all the criticism was favorable. Some readers liked, and others disliked, history so spiced with feeling. Concerning Volume One Arnold Heeren wrote from Germany that it was a "truly inspired history"; Edward Everett, who himself had studied at Göttingen, said that the new *History* would "last while the memory of America lasts, and . . . will take its place instantly among the classics of our language." On the other hand, even liberals, of whom Bancroft's brother-in-law was one, sometimes entreated him "not to let any of the partisan creep into your work." Considering how difficult it is today to find coherency between Bancroft's historical findings and his philosophical beliefs, the comment of John Quincy Adams seems especially right. The ex-presndent said that while the *History of the United States* derived from "transcendent talents and indefatigable industry," nevertheless it was a "diffuse and declamatory panegyric."°

Today another book, bearing the one-word title *Democracy*, which appeared contemporaneously with Tocqueville's second volume and Bancroft's second and third, has an importance which it did not have at the time. Its qualities represent the very phenomenon it set out to depict. It has been forgotten long; the author, George Sidney Camp, is except for an article or two equally unknown. Yet he wrote with fair knowledge of political theory in the West. He did so under commission; the book appeared in 1841, small and unremarkable in appearance, as Volume 138 in Harper and Brothers Family Library series. The publishers, according to a foreword, thought that the need for an adult primer was great, "no work to their knowledge, having ever yet been published, the express design of which is to elucidate democratic *theory*." The aim was to set forth the idea that democracy belongs to all the people, not to one political party or another—it was "to vindicate that grand national party, composed of all republican America, against the aspersions of foreign commentators, and the enmity of European monarchists."°

The text is mild and middle-of-the-road. The present writer guesses from internal suggestions that the author was a Middle State Whig. The book opens with theoretical matters. Camp objected that American political thought honored such Englishmen as Paley, Blackstone, and Burke, and such old continental writers as Burlamaqui and Montesquieu. It respected "arbitrary" power too much. In the same context he remarked derisively that most educated people wished that voting were still restricted to property holders. Insisting that the time had arrived for democracy to be accepted by all, Camp explained that "democracy" and "republic" are overlapping, sympathetic terms. He used them almost interchangeably; to him they signified practical self-government. This is something the United States has but Europe lacks, he said; yet truly it is available to all. Though Camp's language was not fervid it was evangelical in suggestion. "Faith is as necessary to the republican as to the Christian," he insisted. "We must believe in the capacity of man for self-government, or the framework of our Constitution will be altered." Let us reinforce the temple we built in 1787, he was saying: let us extend our foundations of trust to rest on the people at large.

Camp's reasoning about democracy appealed to both moral logic and history. "History yields its final testimony in favor of the practicability of self-government." Here, perhaps affected by Bancroft, he found sustenance for democratic belief not only in the classical Greeks and Romans but in the ways of the "wandering Tartar" and the "primitive Indian." "Modern times" encouraged him too. "Our luxuries, cheapened by science, our territory widely extended by nature, and our habits, modified by Christianity" seemed promising to him, as they did to the economic nationalists. With no stated exceptions, he wanted all adults to vote. "Woman has all the attributes of political freedom in their perfection." Camp welcomed immigrants of every kind, impoverished ones and Roman Catholic ones included. He omitted any discussion of Negroes, either as slaves or as freemen. By inference Camp's vision included the cities, but he made no case for general economic or social democracy.°

Coming to conclusions, the book rests its case mainly on moral sense. Where the vindication of an autocracy may be in a certain practicability, the author acknowledged, the defense of democracy lies in its "moral perfection," its "justice." "The law of justice between man and man establishes the republican principle. . . . A republic is only the application of the law of justice to politics. . . . The just is nothing but the equal." As if someone had interposed a query—"Are you not going too far, relying too heavily on human goodwill?"— Camp observed that it is only "too true that our nature is full of contradictions, errors and infirmities." Yet as Christianity guides believers inwardly, democracy "may be readily comprehended by the plainest minds; it appeals to the first maxims of common-sense morals. . . . Leave every man in the possession of his natural prerogatives, and a republic follows."° European monarchy, the author took a chapter to explain, always traces to a usurpation of power by someone; by contrast democracy always contains a story of justice.

Though there is no intellectual parity between the massive works of Tocqueville and Bancroft, on the one hand, and the primer by Camp, on the other, there does remain to be remarked in conclusion a kind of symmetry among the three. Tocqueville's views, however patrician, belonged essentially to the continuing Enlightenment—to the post-revolutionary phase of the Enlightenment, which was rethinking some of the earlier Enlightenment's ideas. Tocqueville's doubts about the capacity of the people for self-government, for example, did raise matters which Jefferson and Adams had not considered—for instance, the tension of race relations. Yet the large hopes of the philosopher statesmen were truly echoed in Tocqueville's own long-run expectations; and, as we have seen, his incomparable gift was to enrich the world's understanding of democracy.

George Bancroft represented *inter alia* the passionate feeling for the land and the people which sprang up among intellectuals early in the nineteenth century. Undeniably his philosophy was heavily indebted to German scholars. Yet Bancroft did not differ much from the liberal, literary-minded nationalism which rose in Unitarian circles, in distinguished pulpits and journals of Boston and Cambridge where German thought so far had had little reach. Harvard trainee and Unitarian, Bancroft himself was an in-and-out member of those circles. No one sustained more strongly than he did the old Puritan theme of a people specially chosen to rule under God.

George Sidney Camp spoke in lighter tones. The text of *Democracy* shows that his mind moved in the channels of Scottish and English moral-intuitionist philosophy. This factor does not separate him from the others. Scottish common sense still resided at Harvard and within Unitarianism; it was still familiar, where Jefferson discovered it and where Tocqueville knew it, among French liberals. That very set of ideas, moreover, placed Camp close to the generality of contemporary Protestants. Moral intuitionism was the common instrument of American thought. Camp used it to justify the ways of democracy to Americans who were only beginning to think about the condition in which they had arrived.

2 In Jefferson's Country: Flowering and Withering of Confidence

IN the preceding section, where the question is how well public thought comprehended the democratizing processes in Jackson's America, the answer of the national literature is "Not very well." In this period, as in others, political innovation began with trial and error. The systematizing of ideas about it waited a considerable time. As we already know, the colonial-period prehistory of democracy shows a similar lag. Roger Williams is an illustration in miniature. His defiance of the Massachusetts fathers and his founding of Rhode Island occurred soon after his arrival in America; but his writing *The Bloudy Tenent of Persecution* awaited his need to explain things in England. The way in which the colonies achieved legislative autonomy illustrates this point on a broader scale. They were largely self-governing by 1700; but only around 1725 to 1730 did the literature of self-justification noticeably flow, and only after a second generation, between 1763 and 1776, did it fully and famously appear. By nineteenth-century comparison, when the first three volumes of Bancroft's history and Camp's little treatise are viewed together as part of the theory-making process, they resemble the early colonial writers in behalf of autonomy, not the later. Much as John Wise and Daniel Dulany the Elder had made their defenses of colonial self-government a generation or more before John Adams and Thomas Jefferson, Bancroft and Camp defended democracy decades ahead of most of the literature.

Meanwhile, though mass democracy as a condition of society manifested itself in all parts of the nation, the acute expressions of it more often than not occurred in response to local conditions. This takes us first of all to Virginia. In that state, once Jefferson and Madison had led the way into republican self-government, a myriad of expansions created a wide diffusion of culture. The Old Dominion now developed a true port city, as it had not during the colonial period. While traffic did not focus in Norfolk in a way to compete with Baltimore or Philadelphia, the growth there was considerable, and it was matched in the Shenandoah valley by a crop of new market towns. Along with this proliferation of population and commerce, there occurred a proliferation among the churches. Mainly in western parts of the state, Presbyterian, Quaker, Baptist, Methodist, and German church and sectarian elements, which before 1776 though not persecuted had never had opportunity equal to the Anglican establishment, now expanded tremendously. Episcopalianism contracted in proportion; it fell behind not only in number of congregations but in the development of church schools and journals. Presbyterian colleges, Hampden-Sydney and Washington, rose quickly to status equal to William and Mary, though they began as academies. The Methodist college, Randolph-Macon, came a generation later in 1830.

Secular culture flowered. Over and above the fresh beginnings we know in the university at Charlottesville, science—practical science, mainly agricultural—gained throughout the state. Organizations, local and state-wide, were formed; experiments, some of them attempts to meet the hard problem of soil exhaustion, were carried out. The study of economics, indicated by pamphlet and journal literature, increased; the study of law, including much semipolitical writing in that field, advanced. Many handsome new residences, such as Arlington, now famous by reason of General Robert E. Lee's ownership and the national cemetery there, and Monticello and the state capitol designed by Jefferson, illustrate Virginia's preference for architecture in classic republican styles. Even drama and music prospered. To be sure, none of this brightness truly lightened the dark side. Negro slavery persisted, only somewhat curtailed by voluntary manumissions. The state legislature refused during the 1810s as during the 1770s to provide a system of public education; the old structure of social classes continued, much as during the eighteenth century. In those respects the seer of Monticello went to his grave defeated. On the other hand the Old Dominion's many amenities make it impossible not to agree with the expert, Richard Beale Davis, that Virginia during the last quarter century of Jefferson's life belonged especially to him. The Richmond *Enquirer*, a newspaper of national influence which sustained his line of thought and which he read, must have been one of the true comforts of Jefferson's seventies and eighties at home.

The mind of John Taylor of Caroline, rather than Jefferson's own, was the one which most comprehensively reviewed the state's social and political issues and put the findings together in print. The owner of a splendid plantation in Caroline County, Virginia, and a graduate of William and Mary, Taylor belonged by origin, experience, and location to the revolutionary epoch. He had soldiered for independence. As a member of Virginia's ratifying convention of 1788, he opposed entering the Union; he remained always a states' rights man. He served several terms in the House of Burgesses; for his one form of service to the national government, he was three times appointed to fill out an unfinished term in the United States Senate. He completed his books only during his sixties—that is, between 1813 and 1823. This places him in the history of political thought midway between the republicanizing of Virginia during the Revolution and the democratizing of national politics during the age of Jackson. Although Jefferson and Madison alike seem to have withheld open endorsement of Taylor's writings, this appears to have been by reason of the reticence natural to retired great men of the nation and not—at least in Jefferson's case—because of disagreement. "Col. Taylor and myself have rarely, if ever, differed in any political principle of importance," said Jefferson shortly before his own death. "Every act of his life, and every word he ever wrote, satisfies me of this."°

The two books which systematized Taylor's ideas, *Arator* and *An Inquiry into the Principles and Policy of the Government of the United States*, appeared respectively in 1813 and 1814. In the earlier work he went far in agrarianism. Whether or not the scholars are right who find him indebted to the French physiocrats, he forcefully applied that kind of conviction to Virginia and to the nation.

> In the United States, the responsibility of agriculture does not stop at food for all eaters. It extends to the support of government, to the encouragement of commerce, to the sustenance of the learned professions, to the introduction of the fine arts. . . . A common interest ought to suggest the national policy in regard to agriculture. . . . As our country is one great farm, and its inhabitants one great family, in which those who work the least receive the greatest share of the profit, those who are not farmers have a deeper interest for increasing the profit of agriculture, than the farmer himself. . . .

As during the 1790s, when he had pamphleteered against Alexander Hamilton's program of building up business to strengthen the government and against John Adams's politics of balance among economic classes and interests, Taylor attacked the "stockjobbers" rising in America. He represented the country as now being exploited by commercial people who lived off the labor of farmers. Art and morality inhere in the use and the care of the soil, he reasoned as Jefferson reasoned: happiness occurs when men naturally fit "ideas to substance, and substance to ideas" in a "constant rotation of hope and fruition."°

The *Arator*, just quoted, was a series of agricultural essays, with a base in social and political ideas. The *Inquiry into the Principles and Policy of the Government of the United States* was more political and philosophical. As a ten-year member of the House of Burgesses, in line with Jefferson's own hopes, Taylor had sought to have the franchise extended and seats in the legislature redistributed. He had been the introducer of the Virginia Resolutions, and during the 1810s he was still keeping the secret that Jefferson had been the author of the Kentucky Resolutions. Around 1798 had been the time of his closest cooperation with Jefferson and Madison; in later years he grew more states' rightist while they during their presidencies swung the other way. But the *Inquiry* of 1814 spoke mainly of confidence in the people. It returned (after a quarter century) a critical reply to John Adams's *Defence of the Constitutions*, or rather to the acquiescence in social classes contained in that work. From Taylor's almost Marx-like rejection of the business class, from his distaste for Burke and Burke-like fear of social upsets, he took the line of democracy that more and more people should be incorporated in the nation's affairs.

The way to avoid too much human perverseness flowing into the arena of politics, reasoned the *Inquiry*, is to allow no one those large proprietary privileges which government alone can create and grant. Choose the opposite course, Taylor advised: let the state offer fair opportunities to individuals, according to their virtue. "The constitutions [of the states]," he observed with reference to the 1770s, founded "their policy upon the basis of human equality. . . . [They] consider a nation as made of individuals." The writer correctly attributed to John Adams acceptance of the idea that men perform in politics according to their place in society: "Mr. Adams's system is bottomed upon a classification of men." In the same passage Taylor explained that he himself rejected the hierarchical idea of society and that his system rested instead "upon an application of moral principles to human nature."°

Except on the economic side, Taylor's reasoning became quite abstracted from society. Today it is hard to decide how to estimate his antihierarchical argument not simply because he held slaves but also because, though he disliked the institution of slavery, he believed that to change it lay beyond the reach of politics. In respect of training citizens, again Taylor held back: his expectation of education was rather to train up good leaders than to improve the equipment of the people as voters or otherwise. In such matters Taylor stopped far short of his master at Monticello. The merit of his books as a contribution to democratic theory is the tough-minded way in which they reasoned from the American Revolution's promise of equality to the shortcomings of later performance.

Jefferson was in his seventies when Taylor's books appeared. The later 1810s were the time of his making his second great effort for state education. He failed this time as during the 1770s to get enacted a primary- and secondary-school system. But he did succeed in launching the University of Virginia, much the best state university in America up till then. His reputation grew as seer. While he seldom went far from Monticello, he was always being called upon and written to, his political blessing sought. From his correspondence of 1816 Merrill D. Peterson identifies letters written to Samuel Kercheval, of the discontented western part of the state, as representing "the furthest reach of

Jefferson's democratic thought" at any time in his life. Therein the ex-president said that decision making by the people is the "mother principle" and that governments "are republican only in proportion as they embody the will of the people, and advocate it." Thus fifty years after 1776 Jefferson still as always wanted the constitution of Virginia democratized: he wanted all white males to be enfranchised; he wanted the governor to be elected by the people, not by the legislature. But he wanted more than political change. Proposing to cut into what we would now call "the establishment," he proposed to have the county courts eliminated as being "monopolies of county administration" by the squires, and to substitute a more democratic system of local government akin to district school boards. With an intention like that of the revolutionary Pennsylvanians and Vermonters, Jefferson hoped that Virginia would revise its constitution periodically, on the principle that "laws and institutions must go hand in hand with the progress of the human mind." Not during the Revolution or ever before had Jefferson been so ready to apply the principles of 1776 to the reshaping of society.°

Yet while Jefferson represents with his unique authority the continuity of democratic principles during the half century after the Revolution, there are many suggestions of restrictiveness, of strategy executed cautiously or not executed at all. We have caught this in Taylor, and there is more than a hint in Jefferson's own performance. Jefferson had always maintained silence about the resolutions of 1798 he had fathered. Now he asked for secrecy again. He did not think that what he said to Kercheval should be made public. It would seem too much to the voters. When Andrew Jackson of Tennessee and Henry Clay of Kentucky sought his political endorsement, he withheld. Perhaps Jackson came closer than Clay, but neither of those rising leaders of the nation ever received the nod. Somehow the old philosophical democracy and the new political practice never quite blended.

In Virginia, and indeed in the South and nearby Southwest generally, the social extensions of the Revolution were slowed down. Of course the freedoms of 1776 remained inscribed in the statute books. Religion (for example) was as free under law in Kentucky as in Virginia. Not only did evangelicals settle and proselytize in that state as we know, but also Unitarians and Catholics; church colleges were founded, as in Virginia, Transylvania and Center the first and second. But again like Virginia, Kentucky deferred establishing a public-school system; it put off for nearly half a century the founding of the state university.°

In the Old Dominion itself there came political and social tests of the growing power of democracy. During the years after Jefferson's death, the western counties—the Shenandoah valley and the mountain and transmontane region which later became West Virginia—demanded that a constitutional convention be called. At that point, 1829, Jefferson's dozen-years-old letters to Kercheval were publicized. The convention did enact a more liberal franchise, though not quite full manhood suffrage for whites; the western counties were at last given fair representation in Richmond. That is, in 1830 Virginians reached such a stage of practical participation in government as Jefferson had wanted in 1780.

But the western insurgency bore also an antislavery impulse. The first election of legislators under the new constitution sent to the lower house a great number of members who thought that the time had come to reduce the institution of slavery. Opinion varied from those who, in the style of George Wythe and Thomas Jefferson of the preceding generation, thought simply that the institution should be terminated by law, without great effort to taper down, to moderates who proposed schemes for purchasing young slaves for manumission, for African colonization, and the like. Such proposals were gradualist, but in seeking to use state money they were substantial and truly threatened to eliminate the institution. Under the pressures Virginia politics went kaleidoscopic: one of Jefferson's old associates in founding the University of Virginia voted consistently against any steps against slavery; on the other hand Thomas Marshall, son of the chief justice and one of the larger slave owners in the state legislature, took a strong antislavery stand. Unfortunately the most frightening slave insurrection ever, the one led by Nat Turner in lower Virginia in August 1831, intervened between the state election and the vote in the legislature and intruded a factor of panic. Although the Virginia House of Burgesses did not actually come within one vote of taking antislavery action, as the record has sometimes been misread, the balance between attackers and defenders of slavery in the house was about sixty to seventy.°

In the twentieth century this defeat of antislavery in Richmond has the look less of a local event than of a national one, less of a failure of the House of Burgesses to pass a law than failure in continuity of reform in the tradition of the Revolution. One remembers the thin margin by which, not long before the Revolution, the Quakers lost control of the Pennsylvania legislature. After the 1832 decision in Richmond, what had been a moral possibility, within the range of an operating system of legislation, was closed out, practically speaking. Immediately the era opened of southerners defending slavery overtly. Up to 1832 John Taylor's half-apologetic defense of the institution as a form of property holding had been the representative attitude and a yielding one. Thereafter the kind of defense composed by Professor Thomas R. Dew of William and Mary, who drew on the debates and conceptualized slavery as a positive good for the state, became the southern mode. Associated with the new defense, indeed a part of it, Virginia now heard from Abel P. Upshur, one of its young conservatives, a new political doctrine. "There is a majority in *interest*, as well as a majority in number." The proslavery future of John C. Calhoun had dawned.

Altogether we do not have to envisage in old Virginia any failure of voting democracy. The constitution of 1830 did extend the republicanism of 1776 and reinforced it by larger participation by the people. The restriction which did occur was a lowering of democratic horizons. A deterioration began in Virginia, as the distance from Monticello lengthened, a reduction of belief in freedoms and equalities which the generation of the Revolution had said belonged to all men.

3 *West of the Appalachians: Frontier Conditions and Partial Democracy*

THE issues which arose in Virginia did not belong to Virginia alone. The oldest state had been the first in representative government and in Negro slavery, in both conditions since 1619. On these accounts and because of its liberal culture it was a favorable place for equalitarian voices to follow the lead of Jefferson, but it was also natural for conservative voices to resist.

In the younger states of the South—which we may now begin to think of as a region—a like polarization occurred. But, generally speaking, conservative feeling prevailed more quickly. Within weeks of the debate over slavery in Richmond, South Carolina blew up the nullification crisis. As we shall see later in some detail, while the immediate, vocal questions in that state were tariff and states' rights, slavery was also involved. In South Carolina as in Virginia, the bottom question was the survival of the old-plantation hierarchical order of society which took Negro slavery for granted. The success of the old order depended on the state's rallying to the ideas of which John C. Calhoun was the principal, sometimes anonymous, author. More decisively than elsewhere, in South Carolina elitist doctrine came forward and equalitarian dropped out of the discourse. When democracy was defended there it was Greek-style democracy, not the new American mass style. Proposals for social democratization were conspicuously absent—there was no sizable movement to reduce the institution of slavery, or to provide public schools, or to assign land to the landless.

While after 1815 the South—both the seaboard states of colonial origin and the transappalachian states—developed social conditions which were especially adverse to the democratic imagination, it by no means had them all to itself. In a later section we shall see that elsewhere, especially in New York where large property-holding became conspicuous, convictions both for and against democratic equality entered the stream of political thought. And, as Merle Curti's richly statistical study of Trempeauleau County in western Wisconsin suggests, probably no part of the United States ever escaped a crop of social differentiations and antagonisms following its founding period of land-grabbing and immigration. On the other hand, there were real social and ideological differences region by region, and, as Curti concludes persuasively, the prime historian of the West and its influence on democracy, Frederick Jackson Turner, was right to insist that the upper Mississippi valley contained conditions of both nature and society which uncommonly aided democracy.

Certainly the Old Northwest—the region west of New York and Pennsylvania which is bounded on the north by the Great Lakes, on the south by the Ohio River, and on the west by the Mississippi—had been planned that way from the start. While the United States was being organized during the 1780s, the Old Northwest, though it occupied one-third of the nation's territory, had few inhabitants who were not Indians. During the three-quarters of a century before Lincoln it grew incomparably. The region supplied one state out of seventeen when Ohio was admitted to the Union in 1803; it supplied six out of thirty-one, and a president-elect, in 1860. (In 1841 it had supplied a president, William Henry Harrison of Ohio.) The states which arose there—Ohio the first, Indiana and Illinois after the peace of 1815, and Michigan, Wisconsin and Minnesota between 1837 and 1858—all made good the promises of the Northwest Ordinance and the Constitution. Slavery remained outlawed. While the distribution of domain lands did not induce economic equality among the citizens, there certainly did not appear anywhere in the region such a squirearchy, English style, as had developed along the seaboard. No state had a set of appointive local officers. Five of the six states on entering the Union (Ohio was the exception) provided white manhood suffrage. Federal lands were actually assigned to support public schools. In Indiana and Wisconsin state universities were born by constitutional provision at the instant the state governments were. In the case of Michigan, the institution seated at Ann Arbor—at first called a "Catholoepistemiad"—was established in 1817 by the territorial government. Altogether the Old Northwest began as thoroughly patterned in the spirit of the Revolution and the Enlightenment as colonial New England had been patterned by Puritanism.

But settlers of the Old Northwest outdid many times over the Puritan forefathers in founding new communities, creating new congregations, churches, and schools, and fulfilling their designs of government. They set up *de novo* their school districts, townships, and counties, all according to pattern. They broke the soil and developed their farms; they sold, purchased, and speculated in land. They enterprised in every direction: they set up newspapers and law offices early and in large numbers; they went into every kind of business, up to the building of canals and railroads. It was not unusual for a farmer to have created more than one farm, or a newspaperman to have founded more than one newspaper, in a lifetime: the individual was often older than his community or his state. By the 1840s town life had grown in places into real urbanism: Cincinnati passed the 100,000 mark (three or four times the population of Benjamin Franklin's Philadelphia) during that decade. St. Louis and Chicago did so during the 1850s (the decade during which New York City passed 800,000). Only a little less spectacularly than these three inland ports, three others—two lake ports and one river port instead of the other way round—Cleveland, Detroit, and Louisville, all became places of large business. No wonder that across the country sprang up a generation of activists too aggressive for Tocqueville to like very well as he observed them.

South of the Ohio River, where early deed won early celebration for Daniel Boone and John Sevier as the greatest pioneers to open trans-Appalachia, there occurred population movement and social voluntarism on a scale almost equal to that in the Old Northwest, and it occurred a few years earlier. But of course no national ordinance excluded slavery from that region. During the first and second generations of the federal republic the Southwest became slavery's great area of expansion, from Kentucky to Texas and especially along the black belt which paralleled the Gulf coastline a bit inland. The states of the region fell short not on the primary components of democracy—provision in law for freedom and for (white) manhood suffrage—but on the social components contained in the Jeffersonian cluster of ideas and policies. No more than old Virginia itself did the southwestern states provide universal education; unless exception be made for Texas while an independent republic, none matched the Old Northwest in respect of distributing domain lands liberally. Although the southern seaboard states—Georgia, North Carolina, Virginia—had been the principal early ones to provide state universities, the states of the old Southwest lagged behind the Northwest in that respect. Only the University of Tennessee was born when the state was; it proved a slow developer. Among the other southwestern states, the University of Alabama and the University of Mississippi began within a quarter century of statehood. But no other university in any part of the South before 1900 would catch up with the achievement of the one at Charlottesville.

But, while according to Jeffersonian standards the social and cultural desiderata of democratic-republican life lagged in the Southwest, that very region supplied the United States with two presidents, Andrew Jackson and James K. Polk, and two other national leaders, Henry Clay and Thomas Hart Benton. Henry Clay we already know as the public legislative spokesman for the American System. In that respect his mind had a large and generous grasp; it moved toward using the powers of government to serve the people's economic benefit. And of course his prime leadership of the Whig Party does not exclude characterizing him as a political democrat. He was one of the many who in the 1820s sought and failed to receive the blessing of Thomas Jefferson; during the campaign of 1832, when he fought Andrew Jackson most bitterly, he was as completely as anyone else the developer of mass participation in the nation's electoral processes. On the other hand neither Clay's convictions nor his career gives him any general identification with equalitarian belief. In respect of national land-distribution policy he was moderately withholding, more in the line of Hamilton than of Jefferson. Concerning the problems of race and slavery he went no further toward reform than the movement to colonize American free Negroes in Africa. He never objected to slavery as an institution; as a public man he rendered no service to education.

By the same standards of measurement, General Andrew Jackson, though by custom we attach his name to the emergence of nationwide mass democracy, comes out even more short as a social democrat. As long ago as 1932 Thomas Perkins Abernethy of the University of Virginia shattered the illusion that Old Hickory personified the ideals of equality. It is true that his origins were right for that kind of image to get started. The posthumous son of a Scots-Irish immigrant, he grew up on the state boundary between the two Carolinas. At thirteen he served in the Revolution, as a Patriot soldier. He never had much schooling, yet managed somehow to train in law in a North Carolina office; then he went with the migration westward into middle Tennessee. By 1791 at age twenty-four he was already well situated in that territory—a rising lawyer, married, and a favored friend of William Blount, the governor appointed by Washington. In 1795 he served in Tennessee's constitutional convention. (But the forthcoming fundamental law required a property qualification of voters; it was in no way advanced in democracy.) The next year, while Blount went to the Senate, Jackson was elected to the House of Representatives, where he served only one term. On returning to Tennessee he was elected to the bench, one of the state's "superior" judges. But after only five years he resigned in order to accept the commanding major-generalship of the militia of his very large state. That office lay within the choice of the field officers and he received it—the key it would prove to his destiny as a national hero and president—by the casting vote which broke a tied election. So far, up to age thirty-six, whatever else his history may be, it is a story of a poor boy becoming successful, popular, and powerful.

But doubt about much democratic meaning in the story becomes necessary as early as his arrival in Tennessee. Beginning with Blount, he consistently sought the associations of power and wealth, the life of a gentleman. He came with one slave, and through the years increased his slaveholding. At no time in his life did he have anything more adverse to say about slavery than that it depended on benevolence from the masters. His benefactor, Governor Blount, who died in 1800, had been a dishonest land speculator. Jackson himself acquired, sold, lost, and ultimately netted many speculative holdings; his permanent gains included the plantation where he built the home he loved, the Hermitage. Jackson, the lawyer and landowner, strained the letter of the law if no more than that on his way to sizable fortune.

In short, the man who during the 1820s and 1830s became a symbol for democracy had earlier represented the well to do and the office seekers of Tennessee more than the ordinary people. In the final subsection of this chapter we shall return to him, discovering him in the White House. What had in the interval transpired to elevate him, and what he did and said as president, doubtless will reassure us that the legend of Jackson as American democrat has a truthful foundation in history. But the foundation cannot include much beside a rags-to-riches story in the general's background history as citizen of a state of the old Southwest.°

Indeed, of the half-dozen foremost political leaders who emerged from the American West prior to Lincoln, only the least of them, Thomas Hart Benton, came close to making his own a large cluster of democratic convictions, in the way of Thomas Jefferson. Senator Benton, whose nickname "Old Bullion" presents an obstacle to recognizing him as a man of broad principle, began about 1840 to speak in a connected way for policies of equality. He quoted Jefferson often and lovingly. To be sure he was by birth a North Carolinian, was married to a Virginian of eminent family, and as an adult resided always in a slaveholding state. During the 1820s, just after Missouri had entered the Union and had sent him to the Senate, he defended the institution of slavery. Yet during the next decade, while he was in his thirties, he changed his mind. Thereafter, on occasions when he felt that as a servant of his state he could possibly do so, he spoke and voted against the westward extension of slavery. Similarly in the Jeffersonian line he sought moderating decisions on the power issues between state and national government. He was slow to approve the war with Mexico; he hated the ideas and politics which bore toward the theory or practice of secession. Although he rejected the all-out abolitionists, he felt that the Compromise of 1850 conceded too much to the doctrinaires of secession. In these respects his opinions resembled Lincoln's, before the Illinoisan became a figure on the national stage. In the Senate, Benton's free-land positions made him a prophet of the Homestead Act, one of the principal laws Lincoln in due time would sign.

To the main point of the present chapter, the convictions which Benton especially gathered and which made him an early one to favor the liberal decisions the Union would make in crisis, all placed him in the direct line of Jefferson's hopes for the nation. Of course the Missouri senator lacked the intellectual scope of the philosopher statesman he admired. At seventeen he was dismissed from the University of North Carolina; he was one of America's many self-educated leaders. But assistance to education was the only still-lively item in Jefferson's bundle of policy ideas about which he had nothing to say. The broad front on which he actually ranged was exceptional. Especially his antislavery feeling, though moderate, is eloquent because it cost him votes.

Altogether, the main aspects of institutional ideas and the convictions of public leaders in the American West accord with the general proposition of this chapter. That is, in the West as elsewhere democratic political processes preceded democratic theory when mass democracy was born. Were the fact otherwise, had the regional culture or leadership either north or south of the Ohio generously comprehended the moral logic of democracy when national leaders in religion and letters failed to express it, much explanation would be in order. But what we are actually discovering is an equality among many who spoke to the condition of the country. Political leaders on one hand and intellectuals on the other were alike proud of America, were alike in expecting everything of the future, but were alike also in being slow to comprehend and express what ideals of equality had once demanded, and would again demand. The wide range of what democratic republicanism actually called for, or might come to call for, was not closed to any who chose to speculate, but not many—hardly any who were politically prominent—were so bold.°

4   *North and East of Washington:*
Democracy as Source of
Anxiety and Hope

IN the coastal states north and east of the Potomac River, American society was as expansive, mobile, and tense as anywhere else. But while in the transappalachian states all institutions were new, in the cismontane ones much that was old was left over from prerevolutionary times. Although soon after 1820 several states adopted new constitutions—New York, Connecticut, and Massachusetts did so, and theirs turned out to be, like Virginia's, more democratic than before—nowhere in the Northeast was there a new polity and society to be constructed from the ground up. Little matter how radical by the standards of old England their systems had been when founded, all the seaboard states—even Rhode Island and Pennsylvania—now had an established order. In the Northeast demands for reform naturally and usually came piecemeal. Not surprisingly, the expansive, mobile society of old New York, once half feudal, was the principal one to produce thought and politics which contemplated broad-scale democratization.

Indeed, that state's particular background is the striking thing about the one remembered discourse on democracy which we have from a major American writer of the period. When James Fenimore Cooper brought out *The American Democrat* in 1838, he was fifteen years along in his incomparably profitable writing of the Leatherstocking tales, the creator of Natty Bumppo, the perfect pioneer, the hero in whom freedom and self-reliance and separateness from any corrupting social order were thrillingly brought together. But in a nonfictional view, American society did not look like a collection of Natty Bumppos to Fenimore Cooper. Like Tocqueville he half feared the people, both as participators in mass politics and as aggressive individuals. But unlike the French philosopher he held a stake in American life; his heart was invested there. His little book was more than anything else a textbook, advice to young readers on how to behave now that democracy had moved permanently into New York State.

For some years before 1838 Cooper had been warming up to the problem by responding to overseas comment. His *Notions of Americans* answered critics in England; their ideas concerned him more than others' because he spent considerable time in England and felt the pull of English traditionalism. His *Letter . . . to General Lafayette* argued (a line that George Sidney Camp would take in *Democracy*) the superiority of republican to monarchical institutions; he wrote essays in the same vein for the newspapers. Besides doing straight political pieces, Cooper in his novel, *The Monikins*, satirized the antagonisms of social class in England, France, and America. What all this suggests, that the author felt a great anxiety for the stability of society, *The American Democrat* amply confirms.

Yet the book is lacking in anger. Only after forty pages of preliminaries do we reach a section, "On Equality," which is somewhat sharp: "Equality of condition is incompatible with civilization." Later, at the point of discussing the role of women in society, Cooper's resistance again appears: women participating in politics would be mistaken, he said, a violation of the natural order of society. His words sound like a reaction to Frances Wright, the beautiful but outspoken radical Scotswoman who had already been long in American reform and journalism. Cooper came close to Tocqueville in the passage "On Liberty," which warns against overacceptance of the majority principle: "We do not adopt the popular polity because it is perfect, but because it is less imperfect than any other." In the section "On Demagogues," Cooper was likewise moderate. He said that the United States now contained a class of politicians who were "not properly exempt from the imputation of falling into some of [the demagogue's] most dangerous vices." He admonished the press to be responsible; he declared for the civil liberties. Again like Tocqueville, Cooper predicted the end of slavery and a later time of race troubles.

As for his over-all perspective, the novelist acknowledged that England had a higher civilization than the United States. Even so, "Americans excel in humanity" and in providing for "the ordinary comforts" of life, he observed. He represented his own period in believing that the age of the American Revolution had been golden and that ideals since then had declined—"truths" which had once been uppermost now yielded to "sophisms," he said.° Taken as a whole, it is hard to see in *The American Democrat* what our own century's most caustic critic of democracy, H. L. Mencken, saw a generation ago, "a splendid diatribe." The book has the sound rather of a worried citizen trying to prevent young people from being misled.

The sharper words, the actual diatribes, came from the leftward side of the discourse. During the 1820s they came mainly from pro-labor pamphleteers; during the 1830s, from a New York City faction of the Democratic Party; and during the 1840s from the trade-union movement, the part which called itself the National Reform Association. In those three phases New Yorkers outdid all their contemporaries in discussing the social goals of democracy. Where Cooper feared that people in politics would disturb the social order, this sequence of city reformism demanded that very result—political power and economic power joined together in the service of social justice.

A demand for political equality appeared in New York's constitutional convention of 1821, the one in which we have met Chancellor Kent resisting reform. As in the case of Virginia, part of the problem at that time was the stiff property limitation on franchise imposed under the state constitution of 1777. But where in Jefferson's state the discriminations had been against those who lacked property in land and against fair representation of the western counties, in New York it was workingmen in the early industrial cities, especially America's greatest city, who mainly felt the discriminations. Steamboats, railroads, textile and metallurgical factories, lumbering and shipbuilding enterprises were already in business. Immigration, mainly from England, was beginning to build up the nineteenth-century crescendo of social tension. Between 1790 and 1865 the population of New York City multiplied more than thirty-fold, from about thirty thousand to well over a million. (Today's "population explosion" is not as explosive as that.) Under such circumstances the Empire State enacted white manhood suffrage. It did so a decade earlier than Virginia passed a similar reform; the conditions were much more compelling.°

Voting democracy was not the kind of provision, however, to supply a resting place in New York politics. Quite in line with the fears of Chancellor Kent and Fenimore Cooper, class antagonisms did powerfully develop. A man whose career in some ways resembles Franklin's, Langdon Byllesby, who happened to come from Philadelphia, was the earliest to make the new protest in memorable words. A printer and journalist, and personal combiner of the functions of capitalist and laborer, he was also a man of dogmatic mind. The little book for which he is remembered, *Observations on the Sources of Equal Wealth* (1825), attacked problems of economic distribution from a doctrinaire point of view. Premising that every man has a right to life, liberty, and happiness, he attacked New York's law and usage with respect to land-holding, credit, and inheritance. Society conspires, he said, to do injustice to workingmen: labor-saving devices create unemployment. Probably because Byllesby drew from factory situations which anyone could observe and applied to them the doctrine of the Declaration of Independence, he won a hearing at least in New York. On the other hand his book was not at all well timed: it was published during a period of recovery from depression. He blew against the wind of technological development and had no visible result in politics.°

We come close to the heart of our problem, though with an increase of dogmatism, in the case of Thomas Skidmore. This New Yorker's relevance to the intellectual history of mass democracy begins with good timing, for he published in 1829, the year when Jackson entered the White House, and it is enhanced by his being a working machinist. That is, he belonged to that infrequent category of writers whose lives are spent mainly in manual labor. His prose was crude and his title flamboyant, *The Rights of Men to Property! Being a Proposition to Make it Equall among Adults of the Present Generation*. Yet he drew on Jefferson and Paine and also on contemporary social radicals in England: Robert Owen, Thomas Spence, and William Thompson. He developed a coherent argument. Insisting, what many scholars of the nineteenth century would come to say, that titles to land always trace historically to some conquest, and saying that individual titles in America were usually acquired by inheritance, Skidmore proposed that equality in property—in real estate and personal estate both—be made the law of the land. He wanted government to enforce this policy in two ways: first, indirectly, by providing every child with training until he became of age; second, directly, by assigning to every adult an equal share of all property left by owners at death. Although the author lived only three years after his book was published, he managed to bring out a little journal, the *Friend of Equal Rights*, and to help found the New York Workingmen's Party, to which he devoted that paper. A slogan from that party's platform catches the main goals of *The Rights of Men to Property!*: "All children are entitled to equal education; all adults to equal property; and all mankind to equal privileges."°

While this pamphleteering and party building went on, a sympathetic development occurred in the journalism of New York City. Almost simultaneously with the publication of Skidmore's book, a son of Robert Owen, Robert Dale Owen, and his friend Frances Wright launched their own prolabor and reform journal, the *Free Enquirer*. As the organ of young editors who had recently been promoting the New Harmony and Nashoba communities in the West, and who spoke for the abolition of slavery, for free education, and also for women's rights and contraception, the *Free Enquirer* was bound to be radical. Even so, it stopped short of Skidmore. Let workingmen concentrate first on their rights as citizens to organize, it proposed. Let them develop their programs through newspapers and organizations; especially they should press to educate themselves and to have their children educated. Robert Dale Owen, who was well informed about F. W. A. Froebel's kindergarten ideas and generally about Swiss educational reforms, made a great deal of the merits of gradualism. Miss Wright seems to have been less patient, and, returning to Europe, soon abandoned the paper.°

The lives of the *Friend of Equal Rights* and the *Free Enquirer*, though short, began a new element in American journalism. Whereas earlier there had been no labor newspapers, there now began an unending series, journals which were produced either by labor unions or parties or else were independent papers largely devoted to labor's cause. The *New York Tribune*, to be founded in 1841, would of course in time become the most famous independent paper ever to take the prolabor line. Yet a decade before the *Tribune* the eminent New York *Evening Post*, though it had begun as a Hamiltonian party organ, took a strong turn in that direction. In 1825 it appointed the brilliant young Massachusetts nature poet, William Cullen Bryant, to be an editor; four years later it placed him in charge. At about that time a younger poet, also something of an adventurer, William Leggett, joined the staff. The change of style which Bryant's control brought about led into a wonderful half century for the *Evening Post*. Firmly liberal and literary, it advocated over the years one reform after another, including anticorruption in government and antislavery. Also during the 1830s the *Post* became a Democratic Party organ. This gave Andrew Jackson's party, which up to that moment lacked much support from intellectual elements, an unmatched windfall. It helped turn New York reformers somewhat away from utopianism with distant goals toward issues which were coming into national politics.

Antimonopoly was the main idea which this contact of journal with party quickened into political life. Of course, a close look at the origins of antimonopoly would open up a long perspective on the history of English common law and would remind us of the colonies' resistance to English monopolies, especially the Boston Tea Party. What the young editors of the *Post* contributed—Leggett more than Bryant—was to give prime newspaper voice to the protest which was rising—in and out of New York—to credit monopolization. To be sure, this linked the *Evening Post* with Byllesby and Skidmore, the radicalism of the city. But immediately and politically the editors connected their paper with a different kind of hard-money, antibank writers who popped up around 1832, the year Henry Clay espoused and Andrew Jackson vetoed the bill to continue the second United States bank. The fire of the critics was sweeping: to them any bank—national or state-chartered—was objectionable if it held some exclusive authority to issue printed notes, that is, paper money. Leggett, not the most original but one of the most insistent of the objectors—some of them Democrats, some of them Whigs—protested that note issue meant credit manipulation, a power and privilege which no republican government should ever delegate to an unrepresentative, self-interested body. Senator Benton was the principal early national figure to take that line. William Gouge, a clerk in the Untied States treasury and an editor and pamphleteer whose writings would be exhumed by the Populists of the 1890s, was the principal pamphleteer. Among New Yorkers not on the *Post*, the following represent the movement: Clinton Roosevelt, Whig and member of the prominent, then mercantile, family whose name he bore; Dr. Henry Vethake, a medical man and a writer on public questions; and William Leggett's personal friend, Theodore Sedgwick, Jr., son of the famous supporter of Hamilton but himself a persuaded Jeffersonian and an admirer of President Jackson.

In that context of protest, Leggett's work on the *Evening Post* advanced him into being the principal brains man in the New York faction who styled themselves "Equal Rights Democrats" but who are better remembered as the "Locofocos." (The strange nickname was borrowed from the brand of matches with which they lighted a meeting, after Tammany Hall men departing in anger had blown out the lamps.) The Locofocos censured all banks to the degree that they were monopolistic. And, expanding the idea that a just government gives no financial preference to any group, they opposed protective tariffs as well. Their attitudes drew freshly on theory. The Locofocos combined the competitive beliefs of British economics (which were now widely accepted in America) with American attitudes about freedom and individuality. As Merrill Peterson, the historian of the legacy of Jefferson, says with wide application to the period, here the political ideas of Thomas Jefferson and the economic ideas of Adam Smith were proving to be "twin sisters" and "natural champions of freedom."°

Indeed the Equal Rights Democrats went far by contemporary standards in drawing together freedom and equality as fighting ideas. By the middle 1830s, moreover, civil rights issues gave them an added impulse. The rising debate over slavery made that area widely sensitive for the first time since the Alien and Sedition Acts crisis. Leggett wrote strongly against Jackson's Postmaster General Kendall, for permitting southern postmasters to refuse to deliver abolitionist literature. The editor accused Kendall of an outrage against the first amendment. More deeply, Leggett disliked the institution of slavery. Yet he foresaw realistically that any large-scale emancipation which released Negroes onto the free labor market would depress the wages of all. In this connection he emerges as one of several American followers of Malthusian principles; his Malthusianism appears to have held him back as reformer, for he did not press for antislavery. Likewise, though his work associated him with spokesmen for free land and for public schools, he never moved strongly in these lines either. Ill health may have been a factor, for he burned himself out during the middle 1830s. In sum, the Locofocos at once surpassed their contemporaries, in combining and applying current ideals of freedom and equality, and yet stopped short of speaking or acting for the full pattern of equal rights which Jefferson had envisaged.°

Developing parallel with them, however, and reaching full stature during the 1840s after Jackson and Van Buren had departed office, a nearby overlapping group soon pressed farther than they. Once again a bold newspaper, this time the *Workingmen's Advocate*, provided the place for discussion. George Henry Evans, who had been born in England but raised in upstate New York, became the principal spokesman. As a very young man he had become acquainted with Owenite socialism; later he got to know the Rochdale cooperative movement. Much that he had to say resembled Tom Paine's *Agrarian Justice* and the socialist ideas of Thomas Spence. Considering these various resemblances, and remembering the presence in New York of Robert Dale Owen and Frances Wright when the *Workingmen's Advocate* was new, one readily doubts Evans's denial that he and his paper were much influenced by ideas brought over from England.

In any event this editor and writer rose quickly during the 1830s to become the principal second-generation voice of labor reformism in New York and in the country. Evans followed Thomas Skidmore in insisting that labor should go in for independent political action, organized by local parties. He pleaded for "equal republican education." Reasoning from familiar environmentalist principles, he wrote in favor of requiring all children to attend publicly supported schools. Lodging, food, and clothing, all on a basis of equality, were calculated, as well as the training, to remove respect for privilege from the minds of the young. On the economic side the early *Workingmen's Advocate* went along with the liberal, free-trade and antimonopoly doctrines of the Locofocos. Also compatibly with reformist neighbors in New York City and with free-land agitation in the West, Evans proposed legislation by Congress which would make it easy for settlers to take title to arable land in the domain. He made this point years before the Preemption Act was passed in 1841, and a quarter century before the Homestead Act provided free farms for actual settlers.

By the later 1830s the ideas of the *Workingmen's Advocate* were being officially accepted by labor organizations. A number of craft unions gathered in New York City in what they called the National Trades Union. For the time being their reach far exceeded their grasp —there was nothing truly "national" about the National Trades Union, and it fell apart during the depression of 1837. But though the *Workingmen's Advocate* itself temporarily went under, the program survived. In 1841 Evans was able to begin again labor journalism; he named the new paper the *Radical*; he resumed also as labor organizer. Assisted now by two Irish immigrants, Michael Walsh and Thomas Devyr, he founded, still in New York, the National Reform Association. That association launched an entire series of newspapers. The *Workingmen's Advocate* was resurrected, and the *People's Rights* and *Young America* were commenced. A formula offered by the *Radical* in 1841 catches the emphasis of the whole National Reform Association enterprise. The paper reasoned that recourse to the public domain is the one security of workingmen—that free land could be made a form of justice, a compensation for lack of opportunity for employment. In the words of the paper: "If any man has a right on the earth, he has a right to land enough to raise a habitation on. If he has a *right to live*, he has a right to land enough for his subsistence. Deprive anyone of these rights, and you place him at the mercy of those who possess them."°

Thus we discover during the 1840s a new conjunction, a rounding out at last of social-democratic thinking. In a state where the colonial and early republican background had been a patrician order of society, labor voices were now being raised for freedom and equality. The several proposals we have considered, from Byllesby's and Skidmore's through Bryant's and Leggett's to those of George Henry Evans, were sometimes bizarre. Yet, in fact they only reapplied old ideas of natural rights. Manhood suffrage was the starting point. Insistence that labor unions have a right to organize was their new, creative phase of asserting civil rights. Equality of opportunity, in the twin proposals for schools and for lands, was the most advanced demand any of them made. Antimonopoly and antiprivilege with respect to credit and freedom of international trade were their principal proposals for economic legislation.

As we have seen and shall see in other chapters, New York's reformers of labor origin and prolabor purpose were not the most radical reformers of the time. Some who were more radical achieved greater short-run political or social success—the antislavery people and the communitarians did, for example. But the New Yorkers spoke more broadly. They spoke more like Thomas Jefferson, and more like social democrats of the future, than anyone else in America was doing. Theirs was a city base, not a plantation one; their complaints had the reality of known conditions. Perhaps oddly, their background was the busy aggressive society which had welcomed and frightened Tocqueville.

Colonial Philadelphia, beginning with the Quakers and developing during the period of Franklin and Woolman, had long preceded New York as the main American city of hope for workingmen. No other city had come earlier. Only during the 1860s would Bostonians began to make similar social promises, and not before the final quarter of the century would other cities, such as San Francisco and Cleveland, catch on. Yet during the age of Jackson, when mass democracy came alive, it seems prophetic that the most massive city was the one which entertained a group of labor and prolabor writers and program makers. In that city uniquely long-term democratic convictions were somewhat systematized; more than that, some of them were brought into the range of the national political discourse.

5 National Democracy as People Volunteering: Public Action and Public Thought

HAVING now reached the final section of our chapter on the convictions about democracy which were entertained during the age of

Jackson, we can defer no longer our appointment with the president. So far there has been no reason for haste. Before he was elected, Jackson contributed next to nothing to building the system of mass democracy; still less had he served in the planning or the designing. Rather, beginning with the campaigns of 1824 and 1828—or better, beginning with the preliminaries of those campaigns—instead of his molding the system the system first molded him. Thanks to partisans and promoters, people saw in him qualities of a hero as citizen, farmer, and soldier, at once leader and servant of the people. Only after he had accepted that role, different though it was from his past, was Andrew Jackson ready to render services to national democracy, its growth and character development, for which he is sometimes correctly and sometimes incorrectly remembered.

All during his first administration Jackson made three major decisions. Two of them, rotation in federal officeholding and the veto of the second Bank of the United States, were overtly democratic decisions, with ideals of freedom and equality involved. The third decision, President Jackson's complete resistance to nullification by South Carolina, has more the sound of nationalism than democracy. But as we shall see both values came into play: the large question between South Carolina and the United States government was how and by whom the will of the people should be done.

The first of the three decisions was required in 1829. As newly installed chief executive, Jackson had both the power and the occasion to make and to terminate administrative appointments; as leader of a renovated political party and as winner over an incumbent whose judgments were different from his own, he had reason to exercise that authority promptly and broadly. His unforgettable phrase, "To the victor belong the spoils," was only a crude blunt statement of the actual position he held. He picked new men as customs collectors, postmasters, marshals, and clerks; he removed previous appointees at will. Naturally, many were hurt or offended. The complaints they set up, that an officeholder's service improves with experience, and that to dismiss him for political reason does injustice, voiced considerable truth. On the other hand we know now that the actual rotation of 1829 and after was not drastic. In an expanded United States Jackson had more offices to fill than any predecessor. And both the Federalists of the 1790s and the Jeffersonians of 1800 and after had made appointments according to party and preference.

By the 1830s, moreover, short-term service in government had gathered a positive defense. Long-term officeholding at that time still sounded like monarchy and echoed the colonial experience. Before 1776 government "places" had been the gifts of the Crown or the lords proprietors. Jackson was not wrong when he said that office was still too often regarded as "a species of property," more "a means of promoting individual interests than . . . an instrument created solely for the service of the people." And reformers were beginning to demand that the duties of officeholders should be made "so plain and simple that men of intelligence may readily qualify themselves for their performance." Doubtless in saying such things Jackson realized that he was speaking from personal history—having been a judge without legal learning, a general without more than militia experience, a public man without education. He may or may not have known that his explanations corresponded with the opinion of Jeremy Bentham, the English philosopher and reformer, who favored rotation in office on principle. Jackson's own time, after the ideal and practice of the mercantilist state had declined and before the welfare state (or the modern military state) had arrived, was probably the most favorable time ever to argue for rapid rotation in government office.

At any rate the spoils system succeeded, at least in the short-term political sense. Whigs objected to Jackson's practice, but when they were elected to office, and later when the Republicans were, they performed in the same way. Rotation in office became an American habit, one of the most active parts of mass democracy, operating of course at all levels—in local, city, and state governments more numerously than in national. Indeed, after universal manhood suffrage in electing congressmen and the new party operations for choosing the president and vice-president, it was the chief element of the democratic process to impinge on Washington, and the main one to be nationalized, during the Jackson period.°

President Jackson's veto of the bill sponsored by Henry Clay in 1832, which would have extended for twenty years the life of the second Bank of the United States, came chronologically second among the three decisions we are considering and remains, of course, the most debated of anything he ever did in the name of the rights of the people. The bank was an institution altogether Hamiltonian in design, and Jackson had hated it for years. Generally speaking, it resembled Hamilton's own first Bank of the United States, but with the addition of branches which made its services available in all regions of the country. To be sure, the first bank had not disturbed Jackson when in Congress in 1797; and in 1816 the second bank had been approved and signed into existence by the country's number-two Jeffersonian, James Madison, as president. But now, after Clay aggressively made bank renewal a presidential-election issue, Jackson put the fight on constitutional grounds, much as Jefferson had fought Hamilton in 1791. He spoke, that is, as an emphatic strict-constructionist. "Some of the powers and privileges" assigned to the present bank, he said, were "unauthorized by the Constitution" and "dangerous to the liberties of the people." The mere legitimizing of such an institution, he reasoned, sustained a monopoly from which the owners were gainers, and to which all others were payers. The president appealed to natural rights. "Banking, like farming, manufacturing, or any other occupation or profession, is *a business*, the right to follow which is not originally derived from the laws." This led into a statement in favor of *laisser faire* in business and opportunity for all. "It is to be regretted that the rich and the powerful too often bend the acts of government to their selfish purposes. . . . When the laws undertake . . . to make the rich richer and the potent more powerful, the humble members of society—the farmers, mechanics, and laborers—who have neither the time nor the means of securing like favors to themselves have a right to complain of the injustice of their Government." Here the president uttered a kind of credo: "There are no necessary evils in government. Its evils exist only in its abuses. . . . In the act before me there seems to be a wide and unnecessary departure from these just principles."°

In the writings of today's historians President Jackson stands pretty well condemned for having vetoed a successful bank, useful to the economy, and for having pronounced on banking on other grounds than the economic merits of the case. More than that, adds the major historian of the problem, Bray Hammond, the Clay-Jackson dispute did not even rise to high level on the issue of constitutionality. The principals did not consider (what Vice-President Calhoun, for example, understood) that the Constitution supplies solid ground for a national banking act by assigning to Congress control of the nation's currency.° This criticism, adverse though it be to Jackson as an all-around statesman, helps us see the president's success within the grounds of debate he chose. For him the bank debate opened a way to build antimonopolism into the stance of the Democratic Party. Two years after the event he told the Senate what for him the other choice would have been: "If I had been ambitious, I should have sought an alliance with that powerful institution which even now aspires to no divided empire."°

Thus, when we view together the first and second of Jackson's strongest policy decisions, we discover resistance to privilege in the name of fair opportunity. Whether the battle was to remove old holders from office and appoint new or to eliminate a bank which had institutional advantages no other bank could touch, equally the enemy was power and privilege—power and privilege which had been created *de novo* by the national government during its forty years. Bringing down that enemy would restore such a *tabula rasa* of privilege as had followed 1776. Jackson's antimonopolism, like what we have seen in New York City, was built on popular *laisser faire*; his equalitarianism was simply a sentiment—not a general doctrine at all—which he applied (and also withheld) at will. None of this makes a philosophical speaker for democracy out of the earlier Jackson, but it does bring him to the threshold of democratic ideas with his own gift of vigor and relevance.

The third strong stand by the president, taken in 1832 and 1833, while very different in context, resembled the others in being defiant of power. Where on the bank issue Jackson fought his Kentucky rival for the presidency, later that year, when South Carolina nullified a United States tariff law, he fought his own vice-president (also a possible future president), John C. Calhoun. Where earlier he had attacked what he considered to be artificial and mistaken new concentrations of power, now he challenged one of the original states of the Union and tackled a leader of the country whom he had come to detest.

In this case the issue of principle was the most sensitive there is for a head of government—that is, the true location and reach of sovereign power. By 1832 Calhoun had become a stronger asserter of states' rights than any Virginian had been. In the Alien and Sedition Acts crisis Jeffersonians there and in Kentucky had pressed the two state legislatures to condemn federal statutes as contrary to fundamental law and natural law and so not worthy of honor. In the contest of 1832 and 1833, when the analogy with 1800 was perfectly patent, South Carolina followed a similar logic. But what had inspired Jefferson, Madison, and Taylor of Caroline had been a dedication to civil liberties, universal rights pertaining to all men; and though it is impossible to say how far they and their colleagues (in control of the two states) might have thrust if necessary, the facts are that the election of 1800 put their side in control of the nation, whose cause they loved and continued to serve. Calhoun and all the nullificationists reasoned and acted on a lower level. The law they defied was a national tariff. They argued that a state's constitutional rights were at issue, but in their case no one could say a natural right of man was. Their course took them direct to a decision for state-wide civil disobedience to national law. This was a long step psychologically if not logically farther than 1800—farther than Jefferson or Taylor had had to consider, and farther than the doctrinaire states' rights lawyers had gone in response to Chief Justice Marshall.

The background event which tells most about the course the president should have been expected to take is the toast he offered two years before the collision, the most famous toast in American history. The occasion was a Jefferson Day banquet in Washington; the practical object of the evening was to improve the alliance of southerners and westerners within the Democratic Party. The president and vice-president were the guests of honor; Judge Spencer Roane of Virginia was the toastmaster. Recently Senators Webster and Hayne had had their now classic debate over the nature of the Union; and the air of the banquet hall was as electric with feeling about states' rights doctrine as was the air of Congress. Probably every man in attendance knew that Calhoun had four years earlier been the author of the anonymously published *South Carolina Exposition*, the manifesto which was all but creed for Hayne. That paper clearly specified that protective tariffs are unconstitutional, and openly generalized that states may rightly nullify—that is, unilaterally refuse to obey—national laws which they on their own may decide to be unconstitutional. At the Jefferson Day dinner, the story is reasonably well supported, after five hours at table and twenty-four announced toasts, the president was called upon to give a voluntary one. With his incomparable presence, gazing at Calhoun, Jackson uttered a pledge as short as an oath: "Our *Federal Union*—It must be preserved."

Relishing those seven words, we may assume (now as earlier) that Andrew Jackson if asked would not have recognized the names of Jean Jacques Rousseau or Georg Wilhelm Friedrich Hegel; he may not have heard of George Bancroft. Yet in 1830 or in 1832 no long speech would have expressed more sharply than Jackson did the rising doctrine of national will. In South Carolina's actual deed of defiance, the challenge was built up over a period of months. First the governor, then the legislature, then a special convention each made a strong declaration. The collection of tariff duties was stopped. In Washington Congress reacted; passing a Force Act it gave the president power and means. Not even the states which adjoined South Carolina supported her, as they were expected to do. Preparing to move troops if need be, but relying first on a civilian posse, Jackson issued his own declaration: "Disunion by armed force is treason."

Before spring 1833 the episode tapered down. In terms of the economic issue behind the issue of sovereignty, South Carolina had by that time won. Henry Clay introduced a tariff which wiped out the offensive rates; from 1833 to the Civil War, though there were fluctuations, the American tariff went down practically to free-trade level. On the headlong issue of sovereignty, however, South Carolina had to retract. The ordinance of nullification was repealed; Calhoun and those who had acted on his doctrine were humiliated for the time being. By the same token Congress and the president gained. This once even ex-President John Quincy Adams and the great justices of the generation which was fading, John Marshall and Joseph Story, approved of Andrew Jackson.°

Yet Jackson's nationalism was different from theirs. Theirs varied: it was economic and jurisprudential, cultural and somewhat visionary; it waited on the future to become very much realized in life. The president's was more immediate, more social and more administrative: it was much more a people's nationalism. The voters had twice put Jackson in office; now he had several times spoken for them in the language of immediate power and preference. In his career the three spectacular decisions of 1829 to 1833 make a coherent whole: they brought the people into a felt relationship with their government in Washington.

Jackson drew out the people, but also the people drew him. Recent studies by scholars expert in literature and folklore have helped us visualize how Andrew Jackson in spite of himself became fire bringer to American democracy. First people brought fire to him. Little or no time passed after the Battle of New Orleans, according to John William Ward, before a legend was born about the victor, celebrating him as citizen soldier hardly second to General Washington. Jackson admirers said over and over, in speech and column and book, that controlling New Orleans in 1815 had fulfilled a goal of the War of Independence, to possess the Mississippi valley. They loved and dwelled on the thought that General Jackson, himself a farmer, had commanded farmers who rallied to defend their homeland in the style of the Roman republic. No one said this better than Nathaniel Claiborne of Virginia in 1819. The writer was the son of a family distinguished in the American Revolution; he himself helped Jefferson to get the University of Virginia started. At New Orleans "the most obscure soldier in the American lines saw that the hour of peril was at hand, and instead of shrinking from the horrors of the approaching tempest, seemed . . . to wait its coming with the composure and freshness that belongs to cultivated minds. This is not to be wondered at," according to Claiborne, for "they were almost to a man freeholders, or the sons of freeholders; they were not taken from the streets of dissipated and corrupt cities, or enlisted into the army to prevent their becoming victims to the shivering pangs of want."° Thus weaving the threads of old belief in the yeoman into new belief in the nation, popular writers of the age—the age which honored Daniel Boone as a seer and transformed John Chapman into Johnny Appleseed—portrayed Andrew Jackson as the Cincinnatus of the American republic.

This process of transubstantiation continued, indeed was stimulated, as the hero rose to the highest honor and power. "We do not claim for General Jackson the distinction of the academy," said an upstate New Yorker in 1828, "but we do claim for him those higher attributes which an active public life alone can teach, and which can never be acquired in the halls of a university—a knowledge of mankind . . . , an integrity never known to yield to interest or ambition, and a judgment unclouded by the visionary speculations of the academician." Add to such character casting the appreciation which a New York journalist ex-

pressed—fulsomely but in a mode that was romantic and commonplace—
after Jackson had served a full term as president and had hurled the
three defiances we have considered:

> There is a mysterious light which directs his intellect. . . . He arrives
> at conclusions with a rapidity which proves that his process is not
> through the tardy avenues of syllogism, nor over the beaten track of
> analysis, or the hackneyed walk of logical induction. For, whilst other
> minds, vigorous and cultivated, are pursuing these routes, he leaves
> them in the distance, and reaches his object in much less time, and
> with not less accuracy. His mind seems to be clogged by no forms,
> but goes with lightning's flash and illuminates its own pathway.°

Thus, seeing in their national leader gifts which might fall to any man,
contemporaries were fond of attributing to Jackson an unlimited
capacity to serve them. The joy with which his followers identified
both themselves and their president with the nation helps us comprehend ways in which Jackson's term in office was more than a demonstration of strength in the executive branch. Hero worship introduced,
as well as new excitement about liberty and equality, a new feeling of
fraternity among Americans.

There are many reasons which are familiar for considering the age
of Jackson to extend beyond his retirement from office and even
beyond the year of his death, 1845. The processes of mass participation
in the national government unfolded at every election. Jackson's
favored successor, Van Buren, operated party politics with an *expertise*
which Jackson himself never needed to acquire. When in 1840 and
1848 the Whig Party for the two times ever in its history succeeded in
winning the presidency, it did so by nominating army generals. After
Jackson the most conspicuous Democrat to be elected earlier than
Wilson, James K. Polk, was like the model a willful Tennessean, and
the very embodiment of the Manifest Destiny as well. Among all of
America's associationist movements no other was as nationwide and
prevailing, and few others were as passionate, as Manifest Destiny in the
1840s. At home in the Democratic Party, but not a stranger to Whigs
and friendly in many churches, Manifest Destiny as adopted by government suddenly made the United States a transcontinental, a Pacific, and
a Caribbean power. It increased the people's involvement, their identification with the national government, as perhaps nothing else had.

Indeed if the problem of this chapter were to examine the currents
in American society which achieved strength during the 1830s and
soon became very much stronger, we could hardly stop short of 1861,
when the ultimate nullification movement took hold. But our problem
is still the emergent, essential expression of mass democracy. And while
that problem leads direct to many others, we will understand the thing
itself better if we save for later discussion the expansions and the

vulgarizations. Short of much philosophy about it, along with incompleteness and inchoateness of expression everywhere, democracy in the age of Jackson did in fact display institutional strength, did produce insights and foresights, and did give lovely promises for the future. A few actors in politics did contribute practical thinking—the liberals who composed new state constitutions on both sides of the Appalachians, journalists and labor leaders in New York, the incomparable activist in the White House. But a true convergence of democratic thought and action would wait a full generation, until catastrophe demanded it and the president was Abraham Lincoln.

Ruins of a convent burned near Boston, 1834. Anticatholicism spread through a Protestant community stirred to self-consciousness by a new cycle of revivalism, open competition for converts.

Benjamin H. Latrobe's rendering of his aggressively classical design for the Catholic cathedral at Baltimore. Built in 1805 under liberal Bishop Carroll, it was important both as architecture and as an early sign of the Church's assimilation into the national culture.

This frontier revival, which occurred in Kentucky only a few years before the Baltimore cathedral was built, represents a contrasting innovation in religious life. Beginning under Presbyterian leadership about 1800, the Second Great Awakening introduced the days-long camp meeting, and Protestant worship attained a new emotionalism that stirred reform and conversion but was sometimes merely exciting.

Joseph Henry was probably the most gifted scientist in early nineteenth-century America. The nation's religious colleges were not generous to scientific work, and the government had done little for pure science, but he did his basic work on electromagnetism while a professor at Albany Academy and, later, Princeton and in 1846 became the first head of the Smithsonian Institution. Below is his design for an electromagnetic motor (1831), the first to lead to practical development.

John Bartram, friend of Franklin and founder (1728) of the first American botanical garden, stands between Harriot and Audubon as a precise observer and delineator of the New World's fauna and flora. The drawings at left were probably made by him about 1740, perhaps for a never-completed book by the Virginia historian William Byrd.

Spruce grouse

Purple grackle

John James Audubon (below) in a portrait by his sons Victor and John, painted in 1841 when he was 56; and (right) three samples from the extraordinary collection of 435 water colors published in London (1826–1838) as Birds of America. Audubon belongs in the lineage of science which stretches from Harriot through Bartram, Lewis, and Clarke to today's descriptions of the moon. French-educated, he knew the nature appreciation of Rousseau, Buffon, and Lamarck. From the age of twenty, he roamed Pennsylvania, Kentucky, Louisiana, and the Mississippi Valley, observing and painting birds, the plants they fed on. His work has a place in the history of conservation.

White crowned pigeon

The solitary-confinement prison at Cherry Hill near Philadelphia, a costly innovation in penology begun in 1829. Tocqueville studied such reform in America in 1831 and published this plan in a book on the subject. The prison's fortress-like appearance, the inmates' isolation (many went mad or died), may have influenced his adverse view of American individualism.

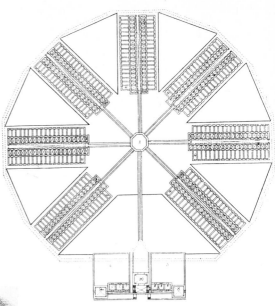

Immigrants (here, New York, 1854) in the 1850s—from Britain, Ireland, France, Germany, Scandinavia—faced both freedom and a hard future: Know Nothingism, social mobility often to a painful degree, and economic exploitation.

New York, Broadway, about 1860. Early America's metropolis had begun to be and to look like lower New York today: filled with people and activity, mixed prosperity and poverty, social mobility and frustration. Education was a leader among the many social problems raised by the explosive growth.

The inscriptions on this New York Building—School Society, 1805, and Board of Education, 1842—sum up the common schools of America's biggest city: first voluntary, then city-and-state-supported. Quite early, by the 1840s, the interchurch common schools became a public school system.

These two New York City common-school classrooms discover early mass-educational instruction in basic subjects. The marching and hand-clapping youngsters (above, 1828) are learning multiplication by rote; the class at right, in the 1840s, is in "phonetics." Common speech and understanding, common readiness to learn the business of citizenship, were the heart and soul of the public-education movement.

Brook Farm, an early paintin
by Josiah Wolcott. George an
Sophia Ripley organized som
of the Transcendentalists o
Fourierist communitarian prin
ciples, in a notable attempt in th
history of social thought to rec
oncile the values of ind
vidual and of community lif

Harmony, Indiana, was found
in 1814 by German religio
leader George Rapp on comm
nitarian and celibate lines.
1825 he sold its 2,000 acres
Robert Owen, a freethinki
Scottish industrialist and soc
theorist who named it New H
mony and made ambitious pla

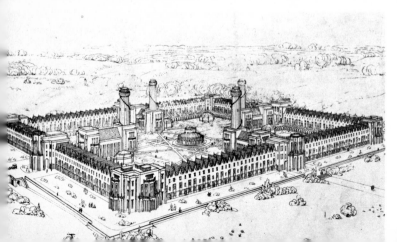

This striking architect's plan f
New Harmony embodied Ow
en's ideas about community o
ganization, labor, and educatio
Communitarian in theory, wi
an industrial base, it promis
unprecedented advantages
its 2,000 members. But a
ter two years, it faile

III–6

An 1867 view of Salt Lake City, the Temple and Tabernacle to right of center. If the Transcendentalists sought freedom from the materialism of cities, the Mormons, country folk, built their city beside a mountain. It was a bigger religious community than any other; and, though not socialist in name, in fact it was no less so than the Owenite and Fourierist experiments, ruled by Latter-Day Saints under divine revelation. Brigham Young's management appears everywhere.

Shakers, engraved in two characteristic activities, as portrayed by nineteenth-century artists: methodically planting corn (above) and worshiping (below). They were chronologically first among the communitarians of the republic, outdoing their German predecessors in completeness of monastic discipline. The ritual dances in the meetinghouses, without music, were probably the closest and most organized relationship the Shakers permitted between the two sexes.

Ralph Waldo Emerson (left) and Henry David Thoreau (in 1854, the year Walden *was published) affirmed the rightness of men's trusting men and nature. Neither systematizers nor activist reformers, they are ultimate figures of perfectionist thought in America, believing in personal renewal but placing little reliance on political democracy.*

In 1856 Emerson helped found the Saturday Club, whose monthly meetings brought together many of the finest minds of the day. Two years later the artist William J. Stillman led several of its members on a camping trip in the Adirondacks and recorded it—an act of nature appreciation—in this remarkable painting: James Russell Lowell is seventh from right, the great scientist Louis Agassiz fourth from left, and Emerson characteristically stands solitary and erect at the center.

CHAPTER XV

The Inculcation of Virtue: Education for a People's Republic

*All mankind are one great family, and the Almighty
Father of us all has made our common mother earth to
produce bountifully. . . . He gives all an equal right
to partake. . . . Equality comprizes everything that
is good; inequality everything that is evil. . . . Equality
is democracy. . . .*

*The cause of the people . . . is now progressing. And
it only needs for us to carry the first, the great
reform which we have proposed, the equal mental
and physical education of all, at the expense of all,
and our emancipation from the power of aristocracy
will be effectual and eternal. . . .*

*When the intellectual faculties of all shall be enlarged
by education, and the productive powers of all shall be
brought into action, a state of independency, comfort,
wealth, happiness, and benevolent feeling will ensue
of which we have not now the power to conceive.*

Frederick Robinson, Oration before the Trades'
Union of Boston and Vicinity, *July 4, 1834*

1   *Republican Education: Obligation of the States*

I N no other institution-building before the Civil War were Americans more ready to improve things than in their institutions of education. Hopes for the children and the future of the country came into focus together as plans were made for schools, colleges, and universities.

Around the turn of the eighteenth into the nineteenth century, planners were often touched by what became known as "republican education." They believed in what Franklin had pioneered and what Jefferson wanted Virginia to provide for her own, schools and colleges especially designed to train the young to be good producers and citizens and to prepare future leaders for public responsibility. Republican education was intended to have a wide appeal, and it did. The spirit of the Enlightenment was in it, but far from being antireligious it encouraged Christian patriotism and gained church support. It had an upper-class sound of experience with politics and perhaps on that account appealed to people and groups who were inexperienced. The declamatory words just quoted in the epigraph, though they sound like Thomas Jefferson, were actually spoken by a trade-union leader.

Of course only some of America's educational idealism sprang from so democratic a mood. To indicate another social background, Dutch Reformed schools using the Dutch language, German sectarian ones speaking German, English-speaking schools operated by Presbyterians and Episcopalians and by Quakers and Catholics—altogether a huge variety of parochial schools from Albany to Atlanta—testify to the determination of the older churches to enlarge in the republic the Christian tradition of education. Conspicuously in the South, where not a single state system of schools was established before the Civil War and only a few city systems were, a sizable share of the school-teaching was done by clergymen, as it had been during the colonial period. But, as the next section will indicate in detail, the churches generally were more involved with colleges than with schools. A side effect of the religious involvement shows up in the way the money was raised. Because American churches were voluntary, their schools like themselves had to depend on fees and donations, the gifts usually much less than endowment size. That is, in the degree to which American education was church controlled, it followed religion into reliance on freewill support, a growing extension into American society of the principle of voluntarism.

Yet there was a countercurrent. Republican education visualized the public interest, and believers in it like Jefferson thought that both nation and state should give aid. The institutional situation was favorable. Those states which as colonies had provided funds for schools continued to do so, acting in a variety of ways. The national government, besides having inherited the commitment made by the Land Ordinance of 1785 to allocate certain western domain lands to schools, soon was concerned about possibly establishing a university in Washington. To many national leaders this was a convincing need. The convention of 1787 had considered a university; and, although no special enabling clause had been put in the Constitution, President Washington early and late asked Congress to act. In his final state-of-the-union message he pleaded: "A primary object of such a national institution should be the education of our youth in the science of *government*. In a republic what species of knowledge can be more important. . . ?"° Regrettably Congress, where states' rights ideas were rising, omitted to act. A memorable thing about the national university idea, however, is the support that it had and kept. Not only the strong-government presidents, Washington and the two Adamses more than a quarter century apart, but also the Virginia Jeffersonians wanted the institution. Among the presidents, as we have seen, though not in Congress, the advancement of higher learning for the good of the republic overrode strict-constructionist doctrine.°

The university which was conceived but not born of national statesmanship is remarkable for both the ends and the means which were contemplated. The other nationally conceived educational enterprise of the early nineteenth century, the American Lyceum, was entirely different: its method was voluntary association, it was entirely decentralized, and it grandly succeeded. The lyceum movement emanated from Connecticut, the state which produced many enterprises of religious and literary, and especially educational, nationalism. Where Noah Webster with spellers and readers and dictionaries had long been and still was the principal nationalizer of the American language, Josiah Holbrook, the founder of the first lyceum in 1826, became the principal educator of adults of his generation in the nature of their national and general culture. Holbrook was trained at Yale (as Webster had been) under Benjamin Silliman, the main establisher of science in the college and the state. After a few years of schoolteaching, he began his entrepreneurship in education in a familiar style, by setting up an agricultural institute on his father's farm near New Haven. But when before forty he got down to his life's main business of operating lyceums, he did so manifestly influenced from overseas; and he soon emerged as American leader of a binational activity. Englishmen had made the start, and their work was known in America by way of their own *Mechanics' Magazine*; likewise the *Franklin Journal and American Magazine*, which after 1826 became the instrument of the Franklin Institute of Philadelphia, promoted the movement. The main intention at first was training craftsmen, giving them an understanding of the scientific or technological base on which their work depended.

That purpose was well timed for Connecticut, better than Holbrook's agricultural institute. It remained always important in cities like Philadelphia and Baltimore, where workingmen and philanthropists joined the movement in numbers. But as the lyceums proliferated across the country, meeting needs widely felt, additional goals took over. Holbrook's organization rapidly reached the Potomac and the Ohio, and soon it reached and crossed the Mississippi River as well. It rooted even in sparsely settled frontier areas, west and south. Suggestively and successfully, when he put out a prospectus to guide local people, he proposed a broad spectrum of lectures. In Barnard's *American Journal of Education*, Holbrook said that if lyceums "could once be started in our villages, and upon a general plan, they would increase with great rapidity, and do more for the general diffusion of knowledge, and for raising the moral and intellectual taste of our countrymen, than any other expedient which can possibly be devised." Thus, though not withdrawing "mutual instruction in the sciences," specifically mechanics, hydrostatics, pneumatics, chemistry, mineralogy, and botany, he offered cultural instruction and instruction for citizenship in rising ratio.

Taking to the people what Carl Bode, the historian of the movement, calls a "gospel," the American Lyceum (as the nationwide organization was duly named) offered instruction in aid of personal and community development. "Personal development" meant improving one's conversation and one's capacity for entertaining; America was no place for manners to correspond to the serving of "loaded decanters and sparkling glasses." Attending a lyceum, Holbrook said further, would improve one's reading and library habits. On the side of community development, the leader's claims were at least as promotional as descriptive, and they were large. Having a lyceum in a town brightened up the teaching in the schools; it brought in the older children; it led to the founding of libraries or even to producing local histories and maps and making collections of minerals. Holbrook's gospel was hardly less than a cultural rejuvenation, locality by locality.

Many of the things Holbrook proposed happened in American towns. But it would be hard to determine how much of the good work was owing to lyceums. Somewhat in the way national missionary boards of that time kept up with their constituent congregations and missions, and also in a way which suggests a modern concert bureau supplying artists to the provinces, the American Lyceum, maintaining a New York office, sent out speakers and literature. It benefited from the common-school movement of the 1830s; it served the movement also, as a kind of interstate lobby. Henry Barnard of Connecticut, the number-two school reformer, worked in the lyceum movement; Horace Mann lectured for it. In one series of lyceum lectures, which seems to have been representative when the movement was a dozen years old, among a total of nineteen offerings three had to do with educational work. From the others the following illustrate the scope and interest of the enterprise: Jared Sparks on "The Causes of the American Revolution," John Wayland on "The Progress of Democracy," C. H. Brewster on "The Sources of National Wealth," Samuel Osgood on "The Satanic School of Literature," Hubbard Winslow on "The Sun," and Simon Greenleaf on "The Legal Rights of Women." But the all-time star of the American Lyceum circuit was Ralph Waldo Emerson. Though Transcendentalism was never a popular doctrine and he himself was always somewhat aloof, Emerson made cold-weather tours across the Ohio and Mississippi valleys, to be well attended and honored. His lectures on nature and on historic and literary figures often turned out to be his forthcoming essays in preliminary form. Whatever help the Concord man's parcels of wisdom gave his listeners, they gave him opportunity to rough-hew his ideas and try out on willing ears the Americanisms he loved.°

The idea of having a national university and the gospel of the lyceum movement conformed, each in its own way, with the ideal of republican education. The one sought to provide leadership; the other served citizenship and the common culture. But neither the one nor the two together at all comprehended the utility which believers saw in the ideal. During the years, roughly from 1790 to 1830, between the appearance of the plan for a public university in Washington and the birth of the American Lyceum, many similarly inspired institutions were born. Partly because we are already familiar with the educational work of the philosopher statesmen of Virginia and Massachusetts, we turn immediately to Pennsylvania, where mid-eighteenth-century culture had especially flowered. During the two generations from Penn to Franklin, that colony had produced mainly denominational schools; only in the case of the College of Philadelphia had it taken a prominent lead. In the wake of national independence the state legislature transformed that institution twice. First it was reorganized as a state university; then, after only a few years and while retaining (somewhat fictionally) the name of the University of Pennsylvania, it was returned to private-trustee control. Thus Pennsylvania's specially strong habit of cultivating institutions apart from the state was honored again.

Yet with an effective leader in Dr. Benjamin Rush, a new institution, soon Dickinson College, became the most specific application of the principles of republican education in the Middle States. Rush was himself professor at the university, one who experienced its transformations firsthand; he had the authority of being the leading teaching and investigating physician in the country. Though an early member of the American Philosophical Society and a rationalist, he took an active role in church life. He passed in and out of Presbyterian, Episcopalian, and Universalist loyalties. A feeling that religious values and morals are necessary to citizenship seems to have impelled his work. In 1788, when he spoke prominently for a national university, he was already, as of four years earlier, the founder of the college in the outlying small town of Carlisle.

The institution was named for John Dickinson, the Pennsylvania statesman of Quaker background and scholarly gifts, a moderate Patriot in the Revolution. Thanks to Rush, Dickinson began as a Presbyterian college; Methodist control came later by bargain purchase. Under conditions which might seem to suggest parochialism, Dickinson College was launched fully in the contemporary spirit which Rush's own words render uncommonly well:

> While we inculcate these republican duties upon our pupil, we must not neglect, at the same time, to inspire him with republican principles. . . . I conceive that it is possible to combine power in such a way as not only to encrease the happiness but to promote the duration of republican forms of government far beyond the terms limited for them by history, or the common opinions of mankind. . . . Our business is to make them men, citizens, and Christians. . . . Above all let our youth be instructed in the history of the ancient republics, and the progress of liberty and tyranny in the different states of Europe.°

During the same end-of-century period, in the same spirit of serving the republic and keeping it Christian, and again like Dickinson in being placed upcountry in their states, a number of independent colleges were founded. Probably the Presbyterian ones in Virginia, Hampden-Sydney and Washington (later Washington and Lee), and the Presbyterian-and-Congregationalist Union College at Schenectady, New York, represent as well as Dickinson an identification of free church with free republic in aid of common goals. But the logic of republican education called for government support, and in certain doctrinaire voices it even resisted church help. Such logic fared best in states which had no colonial Christian college with prestige.

The first proponent of the general policy of having higher education state supported and state controlled, William Livingston, spoke in New York just before King's College was founded. As a member of a great landholding family, a lawyer and essayist, and as a member of the provincial legislature, he had every opportunity to be heard. A Yale graduate and a Presbyterian in a colony where Anglicans were accustomed to preference and wanted a church establishment, he was a natural leader of the opposition. Thus in 1753, in essays published in the New York *Independent Reflector*, Livingston developed the argument—now familiar, then novel in America—that institutions of higher learning which are state supported and supervised are the only kind which assure the people against excessive influence by powerful churches. Where a church has control, he said, "the system of the college is generally taken [by the students] for true, and the sole business is to defend it. . . . Every deviation from the beaten tract is a kind of literary heresy. . . . Hence that dogmatical turn and impatience of contradiction, so observable in the generality of academics. . . . Should our college, therefore, unhappily thro' our own bad policy, fall into the hand of any one religious sect . . . , 'tis easy to foresee, that Christians of all other denominations . . . will . . . rather conspire to oppose and oppress it." Accordingly Livingston proposed that New York's college be set up by a special act of the legislature, in order "that by this means that spirit of freedom . . . may be rendered impregnable to all attacks. While the government of our College is in the hands of the people, or their guardians, its design cannot be perverted. . . . For as we are split into so great a variety of opinions and professions; had each individual his share in the government of the academy, the jealousy of all parties combating each other, would inevitably produce a perfect freedom for each particular party."°

Of course, William Livingston did not succeed in 1753. King's College was launched the next year, its Anglicanism only a little circumscribed—on the curriculum side, memorably, by the provision that the Dutch Reformed could appoint a professor of divinity. After the Revolution the college, renamed Columbia, like the Philadelphia one was transformed by legislation into being (for a short time) a state institution. But more than in Columbia College or in any other teaching institution in the state, some realization of William Livingston's principles is to be found in the University of the State of New York, which the legislature provided in 1784. Uniquely in America, to this state university was assigned an exclusively supervisory function. Along lines already familiar from French education-reform thought—nearly a quarter century before Napoleon set up his Imperial University—in New York's Board of Regents was placed responsibility for approving or disapproving new (private) academies and colleges, that is, for seeing to it that education and republican government were kept compatible.

Differing from Dr. Rush on another point besides reliance on organized Christianity, William Livingston had contemplated bigness of institution, even monopolism, in New York higher education. While objecting to the control of King's College by the Church of England, he spoke as though one college would be the limit for a province, as in fact the American situation was at the time. But he thought that monopolism by government would be principled and correct. In some respects both men were prophetic. Dr. Rush was, in that during his own time, and until the later nineteenth century, most American institutions of higher learning would be small church colleges, and they would educate young men in loyalty to republican institutions in every part of the country. Livingston too was prophetic, in pleading the cause of state universities. While their great strength would be long coming, their origins belonged to the Enlightenment, and before 1800 their practical beginnings marked a new departure in Anglo-American culture.

The earliest actions of the kind were taken by the Southern States, which, all except Virginia, were *tabulae rasae* in higher education. The legislatures of Georgia and North Carolina acted during the 1780s, South Carolina in 1801. Institution building proved slow, but in 1798 North Carolina became the first state university in the country to grant degrees; the other two followed by 1805. Those three institutions struggled along, but neither the three together nor the three plus the state-aided College of William and Mary introduced any grand academic epoch in the South of the early republic. Representative figures are hard to be sure of, but during the 1830s less than two hundred students attended the University of North Carolina; the library there comprised about 3,600 volumes. The University of Georgia, though it was a place where Yale graduates liked to teach and often did, was even less sizable. Even after the opening of the University of Virginia, which was different, it seems clear that the first geographic cluster of American institutions to bear the name of "university" was thinly prepared to live up to their role. (No more was the one northern public institution of the same period, the University of Vermont, which opened at Burlington in 1800.)

The situation excluded stagnation, however. If only by reason of population growth, the state universities expanded. Simultaneously the evangelical churches planted colleges, in the South now as everywhere else. Those institutions expanded more rapidly than the universities; the Second Great Awakening especially caused them to proliferate. Among the new foundations which have proved durable, Baptist Wake Forest and Presbyterian Davidson in North Carolina, Methodist Randolph-Macon in Virginia, and Emory in Georgia were especially healthy in their growth, and occasionally one or another of them had more students than the university of their state. (Five hundred was a large student population in any institution, northern or southern.) Thus competed with and thus stimulated, the state universities probably doubled in total enrollment during the three decades before the Civil War. Buildings were built, not all so lovely as the ones at Charlottesville; sometimes a president or even a professor, conspicuously Francis Lieber, the political scientist at South Carolina, became a force in the community. By mid-century several foundations had been laid which would bear weight in the future—bricks and mortar on the campuses, and emotional foundations in state tradition.°

As we now come to the founding of public universities in the future heartland, then the region of the Old Northwest, hindsight makes it hard not to magnify events. Today those six states are the only region in the country where every state has one or more of the nation's great universities, maintained by the state. Beginning at the beginning, of course the ordinances of the 1780s, programing freedom and farms and schools for the region, were the political and institutional background for educational, as for all democratic, development. But neither the seer of Monticello nor the Congress in Philadelphia made or directly affected the decision to start the state universities. The constitutional conventions and the state legislatures did that on their own and did so with near to complete regularity.

To a degree which might possibly be measured some day by an historian willing to count dozens of legislative votes and to search out the records of hundreds of voters, the Puritan tradition entered the story. While in terms of its political and social institutions the Old Northwest represents the goals of revolutionary Virginia projected into new country, in terms of early population and culture the settlement of at least the northern half of the states between the Ohio and the Great Lakes, and the settlement of most of the three more northerly states of the region, in great part flowed from New England. Yankees often predominated in politics. In religion and education, they kept their habit—rather, their enthusiasm—for building congregations, schools, and colleges, local institutions, wherever they went.

The New England migration was thus both a force for educational voluntarism and a force for state action. One state, the third in the region to enter the Union, represents the voluntarism at fullest degree; alone among its five neighbors, Illinois delayed for many years the founding of a state university. But before the Civil War about twenty church colleges appeared. Illinois College, founded in 1830 at Jacksonville by missionary-minded Yale graduates, and Knox College at Galesburg, a Presbyterian institution of Second Great Awakening origins, illustrate the trend. On the side of state action, Ohio, the first state in the region to enter the Union, led off in the way which would become typical of the region. Just before statehood, the territorial government created the publicly supported university at Athens; just afterward the legislature chartered another state university, at Oxford. The universities of Michigan and Minnesota were launched some years ahead of statehood. And, as we noticed in the previous chapter, Indiana University and the University of Wisconsin were brought to birth by constitutional provision at the same instant as the states.

No more than those in the South did the new universities of the Old Northwest as a cluster reach academic distinction before the Civil War, or indeed before the end of the century. Yet, as in the South, one exception to meagerness occurred: the territorial Catholoepistemiad of Michigania which became the University of Michigan. Appropriately at that institution the principal planner, Augustus B. Woodward, who was a territorial judge and an amateur scientist, came up with schemes which are reminiscent of Jefferson's plans for Charlottesville. He proposed *didaxia* and *didactors* (specialized professorships and professors) across a broad spectrum which was bright on the side of the sciences. In some degree practice corresponded with hope at Ann Arbor. Before the Civil War one president, Lewis Henry Tappan, who was fired by the German university idea and had written a book on it (*University Education*), proposed research in addition to teaching by the faculty, graduate work as well as undergraduate for students who were ready. In a short and exciting administration he improved the library; he made strong appointments in medicine and other sciences and the superb choice of Andrew Dickson White for a chair in history and literature. He established the Detroit Observatory. Probably, as was charged against him, there was more that was Prussian than republican or democratic about his methods. Yet he was placing before the people of Michigan, and before women students as well as men, grand opportunities and freedom to develop their minds as they would. He brought the young university to grapple with the burden which so far only the University of Virginia had broadly assumed.° This was the task—which Harvard and other colleges were only beginning to undertake—of training the youth of the land for many varieties of personal and community growth.

What the universities accomplished despite their frailties affected the states as well as themselves. Thus the two public institutions which stand out were displaying and were enlarging a new responsibility of government in America—a free offering of higher learning in variety, to the young of the state in the interest of the state.

2   *Christian Nurture of Society:*
Obligation of the Colleges

WHILE every phase of education in the republic called for larger and larger provision for the burgeoning population, republican education as a set of principles was applied from the outset to the few rather than the many, to higher education for future leaders rather than to the training of ordinary citizens. On the side of the state institutions, moreover, as the beginnings we have seen at Charlottesville and Ann Arbor indicate, the curricula sought to cultivate high secular skills. At Mr. Jefferson's university, law, government, and history were emphasized as preparation for a public career; at President Tappan's, science was conceived as especially right for young men who would improve their state and community.

While the Christian colleges responded to the principles of republican education as affirmatively as the state universities, they were more concerned to present the country with leaders of religious mind and character than with secular experts. As George Sidney Camp's *Democracy* illustrated in the last chapter, a Protestant layman of the age of Jackson could defend political democracy on principle, could equate it with historical republicanism, even discover in it a fulfillment of religion. Indeed the idea of a Christian commonwealth was as old in America as Puritanism; and the home missionary movement of the nineteenth century renewed on a grand scale the ideal of the Puritan theocrats, that the saved of Christ should control society. Probably the Charles Grandison Finney period of the Second Great Awakening—the time of Jackson in the White House too—was the time in all American history when the churches expected most confidently to dominate national affairs. Under such auspices the Christian colleges of the period came readily to believe that of all institutions they were called on to guide both individuals and society.

The character of the American colleges, as it matured during their period of expansion, will appear the more clearly if, besides remembering their lineage back to 1636 and earlier, we recall their subsequent pattern of development. Several of the colleges founded shortly before the Revolution—certainly the ones we know as Princeton, Columbia, and Pennsylvania—had been educational innovators from the beginning. Although all three suffered setbacks, sometimes traceable to the War of Independence, sometimes to state politics or shortages of church or trustee support, all three managed as Harvard and Yale did to grow in size and in deed. While they required a century or more (until about 1900) to become true universities, they achieved academic distinction along the way—at Princeton, in early success in philosophy and in helping frontier colleges to birth; at Columbia, in economic, legal, and political studies; at Pennsylvania, in science, especially medicine. With occasional exceptions the colleges which were founded after the Revolution developed less thrust. The two of that generation which clearly influenced other institutions, Williams and Union, were both identified with missionary enterprise and westward expansion and served those causes greatly. Union, like its alma mater, Yale, went early into science and engineering, an unusual development in the church colleges. But the usual story is general service rendered to an unspecialized local clientele, on the whole more like that of a large boarding school than that of a small university. Indeed, no college founded since the Revolution has grown in an institutional way to compare with any of six of the colonial colleges—Harvard, Yale, Princeton, Columbia, Pennsylvania, and Brown.° Or, making our comparisons with the motherland of all early American institutions, around 1830 England had just two degree-granting institutions, the same as when Harvard was founded. But the United States, with a population which at thirteen million had still not caught up with England, had about 150 such institutions. By 1850 the number had risen to 250 or so.°

Notwithstanding the costliness of this proliferation, and the high bankruptcy and death rate among young colleges, the ever impressive thing is the durable trail of learning they opened across the continent. Not only is there a familiar roster of colleges of church origin which have succeeded brilliantly in baccalaureate (and sometimes master-of-arts) training, there is also a sizable list of theological seminaries. Tracing these institutions on the map, one discovers first a northerly band, east to west, made up mainly of institutions planted from the Congregationalist seedbeds at New Haven and Andover. Bowdoin and Williams came first during the 1790s; soon Amherst, Middlebury, and Hartford Seminary extended the dispersion in New England. Only a little later but far away in the Old Northwest, Western Reserve, Oberlin, Beloit, and Grinnell were all established before mid-century. During the next twenty-five years Colorado College and the college on San Francisco Bay (which the state legislature soon changed into the

University of California) represented the perseverance of the Congregationalists. Their principle of decentralization, or rather their capacity to honor successfully both decentralization and learning, thus established a stellar chain of colleges all the way from Brunswick, Maine, to Claremont in southern California.

A middle-to-southerly band of colleges and seminaries was begun by Presbyterians and during the first half of the nineteenth century was built by joint action of Presbyterians and Congregationalists under the Plan of Union. We are familiar with the Presbyterian start southwest from Princeton before the Revolution was over. It assisted Dickinson in Pennsylvania and several colleges in Virginia and Kentucky. Beyond Virginia, evangelical colleges and state universities were more alike than their origins would suggest. The early University of Georgia except for state support was hardly different from a small church college; the University of Tennessee was built on the foundation of Blount College. In that region—that is, along the southern edge of college expansion—the Presbyterians acted only a little ahead of the more numerous churches of less academic background, the Methodists and the Baptists. In Georgia during the 1840s, the Presbyterian college, Oglethorpe, and the Methodist one, Emory, were both about the size of the state university, each with about two hundred students.

The combined Calvinist strength of Presbyterians and Congregationalists under the Plan of Union had its greatest effect on education across the state of New York and along the Ohio valley. Union Seminary in New York City and Lane in Cincinnati were the principal theological foundations which represent the union; and Union College in Schnectady and New York University in the city were its products as well. In the Old Northwest, Wooster College in Ohio and Knox College in Illinois have been especially successful among many Presbyterian institutions. Thinking of Calvinist-church leadership in founding the colleges of the nineteenth century, one remembers how Congregational separatism provided the colonies with their main seventeenth-century lesson in independence from English institutions, and how Presbyterianism—by way of its presbyteries, synods, and convention—set America its one object lesson in federalism prior to the Confederation. Against that background of leadership the success in the college movement that the two churches had together seems to have brought to climax their special services to the republic.

Meanwhile other denominations began to catch on widely. Among those as old as the Presbyterians and Congregationalists, but less numerous and less evangelical, the Episcopalians and Quakers founded their colleges mainly along a middle band of westward extension. The Episcopalians placed their first seminary in Alexandria, in the home state of their church near Washington; and they established Trinity, their first college of the republican epoch, in Hartford near where high Anglicans had once upset Yale College Puritans. Hobart College in western New York, and Kenyon in Ohio, more a seminary than a college, followed soon, a challenge to Calvinists; the Episcopal Church's University of the South (called Sewanee), which would import ideas and methods from Oxford, was founded shortly before the Civil War. The Quakers, who true to their tradition did not want seminaries, in the same spirit were slow to found colleges. Yet they began in the Old Northwest with Earlham College; Haverford College, just outside Philadelphia, came second—both institutions near mid-century. Not until after the Civil War did Swarthmore College, with a Quaker name from seventeenth-century England, and Whittier College, with a nineteenth-century one from New England, begin their vigorous lives. Colleges by and for Friends indicate both a practicalizing in Quakerism and a pietizing (as different from evangelizing) in American colleges.

Methodists and Baptists began to participate largely in the college movement during the revivalism of the 1820s and 1830s. Those churches, because they were short on academic experience, had to improvise if they were to serve their very large memberships. As we have already noted, college bankruptcy and closure occurred altogether too frequently. If the Methodists did somewhat better than the Baptists, the reason was probably their centralized church government. Of the several colleges named "Wesleyan," the one in Connecticut had to compete with nearby Trinity and not-very-distant Amherst and Williams, and it did well. In the South, besides Randolph-Macon and Emory, the Trinity College in North Carolina, which would be transformed into Duke University, and also Vanderbilt (soon after the Civil War) began under Methodist auspices. North of the Ohio, Methodists founded Northwestern University near Chicago and Hamline College in St. Paul about mid-century, some years before the universities of their respective states. Methodists acted ahead of all other churches on the Pacific coast. Their College of the Pacific on lower San Francisco Bay and Willamette University in Oregon were established respectively in 1851 and 1853.

The Baptists, whose early disadvantages for organizing colleges included theological discordancies and very little gift for ironing them out, nevertheless gathered enough unity of purpose to found a sizable number of Middle State institutions. Colgate University in upstate New York, Bucknell in Pennsylvania, and Denison in Ohio were all established during the Jackson period, universities in name but colleges in fact and intention. The Baptists made a habit of starting small colleges in large or growing cities like Washington, Rochester, and Chicago.

As for the academic character of the Christian colleges, oddly Yale—although that institution had just passed through a half century of growth in science in a state and region which lacked state universities—became the model. In 1817 the New Haven college was put on a somewhat changed course by a new president, the Reverend Jeremiah Day. Like all his predecessors in the office, Day was a Congregationalist minister—indeed, Andover tried to draw him away to head the seminary. Many strengths made him a natural successor to the more liberal Ezra Stiles and the more dynamic Timothy Dwight. He wrote theology in the Jonathan Edwards sequence; his book, *The Self-Determining Power of the Will*, was his principal contribution to the field. He wrote also on algebra, trigonometry, and navigation. As president he taught mental and moral philosophy to upperclassmen. But in the history of Yale and the history of the college movement, President Day is remembered as part author and executor in his own institution of a famous report on curriculum. It confirmed values and set forth arguments which would be followed at Yale and elsewhere for a century to come.

This Yale report, which was published in 1828, freely acknowledged that universities in Europe were departing from traditions honored since the Middle Ages. In its own words, "Whole sciences have, for the first time, been introduced; chemistry, mineralogy, geology, political economy, etc." It pleaded, on the other hand, that the old studies were more important.

> As in our primary schools, reading, writing, and arithmetic are taught to all, however different their prospects; so in a college, all should be instructed in those branches of knowledge, of which no one destined to the higher walks of life ought to be ignorant. . . . While an academy teaches a little of every thing, the college, by directing its efforts to one uniform course, aims at doing its work with greater precision. . . . It must be obvious to the most cursory observer, that the classics afford materials to exercise talent of every degree, from the first opening of the youthful intellect to the period of its highest maturity. . . . Familiarity with the Greek and Roman writers is especially adapted to form the taste, and to discipline the mind, both in thought and diction, to the relish of what is elevated, chaste, and simple. . . .

Any readers who might think that modern languages would serve as well as ancient were advised to "let a page of Voltaire be compared with a page of Tacitus."°

Paradoxical though it seems, the Yale plea to sustain the old Latin-and-Greek-and-philosophy curriculum for a nation of farmers and businessmen had a certain educational practicability about it over and above the principles it argued. It is hard to estimate what proportion of the college students of the time intended to enter one of the learned professions, but probably within that element the number who ultimately wanted a career in law—or law and politics—was the largest.

Of course a B.A. degree was no prerequisite then for legal training, whether in law school or in law office—Abraham Lincoln is only the most historic illustration of the great majority who lacked a degree. But all lawyers needed some Latin, and the classical curriculum which trained men in logic and rhetoric was desirable for them too. Many took it on the way to professional study. But of course the founders and leaders of church colleges valued more highly than any others the students who wished to be ministers. For them the classical curriculum offered the traditional work: Latin, Greek, and sometimes other Bible languages, and Christian philosophy. Here the college presidents and the professors of divinity and philosophy had a vested interest: what they taught was what their most cherished students needed. Their own services were available; and to meet the demand of an academic market in short supply it was not too hard to train up new minister professors. While to twentieth-century minds their studies may seem archaic, general and unspecific preparation even for the cure of souls, to themselves the legacy they transmitted was on that account more precious, more to the citizens' ultimate need, than anything else.

The traditionalism of the colleges sometimes raised annoyance within. Occasionally faculty or students demanded such modernizations as were occurring in Europe. Besides Harvard and Virginia, reformism appeared at institutions which (though generally conforming) were somewhat apart from evangelical contexts and ways. President James Marsh of the University of Vermont and President Philip Lindsey of the University of Nashville (the future George Peabody College) sought, in the first case, to allow freedom to students to choose their own studies, and in the second to introduce vocational and professional training. Change from the classical curriculum occurred more often, however, as erosion than as reconstruction. For example, during the 1820s, in two upstate New York church colleges, Union and Hobart, a "parallel curriculum," alternative to the classical one, was offered to students; before long Hampden-Sydney, Columbia College, and Wesleyan University did the same. The essential change was a degree without Greek and Latin; this was a reform which spread. Yet sometimes it met successful opposition, for instance from the Amherst faculty. One suspects that in the ancient languages a great deal of backsliding, by faculty men and students alike, often reduced the need for deliberative change.°

Perhaps no other characteristic of the colleges better exemplifies the over-all adjectives our century applies to them, "conservative" and "traditional," than their architectural appearance. But plainly it was not an American tradition which the buildings, especially those of the second and third quarters of the nineteenth century, maintained. While before that time the colleges and universities were built generally on the "Federal period" variation of late Renaissance style which before 1776 we call "Georgian" or "colonial," thereafter academic fashion shifted to neomedieval. In terms of the international history of architecture this was part of the Gothic revival; in terms of academic history it corresponds nicely to the effort being made to keep alive the values and habits of the trivium and the quadrivium. While the word *monastic* would overstate the American collegiate style of building, at least one stone hall with a tower, usually the chapel, and a quadrangle, became a kind of norm. One can view it today in any number of places —for instance, in Burlington, Vermont; in Galesburg, Illinois; in Sewanee, Tennessee—and, if we follow American missionaries overseas to a land where crusaders put up Gothic buildings half a millennium earlier, in Beirut, Lebanon. It all seems strangely appropriate. On the middle-western frontier and in the Middle East alike, American evangelicals chose to create academic seclusion. The American college campus was intended to be a romantic, separated place, a place to prepare men not to yield too much their Christianity when they entered the everyday world.

But we must not narrow our vision too exclusively. Besides "conservative" and "traditional," such adjectives as "enterprising" and "particularist" apply to the church colleges. The records are full of what presidents and others had to say about the superiorities of their own institutions. "There is not a Methodist in America with sufficient learning to fill a professor's chair if it were tendered him," proclaimed one Presbyterian in the Indiana legislature. "Shall it be said that six thousand Presbyterians built a college at Midway and that forty thousand Baptists were unable to build [a college here] at Washington?" chided a Georgia Baptist, referring to town locations in his state.° If attitudes of this kind were uncharitable, one must recognize as well that they came from churchmen who were giving money on a scale that the state governments were not trying to match, in a field which the national government refused to enter, all to raise up citizens and leaders.

As had been true since Harvard was young under Henry Dunster, during the nineteenth century the president was the special genius of the American college. Once the trustees launched the enterprise, how an institution met its environment, whether it tried innovation or relied on tradition, depended peculiarly on him. He held a most interesting and responsible job. He admitted students and dismissed them; he preached and lectured and advised; he planned and executed new buildings; he hired and fired members of the faculty; he raised funds; he became almost ex officio an important citizen, and was likely to be drawn into affairs. Strong presidents fitted the job to themselves. It could be made more or less professorial, more or less administrative, and more or less a work of external relations. It offered rewards of appreciation and honor which few other callings could match. Many a president became beloved, even legendary, in his community: Mark Hopkins of Williams and Francis Wayland of Brown are cases in point. They may have been too wise to take adulation seriously. But one imagines that their ears were human and did not mind hearing what students said, that they were the best men in the world.°

American college lore runs to men and places, but it would be a warped account which failed to speak of the special brand of Christianity the colleges mainly conveyed. There was a chapel service daily, and attendance was required. For the student the course in philosophy, which he took usually during senior year under the minister president but sometimes under a minister professor, was the culmination of the college's service to him. The purpose of the course was to reconcile intellectually what his religion should reconcile spiritually, the good and the evil he was aware of. Everyday life made him acquainted with the hardness and aggressiveness, the evil, of economic existence; he could not help knowing also the boundless, millennial hopes entertained by his culture. Perhaps from his earlier reading in or out of college, certainly in the work of the senior course, he somewhat sensed that economists and other scholars failed to reconcile those opposites. Adam Smith, who explained in the *Wealth of Nations* what economic conditions govern men, and yet said in the *Theory of Moral Sentiments* that altruism can rule, represented that failure. Students must sometimes have known of his case. At any rate the intention of the philosophy course was to eliminate this kind of inconsistency.

In general the procedure was a Socratic demonstration that Christ's law can be man's law. The expectations available to young Christians —based on republican government here and now, and on the millennium either waiting to begin or already begun—were wonderfully fair. (Certain thrilling phrases of the future—Harriet Beecher Stowe's "Mine eyes have seen the glory" sung during the 1860s, and Martin Luther King's "I have been to the mountain" uttered a century later—would carry that kind of hope far outside college circles.) The course often carried the old title, "Moral Philosophy," but some colleges used another title or offered additional ones, such as "Mental Philosophy" or (following the English theologian William Paley) "Evidences of Christianity." The characteristic content was a blending of social studies: history, politics, economics, and social ethics. If the course were in mental philosophy or contained that field, the core subject matter was introspective psychology. Working from Locke, or the Scottish common-sense philosophers or other moral intuitionists, the problem was the "faculties" of the mind. With the aid of texts, but assisted principally by the president or professor in class, students examined their own thought processes concerning behavior—how they best apprehended, assimilated, and decided on questions which had to be acted on. As in the history of Jonathan Edwards and his successors and revisers so famously, the classroom problem returned ever to free will. How should a Christian conceive his freedom? What governs a man, evil or good?

While, as we saw three chapters back, even at the centers of Calvinist orthodoxy nineteenth-century Protestant thought stopped short of the old conviction of total depravity, with exceptions it retained a lively sense of the evil in man. Thus the final problem the minister president or minister professor had to help his students resolve was how to think and act in spite of all like children of God. If he were a Congregationalist or Presbyterian, or by some other route was sympathetic with the main latter-day Edwardsian answer, he had a noble ideal and formula, "disinterested benevolence," with which to respond and explain. Human souls, this refinement of the New England theology taught, are made capable of acting unselfishly, or disinterestedly, according to the great commandment. So acting, they do rise above their own lower impulses, this side of heaven, and do escape the compulsions which press on all men from society. Thus, disinterested benevolence was a hopeful doctrine and a moderate one, which offered the orthodox fresh meaning for Christian conversion. But even if the college teacher of the course in moral or mental philosophy, say a Methodist one, had been reared outside the Calvinist tradition or found Edwardsian argument overdone and distasteful, he could hardly avoid in that era a similar line of conviction. American colleges were so oriented, so built on assumptions of altruism and benevolence, that freedom in Christ to follow Him in serving men was the only meaning of life they had to offer.°

We are able to view American collegiate moral philosophy a little from the inside, not because specialists have discovered and explored a great number of syllabi or students' notes but because the presidents and professors, living in America's first great age of textbook writing, themselves somehow found time to produce great textbooks. Like the better remembered writers on law—Kent, Story, and others—they had a clear service to render. They were surrounded, as well as by a mobile, aggressive, economic society, by mystics and revelationists who to their minds greatly threatened Christian reasonableness. That is, as we shall see in the next chapter, from Brook Farm to Salt Lake City the United States was being dotted with individuals and groups who, if their ideas were ever broadly applied, would upset the social order. By any such standards, academic philosophy naturally sought a moderating course.

So the ministers as presidents and professors poured out their philosophy courses as books to all who would read.° Probably *The Ele-*

ments of Moral Science, by President Francis Wayland of Brown, is as good and representative a choice as any for quotation. It came from a college not of the straight-line Puritan tradition. The writer was a man in whom the generosities of belief and action readily arose. As Christian he supported, though with some criticism, the overseas missionary movement. As a public man, a Jeffersonian Democrat in New England, he assisted many educational reforms. He favored a national university; he promoted a public-school system for Rhode Island. With great success he led his own college in curricular reform: he introduced studies in history and economics, and in sciences and modern languages. He was one of the truly great college presidents.

To the point of presenting college work in moral science as a convergence of social study with Christian commitment, Francis Wayland had the following to say in his *Elements*:

> We frequently cannot requite our actual benefactors, but we may always benefit others less happy than ourselves; and thus, in a more valuable manner, promote the welfare of the whole race to which we belong. . . . This being manifestly an obligation imposed upon us by God, it cannot be affected by any of the actions of men; that is, we are bound by the law of benevolence, irrespective of the character of the recipient. It matters not though he be ungrateful or wicked or injurious. . . . In all cases we are bound to govern ourselves, not by the treatment we have received at his hands, but according to the law by which God has directed our intercourse with him to be governed.°

3 Preparation for Citizenship: Obligation of the Common Schools

IN 1954 a Jesuit scholar, Father Francis X. Curran, examined the rise of public schools in America from a point of view natural to a priest. To him the history of the common-school movement of the 1830s and after revealed an amazing "surrender" by church to state, a concession "unique in the history of Christendom." Not at a time of weakness, Father Curran observed, but while they were strong, Protestant Americans quietly conceded to state and local governments a precious duty the Christian churches had always exercised, that of training their children for life in the world. Instead of surrendering why did they not, the author inquired, keep and develop their control of primary and secondary education? Why did they not spread across America a network of congregational and denominational or interdenominational schools?°

As all who have attended public schools know firsthand, the suppositions on which the schools operate, though not opposed, are removed from Christianity. The children are led into the auditorium to salute the flag en masse, but there is no saying of prayers. The schools suppose that a people's government requires minds which are prepared for citizenship and are ready for work and expression. As is almost equally common knowledge, the first public-school systems were created, with a good deal of philosophy and policy thinking in the creating, during and of the first age of mass democracy. The prime leaders of the movement were Horace Mann and Henry Barnard of New England, but others such as Calvin Stowe of Ohio and DeWitt Clinton of New York rendered services which also were essential. Their principles were essentially the same as those of the republican education movement. Only where the generation of Thomas Jefferson and Benjamin Rush thought first (but not exclusively) of training intellects for public leadership, they thought mainly of the good citizenship of the common man. Where their movement succeeded in the legislatures, the states accepted a responsibility administratively and socially larger than any of the commitments by the colonies during the mercantilist age. Not even the Puritan colonies with their church-state alliances and school-and-college commitments had ever operated on so grand a scale.

Of course questions like Father Curran's—why such an assignment should have been made to government by a free and church-loving people—become the more pointed when considered against the background of voluntarism in higher education. Not forgetting their financial troubles, the colleges were the energetic, dominant institutions of higher education from before the Revolution until after the Civil War; and, allowing for their usual traditionalism, they did sometimes venture radical ways, as when Oberlin admitted women and Negroes. Unaffected by government controls or favors, the colleges exercised considerable freedom simply by being themselves, religiously intense here and less so there, Edwardsian in one place and anti-Calvinist in another. Did or did not the same Christian and moral particularities apply also to primary and secondary education?

As we shall illustrate presently, they applied with force. But other considerations applied simultaneously—practical political and financial considerations. When during the 1830s the public-school movement began to succeed, it was the first successful thrust since the one made by Massachusetts, Connecticut, and New Hampshire, two centuries earlier, to assure primary education for all and to make secondary education widely available. And it began in the same old Puritan region. It did not appear to contemporaries, as it now does to us, to be the beginning of an educational revolution. It was more like toning up, or installing a set of improvements, in the township schools. It made no effort to displace church education. Although in the Jackson period there began to be truth in the formulas which are conventional wisdom today, that church schools characterize older rather than newer communities and that they are attended by the rich, not the poor, those formulas are far from comprehending the situation. During and after the middle third of the nineteenth century, radical denominations, often in westward locations—for instance, the Mormons and the Adventists—set up schools of their own. So have immigrant groups, especially German groups in Wisconsin and in such cities as Chicago and Baltimore. And of course the greatest proliferation ever of parochial schools would follow on, and would be set up by and for, the Roman Catholics of mid-century and later arrival, who were usually impoverished people.

In the period which concerns us, beginning even a little earlier than the public-school legislation, the Sunday-school movement testifies to new Protestant energy entering the mixed economy of education. The case history of a Congregationalist leader, Frederick Packard, tells much of the story. Packard was the son of the minister in a small town in Massachusetts; educated at Harvard, he read law in a Northampton office and as a young man was elected to the state legislature; he worked as a journalist as well as a lawyer. But he did not find his true career until 1827, when he was thirty-four and accepted what in most men would have been an unremarkable assignment, the superintendency of the Sunday school of his own congregation, the First Church of Springfield. Almost at once he was called to Philadelphia to serve as secretary of the American Sunday School Union, a nationwide organization which was part of the Congregationalist and Presbyterian union. During four decades there he held a kind of national pulpit of the written word for children. He himself wrote more than forty books; his office edited and issued more than fifty times that number. (There was an Episcopalian Sunday-school publishing house in the same city.)

Besides the strictly educational work, Packard at head and center of the Sunday-school movement had many demands made on his talent for politics. Some of his people were capable of resisting public-school legislation headlong. For instance in 1845 members of the Presbyterian Synod of New Jersey, century-old home of the New Sides spirit, opposed public-school bills before the state legislature on the ground that "the race of irreligious and infidel youth, such as may be expected to issue from public schools, *deteriorating more and more*, with the revolving years will not be fit to sustain our free [voluntary] institutions." This kind of "religious intransigence," observes Rush Welter, created a greater obstruction to state-government action than did the parsimony of taxpayers. But while Packard himself could be critical, he recognized that Sunday schools are by nature dependent on weekday schools. Old Massachusetts man that he was, he rather sought state help for Sunday schools than church defiance of public ones. But he pushed dangerously far when he asked Massachusetts authorities to place libraries of Sunday-school books in the public schools. Full constitutional separation of church from state was about fifteen years old in Massachusetts at the time; the principle seems not to have deterred him. When the authorities refused his request he started a long campaign of criticism and counterreform against Horace Mann as secretary of the Massachusetts Board of Education. It had little effect. But the resistance indicates that even those who belonged to the culture which produced the public-school movement sometimes had serious misgivings. Their interest in religious training for the children was not easily reconciled.°

But this draws only from the negative side. Both the public-school movement, which was a demand for a public service from government, and the child-development movement, which was a related but different phenomenon, shared—as did the Sunday schools and the lyceums—in the age's restless and boundless propensity for reform. As seems just, the Old Northwest was the region where the earliest start was made in public-school legislation. Ohio, which was the first state there to enter the Union and which had founded two state universities, in 1836 became the first state of all to try to systematize its schools. The representative and leading figure, Professor Calvin Stowe of Lane Seminary, belonged completely to the evangelical movement. Born in Massachusetts into a family of seventeenth-century Puritan origins, he was educated at Bowdoin College and Andover Seminary, and he taught for a while at Dartmouth. In Ohio he married his president's daughter, Harriet Beecher, who was already a writer and already thinking about slavery. Thus when he was appointed state commissioner to investigate the condition of education, the state government placed crucial authority in entirely orthodox Congregationalist hands.

The new commissioner was well acquainted with the state situation. Working with President Beecher he had participated in the Western Institute and College of Professional Teachers, the principal center west of the Appalachians for teachers to consult and lobby for the schools. He was informed about the school centralization which was taking place in Prussia; he knew also that Victor Cousin, the rising reformer of French education, had gone there for ideas. One wonders (and doubts) whether Stowe and his fellow commissioners, making their own pilgrimage according to instructions, felt some irony in going from their frontier land planned for freedom to the Lutheran kingdom of Prussia where church was subordinate to state and all was subordinate to the Hohenzollerns.

The commission's *Report on Elementary Public Instruction*, promptly published in 1837, went straight to the relevant comparisons.

With the curricula and policies of Prussia and Württemberg in mind, it pointed to Ohio's shortage on school requirements beyond the three R's; it condemned the state's failure to insist that teachers be professionally trained. Stowe described with enthusiasm German methods of combining school discipline with Pestalozzian respect for individual differences among the pupils. He insisted that in asking the Ohio legislature to make a similar provision he was pressing "no visionary scheme emanating from the closet of a recluse, but a sketch of the course of instruction now actually pursued by thousands of [German] schoolmasters in the best district schools that have ever been organized. It can be done, for it has been done, it is now done, and it ought to be done. If it can be done in Europe, I believe it can be done in the United States: if it can be done in Prussia, I know it can be done in Ohio."°

By order of the Ohio state legislature, the report was distributed by the thousands. Three other states which took part in the public-school movement, Massachusetts, Michigan, and Pennsylvania, and two states which held back, Virginia and North Carolina, had it reprinted. Although Ohio itself failed to take early action, we have the testimony of Henry Barnard, who knew more than anyone else about the progress of the public-school movement, that the cause was much assisted by the Stowe report.

While preliminaries in the West broke the ground for public-school legislation, preliminaries in New England carried into the field of child study. Bronson Alcott, who is reasonably called the American Froebel, had only one experience with public schools which counted. In his home township of Wolcott, Connecticut, he learned from ache of back on school benches and from the gabble-gabble of group memorization a lifelong lesson in how a school should not be conducted. Unless we call that experience a challenge, there was little in Alcott's background which indicated a career in education. Perhaps thanks to his mother's Episcopalianism he avoided the evangelical spirit of Connecticut; he attended no college. The inspiration of reading *Pilgrim's Progress*, he tells us, was what determined him against settling into a factory job. He took up first as a peddler of tinware. Somehow he discovered the Quaker mystics, Fox, Penn, and Barclay, and the contemporary English poets, Wordsworth and Coleridge. He was a natural Platonist. He thought of teaching in the South where his peddling took him, but when offered them he took short-term appointments near home and one in Germantown, Pennsylvania. His influential career began in 1834, when he became master of Temple School in Boston.

A stranger in the hub city, free spirit in charge of a liberal school, he had the grand luck to acquire as assistant Elizabeth Peabody, who had all the right capacities and connections. She had worked as secretary to William Ellery Channing, principal Unitarian and inspirer of Transcendentalists; with seven years of school experience she had already developed a taste for child-centered education—the taste which would make her, in due time as bookseller and publisher, an introducer to America of the works of Froebel. With such a person to assist in the classroom and to help fill it with paying pupils, Alcott at age thirty-five began with a superb opportunity.

He proceeded with zest and imagination. The most spirited account of the school is the one which was rendered to the children of America in 1871, in the novel *Little Men*, by Louisa May Alcott, the pedagogue's daughter. Although the circumstances described in the book are imaginary, for Temple was a city day school and provided no such home surroundings as improved Miss Alcott's own little men and women, the story contains much philosophy and behavior which are truthful. The actual schoolmaster, like the fictional one, never punished the children corporally. His most unusual method was the "conversations" he conducted with the children, his effort to draw into conscious expression the goodness he believed to be in them.

On quick reading thirteen decades later, those conversations (as selected and edited) sound silly, not at all as they must have sounded when spoken between master and pupils. But Alcott's beliefs and goals, his romantic experimental share in early nineteenth-century child study, are to be glimpsed there. He once said to his class, for instance: "You all appear to think that you have something godlike, spiritual, like Jesus though not so much. And what is this?" The children responded: "Spirit, Conscience." A single voice: "Conscience is God within us." Then the teacher, who favored the idea that the soul's existence precedes the body's: "Behold the Babe! It is a flame of light! Yea its life is as the flame when it struggles amidst the fuel." Later, in his "Orphic Sayings" published in Emerson's *Dial*, Alcott stated in another way the belief that young people—all people—may rely on guidance from within. "Believe, youth, that your heart is an oracle; trust her instinctive auguries, obey her divine leadings; nor listen too fondly to the uncertain echoes of your head. . . . Enthusiasm is the glory and hope of the world. It is the life of sanctity and genius; it has wrought all miracles since the beginning of time." For a final quotation, a passage from *Concord Days* long after Temple School days were over: "Only a God could inspire a child with the intimations seen in its first pulse plays. . . . Were the skill for touching its tender sensibilities, calling forth its budding gifts, equal to the charms the child has for us, what noble characters we would graduate!"°

Alcott was thus saying, to children and about children, that they are and should be guided from within. According to his way of thinking, the role of the school is to evoke goodness, not to establish rules against badness or to depend much on rational controls: children are naturally good. During the 1830s, such doctrine was touchy or more, even in a school community which had no belief in original sin; it was out of key also with the environmentalist and determinist ideas which the Enlightenment had encouraged and which were familiar among Unitarians. Yet what Alcott was saying corresponds to much the nineteenth century was about to believe—from Emerson to John Dewey—concerning human nature, and it is doubtful that the schoolmaster's sentimentality about children alone got him into trouble at Temple School. Like other intuitionists Alcott believed that the child can confront the stresses of life, and he made school business of candid discussion. Not surprisingly when he talked to the children about the pain and risk of childbearing, unpleasant publicity followed. And when a Negro was admitted as a pupil, a number of parents decided that Temple no longer provided the environment they wanted for their children. The school disbanded in 1839, after Alcott had served five years.

It seems as natural that at that point Alcott withdrew finally from schoolmastery as that Emerson withdrew from the ministry. In other ways, for decades indeed at Concord, without a school he would continue to think about children and teach. As member of the Transcendentalist Club, and during the 1880s as founder and leader of the Concord School of Philosophy, he came to bear a relationship toward child study and the philosophy of education which resembled the one Emerson and Thoreau bore toward more general philosophy.

Fortunately for the actual proliferation of schools during the period, two Yankee leaders quite different from Alcott moved into the politics and administration of government-supported schools. Horace Mann and Henry Barnard were fairly different, also, from one another. The Massachusetts man, the prime leader of the whole public-education movement, derived (at least this much like Alcott) from a narrow background he could surmount. For one thing this meant deciding against the Edwardsian religion of his home community and adopting the Unitarian faith. For another it meant a college education, and here he was lucky: he was given assistance his family could not afford, to go during his twenties to Brown. Brilliant performance there led to Judge Dane's law school; thence, the decisive first step in a public career, he moved to Boston to practice. As a successful young lawyer there, also as member of the humanitarian element, one who was especially interested in the peace movement, he rose rapidly in liberal politics. Within ten years he was president of the state senate. In that office he signed the Massachusetts Education Act of 1837—the law which his own administration would make historic.

Henry Barnard's early development ran parallel. It began later but advanced so rapidly as to make their major careers simultaneous. Though his Hartford family was able to send him to Yale and to law school, he too did some rebelling. At thirteen he hated the ways of the district school he attended. In college (he graduated at nineteen) an avid reader, he discovered Pestalozzi. Although he prepared for the law, his heart was fixed on the schools. While traveling in Europe during his twenties he managed to talk with reformers and sympathizers: in England with Lord Brougham and Carlyle and Wordsworth, and in Switzerland with numerous schoolmen. On return he associated himself with Edward Gallaudet's pioneer training of the deaf, in Hartford.

Although he had no solid personal identification with the Congregational Church of his origin—perhaps his marrying a Catholic explains —in general terms he was more conservative than Horace Mann and much more so than Bronson Alcott. He philanthropized in fields Lyman Beecher had opened, and his ideas of character training resembled those of his theologian fellow citizen of Hartford, Horace Bushnell. The salvation of the young, according to Bushnell's famous work, *Christian Nurture*, depends largely on inspired upbringing by family and church. This was a middle way, between guidance from the heart and guidance from environment, a way of love. Barnard's conviction about schools was similar. In Connecticut, moreover, where there was a maximum tradition of church-and-state affinity, a man of that kind of persuasion did not need to hesitate to enter politics. Barnard did so with quick effect. In 1838, though he was fifteen years younger, he was only one year later than Horace Mann in seeing a public-school law through the state legislature.

The educational situations which the two men confronted were essentially the same, and not very different from the one Calvin Stowe had opened up in Ohio. Like the northwestern states, the New England ones began reform with a school-and-state alliance to improve on. Only theirs was two hundred years old, and the reformers were strengthened by the nearness of the bicentennials of the basic Massachusetts and Connecticut school laws of the 1640s. But for a hundred years those ancient provisions had been falling short. Townships came to contain several villages; they were widely spaced, and some of them were distant from the original village and school. Population expansion, and evangelism which raised antagonisms between congregations, made single township schools difficult if not unworkable. Accordingly the townships divided into school districts, each of which made its own provisions for buildings and teachers. But at very least the district suffered the administrative, financial, and appointive problems of atomizing the community. In agricultural areas the normal parsimony, and collisions between the demands of the teacher and the demands of the father for the time of the children, came into play. In port cities and mill towns, though some of the problems were different they were hard. In the parts of those towns inhabited by poor people—the same in principle as in inner-city ghettos today—the school districts had few bootstraps to pull and did not try very hard.

All things considered, the public-school reformers, whether their ideals were more humanitarian in the new mode or were more nationalist and citizenship-minded like old Noah Webster, had many objects for their goodwill. Whether their sense of need was or was not much sharpened by a wish to provide better workers for farm and factory, the situation before them looked inadequate. Yet to their minds it lay within the reach of state action, and both the Massachusetts leader and the Connecticut one acted that way.

The essence of the Massachusetts Education Act was to supply centralizing supervision and aid where there had been none; the natural growing point was the European-style Board of Education provided by the law. The principal author of the legislation, James G. Carter, was a teacher and textbook writer who had been stimulated by the Swiss. He might, except for a twist of state politics, have become the executive secretary of the board and the focal figure of New England school reform. When fortunately Whig Party influences threw the job to Horace Mann, he accepted under personal circumstances which brought an unusual supply of altruism into play. The new secretary was childless and a recent widower; he had so prospered at the law that the salary of fifteen hundred meant little, but he was discontented with practice. The two comments by him which follow, the first from a personal letter early after taking the secretaryship and the second from an official report six or seven years later, tell much about his dedication. "If I can be the means of ascertaining what is the best construction of [school] houses, what are the best books, what is the best mode of instruction; if I can discover by what appliance of means a non-thinking, non-reflecting, non-speaking child can most surely be trained into a noble citizen, ready to contend for the *right*, and to die for the *right*, . . . may I not flatter myself that my ministry has not been wholly in vain?" This represents his hope. The following sentences come from the six-year retrospect: "He who has been a serf until the day before he is twenty-one years of age, cannot be an independent citizen the day after; and it makes no difference whether he has been a serf in Austria or America. As the fitting apprenticeship for despotism consists in being trained to despotism, so the fitting apprenticeship for self-government consists of being trained for self-government."°

Among the prior obligations of the secretaryship, Mann had to lead his colleagues on the board—governor, lieutenant governor, and eight gubernatorial appointees—into active innovation and expenditure.

Hardly separate from that duty was his obligation to the legislature, to bring it information and ideas and persuade it to appropriate money. (His work began coincidental with the depression of 1837.) Here the number-one need was to provide professional training, a normal school, for prospective teachers. Besides his principal obligations in Boston, the secretary had to cross and recross the state: he needed to induce the schools to accept state guidance, to believe in raising their standards. He had to prod school-district officers to appoint well-trained teachers and pay them enough to encourage permanent careers.

Working in the two directions, toward government and toward people and schools, Horace Mann proved superb. By having county teachers' conventions annually, by many official reports and much public speaking, he educated the people about education. By establishing the state normal school at Lexington, the first in the country, he made good the principle that a state government trains up teachers as a national government trains army officers. Mann succeeded also in founding fifty public high schools, sensibly spaced across the state. These were new-style institutions, planned for contemporary society. They differed at once from the old Latin grammar schools and from the recent crop of academies: they abandoned old language requirements and introduced modern and practical courses, some of which verged toward modern vocational training. More important, the distribution of the high schools made widely available (not yet universal or compulsory) public education up to age about seventeen. When, after eleven years, Horace Mann resigned the secretaryship to take the seat in Congress from which death had removed John Quincy Adams, the high schools were requiring more outlay than all the private secondary schools—religious or not—in the state. Thus, thanks in great part to his leadership, the people were already using and paying for a long and broad program for young citizens and a longer one for intended teachers. They were liking it well enough to retain it, and to begin the endless process of growth.°

The second leader made a more diffuse contribution to the common-school movement as a whole. Like Horace Mann, Henry Barnard moved directly from legislative politics into the executive secretaryship of his state board. The terms of the legislation were favorable, and he worked desperately hard for four years. He founded the teachers' institute which would soon be the famous normal school in New Britain; he launched the journal of education which would soon gain a canonical reputation. Unfortunately in 1842, while Mann's successes were accumulating, a Democratic Party victory in Connecticut led to legislating Barnard's secretaryship out of existence. Rhode Island called him immediately; and, although appropriate to its beginnings that state had remained strong in decentralization, it gave him better support. Next

Connecticut invited him home, to be president of the New Britain Normal School and to combine with that office the principal functions of the old secretaryship. Making these moves he was able to lead the two states of lower New England into near equality with Massachusetts public-school achievement. Meanwhile his devotion to the *American Journal of Education* made it the clearinghouse of ideas and programs for the national public-school movement. Experiments in education, whether or not successful and whether American or European, had their hearing. The editor of the journal gradually became known as the wise man and career man who stood at the apex of American education, new profession and new area of thought. This was a new role in society. If it was occupied and maybe created by the individual, Henry Barnard, society itself had called for the role.°

Outside of New England, while the South was deterred by peculiar conditions and institutions and the Middle States had conditions of cultural pluralism to sort out, the Old Northwest was the region most ready for action. Sometimes a bit of local leadership was all that was needed to make the school-district system operate one way or another. For instance in 1843 a district near Racine, in the territory of Wisconsin, elected a recent immigrant from England to be its clerk; he and others from the "English settlement" raised money to pay a teacher. They built a schoolhouse; on Sundays they let it be used by a union Sunday school; Episcopalians and Methodists were allowed it for regular worship. When Roman Catholics objected, they raised voluntary funds for a building for interdenominational Protestant use.°

Michigan went further than any other state to transcend local controls. Affected by Victor Cousin, who became France's minister of education under the Orleanist monarchy, Michigan provided for a state-wide system of graded schools. It transferred the control of school lands from township to state; it created a state superintendency of public instruction. Michigan's total became quickly high: for the schools, funds and central direction over and above the school-district operation; for the people of Michigan, simultaneously a school system in line with the newly reformed systems in Europe and the United States, and a promising state university. Neither Virginia, which had the one state university which was stronger, nor Massachusetts, which had the leading school system, could equal the combination.°

Among the Middle States, where pluralism and voluntarism were more built into institutions and habits than elsewhere, and where during the colonial period (with a fractional exception for Anglicanism) there had been no church establishment, New York responded first and foremost to the new needs for schools. The same incomparable growths and frictions in economic society which impelled labor unions and parties (including labor's own demands for equality in education), impelled likewise but earlier a broad movement for schools. Like the college movement in the state—which gave it Columbia, Union, Hobart, Hamilton, and New York University—the movement to provide common schools began as Christian philanthropy. But while religious it was not denominational; it set out to reach children for whom no single church would provide. And while the movement at first was nonpolitical, again a little different from the college movement it did not hold fully apart from government.

The great port city was the active location. Doing what Philadelphians, Baltimoreans, and Washingtonians—where Thomas Jefferson contributed—also did, but doing it earlier and more grandly, leading citizens founded in 1805 the Society for Establishing a Free School in the City of New York, for the Education of Such Poor Children as Do Not Belong To or are Not Provided for, by Any Religious Society. This society would be active for half a century, and it is better remembered by the short name which describes its final purpose, the Public School Society. From the outset the mayor, the wealthy, principled, and highly political DeWitt Clinton assumed leadership and gave money.

The original plan was inspired alike by emergency and philosophy. The society aimed to educate children who were "wandering about the streets, exposed to the influence of corrupt example." According to Mayor Clinton, Americans could not tolerate in their own midst the "monstrous heresy," familiar in Europe, of confining "the light of knowledge to the wealthy and great." The society raised thirteen thousand dollars, including four thousand contributed by government, to build its first school; it assigned a thousand a year to teachers' salaries. Large expansions followed. According to Ellwood P. Cubberley, by 1853 the society had educated more than six hundred thousand children and had trained twelve hundred teachers. Along the way it introduced, from the English educationist Henry Lancaster, two helpful principles for mass operation. The first was the method of elementary teaching by older student monitors; the other was simply the belief that, for the primary education of Christians, a nondenominational school was as good or better than a denominational one. So persuaded, Free School Society schools taught reverence for God and Bible and urged church attendance and family worship on the children's parents; sometimes they assembled the children at school on Sundays and marched them to the churches of the parents' choice.

Thus in great New York City a huge operation of philanthropic schooling led to mixed private and public financing and into interdenominational Christian effort. Among the leading congregations—the wealthy or sizable Episcopalian, Presbyterian, and Methodist ones—the operation proved satisfactory. While society schools expanded, supporting denominational ones contracted insofar as they served the indigent. Roughly the situation was that when families could pay the children attended the church schools; when families could not, the children attended society schools. Thus class differences were made unfortunately apparent; exclusions and shortcomings became embarrassing. Neither Catholics nor Jews nor unbelievers had a place in the scheme. Among Protestants who did not cooperate, appropriately a Baptist congregation objected to the society's having sole control of public money appropriated to city schools. Thus, when during the 1840s Governor William Henry Seward recommended that the state legislature appropriate no money for private schools, he struck the heart of the school operation in the city. The governor's famous denial accorded with denials already made; it accorded also with the public-school policies which were already succeeding in neighboring states both east and west of New York.°

Under these pressures the New York Society itself shifted to favor a public-school system. Differences among themselves notwithstanding, the Protestants of America's largest city were now ready as a matter of policy to entrust education to government. Of course families who could afford to do so remained always free to send their children to church schools, to any private schools anywhere, as they chose. And neither state nor city approached establishing any such universal, equalitarian boarding schools as prolabor radicals proposed. Yet the state acted with vigor in 1849. The Free School Act of that year matched in importance the Massachusetts law of a dozen years earlier and in principle was the same. It provided that state government and school districts should contribute matching funds for schools. New York State did not need to create a school board; it simply enlarged the responsibility of the half-century-old Board of Regents, the French-style supervising state "university" which so far had had little to supervise.

The whole New York rearrangement brought to national prominence two, perhaps three, main principles. First was the negative principle that "common schools" are not truly "common" if they are privately operated, no matter that the foundation of philanthropy to support them was generously broad. Second was the positive principle that education for all requires support by, and responsibility to, government. The support was a financial necessity in New York. The responsibility was a logical necessity from the public beliefs New Yorkers applied. If schools of private origin were to accord with the ideas of the republican-democratic polity, and were to teach those principles as being universally valid—government under law, authority derived from the people, separation of church from state, power always subject to limitation—they themselves could not reasonably want to remain the servant of two masters. Perhaps the two principles point to a third, or at least to a nearby tendency which was becoming likewise conspicuous. Republican government, which by nature excludes a church establishment and resists private monopolism in school control, by the same nature demands to have an establishment of education under its own authority.

CHAPTER XVI

The Farthest Reaches of Perfectionism: Individualist and Socialist

The key to the period appeared to be that the mind had become aware of itself. Men grew reflective and intellectual. There was a new consciousness. The former generations acted under the belief that a shining social prosperity was the beatitude of man, and sacrificed uniformly the citizen to the State. The modern mind believed that the nation existed for the individual, for the guardianship and education of every man. This idea, roughly written in revolutions and national movements, in the mind of the philosopher had far more precision; the individual is the world.

This perception is a sword such as was never drawn before. It divides and detaches bone and marrow, soul and body, yea, almost the man from himself. It is the age of severance, of dissociation, of freedom, of analysis, of detachment. Every man for himself. . . . The social sentiments are weak; the sentiment of patriotism is weak; veneration is low; the natural affections feebler than they were. People grow philosophical about native land and parents and relations. There is an universal resistance to ties and ligaments once supposed essential to civil society. The new race is stiff, heady and rebellious; they are fanatics in freedom; they hate tolls, taxes, turnpikes, banks, hierarchies, governors, yea, almost laws. . . . They rebel against theological as against political dogmas, against mediation, or saints, or any nobility in the unseen.

The age tends to solitude. . . . The association is for power, merely—for means; the end being the enlargement and independency of the individual.

Every true man is a cause, a country, and an age . . . and posterity seem to follow his steps as a train of clients. . . . An institution is the lengthened shadow of one man; . . . and all history resolves itself into the biography of a few stout and earnest persons.

To believe your own thoughts, to believe that what is true for you in your private heart is true for all men,—that is genius.

Ralph Waldo Emerson, "Historic Notes on Life and Literature in New England" and "Self-Reliance"

1 *Fork in the Road toward Perfection*

I N these chapters under the heading of "The Conscience of the Republic" so far we have considered ideas which Americans applied to a dozen or so institutions or sets of social conditions. From the theories and obligations which attached to nation-size operations such as the federal government, the economy, and the largest churches, we have descended through smaller things, like labor movements and regional traditions, to local sects, colleges, and school districts. But we have no more than gone with Tocqueville in touching on the smallest and most durable of all social units, the one he thought too much regarded and too little disciplined in America, the individual.

Yet the individual had ever and always been honored by Protestant thought and by democratic-republican theory. In Fenimore Cooper's bill of particulars: "Individuality is the aim of political liberty. . . . All greatness of character is dependant on individuality. . . . The pursuit of happiness is inseparable from the claims of individuality."° Looking back from old age on the period in which Cooper said this, and during which he himself matured as philosopher, Ralph Waldo Emerson wrote a memoir on the conditions and ideas which buffeted the individual, making for "a new consciousness." The second quarter of the nineteenth century, he explained, was "the age of severance, of dissociation, of freedom, of analysis, of detachment. Every man for himself. . . . The modern mind believed that the nation existed for the

[497]

individual, for the guardianship and education of every man." Emerson's own opinion, the same late in life as always, favored this idea: "The individual is the world."°

As all who have made acquaintanceship with the Transcendentalists of Concord know, the most memorable of all congregations of American thinkers came early to a division in its road. The first bending led to Emerson on the edge of town on toward Henry David Thoreau's Walden Pond—to the great men who answered Tocqueville's protest that individualism is gross. To the contrary, not only was the individual the world, but "An institution is the lengthened shadow of one man; and all history resolves itself into the biography of a few stout and earnest persons." Or, as Thoreau worded the answer, "Any man more right than his neighbors constitutes a majority of one already." Appropriately, Bronson Alcott said early of Emerson and Thoreau that they practised their preachment: "Forcible protestants against the materialism of their own, as of preceding times, these masterly Idealists substantiate beyond all question their right to the empires they sway—the rich estates of an original Genius."°

All Transcendentalist traffic of the intellect lingered awhile at Emerson's. Much of it passed near Walden, but that was no place for more than one mind to rest. On the other hand, much was attracted down the lane which led to Brook Farm. Perhaps no other Transcendentalists were more consciously devoted to the principle of individual fulfillment than were the Reverend George Ripley, his wife, Sophia Dana Ripley, and his other colleagues in charge. Their aim was to provide an environment which would evoke all good talents. Yet their collectiveness was what interested people, including themselves. It met the eye on arrival and filled the ear with unending talk about arrangements for the day, planning for the farm season, working out schemes for society anywhere in the world. If a visitor were like Emerson, who enjoyed Brook Farm for occasional companionship but was not even tempted to join, he went away with mixed feelings. He honored their values and wished them well. He answered them not by giving them argument but by not coming to stay. (Few married couples became members.) He simply felt that life outside was roomier and more satisfying, externally and internally the same.

Thanks especially to the writings of John William Ward and Yehoshua Arieli, we now understand that the main road of Transcendentalist thinking, the one which led to the grand statements in favor of individualism, had many parallels in less literary routes of expression, ones which were closer to the common mind. A Whig Party pronouncement in the *American Review*, for instance, which was made during the year of General Taylor's success at the polls, insisted that "The doctrine . . . that the whole people, as sole and sovereign source of power, established the Constitution for a guarantee of *individual freedom* and a source of all authority, is the doctrine of liberty." Another contributor to the same journal, which was the opposite number to the *Democratic Review*, said the same thing more firmly: "Your Whig refers all rights and liberties back to their original source in the individual, and holds that society is established for the protection of these rights and liberties." Probably the Whigs, who had less mass democracy on their side than the Democrats, and who were more threatened by the possible tyranny of majorities, were stronger for individuality and individual rights.° But Ward makes no distinction between political parties when he says of America broadly that "the body of assumptions made explicit in Emerson's thought are implicit in contemporary political thought, religious thought, and in the celebration of the Old Hero, Andrew Jackson himself."° Indeed a prominent contemporary theologian, John W. Nevin of Mercersburg Seminary, who as a blender of Calvinist and German religious thought and a speaker for strong churchmanship might have chosen to resist individualism, became both explicit and hopeful. Reacting to Tocqueville's dark feeling, Nevin acknowledged no more than that "the principle of individual liberty has been, in fact . . . carried to an extreme." The greater truth, Nevin insisted, was that a "new stadium is in progress, for the universal life of the world; having for its object now the bold assertion of what may be styled the subjective pole of freedom."°

While we are only just now catching on that Transcendentalist individualism corresponded to an earlier articulate individualism in the general culture, scholars have never been slow to recognize that Brook Farm was matched by many predecessors and contemporaries in utopian socialist life. Quite as that farm was to be found on a lovely side road of Transcendentalist thought, so a great number of side roads led to other communities. From east to west America's culture more than tolerated radical utopias; it created new Lebanons in several states, Red Bank in New Jersey, Oneida in New York, Amana and Salt Lake City beyond the river. Those communities as much as the celebrated Brook Farm—some of them earlier, several of them larger and more successful, but none of them quite so literary and philosophical—came up with collectivist amendments to the norms of American life.

The course of this chapter will be easier if we begin with the communities and do not omit to ask what they did for their members as people. If we view such minorities first, we will understand better American perfectionism where it less rigidly followed some pattern of rules.

2　Utopian Communities and Personal Fulfillment: Secular and Evangelical Goals

THE utopian communities which are about to speak their lines on our stage renewed from earlier centuries some of the prime phenomena of colonization. Their function during a new current of social relocation was to guide people in settling the land. Their specialty was to supply purposes and ideals, to build a community to which members would be drawn and attached.

Intense commitment to a common faith had been almost a necessity, we know, to the seventeenth-century colonizers. Those who lacked it succeeded more slowly. During the transcontinental expansion of the nineteenth century, the need was both similar and different. The long forward reaches made by hunters and miners, the more routine business of extending the contiguous farming frontier, were carried often by individuals or families, in the styles which Daniel Boone and Andrew Jackson and the family of Abraham Lincoln represent. For the great majority of the latter-day settlers, the large-scale prearranging of society was done by territorial, state, and national government—far more than the Crown, Parliament, and assemblies had provided the colonists. Unless the farm-building and town-building habits of the people be called prearrangement, little more was absolutely required. Not to meet organizational needs that were widely felt, of the kinds which Puritanism and Quakerism had met two centuries earlier, but only needs that were quite uncommon, did doctrinaire programming now come into play.

But these needs, when they were in fact strongly enough felt for action, became compelling. What less than Robert Owen's stiff orders for New Harmony would do, if Robert Owen's goals of regular employment, balanced economy, and education were to be met? What less than an Oneida, if a Perfectionist lesson were to be set the world on how to improve human propagation and give free play to life's "amative" impulse? Among leaders who answered such questions affirmatively, moreover, there came readily to hand that old and tried institution in England and America, the voluntary corporation. What the corporation's ancestor, the trading company, had offered the founders of Virginia and New England, the corporation itself now offered American utopians. They could and did use it freely, much as commercial and industrial business was doing, but toward purposes different from money profits.

The first of the leaders in secular communitarianism, and the first of any kind to gain wide attention in the republic, was Robert Owen. He came to America in the 1820s, a short-term loan of social entrepreneurship from the owning and managing sector of Britain's industrial economy. As the famous man of New Lanark, Scotland, a business success in cotton textiles and an epoch maker in providing for his workmen, Owen in America had every advantage for explaining his ideas. Among many speeches on his travels to and from New Harmony, a lecture that he delivered in 1825, the year of launching the community, was the more important because the United States Congress invited him. Perhaps the fact that the House of Representatives had recently debated Henry Clay's American System disposed it to listen to another beneficial program; certainly the attendance of President John Quincy Adams, who himself was an economic nationalist and a believer in public provisions for the common welfare, corresponds to the attention the speaker was commanding wherever he went.

Owen delivered what amounted to a social and economic manifesto; probably Congress has never since heard another exposition of socialism which was half as systematic, certainly not by a foreigner. In America Owen had the advantage of building on suppositions which had been familiar for three generations, the idea that environment greatly determines life and that common sense is the fount of morality. Thus he phrased a line which Thomas Jefferson might have uttered: "The character of man is, without a single exception, always formed for him." But where Americans who believed this were likely to be agrarians, Robert Owen took factory towns for granted as good. He conceived that a community of about twenty-five hundred would be economically ideal: such a population would supply workers for a technologically modern textile mill; it would produce but not overproduce for the accessible market. As planner he wanted the culturally necessary buildings to be placed at the center of his town: the school, the church, and the dining hall. He wanted workshops on the periphery; and the residences between, where they would be convenient to both. Thus, after Major L'Enfant, who came from France to design Washington, Robert Owen journeyed from Scotland to the banks of the Wabash to become America's number-two town planner after the Revolution.

Estimating Robert Owen as a doctrinaire, now when after a century and a half the word "socialism" has gathered many variations of meaning, it is fair to call him a socialist. Admittedly, this is not very informing: Owenism is no closer than a distant older cousin to the Marxism we know; the term "communitarianism," which Arthur E. Bestor as historian of American utopias has revived, signifying local and voluntary but radical reorganization, is a word which fits better. Robert Owen did not need to ask for common ownership of property.

At New Harmony all or most large ownership—land, mills, public buildings—lay in his own hands, thanks to his heavy investment. But he did not operate them for profit in any short-run sense. The productivity and the life of the community were conceived as a whole, and so managed. When the venture broke down it did so at heavy cost to him and his family. This means that more than technically Robert Owen was a private owner, the same at New Harmony as at New Lanark. He had assumed the risks and prerogatives of ownership, and indeed he earned a reputation for being dictatorial at New Harmony. Yet more than nominally he and his son, Robert Dale Owen, were socialists also, for they collectivized production for the benefit of all settlers. Of all the communitarian enterprises in America, theirs was the only one geared to the age's condition of early industrialization.

In their case the bearing of collectivism on individualist goals and values is uncommonly hard to judge. Owen was overtly anti-Christian; that characteristic increased his offensiveness to critics nearby. On the same account, and because of the doctrinaire environmentalism of the scheme as a whole, New Harmony contained no such factor of salvation seeking, or of evoking personal talents, as occurred elsewhere. Yet the community resembled all others in being education-minded: improved schools lay at the heart of the program, and the hope was to set a candle before the world. And, however paradoxical from the point of view of Owen's intentions, the collisions at New Harmony led to counterproposals which were rampantly individualistic after all.

No sooner had a couple of years of life in the community proved that it could not hold out, in the prosperous unarranged economy of Indiana, than amoeba-like separations took place. In one case a scientist originally from Philadelphia, who could not stand Robert Owen, founded a new community, Macluria, named for himself. The successor community which lasted longest, four years, was the one Frances Wright founded at Nashoba in western Tennessee. Intended to give security and training to manumitted Negroes who were at a disadvantage on the free labor market, intended also to provide a place for practising free love, Nashoba was radical by any standards; hence its special vitality. Its goals, however, excluded its even seeking to become a pure model of industrialization, an object lesson to the world of the kind which Robert Owen had wanted.°

Yet Owenite ideas did diffuse in other ways than by a proliferation of communities. Robert Dale Owen, while drawing on family funds to help in the New York phase of his career which we noticed in Chapter XIV, did more than simply second the ideas of Locofocos and agrarians. In his *Free Enquirer* he pushed hard for his own "National System of Equal, Republican, Protective, Practical Education." He publicized it as offering "the sole regenerator of a profligate age, and the only redeemer of our suffering country from the equal curses of chilling poverty and corrupting riches, of gnawing want and destroying debauchery, of blind ignorance and of unprincipled intrigue." In articles on "republican education" and "national guardianship" he went full length with the New York radicals in favor of equality in education: public schools should supply lodging, food, and clothing, he said. His argument became more specially his own when he reasoned about proper curricula. In the line the philosopher statesmen had taken he proposed—but for all pupils—history, modern languages, chemistry, drawing, and music. In accord with schools he had observed in Switzerland, he wanted young Americans trained also in farming and in one manual trade. Here the old Owenite reasoning expanded. Robert Dale Owen was trying to inculcate belief in the dignity of all men and to guide children into freedom to choose how they would express themselves, individuals in the world.°

Where Owenism came to America aggressively, during a cycle of prosperity, with a mission to rationalize industrial ways, Fourierism fifteen years later waited to be invited and finally arrived in a depression period with an almost agrarian philosophy. The basic work containing the program and the philosophy, Charles Fourier's *Théorie des quatre mouvements*, in two volumes, had been published in 1808. The remainder of his life, thirty years, the author devoted to explaining his system: he wrote two more books on the subject; he entered journalism and won a following among journalists; he argued out his ideas with Saint-Simon, his older contemporary in socialism (who was more a technocrat, even a state socialist, than a communitarian), and from a distance argued with Robert Owen himself. Just one disciple in France launched a community. Only in 1832 when he was sixty was he discovered by the wealthy young journalist whose transmittal of Fourierism to America would lead to the founding of dozens of communities.

Albert Brisbane, who did this, chose travel and study in Europe in place of a college education. Because he was an upstate New Yorker it would be convenient to discover in him one who began with firsthand knowledge of the hardships of labor in the new mill towns. But actually a tutor in New York City had given him readings in modern French thought; he went to the Sorbonne to fulfill a personal enthusiasm. There he heard Victor Cousin lecture; thence he went on to Germany as many Americans did. But he continued to prefer the French. "I, imbued with the democratic principles of my native land, saw some progress at least, in the transformation of these old despotisms . . . into the democratic institutions of a republic." On the other hand he tells us that he "found in Hegel and among his disciples no idea of a higher social order than the European civilization." Nothing in German philosophy "satisfied the yearning curiosity of a mind in its restless search for the destiny of humanity."°

In this mood he ran into Charles Fourier. Back in Paris he must have astonished that philosopher when he called and asked to be tutored. The reading and the lessons took beautifully. Eight years later in 1840 Brisbane published his own rendering of Fourierism, *The Social Destiny of Man; or, Association and Reorganization of Industry*. He did better than summarize. The young New Yorker adjusted the system to American modes of thinking; he acquired the timeliness, moreover, of putting out the book during a depression and when America was just entering its first great period of social reform. In agreement with Rousseau and with the Swiss education reformers, in accord also with a feeling common in his own social class, Fourier attributed the wrongdoings of men to bad institutions and habits. Men have a natural goodness within, he believed; and where Owen had spoken for creating opportunity for all within the industrial order, Fourier spoke of providing security and amenity for all, with little regard for industrialization. He conceived a community more like a French village than an English or American one, whence people would go out to the farms or where they would work at home in household manufacturing. His design included a central residence, with more than a touch of Versailles about it. He called the community a "phalanx." He believed that about sixteen hundred persons, settled on four thousand to six thousand acres, would be right. The members would distribute the work according to individual gifts and preferences. Menial tasks would be especially well paid for, to compensate and dignify the doers; the managers would be rewarded less by money than by the satisfactions of responsibility. As to distribution, the total product of the phalanx was pledged first to meet the phalanx's corporate obligations; the residue would be divided among the members. The first round of the members' share was assigned to minimum subsistence for all. On the second round the differentials would begin to apply: five-twelfths to labor, four-twelfths to capital, and three-twelfths to talent. Part of each member's satisfaction was to come from his apartment in the phalanx house: the apartments were to be arranged and decorated with variety; appropriate rentals were to be charged.

In no respect did the Fourier-and-Brisbane plan for communitarianism differ more greatly from Owenism than on the point of human nature and social motivation. As Brisbane introduced the idea of phalanges to Americans, he asked them to place reliance on the operation of the reconciling passions. He made communitarianism sound like the Golden Rule put to work. Approaching by way of the *New York Tribune* the largest readership among reform-minded people, he used the language of conversion. He claimed for Fourierism much more than a road to socialism: he promised that in it lay the key to an over-all social and moral change. A column printed in 1842 had the following to say:

> The Slavery of the Negro Race is but a very small fragment of the universal Servitude which exists. . . . To attack it separately, *leaving the cause of it untouched*, will produce great commotions, perhaps revolutions, without eradicating it. One-tenth part of the efforts and money which are now devoted to the cause of Abolition would, if devoted to the cause of Association and Attractive Industry prove practically their Truth. . . . Attractive Industry will sweep peaceably and by common consent every variety of Slavery and Servitude from the earth.°

Acting out his own optimism, Brisbane in 1843 produced an eighty-page pamphlet, *Association*, which made better, briefer, and more telling propaganda than *The Social Destiny of Man*.

During the mid-forties Fourierism in America generated journalism all its own. Brisbane himself began this with *The Phalanx* of New York, which he edited for a year. Then the Brook Farm Transcendentalists assumed the intellectual leadership of the movement. They wrote for themselves a Fourierist constitution; Elizabeth Peabody, who was good at slogans, composed one to fit the change: "Leisure to live in all the faculties of the soul." They took over *The Phalanx*, renaming it *The Harbinger*; the new journal served in some degree as successor also to Emerson's and Margaret Fuller's *The Dial*, which had just collapsed. Altogether with the practice of Fourierism at the farm, which was limited, and with Transcendentalist talking and writing, which were not, this brand of communitarianism emerged much the most philosophical brand in America.

Meanwhile the movement expanded in action, in the part of the country where Brisbane had begun. Near New York City, and a hundred miles or more northward and five or six hundred miles westward, phalanges arose in numbers. The nearest to the city was at Red Bank, on the New Jersey shore; Brisbane personally helped to found it, and it would last the longest of any, until after the Civil War. Near the northernmost point of the geographic crescent in which volunteering occurred, a strong phalanx developed at Rochester, New York; a cluster of them started near Cincinnati. By the indications the records still contain, the communities delivered real benefits to the members. Their prices sound good: coffee sold at a half cent a cup; a room in a "phalanstice" rented for twelve dollars a year. On such a basis a member's wages considerably exceeded the cost of subsistence; he could pay his room rent with about one-twentieth of his earnings. Doubtless such benefits help account for the durability of the phalanges. Several of them lasted—many times longer than the Owenite communities but not as long as certain religious ones—from ten to thirty years.

Chronologically between the quick waxing and waning of the Owenite communities and the rise of the Fourierist ones, there gathered the grandest of all community movements, the one which after fifteen years' wandering in the Mississippi valley settled beside the Great Salt Lake. And, while there is no basis for questioning the uniqueness of Mormonism either as a faith or an enterprise, equally we are bound to observe that it shared characteristics with several other communities, especially with two famous ones which rose and flourished in the western New England and upstate New York region of its own origin. A half century before Joseph Smith's revelation, the Shakers, and contemporaneously with him the Oneida Perfectionists, began with what they believed to be special revelations from God. Both received divine instructions to reorganize family life and sex practice and to live separately from the sinners of earth. In 1870, after nearly forty years of leading the Perfectionists, John Humphrey Noyes in his *History of American Socialisms* said, what no scholar today is likely to doubt, that utopian movements required both a God-given inspiration and a style of family life peculiar to themselves if they were to survive very long. Certainly during the middle decades of the nineteenth century, sizable numbers of Americans and their European recruits combined religious radicalism, sex radicalism, and communal holding of property in ways which created strong loyalties.

Ann Lee (or Lees), who grew up and married in England before gathering her own cult here, is the first religious leader who requires to be mentioned in these pages who was illiterate, and one of few who were little educated. The daughter of a blacksmith of Manchester, as a girl she worked in a cotton mill, as a hatmaker, and as a cook. At about twenty-two she was converted a "shaking" Quaker—that is, she joined an element among the Friends which was affected by a wave of peasant piety: the Camisard movement from southern France, which held millennialist beliefs and practised physical manifestations of mystical feeling. As a young wife she bore four children and lost them all. Thus it seems more natural than supernatural that, when at age thirty-four she began to have revelations, she denounced carnal love as the source of all sinfulness. Her second revelation explains her entering our story: it told her to go to America and introduce the religion she knew. On that authorization she emigrated in 1774, a politically troubled year; her husband and six other believers crossed with her, but he was one who soon dropped out. Enough of the group settled together in Watervliet, near Albany, however, to set themselves up as the "First Witnesses of the Gospel of Christ's Second Appearing." The conditions of the War of Independence, though not favorable to free wandering and speaking, did not prevent the First Witnesses from evangelizing out of New York into western New England.

Mother Ann Lee lived only to 1784. Direct evidence about what she preached is short; what has come to us is a collection, the *Testimonies of the Life, Character, Revelations and Doctrines of Mother Ann Lee.* Within a quarter century they became a canon to her church; they contained her ideas about the Godhead, about the church, and about life. In place of the Trinity, Mother Ann taught that God is dual, male and female in aspect; that Jesus represents the male aspect, and she herself, the female one. Salvation is explained as doing God's will on earth. Her own coming had been the second "appearing" of Divinity among men. The Inner Order of the church she founded was the true company of saints: members were obligated to live in perfection—that is, in condition of sinlessness in the community houses. The Outer Order belonged in part to the world: for those members marriage, childbearing, and private property were all permitted. But as salvation was beyond their reach from that condition, the benefit of Outer Order membership was transitional only; that element is historically inconspicuous and the Inner Order which created and occupied the communities was the Shaker movement in fact.

Set in that framework, the regimen of the Shakers seems entirely logical. The First Witnesses called the economic part of their system "Christian Communism" and completely shared their property. Their doctrine included a sizable factor of spiritualism: Mother Ann said that a sanctified soul has power over disease, even death, and can converse with souls whose bodies have died. Shakerism disciplined sex expression further than any other community movement. Males and females occupied the same houses, yet were elaborately segregated from each other. All rose early by the call of a bell and worked long hours daily. Conversation between men and women was at all times kept close to zero; they were forbidden to pass on a staircase and met only in groups of three or more. The ritual dances they did in the meetinghouses were shuffling performances without music; they put all participators into a common rhythm but still kept the sexes apart. Appropriate to the dual principle, the Shakers placed community government equally in the hands of elders and eldresses.

Once the communities were operating, the Shakers achieved a superb competency in all they undertook. Their community houses, farms, workshops, and meetinghouses are legendary for cleanliness, orderliness, thrift, and efficiency. After Mother Ann died, their external relationships became easy. Although they depended entirely on recruitment, their proselytizing—the maximum Inner Order membership reached about five thousand—was too limited, apparently, to provoke animus against them. They wanted economic self-sufficiency, and their way of life—all adults, all vegetarians, all wearers of uniform clothing—made them undemanding consumers. But they did produce for the market, and their products became famous for quality: garden seeds, farm appliances, and furniture (including ladder-back chairs) were their specialties.

After Mother Ann Lee's death, the first Shaker community under her rules began in 1787 at New Lebanon, New York, not far from Watervliet and close to the Massachusetts line. During the next few years, before the Second Great Awakening, four societies were founded in Massachusetts, four in New Hampshire and Maine, and one in Connecticut. Only during the evangelical first quarter of the nineteenth century did the movement turn west: a half-dozen communities were founded in Ohio, Indiana, and Kentucky. The name Lebanon recurs wherever they went. Generally speaking a farm of a thousand acres and a membership of fifty was minimum; several communities had two or three hundred members. To people who saw them regularly, the Shaker communities had the quality of a collection of unmarried aunts and uncles who were odd and prim and withdrawn, quiet neighbors who truly minded their own business and kept out of trouble.°

The second nineteenth-century postmillennial movement was the one which settled near Syracuse, New York, at Oneida. But where Mother Ann Lee had been deprived, the leader of the Perfectionists was the son of a well-to-do congressman and the husband of a wife he loved. Brought up in Connecticut River towns in Vermont, John Humphrey Noyes went to Dartmouth, as his father had, and tried the study of law. But he rebelled early against parental agnosticism and, deciding for the ministry, after Dartmouth he went to Andover and to Yale. Especially at Yale the old doctrine of human depravity was being interpreted out of its familiar meaning, and in that area Noyes took an independent course. He decided that Christ had made his second coming in 70 A.D. This amounted to saying that the millennial age was as old as the culture of the West and that sin among Christian churchmen had always been erroneous doctrine. No other American millennialist had ever gone so far with the idea; it was much too far for the Yale Department of Divinity. The college let him go without a degree and with no chance for ordination.

Returning to his home state, Noyes founded a small Bible school of his own. Applying there his ideas of what postmillennial behavior should be, he developed a society of "Bible Communists." Doubtless because he was twenty-five and about to be married, he rapidly formulated his ideas of love without sin. He tackled the same problem as Ann Lee had but came to an opposite answer. Being truly governed by love, he concluded, excludes monogamic or possessive marriage. It calls for sex, commitment, and propagation. He made these affirmations with reference to Matthew 22: 23–30. He preached that what is usually condemned as "free love" is right when the spirit is right—that is, when those who practise it do so as part of a total pledge to Christian perfection. He persuaded Harriet Holton, his fiancée, to accept the theory. In his home community, Putney, Noyes met more criticism on account of his Bible communism than on account of his radical pronouncements on family and sex.

But resistance did not press him quickly, either to migrate or to speak through books. Only in 1848, after ten years of marriage and more years of preaching perfection, did he and his followers settle Oneida, where he began putting his doctrine fully before the world in both practice and print. During the next dozen years, which included his forties, he covered in three volumes his main convictions about communitarianism, economics, and sex. *The Berean, Bible Communism,* and *Male Continence* were the books. Twenty years later, after grand success in building the Oneida community, he enlarged his message to include works on the scientific propagation of the human race and on the history of socialism in America.

On the point which gave Oneida its place in history, Noyes premised that the relationship between the sexes divides into two functions, the "amative" and the "propagative." Where there is Godliness, he explained, amative love should be voluntary, or governed from within and not subject to external law. Propagative love on the other hand requires regulation, according to Noyes. In the practice of Oneida he made it mean very little childbearing at first. Later it meant exact and detailed planning: so many children by such and such unions, at specified times. Given the ideas and the authoritarianism of the system, not surprisingly many of the babies at Oneida were born to the name of Noyes. On the other hand, life in that community is not known to have been marred by such resentments or withdrawals as one might imagine to have occurred.°

At least in small movements—a few thousand Shakers, a few hundred Perfectionists, and yet others less numerous and less remembered—postmillennial thought made possible radical changes in group behavior. What is not often realized, though the evidence is plentiful still in our times, postmillennialism achieved also a sizable result among people who did not at all retire from the world. The principal case is the Adventists, as they called themselves, another movement which traces mainly to "burned over" New York—the upstate region where, beside the communitarianisms discussed in this section, Charles G. Finney's evangelism flourished and spiritualism took unusual hold.

Their leader, William Miller, combined backgrounds and talents which help explain the movement. He was the son of a veteran of the Revolution and grandson of a Baptist minister; he himself was a farmer, a captain in the War of 1812, and an amateur but hard and habitual Bible student. He seized on the millennial idea in the most risk-taking way: his studies brought him to believe that Christ's second coming was literally at hand—according to his book of 1831 it would occur "about the Year 1843." While narrowly this makes him a premillennialist rather than a postmillennialist, and makes his timing eighteen centuries different from John Humphrey Noyes's and seven decades different from Mother Ann's, it seems better to think of him as postmillennial because he and his people were governed by the expectation as if by a current event. Contemporary reports and the histories based on them differ about the preparations the Adventists made for the great day. Whether many or few decided that debts no longer needed paying, that farm chores no longer needed doing, or that ascension robes should be worn on a hilltop on the expected morning are not problems to detain us here. Some people did those things. But the important thing is that many took the message only a little less literally. Believing what other Christians did about the life of Jesus in Palestine, they chose to believe further that He would return to earth in America. When the world outlasted 1843 and the next few years without Christ's visible return, they survived the humiliation and kept to the supposition that sometime He would actually come.

Once the tension over 1843 and amended dates had passed, the Seventh-Day Adventists, still sometimes called Millerites, settled into being one of the more ascetic but less socially revolutionary of American sects. (The "Seventh-Day" part of their name expresses their belief that the last day of the week is the true Sabbath.) They are still known for their temperance in food and drink: they deny themselves coffee and tea as well as spirits; they are vegetarians. This expresses their regard for the body as temple of the soul. In time they became conspicuous builders of church hospitals and sanitariums, and sent medical missions overseas. They set up numerous schools, colleges, and medical schools. In and beyond American soil they seem like a renewal of the Philipp Jakob Spener style of piety and humanitarianism which had expanded out of the Germanies a century and a half before their own time.

The history of the Latter-Day Saints is the most copious story of postmillennial belief, of the reorganization of family life, and of (outsize) communitarianism in the American experience. Joseph Smith, the receiver of most of the revelations, the establisher of the canon and the church, and the first leader in the migrations, derived from the same geographic region as John Humphrey Noyes and William Miller but from a location in society closer to Ann Lee's. Born in Sharon on the Vermont side of the Connecticut River, Smith belonged to a ne'er-do-well family; in 1816 when he was eleven they took him to Palmyra, south of Rochester, New York. His education stopped after common school. In his teens he became a "money digger"; he performed at night with hazel twig and incantation. There was nothing unusual about this: he lived in romantic Indian country where legend was lively and treasure hunting was the same. When he was fifteen and a wave of revivalism was sweeping the countryside, Joseph Smith began to have visions which he took to be revelations from God.

In 1823, only three years later, according to his own account the revelations demanded action. He was visited, he said, by the angel Moroni who told him that he would find buried near his home—on what has since been known as Mormon Hill—inscriptions which would yield the story of the inhabitants of America before the white man. According to the same story, Smith actually unearthed them four years later, golden plates which he took home. He alone was permitted to see them; spectacles (or "peep-stones") which he found with them enabled him to read the unknown language. Thus the *Book of Mormon* entered the world. Many months were required to dictate the English translation—from behind a curtain which separated him from his amanuenses. Produced in 1830, the *Book of Mormon* was received by believers as history and prophecy given by God, practically a third testament and a covenant made with a chosen people.

The *Book of Mormon* says that the Lord instructed Nephi to lead certain tribes of Israel, the famous lost tribes of Bible history, to the western hemisphere. Here, much as in the Old Testament story, they wandered and warred. Christ made His second coming, in America, among them. But—a repetition of Christian history instead of a Christian fulfillment—the people rejected Him again. After another epoch of war and disaster, about 384 A.D. the good people, called Nephites, dwindled away. Only their great leader and the last to die, Mormon, inscribed and buried the plates. The sad history ended with God punishing the destroyers of the Nephites. They became the Indians of American history; their punishment was that God darkened their skins. (Thus did racism enter the new holy book, a blot not yet eradicated from Mormon belief.)

Looked at without piety as folk literature, the *Book of Mormon* makes Joseph Smith a large participator in two of his region's most characteristic operations of the imagination: searching for salvation by way of special revelation, and reworking Indian lore. Belief that the redskins were (benighted) descendants of the ancient Jews was no original idea. Lewis and Clark, among many, had speculated on their possibly having that derivation. But where Indian life supplied the place and time for the drama of the *Book of Mormon*, the Bible provided the theme of death and renewal. According to Woodbridge Riley's analysis in detail, about one-eighteenth of the *Book of Mormon* is borrowed directly from Holy Scriptures: the Sermon on the Mount, the Ten Commandments, eleven chapters from Isaiah, and about three hundred scattered passages from the New Testament all reappear. The same expert finds the *Book of Mormon* eclectic as to religious thought: he finds the first Book of Nephi to be Calvinist in underlying supposition; and the second book to be freewill.°

If Mormon divinity, history, and millennialism are to be found in the *Book of Mormon*, Mormonism's particular social ideas are recorded in the later revelations which Joseph Smith and Brigham Young received and put into practice. Of course the best known of these was the revelation which commended polygamy to Latter-Day Saints. It came to Joseph Smith while the Mormons were at Nauvoo, Illinois, only a year before he died; but he had received earlier revelations which sanctioned individually his own departures from monogamy. Whatever the merits of the provision for the founder of the faith and his colleagues while they moved about in mid-America, it does seem to have proved sensible for the Mormons during the early years in Utah, their stage of maximum isolation from the world. During the four decades there before another revelation repealed polygamy, many more women than men were converted and brought in from Europe and the eastern United States. Any provision different from polygamy, say a convent for women, would have strained religious loyalty and behavior and would have denied childbearing to true believers at a time when children were needed.

Much nearer to the mind and management of the movement was the revelation Joseph Smith received, as early as 1833, concerning church polity. He was told that his two principal associates, Sidney Rigdon and F. C. Williams, were his peers in governing the church. From this Smith derived the tripartite headship of the Church of the Latter-Day Saints—the first, second, and third presidencies which, corresponding to the Trinitarian Godhead, has from then to now given the Mormon leaders effective control at the top. In downward gradations, the twelve apostles of the church, a council of twelve high priests, and local officers known as bishops, elders, preachers, teachers, and deacons rounded out the system. The names of these offices, but not the functions, corresponded to the offices the Mormons knew among the Methodists, Presbyterians, Congregationalists, and Baptists from whom they themselves mainly derived. The two "orders" of the church, called Melchizedek and Aaronic, resemble somewhat the Masons, who had been numerous and notorious in the upstate New York of Joseph Smith's young manhood. But none of this plural background inhibited the centralizing of authority among the Mormons; they even outdid Methodists and Catholics in that respect. Brigham Young, whose first-presidency lasted a third of a century, though less a receiver of revelation than Joseph Smith, added to the tendency to authoritarianism by his charisma and his immense administrative skill.

By design the migration of 1846, which Brigham Young led from the Missouri through the Rocky Mountains to the Great Salt Lake, took the Mormons outside United States territory. Even when the Mexican War extended the American domain to the California coast, they remained essentially free. For a couple of years Brigham Young held simultaneously the offices of first president of the Latter-Day Saints, governor of the Mormon state of Deseret elected by the people, and governor of the territory of Utah, appointed by the president of the United States. Altogether he was a more powerful theocrat—ruler designated by God—than any Massachusetts Puritan had ever been.

During two decades of almost unlimited sovereignty—the prewar and Civil War decades in national history—Deseret and especially the capital city were operated on a basis as collectivist as authoritarian. Then as now the situation between the Great Salt Lake and the Wasatch Mountains was salubrious and wonderfully beautiful. But desert conditions would not allow freehold farming, every man on his own. They required that a system of irrigation be built and administered. With minor exceptions this was a condition unknown to Americans and western Europeans, unless from their Bibles. Yet with Brigham Young in charge they tackled the problem. To begin, eight thousand acres of flatland south of the city were divided into five- and ten-acre lots; all the men were required to help dig the canals; the parcels of irrigated farm land were distributed by lottery. Their system worked, and they extended it: Deseret was made to bloom.

Equally in Salt Lake City life was arranged and cultivated. Residential lots were assigned to families, roughly one acre and a quarter each; tenure was given in usufruct, not in fee; every holder was required to plant fruit trees. As every present-day visitor knows, at the center of the geometrical system of lots and streets, a temple and a tabernacle, stunning buildings, were constructed. In the same vicinity the church established its tithing office. Thither was carted one-tenth of each farmer's produce. That is, a church-and-community granary was established, unique insurance against lean years. Under church supervision, the Zion Cooperative Mercantile Institution (today a department store in appearance and function) did the store business of the community. Their scanty educational backgrounds notwithstanding, the Mormons founded schools and a university promptly. What was less like other evangelical enterprises, they established a theater in Salt Lake City and consistently favored drama and music. For them as distinctly as for the Adventists, salvation meant a healthy life for body and mind.

The last word belongs to the church work, institutionally speaking both the end and the means of the whole enterprise. Where Protestants generally sent out home missions, church deputies from eastern to western congregations, the Mormons spread out from nearby valley to nearby valley. So-called "stakes" or congregations, each with its own "bishop," stretched both north of the Wasatch Mountains and south into the Colorado valley. Church administration grew in proportion; so did the schools and the taking of tithes.

The foreign missions were more conspicuous before the world. For years the Mormon hierarchy made almost a continuous operation of sending missionaries to northern Europe and of bringing to Salt Lake City new settlers for Deseret. To be converted a Latter-Day Saint meant in practice to become a citizen in residence of the theocratic state. The first mass "in-gathering" occurred in England in 1837; that practice was extended to Scandinavia in 1849. The converts made their famous long marches across the continent; the effort, especially the women's, was heroic. On the other hand the church organization helped them with their transatlantic passage and with their fare to the western railhead.°

By Owenite or Fourierist standards, the impressive thing about the Mormon community is the size it attained, a utopia of western-state dimensions. By the measure of other religious communities, the grand achievement is durability and practical relevance to the rest of the world. Eighty-odd years after the tithing office opened in Salt Lake City, the Mormon system of storing grain entered New Deal planning for an "ever normal granary" for the nation. To the general reviewer of the early nineteenth-century efforts for social perfection, the most striking thing of all must be the solidarity—the oneness—of Mormonism's religious independence with its institutional imagination and power. A kind of courage which is not often given a chance to act must have been required of Mormon converts. When that decision was made, say by a working woman of Copenhagen, the convert committed herself to forms of group life previously unknown—all at once to religious and economic ones and to sexual and cultural ones. The reward of entering the millennium was the stake the convert contemplated, salvation here and now on this earth.

3   *Individualism Made Philosophical:*
The Self-assertion of
Ralph Waldo Emerson

THE distance and differences are great between nature's wonders at Walden Pond and those at the Great Salt Lake. The town of Concord, home of the Transcendentalists, differed equally from Salt Lake City, the refuge of the Mormons. On first comparison, what the two had in common were the contemporaneousness of their blooming and their cousinship in being culturally descended from Massachusetts Puritans.

On a second look, however, the wideness of the gap closes. During the 1830s Transcendentalists as much as Mormons experienced renewals which signified to themselves that they were guided by God to live differently from most men. They too disliked the ways of business and government. Though not far in miles, they kept moral distance from State Street, the big-business center of Boston, and believed—on or off Brook Farm—in a different economy. They loved their country but hated politics. In their own high language they said, as well as the post-millennialists, that evil no longer need rule men.

The young mystic and seer, Ralph Waldo Emerson, whose voice proved magisterial among them, began as a churchman and a national-ist. "I dedicate my book to the Spirit of America," he said in 1823, when he was two years out of Harvard. A little later but still under twenty-one, Emerson made a similar pledge to the faith of his father: "I deliberately dedicate my time, my talents, and my hopes to the Church."° When he said "church" at this stage, he meant Congrega-tionalism—the church of the Puritans which just at the time was bi-furcating, many congregations around Boston and Cambridge going into Unitarian liberalism, the rest staying with latter-day Edwardsian orthodoxy.

All the lines of Emerson's background pointed toward the leftward fork. His father, William Emerson, as minister of First Church, Bos-ton, had been early to take that turning; though not a dynamic man, his talents and tastes carried him, well before his premature death, to prominence in Unitarian circles: he became editor of the Anthology Club's journal, overseer of Harvard College, and a leader in philan-thropy. After William Emerson died, his sister, Mary Moody Emerson, more than sustained the same spirit in the mind of the boy. She was a religious genius and had a passion for letters. Tutoring Waldo she taught him criticism, eloquence, and acuteness with the American vocabulary; she had him read authors whom eighteenth-century New England had cherished—Plutarch, Montaigne, and Milton, for example. She must have left something for the Boston Latin School and Harvard to teach him. In college he took courses under some of the rising scholars in language and literature; he had the advantage of studying composition under Edward Tyrrel Channing, the professor whose grand vision of American literature we have noticed. Emerson's head starts toward literary knowledgeability, however, did not veer him away from his churchly intentions. From 1827 to 1832 he served as minister of the Unitarian Second Church of Boston; he won quickly the honor and affection of his people. While there he found, loved, and

married—then lost to the disease he himself had to fight, tuberculosis—
the very lovely, very young Ellen Tucker of Concord, New Hampshire. Her death left him hard injured, but with a legacy of a few
thousand dollars which would help him for years.

Emerson resigned his ministry soon after Ellen's death. He needed a
change, as he said. But for years he had been discovering that he was
ill at ease in his ministerial duties and attitudes. The ways of the
Quakers attracted him, and he probably had their silence in mind when
he confessed to his journal a doubt that a congregation ever truly
unites in a prayer which is spoken from a pulpit. He wished, he said,
that the principle of nonresistance might be tried again, but with more
lasting success than in William Penn's colony. Borrowing from a less
likely source of inspiration, moreover, he came to realize that commitment to truth does not belong exclusively to religious believers. With
reference to Achille Murat, he observed that "I have connected myself
by friendship to a man who with as ardent a love of truth as that
which animates me, . . . is yet that which I had ever supposed only a
creature of the imagination—a consistent atheist—a disbeliever in the
existence . . . of the soul. My faith in these points is strong . . . inde-
structible. Meantime I love and honour this intrepid doubter." When
he came to his showdown with the Second Church, his stated reason for
quitting fell in an historic area of debate in the New England churches,
the communion service. From the early time of the communion's signifying full church membership and therefore citizenship and the right
to vote, it had often had an extra-religious meaning. Now in 1832,
when young Emerson questioned the sacrament, the issue was whether
or not the bread and wine meant anything at all. He said that he could
no longer conduct the service. Thus abandoning his planned career,
Emerson was saying, so early for himself, what he would generalize in
the Divinity School Address five years later. Must a minister call his
people "to the Lord's Supper? He dares not. If no heart warms this rite,
the hollow, dry, creaking formality is too plain. . . . Now the priest's
Sabbath has lost the splendor of nature; it is unlovely; we are glad
when it is done."°

Emerson's exit from the ministry marked much more than his determining on a writing career. It freed him first of all to travel in Europe
and to gather his thoughts. Oddly it seems, for a Transcendentalist, he
avoided Germany. Possibly slowness in the language deterred him;
more probably his unreadiness, even distaste, for ideas which were
systematic and authoritarian counted more heavily. Rather than visit
that heartland beloved of Harvard scholars, he went first to Italy, then
worked his way through Switzerland and France to England and Scotland. Although the trip gave him pleasure, and the end of it made him
great friends, his main insight was to discover that home truths are the

important ones. "The world exists for the education of each man," he would say in his essay on "History" a decade later. "He should see that he can live all history in his own person. He must sit solidly at home, and not suffer himself to be bullied by kings or empires, but know that he is greater than all the geography and all the government of the world; he must transfer the point of view from which history is commonly read, from Rome and Athens and London, to himself, and not deny his conviction that he is the court, and if England or Egypt have anything to say to him, he will try the case."°

Three years passed between his return to America and his settling down and publishing *Nature*, the essay which would become the foundation piece of his philosophy. In 1835 he married Lydia Jackson. Their partnership produced four children and a wealth of devotion, a great source of Emerson's strength. Beginning in the historic Old Manse, they made their home in Concord into a yet more historic workshop and the main location of Transcendentalist talk. While their marriage was young, Emerson completed his shift of career. From having been a minister with a disposition toward letters he became a professional writer, essayist and poet, with a kind of noninstitutional ministry on the side. For years he did considerable free-lance preaching, not very different from his lecturing under lyceum and other auspices. Although neither his speaking nor his writing became profitable in a way to compare with fortunes soon to be made in America, Emerson did passably well in that sense. His essays and poems were promptly published and purchased. With that kind of success, and the benefit of his situation in Concord, he gradually became something of a public man. Always a seer, sometimes a reformer, every facet of his work had power to attract. The expressive presidents aside—Jefferson, Jackson, Lincoln, and the Roosevelts—it would be hard today to name another American upon whom history has conferred an equal charisma.

Although many volumes have been written to sort out the ideas which converged at Concord and went out from there, there is no better choice for us, dealing with the elements of the problem, than to return to Emerson's own account with which this chapter opens. The key to the ferment of the 1820s and 1830s, he said, is that "the mind had become aware of itself. Men grew reflective and intellectual. There was a new consciousness." By the time of this writing Emerson had become more respectful than earlier of German philosophy and letters. He had read much more German. In 1850 he selected Goethe to be "The Writer" in his series of essays in *Representative Men*; now he acknowledged that "Immanuel Kant has made the best catalogue of the human faculties and the best analysis of the mind. Hegel also, especially." One thing that Emerson saw or thought he saw in Germany was "multiplicity" of talent, something "hundred-handed, Argus-eyed, able and happy to cope with all this miscellany of facts and sciences." He makes it seem that Kant and Hegel and Fichte, Goethe and Heine, and the German university scholars were offering America an object lesson, that man can think freshly about nature and man in this world.° He credited also European mysticism. Here he paid generous respects to Emanuel Swedenborg, whom also he had honored with a place in *Representative Men*. Doubtless remembering two Swedenborgians, Henry James (the elder) of New York and Sampson Reed of Boston, who were personal friends but critics of his philosophy, Emerson said of the Swedish seer that he was "a man of prodigious mind . . . as I think tainted with a certain suspicion of insanity, . . . but exerting a singular power over an important intellectual class."° In such ways distributing his credits, Emerson as brief historian of Transcendentalism was strangely silent about the Far Eastern and Near Eastern literature he himself studied and sometimes followed.° But he may have had Oriental borrowings in mind when he jotted of the early Transcendentalists that "the individual is the world."

While he put down specific sources of inspiration and encouragement, he recorded also—what Achille Murat had brought home to him personally earlier—the challenge which came from disbelief in the soul. "The paramount source of the religious revolution was Modern Science." Looking backward and saying this, Emerson was not referring to the great scientists of his own lifetime—neither Baron Cuvier nor Louis Agassiz, not Michael Faraday or Joseph Henry, was part of his calculations. What troubled him was one aspect of the older "Modern Science" and rationalism to which his original Unitarianism was indebted, the eighteenth-century skepticism which sometimes downgraded the spirit in man. Astronomy first, he said, had "taught our insignificance in nature," and very recently geology had completed the lesson. He credited the French with having been foremost in doubting: their "exact, pitiless" minds had slashed down every kind of authority; with them, "Experiment is credible; antiquity is grown ridiculous." The whole modern movement in secular knowledge, he judged, had equipped "young men . . . with knives in their brain, a tendency to introversion, self-dissection, anatomizing of motives." As an example of science with a "rough hand," he mentioned what, imported from Europe, had recently become a fad in America, "Gall and Spurzheim's Phrenology laid a rough hand on the mysteries of animal and spiritual nature." While he admitted to there being "a certain truth in it," Emerson saw in phrenology a vulgar, insensitive, but popular approach to the study of human nature.°

As during his travels Emerson had taken the greatest satisfaction from finding friends in Great Britain and returning home, so again, finding his way with the problem of the soul, the familiar influences were the ones which helped most. To Concord with him from Scotland he had brought the most personal treasure picked up on his journey, his friendship with Thomas Carlyle. Though he would never become as direct a protester as the Scot was against the inhumanities of industrial life, the two now began the long parallel courses which they would keep connected by letters. But more than anyone else, either abroad or at home, William Ellery Channing was the individual who inspired him most and to whom the "Historic Notes" pays greatest tribute. Still the central beloved figure of the Unitarian movement, Channing's external career resembled the one Emerson himself was undertaking: he moved freely from writing desk to lecture platform to occasional pulpit. Although his inner development never impelled him quite inside the Transcendentalist circle, he made the crucial departure from Lockian determinism. In Emerson's own estimation Channing appears to have been a model of human freedom, believer and practitioner both: a man of God, but emancipated from church routines; a humanitarian, but not given to managing other people; supremely an inspirer of letters and thought.°

Yet as none saw better than Emerson did, neither backgrounds nor parallelisms make an awakening. Spiritual leadership was the service he felt called upon, himself, to render. Of course his essay of 1836, *Nature*, was the beginning; in that essay he inserted with intention a phrase from Jonathan Edwards's time, "new light." His own tribulations were still in him, and he came close to saying as much. In the preface he inserted a warning: "Nature is not always tricked out in holiday attire. . . . Nature always wears the colors of the spirit. To a man laboring under calamity, the heat of his own fire hath sadness in it. Then there is a kind of contempt of the landscape felt by him who has just lost by death a dear friend. The sky is less grand as it shuts down over less worth in the population." And in an early passage in the text: "I am glad to the brink of fear."°

As is well known, the total feeling of *Nature* is reassuring, indeed is too cheerful for many present-day tastes. Emerson's recourse, like that of the German philosophers, was to the character of the universe; his purpose, like no one else's in contemporary American expression, was to speak of nature as a whole. Yet he felt that he represented his country. "Our age," he said, "is retrospective. It builds the sepulchres of the fathers. It writes biographies, histories, and criticism. The foregoing generations beheld God and nature face to face; we, through their eyes. Why should not we also enjoy an original relation to the universe? . . . There are new lands, new men, new thoughts. Let us demand our own works and laws and worship." This comes close to the literary Americanism of the two Channings he knew, William Ellery and Edward Tyrrel; it brought him near the old optimism of the agrarian. "What is a farm but a mute gospel?" Emerson himself inquired. But admiring the farmer he observed that "the sailor, the shepherd, the miner, the merchant . . . have each an experience precisely parallel."°

Only in the later passages of the essay, when his subject became more precisely "Nature" than "nature," did Emerson speak strongly in the individualist and mystical vein. "The Universe is composed of Nature and the Soul," he posited, and it is up to the poet and philosopher to speak—"to assert the predominance of the Soul. . . . The sensual man," he reasoned concerning the scientist, "conforms his thought to things; the poet conforms things to his thoughts. The one esteems nature as rooted and fast; the other, as fluid, and impresses his being thereon. . . . The Imagination may be defined to be the use which Reason makes of the material world." This passage, which occurs in the chapter on "Idealism," says that man is given sufficient capacity to comprehend Nature. When he does this he learns that his own soul is a part of the universe and that he is free to govern himself according to Nature's harmonies.

The final step in this reasoning was to add that man, being given so sublime a capacity, will in fact put it to use. This result is not at all predetermined, according to Emerson, for either the few or the many. Even for philosophers and poets, he says, success depends on "love" or "redemption." For them, indeed for all men, the need is to "fasten attention upon immortal" things, or "Ideas." Whoever does so "will think of nature as an appendix to the soul. . . . And no man touches these divine natures, without becoming in some degree, himself divine. . . . No man fears age or misfortune or death in their serene company, for he is transported out of the district of change. Whilst we behold unveiled the nature of Justice and Truth, we learn the difference between the absolute and the conditional, or relative. We apprehend the absolute. As it were, for the first time, *we exist*." Here reaching the apex of his argument, Emerson adds: "The ruin or blank that we see when we look at nature, is in our own eye. . . . The reason why the world lacks unity, and lies broken and in heaps, is because man is disunited with himself. . . . But when a faithful thinker" —a Transcendentalist, the writer is saying—"resolute to detach every object from personal relations and see it in the light of thought, shall, at the same time, kindle science with the fire of the holiest affections, then will God go forth anew into the creation."°

To go with God into the world anew meant taking departures from old bases as well as selecting fresh goals. For Ralph Waldo Emerson Harvard College was the natural Greenwich for recalculating his spiritual longitude; the young men there, about fifteen years younger than himself in the middle 1830s, were the natural people to hear his results practically stated. His alma mater gave the right invitations and he accepted. In 1837, when *Nature* was one year old, he spoke before the chapter of Phi Beta Kappa of which he was a member; and in 1838 he spoke before the Divinity School, where he had been a student ten years earlier.

In the Phi Beta Kappa address, which the world knows as the essay on *The American Scholar,* Emerson applied his guiding principles to academic ways. Specialization of any kind or degree, no matter how necessary or familiar, he reasoned, separates people from one another at risks which need to be understood. Whatever life may demand to the contrary, the search for goodness leads in the opposite direction. "Man is not a farmer, or a professor, or an engineer, but he is all. Man is priest, and scholar, and statesman, and producer, and soldier." Unhappily in the present state of society, "the members have suffered an amputation from the trunk, and strut about so many walking monsters,—a good finger, a neck, a stomach, an elbow, but never a man. . . . The priest becomes a form; the attorney a statute book; the mechanic a machine; the sailor a rope of the ship. In this distribution of functions, the scholar is the delegated intellect. In the right state he is *Man thinking.*"

Emerson especially disliked delegated thinking when it broached moral and spiritual matters. Explaining things to the students, he took middle courses. In the direction of the Harvard faculty, he paid his disrespects to the more narrow scholars, the men who were satisfied to be "restorers of readings," the emendators, the bibliomaniacs. On the other hand, he acknowledged that specialized academic drudgery is not to be avoided: certain aspects of knowledge, the facts of science and history for example, and other "elements," require drill. For the students, he urged the timeless "best books." More than a little of what the next century would call "instrumentalism" appears at this point in *The American Scholar:* "Each age, it is found, must write its own books." And thinkers are actors. "Action is with the scholar subordinate, but it is essential. Without it, he is not yet a man. . . . The preamble of thought, the transition through which it passes from the unconscious to the conscious, is action. Only so much do I know, as I have lived."°

The Phi Beta Kappa address proved not too upsetting at Harvard, which as a college becoming a university was itself in a stage of taking new directions and turning out new books. It could well absorb that kind of criticism from an alumnus of rising fame. But when 1838 came and Emerson on the second invitation delivered a more specific message, his objections to academe became suddenly painful. As he stood before professors and students in the Divinity School, the speaker said, what would destroy the institution if accepted, "that no man can go with his thoughts about him into one of our churches, without feeling that what hold public worship had on men is gone, or going. . . . It is already beginning to indicate character and religion to withdraw from the religious meetings." Evidently intending to kill any supposition among his hearers that he might allow an exception for the Unitarians, Emerson deplored the modern "error that corrupts all attempts to communicate religion. . . . It has dwelt, it dwells, with noxious exaggeration about the *person* of Jesus." This referred to the habit of New England liberals, as they rejected the idea of the Trinity, of stressing— what orthodox Christians stressed differently—the exact example, the performance on earth, of Jesus.

Emerson was speaking for a religion of principle, not personality.

> The soul knows no persons. It invites every man to expand to the full circle of the universe, but will have no preferences but those of spontaneous love. . . . Good is positive. Evil is merely privative, not absolute: it is like cold which is the privation of heat. . . . The intuition of the moral sentiment is an insight of the perfection of the laws of the soul. These laws execute themselves. They are out of time, out of space, and not subject to circumstance. . . . If a man is at heart just, then so far is he God; the safety of God, the immortality of God, the majesty of God, do enter into that man with justice.°

For 1838 and for many years—thirty years would pass before he would be invited to speak there again—this was too much for Harvard. And indeed it would be hard, even in our own times of individualist feeling against one form of establishment or another, to imagine how Emerson could have gone further than he did to incite students to secede from the church. His secessionism put him, we can now see, in direct line with Anne Hutchinson and all antinomians. Like her, being prompted as he believed in a holy way from within, he denied all other authority. But different from hers, his denials were made in a context of freedom. The polity and culture in which he lived allowed him to speak and act subversively among those institutions—church and college—which were no longer allied with the state. The self-assertion of Ralph Waldo Emerson needs to be remembered, accordingly, for the external opportunity which it enjoyed but did not create, as well as for its acuteness and integrity.

4 Transcendentalism and Society: Emerson, Thoreau, and Others

RALPH Waldo Emerson and his friends in and out of Concord thought a great deal about society, in both the two common meanings of that word. In the meaning of desirable and compatible company, they acted at about the time of his second marriage. Emerson joined Frederic Henry Hedge and George Ripley, who were Unitarian ministers of his own age and who knew German philosophy, and a dozen or so others to form what they called the "Symposium" or the "Hedge Club"—the Transcendental Club as history knows it. Among people who have appeared earlier in these pages, Bronson Alcott and Elizabeth Peabody of the Temple School were members. Young essayists and poets they nearly all were; women members were few, but few of the men achieved more than Margaret Fuller and Elizabeth Peabody. Several were still in their twenties. Henry David Thoreau is the most remembered of this group; but Jones Very, whose mystical poetry has won increasing regard in our times, and William Ellery Channing, a nephew of his eminent namesake, were also among them. Not since Franklin's Junto a century earlier, not again until the Metaphysical Club in Cambridge around 1880, does the American record show an equal gathering devoted to discussing and applying ideas.

According to Emerson's own testimony, while the club flourished in personal affinity and the excitement of shared convictions, it intentionally avoided taking collective action. In his words, "As these persons became in the common chances of society acquainted with each other, there resulted certainly strong friendships, which of course were exclusive in proportion to their heat." Emerson doubtless was remembering the devotion between Thoreau and himself as he said this, but he had outgoing goodwill for all. Bronson Alcott, he recorded, was their "pure idealist, who read Plato as an equal, and inspired his companions only in proportion as they were intellectual"; Theodore Parker, so different from himself yet intellectually sympathetic, was their "Savonarola, an excellent scholar, . . . [and] the tribune of the people, and the stout Reformer to urge and defend every cause of humanity." It is true, the same authority explained, that Bostonians believed that in Concord "there was some concert of *doctrinaires* to establish certain opinions and inaugurate some movement in literature, philosophy and religion." But such opinions were uninformed: "the supposed conspirators were quite innocent; for there was no concert and only here and there two or three men or women who read and wrote, each alone, with unusual vivacity. Perhaps they only agreed in having fallen upon Coleridge and Wordsworth and Goethe, then on Carlyle, with pleasure and sympathy. Otherwise their education and reading were not marked, but had the American superficialness, and their studies were solitary."

The one appeal to the world which Emerson acknowledged that the club made was "the modest quarterly journal called *The Dial*, which . . . enjoyed its obscurity for four years. . . . Yet it contained some noble papers by Margaret Fuller, and some numbers had an instant and exhausting sale, because of papers by Theodore Parker."° Of course Emerson speaks too modestly of *The Dial*; besides the authors he mentions, he himself, Thoreau, Alcott, George Ripley (who served as assistant editor), and Elizabeth Peabody were early contributors. And though the Transcendentalists' "studies were solitary" as he said, the Bostonians were hardly wrong in supposing that a deep community joined them in ideas and purposes. To offer just four illustrations, apart from the central figure: Bronson Alcott produced his "Orphic Sayings"; Margaret Fuller, her *Woman in the Nineteenth Century*; Theodore Parker, his *Discourse of Matters Pertaining to Religion* and his *Touching the Matter of Slavery*; and Thoreau, his *Essay on Civil Disobedience*, all between 1842 and 1848. In the hindsight of today all those writings seem to have been American firsts during their period: respectively first in child-study speculation, first in expressing the woman movement, first in socially radical religion, and first in the philosophical defiance of state power. With so much that was dedicated to an emancipation of one kind or another and was intellectually coherent with Emerson's own positions, any contemporary who saw some concert in Transcendentalist writings would seem to have been correct.

As we have seen briefly, looking at Brook Farm through a telescope focused on the Fourierist movement, Transcendentalism had a sideline which led to communitarian organization. Yet the Transcendentalists who refused to take it, who at most went to the farm to visit, are so conspicuous that there is no cause to imagine it truly lay on the main line, although that error has been made. Emerson and Thoreau refused; Bronson Alcott, who would seem to have been natural for membership, visited England during the early period of the farm and later founded his own community, Fruitlands. The Transcendentalists who were the most active in reform and affairs, Theodore Parker, Elizabeth Peabody, and Margaret Fuller, like Emerson were sympathetic and sometimes visited awhile. Nathaniel Hawthorne, who was not a member of the Transcendental Club or entirely of its philosophy, was the most distinguished—indeed the only still-remembered—Brook Farm member and resident of that kind. The president of the organization, the Reverend George Ripley, was of course an early member of the Transcendentalist Club. He had served fifteen years as a Unitarian minister and had followed Emerson out of the ministry. But his gift, and that of his wife Sophia, was more for organizing and editing than for writing.

Much that is telling about the ideas, the suppositions, and tastes of the Transcendentalists occurred at Brook Farm. Their romantic anti-materialism contained anti-urban and anti-industrial components: this seems implicit in their choosing collectivized farming and a rough-hewn Fourierism of their own, before they adopted Fourier, as the best way to live. The Brook Farmers hired an experienced farm manager. The work they did under his direction, having assigned him to keep them at proper duty, and especially the trials the Ripleys suffered to keep the enterprise afloat, speak of the seriousness, even the heroism, of the six years on the farm. Yet as at the time of recruiting, many of the best men did not volunteer, so during the operation proper, somewhat less than full commitments were acted out. The Brook Farmers would not have been Transcendentalists (mainly) if they had not talked a great deal of the time, and if, with or without Miss Peabody's slogan, they had not cared more for their "Leisure to live in all the faculties of the soul" than for hoeing their rows. Hawthorne's famous fictionized history, *A Blithedale Romance*, catches a comic element at the farm. And Emerson himself, though he criticized that novel as being unworthy of the author, voiced a detachment about Fourierist-style organization which says more than his simple nonparticipation. "I regard these [communitarian] philanthropists as themselves the effects of the age in which we live. . . . They were not the creators they believed themselves, but were the unconscious prophets of a true state of society. . . . The large cities are phalansteries."° Altogether the plainest characteristic of Transcendentalism embodied in Brook Farm was its instrumentalism. The farm gave individuals a chance to be themselves in mutual experimentation. It was an adventure in, not a large fulfillment of, the intellectual movement.

More like a fulfillment of Transcendentalist imperatives, indeed very much like completions of Emerson's secessions from church and university during the 1830s, were the exits from society made by Henry Thoreau during the following decade. The starting point of this part of our story is the youth of Thoreau: he was at Harvard and only nineteen when Emerson's *Nature* appeared in 1836; the next year, about to graduate, he may well have been present (we do not know surely) as a member of Phi Beta Kappa when Emerson delivered his address, *The American Scholar*. There is no doubt that he accepted Emerson's messages or that, as he now lived mainly in his parental home at Concord, his friendship with Emerson utterly inspired him. There is equally no doubt that he had to be a Transcendentalist of his own kind. During the eight or nine years between finishing college and his memorable separations from society—going to live alone at Walden Pond in 1845, going the next year to jail—he wrote a nature book which would be published later, *A Week on the Concord and Merrimack Rivers*. It was a dull performance, but it set a mode. During the fourteen years which remained to him after living at Walden, his writings, generally speaking, combined in one way or another a fondness for life close to nature with ideas of protest. His books and essays on camping were also philosophical declarations; and his essays on politics and economics were also moral writings, with practical reconciliation to nature the basic impulse. His masterpiece of 1854, *Walden*, displays all these qualities; his prime essay on political protest, *Civil Disobedience*, is only to a degree an exception. That little book, published in 1849 after his second (very brief) departure from society, is what first made him a public thinker.

As far as he could arrange things, Thoreau created for himself the situation of 1846 which led to his being jailed. He had omitted for four years to pay the poll tax; Bronson Alcott had done this and had been arrested (but not jailed), and he wanted to make the same gesture with all possible effect. One of the reasons for the defiance was the Massachusetts way of still having tax collectors collect church dues; this seems objectionable enough now that the state's old alliance with the church had been abandoned. But by the summer of 1846, with the Mexican War in progress, abolitionists were advocating tax refusal as a way of resisting any toleration of slavery and any expansion of slavery beyond Texas. All this so affected Thoreau that when, on a chance meeting with the constable of Concord, that official said, "Henry, if you don't pay, I'll have to lock you up pretty soon," he replied, "As well now as any time, Sam." Such an event had not occurred earlier because Constable Sam Staples liked the delinquent and kept postponing action. The event ended as satisfactorily as possible: it bestowed on Thoreau freedom to write of having defied government on principle. By his own account, the night in jail gave him an agreeable opportunity to talk with his cell mate. Not altogether "unfortunately," although that was his own word, his aunt paid the tax the next morning and he was able to return to Walden.

At least the incarceration lasted long enough to give rise to the story, which is possibly true but not established, that Emerson visited the jail and asked, "Henry, why are you there?" To which Thoreau replied, "Why are you not here?" There is no doubt about the older man's appreciation and understanding of the younger:

> It cost him nothing to say No; indeed he found it much easier than to say Yes. . . . [He was] a protestant *a outrance*, and few lives contain so many renunciations. He was bred to no profession; he never married; he lived alone; he never went to church; he never voted; he refused to pay a tax to the State; he ate no flesh; he drank no wine; he never knew the use of tobacco; and, though a naturalist, he used neither trap nor gun. He chose, no doubt wisely for himself, to be a bachelor of thought and Nature.°

The essay which was first called *Resistance to Civil Government* and later *On the Duty of Civil Disobedience* followed the night in jail by three years. The question which bore on the author was how to live with a government which sustained slavery—that is, a basic public injustice. In part he answered with counter questions:

> Can there not be a government in which majorities do not virtually decide right and wrong, but conscience? . . . Practically speaking, the opponents to a reform in Massachusetts are not a hundred thousand politicians at the South, but a hundred thousand merchants and farmers here, who . . . are not prepared to do justice to the slave and to Mexico, cost *what* it *may*. I quarrel not with far-off foes, but with those who, near at home, coöperate with, and do the bidding of, those far away, and without whom the latter would be harmless. . . . I do not hesitate to say, that those who call themselves Abolitionists should at once effectually withdraw their support, both in person and property, from the government of Massachusetts and not wait till they constitute a majority of one, before they suffer the right to prevail through them. . . . Moreover, any man more right than his neighbors constitutes a majority of one already. . . . Under a government which imprisons any unjustly, the true place for a just man is also a prison. The proper place to-day, the only place which Massachusetts has provided for her freer and less desponding spirits, is in her prisons.

His night in prison had taught Thoreau that the state is by no means all-powerful.

> I saw that the State was half-witted, that it was timid as a lone woman with her silver spoons, and that it did not know its friends from its foes, and I lost all my remaining respect for it, and pitied it. . . . The State never intentionally confronts a man's sense, intellectual or moral, but only his body, his senses. It is not armed with superior wit or honesty, but with superior physical strength. I was not born to be forced. . . . I have never declined paying the highway tax, because I am as desirous of being a good neighbor as I am of being a bad subject; and as for supporting schools, I am doing my part to educate my fellow-country-men now. . . . I do not care to trace the course of my dollar, if I could, till it buys a man or a musket to shoot with,—the dollar is innocent,—but I am concerned to trace the effects of my allegiance. In fact, I quietly declare war with the State, after my fashion, though I will still make what use and get what advantage of her I can, as is usual in such cases. . . . I please myself with imagining a State at last which can afford to be just to all men, and to treat the individual with respect as a neigh-bor. . . . A State which bore this kind of fruit, and suffered it to drop off as fast as it ripened, would prepare the way for a still more perfect and glorious State, which also I have imagined, but not yet anywhere seen.°

Thoreau's *Walden* followed by seven years his period of living in the woods, by the waterside, in calculated separation from the economic community. Published in 1854, in the climax time of the whole Transcendentalist-Hawthorne-Melville-Whitman literary epoch, it was the one full book-size performance by any of the major Transcendentalists. Not the least of its achievements, and entirely in line with *A Week on the Merrimack* and his articles on the Maine woods and Cape Cod (which would reach book form only posthumously), the book bespeaks the wonder of wilderness living. To its unsurpassed verbalizing of the sights, sounds, and smells of the woods it owes a large part of its century-long popularity. There is much of intimacy with nature, nothing of conquest of nature, about it. The land whereon Thoreau found this kind of inspiration belonged legally to Emerson; the younger man lived on it in a kind of extension of both Emerson's possession and his thought. Thoreau returned frequently enough to Lydia Emerson's table to keep the unending discourse from flagging. The primary idea of the withdrawal was that "the order of things should be somewhat reversed." As he had said when he was twenty, "The seventh should be man's day of toil, wherein to earn his living; the other six the Sabbath of the affections and the soul—in which to range this widespread garden, and think."

Many famous pages of the opening chapter, on "Economy," explain how he actually lived that way. He accounts among many items for the $28.12½ he paid for the materials he used on his cabin, and for the $8.74 he laid out for provisions for eight months; on the credit side he is equally exact about, selecting again, the $36.78 he took from selling vegetables and doing odd jobs. Finding that he fell behind $25.21¾ during the twenty-six months, he balanced that loss against "the leisure and independence and health thus secured, a comfortable home for me as long as I chose to occupy it." He made comparisons and reinforced them with his insight.

> I see young men, my townsmen, whose misfortune it is to have inherited farms, houses, barns, cattle, and farming tools. . . . Who made them serfs of the soil? . . . The mass of men lead lives of quiet desperation. . . . From the desperate city you go to the desperate country, and have to console yourself with the bravery of minks and muskrats. A stereotyped but unconscious despair is concealed even under what are called the games and amusements of mankind. There is no play in them, for this comes after work. But it is a characteristic of wisdom not to do desperate things. . . . I have lived some thirty years on this planet, and I have yet to hear the first syllable of valuable or even earnest advice from my seniors. . . . Confucius said, "To know that we know what we know, and that we do not know what we do not know, that is true knowledge." When one man has reduced a fact of the imagination to be a fact to his understanding, I foresee that all men will at length establish their lives on that basis.°

Sixteen very short chapters on "Where I Lived and What I Lived For," on "Sounds" and "Solitude," "The Bean-Field," "The Ponds," and "Brute Neighbors" and "Winter Animals," make good on the promise given in the long first chapter that health, sanity, and sense are the rewards of living simply in accord with the laws of nature. But the point of protest in *Walden* had been made earlier, as we have just seen. Much as in *Civil Disobedience* Thoreau had quietly declared war against the state, a position which *Walden* reiterates, in the later book he declared war on the economy, more on the mind and the taste of the economy than on its operating institutions. He had insisted that a state could possibly be dedicated to justice and that, with that goal achieved, yet better might come. He now asked for an economy based on something more human than raw competition to acquire and retain goods. When men understand themselves and love nature outside themselves, *Walden* tells us, they truly enjoy simple living. Given beauty and moral sense, honoring the Sabbath six days of the week, they will not be driven by the market.

5   Perfectionism and Democracy

WHEN Owenite, Fourierist, Shaker, Mormon, or any other kind of communitarian reached for the future, his goals in his own judgment were quite perfect. But he was guided by a book. That is to say, though he reached beyond the expectations of politics, economics, and morality, his ceiling was not unlimited. Even were he one who believed in the millennium, he believed also that Christ would soon return, or had already returned, to begin his rule on this so familiar earth. The communitarians made plans for the morrow and laid up all the treasures they could.

In this respect the Transcendentalists differed. As a group they were more perfectionist, at any rate more idealist, than Owenites or Fourierists generally; among themselves, Emerson and Thoreau were more so than the Brook Farmers. Emerson began by denying the church in order to serve true religion. In hard days of grief and self-assertion, he discovered that not Jesus alone but any man, if he served Justice and Truth, took on divinity. Thoreau declared war on his government; he denounced the state so soundly that *Civil Disobedience* would during the next century thrill defiers of the British raj in India and unwilling American draftees. Yet he envisaged a state which would be governed, and would govern, well; he glimpsed beyond that a yet better system, its constitution not divulged, but he meant government by love.

Thoreau hated what work six days a week, getting and gaining, did to men. It is fair to call him anti-industrial, probably not fair to call him anticapitalist. A critique of his in 1843 for the *Democratic Review* of a book by a German immigrant in Pittsburgh, J. A. Etzler, about whom little is known except the technocratic writing which Thoreau considered, tells why he distrusted technology and factories in the present condition of society:

> How meanly and grossly do we deal with nature! Could we not have a less gross labor? What else do these fine inventions suggest,—magnetism, the daguerreotype, electricity? Can we not do more than cut and trim the forest, can we not assist its interior economy, in the circulation of the sap? . . . It will be seen that we contemplate a time when man's will shall be law to the physical world, and he shall no longer be deterred by such abstractions as time and space, height and depth, weight and hardness, but shall indeed be the lord of creation.

Making fun of perpetual motion, and of the surplus products Etzler called the "Paradise within the Reach of All Men, Without Labour, by Powers of Nature and Machinery," the reviewer concluded: "The chief fault of this book is, that it aims to secure the greatest degree of gross comfort and pleasure merely. It paints a Mahometan's heaven. . . . There is far too much hurry and bustle, and too little patience and privacy, in all our methods, as if something were to be accomplished in centuries. . . . What is time but the stuff delay is made of?" Judging, Thoreau appealed to Hindu wisdom: "He whose mind is at ease is possessed of all riches." But his final quotation was from Sir Walter Raleigh: "The souls of men loving and fearing God receive influence from that divine light itself, whereof the sun's clarity, and that of the stars, is by Plato called but a shadow."° On this more particular testimony, as well as on that of *Walden*, Thoreau seems more like a scourge of economic materialism than an opponent of any economic system.

Much the same quality inheres in the radicalism, the anarchist factor, of his political convictions. Even in *Civil Disobedience*, in the fourth paragraph following the declaration of war on the state, Thoreau acknowledged that the American "Constitution, with all its faults, is very good; the law and the courts are very respectable; even this State and this American government are, in many respects, very admirable, and rare things, to be thankful for, such as a great many have described them." But this concession carried the author to no reconciliation; it led simply to restating his doubts. "Seen from a point of view a little higher, [State, law, and government] are what I have described them; seen from a higher still, and the highest, who shall say what they are, or that they are worth looking at or thinking of at all?"° By Thoreau's standards of justice and love, the state as protector of slavery and wager of war invited the most eloquent doubts. These he could put in words. Any other political system than the American one, however, like some possible alternate economic system, was nothing his mind reached for. Institutions were not the answer.

Emerson's mind unfolded more gradually in these directions, and more toward politics than toward economics. Within the sovereign, involuntary institution of the state during the 1840s, as within the disestablished, voluntary institution of the church during the 1830s, he felt uneasy but not defiant of ultimate goals. The "rank rabble Jacksonism of the country," as he spoke of it, offended him. Yet he admitted to himself, as his journal indicates, that Transcendentalism and democracy begin on the same footing. "The root and seed of democracy is the doctrine, Judge for yourself." And again: "Democracy, freedom has its roots in the sacred truth that every man has in him divine reason, or that . . . all men are capable of so doing. That is the equality and the only equality of man. To this truth we look when we say, Reverence thyself; Be true to thyself."°

In "Man the Reformer," the lecture he gave before a workingmen's library association in 1841, Emerson posed the question so often quoted, "What is a man born for but to be a Reformer, a Re-maker of what man has made?" The answer for him was not to be a do-gooder; in that disinclination he resembled Thoreau entirely. "The idea which now begins to agitate society has a wider scope than our daily employments, our households, and the institutions of property. We are to revise the whole of our social structure, the state, the school, religion, marriage, trade, science, and explore their foundations in our own nature; we are to see that the world . . . fits us, and to clear ourselves of every usage which has not its roots in our own mind."° Other speakers might have offered an audience of mechanics more specific advice. But once he had ventured—what accorded with current labor thinking—that, farm life apart, "the whole of our social structure" was altogether too far severed from "our own nature . . . our own mind," he left his listeners with scanty advice.

Only during the middle 1840s and after did Emerson become very particular about affairs; doubtless he was affected by the events which affected Thoreau and by Thoreau himself. His essay on "Politics," 1844, argued against investing much faith in that field. "In dealing with the State we ought to remember that its institutions are not aboriginal. . . . The State must follow and not lead the character and progress of the citizen. . . . The history of the State sketches in coarse outline the progress of thought, and follows at a distance the delicacy of culture and of aspiration. . . . Every actual State is corrupt. Good men must not obey the laws too well." Saying so much, though, the prime Transcendentalist did not secede from the state or declare war. "The philosopher, the poet, or the religious man, will of course wish to cast his vote with the democrat, for free-trade, for wide suffrage, for the abolition of legal cruelties in the penal code, and for facilitating in every manner the access of the young and the poor to the sources of wealth and power. But he can rarely accept the persons whom the so-called popular party propose to him as representatives of these liberalities. . . ."° At the end of the decade, writing his *Representative Men* essay on "Napoleon; or the Man of the World," Emerson estimated that the emperor of France had been accepted so widely across Europe because he imposed with grandeur what the people of the times loved. Napoleon was honored, in short, because he stood for the power and corruption of a revolution, and his system promoted the making of money. Emerson came close to indicting middle-class culture in this essay.

Coming now to our final drafts on Emerson, we need return to 1841 when he was midway between the hard years of self-discovery, writing *Nature* and the Harvard defiances, and the time of increasing preoccupation with public events. Not all his prose at that time was the strongest: "Man the Reformer" is vague, and "Compensation" makes the moral life seem too easy to accord with the author's own values. But there is no doubt about "Self-Reliance," the essay which seems to draw the whole moral vision of the Transcendentalist movement into one focus. "To believe your own thought, to believe that what is true for you in your private heart is true for all men,—that is genius," he observed at the beginning. "The highest merit we ascribe to Moses, Plato, and Milton is, that they set at naught books and traditions, and spoke not what men but what *they* thought. . . . Great men have always done so. . . . And we are now men. . . . Good and bad are but names readily transferable to that or this; the only right is what is after my constitution; the only wrong is what is against it." What is needed, the sage was saying, is capacity for ideals, strength not to be misled. He warned equally against "the rage of the cultivated classes" and "the indignation of the people . . . the unintelligent brute force that lies at the bottom of society." He asserted: "The soul raised over passion beholds identity and external causation, perceives the self-existence of Truth and Right."° If there is a single sentence in American literature which answers Tocqueville's derogation of individualism, this sentence, wherein Emerson said he tried for "the highest truth on this subject," is the one.

Not to be ruled by a book and a leader, but by the spirit and the mind, was the difference between the Transcendentalists and the other perfectionists of the day. Not to be ruled by the market place or even the forum, but by conscience and thought, was the Transcendentalist answer, not entirely defiant, to the democracy of Andrew Jackson.

From Expansion to Crisis at Mid-century: In Third Cycle of Public Thought

Always planning to close the present volume at mid-century, the writer at one time was uncertain whether the final chapter should be peopled as it now is with perfectionists, men who were sometimes quite unpolitical but were universally assertive of individual or community freedom, or with attackers and defenders of Negro slavery, some of them very thoughtful, who were increasingly taking control of affairs. Ralph Waldo Emerson's saying that the Transcendentalists resembled the New Lights of one century earlier and the Puritan Platonists of two centuries earlier than themselves points to the reasons for choosing the perfectionists. Neither the men of Concord nor the communitarians, who were dispersed from Maine to Utah, were numerous or popular. Yet they do supremely represent a great part of the past which has been the burden of this history: the expression, in words, actions, and institutions, of goals of self-realization.

But while our closing Chapter XVI is governed by the two-hundred-fifty-year past of 1850, the very recent past demands mention, and estimation for historical size and significance, at the end. There is no room for doubt about size. Even while this volume stands back from the brink of 1861, and after 1833 avoids the complex story of slavery and antislavery which connects in a thousand ways with matters we do mention, the very absence of that story is conspicuous. But the apology for absence is simple and I hope complete. To have included at the end of this volume the growth of convictions for and against slavery, and ideas about federalism, states' rights, and nationalism, and about race and race relations, would have both destroyed the coherency of this volume and thrown those things themselves out of the centrality they demand. They are huge and serious business, indeed, in the history of public thought, but they belong elsewhere.

Yet mere mention of the problem is to notice, in addition, that for the third time in this history, great expansion and great outlay of cultural energy in America was immediately accompanied by doubts and challenges, and before long by political disintegration and violence. Emotional intensities are hard to compare from period to period, but we have met with the pessimism of the Boston Puritans before the Revolution of 1688, and later with the forebodings thrown at the establishment by the Puritan New Lights before the American Revolution. So again now, in the same region but having to do with the issue of slavery—even while for most people the Great Compromise of 1850 eased moral and political anxiety—foresight and concern bred fear and doubt. A visitor to political-party headquarters in Massachusetts during election year 1848, or thereafter, could not have escaped the feeling which spread that both the Democrats and the Whigs, whose leaders—Daniel Webster the greatest—were accustomed to being taken seriously on grounds of principle, had fallen out of touch with moral reality. Were national politics incapable of doing right? As we know, the people had heard that doubt recently from Transcendentalists and sectarians; they had heard it earlier, to the point of nullification, from South Carolinians. It was not a prevailing doubt in 1850, but it tells us that then, as in earlier centuries, tensions which were building toward large upheaval cast shadows ahead, across people's vistas of foresight.

Indeed, to look backward from the 1970s to the years surrounding 1850 may readily become an exercise in poignancy. On the bright side is the once satisfying record of population and economic growth, and the corresponding habit of common belief in social and national progress. More specifically: the recent, successful, adventurous, and acquisitive War with Mexico, and the spirit of Manifest Destiny; the acquirement of the Pacific seaboard and a promising port for Oriental trade; the rapid agricultural and commercial occupation of the wide Mississippi valley; the growth of cities in every region; the manifold growth of technology with steam technology, especially as realized in railroads and riverboats, acquiring a mystique from its hoped-for capacity to link together the parts of the nation. On the dark side, apart from politics, was the more than beginning process of population redistribution. New York had already become massive. Partly owing to enormous immigration both before and after 1850, that city was soaring from its recently achieved population of half a million to the well over a million it would reach before Appomattox; half the size of contemporary London, New York was now several times the size of the London from which colonizers had sailed during the 1630s—which was the last time for two centuries when men who have roles in this book resided in a city larger than one hundred thousand. Meanwhile massiveness, not equal to New York's but counted in six digits, was happening to Philadelphia, Baltimore, Boston, and New Orleans; perhaps even more dramatically, river and lake ports in the West were achieving populations (though still under one hundred thousand) which were much larger than the colonial capitals and seaports in their period of brilliance had ever achieved—Philadelphia, New York, Boston, Providence, and Charleston. Through the nation as a whole, where, when the republic was new, the ratio of urban population had been one in thirty, now it was approaching one in six and would become that before the firing on Sumter; it would rise to one in three during the expansive but often depression-marked years between then and the end of the century. While all this growth multiplied zest and self-congratulation among contemporaries, in today's situation one notices that the largest cities often fermented Know Nothing intolerance. One notices also that, while cities gave some opportunity for living to free blacks and in the South provided diversified employment for slaves who were brought in from plantations, these situations evoked new racial barriers which were harsh. Already Negro ghettos were forming in cities in all parts of the land.

But for present purposes we are less concerned to view the beginning of modern social problems during the middle of the nineteenth century than we are to visualize the fact that, once again as during the seventeenth and eighteenth centuries, social strains immediately followed a great expansion and shortly preceded an upset of government. More specifically, our final problem is to envisage as a continuity the recurrences of public situation and public response which we have met, over the course of two and one-half centuries, in cycles of about ninety years. Some of the recurrences are plainly marked in the text, especially the ones which affected political ideas, where precedent and renewal— say between the Glorious Revolution and the American Revolution— are conspicuous. But no earlier place in this volume has been the right place to view the continuity from first to last, and to make over-all comparisons from cycle to cycle.

Let us draw such an outline of the content, or the phases, of the cycles as our data will sustain. In the period of primary colonization, the early seventeenth century, the 1630s the principal decade, (1) the occupation of spacious territories by settlers who had considerable freedom for self-organization—indentured servants and slaves excepted—was the essential work, a process which immediately affected thought. Even though a great reason for founding a colony may have been a wish to achieve some religious or political or economic liberation not to be had at home, settlers arriving on the edge of the wilderness had to think of organization—of security, of food, of law and order. The voluntary agreement which the Pilgrims made among themselves, the Mayflower Compact, is only the most eloquent case of freedom men turning to organization when they started life in the New World. Virginia's representative assembly of 1619, and Massachusetts's theocratic commonwealth of the 1630s, represent the same priority. This was the most imaginative period in the building of communities, and in thought about community-building, in all American history.

Even so, we have seen two comparable times, the first of them early in the eighteenth century. Of course the non-English settlers who came at that time were granted no such freedoms and powers of self-government as the primary colonists had been given. Yet the Germans, though they were the most politically passive of all colonial settlers, constructed the institutions they cherished most, their churches, quite in the ways they desired; and the Scots Irish, who dispersed themselves the full length of the seaboard, at once dominated certain communities and, by way of the federative principles of the Church of Scotland, became the first Americans to succeed in north-to-south and east-to-west institutional organization.

Land occupation, both on the frontier and behind it, was a process which never quite stopped. The second wave of immigration and settlement which bears comparison with the original one waited for national independence, and indeed for peace on the frontiers which did not come before 1815. Carrying first into the Tennessee and the Ohio valleys, then into the wider basin of the Mississippi, this became the most massive of all American agricultural migrations. Paradoxically it may seem in the long view, occupiers of unoccupied territory at this time entered a more structured situation, as to the organization of government and the distribution of land, than had the colonial fathers. The structuring had been part of the great political work of the 1780s. The American republic seemed to newcomers to offer almost the earth: always and everywhere, civil rights and republican government; north of the Ohio, uncommon encouragement to education, and exclusion of slavery; everywhere, land to live on, and earn a living on, on terms which at first were rather restrictive but after 1825 became favorable. Within this framework, those settlers who came with utopian programs had as much self-organizing to do as they wished; those whose precommitment took the shape of ambitions for wealth and power could proceed either politically or economically, nearly always using institutions they helped to form: partnerships or corporations, school boards or constitutional conventions, churches or political parties, or frequently a combination of many. Where, during the seventeenth century, imagination which was often religiously inspired had been the special characteristic of thought and feeling about organizing life in the New World, now, during the early nineteenth century, secular and religious variety in social ideas outdid all previous experience.

The second phase which appears in all three cycles began in every case while the first was still in process: it was more like an early second-thinking than like a later thinking of public needs and goals. (2) We may call it the volunteering of public thought, constructive and critical. In the seventeenth century the constructive part was doing the business of the new colonies; it included extensions and amendments, but consisted essentially in fulfilling the accepted plan. In Massachusetts this phase came with the reaction after the Antinomian controversy: the theocracy was then made firm; the schools were established. In Maryland, passing the Toleration Act, which made virtuous provincial policy out of necessary practice, represented the phase; in Virginia, the full assimilation and acceptance of the legislature into government, with sizable powers and pretensions, did so. During the second cycle, which as a whole may be dated from about 1715 to the close of the century, the Great Awakening of the 1730s and the 1740s did much of the work of voluntarism; Presbyterian congregations, presbyteries, synods, academies, and college were the principal product. But meanwhile the early Enlightenment in America produced in parallel its own kinds of volunteering; the civic and scientific organizations founded by Benjamin Franklin and his contemporaries represented that phase of fulfillment. During the third cycle, the many-sided reform movement of the early nineteenth century was the most effective product, so far, of voluntarism on the constructive side.

The critical side of this phase displays, in all three cycles, the most purely individualistic performances which appear anywhere in this volume. Though the constructive side produced superb and original spokesmen—John Winthrop and Horace Mann, Benjamin Franklin and Henry Carey, for examples—in the nature of the case deep criticism of society's standards seems regularly to have demanded persons of uncommon gifts, which perhaps began with moral acumen.

At any rate it is impossible to think of public thought in America, during any one of the three cycles, without a few such individuals. During the 1630s and after, Roger Williams and Anne Hutchison became the peerless speakers, before Jefferson, for freedom of conscience and religious conviction. Their defiances struck the root of the Puritan church-state alliance; their arguments still exhibit integrity and thought, as well as courage. From mid-eighteenth century, before and apart from the political crises which led to the American Revolution, top distinction in defiant criticism is not so easily determined; some would think first of John Peter Zenger and Andrew Hamilton. Yet it would be hard to deny to either Jonathan Edwards or John Woolman an estimate of courage and integrity equal to any, or credit for an effective intellectual attack on standards and usages which prevailed in their own communities. After Edwards the Puritan tradition would be always divided, and more fruitful on that account; after Woolman the English-speaking world would never lack an antislavery movement, until the institution was destroyed. Finally, so far as concerns the critical side, during the mid-nineteenth-century years of the third cycle, Emerson and Thoreau now seem to have achieved pre-eminence in their own century equal to that, or greater than that, of any of their predecessors in individual protest. The breadth of their defiances—against misplaced effort in higher education and in church, and against injustice in the system of government and false values in economic theory and practice—makes the Transcendentalists different from those predecessors but, quite as Emerson said, of the same spirit.

The third and fourth phases, which occur in all the cycles, were mainly political, and they require hardly more than recollection and mention here. (3) The third is the phase of widespread rejection of the authority of the national sovereign, and of political and social upset with violence, which has happened three times in America, beginning in 1688, 1775, and 1861. (4) And the fourth is the phase of reconstruction which, in the two cycles this volume has covered, not different from the third one which we may now anticipate under the familiar name, "Reconstruction," has required many years. To speak of the third and fourth phases of the first cycle together, the protest in New England and New York, of 1688 and 1689, which threw Governor Sir Edmund Andros out of the consolidation of autocratic power in which James II had placed him, was of course the American colonial phase of the Glorious Revolution in England. The memorable political theorizing of that revolution was done mainly at home, by John Locke and Algernon Sydney, and only little and late in the colonies, by John Wise in particular. But where the Glorious Revolution in England merely confirmed representative and constitutional government which the Puritan Revolution had essentially established, in the New World it restored legislative autonomy in the great area where it had been eliminated. During the years which followed, to be sure, government directly under the Crown was extended: this occurred colony by colony in Massachusetts, New York, New Jersey, and the Carolinas. And Virginia's previously unique system of government and society—an Anglican church establishment; provincial control balanced between royally appointed governor and representative assembly—became, for about half the colonial world, the norm of life. But the main features of this reconstruction, Anglicanization and royalization, were never consolidated, and—at least until 1765, when Parliament began to act drastically—the colonies managed their own affairs. Again they were free to practice the English tradition of uncentralized representative self-government, very much as when they were new.

In the second or eighteenth-century cycle, the phase of widespread rejection of the national sovereign was of course the phase of 1776—of Jefferson and Adams, independence and the Revolution, the state bills of rights, the disappearance of all but two of the church-state alliances, and of other reductions of the old establishments of power. And, immediately following in that same cycle, the phase of reconstruction is represented, not alone by the replacement of provincial and imperial controls by state and federal, but by constitutions for the nationwide churches, by programs for land occupation, and by economic, educational, and immigration policy which national and state governments put into effect between, approximately, 1787 and 1816.

To recall these phases of the second cycle is to return at the end to the third cycle, which the end of this volume breaks in the middle, between the volunteering of constructive and critical public thought before 1850 and, soon after that date, crisis with region-wide denials of the system of sovereignty, and then violence and devastation.

This anticipation of our Civil War notwithstanding, to the writer, and I hope to the reader, there is comfort, during our own time of trouble, to be taken from contemplating the three cycles, each in four phases of public situation and public thought, like the others. Including politics, but much bigger than politics, and containing economic development, but not dominated by economic affairs, and affected by religion, but not governed by churches, these cycles and phases speak of durability in society and thought about society—of continuity, and crisis, and renewal, over two and one-half centuries in the New World.

Bibliographical Notes

Part One

TRANSATLANTIC OLD REGIME, 1600–1750

The histories of society and culture which apply broadly to the area of Part One have mostly been written since 1925. They have a noble predecessor, now often overlooked: Edward Eggleston, *The Transit of Civilization from England to America in the Seventeenth Century* (1901). The first three volumes of the thirteen-volume *History of American Life* (1928–1948) have bearing and still have usefulness: Herbert I. Priestley, *The Coming of the White Man, 1492–1848* (1929); Thomas Jefferson Wertenbaker, *The First Americans, 1607–1690* (1927); and James Truslow Adams, *Provincial Society, 1690–1763* (1927). Louis B. Wright, whose first concern is the history of literature, is the broadest cultural historian of the colonial epoch as a whole. He has two survey works: *The Cultural Life of the American Colonies, 1607–1763* (1957) in the New American Nation series and *The Atlantic Frontier: Colonial American Civilization, 1607–1763* (1947). Less scope but greater depth and particularity are achieved in the three-volume series by Thomas Jefferson Wertenbaker on *The Founding of American Civilization*—namely, *The Middle Colonies* (1938), *The Old South* (1942), and *The Puritan Oligarchy* (1947).

The basic literary histories of the United States, several of them multivolume and multiauthor, illuminate aspects of the colonial old regime. The principal ones are: Moses Coit Tyler, *History of American Literature, 1607–1765* (2 vols., 1878; one vol., 1949); *The Cambridge History of American Literature*, I, *Colonial and Revolutionary Literature; Early National Literature* (1917); Vernon Louis Parrington, *Main Currents in American Thought*, I, *The Colonial Mind* (1927); and Robert E. Spiller and others,

[541]

eds., *Literary History of the United States* (3 vols., 1948), I, Chapters I–VIII.

CHAPTER I *The Birthright of English Colonies:*
Freedom and Organization

The problem for the American reader is to find general works on English history which consider England as the source of his own culture, a valid but one-sided point of view. From this angle, American scholars have done best. Concerning English society and popular culture, see Carl Bridenbaugh, *Vexed and Troubled Englishmen, 1590–1642* (1968). For deeper background, Lawrence Stone, *The Crisis of the Aristocracy, 1558–1641* (1965). See the introductory volumes of the old and the New American Nation series: Edward P. Cheyney, *European Background of American History, 1300–1600* (1904), and Wallace Notestein, *The English People on the Eve of Colonization, 1603–1630* (1954). Among English scholars, the following help: George S. R. Kitson Clark, *The English Inheritance* (1950); Joseph R. Tanner, *English Constitutional Conflicts of the Seventeenth Century* (1928); John William Allen, *History of Political Thought in the Sixteenth Century* (1928); George N. Clark, *The Seventeenth Century* (1929); Basil Willey, *The Seventeenth Century Background* (1934); and Charles Ogilvie, *The King's Government and Common Law, 1471–1641* (1958).

1 *England: Prime Source of American Thought*

p. 6 Melville quotation from *Redburn: His First Voyage* (1924 ed.), pp. 190–191.

2 *Factors of Tradition: Language and Social Structure*

On English economic society, besides the titles just above, see Alfred L. Rowse, *The England of Elizabeth* (1951); Richard H. Tawney, *The Agrarian Problem in the Sixteenth Century* (1912); and Mildred Campbell, *The English Yeoman under Elizabeth and the Early Stuarts* (1942).

p. 15 Passage from *Troilus and Cressida*, among many others which indicate Elizabethan
l. 14 belief in hierarchy and order, is discussed in Eustace M. W. Tillyard, *The Eliza-*
bethan World Picture (1944), pp. 7–8. For John Adams's knowledge of such matters, see Zoltan Haraszti, *John Adams and the Prophets of Progress* (1952), p. 170.

p. 15 Lines from Hooker, Book I, *Of the Laws of Ecclesiastical Polity* (London, 1882
l. 34 ed.), pp. 106, 58.

p. 18   On parliamentary privilege, see Josef Redlich, *The Procedure of the House of Commons: A Study of Its History and Recent Form* (3 vols., 1908); Mary P. Clarke, *Parliamentary Privilege in the American Colonies* (1943); Leonard W. Levy, *Legacy of Suppression: Freedom of Speech and Press in Early American History* (1960); John E. Neale, "The Commons' Freedom of Speech in Parliament," in Robert W. Seton-Watson, *Tudor Studies* (1924), pp. 257–286; Harold Hulme, "The Winning of Freedom of Speech by the House of Commons," *American Historical Review*, 61 (1955–1956):825–853.

p. 20   For Coke as person, see Catherine Drinker Bowen, *The Lion and the Throne: The Life and Times of Sir Edward Coke (1552–1634)* (1956), from which, p. 484, I quote Coke. For Coke in close context of constitutional history, see Joseph R. Tanner, *English Constitutional Conflicts of the Seventeenth Century, 1609–1683* (1937), especially pp. 35–42, 61–63; and, for another specialized view, William S. Holdsworth, *History of English Law*, V (1924), 423–494.

p. 22   On the idea of toleration in England, Wilbur K. Jordan, *Development of Religious Toleration in England, III, ... 1640–1660* (1940).

CHAPTER II *The Old Order in The New World*

1 *English Ways in American Regions*

p. 30   English sermon and Virginia law are quoted from Perry Miller, *Errand into the Wilderness* (1956), pp. 131–133.

2 *The Old Order Brought Overseas*

The historiographically conservative position concerning continuities of feudalism in America which I adopt in this section has long since been challenged by Louis Hartz, *The Liberal Tradition in America* (1955), Part One. Robert E. Brown, in his *Middle-Class Democracy and the Revolution in Massachusetts, 1691–1780* (1955) and elsewhere, comes up with sustaining fact and idea; many scholars accept this position. Yet I think that the older position is truer, or at least is in such measure true as to sustain my discussion here. It is to be found throughout the works of the "imperial school" of colonial historians, especially Charles M. Andrews and Herbert L. Osgood; the suggestion of their work as to social presupposition is encapsulated nowhere, but Leonard W. Labaree, *Conservatism in Early American History* (1948; paperback, 1959) helps.

p. 33   Quotations from Cotton and Winthrop in Perry Miller and Thomas H. Johnson, eds., *The Puritans* (1938), pp. 210, 183, 206.

p. 34   Malynes, *A Treatise of the Canker of Englands Commonwealth*, and Davenant, *Discourse upon Grants and Resumptions (1700)*, quoted from Philip W. Buck, *The Politics of Mercantilism* (1942), pp. 72–73, 130.

p. 36   See Hartz, *Liberal Tradition*, especially pp. 3–7, 21–27.

p. 39   See Abbot Emerson Smith, *Colonists in Bondage: White Servitude and Convict Labor in America, 1607–1776* (1947), especially Chapter XIII (p. 306 quoted).

p. 40   See Oscar and Mary Handlin, "The Origins of the Southern Labor System," in *Race and Nationality in American Life* (1957), pp. 1–22.

p. 41   See Winthrop Jordan, *White Over Black: American Attitudes Toward the Negro, 1550–1812* (1968; paperback, 1969), especially Chapters I–II. See also Louis Ruchames, "The Sources of Racial Thought in Colonial America," *The Journal of Negro History*, 52 (1967):251–272.

3   English Freedoms Transplanted to Chesapeake Shores

In regard to the three areas of freedom traditionalized in England which concerned us in Chapter I, the history of only one of them has been examined as something directly and consciously transmitted to America; see Mary P. Clarke, *Parliamentary Privilege in the American Colonies* (1943). Evarts B. Greene, *Religion and the State, the Making and Testing of an American Tradition* (1941; paperback, 1959), performs a somewhat similar service, however, in a broad treatment of the separation of church from state; see especially Chapters I–III. There is no one work on English law in early colonial America equivalent to these in breadth. George L. Haskins's *Law and Authority in Early Massachusetts: A Study in Tradition and Design* (1960) comes nearest. The fact that the one colony which it studies is Massachusetts makes it regional in meaning, but the sweep of its analysis, from medieval backgrounds to Bible influences and American foregrounds, and from questions of authority to those of freedom, makes it more than regionally suggestive. See Chapter IV, Section 1.

p. 44   See Thomas J. Wertenbaker, *Give Me Liberty: The Struggle for Self-Government in Virginia* (1958), and Stanley M. Pargellis, "The Procedure of the House of Burgesses," *William and Mary Quarterly*, 2nd Series, 7 (1927):73–86, 143–157.

p. 46   On the Anglican church in Virginia to about 1700, see George M. Brydon, *Virginia's Mother Church and the Political Conditions Under Which It Grew* (2 vols., 1947–1952), I, especially Chapters X–XVIII.

p. 48   For a recent Catholic comment on Maryland toleration, see Thomas O'Brien Hanley, *Their Rights and Liberties: the Beginnings of Religious and Political Freedom in Maryland* (1959). For Charles M. Andrews's comment, see *The Colonial Period of American History* (1935–1938), II, 291; see also Gerald W. Johnson, *The Maryland Act of Religious Toleration, an Interpretation* (1949).

CHAPTER III   *The Puritan Amendment*

Although the Massachusetts tercentennials of the 1930s provided stimulation to scholarly work on seventeenth-century Puritanism with grand results at Harvard, the twentieth-century interest began early and since then has been sustained also at Columbia and other universities. Herbert W. Schneider, *The Puritan Mind* (1930), is the broadest of the twentieth-century revisionist treatments. William Haller's *The Rise of Puritanism* (1938) and *Liberty and Reformation in the Puritan Revolution* (1955) are confined to Puritanism in England. For current English scholarship, see Christopher Hill, *Intellectual Origins of the English Revolution* (1965) and *Society and Puritanism in Pre-Revolutionary England* (1964).

Kenneth B. Murdock's *Increase Mather* (1925) and Samuel Eliot Morison's *Builders of the Bay Colony* (1930) and *The Puritan Pronaos* (1936) were the starters of Harvard's modernism about the Puritans. Perry Miller's *Orthodoxy in Massachusetts, 1630–1650* (1933) began his distinguished series of intellectual and institutional studies, with first attention to the institutional side. Then *The New England Mind: [I] The Seventeenth Century* (1939; paperback, 1961) changed the stress, treating elaborately "Religion and Learning," "Cosmology," "Anthropology," and "Sociology" among the Puritans of old and New England, while letting institutions go. But *The New England Mind: [II] From Colony to Province* (1953; paperback, 1961) combined the story of intellect and institution during the late seventeenth and early eighteenth centuries. For beginners with Miller's works, his *Errand into the Wilderness* (1956), some essays of which were starting points for sizable books, should be helpful; readers may well tackle first Chapter III, "The Marrow of Puritan Divinity." Edmund S. Morgan's *The Puritan Dilemma: The Story of John Winthrop* (1958) revises a little the tendencies of Harvard interpretation in which he was trained; his book is for the general reader. From outside that school, Alan Simpson, *Puritanism in Old and New England* (1955), brings a different point of view to bear.

Selections from some of these historians and from others are conveniently put together in George M. Waller, ed., *Puritanism in Early America* (1950). But there is no substitute for acquaintanceship with the Puritans' own writings; Perry Miller and Thomas H. Johnson, eds., *The Puritans* (1938), is a remarkably full anthology, from which I draw.

1 A Reformation of the Old Order

p. 54 See Ralph Barton Perry, *Puritanism and Democracy* (1944); and, for an explicit statement of his purposes, see Perry Miller, *Errand into the Wilderness*, pp. vi–ix.

2 English Puritan Politics: Recapitulation of Protestant Demands

p. 56 See Marshall M. Knappen, *Tudor Puritanism, A Chapter in the History of Idealism* (1939), pp. 195–196, 218–219, 257–258 *et passim*. For a discussion which stresses the Rhineland backgrounds of Puritan thought, see Leonard J. Trinterud, "Origins of Puritanism," *Church History*, 20 (1951):37–57.

p. 57 For much about Emmanuel College and other Puritan aspects of Cambridge Uni-
l. 4 versity, see Samuel Eliot Morison, *The Founding of Harvard College* (1935); the Sir Walter Mildmay story, p. 93.

p. 57 See Alfred L. Rowse, *The England of Elizabeth, the Structure of Society* (1950),
l. 35 pp. 267–272.

p. 58   See A. F. Scott Pearson, *Thomas Cartwright and Elizabethan Puritanism, 1535–1603* (1925).

p. 61   Concerning the nonseparating congregationalists, Perry Miller is the master. See his *Errand into the Wilderness*, Chapter III, "The Marrow of Puritan Divinity"; and *The New England Mind: The Seventeeth Century*, especially Book IV.

3   The Vision of the Puritan: American Glimpses

p. 62   On the Augustinian strain, see Miller, *The New England Mind: The Seventeenth Century*, especially Chapter I.

p. 64   Miller, *Errand into the Wilderness*, p. 62.

p. 65   Wigglesworth, "God's Controversy," in Miller and Johnson, *The Puritans*, pp. 611,
l. 17   612, 616.

p. 65   Taylor, "The Ebb and Flow," in Miller and Johnson, *The Puritans*, p. 652.
l. 39

4   Church and State in Early New England

Recent scholarship centering on the question of theocracy in New England differs from James Truslow Adams, *The Founding of New England* (1921), but it owes to that work much stimulation to discover wherein Adams's critical findings could be improved. See Morison, *Builders of the Bay Colony*, Appendix. For background see George L. Mosse, *The Holy Pretence, a Study in Christianity and Reason of State from William Perkins to John Winthrop* (1957). Morgan, *The Puritan Dilemma* (1958), is informative for this section.

p. 67   On the two covenants, see Ola E. Winslow, *Meetinghouse Hill, 1630–1783* (1952), p. 22, and George L. Haskins, *Law and Authority in Early Massachusetts, A Study in Tradition and Design* (1960), p. 87.

p. 68   For recent discussions of the congregations as enforcers of law and order, see Haskins, *Law and Authority in Early Massachusetts*, especially pp. 88–90, and Emil Oberholzer, Jr., "The Church in New England Society," in James M. Smith, ed., *Seventeenth-Century America* (1959). Sumner Chilton Powell's *Puritan Village: The Formation of a New England Town* (1963), a study of Sudbury, Massachusetts, evokes the practical freedom of the Puritan as town builder, churchman, and doer of justice.

p. 69   For discussions of high order, one of which preceded and one of which followed the disagreements of about 1930, see Horace E. Ware, "Was the Government of the Massachusetts Bay a Theocracy?" *Publications* of the Colonial Society of Massachusetts, X (1904–1906): 151–180; and Aaron Seidman, "Church and State in the Early Years of the Massachusetts Bay Colony," *New England Quarterly*, 18 (1945):211–233. Unfortunately both arguments hinge on questions of the authority in affairs of state exercised by the *clergy*. The writers resist the concept of "theocracy" for New England, because (surely correctly) they find that clergymen were neither officeholders nor otherwise in control of politics. But this seems to me to be a *non sequitur*. The question of theocracy depends on whether or not visible saints, *God's elect* as surely as the Puritans could tell, had power.

Part Two

THE SHAPING OF AMERICAN CHRISTIANITY, 1630–1760

Until after World War II, the personality of the American Clio was pretty well split; the history of religion, especially religious thought, was an area of existence she almost succeeded in separating from the rest of life. The exceptions were the points where religious history is closely interwoven with secular, especially political history and literary history. The Puritans, the antislavery people, the Transcendentalists, the Social Gospelers simply would not be blanked out. Otherwise only a part of the mind of our national Clio, especially the fraction which resides in schools of divinity, sustained religious history as a fairly distinct topic. The American Church History series, edited by Philip Schaff and others (1893–1897), devoted all or part of each volume—except one, Leonard W. Bacon, *History of American Christianity* (1897)—to the history of a denomination or a cluster of denominations, considered apart. Although Bacon's generalizing volume was based on remarkable learning, and was inspired by a wish to help inter-church understanding, it shared with the other volumes of the series the assumption that God entertains a special interest in Christian ecclesiastical institutions. Some of the volumes of the series remain about the only thing historical we have on the denominations in question. Williston Walker's *A History of the Congregational Churches* (1894) is still useful, even though it concerns the church which has been most written about since his time; his *Creeds and Platforms of Congregationalism* (1893; 1964 ed. by Douglas Horton) is a first-class source book. But Christian history conceived mainly as denominational history, and conceived as though churches have a spark of divinity in them which synagogues and other institutions lack, does not engage interest among today's historians.

The prolific work of William Warren Sweet stands in the middle between the old preference for denominational history and the new preferences. His *Story of Religion in America* (1939) is pretty much a survey of church history. But it is organized less according to the denominations and more according to the conventional periods of secular history than the earlier histories were. His *Religion in Colonial America* (1943) incorporates considerable material from the history of thought and is the one of his writings which has much bearing on Part Two.

Very recently the newer interest in religious thought has been greatly advanced by the studies of Puritanism which are discussed in the notes to Chapters III and IV and by several general works, listed under Chapters V, VI, and VII; see especially those on intercolonial Anglicanism by Carl Bridenbaugh, on Presbyterianism by Leonard J. Trinterud, and on Quakerism by Frederick B. Tolles. Of the four splendid volumes edited by James Ward Smith and A. Leland Jamison under the general title *Religion in American Life* (1961), Volume I, *The Shaping of American Religion*, contains chapters which concern the data of Part Two, especially three by H.

Richard Niebuhr, Henry J. Browne, and Sidney E. Ahlstrom. Volume IV, *A Critical Bibliography of Religion in America*, by Nelson R. Burr, surpasses all other bibliographies in the field. The best recent collection of documents, set forth with interpretations, is H. Shelton Smith and others, *American Christianity: An Historical Interpretation with Representative Documents* (1960). Peter G. Mode, ed., *Source Book and Bibliographical Guide to American Church History* (1921), is not displaced, however, in its function as a convenient collection of documents. In the recent survey by Clifton E. Olmstead, *History of Religion in the United States* (1960), Chapters III–IX cover the time span of Part Two of this book. Edwin S. Gaustad, *Historical Atlas of Religion in America* (1962), gives uncommon information about church distribution.

CHAPTER IV *Orthodoxy and Freedom In Early New England*

The works listed at the head of the notes for Chapter III apply again here; those by Samuel Eliot Morison and Perry Miller are the essential ones.

I *The Theocracy: From Settlement to Commonwealth*

On the development of the theocracy, besides the works cited for Chapter III, see two recent studies of the leaders: Richard S. Dunn, *Puritans and Yankees: The Winthrop Dynasty of New England, 1630–1717* (1962); Larzer Ziff, *The Career of John Cotton: Puritanism and the American Experience* (1962).

p. 80   On the Remonstrance see George L. Kittredge, "Dr. Robert Child the Remon-
l. 18   strant," *Publications* of the Colonial Society of Massachusetts, XXI (1919):1–146;
        the Remonstrance is quoted, p. 18. There is a modern discussion in Edmund S.
        Morgan, *The Puritan Dilemma: The Story of John Winthrop*, pp. 199–202.

p. 80   For text of Cambridge Platform, see Williston Walker, *Creeds and Platforms of
l. 40   Congregationalism*, pp. 193–237.

p. 81   Ward quotation from "The Simple Cobbler of Aggawam" in Perry Miller and
        Thomas S. Johnson, eds., *The Puritans*, p. 236. Ward's "Body of Liberties" is
        quoted and discussed in Morgan, *Puritan Dilemma*, pp. 169–173, and discussed in
        Samuel Eliot Morison, *Builders of the Bay Colony*, pp. 229–234.

p. 82   *The Laws and Liberties of Massachusetts* were reprinted from the 1648 edition,
l. 13   with an introduction by Max Farrand, in 1929; the passages quoted are from
        pp. 1, 35. This code is discussed in Morison, *Builders of the Bay Colony*, pp. 261–
        265; and in George L. Haskins, *Law and Authority in Early Massachusetts*, pp. 69,
        129–130.

p. 82   See Samuel Eliot Morison, *Harvard College in the Seventeenth Century* (2 vols.,
l. 33   1936), I, 70.

2   Radical Piety and the Impulse to Freedom

The best roads to the Puritan individualists discussed in this section are their own writings and the recent biographies. Roger Williams comes off much the best as to biographies and studies. See those by James E. Ernst (1929), Samuel H. Brockunier (1940), Perry Miller (1953; paperback, 1962), and Ola E. Winslow (1957). Williams's writings, which were published a century ago (1866–1874) by the Narragansett Club, in six volumes, have been republished as *The Complete Writings of Roger Williams* (7 vols., 1963). The report on Anne Hutchinson's trial is reprinted from Thomas Hutchinson's *History of the Colony and Province of Massachusetts Bay*, with other rare materials, in Charles Francis Adams, ed., *Antinomianism in the Colony of Massachusetts, 1636–1638* (1894); Adams's own account of the affair appears in *Three Episodes of Massachusetts History* (2 vols., 1892), pp. 363–578. The several biographies of the 1930s are now superseded by Emery Battis, *Saints and Sectaries: Anne Hutchinson and the Antinomian Controversy in the Massachusetts Bay Colony* (1962), which ventures social and psychological interpretations. Edward Taylor's *Poetical Works* were edited by Thomas H. Johnson and published in 1939, two and a half centuries after writing; there is a biography (1961) by Norman S. Grabo. George A. Cook has written a good biography of John Wise (1952).

p. 86 l. 9   On the Providence town government, see Ola E. Winslow, *Master Roger Williams*, pp. 35–40; p. 117 quoted.

p. 86 l. 20   Williams's observations on the nature of a church are from *The Bloudy Tenent*, in *Complete Writings of Roger Williams*, III, 73.

p. 87   Lines, again from *The Bloudy Tenent*, *op. cit.*, 3–4, 147, 152, 160–161.

p. 90   For a lively account of Mrs. Hutchinson's trial from a procedural rather than a theological or a libertarian point of view, see Richard B. Morris, *Fair Trial: Fourteen Who Stood Accused, from Anne Hutchinson to Alger Hiss* (1952), Chapter I. Quotations of Mrs. Hutchinson from Adams, ed., *Antinomianism*, pp. 269, 270–271, 274. For the theology of the controversy, see Norman Pettit, *The Heart Prepared: Grace and Conversion in Puritan Life* (1966), Chapter 5.

p. 91   Taylor, "Meditation Three" in Miller and Johnson, *The Puritans*, pp. 656–657.

p. 93   Quotations from Wise, "Vindication," in Miller and Johnson, *The Puritans*, pp. 258, 260–261, 262.

3   Puritan Commitment and New England Education

For an introduction to the history of Puritan education and the full sweep from elementary to advanced training, see Samuel Eliot Morison, *The Puritan Pronaos*, Chapters II–IV. For a college history which is in a class by itself as being an intellectual history of broad bearing also, see Morison's massive volumes: *The Founding of Harvard* (1935) and *Harvard College in the Seventeenth Century* (2 vols., 1936).

p. 94   See Pauline Holmes, *A Tercentenary History of the Boston Public Latin School, 1635–1935* (1935), especially Chapter I.

p. 96   On the operations of early Puritan schools, see Robert F. Seybolt, *The Public*
l. 17   *Schools of Colonial Boston, 1635–1775* (1935), especially pp. 70, 71, 74.

p. 96   For eight well-chosen contemporary documents of early Harvard, see Richard
l. 21   Hofstadter and Wilson Smith, *American Higher Education: A Documentary History* (2 vols., 1961), I, 1–32.

p. 97   For the Harvard presidents on philosophy, see Morison, *Harvard College in the Seventeenth Century*, I, 167, 168.

4   *After 1660: From Theocracy to Tradition*

Perry Miller, *The New England Mind:* [II] *From Colony to Province*, and Kenneth B. Murdock, *Increase Mather*, are so special here that they require repeated mention.

p. 99   The text of the Halfway Covenant is in Walker, *Creeds and Platforms*, pp. 301–339.

p. 101 Wigglesworth, "Day of Doom," is in Miller and Johnson, *The Puritans*, pp. 587–606. On the jeremiads of 1660–1710, see Miller, *The New England Mind: From Colony to Province*, Chapter II. For some discussion of the moral waywardness which actually accompanied, but not so surely justified, the jeremiads, see Emil Oberholzer, *Delinquent Saints: Disciplinary Action in the Early Congregational Churches of Massachusetts* (1956), especially Chapter XV.

p. 104 On Solomon Stoddard, see Perry Miller, "Solomon Stoddard, 1643–1729," *Harvard Theological Review*, 34(1941):277–320; quotations from *The Doctrine of the Instituted Churches*, p. 310.

CHAPTER V *Leveling the National Churches*

Although the ideas of this chapter are, I believe, in line with the accepted scholarship on which it is based, I have found it more of an innovation than I expected to undertake a comparative story of the main institutional practices, presuppositions, and ideas of the colonial churches. The old procedure, of course, was to think of the histories of the several churches as quite separate, as the American Church History series of the 1890s did; the more recent procedure in religious history is by topics, concerning ideas or regions. Neither of those methods quite meets the need of this book. Two recent surveys, Clifton E. Olmstead, *History of Religion in the United States* (1960), Chapters I, III–IX, and Franklin H. Littell, *From State Church to Pluralism: A Protestant Interpretation of Religion in American History* (1962), Chapter I, seem close to my point of view.

2   *The Truncated Church of England*

The Anglican church in America was regionally divided in its history along the Mason-Dixon line. Although the two-volume history by George M. Brydon, *Virginia's Mother Church and the Political Conditions under*

Which It Grew (2 vols., 1947–1952), is a one-colony history, Virginia Anglicanism is so large a part of southern-colonial Anglicanism that the book has regional suggestiveness. The recent work by Carl Bridenbaugh, *Mitre and Sceptre: Transatlantic Faiths, Ideas, Personalities, and Politics, 1689–1775* (1962), places fresh and illuminating stress on intercolonial and transatlantic aspects of Church of England history during the eighteenth century. Because this means the missionary and power-building effort of the church, Bridenbaugh's book applies more to Anglican efforts to get a footing in New England and the Middle Colonies than to its work in the Southern Colonies. Thus Brydon and Bridenbaugh supplement each other admirably. For a lively treatment of one facet of our problem, see P. H. Haffenden, "The Anglican Church in Restoration Colonial Policy," in James M. Smith, ed., *Seventeenth-Century America, Essays in Colonial History* (1959), Chapter VIII. On the distribution of Anglicans, see Edwin S. Gaustad, *Historical Atlas of Religion in America* (1962), pp. 2, 6–10.

p. 118   On the condition of the Virginia church, on both sides of the year 1700, see Brydon, *Virginia's Mother Church*, I, Chapters XVII–XVIII, XXII. For a more general treatment, Richard L. Morton, *Colonial Virginia* (2 vols., 1960), II, 30. About the Coventry insurgency, see Charles A. Barker, *Background of the Revolution in Maryland* (1940), pp. 278–281. Bland quotation from Bridenbaugh, *Mitre and Sceptre*, p. 319.

p. 119   For the charter (in abbreviated form), 1693, and the college statutes of 1727, see Richard Hofstadter and Wilson Smith, eds., *American Higher Education: A Documentary History* (2 vols., 1961), I, 33–49. See Herbert Baxter Adams, *The College of William and Mary* (1887).

p. 121   On the Yale drama of 1722, see Bridenbaugh, *Mitre and Sceptre*, p. 69; the book discusses the whole forward movement of the Church of England, and this event places the S.P.G. in that perspective.

p. 122 l. 27   Johnson is quoted from his *Autobiography* in Herbert W. and Carol Schneider, eds., *Samuel Johnson, President of King's College: His Career and Writings* (4 vols., 1929), I, 7, 13.

p. 122 l. 44   On American interest in having a bishop see (besides Bridenbaugh, *Mitre and Sceptre*) Arthur L. Cross, *The Anglican Episcopate and the American Colonies* (1902), especially pp. 103–108.

p. 123 l. 3   See "On the Beauty of Holiness," 1761, in Schneider, eds., *Samuel Johnson*, III, 515–537.

p. 123 l. 19   Johnson's *Elementa Philosophica* is in Schneider, eds., *Samuel Johnson*, II, 357–515. H. W. Schneider discusses Johnson at length in "The Mind of Samuel Johnson," *Samuel Johnson*, II, 3–22; and briefly in *History of American Philosophy* (1946), pp. 21–26. See also I. Woodbridge Riley, *American Philosophy: The Early Schools* (1907), pp. 113–118.

p. 123 l. 35   Laws and Orders of King's College, 1755, are in Hofstadter and Smith, *American Higher Education*, I, 117–121.

3   The Independent Presbyterians

Where scholarship on Puritanism has been abundant, and that on colonial Anglicanism and Catholicism occasional, until recently scholarship on colonial Presbyterianism has been in short supply. The principal work is

Leonard J. Trinterud, *The Forming of an American Tradition: A Re-examination of Colonial Presbyterianism* (1949). This work, and an excellent article by Alice M. Baldwin, "Sowers of Sedition: Political Theories of Some of the New Light Presbyterian Clergy of Virginia and North Carolina," *William and Mary Quarterly*, 3rd Series, 5 (1948):52–77, are our best discussions of thought in this energetic church. Katherine Lowe Brown, "The Role of Presbyterian Dissent in Colonial Virginia, 1740–1785" (1969), a Johns Hopkins doctoral dissertation in history, is more a social and educational than an intellectual history, but it informs every aspect of Presbyterian and Anglican existence in Virginia. In Bridenbaugh's *Mitre and Sceptre*, wherein Presbyterianism is an important sideline, there are fresh data and suggestions.

On the Scots-Irish, with incidental information on their church and their faith, since the old compilations by Charles A. Hanna, *The Scotch Irish* (2 vols., 1902), and by Henry J. Ford, *Scotch-Irish in America* (1915), we have the excellent Wayland F. Dunaway, *The Scotch-Irish of Colonial Pennsylvania* (1944), which has more than one-colony meaning, and James G. Leyburn, *The Scotch-Irish, a Social History* (1962), which brings a lively sociological mind to bear on those people (see especially Chapter 4, pp. 117–119, and Chapter 15). On Presbyterian immigration from Scotland direct, although it was too late and too loyalist to have much influence on American Presbyterianism, see Ian C. C. Graham, *Colonists from Scotland: Emigration to North America, 1770–1783* (1956). On the distribution of Presbyterians, see Gaustad, *Historical Atlas*, pp. 19–21.

p. 125   On the Makemie trial, see Trinterud, *The Forming of an American Tradition*, pp. 32–33.

p. 126   On Virginia Presbyterianism Mrs. Brown's work, not yet published, is amplest. See Brydon, *Virginia's Mother Church*, II, Chapter VII; and Morton, *Colonial Virginia*, II, Chapter XVI.

p. 128   *Renewal of the Covenants*, quoted in Baldwin, "Sowers of Sedition," *William and Mary Quarterly*, 3rd Series, 5 (1948):71.

4   Dutch and German Churches Expatriated

There is one old, and there is one new, compendious work on German culture in America, religious history somewhat included: Albert B. Faust, *The German Element in the United States* (2 vols., 1909), and Henry A. Pochmann, *German Culture in America: Philosophical and Literary Influences, 1600–1900* (1957). On the distribution of Catholics, Lutherans, and Reformed, see Gaustad, *Historical Atlas*, pp. 16–19, 26–29, 34–36.

p. 130   My remarks on the German churches are guided by the unpublished doctoral dissertation by Charles H. Glatfelter, "The Colonial Pennsylvania German Lutheran and Reformed Clergyman" (1952, in the Johns Hopkins University Library).

p. 131   On the founding of Rutgers, see William H. S. Demarest, *History of Rutgers*
l. 20   *College* (1924), Chapters I–V.

p. 131 When Franklin College joined with John Marshall College, the church affiliation
l. 29 of the new institution was Evangelical Reformed, a nineteenth-century blend of
early American Lutheran and Reformed traditions.

5 Church Leveling and Christian Voluntarism

p. 132 For charts and figures which compare the growth of the churches, see again
l. 19 Gaustad, *Historical Atlas*, pp. 3–5.

p. 132 For a strong statement about the church as community-builder, see Timothy L.
l. 33 Smith, "Congregation, State, and Denomination: The Forming of the American
Religious Structure," *William and Mary Quarterly*, 3rd Series, XXV (1968):
155–176.

CHAPTER VI *The Expansion of Pietist Faith*

Broad scholarship in or near the area of this chapter falls into two groups,
the first of which is the intellectual history of mystical Christianity in early-
modern times. Rufus M. Jones was the master in this field: his *The Quakers
in the American Colonies* (1911) is still basic; he covers backgrounds in
Studies in Mystical Religion (1909) and in *Spiritual Reformers in the 16th
and 17th Centuries* (1928). See also Ernst Troeltsch, *The Social Teaching
of the Christian Churches* (2 vols., translated from the German by Olive
Wyon, 1931), and Ronald A. Knox, *Enthusiasm: A Chapter in the History
of Religion* (1950), which are highly suggestive.

Distinguished regional and topical scholarship forms the second group.
Thomas Jefferson Wertenbaker, *The Founding of American Civilization:
The Middle Colonies*, and Carl Bridenbaugh, *Cities in the Wilderness: The
First Century of Urban Life in America, 1625–1742* (1938) are the principal
regional works. Frederick B. Tolles, *Meeting House and Counting House*
(1948), and Peter Brock, *Pacifism in the United States: From the Colonial
Era to the First World War* (1968), are both more informative than the
titles suggest; and their quality raises the scholarship of American pietism
high. Brock's Part One, "Pacifism in Colonial America and the American
Revolution," comes close to being a compendious history of early pietist
thought in America.

2 English Friends and American Colonies

There are old editions of the collected writings of Fox and Penn (but
strangely, these days, no modern ones): *The Works of George Fox* (8 vols.,
1831), *A Collection of the Works of William Penn*, ed. by Joseph Besse
(12 vols., 1726), and *The Select Works of William Penn* (London, 1782).
Much the most complete treatment of Penn from a point of view which
informs this book is Edward C. O. Beatty, *William Penn as Social Philosopher* (1939), on which I draw. William I. Hull, *William Penn: A Topical*

Biography (1937), is the principal biography; William W. Comfort, *William Penn, 1644–1718, a Tercentenary Estimate* (1944), is useful. Recently Vincent Buranelli, *The King and the Quaker: A Study of William Penn and James II* (1962), has explained freshly a relationship which has been puzzling.

p. 138 See Thomas C. Hall, *Religious Background of American Culture* (1930).
l. 2

p. 138 Historians estimate more than 15,000 Quakers jailed between 1661 and 1685, and
l. 19 450 deaths in prison. See Edwin B. Bronner, *William Penn's "Holy Experiment": The Founding of Pennsylvania, 1681–1701* (1962), p. 15.

p. 140 *No Cross, No Crown* in *The Select Works of William Penn*, II, 24–25, 28, 29, 30,
l. 7 31.

p. 140 *A Brief Account*, in Joseph Besse, ed., *The Peace of Europe, the Fruits of Soli-*
l. 22 *tude and Other Writings by William Penn* (Everyman's Library, 1938), pp. 175, 176, 186.

p. 141 Penn quoted from Beatty, *William Penn as Social Philosopher*, pp. 46, 163. On
l. 15 Penn as squire, see Beatty, *William Penn as Social Philosopher*, Chapters VII–VIII; on his economic thinking, Joseph Dorfman, *Economic Mind in American Civilization, 1606–1865* (1946), I, Chapter VI.

p. 141 Barclay's *Theses Theological*, stating the Quaker position, and *An Apology for*
l. 42 *the True Christian Divinity Held by the Quakers* were published, respectively, in 1675 and 1678.

p. 142 Frame of Government, quoted from Bronner, *William Penn's "Holy Experiment,"* p. 11.

p. 143 Penn quoted from Beatty, *William Penn as Social Philosopher*, pp. 29, 25, and
l. 6 Tolles, *Meeting House and Counting House*, p. 12.

p. 143 For observations on the monthly meetings assuming the usual duties of local gov-
l. 29 ernment, see Tolles, *Meeting House and Counting House*, p. 64.

p. 144 Declaration incorporated in the Great Law, quoted from Beatty, *William Penn*
l. 18 *as Social Philosopher*, p. 161.

p. 144 Penn quoted from Beatty, *William Penn as Social Philosopher*, p. 103.
l. 41

p. 145 On Penn's actions and failures to act concerning war, and his attitude on Indian relations, see Beatty, *William Penn as Social Philosopher*, pp. 112–115. See also Robert L. D. Davidson, *War Comes to Quaker Pennsylvania, 1682–1756* (1957), Chapter I; Tolles, *Meeting House and Counting House*, pp. 17–19, from which I quote; and Brock, *Pacifism in the United States*, pp. 81–88.

3 *German Sectarian Pietists*

For European origins and developments of German sectarian convictions, see Troeltsch, *Social Teaching of the Christian Churches*, II, Chapter III, Part 4. For developments in eighteenth-century America: Albert B. Faust, *The German Element in the United States*, Volume I, Chapters II, V; Volume II, pp. 409–410; Julius F. Sachse, *German Sectarians of Pennsylvania* (2 vols., 1899–1900); Jacob J. Sessler, *Communal Pietism among Early American Moravians* (1933); and Brock, *Pacifism in the United States*, Chapter IV.

Concerning Quakers as rejecters of the military system (and compromisers with it), I am indebted to Davidson, *War Comes to Quaker Pennsylvania*, especially pp. 5, 20, 117, 168, 187. But for a more recent treatment with greater detail, especially concerning the German pacifists, see Brock, *Pacifism in the United States*, Chapters II–IV.

p. 150 Lawrence H. Gipson, *The British Empire Before the American Revolution:* [VI] *The Great War for the Empire, the Years of Defeat, 1754–1757* (1956), p. 67; Boorstin, *The Americans: The Colonial Experience*, pp. 33–70.

p. 151 Among several editions of Woolman's *Journal*, some of them including some of
l. 13　the pamphlets, John G. Whittier edited one with an appreciative introduction (1871); Amelia M. Gummere, ed., *The Journal and Essays of John Woolman* (1922), is the fullest and contains a biographical introduction. The passages quoted are from pp. 159–160, 167. See the following studies: Janet Whitney, *John Woolman* (1942), and Edwin H. Cady, *John Woolman* (1966).

p. 151 On the early antislavery movement, see Mary S. Locke, *Anti-Slavery in America*
l. 35　(1901), from which I draw. See also George S. Brookes, *Friend Anthony Benezet* (1937), from which, pp. 81–82, I quote Benezet; and Sidney V. James, *A People Among Peoples: Quaker Benevolence in Eighteenth-Century America* (1963).

p. 152 Woolman Journal quoted from Gummere, ed., *Journal and Essays*, pp. 204, 212, 206, 207.

p. 153 See Merle E. Curti, *Peace or War: The American Struggle, 1636–1936* (1936), p. 22; Brock, *Pacifism in the United States*, Chapter V.

p. 154 Woolman, *Plea for the Poor*, quoted from Gummere, ed., *Journal and Essays*, pp. 417, 419, 409–410, 404.

CHAPTER VII　*The Great Awakening*

There are three regional histories of the Great Awakening: Charles H. Maxson, *The Great Awakening in the Middle Colonies* (1920); Edwin S. Gaustad, *The Great Awakening in New England* (1957); Wesley M. Gewehr, *The Great Awakening in Virginia, 1740–1790* (1930). Of the three, only Gaustad makes much contribution to intellectual history. Maxson is now better than supplemented by Leonard J. Trinterud, *The Forming of an American Tradition: A Re-examination of Colonial Presbyterianism* (1949); Katherine L. Brown's unpublished study of Presbyterian dissent in Virginia, cited in the note on Chapter V, Section 3, supplements Gewehr. The best works on strictly intellectual matters, whether contributing to the awakening or deriving from it, are the biographical and topical studies of Jonathan Edwards, listed in Section 3 of this chapter.

Although a general history of the Great Awakening is still lacking, Alan Heimert and Perry Miller, eds., *The Great Awakening: Documents Illustrating the Crisis and Its Consequences* (published in 1967 after this chapter was written) helps. Heimert's introduction surveys the movement roundly; the documents are all contemporary and mainly doctrinal.

1 A Situation for Religious Renewal

p. 157 For a generation-old but basic statement about business-cycle theory, see the article by Wesley C. Mitchell in *Encyclopedia of the Social Sciences* (1930), III, 92–107. Arthur M. Schlesinger, Sr., developed the idea of alternations in national politics in *Paths to the Present* (1949), Chapter IV. For cycles in American letters, see Robert E. Spiller, *The Cycle of American Literature* (1955).

p. 158 On the periodization of religious renewals, see William G. McLoughlin, *Modern*
l. 13 *Revivalism: Charles Grandison Finney to Billy Graham* (1959), p. 8. For a topical treatment, see William Warren Sweet, *Revivalism in America, Its Origin, Growth and Decline* (1944).

p. 158 On colonial population growth, see Evarts B. Greene and Virginia D. Harrington,
l. 39 *American Population before the Federal Census of 1790* (1932), and Stella H. Sutherland, *Population Distribution in Colonial America* (1936).

2 Galvanizing the Calvinist Churches: The Middle Colonies

Besides Trinterud, *The Forming of an American Tradition*, see the works listed for Chapter V, Section 3; in addition, see Dietmar Rothermund, *The Laymen's Progress: Religious and Political Experience in Pennsylvania, 1740–1770* (1961).

p. 160 On Frelinghuysen, see Maxson, *The Great Awakening in the Middle Colonies*,
l. 5 Chapter II; and a book published after this chapter was written, James Tanis, *Dutch Calvinistic Pietism in the Middle Colonies: A Study in the Life and Theology of Theodorus Jacobus Frelinghuysen* (1967).

p. 160 Tennent and Finley quoted in Trinterud, *The Forming of an American Tradition*,
l. 38 pp. 89–90; full text of Tennent sermon in Heimert and Miller, *Great Awakening*, pp. 72–99; pp. 77, 78 quoted.

p. 163 On the College of New Jersey, the official name of which became Princeton University only in 1896, see Thomas J. Wertenbaker, *Princeton, 1746–1896* (1946). The charter is printed in Richard Hofstadter and Wilson Smith, *American Higher Education: A Documentary History* (2 vols., 1961), I, 82–91. See also George P. Schmidt, *Princeton and Rutgers: The Two Colonial Colleges of New Jersey* (1964).

3 The New England Way Divided: Eighteenth-Century Puritanism

Besides Gaustad's *Great Awakening in New England*, see C. C. Goen, *Revivalism and Separatism in New England, 1740–1800: Strict Congregationalists and Separate Baptists in the Great Awakening* (1962).

Of the many studies of Edwards, Ola E. Winslow, *Jonathan Edwards, 1703–1758, a Biography* (1940) is the fullest biography and still a very useful one. Perry Miller, *Jonathan Edwards* (1949; paperback, 1959), is a brilliant gem with many facets. One may wonder whether Edwards contained in himself as much of the eighteenth century (and after) as Miller says, yet not doubt that this is the basic and best book. Paul K. Conkin, *Puritans and Prag-*

matists: Eight Eminent American Thinkers (1968), Chapter II, "Jonathan Edwards: Theology," is a good summary.

p. 165 Both the sermons discussed, "God Glorified in Man's Dependence" and "A Divine and Supernatural Light," are printed in the two modern anthologies of Edwards: Clarence H. Faust and Thomas H. Johnson, eds., *Jonathan Edwards, Representative Selections* (1935), pp. 92–111, quotations from pp. 109–111; and Vergilius Ferm, ed., *Puritan Sage: Collected Writings of Jonathan Edwards* (1953), pp. 144–163. The sermons are treated at length in Miller, *Jonathan Edwards*, chapters on "Trial of a Successor" and "The Inherent Good"; I quote Edwards from p. 31.

p. 167 "Personal Narrative," in Faust and Johnson, *Jonathan Edwards*, pp. 60–61, 58–59.

p. 168 Edwards quoted from Gaustad, *Great Awakening in New England*, p. 18.

p. 169 Edwards quoted from his "Narrative of Surprising Conversions," a more or less public letter to the Reverend Benjamin Colman of Boston, May 30, 1735, in Faust and Johnson, *Jonathan Edwards*, pp. 74–78. The *Narrative*, as published under the long title given in the text, dated by the author November 6, 1736, is reprinted in Ferm, *Puritan Sage*, pp. 164–218.

p. 171 Enfield sermon and Wheelock comment in Faust and Johnson, *Jonathan Edwards*, pp. 155–172, 422.

4 *Religious Renewal and Religious Enlightenment:*
    The System of Jonathan Edwards

p. 173 *A History of the Work of Redemption* is reproduced in part in Ferm, *Puritan*
l. 10   *Sage*, pp. 602–613; Miller discusses it elaborately in *Jonathan Edwards*, chapter on "History." See also Herbert L. Osgood, *American Colonies in the Eighteenth Century* (4 vols., 1924–1925), III, 407–427.

p. 173 Edwards's Brainerd sermon and farewell sermon are in Faust and Johnson, *Jona-*
l. 39   *than Edwards*, pp. 173–202, my quotations from pp. 175, 191, 192, 194; his sermon on Colonel Stoddard is discussed in Miller, *Jonathan Edwards*, pp. 246–248, and in the same author's "Jonathan Edwards and the Great Awakening," in Daniel Aaron, ed., *America in Crisis* (1952), pp. 15–17.

p. 174 On the writings from which the author drew, see the work itself: Jonathan Edwards, *A Treatise Concerning Religious Affections*, edited by John E. Smith (1959), pp. 55–60 *et passim;* see also Miller, *Jonathan Edwards*, pp. 185–186 *et passim.*

p. 175 *Some Thoughts* is included in part in Ferm, *Puritan Sage*, pp. 379–414; pp. 379, 382, 390 are quoted.

p. 176 The Smith edition of *Religious Affections*, cited previously, is the one modern
l. 19   and complete one, from which I quote p. 396; the work is reproduced in small part in Faust and Johnson, *Jonathan Edwards*, pp. 206–254, and in Ferm, *Puritan Sage*, pp. 415–450.

p. 176 For comment on Edwards's problem of Christian practice, see Rufus Ruter, "The
l. 29   Concept of Morality in the Philosophy of Jonathan Edwards," *Journal of Religion*, 14 (1934):265–272.

p. 177 *The Nature of True Virtue* is included, in part, in Faust and Johnson, *Jonathan*
l. 14   *Edwards*, pp. 349–357, p. 350 quoted; and in Ferm, *Puritan Sage*, pp. 578–594.

p. 177 Quotations from *Original Sin* and *The End for Which God Created the World*
l. 36   in Faust and Johnson, *Jonathan Edwards*, pp. 325–326, 348.

p. 177   The original title is *A careful and strict Enquiry into The modern prevailing*
l. 40   *Notions of that Freedom of Will Which is supposed to be essential to Moral*
          Agency, Vertue and Vice, Reward and Punishment, Praise and Blame. Jonathan
          Edwards, *Freedom of the Will*, edited by Paul Ramsey (1957), is Volume I of
          The Works of Jonathan Edwards, Perry Miller, general editor. Selections from
          earlier editions occur in many anthologies: generous ones in Faust and Johnson,
          Jonathan Edwards, pp. 263–309, and Ferm, *Puritan Sage*, pp. 480–515.

p. 180   In the order of the text, quotations from *The Freedom of the Will*, Ramsey
          edition, are from pp. 137, 164, 141, 159, 160, 172, 431, 432, 439.

5   American Christianity Rough-hewn

p. 182   Gaustad, "The Theological Effects of the Great Awakening in New England,"
          Mississippi Valley Historical Review, 40 (1953–1954):706.

p. 183   On the later directions of Edwardsianism, see Frank H. Foster, *Genetic History
          of the New England Theology* (1907); Heimert and Miller, *Great Awakening*,
          pp. lii–lxi, Parts V–VII; and Alan S. Heimert, *Religion and the American Mind:
          From the Great Awakening to the Revolution* (1966).

Part Three

THE ENLIGHTENMENT AND THE REVOLUTION:
THE EMERGENCE OF NATIONAL CONVICTIONS,
1740–1800

Although there is yet no over-all history of the Enlightenment in America,
while there are many histories of the colonies and many of the Revolution,
the situation of scholarship concerning the history of the mind during the
eighteenth century is not so short as that fact suggests.

An interest in the field of the American Enlightenment as a whole, and an
illumination of the pragmatic factor in the public thought of the age, are to
be found in Adrienne Koch's volume, *Power, Morals, and the Founding
Fathers, Essays in the Interpretation of the American Enlightenment* (1961).
Less fortunately, while Mrs. Koch's *American Enlightenment: The Shaping
of the American Experiment and a Free Society* (1965) has many excel-
lences, the title promises more than the documents deliver; they are almost
all political. Max Savelle, *Seeds of Liberty: The Genesis of the American
Mind* (1948), is confined to the middle two decades of the eighteenth century, and concentrates on cultural nationalism, but is otherwise broad.
Though I estimate Daniel J. Boorstin, *The Americans: The Colonial Experience* (1958), to represent undue skepticism about the existence of the
Enlightenment, or at least of anything historically important in America
which is well expressed by that name, Books Two and Three of his volume
make lively and critical contributions to understanding it. Moses Coit Tyler's
old but still splendid *Literary History of the American Revolution, 1763–
1783* (2 vols., 1897, 1941) comes close to being a literary history of the

Enlightenment, too; Thomas J. Wertenbaker, *The Golden Age of Colonial Culture* (1942), and Evarts B. Greene, *The Revolutionary Generation, 1763–1790* (1943), are social histories. Among the treatments of the field in the leading national histories of thought, Merle E. Curti, *Growth of American Thought* (1964 ed.), Chapters 4–7, and Herbert W. Schneider, *A History of American Philosophy* (1946), Chapter II, are masterful.

The best scholarship within the area of Part Three is specialized scholarship; the kind of specialized work which ranges most effectively across the activities of the Enlightenment and the Revolution is, naturally, biographical. At least one figure demands attention in all four of the next chapters; Thomas Jefferson. Four require it in three chapters: Benjamin Franklin, John Adams, Alexander Hamilton and James Madison. The papers of every one of the five—men of the Enlightenment, men of the Revolution, fathers of the republic, all—are being superbly edited and published at length while this book is being written. Full-length biographies of all five have appeared during the last generation: Carl Van Doren, *Benjamin Franklin* (1938); Page Smith, *John Adams* (2 vols., 1962); Dumas Malone, *Jefferson and His Time* (3 vols., 1948–1962); Marie Kimball, *Jefferson* (3 vols., 1943–1950); Broadus Mitchell, *Alexander Hamilton* (2 vols., 1957–1962); John C. Miller, *Alexander Hamilton, Portrait in Paradox* (1959); Irving Brant, *James Madison* (6 vols., 1941–1961). Each tells the story of a man for whom to act was, first, to study and write.

CHAPTER VIII *The Enlightenment in America*

1 *With the Enlightenment at Peak in Europe*

Either the history of the international Enlightenment or of the American phase of it would be a proper object for a career-long study, but not my own. I have taken certain points of departure from the writings of three major scholars: Ernst Cassirer, *The Philosophy of the Enlightenment* (1932 in German original; English translation by F. C. A. Koelln and J. P. Petergrove, 1951; paperback, 1955), and Cassirer's superb article, "Enlightenment," in the *Encyclopedia of the Social Sciences* (1931), V, 547–552; Preserved Smith, *The Enlightenment, 1687–1776* (1934), Volume II of his *History of Modern Culture*; and Leslie Stephen, *History of English Thought in the Eighteenth Century* (2 vols., 1876). Peter Gay's splendid volumes, *The Party of Humanity: Essays in the French Enlightenment* (1964) and *The Enlightenment: An Interpretation: The Rise of Modern Paganism* (1967) focus on the philosophes in France; American figures appear only in the background but, as they do have a place, are given in telling perspective. The following science histories, which have no special regional bearing, apply to this and the following sections: Whitfield J. Bell, *Early American*

Science, Needs and Opportunities for Study (1955); Bernard Jaffe, *Men of Science in America* (1944); Brooke Hindle, *The Pursuit of Science in Revolutionary America, 1735–1789* (1956); G. Brown Goode, *The Beginnings of Natural History in America* (1886); William M. Smallwood, *Natural History and the American Mind* (1941).

p. 190   For Boorstin's elaborate statement of his judgment against originality in colonial science, see *The Americans*, I, Part 9.

2   *Scientific and Humanistic Interests in the Plantation Colonies*

For the southern seaboard areas, where events and conditions in the history of thought were most closely connected with the ruling order, political and general histories are uncommonly useful. The following supply background, and some foreground, of our field: Carl Bridenbaugh, *Myths and Realities: Societies of the Colonial South* (1952); Thomas Jefferson Wertenbaker, *Golden Age of Colonial Culture;* Charles A. Barker, *The Background of the Revolution in Maryland* (1940).

Louis B. Wright is the historian of southern colonial humanistic thought and feeling. His general books, *The Atlantic Frontier, Colonial American Civilization, 1607–1763* (1947) and *The Cultural Life of the American Colonies, 1607–1763* (1957) inform us not disproportionately but with special control of southern matter; his *The First Gentlemen of Virginia: Intellectual Qualities of the Early Colonial Ruling Class* (1940) is his masterwork. Other principal work which concerns the thought of the region is biographical; see, besides the biographies of Jefferson and Madison, Louis Morton, *Robert Carter of Nomini Hall, A Virginia Tobacco Planter of the Eighteenth Century* (1941), especially Chapter IX, and David J. Mays, *Edmund Pendleton* (2 vols., 1952).

p. 194   The usually anonymous role of the tutor is brought to clear light, as is much about Potomac River society, in Philip Vickers Fithian, *Journal and Letters*, I (1900).

p. 196   Jones's point is explained in his *Ideas in America* (1944), Chapter 8, especially pp. 141–143.

p. 198   The modern editions of Byrd's history are: Mark Van Doren, ed., *A Journey into the Land of Eden and Other Papers* (1928), and William K. Boyd, ed., *Histories of the Dividing Line* (1929). On him see Moses Coit Tyler, *History of American Literature, 1607–1765* (1949 ed.), II, from which, p. 273, I quote Byrd.

p. 199   Tuesday Club manuscripts are located mainly in the Johns Hopkins University
l. 10   Library, but I quote from a fragment in Dulany Papers in the Maryland Historical Society.

p. 199   The habit of satire belongs no more to the southern than to the other colonies,
l. 39   but it seems uncommonly representative of the plantation elite; Hennig Cohen, *The South Carolina Gazette, 1732–1775* (1953), gives ample illustrations, among which the one quoted appears on p. 197. See also Elizabeth C. Cook, *Literary Influences in Colonial Newspapers, 1704–1750* (1912), which discovers satire to have been the principal genre, from Boston to Charleston, over the entire period.

p. 200   Leonard W. Levy, *Legacy of Suppression: Freedom of Speech and Press in Early American History* (1960), discusses the common-law limitations on freedom and the ways in which they worked; Levy's *Freedom of the Press from Zenger to Jefferson* (1966) supplies much contemporary libertarian literature.

3   Scientific and Secular Thought in the Northern and Middle Colonies

The urban and institutional background is essential for understanding these two regions, and that means the incomparable work on colonial urbanism by Carl Bridenbaugh, *Cities in the Wilderness: The First Century of Urban Life in America, 1625–1742* (1938); *Cities in Revolt: Urban Life in America, 1743–1776* (1955), especially Chapters V and X; and, with Jessica Bridenbaugh, *Rebels and Gentlemen: Philadelphia in the Age of Franklin* (1942), especially Chapters II, III, IX. Ideally, histories of educational institutions belong on this list, but the fact is that Samuel Eliot Morison's large treatment of Harvard in the seventeenth and late nineteenth centuries is unmatched for the eighteenth century in his *Three Centuries of Harvard* (1936) or elsewhere; the modern Yale history does not touch the eighteenth century; and the middle colleges, King's, New Jersey, and Philadelphia, still lack big treatment. For topics especially important in the two regions, however, Hindle's *Pursuit of Science* and Smallwood's *Natural History* supply modern breadth. On the points of physics and astronomy, I. Bernard Cohen's volumes supply depth: *Some Early Tools of American Science: An Account of the Early Scientific Instruments and Mineralogical and Biological Collections in Harvard University* (1950); *Franklin and Newton: An Inquiry into Speculative Newtonian Experimental Science and Franklin's Work in Electricity as an Example Thereof* (Vol. XLIII of *Memoirs of the American Philosophical Society*, 1956); *Benjamin Franklin's Experiments* (1941); *Benjamin Franklin: His Contribution to the American Tradition* (1953).

p. 201   On John Winthrop, Jr., see Samuel Eliot Morison, *Builders of the Bay Colony*
l. 8   (1930), Chapter IX.

p. 201   Morison, *Harvard College in the Seventeenth Century*, II, discusses the earliest
l. 17   astronomy at Harvard; on the scientific achievements of the Mathers I am indebted to Dr. Michael G. Hall for permission to draw on unpublished articles. See Richard S. Shryock and Otho T. Beall, Jr., *Cotton Mather: The First Significant Figure in American Medicine* (1954).

p. 202   James Bonar first informed me about Clap's interest in science; I draw on his findings and on Louis L. Tucker, *Puritan Protagonist: President Thomas Clap of Yale College* (1962).

p. 203   Verse quoted from I. Bernard Cohen, *Some Early Tools of American Science*, p. 2.

p. 205   On the Quaker affinity for science, and on Logan, see Frederick B. Tolles, *Quakers and the Atlantic Culture* (1960), and *James Logan and the Culture of Provincial America* (1957).

p. 206   On John Bartram, besides Smallwood's *Natural History*, see Ernest P. Earnest, *John and William Bartram, Botanists and Explorers* (1940).

p. 209 On Franklin's electrical work, I. Bernard Cohen, *Benjamin Franklin's Experiments* and *Franklin and Newton*.

p. 210 Franklin's *Proposals Relating to the Education of Youth* is handy in Frank Luther Mott and Chester E. Jorgenson, eds., *Benjamin Franklin: Representative Selections* (1936); pp. 202, 206 are quoted. I. Bernard Cohen, *Benjamin Franklin: His Contribution to the American Tradition* is more science-oriented. Leonard W. Labaree and others, eds., *The Papers of Benjamin Franklin* (1959–   ) far outdoes earlier collected editions.

4 The Reach of the Enlightenment in the Colonies

For the reach of rationalism as belief, I. Woodbridge Riley, *American Philosophy, The Early Schools* (1907), remains unsurpassed; Parts III and IV discuss, respectively, leading deists and leading materialists (among whom Colden was the one sizable figure before 1776). Herbert W. Morais, *Deism in Eighteenth Century America* (1934), is principally concerned with the effect of the movement and stresses its lateness and weakness as radicalism in America. For the reach of the Enlightenment as inciter of new interests and organizations, see Hindle, *Pursuit of Science*, and *David Rittenhouse* (1964).

p. 213 Ames's patriotic prophecy is reprinted from his almanac in Ola E. Winslow, ed., *Harper's Literary Museum* (1927), pp. 30–35.

p. 214 Franklin's "Articles of Belief and Acts of Religion" is in Mott and Jorgenson, *Benjamin Franklin*, quotations from pp. 130–137.

p. 215 The quotation from Bacon is from my *Background of the Revolution in Maryland*, p. 50; for Fithian's comment, see Hunter D. Farish, ed., *Journal and Letters of Philip Vickers Fithian, 1773–1774* (1943), *passim*.

p. 216 For revisionist ideas on Cotton Mather's incipient deism, I am again indebted to Michael G. Hall; the quotation of Cohen is from "The *Compendium Physicae* of Charles Morton," *Isis*, 33 (1942):659.

p. 217 For the carry-over from rationalistic Puritanism and Presbyterianism to political doctrine, see Alice M. Baldwin, *New England Clergy and the American Revolution* (1928), and "Sowers of Sedition, Presbyterian Clergy," *William and Mary Quarterly*, 3rd Series, 5 (1948):53. For a detailed close history of these continuities and related matters, see again Alan S. Heimert, *Religion and the American Mind: From the Great Awakening to the Revolution* (1966).

CHAPTER IX *First Gathering of Political Convictions: Freedom for Persons and Peoples*

Until about 1965 the history of political thought before and during the Revolution was habitually related closely to such crises as 1765, 1774, and so on. In that way the field of this chapter was largely covered by two renowned works: Randolph G. Adams, *Political Ideas of the American Revolution, Brittanic-American Contributions to the Problem of Imperial Organization, 1765 to 1775* (1922; paperback edition, with commentary by Merrill Jensen, 1958); and Clinton L. Rossiter, *Seedtime of the Republic:*

The Origin of the American Tradition of Political Liberty (1953). Up to that time the shortage we were aware of was just discussion of pro-imperial thought. But some historians performed very fairly: R. G. Adams himself did; long before him Moses Coit Tyler, *Literary History of the American Revolution, 1763–1783* (2 vols., 1897; reprint 1941) had done so; and after him so did Edmund and Helen Morgan, *The Stamp Act Crisis, Prologue to Revolution* (1953).

Recently the attack has altered. Bernard Bailyn has been the leading revisionist, with three volumes. First came his *Pamphlets of the American Revolution, 1750–1776*, Volume I, 1750–1765 (1965), an edition of 14 pamphlets illuminated by a long introduction; this he soon amplified and published in a separate volume, *The Ideological Origins of the American Revolution* (1967). And now his *Origins of American Politics* (1968) sustains those two. Simultaneously Staughton Lynd, *Intellectual Origins of American Radicalism* (1968), further changes things. Stressing the quantity and impact of the literature, Bailyn gives us a kind of historical sociology of Revolutionary thought; stressing the emotional intensity of the same literature, Lynd gives a kind of historical psychology. For a yet further step in examining the arrival of American national awareness, using quantitative symbol analysis, see Richard L. Merrit, *Symbols of American Community, 1735–1775* (1966).

1 *The Enlightenment and Concern for Public Affairs*

p. 222   For the story of Franklin's decision between science and politics, see I. Bernard Cohen, *Benjamin Franklin's Experiments* (1941), pp. 6–7.

p. 224   The histories mentioned are: Cotton Mather, *Magnalia Christi Americana* (2 vols., 1702, 1853); Thomas Prince, *Chronological History of New England in the Form of Annals* (1736); William Stith, *The History of the First Discovery and Settlement of Virginia* (1747); Robert Beverley, *The History and Present State of Virginia* (1705; ed. by Louis B. Wright, 1947); William Smith, *A Brief State of the Province of Pennsylvania . . .* (1755); William Smith, *The History of the Province of New York From the First Discovery to the Year 1732* (1757, 1792, 1814); Thomas Hutchinson, *History of the Colony and Province of Massachusetts Bay* (3 vols., 1764–1828; ed. by Lawrence S. Mayo, 1936). See Mayo edition, I, 352, 362, 49–52, 333, 297, for Hutchinson's judgments cited in the text. Much of what the eighteenth-century historians reveal about colonial loyalties is suggested in the Morgans' *Stamp Act Crisis*, from which I borrow.

p. 225   On colonials at the Inns of Court, see Charles Warren, *A History of the American Bar* (1911), p. 188. See also Richard B. Morris, *Studies in the History of American Law: With Special Reference to the Seventeenth and Eighteenth Centuries* (1930) and Daniel Boorstin, *The Americans: The Colonial Experience* (1958), especially Chapter 32, which is altogether informative. I borrow largely from Alan M. Smith, "Virginia Lawyers, 1680–1776: The Birth of an American Profession," unpublished doctoral dissertation in History, Johns Hopkins University, 1967. For a lively case study exhibiting the affinity of law and history in the mind of a colonial intellectual, see H. Trevor Colbourn, "John Dickinson, Historical Revolutionary," *Pennsylvania Magazine of History and Biography*, 83 (1958–1959):271–292.

Professional historians of the late nineteenth and early twentieth centuries were slow to get down to work on late-colonial history. Their habit was to jump from the founding fathers of the colonies to the founding fathers of the republic, as though nothing that mattered happened during the hundred and fifty years between. Since 1918, when Herbert L. Osgood, *The American Colonies in the Eighteenth Century* (4 vols.) appeared, the situation has been different; more recently Lawrence H. Gipson's masterful *The British Empire Before the American Revolution* (12 vols., 1936–1965) has completed the alteration on the political side. Yet, because these works represent (and fulfill) the thought of the "imperial school" of colonial history and are concentrated on crown institutions and major politics, they supply nuggets rather than veins in the line of the present work. More to the point which concerns us, even though the author confined her researches to the English side and suggests only some bearings on American history, is Caroline Robbins's superb *The Eighteenth-Century Commonwealthman* (1959). Bailyn's important volumes, mentioned near the head of these notes, expand the commonwealthman story.

p. 230   On the Zenger case, Osgood, *The American Colonies in the Eighteenth Century*, II, 453–462, is a good starting point; so too is Richard B. Morris, *Fair Trial: Fourteen Who Stood Accused, from Anne Hutchinson to Alger Hiss* (1952), Chapter III. A full and literal reprint of the principal contemporary account of the trial is given in Livingston Rutherfurd, *John Peter Zenger, His Press, His Trial, and a Bibliography of His Imprints* (1904). A fresh rendering of the same document, edited with introduction, "A Note on the Text," and appendices by Stanley Nider Katz, was published in 1963 as follows: James Alexander, *A Brief Narrative of the Case and Trial of John Peter Zenger, Printer of the New York Journal.* For recent comment, see Arthur M. Schlesinger, Sr., *Prelude to Independence* (1958), p. 63; and especially Leonard W. Levy, *Legacy of Suppression: Freedom of Speech and Press in Early American History* (1960), and *Freedom of the Press from Zenger to Jefferson* (1966), and "Did the Zenger Case Really Matter?", *William and Mary Quarterly*, 3rd Series, 17 (1960):35–50. But Zenger is given a different new look in Joseph Sax, "Conscience and Anarchy: The Prosecution of the War Resisters," *Yale Review*, July 1968.

p. 231   On the Parsons' Cause, see, besides biographies of Patrick Henry, Hamilton J. Eckenrode, *Separation of Church and State in Virginia* (in Special Report of the Department of Archives and History, Virginia State Library, 1910), Chapter II. About the bearng of this bit of Anglican history on Virginia opposition to Anglicanism, see Wesley M. Gewehr, *The Great Awakening in Virginia, 1740–1790* (1930), p. 99.

p. 233   On the protest involved in the antiproprietary movements, see Charles H. Lincoln, *The Revolutionary Movement in Pennsylvania, 1760–1776* (1901), and my own *Background of the Revolution in Maryland* (1940), Chapters IV–V, VII. Aubrey E. Land, *The Dulanys of Maryland* (1955), gives the best account of the authors and their pamphlets; see p. 83. St. George L. Sioussat, *The English Statutes in Maryland, 1720–1750* (1903), reprints *The Right of the Inhabitants*, pp. 79–104; from which I quote pp. 81–82, 83, 90.

All histories of the American Revolution give place to the crisis of 1763–1766, which came to a head with the Stamp Act. For the classical interpretation of the transformation of the British system from something originally commercial into a territorial empire, see Charles M. Andrews, *The Colonial Background of the Revolution* (1924). On the principles of American resistance, the works by Clinton L. Rossiter and Randolph G. Adams are still basic. But all else on the Stamp Act crisis is superseded by the Morgans' *The Stamp Act Crisis*, from which I borrow again. For comparative information on the economic burden (or lightness) of American taxation, see Robert R. Palmer, *The Age of the Democratic Revolution*, I (1959), 156–157.

p. 234   For statements which are sympathetic about the Stamp Act, see *Cambridge History of the British Empire*, I (1929), 644–646; Lawrence H. Gipson, *The Coming of the Revolution, 1763–1775* (1954), pp. 76–80.

p. 235   Some of Sir Francis Bernard's letters were published within a decade of writing: *Letters to the Right Honorable Earl of Hillsborough* . . . (Boston, 1769) and *Select Letters on the Trade and Government in America* (London, 1774). By the time of publication the author's reform suggestions were too late to have much relevancy.

p. 236   Labaree's discussion of Pownall is in the *Dictionary of American Biography* (hereinafter referred to as *D.A.B.*), XV (1935), 161–163.

p. 237   The newspaper essay is quoted from the Morgans' *Stamp Act Crisis*, p. 82.

p. 239   Dulany, *Considerations*, quoted from Samuel Eliot Morison, ed., *Sources and Documents Illustrating the American Revolution, 1764–1788, and the Formation of the Federal Constitution* (1923), p. 27. Full text in Bailyn, *Pamphlets*, I, no. 13.

4   *Independence of Parliament and King: The Ultimate Reasoning*

Clinton L. Rossiter, *Seedtime of the Republic*, and Randolph G. Adams, *Political Ideas of the American Revolution*, are important; see references below. And, while the new works by Bailyn and Lynd have earlier reference, the late 1760s and the 1770s are the time of their full meaning. Carl L. Becker's *The Declaration of Independence, A Study in the History of Political Ideas* (1922), long since become a classic, helps with the earlier crises as well as with 1776.

p. 242   On the acute stage of the question of an Anglican episcopate, see Arthur L. Cross, *The Anglican Episcopate and the American Colonies* (1902), Chapters VI–XI, and especially Carl Bridenbaugh, *Mitre and Sceptre* (1962), Chapters X–XI.

p. 244   There is a generous passage from Wilson's *Considerations* quoted in Morison, *Sources and Documents, 1764–1788*, pp. 104–115; see also Page Smith's informative biography, *James Wilson: Founding Father, 1742–1798* (1956), pp. 55–57. I have drawn from both.

p. 245   Adams's *Dissertation on the Canon and Feudal Law* has not yet appeared in the superb Lyman H. Butterfield edition of *The Adams Papers* (1961–   ); it is to be found in Charles Francis Adams, ed., *The Works of John Adams,* III (1851), 445-464.

p. 246   Adams's *Novanglus Papers* appear handily and at some length in Samuel Eliot Mori-
l. 11   son, *Sources and Documents, 1764-1788;* my quotations are from pp. 125-126, 128-
         129, 130, 131, 136. The *Papers* are discussed in Page Smith, *John Adams,* (2 vols.,
         1962) I, 189-195.

p. 246   Jefferson's *Summary View,* published in Williamsburg (n.d.) and in London,
l. 28   1774, appears in Julian P. Boyd, ed., *The Papers of Thomas Jefferson,* I (1950),
         121-137. On Jefferson's thought as infused and influenced by early Whig historians
         of England, I am indebted to H. Trevor Colbourn, *The Lamp of Experience: Whig
         History and the Intellectual Origins of the American Revolution* (1965).

p. 247   For Randolph G. Adams's estimation, see his *Political Ideas of the American Revo-
         lution,* Chapters V-VII.

p. 248   For a fresh word on Paine: Alfred Owen Aldridge, *Man of Reason: The Life of
         Thomas Paine* (1959); see Chapter III. *Common Sense* is quoted from the standard
         edition: Moncure D. Conway, ed., *Complete Writings of Thomas Paine* (4 vols.,
         1894-1896), I, 92, 75, 73, 83.

p. 249   For one scholar's attack on the problem of colonial coolness toward the monarch:
         Stella F. Duff, "The Case Against the King, the *Virginia Gazettes* Indict George
         III," *William and Mary Quarterly,* 3rd Series, 6 (1949):383-397.

p. 250   Becker's analysis appears in *The Declaration of Independence,* Chapter I. Edward
         Dumbauld, *The Declaration of Independence and What It Means Today* (1950),
         picks up key phrases from first to last, for instance, "life, liberty, and the pursuit
         of happiness," and explains the issues and idea behind them. On the egalitarian mo-
         tive, see Henry A. Myers, *Are Men Equal? An Inquiry into the Meaning of
         American Democracy* (1945), especially Chapters I-III.

CHAPTER X   *The Principles of the Revolution*

At the time of sending these Bibliographical Notes to press, and after the text had gone, Gordon S. Woods, *The Creation of the American Republic, 1776-1787* (1969) was published. Here at last seems to be a truly comprehensive study of the political institutions and ideas of the early republican years.

1   *Commonwealth Ideas Applied* and
2   *State Sovereignty and the Rights of Man*

The matter of Sections 1 and 2, from 1776 to 1785, is (except for Woods) short on scholarly treatments which are at all comprehensive. The strongest sizable work is Elisha P. Douglass, *Rebels and Democrats: The Struggle for Equal Political Rights and Majority Rule During the American Revolution* (1955), from which I have gratefully borrowed. Thirty years older are two classics: John Franklin Jameson, *The American Revolution Considered as a Social Movement* (1926), and Allan Nevins, *The American States During and After the Revolution, 1775-1789* (1927). For recent comment, the earlier one more adverse to Jameson's findings and the second more approving, see Frederick B. Tolles, "The American Revolution Considered as a

Social Movement: A Re-Evaluation," *American Historical Review*, 60 (1954–1955): 1–12; and Richard B. Morris, "Class Struggle and the Revolution," *William and Mary Quarterly*, 3rd Series, 19 (1962):3–29. Two topical works are important: Benjamin F. Wright, *American Interpretations of Natural Law, A Study in the History of Political Thought* (1931), and Gilman M. Ostrander, *The Rights of Man in America, 1606–1861* (1960). And just now the field is enriched by Bernard Bailyn, *Ideological Origins of the American Revolution* (1967), Chapters V and VI.

p. 256
l. 19
Corwin's comment is in "The 'Higher Law' Background of American Constitutional Law," *Harvard Law Review*, 42 (1928–1929):403.

p. 256
l. 32
John Adams's letter, accompanying his *Thoughts on Government*, was to Richard Henry Lee, and is in Charles Francis Adams, ed., *The Works of John Adams* (1850–1856), IV, 187, 200.

p. 258
l. 10
Jefferson quoted from Douglass, *Rebels and Democrats*, p. 293.

p. 258
l. 26
The English Declaration of Rights, 1688, and the Virginia one, 1776, appear between the same covers in Wilson O. Clough, ed., *The Intellectual Origins of American National Thought* (1955; paperback, 1961), pp. 163–164, 269–270.

p. 260
On the governing class in Virginia, see Charles S. Sydnor, *Gentlemen Freeholders, Political Practices in Washington's Virginia* (1952). Robert E. Brown explains in *Virginia, 1705–1786: Democracy or Aristocracy* (1964) that the male franchise was so wide open as to have been well advanced toward democracy in colonial Virginia. On the politics of the Revolution there, see Hamilton J. Eckenrode, *The Revolution in Virginia* (1916).

p. 261
l. 29
On Jefferson's revolutionary role, Dumas Malone, *Jefferson and His Time* (3 vols., 1948–1962), I–II, is best. Jefferson quoted from Douglass, *Rebels and Democrats*, p. 295.

p. 261
l. 43
On Jefferson's penological proposal, Gilbert Chinard, *Thomas Jefferson: The Apostle of Americanism* (1929; paperback, 1957), p. 94.

p. 262
l. 9
On manumissions by will, see Luther P. Jackson, *Free Negro Labor and Property-Holding in Virginia, 1830–1860* (1942).

p. 262
l. 30
For downward revision of the old belief that entail and primogeniture were important in America, see Douglass, *Rebels and Democrats*, pp. 300–301, and (for a different estimation from my own) Louis Hartz, *The Liberal Tradition in America* (1955), pp. 68–72.

p. 262
l. 41
Letter to Bishop Madison, October 28, 1785, in Paul L. Ford, ed., *Writings of Thomas Jefferson* (10 vols., 1892–1899), VII, 36.

p. 264
l. 21
Conant's view appears in his *Thomas Jefferson and the Development of American Public Education* (1962), Chapter I.

p. 264
l. 27
Jefferson quoted from Roy J. Honeywell, *The Educational Work of Thomas Jefferson* (1931), p. 150.

p. 265
On the enactment of the statute of religious freedom, see Irving Brant, *James Madison* (6 vols., 1941–1961), II, Chapter XXII; the text is in Ford, ed., *Writings of Thomas Jefferson*, II, 237–238.

p. 267
The comment on Cannon is by Alexander Graydon, quoted from Douglass, *Rebels and Democrats*, p. 264. See also John P. Selsam, *The Pennsylvania Constitution of 1776: A Study in Revolutionary Democracy* (1936). Although Franklin far from managed the Pennsylvania convention, his spirit was there. On his ideas, see Paul W. Conner, *Poor Richard's Politicks: Benjamin Franklin and His New American Order* (1965; paperback, 1969).

p. 269　The quotations from Massachusetts pamphleteers and preachers are from Douglass, *Rebels and Democrats*, pp. 153–154.

p. 270　Concord's resolution is printed in Samuel Eliot Morison, ed., *Sources and Documents Illustrating the American Revolution* (1923), pp. 176–177.

p. 271　For John Adams on his own reading and for the quotation about representation, see his *Thoughts on Government* in C.F. Adams, ed., *Works*, IV, 194, 195. For his reminiscence of Paine and the Pennsylvanians, his *Autobiography* in Lyman H. Butterfield, ed., *The Adams Papers*, III (1961), 333. For systematic treatments of his political ideas, see Correa M. Walsh, *The Political Science of John Adams* (1915), and John R. Howe, Jr., *The Changing Political Thought of John Adams* (1966); see also Page Smith, *John Adams* (2 vols., 1962), I, 438–444.

p. 272　The quotations from Hawley and the town of Middleboro are from Douglass,
l. 3　*Rebels and Democrats*, pp. 205–206, 207.

p. 272　The studies here drawn on are: Oscar and Mary F. Handlin, *Commonwealth, A*
l. 31　*Study of the Role of Government in the American Society: Massachusetts, 1774–1861* (1947), Chapter I; Samuel Eliot Morison, "The Struggle over the Adoption of the Constitution of Massachusetts, 1780," Massachusetts Historical Society *Proceedings*, 50 (1916–1917):353–412; J. R. Pole, "Historians and Early American Democracy," *American Historical Review*, 67 (1961–1962):626–646; Robert E. Brown, *Middle-Class Democracy and the Revolution in Massachusetts, 1691–1780* (1955).

3　Federalism and the Control of Power

After a long wait, the philosophical and intellectual history of the United States Constitution has begun to receive considerable attention. Recently the Benjamin F. Wright edition of *The Federalist* (1961) has especially helped; and, while these notes were being prepared, a new and promising work appeared: Paul Eidelburg, *The Philosophy of the American Constitution: A Reinterpretation of the Intentions of the Founding Fathers* (1968).

p. 273　Lucien Price, ed., *Dialogues of Alfred North Whitehead* (1954), pp. 157, 158.

p. 274　On the *Defence* and its influence, see Page Smith, *John Adams*, II, 690–702; and John R. Howe, *The Changing Political Thought of John Adams*, pp. 66–67.

p. 275　Beard's *Economic Interpretation* was first published in 1913 (paperback, 1961). The criticisms referred to are Robert E. Brown, *Charles Beard and the Constitution* (1956), and Forrest McDonald, *We the People: The Economic Origins of the Constitution* (1958).

p. 277　For discussion of the early use of nationalizing words, see Charles A. and Mary R.
l. 15　Beard, *The American Spirit* (1942), and Daniel Boorstin, *The Americans: The Colonial Experience* (1958), Part 10.

p. 277　For a clear statement of Hamilton's convictions of the mid-1780s about the people
l. 29　in government and about American nationality, see Broadus Mitchell, *Alexander Hamilton* (1957–1962), I, 448–449.

p. 278　For Wright's comments on the ratifying conventions and *The Federalist* (which seem to me correct), see his introduction to the John Harvard Library edition of *The Federalist* (1962). See also Gottfried Dietze, *The Federalist* (1960); Robert R. Palmer, *The Age of the Democratic Revolution*, I, 214–228; and Cecilia M. Kenyon, "Republicanism and Radicalism in the American Revolution: An Old-Fashioned Interpretation," *William and Mary Quarterly*, 3rd Series, 19 (1962):158–182.

p. 279   The most substantial works interpreting ratification are: Orin G. Libby, *The Geographical Distribution of the Vote of the Thirteen States on the Federal Constitution, 1787–1788* (1894); Beard, *Economic Interpretation*, and the works by Robert E. Brown and Forrest McDonald in criticism cited previously; and Jackson T. Main, *The Antifederalists, Critics of the Constitution, 1781–1788* (1961). Among the many achievements of this last work is an appendix which settles it, as nearly as any such thing can be settled, that Virginia's ratification represented minority opinion in that state.

p. 280   For a topical treatment of the knowledge of the classics drawn on by the authors of the Constitution, see Richard M. Gummere, "The Classical Ancestry of the United States Constitution," *American Quarterly*, 14 (1962):3–18, from which I borrow a good deal, including the Hamilton quotation from the *Continentalist*. Wilson O. Clough, *Intellectual Origins of American National Thought*, pp. 19–92, contains interesting selected translations from Greek and Roman writers known and followed by the revolutionary fathers.

p. 281   Professor Schuyler's article, "British Imperial Theory and American Territorial Policy, A Suggested Relationship," *Proceedings* of the American Philosophical Society, Volume 97 (1954), no. 4, is far more sweeping than its title suggests.

4   *How Revolutionary Was American Revolutionary Thought?*

See Jameson, *American Revolution Considered as a Social Movement*, and articles by Frederick B. Tolles and Richard B. Morris, listed at the beginning of the note for this chapter.

p. 283   For this estimation of the American Revolution, Robert H. Palmer, *The Age of the Democratic Revolution*, I, 232–235 *et passim*.

p. 284   For discussions of religious freedom, see Evarts B. Greene, *Religion and the State: The Making and Testing of an American Tradition* (1941; paperback, 1959), especially Chapter IV; and Anson Phelps Stokes, *Church and State in the United States* (1950), I.

p. 286   On the egalitarian question, Henry A. Myers, *Are Men Equal? An Inquiry into the Meaning of American Democracy* (1945), Chapter I. For the successes of revolutionary-age antislavery, see Arthur Zilversmit, *The First Emancipation: The Abolition of Slavery in the North* (1967); for the broader situation, Winthrop Jordan, *White over Black* (1969), pp. 323 (from which I quote Madison; the italicization of a phrase is mine), 345, 350–352, 430–440, *et passim*.

CHAPTER XI   *The Goals of the Philosopher Statesmen: Hamilton, Adams, Jefferson and Madison*

Adams, Hamilton, Jefferson, and Madison escape any very particular treatment in the survey histories of American thought produced during the last two decades. There are memorable collective treatments, however, in Vernon L. Parrington, *Main Currents in American Thought*, I, *The Colonial Mind* (1927; paperback, 1956), 292–320, 342–356, and in Joseph Dorfman, *The Economic Mind in American Civilization*, I (1946), Chapter XVII. Adrienne Koch's *Power, Morals, and the Founding Fathers* (1961) draws threads together, also. For the chapter as a whole, the reader may be reminded of the major modern biographies: of Hamilton, by Broadus Mitchell and John C. Miller; of Adams, by Page Smith; of Jefferson, by Dumas Malone and Marie Kimball; of Madison, by Irving Brant.

2 Alexander Hamilton: To Create Strength from Weakness

p. 294   For Broadus Mitchell's speculation about the result of Hamilton's attending King's College, see his *Alexander Hamilton* (1957–1962), I, 52.

p. 295   For the analogy with Hobbes, Mitchell, *Alexander Hamilton*, I, 385–387.
l. 6

p. 295   As economist historian, Mitchell is the expert on Hamilton's economic ideas; see
l. 32   his *Alexander Hamilton*, I, 100.

p. 297   On Hamilton the spokesman for judicial review, see Miller, *Alexander Hamilton*, Chapter XIII, especially p. 202.

p. 298   As the John Harvard Library edition of *The Federalist* (1961) has the special advantage of Benjamin F. Wright's introduction, the edition by Jacob E. Cooke (1961) has that of special Hamilton *expertise*, which includes textual annotations. For a fresh interpretation of Hamilton's *Federalist* papers, stressing "free government," see Gottfried Dietze, *The Federalist: A Classic on Federalism and Free Government* (1960), Chapter VI. For the biographers' treatment, see Mitchell, *Alexander Hamilton*, I, Chapter XXV; Miller, *Alexander Hamilton*, Chapters XII–XIII.

p. 301   For a handy compilation of the principal Hamilton documents with comment, see Richard B. Morris, *Alexander Hamilton and the Founding of the Nation* (1957); his main reports as secretary of treasury are in Henry Cabot Lodge, ed., *Works of Alexander Hamilton* (12 vols., 1904), as follows: "Public Credit," first report, II, 227–291; "National Bank," III, 388–493; "Manufactures," IV, 70–198. I have borrowed from E. C. Lunt, "Hamilton as a Political Economist," *Journal of Political Economy*, 3 (1894):289; and from Mildred B. Otanesek, "Alexander Hamilton's Financial Policies" (doctoral dissertation, Johns Hopkins University, 1939). For the recent biographers on the reports, see Broadus Mitchell, *Alexander Hamilton*, II, Chapters I–V; Miller, *Alexander Hamilton*, Chapters XV–XX.

p. 302   For perspective on Hamiltonianism, certain biographies of a century after Hamilton are helpful: Henry Cabot Lodge, *Alexander Hamilton* (1882) and William Graham Sumner, *Alexander Hamilton* (1890). Louis M. Hacker's *Alexander Hamilton in the American Tradition* (1957) is altogether approving. For a recent caveat, a little antidotal to this attitude and to Mitchell's admiration and Miller's appreciation, see Joseph Charles, *The Origins of the American Party System* (1956; paperback, 1961), essay I. The unpublished doctoral study by Lynn H. Parsons, "The Hamiltonian Tradition in the United States" (Johns Hopkins University, 1967), contains a systematic treatment.

3 John Adams: To Fit Government to Human Nature

p. 303   Letter of 1809 quoted from Zoltan Haraszti, *John Adams and the Prophets of Progress* (1952), p. 6. On Adams's role in the enactment and enforcement of the Sedition Act, see Page Smith, *John Adams* (1962), II, 975–978.

p. 305   The quotations from Adams on the mechanistic nature of politics, several of which
l. 2   I owe to Francis Haber, are: the 1776 one, C. F. Adams, ed., *Works of John Adams*, IX, 376; 1787, Adams, ed., *Works*, I, 432; 1796, Adams, ed., *Works*, I, 488; 1821, Lester J. Cappon, ed., *Adams-Jefferson Letters* (1959), II, 573. See again

Correa M. Walsh, *Political Science of John Adams* (1915) and John R. Howe, Jr., *The Changing Political Thought of John Adams* (1966). Besides these works, Manning, J. Dauer, *The Adams Federalists* (1953), Chapters III and IV, concerns Adams's thought.

p. 305
l. 23
For Adams on Locke as prober of human nature, see C. F. Adams, ed., *Works*, I, 53.

p. 306
For the passage from the *Autobiography*, see Lyman H. Butterfield, ed., *Adams Papers*, III (1962), 254n.

p. 307
l. 10
On Adams as student of Bolingbroke, see Haraszti, *John Adams and the Prophets of Progress*, Chapter IV. On Adams the student in general see also Alfred Iacuzzi, *John Adams, Scholar* (1952). On the question of library and motive, see *Diary*, 30 January 1768, in Butterfield, ed., *Adams Papers*, I, 337–338.

p. 307
l. 31
For a discussion of Adams's pamphlet as part of the American resistance to an Anglican bishop, see Carl Bridenbaugh, *Mitre and Sceptre* (1962), pp. 237–238.

p. 308
The quotations from *A Dissertation of Canon and Feudal Law* are from Adams, ed., *Works*, III, 448, 451–453, 457, 467.

p. 309
The text of the *Defence* is in Adams, ed., *Works*, IV, V, and VI, 3–220. On Turgot's ideas and Adams's response, see Haraszti, *John Adams and the Prophets of Progress*, Chapters VIII–IX; I borrow from p. 164. See also Page Smith, *John Adams*, II, 690–702.

p. 310
On Adams's borrowing from Adam Smith, see Haraszti, *John Adams and the Prophets of Progress*, pp. 169–170.

p. 311
The text of the *Discourses on Davila* is in C. F. Adams, ed., *Works*, VI, 221–399; the quotations are from pp. 285–286, 234, 238, 252, 274, 399. Haraszti's discussion, *John Adams and the Prophets of Progress*, Chapter X; see Page Smith, *John Adams*, II, 797–802.

4   *Thomas Jefferson and James Madison: To Fit Government to the Goodness of Man*

p. 314
For a formal discussion of Madison's political ideas, see Edward M. Burns, *James Madison, Philosopher of the Constitution* (1938). Irving Brant supplies much information about Madison the intellectual, in the six volumes of his *James Madison* (1941–1961).

p. 315
l. 8
On Jefferson's philosophical "debut" in Paris, see Adrienne Koch, *Philosophy of Thomas Jefferson* (1943), Chapter VI, from which, pp. 16, 49, I borrow Jefferson quotations.

p. 315
l. 37
The discussion of Jefferson's responses to France is very keen in Gilbert Chinard, *Thomas Jefferson: Apostle of Americanism* (1929; paperback, 1957), Book Three, whence, pp. 174, 217, I borrow Jefferson quotations.

p. 316
l. 19
Jefferson letter quoted from Roland Van Zandt, *The Metaphysical Foundations of American History* (1959), p. 152.

p. 316
l. 40
On the Sedition Act in the light of modern realism, see again the writings of Leonard W. Levy, *Jefferson and Civil Liberties: The Darker Side* (1963), and especially *Legacy of Suppression* (1960), Chapter VI, where he points out that English libertarian theory during the 1790s had advanced further than American, that Jefferson and Madison allowed *to the states* the control of sedition, and that American civil libertarianism really began in 1798. Levy's case, that Jefferson was consistently libertarian only with respect to religion and that under political pressure he sometimes became quite unlibertarian, tells against the philosopher statesman. But it affects the story of the unfolding of his ideas rather by saying that they

developed politically, without his always comprehending the legal issues, than by indicating that they lacked integrity. For full political accounts of the episode, see John C. Miller, *Crisis in Freedom* (1952), and James M. Smith, *Freedom's Fetters* (1956). See also Page Smith, *John Adams*, II, 975–978.

p. 317   Letter, Jefferson to Abigail Adams, 22 July 1804, in Cappon, ed., *Adams-Jefferson Letters* (1959), I, 275.

p. 318   On the liberal motive, and the other motives, of France's giving up Louisiana, see
l. 34   Chinard, *Jefferson*, pp. 400–401.

p. 318   For a realistic account of "Jefferson's Farmer before Jefferson," which indicates
l. 38   that Jefferson's own view was idealized to the point of utopianism, see the article by that title by Richard Bridgman, *American Quarterly*, 14 (1962):567–577. A. Whitney Griswold, *Farming and Democracy* (1948), Chapter II, "The Jeffersonian Ideal," summarizes critically Jefferson's agrarianism.

p. 319   Letter to Peale, 20 August 1811, quoted from Griswold, *Farming and Democracy*,
l. 2   p. 24.

p. 319   Letter to Madison, 28 October 1785, Julian P. Boyd, ed., *Papers of Thomas Jeffer-*
l. 42   *son*, VIII (1955), 681–683.

p. 320   On Jefferson's view of Louisiana, see Daniel J. Boorstin, *The Lost World of Thomas Jefferson* (1960), p. 24. See also Albert K. Weinberg, *Manifest Destiny, A Study in Nationalist Expansionism in American History* (1935), pp. 102–103, 121–122, et passim.

p. 324   For moving words by Jefferson and to Jefferson on his university, see Richard
l. 3   Hofstadter and Wilson Smith, eds., *American Higher Education: A Documentary History* (2 vols., 1961), I, 193–199, 224–232, 266–268. On the history of the University of Virginia, see Philip A. Bruce, *History of the University of Virginia, 1819–1919* (5 vols., 1920–1922), I–II; Herbert B. Adams, *Thomas Jefferson and the University of Virginia*, U. S. Bureau of Education, Circular of Information, No. 1 (1888). Brief data in: Chinard, *Jefferson*, pp. 509–512; Adrienne Koch, *Jefferson and Madison* (1950), p. 263; Brant, *James Madison*, VI, Chapter XXXIV.

p. 324   Letter to Du Pont de Nemours, 24 April 1816, in Gilbert Chinard, ed., *Corre-*
l. 37   *spondence of Jefferson and Du Pont de Nemours* (1931), pp. 256–258.

Part Four

THE CONSCIENCE OF THE REPUBLIC, 1800–1850

There are no general treatments of American thought or culture which correspond closely to the coverage of Part Four. The book which comes nearest is Alice Felt Tyler, *Freedom's Ferment: Phases of American Social History to 1860* (1944). But the three scholars who principally launched American intellectual history as an academic enterprise did so as experts in the early nineteenth century, and in that period their surveys are still especially strong. See again: Vernon L. Parrington, *Main Currents in American Thought*, II, *The Romantic Revolution in America, 1800–1860* (1927; paperback, 1954); Ralph H. Gabriel, *The Course of American Democratic Thought* (1940), especially Chapters 1–8; and Merle E. Curti, *The Growth of American Thought* (1943), especially Parts II–IV.

CHAPTER XII *The Reinforcement of*
American Christianity

Concerning the whole or large parts of this chapter, William W. Sweet's *Religion in the Development of American Culture, 1765–1840* (1952) has the broadest application; by being less narrowly focused on church institutions, this volume improves on his *Religion in Colonial America* (1943), which it follows in series. In the *Religion in American Life* series, Volume I, *The Shaping of American Religion* (1961), ed. by James W. Smith and A. Leland Jamison, several of the topical chapters are relevant, but none undertakes to synthesize the story of the evangelical renewal which is our central problem. Volume IV in that series, Nelson R. Burr, *A Critical Bibliography of Religion in America* (1961), treats discursively the historiography of most topics in this chapter in Part 2, pp. 210–237, 272–305, 677–683, 987–1035. Certain chapters in Kenneth Scott Latourette's multivolume histories come nearer. See his *History of the Expansion of Christianity*, IV, *The Great Century, A.D. 1800–A.D. 1914, Europe and the United States of America* (1941), Chapters VI–IX; and his *Christianity in a Revolutionary Age: A History of Christianity in the Nineteenth and Twentieth Centuries* (1958), III, *The Nineteenth Century Outside Europe* (1961), Chapters II–IV. This chapter was drafted before Perry Miller's *The Life of the Mind in America, from the Revolution to the Civil War* (1965) appeared, but it is magisterial and I have borrowed at places. Although Alan Heimert, *Religion and the American Mind: From the Great Awakening to the Revolution* (1966) discusses an earlier period than ours here, the data are often relevant.

Two source books, one old and one new, are repeatedly useful: Peter G. Mode, ed., *Source Book and Bibliographical Guide for American Church History* (1921), Chapters XVII–XXII; H. Shelton Smith and others, *American Christianity: An Historical Interpretation with Representative Documents*, I, *1607–1820* (1960), Period III, 1765–1820, Chapters VIII–XI.

1 *Independence and Constitutions for Churches*

p. 334 Discussion of Allen in I. Woodbridge Riley, *American Philosophy: The Early*
l. 22 *Schools* (1907), pp. 48 ff.

p. 334 Arthur L. Cross, *The Anglican Episcopate and the American Colonies* (1902), p.
l. 41 104.

p. 336 On Palmer and his movement, see Gustav A. Koch, *Republican Religion: The*
l. 7 *American Revolution and the Cult of Reason* (1933).

p. 336 On national church building see besides William W. Sweet, *Religion in the De-*
l. 24 *velopment of American Culture*, William P. Trent, "Constitution-Making in American Churches," in John F. Jameson, *Essays in the Constitutional History of the United States in the Formative Period, 1775–1789* (1889), which, though old and technical, is comparative and still useful. See also Mark A. de W. Howe, *The Garden in the Wilderness: Religion and Government in American Constitutional History* (1965).

p. 339   For readily available selections from the Methodist *Form of Discipline* from which the present quotations are borrowed, see H. Shelton Smith and others, *American Christianity*, I, 456–459. For the history of Methodism, see especially William W. Sweet, *Methodism in American History* (1933) and *Religion on the American Frontier*, IV, *The Methodists, A Collection of Source Materials* (1946).

p. 342   Though American Episcopalianism still awaits proportionate treatment by historians, the monographic literature is growing and is of high order. For institutional problems of the 1780s, see Clara O. Loveland, *The Critical Years: The Reconstitution of the Anglican Church in the United States of America* (1956). White's early plan for the church, *The Case of the Episcopal Churches in the United States Considered* (1782), is excerpted in H. Shelton Smith and others, *American Christianity*, I, 450–455. For background, Carl Bridenbaugh's *Mitre and Sceptre* (1962), though a colonial-period study, is again useful.

p. 343   On the Presbyterians in the 1780s, see again Leonard J. Trinterud, *The Forming of an American Tradition* (1949).

p. 344   On the Quaker situation in the early republic, see Thomas E. Drake, *Quakers and Slavery in America* (1950).

p. 345   On early republican Catholicism, see John T. Ellis, *American Catholicism* (1956), Chapters I–II, which stresses Bishop Carroll's liberalism; and see Theodore Maynard, *The Story of American Catholicism* (2 vols., 1941; paperback, 1960), wherein reservations appear about religious freedom as Catholic policy, I, 146–149. The amplest and most scholarly life of Carroll is Peter Guilday, *The Life and Times of John Carroll, Archbishop of Baltimore, 1735–1815* (1922); Annabelle M. Melville, *John Carroll of Baltimore, Founder of the American Catholic Hierarchy* (1955), especially stresses the archbishop's liberalism and nationalism.

p. 346   Letters of 12 July and 1 August 1780, quoted from *The Literary Diary of Ezra*
l. 12   *Stiles*, edited by Franklin B. Dexter (3 vols., 1901), II, 445, 447.

p. 346   Quotations from the 1783 sermon are from Stiles, "The United States Elevated to
l. 43   Glory and Honor," in John W. Thorngate, ed., *The Pulpit of the American Revolution* (1876), pp. 431, 437, 467. For passages from Stiles's "Discourse on Christian Union," and for discussion of that sermon, see Carl Bridenbaugh, *Mitre and Sceptre*, Chapter I. On Stiles generally see, as always, Edmund S. Morgan, *The Gentle Puritan, A Life of Ezra Stiles, 1727–1795* (1962).

2   *Widening Goals of Christian Perfectionism*

Among the works listed above as applying to the chapter as a whole, Perry Miller, *The Life of the Mind in America*, Book I, has special application to this section. Miller discovered in "the sublime" in Christian thought much the same impulse and taste as I denominate "perfectionism." See also Sidney E. Mead, *The Lively Experiment, the Shaping of Christianity in America* (1963), especially Chapter VI, "When 'Wise Men Hoped': An Examination of the Mind and Spirit of the National Period."

p. 348   Letter of 11 September 1804, Lester J. Cappon, ed., *Adams-Jefferson Letters*, I, 280.

p. 349   On Universalism, see Richard Eddy, *Universalism in America* (2 vols., 1884–1886); the movement has received little attention from historians, a habit to which a useful exception is Ernest Cassara, *Hosea Ballou, The Challenge to Orthodoxy* (1961).

p. 352   Channing's Baltimore sermon, printed in many places, is excerpted with surrounding documents in David B. Parke, *The Epic of Unitarianism: Original Writings from the History of Liberal Religion* (1957), pp. 87–93. For philosophical aspects of the Unitarian emergence, see Wilson Smith, "John Locke and the Great Unitarian Controversy," in Harold Hyman and Leonard Levy, eds., *Freedom and Reform: Essays in Honor of Henry Steele Commager* (1967), pp. 78–100. On Unitarian history before 1805, see Conrad Wright's thorough *The Beginnings of Unitarianism in America* (1955). See also the classic by a participator, Octavius B. Frothingham, *Boston Unitarianism, 1820–1850* (1890); and the modern surveys by Wilbur E. Morse, *A History of Unitarianism* (2 vols., 1945–1952) and *Our Unitarian Heritage* (1943). See also George Huntston Williams, ed., *The Harvard Divinity School: Its Place in Harvard University and in American Culture* (1954), and Joseph Haroutunian, *Piety versus Moralism: The Passing of the New England Theology* (1932), Chapter VIII.

p. 353
l. 19
See Evarts B. Greene, "A Puritan Counter-Reformation," American Antiquarian Society *Proceedings*, 42 (1932):17–46; and Dixon R. Fox, "Protestant Counter-Reformation in America," *New York History*, 16 (1935):19–35. On leaders and aspects of the Counter-Reformation, see James K. Morse, *Jedidiah Morse: A Champion of New England Orthodoxy* (1939); Frank H. Foster, *Genetic History of the New England Theology* (1907), especially Chapters X, XII, XV; Henry K. Rowe, *History of Andover Theological Seminary* (1933).

p. 353
l. 32
See Sidney E. Ahlstrom, ed., *Theology in America: The Major Voices of American Protestantism from Puritanism to Neo-Orthodoxy* (1967), pp. 41–45, and selection from N. W. Taylor, pp. 210–249; see also Ahlstrom's "Theology in America: A Historical Survey," in James Ward Smith and A. Leland Jamison, eds., *Religion in American Life*, I, *The Shaping of American Religion*, pp. 254–260. For more detail, see Sidney E. Mead, *Nathaniel William Taylor, 1786–1858, A Connecticut Liberal* (1942).

p. 354
Park quotation from Perry Miller, *The Life of the Mind in America*, p. 58.

p. 355
For an account of this anxiety, and an estimate of Connecticut in general, see Richard J. Purcell, *Connecticut in Transition, 1775–1818* (1918), Chapter I; see also M. Louise Greene, *The Development of Religious Liberty in Connecticut* (1905).

p. 356
On Dwight at Yale, as for every phase of his life, see Charles E. Cunningham, *Timothy Dwight, 1752–1817, A Biography* (1942); on his theology see Williston Walker, *History of the Congregational Churches*, pp. 301–303, and Frank H. Foster, *Genetic History of the New England Theology*, pp. 361–366.

p. 357
l. 17
On Connecticut revivalism and humanitarianism, see Charles R. Keller, *The Second Great Awakening in Connecticut* (1942); the quotation from the Hartford speaker, the Reverend Thomas Morton, is on p. 173.

p. 357
l. 32
For a characterization of Princeton orthodoxy, and for a sample of Hodge's writing, see Ahlstrom, ed., *Theology in America*, pp. 251–292.

3 *Main Phases of Evangelical Expansion*

p. 358
l. 7
Stiles, in Thorngate, *Pulpit of the American Revolution*, p. 440.

p. 358
l. 21
Dwight quoted from Colin B. Goodykoontz, *Home Missions on the American Frontier* (1939), p. 24.

p. 359
l. 12
For figures and maps portraying church expansion, 1740–1860, see Edwin S. Gaustad, *Historical Atlas of Religion in America* (1962), pp. 4, 43.

p. 359
l. 39
See William G. McLoughlin, "Pietism and the American Character," in *American Quarterly*, 17 (1965):163–186; and Timothy L. Smith, "Historic Waves of Religious Interest in America," *Annals* of the American Academy of Social and Political Science, 332 (1960):10–19, and his *Revivalism and Social Reform* (1957),

Chapters I–III. See also Donald G. Mathews, "The Second Great Awakening as an Organizing Process, 1780–1830: An Hypothesis," *American Quarterly*, 21 (1969):22–43.

p. 360
l. 15   For contemporary accounts of the Kentucky revivals, see the source book by H. Shelton Smith and others, *American Christianity*, I, 566–570; and the old one by Peter G. Mode, *Source Book and Bibliographical Guide for American Church History*, pp. 336–339.

p. 360
l. 37   On western revivalism, in the traditional view or close to that view, see William W. Sweet, *Revivalism in America* (1944); F. M. Davenport, *Prmitive Traits in Religious Revivals* (1905); and Catherine C. Cleveland, *Great Revival in the West 1797–1805* (1916). Charles L. Wallis, ed., *Autobiography of Peter Cartwright, The Backwoods Preacher* (1956), is the classic contemporary work, by a Methodist circuit rider.

p. 361   Charles A. Johnson's revisionism appears in compact form in his "The Frontier Camp Meeting: Contemporary and Historical Appraisals, 1805–1840," *Mississippi Valley Historical Review*, 37 (June, 1950):91–110 (Eggleston quoted from p. 94); it is elaborated in *The Frontier Camp Meeting: Religion's Harvest Time* (1955), which includes interesting passages from the hymns. Bernard A. Weisberger, *They Gathered at the River: The Story of the Great Revivalists and Their Impact upon Religion in America* (1958), sweeps through colonial and western revivals to discuss later revivals in the cities.

p. 362   For a modern edition with introduction, see Charles G. Finney, *Lectures on Revivals of Religion*, edited by William G. McLoughlin (1960).

p. 364
l. 17   On early Oberlin College, see Robert S. Fletcher, *A History of Oberlin College, From Its Foundations through the Civil War* (1943). For a historical discussion of the Oberlin theology, Frank H. Foster, *Genetic History of the New England Theology*, Chapter XVI.

p. 364
l. 34   Although Finney still lacks a worthy biography, two excellent monographs supply much information on his revivals, from which I draw: Whitney R. Cross, *The Burned-Over District: The Social and Intellectual History of Enthusiastic Religion in Western New York, 1800–1850* (1950), Chapter IX *et passim*; Charles C. Cole, Jr., *The Social Ideas of the Northern Evangelists, 1826–1860* (1954). For a brief statement about Finney by Perry Miller, see *The Life of the Mind in America*, pp. 30–35. This passage identifies Finney tightly with the "sublime" in American thought; the treatment which Miller would have given Finney in the unwritten part of the book on "Theology" is a sad incompleteness of this posthumous work.

4   "The Broken Body of Christ": American Fractures

Denominationalism, as a condition brought on by many backgrounds and impulses, is discussed in a minor classic, H. Richard Niebuhr, *The Social Sources of Denominationalism* (1929; paperback, 1954); in Sidney E. Mead, *The Lively Experiment*, especially Chapter VII; and in T. Scott Miyakawa, *Protestants and Pioneers: Individualism and Conformity in the American Frontier* (1964). More specialized are the works of William W. Sweet on Christianity on the frontier.

p. 366   For the text of the Plan of Union, see H. Shelton Smith and others, *American Christianity*, I, 545–547; see also Whitney R. Cross, *The Burned-Over District*, Chapters I–III.

p. 367
l. 19   On the various missionary enterprises and their collaterals, see Latourette, *History of the Expansion of Christianity*, IV, pp. 218–223 *et passim*.

p. 367 On Christian benevolence, national and international, as something more and
l. 35   other than missionary enterprise, see two recent works: Clifford S. Griffin, *Their Brothers' Keepers: Moral Stewardship in the United States, 1800–1865* (1960), and Charles I. Foster, *An Errand of Mercy: The Evangelical United Front, 1790–1837* (1960).

p. 368 The standard work on anti-Catholic nativism is Ray A. Billington, *The Protestant Crusade, 1800–1860: A Study of the Origins of American Nativism* (1938); paperback, 1964); see especially Chapters II–V.

p. 369 On high-church and other varieties of Episcopal feeling, see E. Clowes Chorley,
l. 2   *Men and Movements in the American Episcopal Church* (1946), Chapters VII–X; and George E. DeMille, *The Catholic Movement in the American Episcopal Church* (1950).

p. 369 On Mercersburg, see James H. Nichols, *Romanticism in American Theology*
l. 18   (1961).

p. 369 On Bushnell, see Barbara M. Cross, *Horace Bushnell, Minister to a Changing*
l. 26   *America* (1958), especially Chapter V.

p. 370 For religious statistics and maps, see again Gaustad, *Historical Atlas of Religion in America*, pp. 4, 43.

p. 371 See Mead, *The Lively Experiment*, Chapter VII.

CHAPTER XIII *Working Goals of National Ambition*

The bigness and complexity of the phenomenon of American nationalism is perhaps the reason why few scholars have tried to separate it from general history. But Merle E. Curti has pioneered in this as he has in other fields, in *The Roots of American Loyalty* (1946). Curti's *expertise* in Americanism is matched by Hans Kohn's *expertise* in seeing our nationalism comparatively with European nationalisms, in *American Nationalism, an Interpretative Essay* (1957). Recently Paul C. Nagel, in *One Nation Indivisible: The Union in American Thought, 1776–1861* (1964), and Yehoshua Arieli, in *Individualism and Nationalism in American Ideology, 1776–1865* (1964), have by analysis enlarged our knowledge of nationalist thought.

i *Toward a People's "Intellectual Action": Bases in Science and Publication*

p. 376 On the wave of organizing the interest in science, see Ralph S. Bates, *Scientific*
l. 22   *Societies in the United States* (1945), Chapters I–II.

p. 376 On characteristic deficiencies in our scientific achievement, see Richard H. Shry-
l. 42   ock, "American indifference to basic science during the nineteenth century," *Archives Internationales d'Histoire des Sciences*, 5 (1948):50–65; and John C. Greene, "Science and the Public in the Age of Jefferson," *Isis*, 49 (1958):13–25. But in an article of a decade later Greene represents 1820 as the time when American science ceased to be "any longer dependent on Europe for the bare essentials." See "American Science Comes of Age," *Journal of American History*, 55 (June 1968):22–41.

p. 378 Here I borrow from A. Hunter Dupree, *Science in the Federal Government, A History of Policies and Activities to 1940* (1957; paperback, 1964), Chapters I–IV.

p. 379   On J. Q. Adams and science see, besides Dupree, Samuel Flagg Bemis, *John Quincy Adams and the Union* (1956), Chapter XXIII.

p. 380   On the Columbian Institute, see John W. Oliver, "America's First Attempt to Unite the Forces of Science and Government," *Scientific Monthly*, 53 (September 1941):253–257; Constance M. Green, *Washington*, [I,] *Village and Capital, 1800–1878* (1962), pp. 69, 103.

p. 381   On Witherspoon's findings, and those of several contemporaries, see Mitford McL. Mathews, ed., *The Beginnings of American English: Essays and Comments* (1931).

p. 382   Murdock's opinion is in the *D.A.B.*, XIX (1936), 597; my treatment of Webster
l. 11   depends on Ervin C. Shoemaker, *Noah Webster, Pioneer of Learning* (1936), and Harry R. Warfel, *Noah Webster, Schoolmaster to America* (1936), from which I quote Webster, p. 59.

p. 382   On Americanisms which bore civic suggestion, see Charles A. and Mary R.
l. 31   Beard, *The American Spirit: A Study of the Idea of Civilization in the United States* (Vol. IV of *The Rise of American Civilization*, 1942), Chapters II–IV *et passim*; Arthur A. Ekirch, Jr., *The Idea of Progress in America, 1815–1860* (1944), Chapter I; and again, Mathews, *Beginnings of American English*, Index *et passim*.

p. 383   On newspapers, 1780–1850, see the standard work, Frank L. Mott, *American*
l. 5   *Journalism, A History, 1690–1960* (1962 ed.), pp. 184, 186, *et passim*.

p. 383   On magazine history, 1780–1850, see Mott's very elaborate *History of American*
l. 44   *Magazines*, I, *1741–1850* (1930), especially pp. 67, 119, 123–124, 210, 339–342.

p. 385   On the economics of book publication, see William Charvat, *Literary Publishing in America, 1790–1850* (1959); on best-selling, Frank L. Mott, *Golden Multitudes, The Story of Best Sellers in the United States* (1947), pp. 66–67 *et passim*.

2   *A Fitting National Literature: Beginnings and Hopes*

Besides the titles given at the head of this note for the chapter as a whole, a number of studies consider literary nationalism broadly but apart from other phases of cultural history. For general treatments, see Robert E. Spiller and others, *Literary History of the United States* (1946), I, especially Chapters 13–22; Van Wyck Brooks, *Makers and Finders: A History of the Writer in America, 1800–1915* (1936–1952), [I,] *The World of Washington Irving* (1944); Benjamin T. Spencer, *The Quest for Nationality, An American Literary Campaign* (1957), especially Chapters II–IV. See also discussions by Howard Mumford Jones in *A Theory of American Literature* (1948), Chapter III, and in *O Strange New World: American Culture: The Formative Years* (1964), especially Chapters IX–X.

p. 386   For a recent discussion of the Washington legend, see Paul C. Nagel, *One Nation*
l. 1   *Indivisible*, pp. 224–231.

p. 386   See J. J. McCloskey, "The Campaign of Periodicals after the War of 1812 for
l. 6   National American Literature," *Publications* of the Modern Language Association, 50 (1935):262–273.

p. 386   On the urban and regional backgrounds of early national literature, see Brooks,
l. 17   *The World of Washington Irving*.

p. 387   On Brackenridge, see Claude M. Newlin, *The Life and Writings of Hugh Henry Brackenridge* (1932).

p. 389　On Freneau, see Lewis Leary, *That Rascal Freneau, A Study in Literary Failure* (1941). The poems quoted are from Fred L. Pattee, ed., *The Poems of Philip Freneau, Poet of the American Revolution* (3 vols., 1902–1907), in the order of quotation, II, 38; III, 99–100; II, 333–334.

p. 391　Trumbull quotations are from Leon Howard, *The Connecticut Wits* (1943), p.
l. 11　55; see also Alexander Cowie, *John Trumbull, Connecticut Wit* (1936).

p. 391　On Barlow as deviator from Connecticut norms, see M. Ray Williams, "Joel Bar-
l. 38　low, Political Romanticist," *American Literature*, 9 (1938):113–152.

p. 392　On the ideas of "The Columbiad" I borrow from Howard, *Connecticut Wits*, pp. 139–159; Barlow quoted from p. 157.

p. 393　Concerning the Anthology Club's journal and ideas, I am indebted to suggestions
l. 19　from Mrs. Sue Neuenswander Greene, as author of "The Contribution of *The Monthly Anthology and Boston Review* to the Development of the Golden Age of American Letters" (Ph.D. dissertation, Michigan State University, 1964).

p. 393　On the introduction of romantic literary nationalism, see Benjamin T. Spencer,
l. 43　*The Quest for Nationality, An American Literary Campaign* (1957), pp. 35, 82–83, 90–91 *et passim*. See also William Charvat, *The Origins of American Critical Thought: 1810–1835* (1936), pp. 59–71, 173–201, *et passim*.

p. 394　E. T. Channing's address, the text of which was long lost, is printed with intro-duction by Richard B. Davis, in the Phi Beta Kappa *Key Reporter*, 26 (Spring, 1961):1–4, 6, 8.

p. 395　Bryant's nationalist ideas were contained in a book review, "American Society as
l. 10　a Field of Fiction," in the *North American Review*, 1825, reprinted in William Cullen Bryant, *Prose Writings*, edited by Parke Godwin (1884), pp. 357, 358.

p. 395　Channing's essay has often been reprinted from contemporary editions of his
l. 23　works; here I draw from the sizable one-volume selection, *The Works of William E. Channing* (1903), pp. 124–138.

3　A Resourceful National Economy

For this, as for other periods of our economic thought, there is only one general work of size and quality: Joseph Dorfman, *The Economic Mind in American Civilization* (1946). See Volumes I and II, to 1860.

p. 396　J. Q. Adams quoted from Lynn H. Parsons, "Continuing Crusade: Four Genera-tions of the Adams Family View Alexander Hamilton," *New England Quarterly*, 37 (March, 1964):53.

p. 397　The Humphreys quotation and other data on early industrial propagandizing are taken from Samuel Rezneck, "Rise and Early Development of Industrial Con-sciousness in the United States, 1760–1800," *Journal of Economic and Business History*, 4(1931–1932):792.

p. 398　Quotations from *Niles' Weekly Register* are taken from Norval N. Luxon, *Niles' Weekly Register: News Magazine of the Nineteenth Century* (1947), pp. 18, 26, 31, 32. This is the amplest book on Niles; I borrow also from Richard G. Stone, *Hezekiah Niles as an Economist* (1933).

p. 399　Niles quotations from Stone, *Hezekiah Niles*, p. 61 and from Luxon, *Niles' Weekly Register*, p. 111.

p. 400　For Raymond's ideas, besides his own easily read but not readily available works, see Charles P. Neill, *Daniel Raymond: An Early Chapter in the History of Eco-nomic Theory in the United States* (1897). See also Herbert W. Schneider, *A*

History of American Philosophy, pp. 107, 110–111; Ernest Teilhac, *Pioneers of American Economic Thought in the Nineteenth Century*, translated by E. A. J. Johnson (1936), Chapter I; Dorfman, *Economic Mind in American Civilization*, II, 566–574.

p. 401   List quoted from Abraham D. H. Kaplan, *Henry Charles Carey: A Study in American Economic Thought* (1931), pp. 29–30.

p. 403   Concerning H. C. Carey I have consulted the three works mentioned and have been guided by Kaplan, *Henry Charles Carey;* by Dorfman, whose adverse comment is telling, *Economic Mind in American Civilization*, II, 789–805; and by Charles H. Levermore, "Henry C. Carey and His Social System," *Political Science Quarterly*, 5 (1890):553–582. Throughout this section I have borrowed from Broadus Mitchell's *expertise* concerning the economic nationalists. For an old but informative general comment, see Frank A. Fetter, "Early History of Political Economy in the United States," *Proceedings of the American Philosophical Society*, 87 (1943):51–60. On the less economic side, see Arnold W. Green, *Henry Charles Carey, Nineteenth-Century Sociologist* (1951).

4   *A More Perfect Union: Convictions About Justice and Peace*

p. 405   On codification as a possible but little-successful area for early government action, see Roscoe Pound, *The Formative Era of American Law* (1939), Chapters II, IV.

p. 407   Text of speech, undated in *The Works of James Wilson*, edited by James D. Andrews (2 vols., 1896), I, 1–48; discussed in Page Smith, *James Wilson* (1956), Chapters XXI–XXII; Morris R. Cohen, *American Thought* (1954), pp. 139–140.

p. 408   The Farewell Address, which has been reprinted many times, is handily available
l. 26   in Richard B. Morris, ed., *Great Presidential Decisions: State Papers That Changed the Course of History* (1960), pp. 29–47; the foreign-policy and intellectual background is treated in Felix Gilbert, *To the Farewell Address: Ideas of Early American Foreign Policy* (1961). The earlier Washington addresses quoted are from Paul C. Nagel, *One Nation Indivisible*, pp. 170–171, which is a kind of source book for this section.

p. 408   Jefferson letters in this paragraph are quoted in Nagel, *One Nation Indivisible*,
l. 44   pp. 219, 216.

p. 409   Nagel discusses Madison's sovereignty essay, *One Nation Indivisible*, 33. The text is in Gaillard Hunt, ed., *The Writings of James Madison*, IX (1910), 568–573; the comments on nullification are on pp. 573–603; quotations are from pp. 572, 606–607.

p. 410   For two solid studies of economic policy in the original states, see Oscar and Mary F. Handlin, *Commonwealth, A Study of the Role of Government in the American Economy: Massachusetts, 1774–1861* (1947), and Louis Hartz, *Economic Policy and Democratic Thought: Pennsylvania, 1776–1860* (1948). For a review which generalizes the role of the states, see Robert A. Lively, "The American System: A Review Article," *Business History Review*, 29 (1955):81–96.

p. 412   The idea of Marshall as a fulfiller of Hamilton has been developed by Samuel J. Konefsky in *John Marshall and Alexander Hamilton, Architects of the American Constitution* (1964), from which I borrow; for a treatment of *Marbury versus Madison*, see pp. 3, 111–112. My paragraphs on Marshall derive also from older standard works: Albert J. Beveridge, *The Life Of John Marshall* (4 vols., 1916–1919); Charles Warren, *The Supreme Court in United States History* (3 vols., 1924), I–II; Charles G. Haines, *The Role of the Supreme Court in American Government and Politics, 1789–1835* (1944); William Melville Jones, ed., *Chief Justice John Marshall, A Reappraisal* (1956).

p. 413   Roane quoted from Warren, *Supreme Court*, I, 448.

p. 416   Kent autobiography quoted, *D.A.B.*, X, 345. The widespread legal nationalism of
l. 10   the middle period (1815 to 1850) is beautifully represented by twenty-one of the
twenty-three addresses and essays by lawyers contained in Perry Miller, ed., *The
Legal Mind in America, from Independence to the Civil War* (1962). According
to the editor, pp. 136–137, "These manifestoes record a fundamental chapter in the
history of the American intellect: the emergence, the formulation, and the inner
divisions of an American legal mentality." The "manifestoes" themselves, though
they reveal "inner divisions" aplenty, reveal with all else a common determination
among judges and lawyers to have an American law which would follow but improve on English. "The law is *artificial and technical* to an extent very much
beyond what is required by the reason or nature of the case," observed Henry
Dwight Sedgwick in the *North American* in 1824. "This remark, so far as it includes the principles of the Common Law, is applicable to England and to all the
states of the Union, which have adopted the Common Law, but so far as it relates
to the *practice* of the law so called, or to its modes and forms of proceeding, it
is applicable only to England, and to such of the United States, probably a small
proportion of the whole, as have adopted in mass the English practice of the
Common Law."

p. 416   Kent, "A Lecture, Introductory to a Course of Law Lectures in Columbia Col-
l. 32   lege," 1824, in Miller, *Legal Mind in America*, pp. 95–104.

p. 417   The best edition of Kent's *Commentaries* is the one edited by Oliver Wendell
Holmes, Jr., in 1873. My discussion borrows from John T. Horton, *James Kent: A
Study in Conservatism, 1763–1847* (1939), Chapter VII; the borrowing includes
quotations from Kent, pp. 271, 275.

p. 418   Story, "Discourse . . . Upon the Inauguration of the Author as Dane Professor,"
in Miller, *Legal Mind in America*, p. 180.

p. 419   On the "doctrinal" writing of law, see Roscoe Pound, *The Formative Era of
American Law*, pp. 138–162.

CHAPTER XIV   *The Arrival of Democracy:
In Experience and in Thought*

There is no need to repeat from the text my argument that democracy as
a process was too big and too new for contemporary scholars to assimilate
in history or theory. But Clement Eaton's excellent and representative
compilation of documents, *The Leaven of Democracy: The Growth of the
Democratic Spirit in the Time of Jackson* (1963), a volume in the American
Epochs series (Frank Freidel, general editor), illustrates the argument. Although Eaton found numerous lively materials which display facets of
democratic life, he included no contemporary over-all discussion of theory
of the democratic process. Such writings are few and far between, and I
suppose that infrequency explains the omission. Even Joseph L. Blau's *Social
Theories of Jacksonian Democracy: Representative Writings of the Period,
1825–1850* (1947), to which I am indebted, though full of doctrinaire statements, contains no significant general theorizing.

Frederick Jackson Turner's volume of essays, *The Frontier in American
History* (1920), and Vernon Louis Parrington's *Main Currents in American
Thought*, II, *The Romantic Revolution in America* (1928; paperback, 1954)
are still the classics we must turn to, to find the modern discovery, or

rather the primary explorations, of democracy as a main part of our history. For Turner, democracy was not to be separated from the soil of America, and, despite all the critiques and corrections his essays have endured, they are unforgettable and still give insight, as Robert Frost's poem "The Gift Outright" should remind us. Parrington too is dated, and Parrington likewise persists. His chapters on "The Heritage of Jeffersonianism" and "Two Spokesmen of the West" (pp. 10–19; 145–152) also brought democracy alive to Americans at the time when their loyalties and thought processes were at last beginning to be seriously studied.

After Turner and Parrington, Ralph H. Gabriel and Merle E. Curti both made contributions to understanding democracy and intellectual life as they were each related to the other. Although I am indebted to Gabriel, I have never been reconciled to the lateness of the time, about 1840, when *The Course of American Democratic Thought* (1940) picks up, or to the way in which the chapter on "The American Faith" disregards Jefferson. Curti, whose studies began in the Jackson period and whose discussion of it in his survey, *The Growth of American Thought* (1943), displays his wonderful knowledge, does not do much with political thought. His special achievement here is his demonstration of the connections of intellectual life with other social life at the time when mass democracy arrived. He analyzes those and nearby interconnections in great depth, testing the Turner idea, in *The Making of an American Community: A Case Study of Democracy in a Frontier County* (1959).

Since World War II several generalizing works on American politics or political thought have treated historical democracy in ways which reveal its limitations and adversities. Richard Hofstadter's *The American Political Tradition and the Men Who Made It* (1948) cuts Jefferson ("The Aristocrat as Democrat") and Jackson to the size of their economic-social attachments. The lowest estimate by a historian of the contribution of the Enlightenment to democracy appears in Daniel J. Boorstin's *Lost World of Thomas Jefferson* (1948; paperback, 1960) and *The Genius of American Politics* (1953). Though not conceiving my problem that way, I probably am responding to Boorstin's denial of the importance of ideas when I reason that, although over-all political comprehension was in very short supply during the rise of mass democracy, ideas did count in infinite ways.

In Louis Hartz, *The Liberal Tradition in America* (1955), a treatment of "The Emergence of Democracy" makes telling comparisons, of a kind not usually made, between situations in America and those in Europe. Though the book is probably the most philosophical brief modern discussion we have, unfortunately for the reader who needs facts there is very little illustration from actual events. In *The American Democratic Tradition: A History* (1963), the most recent general work, Arthur A. Ekirch, Jr., finds democracy not too good to have been true, but always in danger of disintegration (and never more so than today).

1 Concerning Democratic Doctrine: The American Shortage

p. 425
l. 17
Allan Nevins, ed., *American Social History as Recorded by British Travellers* (1923), reissued as *America Through British Eyes* (1948), which selects sizable passages from about forty authors, is still the best anthology.

p. 425
l. 32
The best American edition (among a flood of printings of parts of the text) is a revision of the Reeve translation, with sizable scholarly commentary, by Phillips Bradley (2 vols., 1945). See II, 385–391, for an account of the many editions.

p. 426
Quotation from the biography by Jacob P. Mayer, *Prophet of the Mass Age: A Study of Alexis de Tocqueville* (1939; paperback, 1960), p. 29. On Tocqueville's American visit see George W. Pierson's ample *Tocqueville and Beaumont in America* (1938), abridged in paperback by Dudley C. Lunt as *Tocqueville in America* (1959).

p. 427
l. 12
See Tocqueville, *Democracy in America* (Bradley edition), I, Chapter XVIII, "The Present and Probable Future Condition of the Three Races that Inhabit the Territory of the United States," especially pp. 356–381.

p. 427
l. 43
For Tocqueville letters reporting, and comment concerning, his first impressions, see Pierson, *Tocqueville in America*, pp. 50–56.

p. 429
On the German background which bore generally on democratic thought in America, see Thomas I. Cook and Arnaud B. Leavelle, "German Idealism and American Theories of the Democratic Community," *Journal of Politics*, 5 (August, 1943):213–236. For Bancroft in this respect, see Russel B. Nye, *George Bancroft, Brahmin Rebel* (1944), especially Chapter II; and Henry A. Pochmann, *German Culture in America: Philosophical and Literary Influences, 1600–1900* (1957), especially pp. 73–75.

p. 430
l. 8
Bancroft, *History of the United States*, I (3rd edition, 1843), vii; IV (1852), 10, 12; VIII (1860), 247–249.

p. 430
l. 26
For the early reception and criticism of Bancroft's *History*, see Nye, *George Bancroft*, pp. 102–104; for later criticisms, *passim*.

p. 430
l. 23
"Advertisement" in Camp, *Democracy* (New York, 1841), pp. iii, v.

p. 431
Quotations and paraphrases in this and the preceding paragraphs from Camp, *Democracy*, pp. 10, 12, 20, 72, 84, 85, 155.

p. 432
Quotations and attributions in this paragraph, Camp, *Democracy*, 10, 54, 64, 88, 89.

2 In Jefferson's Country: Flowering and Withering of Confidence

Although none of the three works below—a regional study, a state study, and the study of a tradition—corresponds closely to the content of this section, all supply background material, and each is a first-class book: Wilbur J. Cash, *The Mind of the South* (1941; paperback, n.d.); Richard B. Davis, *Intellectual Life of Jefferson's Virginia, 1790–1830* (1964); Merrill D. Peterson, *The Jefferson Image in the American Mind* (1960).

p. 435
l. 9
On Taylor, see Eugene T. Mudge, *The Social Philosophy of John Taylor of Caroline: A Study in Jeffersonian Democracy* (1939); Charles A. Beard, *Economic Origins of Jeffersonian Democracy* (1915), 197–211, Chapter XII; Benjamin F. Wright, "The Philosopher of Jeffersonian Democracy," *American Political Science Review*, 22 (November, 1928), 870–892. Jefferson quotation from Mudge, *The Social Philosophy of John Taylor*, p. 3.

p. 435 *Arator* quoted, Mudge, *The Social Philosophy of John Taylor*, pp. 155–156.
l. 33

p. 436 See Taylor, *Inquiry into the Principles and Policy of the Government of the United States,* with introduction by Roy F. Nichols (1950), pp. 101, 102.

p. 437 For Peterson's discussion of the Kercheval letters, see *The Jefferson Image,* pp.
l. 18 40–46; the letters, Jefferson to Samuel Kercheval, 12 July, 5 September, 8 October 1816, and 5 September 1824, are in Paul L. Ford, ed., *Writings of Thomas Jefferson,* X, 37–47, 319–320.

p. 437 On conditions in the first transappalachian state, see Niels H. Sonne, *Liberal*
l. 41 *Kentucky, 1780–1828* (1939).

p. 438 On this episode I follow Joseph C. Robert, *The Road from Monticello, A Study of the Virginia Slavery Debate of 1832* (1941), voting summary, p. 118 *et passim.* For background, see again Peterson, *The Jefferson Image,* pp. 39–46.

3 *West of the Appalachians: Frontier Conditions and Partial Democracy*

Since Frederick Jackson Turner's writings, except for the textbook surveys there have been few studies which comprehend the culture of the several "Wests." But thanks to efforts made at the state universities of the Old Northwest, there have been many studies, local, state, and general, of the culture of that region. See especially: Beverley W. Bond, Jr., *The Civilization of the Old Northwest: A Study of Political, Social, and Economic Development, 1788–1812* (1934); R. Carlyle Buley, *The Old Northwest: Pioneer Period, 1815–1840* (1951); John D. Barnhart, *The Valley of Democracy: The Frontier versus the Plantation in the Ohio Valley, 1775–1818* (1953); and again Merle E. Curti, *The Making of an American Community.*

p. 443 On the prepresidential history of Jackson, see the biographies by John Spencer Bassett and Marquis James and particularly Thomas P. Abernethy, *From Frontier to Plantation in Tennessee: A Study in Frontier Democracy* (1932), especially pp. 121, 136, 142, 244, 248, Chapter XVII.

p. 444 This paragraph was written before I saw Fred Somkin's *Unquiet Eagle: Memory and Desire in the Idea of American Freedom, 1815–1860* (1967). Somkin probes deeply into the expression of hope for freedom and prosperity in America, and of anxiety on those same points.

4 *North and East of Washington: Democracy as Source of Anxiety and Hope*

Much of the recent reconsideration of Jacksonian democracy hinges on social studies of New York. Generally speaking they are light on the history of thought. The following main ones impinge on the present argument: Dixon R. Fox, *The Decline of the Aristocracy in the Politics of New York, 1801–1840* (1919); Lee Benson, *The Concept of Jacksonian Democracy: New York as a Test Case* (1961); Walter Hugins, *Jacksonian Democracy and the Working Class: A Study of the New York Workingmen's Move-*

ment, 1829–1837 (1960); Douglas T. Miller, *Jacksonian Aristocracy: Class and Democracy in New York, 1830–1860* (1967); Edward Pessen, *Most Uncommon Jacksonians: The Radical Leaders of the Early Labor Movement* (1967).

p. 446   Quotations in this and the preceding paragraph from the 1956 edition of Cooper, *The American Democrat*, with introduction by H. L. Mencken and explanatory note by Robert E. Spiller (Cooper's biographer), pp. 41, 51, 99, 162. For an expert commentary on Cooper's essay, see Marvin Meyers, *The Jacksonian Persuasion: Politics and Belief* (1957; paperback, 1960), pp. 97–100.

p. 447   For general economic background of New York's development during the first
l. 9   third of the nineteenth century, see George R. Taylor, *The Transportation Revolution, 1815–1860* (1951), various passages on the city and the state. For specific New York backgrounds: Dixon R. Fox, *The Decline of the Aristocracy in the Politics of New York*, especially Chapter VIII; and Douglas T. Miller, *Jacksonian Aristocracy*. Although the analyses in Lee Benson, *The Concept of Jacksonian Democracy*, are concerned mainly with political parties and voting, I borrow from it, especially the first chapter.

p. 447   For a selection from Byllesby, see Joseph L. Blau, ed., *Social Theories of Jackson-*
l. 29   *ian Democracy: Representative Writings of the Period, 1825–1850* (1947), pp. 343–354; concerning him see Arthur M. Schlesinger, Jr., *Age of Jackson* (1945), pp. 180–181; and Joseph Dorfman, *The Economic Mind in American Civilization* (1946), II, 638–641.

p. 448   For a selection from *The Rights of Men to Property* see Blau, *Social Theories*
l. 12   *of Jacksonian Democracy*, pp. 355–364; on Skidmore, see John R. Commons and others, *History of Labour in the United States* (4 vols., 1918–1935), I, 235–238; Dorfman, *Economic Mind*, II, 641–645; and Walter Hugins, *Jacksonian Democracy and the Working Class*, pp. 13, 18.

p. 448   On Owenite ideas and activities in New York, see Richard W. Leopold, *Robert*
l. 30   *Dale Owen, A Biography* (1940), *passim*.

p. 450   Peterson, *The Jefferson Image*, p. 80.
l. 10

p. 450   The social-equalitarian interpretation of Jacksonian democracy, in which the
l. 31   Locofocos and their kind are identified with working-class backgrounds and purposes, belongs especially to Arthur M. Schlesinger, Jr., *The Age of Jackson*. The opposing, small-capitalist interpretation belongs mainly to scholars of Columbia University origin. See Richard Hofstadter, "William Leggett, Spokesman of Jacksonian Democracy," *Political Science Quarterly*, 58 (December 1943):581–594; Marvin Meyers, *The Jacksonian Persuasion*, Chapter IX; Dorfman, *Economic Mind*, II, 650–661 *et passim*; and Pessen, *Most Uncommon Jacksonians*. (This last book, though it appeared after this chapter had been drafted, is the more welcome because it shows the labor radicals in their qualities as social realists and as legatees of the Enlightenment.)

p. 451   Quotation from Helene Zahler, *Eastern Workingmen and National Land Policy, 1829–1862* (1941), p. 34n. On Evans and his associations I borrow from this work, and from Commons, *History of Labour*, II, 326–331, 466–469.

5   National Democracy as People Volunteering: Public Action and Public Thought

Concerning the central figure of this section, there have been three multi-volume biographies of quality: James Parton, *Life of Andrew Jackson* (3 vols., 1860); John Spencer Bassett, *Life of Andrew Jackson* (2 vols., 1911); Marquis James, *Andrew Jackson* (2 vols., 1933, 1937). The following five more recent books, given in chronological order, are the principal interpretative works since World War II: Arthur M. Schlesinger, Jr., *The Age of Jackson;* John William Ward, *Andrew Jackson, Symbol for an Age* (1955; paperback, 1962); Marvin Meyers, *The Jacksonian Persuasion;* Bray Hammond, *Banks and Politics in America, from the Revolution to the Civil War* (1957); Lee Benson, *The Concept of Jacksonian Democracy.*

For help with much of this, and with the earlier literature, see Charles G. Sellers, "Andrew Jackson versus the Historians," *Mississippi Valley Historical Review,* 44 (March, 1958):615–634; and John W. Ward, "The Age of the Common Man," in *The Reconstruction of American History* (1962), edited by John Higham. For a handy selection of passages from the interpreters, James L. Bugg, ed., *Jacksonian Democracy, Myth or Reality* (1962).

p. 454 Carl R. Fish, *The Civil Service and the Patronage* (1905), from which I quote Jackson, pp. 111, 112, is the book which first resisted the flow of scholarly opinion against Jackson's appointment policy. Sidney H. Aronson, *Status and Kinship in the Higher Civil Service: Standards of Selection in the Administrations of John Adams, Thomas Jefferson, and Andrew Jackson* (1964), says that Jackson, like Adams and Jefferson, made many appointments from the educated elite. He appointed self-made men also. But he brought about no great change either in the social status or in the level of competence of the government's service. See also Leonard D. White, in his studies of administrative history, *The Jeffersonians* (1954), pp. 397–398, and *The Jacksonians* (1956).

p. 455   The veto message, 10 July 1832, is in James D. Richardson, ed., *Compilation of*
l. 16   *the Messages and Papers of the Presidents, 1789–1897* (10 vols., 1897), quotations from III, 576, 587, 1139, 1150, 1153; Meyers, *Jacksonian Persuasion,* Chapter II, gives a full and critical elucidation.

l. 26   Bray Hammond, *Banks and Politics in America,* p. 111.
p. 455

p. 455   Jackson message of April 15, 1834, in Richardson, *Messages of the Presidents,* III,
l. 33   1311.

p. 457   For an acute brief treatment of nullification by a writer greatly concerned with theory, see Louis Hartz, "South Carolina vs. the United States," essay IV in *America in Crisis,* edited by Daniel Aaron (1952). For the biographical two sides of the story, see: Charles M. Wiltse, *John C. Calhoun, Nullifier, 1829–1839* (1944), pp. 67–73, 187, Chapter XIV, *et passim;* and Marquis James, *Andrew Jackson,* II, Chapters XII, XIV. For extended treatments, see Chauncey S. Boucher, *The Nullification Controversy in South Carolina* (1916), and William W. Freehling, *Prelude to Civil War: The Nullification Crisis in South Carolina, 1816–1836* (1966).

p. 458   Quotation from Ward, *Andrew Jackson,* p. 28.

p. 459   Quotations from Ward, *Andrew Jackson,* pp. 52, 53.

In the recent historiography of American education, which naturally has been affected by the same mood of reconstruction as affects the operation itself, two scholars have had the most to say about the researches which need to be done. Bernard Bailyn of Harvard has focused on the early period. His *Education in the Forming of American Society, Needs and Opportunities for Study* (1960) gives a running start from the eighteenth into the nineteenth century and bears on all three sections of the present chapter. Lawrence A. Cremin of Teachers College, Columbia, whose scholarship concentrates on late-nineteenth century and recent education, is more closely connected here, because his bright *Wonderful World of Ellwood Patterson Cubberley, an Essay on the Historiography of American Education* (1965), which tackles the work of an old master, is part of his own revisionism.

While the contemporaneousness and connectedness between college-and-university history and school history is no new discovery, those two fields are not often surveyed together. Yet, thanks to Frederick Rudolph, ed., *Essays in Education in the Early Republic* (1965), one can now begin to make one's own survey; the two essays by Benjamin Rush, the one by Noah Webster, and the five others by less familiar writers, discuss all phases of education in the spirit of the young republic. Again, while there is no broad bibliography or textbook to help very much with such a union of the two as the present chapter undertakes, the recent standard work by R. Freeman Butts and Lawrence A. Cremin, *A History of Education in American Culture* (1953), Part 2, "The Development of a Distinctive American Education (1779–1865)" helps. And Alice Felt Tyler, *Freedom's Ferment: Phases of American Social History to 1860* (1944), puts the two together in a set of connections quite different from the ones we follow.

I *Republican Education: Obligation of the States*

I borrow heavily here from Rush Welter, *Popular Education and Democratic Thought in America* (1963). And in this and the second section Frederick A. Rudolph's *The American College and University, A History* (1962) is indispensable for facts and ideas alike. Supplying key documents, Richard Hofstadter and Wilson Smith, eds., *American Higher Education: A Documentary History* (2 vols., 1961), supplies also a splendid sense of main developments—stronger for private than public institutions.

p. 464   Message of 7 December 1796, James D. Richardson, *Compilation of the Messages*
l. 31   *and Papers of the Presidents, 1789–1897* (10 vols., 1897), I, 194.

p. 464   On the national-university proposal, see Allen O. Hansen, *Liberalism and Ameri-*
l. 38   *can Education in the Eighteenth Century* (1926), and David Madsden, *The National University: Enduring Dream of the USA* (1966).

p. 466   On the lyceum movement I follow the definitive work, Carl Bode, *The American Lyceum: Town Meeting of the Mind* (1956); quotations from pp. 11, 12, 48.

p. 467   Rush quoted from Howard Mumford Jones, *O Strange New World* (1964), p. 342; on Rush in this aspect, see Welter, *Popular Education and Democratic Thought*, pp. 25–28. See also Rush's "Plan for a Federal University" in Hofstadter and Smith, *American Higher Education*, I, 152–157.

p. 468   Livingston essays reprinted, Hofstadter and Smith, *American Higher Education*, I, 99–103; quotations from pp. 99, 100, 102–103.

p. 470   On the Universities of Georgia and North Carolina, see E. Merton Coulter, *College Life in the Old South* (1928), and Robert Preston Brooks, *The University of Georgia under Sixteen Administrations, 1785–1955* (1956); and Archibald Henderson, *The Campus of the First State University* (1949), especially pp. 146–149.

p. 471   See Howard H. Peckham, *The Making of the University of Michigan, 1817–1967* (1967), Chapter III.

2   Christian Nurture of Society: Obligation of the Colleges

Besides the especially strong Chapters 3 through 10 in Rudolph's general history, there are several works which, treating more than one institution, are invaluable for present purposes. Donald G. Tewksbury, *The Founding of American Colleges and Universities Before the Civil War, with Particular Reference to the Religious Influences Bearing Upon the College Movement* (1932); R. Freeman Butts, *The College Charts Its Course: Historical Conceptions and Current Proposals* (1939), and George P. Schmidt, *The Liberal Arts College: A Chapter in American Cultural History* (1957), are three of that kind. For the inner intellectual history of the colleges, Richard Hofstadter and Walter P. Metzger, *The Development of Academic Freedom in the United States* (1955), and Wilson Smith, *Professors and Public Ethics: Studies of Northern Moral Philosophers before the Civil War* (1956), are narrower but deeper and more modern in interest.

p. 473   If there are exceptions to this observation, the cases in point are eight or ten of
l. 24   today's secular universities, institutions which were suddenly transformed rather than developed out of their original characters as small colleges. Either state legislation or great gifts of money usually made the change. The Universities of Rochester and Chicago, the University of California at Berkeley, and Duke University are prime examples.

p. 473   See Tewksbury, *Founding of American Colleges and Universities*, pp. 23–28.
l. 29

p. 476   Yale Report of 1828, in Hofstadter and Smith, *American Higher Education*, I, 275–297; quotations from pp. 277, 283, 286, 289, 290.

p. 477   For informative discussions of the inner operations of the colleges, this side of the many one-college histories, see Rudolph, *The American College and University*, Chapters 1–10.

p. 478   Quotations from Rudolph, *The American College and University*, p. 71.

p. 479   On the office and the holders of it, see George P. Schmidt, *The Old-Time College President* (1930) and *The Liberal Arts College: A Chapter in American Cultural History*, especially Chapter 5.

p. 480 The mental and moral philosophy courses are described concisely in Herbert W.
l. 28   Schneider, *A History of American Philosophy*, Chapters 19–22. They are discussed also in Schmidt, *The Old-Time College President;* Wilson Smith's more
detailed *Professors and Public Ethics* analyzes in helpful plurality, and comparatively, the ideas of four of the stronger philosophers.

p. 480 For a bibliography of the texts, see Schneider, *History of American Philosophy*,
l. 44   pp. 254–256.

p. 481 Francis Wayland, *The Elements of Moral Science*, edited by Joseph L. Blau
(1963), p. 340. See Blau's introduction to this volume (pp. ix–xix) for comment
on Wayland.

3 Preparation for Citizenship: Obligation of the Common Schools

Ellwood P. Cubberley, *Public Education in the United States, A Study and
Interpretation of American Educational History* (1919), the book deeply
challenged by Benard Bailyn and Lawrence A. Cremin, held up for three
decades as the standard text. It remains a mine of data, and the statement
of a classic progressive point of view. Cremin's treatise on the public primary school, *The American Common School, An Historic Conception*
(1951), outdoes all other treatments of that subject.

p. 481 Francis X. Curran, *The Churches and the Schools: American Protestantism and
Popular Elementary Education* (1954).

p. 484 On this issue, see Welter, *Popular Education and Democratic Thought*, p. 105.

p. 485 Stowe's *Report* printed in E. W. Knight, ed., *Reports on European Education by
John Griscom, Victor Cousin, and Calvin E. Stowe* (1930), pp. 248–316; quotation
from p. 307.

p. 486 Alcott quotations, in order of occurrence in text: from *Conversations*, in Odell
Shepard, *Pedlar's Progress: The Life of Bronson Alcott* (1937), pp. 181–182, 143;
from "Orphic Sayings," in Perry Miller, ed., *The American Transcendentalists:
Their Prose and Poetry* (1957), p. 87; from *Concord Days*, in Octavius B. Frothingham, *Transcendentalism in New England, A History* (1876; paperback, 1959), p.
261. For surrounding data, see Bernard W. Wishy, *The Child and the Republic:
The Dawn of Modern American Child Nurture* (1968), pp. 3–80.

p. 489 Mann quotations from Merle E. Curti, *Social Ideas of American Educators* (1935),
p. 108; Welter, *Popular Education and Democratic Thought*, p. 98.

p. 490 For brief treatments of Horace Mann and his work by experts, see Curti, *Social
Ideas of American Educators*, Chapter III; and Howard M. Jones, "Horace Mann's
Crusade" in Daniel Aaron, ed., *America in Crisis* (1952). For a French view,
Gabriel Compayré, *Horace Mann and the Common School Revival* (1907).

p. 491 On Barnard as educational publicist, and on his famous journal, see Richard E.
l. 13   Thursfield, *Henry Barnard's American Journal of Education* (1945); on him as a
thinker, Curti, *Social Ideas of American Educators*, Chapter IV.

p. 491 Racine case reported in Timothy L. Smith, "Protestant Schooling and American
l. 25   Nationality, 1800–1850," *Journal of American History*, 53 (1967):679–695.

p. 491 For comparative data on state educational policies and establishments, see Cub-
l. 37   berley, *Public Education in the United States*, pp. 247–250, 273.

p. 493 On the New York situation, see again Smith's article in the *Journal of American
History*, 53:682–685, and Glyndon G. Van Deusen, "Seward and the School Question Reconsidered," *Journal of American History*, 52 (1966):314–319.

CHAPTER XVI

The Farthest Reaches of Perfectionism:
Individualist and Socialist

Although surveys of American history have done so, few bibliographies or special studies have consolidated what this chapter sets outs to consolidate, the individualist and the collectivist phases of early-century perfectionism in America—also the secular and religious ones, the preromantic and the romantic. But, as the realization of the individual was the goal among all, and as with most of the perfectionists this meant the salvation of the soul, appropriately the most nearly over-all bibliography of a specialized nature is Nelson R. Burr, *A Critical Bibliography of Religion in America* (2 vols., 1961).

1 *Fork in the Road Toward Perfection*

Alice Felt Tyler's *Freedom's Ferment* (1944) and Yehoshua Arieli's *Individualism and Nationalism in American Ideology* (1964) help with the problem of the forking road we explore.

p. 497
l. 18   Cooper, *American Democrat* (1956 edition), pp. 180–181.

p. 498
l. 3   Emerson quoted from "Historic Notes on Life and Literature in New England," *The Complete Works of Ralph Waldo Emerson* (Centenary edition, 12 vols., 1903-1904), X, 326. Hereafter all Emerson quotations, unless otherwise credited, will be from this principal edition, cited as Centenary edition.

p. 498
l. 18   Emerson quotation from "Self-Reliance," Centenary edition, II, 61; Thoreau one from "On the Duty of Civil Disobedience," in *Walden and Other Writings of Henry David Thoreau,* edited with an Introduction by Brooks Atkinson (1937), p. 645; Alcott one from "Concord Days" in *The American Transcendentalists: Their Prose and Poetry,* edited by Perry Miller (1957), p. 101.

p. 499
l. 10   Journal quotations (italics mine) and ideas from Arieli, *Individualism and Nationalism,* p. 203.

p. 499
l. 14   Ward quoted from Stanley Elkins, *Slavery: A Problem in American Institutional and Intellectual Life* (1959), p. 158; see also Ward, *Andrew Jackson,* pp. 188, 210, 213.

p. 499
l. 24   Nevin quoted from Arieli, *Individualism and Nationalism,* pp. 201–202.

2 *Utopian Communities and Personal Fulfillment:*
Secular and Evangelical Goals

Under this heading, Donald Drew Egbert and Stow Persons, eds., *Socialism and American Life* (1952) is the only fully appropriate modern general entry. But three contemporary works must be mentioned, good source documents too: John Humphrey Noyes, *History of American Socialisms* (1870, 1961); Charles Nordhoff, *The Communistic Societies of the United States*

(1875, 1965); and William Alfred Hinds, *American Communities* (1878; paperback, 1961). Arthur E. Bestor, Jr., *Backwoods Utopias: The Sectarian and Owenite Phases of Communitarian Socialism in America, 1663–1829* (1950), is definitive and in a class by itself, but it goes only so far. A connected comparative history of the religious communitarians, including the Mormons, is needed.

p. 502   On Owenite theory and practice in America, see Arthur E. Bestor, Jr., *Backwoods Utopias:* and Richard W. Leopold, *Robert Dale Owen, A Biography* (1940), especially Chapters III–IV. On the original Owen and Owenism in general, see A. L. Morton, *The Life and Ideas of Robert Owen* (1963).

p. 503   On R. D. Owen's ideas of education and reform outside communitarianism, see Leopold, *Robert Dale Owen,* Chapter VI.

p. 504   Brisbane quoted from Arthur E. Bestor, Jr., "Albert Brisbane, Propagandist for Socialism in the 1840s," *New-York History,* 28 (April, 1947):133.

p. 505   Bestor, "Albert Brisbane," *New-York History,* 28 (April, 1947):147.

p. 508   On the Shakers, see Marguerite F. Melcher, *The Shaker Adventure* (1941), and Arthur F. Joy, *The Queen of the Shakers* (1960).

p. 509   Besides J. H. Noyes's own *History of American Socialisms,* see: Pierrepont Noyes, *My Father's House: An Oneida Boyhood* (1937), and *A Goodly Heritage* (1958); and Robert A. Parker, *A Yankee Saint: John Humphrey Noyes and the Oneida Community* (1935).

p. 512   For this critique, see I. Woodbridge Riley, *The Founder of Mormonism: A Psychological Study of Joseph Smith, Jr.* (1902), pp. 107–142. For my own comment on the *Book of Mormon,* I draw on some reading of the text but rely especially on William A. Linn, *The Story of the Mormons: From the Date of Their Origin to the Year 1901* (1902), Chapter XI. Fawn M. Brodie, *No Man Knows My History: The Life of Joseph Smith* (1945), supplies the best biographical information.

p. 514   On the Mormon economy and culture, see Nels Anderson, *Desert Saints: The Mormon Frontier in Utah* (1942); Ephraim G. Ericksen, *Psychological and Social Aspects of Mormon Group Life* (1922); William J. McNiff, *Heaven on Earth; A Planned Mormon Society* (1940).

3   *Individualism Made Philosophical: The Self-assertion of Ralph Waldo Emerson*

The bibliography of Transcendentalism, and even of Emerson alone, is too vast for recapitulation; even if it could be summarized here the summary would bear a false suggestion concerning the present work. So I simply remind the reader that Robert E. Spiller and others, *Literary History of the United States* (1948), III, *Bibliography,* is basic; see especially pp. 106–107, 346–348, 492–501. The standard biography is Ralph Leslie Rusk, *The Life of Ralph Waldo Emerson* (1949). As the notes indicate, I have gone to the best edition, *The Complete Works of Ralph Waldo Emerson* (Centenary edition, 12 vols., 1903–1904) for the early writings I draw on; among many selected editions, I have liked and used Frederic I. Carpenter, ed., *Ralph Waldo Emerson: Representative Selections, with Introduction, Bibliography and Notes* (1934), in the American Writers Series edited by Harry Hayden Clark.

p. 515   The quotations from Emerson's journals are taken from Bliss Perry, ed., *The Heart of Emerson's Journals* (1926), pp. 11, 17.

p. 516   Diary quotation from Perry, ed., *Heart of Emerson's Journals*, p. 36; *Divinity School Address*, Centenary edition, I, 119–151, pp. 140, 137 quoted.

p. 517   "History," Centenary edition, II, 1–41; p. 8 quoted.

p. 518   "Historic Notes," in Centenary edition, X, 325–370; pp. 326 and 328 quoted. For
l. 5   a modern treatment of the German impact, Stanley M. Vogel, *German Literary Influences on the American Transcendentalists* (1955).

p. 518   "Historic Notes," Centenary edition, X, 330.
l. 13

p. 518   Modern scholars have examined the problem. See Frederic I. Carpenter, *Emerson*
l. 16   *and Asia* (1930) and Arthur I. Christy, *The Orient in American Transcendentalism, A Study of Emerson, Thoreau, and Alcott* (1932).

p. 518   Emerson quotations from "Historic Notes," Centenary edition, X, pp. 328–329,
l. 41   327. He did well to concede something to the phrenologists; we know now that they and the followers of Dr. F. A. Mesmer, the animal-magnetism man, did stimulate taking sound approaches to the study of psychology. See John D. Davies, *Phrenology: Fad and Science. A Nineteenth Century American Crusade* (1955).

p. 519   "Historic Notes," Centenary edition, X, 339–342.
l. 18

p. 519   Emerson, *Nature*, in Centenary edition, I, 1–78; these quotations, pp. 11, 9. For
l. 31   recent scholarship on Emerson's convictions about the soul, see: Sherman Paul, *Emerson's Angle of Vision: Man and Nature in American Experience* (1952) and Jonathan Bishop, *Emerson on the Soul* (1964).

p. 520   *Nature*, Centenary edition, I, 3, 42.
l. 4

p. 520   *Nature*, Centenary edition, I, 52, 54, 56, 57, 73, 74 are quoted in the present and
l. 39   preceding paragraphs.

p. 521   *The American Scholar*, in Centenary edition, I, 79–115; pp. 83–84, 88, 94, 95 are quoted.

p. 522   *Address*, Centenary edition, I, 117–151; pp. 142–143, 130, 124, 122 quoted.

4 *Transcendentalism and Society: Emerson, Thoreau and Others*

To the references above, as we consider the social ideas of Transcendentalism generally, two classics two-thirds of a century apart need be added: Octavius B. Frothingham, *Transcendentalism in New England: A History* (1876) and Van Wyck Brooks, *The Flowering of New England* (1936). Though it omits the basic essays by Emerson and Thoreau, Perry Miller, ed., *The Transcendentalists: An Anthology* (1950), which is reduced for paperback publication as *The American Transcendentalists: Their Prose and Poetry* (1957), is the best general anthology and contains a basic bibliography. For Thoreau, the best biography is Walter Harding, *The Days of Henry Thoreau* (1965). For a larger bibliography, see again Spiller's *Literary History of the United States*, III, 742–746 for Thoreau; pp. 381–382 for Alcott; pp. 522–525 for Margaret Fuller. Making my selections from the number-two Transcendentalist, I have drawn on a Modern Library volume, *Walden and Other Writings of Henry David Thoreau*, edited with an Introduction by Brooks Atkinson (1937), rather than go back to the standard Riverside edition in 10 volumes (1884–1894) or its reissues. This is one of many one-volume selected editions; besides containing in full the two writings I draw on principally, *Walden* and *Civil Disobedience*, it contains other nature and antislavery writings. I am indebted also to Bartholow V. Crawford, ed., *Henry David Thoreau: Representative Selections with Introduction, Bibliography, and Notes* (1934).

p. 524   "Historic Notes," Centenary edition, X, 343, 341, 344, 342.

p. 525   "Historic Notes," Centenary edition, X, 357. Lindsay Swift, *Brook Farm: Its Members, Scholars, and Visitors* (1900; paperback, 1961, edited by Joseph Schiffman) is the standard history.

p. 526   Emerson, "Thoreau," Centenary edition, X, 449–485; quotations from pp. 456, 454.

p. 527   Quotations of *Civil Disobedience* from Modern Library edition, pp. 636, 640, 645, 646, 650, 659.

p. 528   Quotations of *Walden* from Modern Library edition, pp. 4, 5, 7, 8, 10.

5   Perfectionism and Democracy

p. 530   Thoreau, "Paradise (to be) Regained," in Crawford, ed., *Henry David Thoreau*,
l. 24   pp. 32–56; pp. 34–35, 36, 51, 55, 56 quoted.

p. 530   Modern Library edition, p. 656.
l. 38

p. 531   Emerson quotations from Arieli, *Individualism and Nationalism*, p. 281.
l. 13

p. 531   "Man the Reformer," Centenary edition, I, 225–256; pp. 246–248 quoted.
l. 24

p. 532   "Politics," Centenary edition, III, 197–221; pp. 200–201, 208, 209–210 quoted.
l. 3

p. 532   "Self-Reliance," Centenary edition, II, 43–90; pp. 45, 47, 50, 56, 69 quoted.
l. 32

Index

Boorstin, Daniel J., 150, 190, 209
Boston, 78, 158–159, 191, 376, 377, 452; center of religious liberalism and rationalism, 174, 182–183, 216, 334–335; focus of revolutionary conflict, 268; King's Chapel, 102, 121, 334–335; Latin School, 94, 96; population, 158, 386; publishing, 384; Temple School, 485–487
Boston Atheneum, 351
Boston Tea Party, 242
Botany, 205–206; 379
Bowdoin College, 473
Boyle, Robert, 119
Boylston, Zabdiel, 201, 211
Brackenridge, Hugh Henry, 386–387, 389, 391, 392
Bracton, Henry de, 196; quoted, 19–20
Bradford, William, 222
Brafferton, the, 119, 120
Brainerd, David, 173, 175
Bray, Thomas, 121
Brethren (Dunkers), 146, 147–148
Brethren of the Common Life, 136
Brief Account of the Rise and Progress of People Called Quakers, A, Penn, 140
Brisbane, Albert, 503–505; quoted, 505
"The British Prison Ship," Freneau, 388
Brook Farm, 348, 498, 499, 505, 524–525, 529
Brown, Charles Brockden, 383, 389
Brown, Robert E., 272
Brown University, 182, 345, 473, 479
Browne, Robert, 59, 60
Brownism, 59, 60
Bryan, George, 267
Bryant, William Cullen, 389, 394, 404, 448–449, 452; quoted, 395
Bucer, Martin, 58, 61
Buckminster, Joseph, 351, 393
Bucknell University, 475
Burke, Edmund, 242, 309, 418, 431, 436
Burlamaqui, Jean Jacques, 195, 431
Burr, Aaron (the father), 127, 163
Bushnell, Horace, 369, 488
Butler, Samuel, 195, 199
Byllesby, Langdon, 447, 449, 452
Byrd, William, II, 193, 195, 196; quoted, 197–198

Calculus, 190, 192
Calhoun, John C., 292, 380, 410, 439, 455, 456–457
California, University of, 474
"The Call," Herbert, 110
Calvin, John, 57, 58, 61, 140
Calvinism, 353, 357, 371; Augustinianism of, 62; doctrine of depravity of natu-

ral man, 179, 349, 480, 508; predestination, 161, 174
Calvinist-descended churches, 115; Great Awakening, 151; interchurch cooperation during Second Great Awakening, 365–366, 371; 19th-century schisms, 369–370
Cambridge Platform of Church Discipline, 80
Cambridge University, 11, 28, 56, 60, 96, 97
Camp, George Sidney, 430–432, 433, 445, 472; quoted, 430, 431–432
Camp meetings, revivalist, 358, 359–361
Campbell, Alexander, 370
Campbell, Thomas, 370
Campbellites, 370
Cane Ridge revival meetings, 358, 359
Cannon, James, 267, 271
Capital crimes, Massachusetts, 81, 82
Carey, Henry C., 401–403
Carey, Mathew, 397, 401
Carlyle, Thomas, 488, 519
Carolina: Locke's plan for, 36; royal land grants, 35
Carroll, Charles, of Carrollton, 31, 195, 225, 241, 344
Carroll, Charles, of Doughoregan, 129
Carroll, Father John, 129, 344, 345
Carter, James G., 489
Cartwright, Peter, quoted, 371
Cartwright, Thomas, 57–58, 59, 60
Catholicism. *See* Roman Catholicism
Causes of the Greatness and Decadence of the Romans, Montesquieu, 195
Center College, 437
Chaderton, Lawrence, 60
Channing, Edward Tyrrel, 394, 515, 519
Channing, William Ellery (cleric), 351–352, 393, 394, 417, 486; Emerson and, 519; quoted, 352, 395
Channing, William Ellery (poet), 523
Chapman, John, 457
Charles I, King, 9, 16, 17, 18, 20, 47, 54, 55, 66, 79
Charles II, King, 16, 46, 91, 99, 114, 117, 140, 191
Charleston, 386; Library Society, 377
Charter of Privileges (1701), Pennsylvania, 143, 144
Chase, Samuel, 387
Chatham, Earl of. *See* Pitt, William
Chauncy, Charles, 174, 183, 216, 335, 350
Chautauqua (New York) camp meetings, 361
Checks and balances, 274, 275–276, 279–280, 286; Adams's emphasis on, 303
Cheever, Ezekiel, 96

Chemical Society of Philadelphia, 376
Chicago, 441
Child, Robert, 79, 125
Child-study and -development movement, 484, 485–487, 524
Chinard, Gilbert, 320
Chosen-people concept, 53, 63, 67, 99, 222, 354, 355, 356, 391, 432, 511
Christian Communism, Shaker, 507
Christian Examiner, The, 353
Christian Nurture, Bushnell, 369, 488
Christian Philosophy, Mather, 216
"On Christian Union" (sermon), 345
Chronological History of New England in the Form of Annals, Prince, 223
Church and state, 21, 65–66, 111–116, 346. *See also* Taxation, church
–colonial Maryland, 30, 43, 116
–colonial Virginia, 30, 32, 42, 115–116
–Connecticut, 111, 180, 283–284, 355–356, 488; Saybrook Platform, 102, 171
–*cujus regio ejus religio*, 112, 113, 114, 129; New World exceptions, 121
–Erastianism, 66
–establishment: absent in Puritan colonies, 69; ended, 284, 333; multiple, 264–265; Southern Colonies, 32, 42, 43, 49, 115–116
–in Europe, 112–113
–post-Revolutionary conditions, 264, 271, 272, 283–284
–Puritan approach, 65–66, 68–70, 181; theocracy, 69–70, 77–82, 85, 100–102, 105–107
–Roger Williams's views, 84–85, 87
–separation of, 21, 283, 327, 334, 484
Church elders, 58, 68
Church government: Anglican, local control, 117–118; congregationalism, 59–60, 67–69, 92–93; episcopal, 58, 122, 339–342; Methodists, 337–338, 340; Mormons, 512–513; moves toward national federation, 128, 164; national constitutions, 273, 336, 337, 341–342, 343; presbyterian, 58, 126, 343; proposals for intercongregational federation, 103; Quaker, 141
Church membership:
–Anglican, 105
–Catholic, 105
–Presbyterian, New Side conversions, 162
–Puritan, 67–70, 100; birthright, 100; conversion required, 71, 182; conversion required by Separates, 171; Halfway (confederate), 100; meaning shift from salvation achieved to salvation hoped for, 105; "natural condition" sufficient, 104–105; "visible saints," 70, 80, 100; voluntarism introduced, 104–105
–Quaker, 141
–Unitarian abandonment of Puritan exclusiveness, 352
Church of England, 15, 70–71, 114, 115–123; clergy, 116–118, 126; converts to, 121–123; disintegration in America, 333–337, 339; education efforts, 118–120, 123–124; in England, 16, 21, 23, 28, 79, 99, 112, 116; establishment in South, 32, 42, 43, 49, 115–116; establishment ended, 264, 284, 333; high vs. low church, 339, 340; institutional privileges, 21, 23, 115; missionary work, 116, 121, 122; in New York, 114, 121, 284, 339; nonseparating Puritan dissent within, and loyalty to, 57–61, 70–71, 80; in Southern Colonies, *see* Southern Colonies; unestablished north of Maryland, 120. *See also* Anglicans
Church of Scotland, 58, 112, 343
Churches: first six in America, 114–115, 131–132; 19th-century cooperation, 365–367, 369; 19th-century schisms, 369–371; presumed order of wealth and size, 132. *See also* individual churches
Churches Quarrel Espoused, The, Wise, 92
Cicero, 18, 96, 195, 294, 319
Cincinnati, 441
Cities, growth of, Middle Colonies, 32, 33; Old Northwest, 441; population figures, 158, 386, 441, 447; religious diversity of, 158–159
Citizenship, preparation for, 262–263
Civil disobedience, 229, 231, 237, 242, 526–527; statewide (nullification), 456
Civil Disobedience, Thoreau, 524, 526–527, 529, 530
Civil liberties. *See also* Franchise; Natural law and rights; Religious freedom; Speech, freedom of
–abrogations of, in colonies, and court cases, 227–231
–due process, 82
–free assembly, 284
–free press, 259, 284–285
–guarantees of: colonial Pennsylvania, 142, 144; federal bill of rights, 284–285; Massachusetts codes, 81–82; state bills of rights, 258–259, 264, 271, 284
–New York's liberal champions, 446–452
–property, 237, 258, 275, 418
Claiborne, Nathaniel, quoted, 458
Clap, Thomas, 202

Clark, George Rogers, 281
Clark, William, 321, 511
Clarke, Mary P., 45
Clay, Henry, 380, 398, 424, 437; American System, 399, 400, 442, 501; and Bank, 399, 449, 454; political beliefs, 442; tariff of, 457
Cleaveland, John, 183
Clergy: Anglican, 116–118, 126; calling of, New Side–Old Side controversy, 160–161; lay, German churches, 129–130; Methodist, ordination, 337; participation in Enlightenment, 189; Presbyterian, 58, 126–127, 160–161; Protestant Episcopal, 341; Puritan, 68, 69; revivalists, 362
Clinton, DeWitt, 482, 492
Coddington, William, 88
Coercive Acts, 242–243; repudiations of, 243–247, 250
Cohen, Hennig, 199
Cohen, I. Bernard, 208, 216
Cohens versus Virginia, 413–414
Coke, Sir Edward, 19–20, 81, 83, 84, 190, 196, 233; *Institutes of the Laws*, 17, 20; legal idealism, 19–20, 348; quoted, 19–20; mentioned, 22, 23, 92, 287, 306, 405, 416
Coke, Thomas, 337
Colden, Cadwallader, 204, 218, 221
Colgate University, 475
Collectivism, 498, 499, 502, 513. *See also* Utopian communities
Colleges. *See also* Universities
—curricula, 96–97, 119–120, 123–124, 211, 264, 476–477; classical, in 19th century, 476–477; philosophy, 479–481; science, 163, 194, 201, 202–204, 211, 356, 376, 473, 476
—degrees, early, 82, 97, 162, 211, 473
—denominational, 131, 132, 366, 467–468, 469, 470, 471, 472–481, 482; Anglican (Episcopalian), 118–120, 123–124, 468, 474–475; Baptist, 345, 475; Catholic, 132; College of Philadelphia an early exception, 129, 131, 149, 210; Congregationalist, 366, 468, 473–474; enrollment, 470; Livingston's warning against, 468; Lutheran and Reformed, 131, 365; Methodist, 434, 467, 474, 475; Presbyterian, 127–128, 162–163, 182, 365–366, 434, 467–468, 474; presidents' role, 478–479; Puritan, 96–98, 106; Quaker, 475; traditionalism of, 476–477
—Great Awakening impetus, 181–182, 183
—Middle Colonies, 123–124, 127–128, 131, 162–163, 210–211

—Middle States, 467–468, 474, 475
—multiformity of thought emerges, 203
—Negro admission, 363–364, 482
—New England, 32, 94, 96–98, 106, 202–204, 473
—Old Northwest, 366, 471, 473, 474, 475
—proliferation of, 473
—public support of private, 263
—reformism, 477
—religious freedom, 102, 106, 162–163, 203
—Second Great Awakening impetus, 366, 470, 471
—Southern Colonies, 118–120, 194–195
—Southern states, 470, 474
—women admitted, 364, 471, 482
Collinson, Peter, 205, 207, 209
Colman, Benjamin, 103
Colorado College, 473
Columbia College (later University), 468–469, 473, 477, 492. *See also* King's College
"The Columbiad," Barlow, 392
Columbian Institute, 379–380, 399
Commentaries, Blackstone, 196
Commentaries, Story, 418
Commentaries on American Law, Kent, 416–417, 418
Common Law. *See* Law
Common Sense, Paine, 247–249, 271, 384
Common-sense philosophy, 163, 191, 314, 392, 432, 479, 501
Commonwealth government, 255–259; Christian, idea of, 472; Connecticut, 111, 260; Cromwell, 82, 255; Massachusetts, 82, 98, 102, 269, 272; Pennsylvania, 142; Rhode Island, 260. *See also* Republican government.
Communion (Lord's Supper): abandoned by Quakers, 141; as aid to salvation, 336; Emerson on, 516; Methodist use of, 336–337; Puritan use of, and qualification for, 68, 104–105, 172; as symbol of salvation achieved, 105, 172, 336
Communitarianism, 529; religious, 146–147, 506–514; secular, 500–502, 504–506. *See also* Utopian communities
"Compensation," Emerson, 532
Compton, Henry, 116, 118, 119, 121
Conant, James R., quoted, 264
Concord Days, Alcott, 486
Concord School of Philosophy, 487. *See also* Transcendentalism
Condorcet, Marquis de, 191, 335
Confederation, 276, 281–282, 296, 321
Confessional system of education, 149
Congregation of God and the Spirit, 130, 147

Cooper, Myles, 294
Cooper, Thomas, 323
Cornbury, Lord (Edward Hyde), 36, 125
Corwin, Edward S., quoted, 256, 412
Cosby, William, 227–229
Cotton, John, 67, 80, 85, 88, 92, 100; quoted, 33, 79
Council of Censors, 268, 415
Counter Reformation, orthodox Congregationalist, 353–354
Country Justice, Dalton, 196
Courts. See Judiciary; Supreme Court
Cousin, Victor, 484, 491, 503
Covenant:
—Mormons, 68, 511
—Puritans: church, 66–69, 86, 105; of grace, 63–64, 67, 88, 104–105, 165; Halfway, 100–101, 104, 171; national, 63, 67, 71; vs. "natural condition" and voluntarism, 104–105
Covenant (federal) theology, 60, 61, 63–64, 66–69, 80, 100–101, 104–105, 127; repudiated by Yale teachers (1722), 121
Coxe, Tench, 300, 397
Crashaw, William, 30, 46
Credit monopolization, 447, 449–450
Crèvecoeur, J. Hector St. John de, 227
Critical deism, 213, 217
Cromwell, Oliver, 9, 17, 79, 82, 255
Crown government, 31, 33–35, 42
Cubberley, Ellwood P., 492
Cujus regio ejus religio doctrine, 112, 113, 114, 129; New World exceptions to, 121
Culpeper, Lord, 35
Cumberland Synod, 370
Curran, Francis X., 481, 482
Curti, Merle, 440
Cutler, Timothy, 121, 122, 168
Cuvier, Baron Georges, 376, 518
Cycle theory of history, 157–158, 172–173

Dalton, Michael, 196
Dana, Richard Henry, 394
"The Danger of an Unconverted Ministry" (sermon), 160, 170
"The Dangers and Duties of Men of Letters," Buckminster, 393
Dartmouth College, 183
Dartmouth College case, 414
Davenant, Charles, quoted, 34
Davenport, James, 171, 175, 183
Davenport, John, 67; quoted, 69
Davidson College, 470
Davies, Samuel, 126, 128, 163, 181, 230, 343
Davis, Richard Beale, 434

Day, Jeremiah, 476
"Day of Doom," Wigglesworth, 101
Declaration of Independence, 6, 244, 257–258, 285, 447; quoted, 249–251
Declaratory Act, 239, 240
Decline and Fall of the Roman Empire, Gibbon, 190
Defence of the Constitution of the United States of America, Adams, 273, 304, 308–310, 436
Deism, 211, 213–217, 334, 336, 359
De La Warr, Thomas Lord, 30
Democracy, 283, 423–460. See also Majority rule; Representative government; Self-government
—vs. aristocracy, Tocqueville on, 428
—Benton's championship of, 443–444
—churches: Lutherans, 130; Protestant Episcopal Church, 341–342; Universalists, 349
—constitutional conventions a step toward, 257, 266, 270
—equated with republicanism, 431, 472
—Jacksonian, 423–424, 442–443, 453–456, 458–460
—Jeffersonian, 324, 327, 428–429, 436–437, 443–444
—mass participation, 423–424, 425, 428, 433, 442, 446–447, 452, 454, 459
—and perfectionism, 529–532
—practice, 423–424, 459–460; lagging in South, 436–439; lagging in Southwest, 441–443; Northeast, 445–452; office rotation, 453–454; Old Northwest, 440–441; political conventions, 424, 454; suffrage extensions, 424, 438, 440, 446–447, 454
—Puritan foreshadowings of, 54, 60–61, 71, 93, 130
—social, 451–452
—in state government, 260, 266, 272, 424
—thought and theory: Bancroft, 422, 429–430; Byllesby, 447; Camp, 430–432; Cooper, 445–446; dearth of, 423–425, 433, 444; Emerson, 531; New York prolabor journalists, 448–452; Niles, 398; Skidmore, 447–448; Taylor, 435–436; Tocqueville, 425–429
Democracy, Camp, 430–431, 445, 472
Democracy in America, Tocqueville, 425, 426–428, 429
Democratic Party, 383, 446, 449, 455, 459
Democratic-Republican (later Democratic) Party, 424
Democratic Review, 499, 529
Denison University, 475
Deseret, Mormon state, 513–514

Destutt de Tracy, Comte Antoine, 314, 315

Determinism, 487, 519; economic, Hamilton's, 296; no part of Edwards's theology, 178, 180; rejected by Emerson, 520

Dew, Thomas R., 438

Dewey, John, 292, 487

Dial, The, 486, 505, 523–524

Dickinson, John, 225, 240–241, 266–267, 467; *Letters of a Pennsylvania Farmer,* 240

Dickinson, Jonathan, 127, 163

Dickinson College, 467, 468

Disciples of Christ, 370

Discourse of Matters Pertaining to Religion, Parker, 524

Discourses Concerning Government, Sydney, 17

Discourses on Davila, Adams, 309–312

Disinterested benevolence, 183, 480, 481

Dissertation Concerning the End for Which God Created the World, Edwards, 176, 177

Dissertation on Liberty and Necessity, Pleasure and Pain, A, Franklin, 213

Dissertation on the Canon and Feudal Law, A, Adams, 245, 262, 307–308, 309

Divided sovereignty. *See* Multiple sovereignty

"A Divine and Supernatural Light" (sermon), 165, 166

Divine law, 19, 216, 348

Divine right of government. *See* Government

Doctrine of Original Sin Defended, The, Edwards, 176, 177

Doctrine of the Instituted Churches, The, Stoddard, 104

Dominion of New England, 91, 101–102

Dorfman, Joseph, 414

Douglass, Elisha P., quoted, 257

Dryden, John, 199, 207

Dudley, Joseph, 224

Due process, Massachusetts code, 82

Dulany, Daniel, the Elder, 226, 232–233, 433; quoted, 233

Dulany, Daniel, the Younger, 218, 238–239, 240; quoted, 238

Dunkers, 146, 147–148

Dunster, Henry, 82, 96–97, 98

Du Pont de Nemours, Pierre Samuel, 314, 322, 324

Dutch Reformed Church, 114, 126, 130, 131, 161, 365, 463; revivalism, 159–160

Dutch settlers, 28, 29, 32, 113–114

Duty of Americans at the Present Crisis, The, Dwight, 356

Dwight, Timothy, 183, 353, 355–356, 359, 377, 392, 476; quoted, 334, 358; writings of, 355, 356, 390, 391

Earlham College, 475

East India Company, 12, 13, 35, 242

"The Ebb and Flow," Taylor, 65

Eckenrode, Hamilton J., 231

Economic Interpretation of the Constitution of the United States, An, Beard, 275

Economic materialism, 530

Economic theory, 295; Carey, 401–403; of cycles, 157; Dulany, on taxing of colonies, 238–239; Enlightenment, 190; Hamilton, 295–296; 299–301, 396, 400; List, 400–401; Owenite, 501; Raymond, 399–400; Woolman's thought, 153–154

Economy: factor in regionalism, 31–33; government role in, 295–296, 299–301, 400, 402, 409–410; liberal reform proposals, 449–450, 451, 452; national, 299–301, 302, 396–403; Old Northwest, 441; protectionism, 396, 402, 403 (*see also* Tariff); Supreme Court decisions bearing on, 414

Eddy, Mary Baker, 89

Education. *See also* Colleges; Schools; Universities

—adult (lyceum), 464–467

—child-centered, 485–487

—church efforts, 132, 366, 463–464, 467–468, 469, 470, 471, 472–481, 483; Anglican (Episcopalian), 118–120, 123–124, 463, 468, 474–475; Baptist, 181, 345, 475; Catholic, 132, 345, 483; Congregationalist, 366, 468, 473–474; failure to preserve church monopoly, 481–483; German pietists, 146, 147, 149; interdenominational, 366, 474, 492–493; Lutheran and Reformed, 131, 365; Methodist, 434, 467, 474, 475; Mormons, 483, 513; Presbyterian, 127–128, 162–163, 181–182, 365–366, 434, 467–468, 474; Puritan commitment, 93–98, 106; Quakers, 148–149, 475; Sunday-school movement, 483–484

—communitarians' efforts, 147, 502, 510, 513

—confessional system of, 149

—early curricula, 95, 96–97

—elementary, 95, 120, 194–195, 481–482, 484–485, 492

—equalitarianism, 322, 363–364, 448, 451, 452, 462, 502–503

—federal involvement, 321–322, 464

—higher, 466–481; closed to Catholics, 129; denominationalism, 131, 132, 472–

—writings of, 517, 532; "Historic Notes on Life and Literature in New England," 496, 519; *Nature,* 517, 519–520; "Politics," 531; *Representative Men,* 517, 518, 532; "Self-Reliance," 496, 532

Emerson, William, 351, 515

Emmanuel College (Cambridge), 56, 60, 96

Emmons, Nathaniel, 363

Emory College (Georgia), 470, 474, 475

Endicott, John, 84

England. *See also* Church of England; Parliament
—church and state, 21, 23, 112
—Commonwealth, 82, 255
—Enlightenment in, 190–191; deist movement, 213, 215
—Glorious Revolution, 8–9, 16, 23, 92
—its government form discussed by Adams, Paine, 245–246, 248–249, 307
—Protestantism, character of, 137–138
—Puritan Revolution, 8–9, 13, 17, 22, 28, 46, 55, 56–59, 60–61, 70
—reconstruction policy of, 234–243
—Reformation in, 7, 11, 64; Puritan phase, 55, 57–61, 70; Quaker phase, 70, 137–140
—Renaissance in, 7
—revivalism, 158, 169
—social radicals, 447
—Tudor and Stuart, 7–22, 55, 112; Elizabethan culture, 6–7, exploration and expansion, 11–12; feudalism and manorialism, 7, 13, 37; language, 10–11; law, 19–20; monarchism, 15–16; parliamentary privilege, 18; political developments, 8–9, 16, 18, 61; political philosophy, 16–18, 23; religious persecutions, 21, 22, 138–139; religious toleration, 20–22, 45, 46; Restoration, 99; social hierarchy, 13–15; social mobility, 14
—Wesleyans, 116, 158

Enlightenment, 189–218, 323, 348, 406, 415, 432, 463, 487; deism, 211, 213–217; furthers intercolonial contacts, 211–212, 217–218; ideas applied in state reconstruction, 261–266; ideas embodied in Declaration of Independence, 251; nature of American participation in, 189, 191–192, 211–212; Old Northwest patterned in spirit of, 440; Puritan foreshadowings, 87, 93; religious divergencies, 216–217, 333–335 (*see also* Liberalism, religious); science, 189, 190, 191, 192, 193–194, 201–206, 208–209, 211–212, 217–218; Scottish influence, 163, 191, 386, 479 (*see also* Common-sense philosophy; Moral intui-

tionism); Southern Colony culture, 195–200

Entail, 262

Environmentalism, 210, 451, 487, 501, 502

Ephrata community, 146–147

Episcopacy, as form of church government, 58, 122, 339–341

Episcopal Academy of Philadelphia, 149

Episcopalians, 102, 339–342; separation of Methodists from, 336, 337. *See also* Protestant Episcopal Church

Equal Rights Democrats, 449–450

Equality, 285, 424; Benton's championship of, 443–444; commitment to, in Old Northwest, 282, 327, 440; Declaration of Independence pronouncement on, 250–251, 285; of education, 322, 363–364, 448, 451, 452, 462; Emerson on, 531; Jackson's championship disputed, 442–443, 455; legislative, of colonies, doctrine of, 244, 247; limited, Adams's view, 310; Locofoco championship of, 449–450; of opportunity, 448, 451–452; political, 431, 446–447 (*see also* Franchise); in property, 447–448; Quaker belief in, 138, 248; questioned by Cooper, 445; and slavery, 262, 285–286, 438–439; vs. social hierarchy, basic dispute, 48; thrust slowed in Virginia, 436–439; Virginia Bill of Rights on, 258

Erastianism, 66

Essay Concerning Human Understanding, An, Locke, 174, 178, 190, 202

Essay on Field Husbandry in New England, Eliot, 202

Essay on the Rate of Wages, Carey, 402

Essay Towards the Present and Future Peace of Europe, Penn, 144

Essays Concerning the English Nation, Voltaire, 190

Etzler, J. A., 529, 530

Evangelism, 158, 358–365; Baptist, 181, 360; community-building impulse, 361; Congregationalist, 354, 362; Dutch Reformed, 159–160; interchurch, 365–367; Methodist, 338, 347, 358–359, 360; Presbyterian, 160–162, 181, 358, 359–360, 361–362; Puritan, 99, 103–106, 168–169, 172. *See also* Great Awakening, Missionary work; Revivalism; Second Great Awakening

Evans, George Henry, 450–451, 452

Everett, Edward, quoted, 374, 375, 430

Executive branch: council, Pennsylvania, 268; federal, 279, 280, 408–409;

Executive branch (*continued*)
independence of, 258–259; state government, 259, 271

Familists, 83
Family life, utopians, 506, 509, 510
Fauquier, Francis, 194
Federal theology. *See* Covenant theology
Federalism: centripetal vs. centrifugal principles of power, 413, 414; of Hamilton, 286, 296–299; Jefferson on, 408; Madison on, 286, 409; multiple sovereignty, 247, 276, 280–282, 286, 296, 297; Newtonian thought, 286–287, 297, 325, 408; Presbyterian example, 128, 164, 342; proponents and opponents at 1787 constitutional convention, 273–274; Protestant Episcopalians, 341–342; strengthened by Supreme Court decisions, 412–414; Whig Party, 396, 424
Federalist, The, 274, 277, 278, 285, 286, 296–298, 313, 408, 409, 412
Federalist Party, 301, 315, 408
Fell, Margaret, 138
Fenno's *Gazette*, 312
Feudalism: Adams on, 245, 308; in early colonies, 35–37, 40; in England, 7, 13, 37
Fichte, Johann Gottlieb, 518
Filmer, Sir Robert, 16, 196, 325
Finley, Samuel, 128, 163; quoted, 160
Finney, Charles Grandison, 361–364, 472, 509; on slavery, 362
Fithian, Philip Vickers, 215
Fletcher versus Peck, 413
Force Act, 457
Foreign affairs, 318, 320–321, 408
Form of Discipline for the Methodist Episcopal Church in America, 337, 338, 340, 347
Fourier, Charles, 503, 504; quoted, 503
Fourierism, 503–506, 524, 525, 529
Fox, George, 137–138, 141, 144
Frame of Government, Pennsylvania, 142
France, Enlightenment in, 190–191, 518
Franchise, 20
—adult white male, 424, 440, 447, 452, 454
—bills of rights on, 259, 260
—general, Camp on, 431
—Jamestown (1619), 43
—John Adams's views, 303
—liberalizations, 424; Massachusetts, 270; New York, 416, 446–447; Pennsylvania, 257, 266, 267; Virginia, 438
—Old Northwest, 440

—restrictions, 424; to church members, in New England, 68–69, 79–80, 100–101; property, 102, 143, 257, 260, 261, 271–272, 424, 442, 446
Franklin, Benjamin, 31, 144, 206–211, 221, 227, 228
—and American Philosophical Society, 217, 218
—deism of, 213–215, 217
—Fellow of Royal Society, 191, 209
—printer and publisher, 191, 203, 206, 207–208, 229, 385
—public service, 207, 209–211, 221–222, 232, 266–268; College of Philadelphia founded, 149, 210–211; 1787 constitutional convention, 274, 275
—quoted, 221–222; on education, 210; on the Junto, 207; on his religious beliefs, 213–214
—scientific work, 208–209
—writings of: "Articles of Belief and Acts of Religion," 213–214; *Autobiography*, 206–207, 213, 214; *A Dissertation on Liberty and Necessity, Pleasure and Pain*, 213; *Education of Youth in Pensilvania*, 210; *The Way to Wealth*, 208
—mentioned, 123, 147, 161, 204, 212, 235, 246, 248, 304, 314, 376, 428, 452, 463
Franklin, James, 228
Franklin (and Marshall) College, 131
Franklin Institute, 465
Free Enquirer, 448, 502
Free School Society, New York, 492–493
Free trade, 295, 450, 451, 452
Free-will doctrine, 161, 480; Arminian belief, 174, 178; Edwards's views, 174, 177–179; Methodist belief, 336, 347
Freedom: abrogations of, in colonies, and court cases, 227–231; achievements of the Revolution, 283–285, 327; colonies' struggle for, 226–251; commitment to, in Old Northwest, 282, 327; English legacy, 5–6, 8–9, 16–23, 42, 44, 46, 48–49; individual, 258, 299, 496, 497, 498–499, 503 (*see also* Individualism); under law, 9, 17–20, 23, 81, 327; New York labor-reformist championship of, 452, 503; vs. organization, in government, 8–10, 23, 61, 81; parliamentary, 18, 23, 45, 48; vs. social hierarchy, a basic dispute, 48; sources of, 6. *See also* Civil liberties; Religious freedom; Speech, freedom of
Freedom of the Will, The, Edwards, 176, 177–179, 180

Jefferson, Thomas (*continued*)
327, 428–429, 436–437; agrarian republicanism, 302, 319; states' rights vs. federal power, 316–318 (*see also* quoted, *below*)
—as president, 317, 318–321, 396, 407
—proposal for Old Northwest, 282
—quoted, 315, 323, 414, 435; on Adams, 270, 303; on belief, 134; on constitutions, 258; on democracy and republicanism, 324, 437; on direct popular vote, 261; on education, 264, 322; on federalism, 408; on land ownership, 262, 319; on his love of rural life, 262, 318–319; on public opinion and morality, 220; on religious freedom, 265–266; on Sedition Act, 317, 348; on self-government, 246–247, 324; on state vs. federal power, 316
—reform efforts in Virginia, 261–266, 437
—and Unitarianism, 315
—writings: *Notes on Virginia*, 192, 261, 318, 382; *A Summary View of the Rights of British America*, 5, 246, 249
—mentioned, 120, 154, 194, 195, 196, 225, 226, 303, 388, 392, 398, 411, 413, 432, 434, 442, 443, 447, 452
Jeffersonianism, 291, 324, 327, 428–429, 443–444, 450
Jesuits, 30, 129, 345
Jews, 76, 143; toleration in Rhode Island, 85
Johnson, Charles A., 360
Johnson, Samuel, 121, 122–124, 163; president of King's College, 123–124; quoted, 122; mentioned, 168, 368
Johnson, Samuel (English author), 382
Jones, Howard Mumford, quoted, 196, 197
Jones, Hugh, quoted, 116–117, 120
Jones, Rufus, quoted, 135
Jordan, Wilbur K., 22
Jordan, Winthrop, 40, 285
Journal of John Woolman, 150, 152
Journalism, 382–383, 397; business, 397–398; Fourierist, 505; literary, 199, 383, 393, 523–524; prolabor, 448–451; religious, 351, 353, 383; science, 377, 383. *See also* Magazines; Newspapers
"Judges' oath" controversy, 232
Judicial review, 279–280, 296–297, 410–414, 415
Judiciary: colonial, 35, 37, 225; federal, 279–280, 406, 410–415; independence of, 259; selection of judges, 259, 267–268, 271, 280; states, 259, 406, 410, 415–416. *See also* Privy Council; Supreme Court

Junto, Philadelphia, 206–207, 428

Kames, Lord (Henry Home), 391
Kant, Immanuel, 429, 517, 518
Kendall, Amos, 450
Kent, James, 259, 399, 415–417, 418, 446, 447; *Commentaries on American Law* quoted, 416, 417
Kentucky: church activities, 345, 437; education, 437; revivals, 358, 359, 370; settling of, 342
Kentucky Resolutions (1798), 317, 408, 410, 435, 456
Kenyon College, 475
Kercheval, Samuel, 436, 437, 438
King George's War (1744–1748), 149, 158, 209
King in council, 35, 231, 232, 249
King Philip's War, 100, 104
King William's War (1689–1697), 144, 145
King's College, 123–124, 163, 204, 469; curriculum, 123–124, 468; founding of, 123, 468. *See also* Columbia College.
Knickerbocker *History of New York*, Irving, 384
Knox, John, 58, 112
Knox College, 366, 471, 474
Koch, Adrienne, 313; quoted, 312
Kometographia, Mather, 201, 215
Konefsky, Samuel J., 412
Kraus, Michael, 212
Kuhn, Adam, 206

Labaree, Leonard W., quoted, 235–236, 242
Labor: child, 300, 397; division of, 295, 300; early-Republican theories, 400, 402–403; journals and papers, 448–451; reformism, 446–448, 451–452; union movement, 446, 448, 451; women, 300
Lafayette, Marquis de, 314, 401
Laisser faire, 455
Lancaster, Henry, 492
Land distribution: in early colonies, 35–38, 39, 41–42, 86, 143; in England, 13; entail, 262; feudal-manorial, 13, 35–37, 283; free-land champions, 444, 450, 451; headright, 39; Jefferson on, 262, 319; New York estates, 36, 440, 447; Old Northwest, 282, 440, 441; primogeniture, 262; Quaker views on land rents, 140–141, 153; reforms in Virginia, 262; Revolutionary changes, 262, 282, 283; Roger Williams's protests, 84; seignorial grants in colonies,

35–36, 140; western domain, early Republic, 301, 320
Land Ordinance (1785), 282, 464
Lane Theological Seminary, 363, 364, 366, 474
Language(s), 380–382; Americanisms, 381, 382; ancient, study of, 11, 96, 97, 120, 381, 476–477; blending of foreign elements, 12–13, 381; emergence of vernacular, 10–12. *See also* Latin
Latimer, Hugh, 17
Latin: eclipsed by vernacular, 10–11; emphasis retained at 19th-century church colleges, 476–477; scholar's language, 11, 97, 120
Latin grammar schools, 95–96, 490
Latourette, Kenneth Scott, quoted, 367
Latrobe, Benjamin Henry, 344
Latter-Day Saints. *See* Mormons
Laud, Archbishop William, 23, 46, 55
Law. *See also* Judiciary; Legal profession; Legal writing; Moral law; Natural law and rights
—codification: attempts, 232–233, 405; common law unsuited for, 405; Louisiana, 405; Massachusetts, 80–82; Virginia, 261–262, 405
—Coke's idealism, 19–20
—common: inadequacies of, in early Republic, 404–406; Kent on, 416, 417; pressure for incorporation in colonial statutes, 232–233; usages in early Republic, 415; viewed as divine law, 19, 348
—constitutional, 407; paramount, 268, 297–298, 412
—criminal: capital crimes, 81, 82; Louisiana codification, 405
—equity, 404, 416
—federal level, 410–415
—land, 36, 48, 81, 224–225
—of seditious libel, 200, 227–230, 259, 285, 316
—state level, 415–416
Laws of Ecclesiastical Polity, Of the, Hooker, 15
Leatherstocking tales, Cooper, 390, 445
Lebanons (towns), 499, 508
Lectures on Revivals of Religion, Finney, 362, 364
Lectures on Systematic Theology, Finney, 364
Lee, "Light-Horse" Harry, 385
Lee, Mother Ann, 89, 506–507, 508, 510
Legal profession, 224–226, 259, 404; training, 225, 323, 476–477
Legal writing: Kent, 416–417; Story, 417–418; Wheaton, 419

Leggett, William, 448, 449–450, 452
Legislative branch: bicameralism vs. unicameralism, Adams, 303, 304, 309; independence of, 258–259; limitations on, 237, 298; priority of, 17, 23, 232–233, 259, 327, 410. *See also* Assemblies, colonial; Congress, Parliament; State legislatures
Legislative equality, colonial, doctrine of, 244, 247
L'Enfant, Pierre Charles, 501
Letter . . . to General Lafayette, Cooper, 445
Letters of a Pennsylvania Farmer, Dickinson, 240
Leverett, John, 98; quoted, 97
Leviathan, Hobbes, 295
Levy, Leonard W., 200, 227, 229
Lewis, Meriwether, 321, 378, 511
Lewis and Clark expedition, 321, 378
Libel, seditious, 200, 227, 259, 285, 316; Zenger case, 227–230
Liberalism:
—literary, 393
—New York leaders of, 446–452, 503
—religious, 349–353; Anglican, 334–335; Congregationalist, 182–183, 216, 217, 351; Presbyterian, 343, 371; Unitarianism, 183, 216, 335, 349–353, 522; Universalism, 349, 350
Liberty. *See* Freedom
Libraries: private, colonial America, 195–196, 201, 205; public, 205, 207
Library Company of Philadelphia, 207
Lieber, Francis, 470
Lilburne, John, 17
Lincoln, Abraham, 292, 444, 477, 500, 517
Lindsey, Philip, 477
Linnaeus, Carl, 190, 194, 218
List, Georg Friedrich, 400–401, 403
Literacy, 94–95
"Literary Independence," Channing, 394
Literary journals, 383, 393, 523–524
Literature, 385–395; emergence of vernacular, 10, 11–12; lag in colonial America, 192; romantic, 390; romantic-nationalistic, 393–395; tastes in content, 384, 393; tastes in style, 393, 395; Transcendentalist, 523–524, 527, 528 (*see also* Emerson; Thoreau). *See also* Historiography; Novels, Poetry; Satire
Little Men, Alcott, 486
Livingston, Edward, 405
Livingston, Robert, 405
Livingston, William, 468, 469; quoted, 468

Minorities: colonial America, 29; protection of, 298, 299
Missionary work: Baptist, 366–367; Catholic, 30, 345, 359; Congregationalist, 354, 365, 366, 367–368; foreign, 366–368, 514; home, 358, 367; among Indians, 30, 99, 121, 172, 173, 175, 366; Methodists, 338, 347, 358–359, 367; Mormons, 514; New Sides Presbyterian, 162; Presbyterian, 358, 366, 367–368; Puritan, 99, 173, 175; societies, 366–368; S.P.G., 116, 121, 122. *See also* Evangelism
Mississippi, University of, 441
Missouri, 443
Mitchell, Broadus, 294
Modern Chivalry, Brackenridge, 387
Monarchy, 15–16, 325–326; constitutional, 16, 23, 249; divine-right vs. limited, 16; early colonial attitudes toward, 33–34, 63; Paine on, 248; pre-Revolutionary attitudes toward, 244, 245, 247–250; subservient to law, 19–20. *See also* Crown government
Monasticism, Protestant, 146–147
Monikins, The, Cooper, 445
Monroe, James, 315, 322, 377
Montaigne, Michel Eyquem de, 207
Montanists, 136
Montesquieu, Baron Charles Louis de, 195, 261, 281, 286, 294, 306, 431; *Spirit of the Laws*, 190, 196
Monthly Anthology and Boston Review, 351, 353, 383, 393
Moral intuitionism, 163, 314, 386, 432, 479
Moral law, 19, 81; Enlightenment belief in, 190
Moral philosophy, collegiate, 479–481
Moravian College for Women, 147
Moravians, 130, 146, 147, 149
Morgan, Edmund S., quoted, 99, 248
Morgan, John, 211
Morison, Samuel Eliot, 82, 96, 272
Mormons (Latter-Day Saints), 112, 506, 510–514, 515, 529; beliefs, 511–512; church covenant, 68, 511; church government, 70, 512–513; missionary work, 514; polygamy, 512; schools of, 483, 513
Morris, Gouverneur, 274, 282
Morris, Richard, quoted, 229
Morris, Robert, 266, 295, 347
Morse, Jedidiah, 352–353, 354, 358
Morse, Samuel F. B., 377
Mott, Frank Luther, 383
Mühlenberg, Ernst, 131
Mühlenberg, Henry Melchior, 130, 131

Multiple (divided, plural) sovereignty, 247, 276, 280–282, 286, 296, 297; judicial review of conflicts, 412–414
Murdock, Kenneth, 382
Murray, John, 349, 350
Music: camp meetings, 361; church, German, 147
Mysticism, Christian, 62, 90–91, 98, 135–137, 147, 506; of Anne Hutchinson, 90, 135, 136; of Emerson, 515, 520; Europeans, 518; Penn quoted, 139–140; and scientific inquiry, 200

Napoleon Bonaparte, 318, 393, 532
Narrative of Surprising Conversions, A, Edwards, 169, 174–175
Nashoba community, 448, 502
Nashville, University of, 477
Nassau Hall, 163
National Bank. *See* Bank
National debt, 295, 299, 301, 400
National Gazette, 388
National Intelligencer and Washington Advertiser, 383, 397
National Reform Association, 446, 451
National System of Political Economy, The, List, 401, 403
National Trades Union, 451
Nationalism, 396, 398, 419; Adams, 307, 308, 312; economic, 299–301, 396–403; educational, 321, 463–464, 472, 482, 489; emerging awareness, 212–213, 217–218, 277; Hamilton, 295–301, 347; Jackson, 453, 457–458; literary, 385, 393–395, 404; and Manifest Destiny, 459; of Marshall Court, 412–415; religious, 336–343, 345–347, 355–356, 404; Unitarian, 393, 394, 395, 396, 432. *See also* Federalism
Natural Condition, 104, 105. *See also* Natural man
Natural law and rights, 23, 92–93, 216, 266, 327, 406; basis of Declaration of Independence, 250–251; espoused by labor reformers, 452; in "judges' oath" controversy, 233; in Parsons' Cause, 231; pre-Revolutionary disobedience justified by, 237, 241, 246, 294; in Zenger case, 229
Natural man, 349; Edwards's view, 179–180; Stoddardian, 104–105; Unitarian view, 352
Natural religion, 213. *See also* Deism
Nature, Emerson, 517, 519–520
Nature of True Virtue, The, Edwards, 176, 177
Nazareth, Pennsylvania, 146
Negroes: African colonization plans for, 366, 438, 442; franchise, 424; hu-

Parties, political: emergence of, 301, 315–316, 383; national conventions, 424, 454; patronage, 453–454; Tocqueville on, 427
Pastorius, Francis Daniel, 146
Patriarcha, Filmer, 16, 196
Patriot King, The, Bolingbroke, 306
Patronage system, 453–454
Peabody, Elizabeth, 485–486, 505, 523, 524, 525
Peace societies, 367
Peale, Charles Wilson, 318
Pendleton, Edmund, 261
Penn, William, 137, 138, 139–145, 148, 153, 154, 172
—biographical notes, 139, 143
—liberalism of, 142–144
—pacifism of, 144–145, 148
—proprietor of Pennsylvania, 35, 140–142
—quoted: on the Christian way, 134, 139–140; condemnation of Christendom of his age, 139; on divine-right government, 142; on Reformation, 140; on religious liberty, 144; on rural life, 141; on study of nature, 205; on war, 144–145
—writings of: *Rise and Progress of People Called Quakers*, 140; *Essay Towards the Present and Future Peace of Europe*, 144; *No Cross, No Crown*, 134, 139–140; *Sandy Foundation Shaken*, 139; *Some Fruits of Solitude*, 141
—mentioned, 121, 204
Pennsylvania:
—colonial charter (1861), 36, 140; decline of Quaker control of, 149, 150; franchise, 143; government, 142–143, 148; land distribution, 37, 42, 143; legislature, 142–143, 149, 231, 323; military obligations vs. pacifism, 140, 144–145, 148, 149–150; proprietary colony, 140, 142, 231–232; royal land grants, 35, 36, 140; weak local government, 143
—economic growth: colonial, 32–33; early Republic, 400
—education, 147, 148–149; 210–211, 467; confessional system, 149; public-school movement, 485, 492
—German settlers, 129, 142, 146–148, 149
—Quakers, 29, 140–141, 143, 145–146, 148–150, 344
—Presbyterians in, 115, 124, 126
—religious diversity, 204
—religious freedom, 143–144, 204
—sectarian pietists of, 146–148

—state, 266–268, 272; abolition law, 285; constitution, 260, 267–268, 284; constitutional convention, 257, 266–267; Council of Censors, 268, 415; franchise, 257, 266, 267; government, 267–268
Pennsylvania, University of, 376, 467, 473. See also Philadelphia, College of
Pennsylvania Gazette, 206, 207, 208
Pennsylvania Society for the Encouragement of Manufactures and the Useful Arts, 300, 397, 401
People's Rights, 451
Pequot War, 78, 89, 96
Perfectionism, 347–357, 497–499; academic sources of, 350–351, 353–357; of communitarians, 499, 500–514, 529, 532; conservative Calvinists, 353–357; definitions, 347–348; and democracy, 529–532; individualist, 497–499, 532; liberal (Universalists, Unitarians), 349–353; Methodists, 338, 347, 363; Oneida, 364, 500, 506, 508–509; "Post-Christian," 348; Shaker Inner Order, 507; social, 348, 357, 364, 514; of Transcendentalists, 529, 532
Perfectionist theology, Finney, 363
Perkins, William, 60
Perry, Ralph Barton, 54
Pestalozzi, Johann Heinrich, 485, 488
Peterson, Merrill D., 436, 450
Petition of Right, England, 9, 20
Phalanges, Fourierist, 504, 505–506
Phalanx, The, 505
Philadelphia, 32, 126, 452; Christ Church, 121, 341; as cultural and scientific center, 191, 204–207, 209–211, 376, 377, 400; population, 158, 386; publishing, 206, 384, 386
Philadelphia, College of, 210–211, 375, 467; charter, 210; curriculum, 211; nondenominational, 129, 131, 149, 210. *See also* Pennsylvania, University of
Philadelphia Academy, 210, 211
Philadelphia *Port-Folio*, 383, 393
Philadelphia Society for the Promotion of Agriculture, 376, 377
Philosophes, 308, 309, 314
Philosophical Transactions, 191, 193
Philosophy, moral, college course, 479–481
Phrenology, 518
Physiocrats, 295, 308, 314, 435
Pietism, 32, 135–137, 145–148, 158, 358
Pilgrims, 12, 61, 113; Mayflower Compact, 61; Separatists, 59, 60, 61
Pitt, William, Earl of Chatham, 234, 239, 242

Plan of Union, Congregational and Presbyterian Churches, 365–366, 371, 474

Plato and Platonism, 16, 18, 136, 195, 197; in Puritanism, 62, 64, 177

Plea for the Poor, A, Woolman, 153

Plural sovereignty. *See* Multiple sovereignty

Plutarch, 195, 281, 294

Plymouth Colony: absorbed by Massachusetts, 32; in Dominion of New England, 91, 101–102; Separatists, 27, 59, 61

Plymouth Company for Virginia, 12

Poetry: epic, 390, 391; nationalist, 386, 388–389, 391–392, 394; Puritan, 64–65, 91, 101

Poinsett, Joel R., 380

Pole, J. R., 272

Political Justice, Godwin, 335

Political writing: English 17th-century, 16–18; of the Enlightenment, 190; lag due to libel laws, 199–200; lags behind events, 433

"Politics," Emerson, 531

Politics: mass participation, 423–424, 425, 446–447; prevalence of lawyers in, 225–226, 259, 404; Tocqueville on, 426–427

Polk, James K., 442, 459

Polybius, 280, 281

Polygamy, 512. *See also* Sex practice, utopians

Poor Richard's Almanack, 207–208, 384

Pope, Alexander, 199, 306; quoted, 15

Popular sovereignty, doctrine of, 429. *See also* Government, derived from the people; Self-government

Population: cities, statistics, 158, 386, 441, 447; 18th-century growth, 158; variety of national and religious origins, 27–29

Population-growth theories, 402–403

Portico, The, 385–386

Post-Christian Perfectionism, 348

Postelthwayt, Malachy, 295

Postmillennialism, 509; Adventists, 509, 510; Mormons, 510, 511; Oneida Perfectionists, 508; Shakers, 507

Pound, Roscoe, 405, 418, 419

Pownall, Thomas, 234, 235–236, 238

Predestination, Calvinist doctrine of, 161, 174; vs. free will, Edwards, 174, 178–179

Preemption Act, 451

Presbyter, defined, 58

Presbyterian Church, 58, 124–128, 132, 336; Church of Scotland, 58, 112, 343; clergy, 58, 126–127, 160–161; education efforts, 127–128, 162–163, 181–182, 365–366, 434, 463, 467–468, 470, 471, 474, 483; emergence in America, 115, 126–127; evangelism, 160–162, 181, 358, 359–360, 361–362; first presbytery and synod established, 126; General Assembly, 126, 342–343; missionary work, 162, 358, 366, 367–368; independence from Europe, 184; its national federation an example for federalizers, 128, 164, 342; New Side vs. Old Side controversy, 160–161, 162; New Sides, Old Sides reunited, 162, 181, 342; 19th-century fragmentation, 369, 370; number of congregations, 342, 370; Plan of Union, with Congregationalists, 365–366, 371, 474; reorganization of 1789, 342–343; in Southern Colonies, 115, 181–182; split over slavery issue, 369

Presbyterianism, as form of church government, 58, 126, 343; efforts in Massachusetts, 79, 124; federating institutions of, 126, 343

Presbyterians, 158, 357; covenant theology, 127; in England, 66, 103; favor multiple church establishment, 264–265; in Middle Colonies, 32, 78, 115, 124, 126; in New England, 32, 79, 111, 115, 126; Patriots, 342; in Pennsylvania, 115, 124, 126, 146; in Southern Colonies, 115, 125, 181; in United Brethren, 103; in Virginia, 46, 124–125, 433; voluntarism, 128

Presbytery, 126, 343; Conjunct, 162

President, powers of, 280

Press, freedom of, 280

Press, freedom of, 259, 284–285

Priestley, Joseph, 322, 323, 376

Primogeniture, 262

Prince, Thomas, 223, 304

Princeton College (later University), 357, 473. *See also* New Jersey, College of

Princeton Theological Seminary, 357

Principal Navigations, Voyages, Traffics, and Discoveries of the English Nation, Hakluyt, 12

Principia Mathematica, Newton, 190, 202, 207

Principles of Political Economy, The, Carey, 402

Principles of Social Science, The, Carey, 402, 403

Printing, 189, 191–192, 199–200; Franklin, 206, 207–208; freedom restricted by libel actions, 200, 227–230

Privy Council, 11, 37, 280, 410, 412

"The Progress of Dulness," Trumbull, 391

Property, forms of: communal, 504, 506, 513; feudal landed, 13, 35–37; commercial, 13–14, 35; in England, 13–14; early colonial, 35–38

Property rights, 258, 275; democratic distribution demands, 447–448; Kent on, 417; Story on, 418; and taxation, 237

Proprietary provinces, 42, 115, 140, 142, 231–232

Protestant Episcopal Church, 113, 336, 339–342; constitution, 341; education efforts, 463, 474–475, 483; evangelism, 369; high vs. low church, 339, 340, 368–369; number of congregations, 342, 359

Protestant Reformation. See Reformation

Protestantism and Protestants: Augustinianism of, 62; English, character of, 137–138; interchurch cooperation, 365–367; interchurch rivalry, 371; interdenominational rapprochement, 345–347; in Maryland, 46–48; monasticism, 146–147. See also *individual denominations*

Providence, Rhode Island, 85–86, 159

Province, defined, 42. See also Proprietary provinces; Royal provinces

Provoost, Samuel, 340, 341, 342

Psychology, origins of science of, 174, 190

Public School Society, New York, 492–493

Publishing, 380, 382–384, 385; Franklin, 206, 207–208; lag in colonial America, 191–192, 199–200. See also Journalism; Newspapers

Pufendorf, Baron Samuel von, 92, 124, 196, 207

Purcell, Richard, 356

Purchas, Samuel, 12

Puritan Revolution, 8–9, 13, 17, 28, 46, 55–61, 307; causes and origins, 22, 56–57

Puritanism and Puritans, 53–71, 77–107
—achievements assessed, 53–54, 106–107
—beliefs, 57, 61–65; Augustinian influence, 62, 63; chosen-people concept, 53, 63, 67, 99, 222, 354, 355, 356; covenant of grace, 63–64, 67, 88, 104–105, 165; expressed in analogies from nature and politics, 62–63; means of salvation, 57, 62, 63–64, 105, 165
—Bible scholarship and faith, 56, 63–64, 94

—church-state relationship, 65–66, 68–70, 181; theocracy, 69–70, 77–82, 85, 105–107; theocracy declines, 100–101, 148; theocracy ended, 102, 104
—clergy, 68, 69
—compared with Quakerism, 138, 141–142
—congregationalism, 32, 92–93; nonseparating, 60–61, 80; proposals for intercongregational federation, 103
—congregations, 67–68, 100, 104–105, 171 (See also Church membership, Puritan Revolution)
—Connecticut, 59–60, 103, 354–357
—covenant (federal) theology, 60, 61, 63–64, 66–69, 80, 100–101, 104–105 (see also Covenant)
—defections to Anglicanism, 121–122
—democracy foreshadowed, 54, 60–61, 71, 93
—dominance in New England, 32, 67, 111–112; dominance weakened, 102–107
—and education, 93–98, 106
—Edwardsian, 164–165, 167–179
—in England, 28, 55–61, 66, 70, 138
—evangelism and revivalism, 99, 101, 103, 106, 216–217; Edwards, 168–169, 172; Stoddard, 103–105, 106
—factionalized, 171, 182–183, 216–217
—late-phase perfectionism, 353–357
—liberal, 182–183, 216, 217
—Massachusetts Bay Colony, 27, 29, 59–60, 66–70, 77–85, 87–90, 98–107
—and mysticism, 62, 89–90, 98
—New Hampshire, 59–60
—New Haven Colony, 28, 32, 60
—Platonism in, 62, 64, 177
—Plymouth Colony, 32, 59, 60, 61
—presbyterian phase, in England, 58
—reform goals of, 57–58
—religious orthodoxy, 78–80, 82, 83
—religious persecution by, 85, 89–90, 98, 138
—second-generation accommodation, 98–101
—Separatist wing, 55, 59, 61, 66, 84
—Stoddardian broadening of, 103–106
—in Virginia, 46

Putnam, James, 225

Pym, John, 17, 60

Quadrivium, in college curriculum, 96–97, 119, 120, 123, 478

Quakers, 32, 94, 135, 136, 137–146, 148–154, 284, 358, 433
—beliefs of, 135, 137, 139–140, 147; in equality of men, 138, 248; sacraments abandoned, 141

Quakers (*continued*)
—Camisard movement (England), 506
—church membership, 141
—compared with Puritans, 138, 141–142
—contributions to science, 205–206
—criticisms of Reformation emphasis on external, over spiritual, reform, 137, 140
—defections to Anglicanism, 121
—and education, 148–149, 463, 475
—in England, 22, 70, 137–140, 506
—meetings, 141, 143
—in New England, 32, 85, 102, 111; Puritan persecution of, 98, 138
—oppose multiple church establishment, 265
—origin of term, 137
—pacifism of, 32, 144–145, 146, 148, 149, 152–153
—Penn, 139–145
—in Pennsylvania, 29, 140–141, 143, 145–146, 148–150; political decline, 149–150, 343–344
—persecutions of, 22, 98, 138–139
—slavery opposed by, 41, 102, 146, 151–152, 285
—theological system lacking, 141–142
—Woolman, 150–154
Quebec Act, 243
Queen Anne's War (1702–1713), 145, 158
Queen's College, 131
Quincy, Josiah, 350

Racism, 40–41, 285; in Mormon belief, 511; 19th-century predictions of future problems, 427, 446
Radical, 451
Rafinesque, Constantine, 378
Raleigh, Sir Walter, 12, 192, 193, 530
Ramée, Pierre de la, 93
Randolph, Edmund, 274, 407
Randolph-Macon College, 434, 470, 475
Ranters, 85
Rationalism, 215, 217, 333, 334–336, 341, 359; attacked by Edwards, 174, 183; attacked by Emerson, 518
Raymond, Daniel, 399–400, 401
Read, George, 274
Reason the Only Oracle of Man, Allen, 334
Red Bank, New Jersey, 499, 505
Redburn, Melville, 6
Reed, Sampson, 518
Reeve, Henry, 425, 427
Reeve, Tapping, 399
Reflections on the French Revolution, Burke, 309

Reformation:
—continental Europe, 112–113
—in England, 7, 11, 64; Puritan phase, 55, 57–61, 70; Quaker phase, 70, 137–140
—Quaker criticism of, 137, 140
Reformed Church, 29, 78, 113, 114–115, 132, 158; Dutch, 114, 126, 130, 131, 159–160, 161, 365, 463; education efforts, 131, 365, 463; in Europe, 58, 66, 112; German, 130–131, 146; independence from Europe, 184
Regionalism, 27, 31–33; in journalism, 383
Religion: diversity, 27–29, 114–115, 131–132, 159, 182–184, 216–217, 333–335; as impetus to colonization, 8, 12; martyrdom for, 17; natural, 213; and science, attempts at reconciliation of, 213, 216; spiritual, 135–137, 146, 150, 344 (*see also* Mysticism, Christian; Pietism)
Religious discrimination, 227; anti-Catholicism, 129, 227, 368; England, 21, 23; Puritan orthodoxy, 79–80. *See also* Religious persecution
Religious freedom, 184, 327, 345; at colleges, 102, 106, 162–163; defined, 21; federal bill of rights on, 284; a natural right, 266; Penn's commitment to, 143–144; protection in state constitutions and bills of rights, 259, 260, 264, 284; spurred by population growth and variety, 159; Virginia statute, 265–266
Religious persecution, 21, 227; Massachusetts, 85, 89–90, 98, 138; of Quakers, in England, 22, 138–139
Religious toleration, 20–21
—in England, 20–22, 23, 45, 46, 114
—in Maryland, 43, 46–48, 227, 260
—in Netherlands, 113
—in Rhode Island, 85–87, 227
—Roger Williams on, 76, 86, 87
—spreads in New England, 102–103, 106–107
—struggle for: Makemie case, 125; Massachusetts Remonstrance, 79–80, 125; Williams and Hutchinson, 83–90
—in Virginia, 45–46
"Remarks on National Literature," Channing, 395
Remonstrance, Massachusetts (1645), 79–80
Renaissance, 64; in England, 7; influences in New England, 93–94, 96; traditions in Southern Colony culture, 194, 195, 196–197

Renewal of the Covenants, National and Solemn League, 128

Representative government: Adams on, 270; colonial, 43–45, 231; Jefferson on, 324; pre-Revolutionary arguments for, 231–233, 243–247; "virtual representation," 238, 239, 240. *See also* Legislative branch

Representative Men, Emerson, 517, 518, 532

Republican education, 463–472, 482, 493–494, 502–503; aims of, 472; Mann on, 489

Republican government, 102, 255–259, 260, 327, 494; Camp on, 431–432; England, 245–246, 248, 249; mass participation, 423–424, 425 (*see also* Democracy); Montesquieu, 281, 286; United States, 280–281, 286, 297, 423–424. *See also* Commonwealth government

Republican (later Democratic) Party, 313, 316, 408, 424

Republicanism: agrarian, 302, 319, 435; Christian, 341–343, 344, 346–347, 365, 472; equated with democracy, 431, 472; Jefferson's, 302, 316, 327, 428–429, 437

Revivalism, 358–365; camp meetings, 358, 359–361; coincidence with political upsets, 158; condemnations of, 174; cyclical occurrence, 157–158, 359; Presbyterian, 160–162, 361–362; in Puritan institutional life, 101, 103; Stoddardian, 103–106, 169. *See also* Evangelism; Great Awakening; Second Great Awakening

Revolution, American: assessment of, 283–287, 325–327; justification of, 240–251

Rhode Island:
—colonial, 27, 32, 85–87, 234; charter (1663), 34–35, 99, 101–102, 260; land grant, 86
—in Dominion of New England, 91, 101–102
—founding of, 85
—public schools, 490–491
—religious toleration, 85–87, 227
—slave-trade center, 42, 151
—state: abolition law, 285; constitution, 260
—unrepresented at 1787 constitutional convention, 274

Rhode Island, College of, 181–182, 183, 345. *See also* Brown University

Richmond Enquirer, 383, 434

Rigdon, Sidney, 512

Right of the Inhabitants of Maryland to the Benefit of the English Laws, The, Dulany, 232–233

Rights of Men to Property, The, Skidmore, 447–448

Riley, Woodbridge, 511–512

Ripley, George, 498, 523, 524–525

Ripley, Sophia Dana, 498, 524–525

"The Rising Glory of America," Brackenridge and Freneau, 386

Rittenhouse, David, 217, 218, 267, 376, 378

Rittenhouse, James, 212

Roane, Spencer, 259, 413, 415, 456

Roanoke colony, 192–193

Robertson, William, 196

Robinson, Frederick, quoted, 462

Robinson, John (Bishop of London), 116

Robinson, John (Pilgrim), 59, 92

Rodgers, John, 343

Roger-Collard, Pierre Paul, quoted, 426

Rolfe, John, 193

Roman Catholicism, 99, 114, 129, 132, 136, 344–345; in continental Europe, 112–113, 307; discriminations against, 129, 227, 368; education efforts, 132, 345, 463, 483; first American bishop and archbishop, 344; in Maryland, 27, 30, 43, 46–48, 129, 150, 227, 260, 344–345; missionary work, 30, 345, 359; in New World non-English colonies, 113; number of congregations, 359; orders, 345; and sacraments, 57, 62

Romanticism, 352, 390, 393–395

Roosevelt, Clinton, 449

Roosevelt, Franklin D., 292, 299, 517

Roosevelt, Theodore, 292, 299, 517

Rousseau, Jean Jacques, 191, 457, 504

Rowse, A. L., 57

Royal African Company, 40

Royal charters: Connecticut (1662), 34–35, 99, 101–102, 111, 260; Maryland (1632), 36, 231; Massachusetts (1629), 66, 101, 111; Massachusetts (1691), 102, 269; Pennsylvania (1681), 36, 140; Rhode Island (1663), 34–35, 99, 101–102, 260

Royal provinces, 31, 33–35, 42

Royal Society of London, 191, 193–194, 201, 203, 209

Rush, Benjamin, 376, 467, 469, 482; quoted, 467

Rutledge, John, 274

Sabbatarians, 85

"Sacramental Meditation," Taylor, 91

Sacraments: Catholic use of, 57, 62; Episcopalian use of, 342, 368; as means of salvation, 57, 62, 336; Mercersburg

Sacraments (*continued*)
discussions of, 369; Puritan use of, 68, 104–105, 172; Quaker abandonment of, 141. *See also* Baptism; Communion

St. Mary's Sulpician Seminary, 132, 345

St. Louis, 441

Saint-Simon, Claude Henri de, 503

Salt Lake City, 499, 506, 513, 514

Salvation: for all, Universalist view, 349; Arminian view, 174; Bushnell on, 369; Edwards's view, 165, 172, 174, 179, 180, 182; by good works, 57, 105, 174, 347; by grace, 57, 62, 63–64, 88, 105, 165, 172, 174, 362, 363; Methodist view, 336, 338, 347; Mormon belief, 511, 513, 514; by sacraments, 57, 62, 336; Shaker belief, 507; Unitarian view, 350, 352

"The Salvation of All Men" (sermon), 350

Sanctification theology, Finney, 363, 364

Sandy Foundation Shaken, Penn, 139

Santayana, George, quoted, 4

Satire, 199–200, 387, 390, 392

Saybrook Platform (1708), 102, 171

Schaff, Philip, 369

Schlatter, Michael, 130–131

Scholasticism, medieval, 62, 64

Schoolcraft, Henry R., 379

Schools: academies, 210, 211, 490; early New England, 94–96, 482; land grants, 321, 440, 464; Latin grammar, 95–96, 490; Moravian, 147, 149; parochial, 463–464, 481, 483, 493, 510; Southern Colonies, 120, 194–195. *See also* Colleges; Education, elementary, public, secondary

Schools of the prophets, 127, 160

Schuyler, Robert Livingston, 281

Schwenkfeld, Kaspar, 147

Schwenkfelders, 146, 147

Science: American voluntarism, 428; at colleges, 163, 194, 201, 202–204, 211, 356, 376, 472, 473, 476; earliest colonists, 193, 200–201; in early Republic, 375–380, 403–404; Emerson on, 518, 520; of the Enlightenment, 190; of the Enlightenment, American participation, 189, 191, 192, 193–194, 201–206, 208–209; institutionalization of, 376–380; intercolonial contact furthered by, 211–212, 217–218; journals, 377, 383; Quaker contributions to, 205–206; and religion, attempts at reconciliation of, 213, 216

Science and the Modern World, Whitehead, 200

Scots settlers, 28, 78, 115, 128

Scots-Irish settlers, 28, 32, 116, 146, 149, 181, 342; Presbyterianism, 115, 124–128, 161, 164

Scott, Sir Walter, 384–385, 390

Seabury, Samuel, 294, 335, 339, 340, 342, 368

Seasonable Thoughts on the State of Religion in New England, Chauncy, 174

Secession, 317, 444

Second coming of Christ: Adventist belief, 510; Mormon belief, 511; Noyes, 508; Shaker belief, 507. *See also* Millennialist beliefs; Postmillennialism

Second Great Awakening, 158, 359–365, 472; camp meetings, 359–361; impetus to colleges, 366, 470, 471; interchurch cooperation, 365–367

Second Treatise of Government, Locke, 17, 23, 25

Sectarianism, 135–137, 145–148, 184; Puritan persecution of, 98

Sedgwick, Theodore, Jr., 449

Seekers, 138

Self-Determining Power of the Will, The, Day, 476

Self-government: Bancroft on, 422, 423, 429; Camp on, 431; colonial, 43–45, 66, 106, 107, 226, 429, 433; Jefferson on, 246–247, 324; John Adams on, 245; Madison on, 43; a natural right, 246; proprietary provinces' fight for, 231–233; Tocqueville's doubts, 432; Wilson on colonial legislative equality, 244

Self-Reliance, Emerson, 496, 532

Separates (Congregationalist), 171, 175, 355

Separation of powers in government, 258–259, 275, 279–280

Separatism, Puritan, 55; Brownism, 59, 60; Plymouth Colony Pilgrims, 27, 59, 60, 61; Roger Williams, 84

Servitude, 38, 39, 42. *See also* Slavery

Seton, Mother Ann, 345

Seventh-Day Adventists, 483, 509–510

Sevier, John, 441

Sewall, Samuel, 151, 417

Seward, William Henry, 493

Sex practice, utopians, 500, 502, 506, 507, 508–509, 512

Shaftesbury, Earl of (Anthony Ashley Cooper), 35

Shakers, 506–508, 509, 529

Shakespeare, William, 7, 10, 306; *Troilus and Cressida* quoted, 14–15

Sharpe, Horatio, quoted, 41

Picture Credits

Insert Page

I–6 *Center*   The Metropolitan Museum of Art, Harris Brisbane Dick Fund, 1925.

I–6 *Bottom*   I. N. Phelps Stokes Collection; Prints Division; The New York Public Library; Astor, Lenox and Tilden Foundations.

I–7 *Top*   The Metropolitan Museum of Art, Gift of William H. Huntington, 1883.

I–7 *C, B*   By courtesy of the Trustees of the British Museum.

I–8 *T*   National Portrait Gallery, London.

I–8 *B*   The Quaker Collection, Haverford College Library.

II–1   Rare Book Division; The New York Public Library; Astor, Lenox and Tilden Foundations.

II–2 *T*   Courtesy of Harvard University.

II–2 *B*   Princeton University Library, Department of Rare Books and Special Collections.

II–3 *T*   The Metropolitan Museum of Art, Bequest of Charles Allen Munn, 1924.

II–3 *B*   Rare Book Division; The New York Public Library; Astor, Lenox and Tilden Foundations.

II–4 *T*   The Massachusetts Historical Society.

II–4 *B*   The National Gallery of Art, Washington, D.C., Gift of Mrs. Robert Homans.

II–5   Bowdoin College Museum of Art, Brunswick, Maine.

II–6 *T, Left*   Information Division; The New York Public Library; Astor, Lenox and Tilden Foundations.

II–6 *B, Left*   The Massachusetts Historical Society.

II–6-7 *T*   I. N. Phelps Stokes Collection; Prints Division; The New York Public Library; Astor, Lenox and Tilden Foundations.

II–*6*-7 *B*	Virginia State Library, Richmond, Virginia.
II–*8 T*	Bowdoin College Museum of Art, Brunswick, Maine.
II–*8 B*	Courtesy, Art Commission, City of New York.
III–*1 T*	Courtesy, The Bostonian Society, Old State House.
III–*1 C*	From the Collections of the Maryland Historical Society.
III–*1 B*	Historical Pictures Service, Chicago.
III–2 *T*	Culver Pictures
III–2 *C*	The Smithsonian Institution.
III–2 *B*	I. N. Phelps Stokes Collection; Prints Division; The New York Public Library; Astor, Lenox and Tilden Foundations.
III–*3 T, Left*	The New-York Historical Society.
III–*3 T, Right*	The Metropolitan Museum of Art, Harris Brisbane Dick Fund, 1945.
III–*3 C, Right*	The New-York Historical Society.
III–*3 B*	Courtesy of the American Museum of Natural History.
III–*4 T*	Information Division; The New York Public Library; Astor, Lenox and Tilden Foundations.
III–*4 C*	The New-York Historical Society.
III–*4 B*	Museum of The City of New York.
III–*5 T*	The Metropolitan Museum of Art, Bequest of Charles Allen Munn, 1924.

DATE DUE

11/30			
DEC 14 1971			
			PRINTED IN U.S.A.